Cinema, Culture, Scotland

Frontispiece: Scotland meets Hollywood. This collage encapsulates two central themes of the book: Scottish culture and Hollywood cinema. Artist: Murray Grigor.

Cinema, Culture, Scotland
Selected Essays

Colin McArthur and Jonathan Murray

EDINBURGH
University Press

Edinburgh University Press is one of the leading university presses in the UK. We publish academic books and journals in our selected subject areas across the humanities and social sciences, combining cutting-edge scholarship with high editorial and production values to produce academic works of lasting importance. For more information visit our website: edinburghuniversitypress.com

© Colin McArthur and Jonathan Murray, 2024, 2025

Grateful acknowledgement is made to the sources listed in the List of Illustrations for permission to reproduce material previously published elsewhere. Every effort has been made to trace the copyright holders, but if any have been inadvertently overlooked, the publisher will be pleased to make the necessary arrangements at the first opportunity.

Edinburgh University Press Ltd
13 Infirmary Street
Edinburgh EH1 1LT

First published in hardback by Edinburgh University Press 2024

Typeset in 11/13 Monotype Ehrhardt by
IDSUK (DataConnection) Ltd

A CIP record for this book is available from the British Library

ISBN 978 1 3995 1286 2 (hardback)
ISBN 978 1 3995 1287 9 (paperback)
ISBN 978 1 3995 1288 6 (webready PDF)
ISBN 978 1 3995 1289 3 (epub)

The right of Colin McArthur and Jonathan Murray to be identified as the author of this work has been asserted in accordance with the Copyright, Designs and Patents Act 1988, and the Copyright and Related Rights Regulations 2003 (SI No. 2498).

Contents

Figures and Tables   vii
Acknowledgements of Original Publishers   ix
Personal Acknowledgements   x
Contributors   xi

    Editor's Introduction: Jonathan Murray   1
1. *Ashes and Diamonds*   29
2. The Roots of the Western   35
3. *Pickup on South Street*   45
4. Extract from *Underworld U.S.A.*   49
5. Politicising Scottish Film Culture   69
6. *Crossfire* and the Anglo-American Critical Tradition   77
7. Breaking the Signs: *Scotch Myths* as Cultural Struggle   85
8. Scotland and Cinema: The Iniquity of the Fathers   97
9. *The Maggie*   121
10. National Identities   133
11. TV Commercials: Moving Statues and Old Movies   139
12. Tele-history: *The Dragon Has Two Tongues*   143
13. *Scotland's Story*   151
14. The Dialectic of National Identity: The Glasgow Empire Exhibition of 1938   159
15. The New Scottish Cinema?   171
16. The Rises and Falls of the Edinburgh International Film Festival   181
17. A Dram for All Seasons: The Diverse Identities of Scotch   195
18. Scottish Culture: A Reply to David McCrone   205
19. In Praise of a Poor Cinema   219
20. Wake for a Glasgow Culture Hero   229
21. The Cultural Necessity of a Poor Celtic Cinema   235
22. Culloden: A Pre-emptive Strike   249
23. *Casablanca*: Where Have All the Fascists Gone?   273
24. The Scottish Discursive Unconscious   279
25. Chinese Boxes and Russian Dolls: Tracking the Elusive Cinematic City   289

26. Artists and Philistines: The Irish and Scottish Film Milieux — 317
27. *Braveheart* and the Scottish Aesthetic Dementia — 331
28. The Exquisite Corpse of Rab(elais) C(opernicus) Nesbitt — 349
29. *Mise-en-scène* Degree Zero: Jean-Pierre Melville's *Le Samouraï* — 371
30. The Critics Who Knew Too Little: Hitchcock and the Absent Class Paradigm — 385
31. Caledonianising *Macbeth*, or, How Scottish is 'The Scottish Play'? — 403
32. Two Steps Forward, One Step Back: Cultural Struggle in the British Film Institute — 427
33. Transatlantic Scots, Their Interlocutors and the Scottish Discursive Unconscious — 449
34. *Scotch Myths*, Scottish Film Culture and the Suppression of Ludic Modernism — 469
35. Bring Furrit the Tartan-Necks! Nationalist Intellectuals and Scottish Popular Culture — 487
36. Vanished or Banished? Murray Grigor as Absent Scots Auteur — 503
Author's Afterword: Colin McArthur — 513

Select Bibliography — 523
Indexes — 527

Figures and Tables

Figures

Frontispiece: Scotland meets Hollywood. This collage encapsulates two central themes of the book: Scottish culture and Hollywood cinema. Artist: Murray Grigor.   ii

1.1	Maciek, having shot Szczuka, catches his falling body in a 'filial' embrace	31
2.1–2	Agrarianism versus Industrialism. The wagon train divides and the 'holy plow' is discarded	42
3.1	Nationalism in the *mise-en-scène*. Skip's final confrontation with Joey shot against a recruiting poster for the US Army	46
4.1	Recurrent trope of the genre: the gangster lies dead in the street in *Odds Against Tomorrow*	60
4.2	The influence of the Kefauver Committee on the gangster film: *Hoodlum Empire*; the character of Senator Stephens (centre) in the 'Kefauver' role	65
6.1	The opening image of *Crossfire*: an anti-Semite murders a Jew. Film noir or 'social problem' film?	79
7.1	From 'Here be dragons' to the picturesque: from the late eighteenth century on, the Scottish Highland landscape became a fit subject for artists and tourists	88
7.2	Cynicus deconstructs the iconic Scottish symbol and motto	92
8.1	Italy absorbs the Scottish Discursive Unconscious: *7 pistole per i MacGregor*	98
8.2–3	The River Clyde functions in two discourses within *Floodtide*: the Scotland of beautiful hills and lochs and the Scotland of bustling industry	105
9.1–2	Sheena, the Spirit of Scotland, advances with open arms and leads Marshall into the dance	130
14.1	Scotland as Janus. Past and future as the modernist Tate tower looms over the Clachan	167

17.1	Contrary to popular belief, whisky's historical advertising did not always contain representations of Scotland or Scots	198
18.1	Unlike the dominant discourse about Glencoe, this collage evokes laughter rather than tears. Artist: Murray Grigor	214
22.1	Poster advertising an exhibition of the authorial photomontages included in the original version of this essay. The photomontage reproduced here is entitled 'Imagined Community'	251
23.1	The design of this fiftieth-anniversary poster reflects the marginalisation of the Second World War in modern accounts of *Casablanca*	274
25.1	City versus Country in *The Barkleys of Broadway*. Fred Astaire and Ginger Rogers drag Oscar Levant for a weekend in the country	293
27.1	Romanticism and Caspar David Friedrich in *Braveheart*: Wallace atop a mountain	335
28.1	'Ich bin ein sheep-shagger!' *Rab C. Nesbitt*'s Cotter moved to tears on hearing 'Flower of Scotland', expresses solidarity with Highland Scots	363
29.1–2	Jean-Pierre Melville's Cinema of Process: Jef, stealing a car, searches for a compatible ignition key in *Le Samouraï*	380
33.1	The Scottish Discursive Unconscious	453
33.2	1950s Scots-Americans wholly enmeshed in the Scottish Discursive Unconscious	459
34.1	Scotland meets Hollywood once again: Murray Grigor directs Sam Fuller in *Scotch Myths*	473

Tables

9.1	Celt/Anglo-Saxon	126
13.1	*Homo Oeconomicus/Homo Celticus*	152
14.1	Core/Periphery	161
18.1	English/Scottish	208
21.1	*Homo Oeconomicus/Homo Celticus*	240
24.1	*Homo Oeconomicus/Homo Celticus*	282
25.1	City Girl/Country Girl	292
25.2	Metropolis/Small Town	293
25.3	City-Cape Cod/Midwest Town	295

Acknowledgements of Original Publishers

Thanks are due to the following publishers for granting permission to reprint the writings listed here: Bloomsbury for 'Scotland and Cinema: The Iniquity of the Fathers', 'National Identities', 'The Rises and Falls of the Edinburgh International Film Festival', 'The Cultural Necessity of a Poor Celtic Cinema' and the extract from *Underworld U.S.A.*; *Sight and Sound* for 'In Praise of a Poor Cinema'; Wayne State University Press for '*Scotland's Story*'; Glasgow Film Theatre for 'The New Scottish Cinema?'; Rivers Oram Press for '*Casablanca*: Where Have All the Fascists Gone?'; Glasgow University Library for 'The Scottish Discursive Unconscious'; Narr Francke Attempto Verlag GmbH for 'Artists and Philistines: The Irish and Scottish Film Milieux'; Ian Christie and *Film Studies* for 'The Critics Who Knew Too Little: Hitchcock and the Absent Class Paradigm'; University of Alabama Press for 'Transatlantic Scots, Their Interlocutors and the Scottish Discursive Unconscious'; Cambridge Scholars Publishing for '*Scotch Myths*, Scottish Film Culture and the Suppression of Ludic Modernism'; Intellect Books for 'Vanished or Banished? Murray Grigor as Absent Scots Auteur'; Routledge for 'Chinese Boxes and Russian Dolls: Tracking the Elusive Cinematic City' and '*Mise-en-scène* Degree Zero: Jean-Pierre Melville's *Le Samouraï*'; Pluto Press for 'The Exquisite Corpse of R(abelais) C(opernicus) Nesbitt'; and Praeger for '*Braveheart* and the Scottish Aesthetic Dementia'.

Personal Acknowledgements

Any book is never less than a collective enterprise. Among those who have provided valuable information and/or hard-to-find references are: the staff of the British Film Institute Reuben Library (especially Ian O'Sullivan), Karl McGee (University of Stirling Archive), Mark McLean (National Records of Scotland), Bernie Regan (Creative Scotland), Christie Young and Amanda Wade-Charters (Perth Theatre). The author and editor have been sustained by the enthusiasm and support of Gillian Leslie, Commissioning Editor at Edinburgh University Press, and her team, particularly Sam Johnson, Anita Joseph, Grace Balfour-Harle, and Bekah Dey. The author and editor would also like to register their appreciation of Aidan Cross's proofreading. Special thanks to Murray Grigor for permission to reproduce his collages (the Frontispiece and Figure 18.1). The initial proposal for this book also benefitted greatly from the suggestions of the anonymous peer reviewers. The act of writing is best conducted in a stable and supportive milieu, provided over the years, in the original writing and the present anthologising, by the author's wife, Tara, whose labour, no less than that of the author and editor, is in this book. The author wishes to stress that the project would never have come to fruition without the 'ramrodding' of its editor, Jonathan Murray. Both author and editor, early on in the book's gestation and as a matter of convenience, had begun to refer to it as 'our book'. Through its various phases that phrase took on an altogether more profound meaning. To the extent that the book approaches the highest standards of scholarship and the protocols of academic publishing, this is due primarily to the cultural and formal meticulousness of the editor, who transformed a diverse set of essays written over almost half a century into something approaching a serious academic work.

The author's dedication is to his grandchildren, Rosa (11), Callum (6) and Blythe (2) in the hope that their generation will make a better job of tackling the toxicity of the natural and politico-economic worlds than did that of their grandfather.

Contributors

Colin McArthur was born in Glasgow in 1934 and left school at fifteen to become a craft apprentice. Following national service in the Army, he had a variety of casual jobs before entering university as a mature student, after which he taught in secondary, further and higher education before joining the British Film Institute in 1968 where, becoming Head of the Distribution Division, he remained until 1984. Writing extensively on Hollywood cinema, British television and Scottish culture, he also lectured widely in the UK, continental Europe and the Americas, becoming Visiting Professor at Glasgow Caledonian University and Queen Margaret University College in Edinburgh. His most recent book is *Along the Great Divide: High Art, Mass Art and Classical Hollywood Narrative* (2020).

Jonathan Murray is Senior Lecturer in Film and Visual Culture at Edinburgh College of Art, University of Edinburgh. He is the author of *The New Scottish Cinema* (2015) and *Discomfort and Joy: The Cinema of Bill Forsyth* (2011), co-editor of several scholarly anthologies, including (with Nea Ehrlich) *Drawn from Life: Issues and Themes in Animated Documentary Cinema* (Edinburgh: Edinburgh University Press, 2019), a Contributing Writer on the permanent staff of *Cineaste* magazine and co-Principal Editor of *Journal of British Cinema and Television*.

For Rosa, Callum and Blythe

Editor's Introduction

Jonathan Murray

Cinema, Culture, Scotland: Selected Essays anthologises thirty-seven scholarly essays written by Colin McArthur between 1966 and 2022. Organised chronologically, containing works published in all decades between the 1960s and 2020s, and including twenty-one essays hitherto out-of-print and a new authorial afterword, the book identifies and illustrates the central strands of critical enquiry and approach animating one of British Film Studies' and Scottish Cultural Studies' most pioneering, prolific and polemic careers. McArthur's multifaceted interests and achievements include: his role in legitimising the analysis of Classical Hollywood genre cinema within Anglophone Film Studies; his leadership, inspirational and controversial in equal parts, in establishing Scotland's cinematic representation as an accepted and widely practiced object of study; and his imaginative and informed interrogation of Scotland's distinctive identity and presence as a visual and material cultural signifier within a diverse range of domestic and international popular cultural traditions from the eighteenth century until the present. As well as showcasing an important individual contribution to the disciplines of Film Studies and Scottish Cultural Studies, therefore, collecting these essays together also illuminates key aspects of those disciplines' respective post-1960 histories and trajectories.[1] Many of the following essays contain new authorial and editorial annotation that aims to illustrate and explain the ways in and extent to which this is so.

McArthur's publishing career incorporates numerous monographs, edited anthologies, print journalism, scholarly book chapters and academic journal articles. Because they have until now represented perhaps the most logistically dispersed and least practically accessible areas of his oeuvre, this volume focuses (with four exceptions) exclusively on the latter two categories.[2] The exceptions to that editorial rule are as follows. An extended extract from McArthur's 1972 monograph *Underworld U.S.A.* is presented to underscore his significance as a pioneering Anglophone historian and theorist of Classical Hollywood cinema and to illustrate a transitional moment in early-1970s Anglophone Film Studies where auteurist theoretical approaches of the previous decade came into initial contact with structuralist and semiological counterparts that shaped the discipline's evolution during the 1970s. A transcript of a 1988 invited lecture, 'The New Scottish Cinema?' makes that work generally available for the first time and provides a useful snapshot of McArthur's thinking at the end of a decade during which his better-known published works on Scottish cinema history and theory comprehensively transformed academic awareness of and approaches to that subject. Finally, two examples of McArthur's journalistic practice, 'In Praise of a Poor Cinema' and 'Wake for a Glasgow Culture Hero' (both from 1993), illustrate not only its characteristic literary style and critical approach, but also its importance as a vehicle through which he has regularly rehearsed and disseminated the critical arguments and approaches defining his scholarly oeuvre. The various works presented here constitute a comprehensive illustration of McArthur's critical identity and influence and, hopefully, an invitation to also discover or revisit the substantial body of his writings not collected within these pages. The following editorial introduction briefly introduces each of the thirty-seven essays which are included here.

Although Polish cinema would not become a long-term concern within McArthur's writing,[3] *'Ashes and Diamonds'* (1966), an extended narrative and formal analysis of Andrzej Wajda (1926–2016)'s 1958 film of that name, usefully flags the existence of several critical and political preoccupations that did: most centrally, the moving image's status as an influential vehicle through which images of and ideas about national identities and histories emerge and circulate, both locally and globally. This early essay is also suggestive in displaying McArthur's career-long close attention to questions of cinematic form: if he aims to establish the nature of *Ashes and Diamonds*'s 'central politico-social statement', he simultaneously asserts that Wajda's 'superb technique'[4] is in large part the vehicle that creates, then communicates the former. While many of his later, better-known writings explore wide-ranging theoretical, methodological and institutional questions, McArthur has regularly undertaken extended formal analyses of particular moving image artists and texts that he deems of especial cultural and political significance and that broadly follow the critical model already sketched out in this early essay. Examples of that critical approach in the present volume include: '*Crossfire* and the Anglo-American Critical Tradition' (1977); '*The Maggie*' (1983); and '*Mise-en-scène* Degree Zero: Jean-Pierre Melville's *Le Samouraï*' (2000).

'The Roots of the Western' (1969) illustrates that the United States and France are perhaps the two nations which figure at most length, alongside his native Scotland, within McArthur's multi-decade interest in the relationship between the moving image and discourses of national identity. On one hand, and as several of the 1960s and 1970s essays republished here show, McArthur's early work was one pioneering vehicle through which the emergence and early evolution of Anglophone Film Studies were centrally informed by mid-twentieth-century French theorists such as André Bazin (1918–58) and French publications such as *Cahiers du cinéma*.[5] But, on the other, such Continental influences were originally applied by McArthur and his peers[6] in order to develop path-breaking accounts of a range of Classical Hollywood genres, including the Western, film noir and gangster cycles. In addition, 'The Roots of the Western' also illustrates distinctive aspects of McArthur's individual critical identity within that wider intellectual phenomenon. In McArthur's case, the late-1960s/early-1970s creation of theoretically informed histories of specific American film genres extends out into an extensive exploration of wider American cultural and intellectual eighteenth- to twentieth-century histories. Like several other essays in this volume, 'The Roots of the Western' is a work of cultural history as well as film theory.

An extended contextual and formal analysis of the 1953 Samuel Fuller (1912–97) film of the same name, '*Pickup on South Street*' (1969) is another early instantiation of critical strategies and preoccupations that structure several of this volume's later essays. These include McArthur's already-noted concern with cinema's illumination of and intervention within debates around particular national identities at particular historical moments and his firm conviction regarding the aesthetic, historical and ideological significance of 'low' (and thus, potentially overlooked) cultural texts, traditions and artists. As one seminal influence on McArthur during his early career framed matters, 'the struggle between what is good and worthwhile and what is shoddy and debased is not a struggle *against* the modern forms of communication, but a struggle *within* those media'.[7] Or, as McArthur puts it in a 2001 essay that looks back on the late-1960s British Film Studies milieu within which '*Pickup on South Street*' was written, 'to promote discussion of authorship and genre centred on popular Hollywood cinema was to us as much a political as an aesthetic act'.[8] On one hand, McArthur's argument that '*Pickup* is [. . .] a political film in the sense that it emanates from its author's intense nationalism and connects with the recurrent theme in Fuller's work of the demands of nationality'[9] explains his critical interest, as an assiduous student of cinema's relationship with national identity discourses, in this film and filmmaker. On the other hand, however, it also exemplifies certain structuring terms within a wider contemporaneous turn within British Film Studies towards recuperation and re-evaluation of popular film traditions and artists, most especially, ones associated with Classical Hollywood.[10] McArthur concludes that 'the connection between the bleak underworld of *Pickup* and the political structure of [the film's] contemporary America [. . .] is not one that Sam Fuller perceives. Because he fails to make the connection, however, is no good reason for undervaluing [. . .] his work.'[11] He thus speaks eloquently of the late-1960s British turn towards Hollywood while that turn speaks eloquently through him.

'*Pickup on South Street*' appears like a microcosmic dry run for several elements of one of McArthur's most significant works: his 1972 monograph, *Underworld U.S.A.*[12] Both are centrally concerned with the mid-twentieth-century Hollywood gangster film, auteurist evaluations of individual directors prominent within that tradition and unapologetic assertion of the intellectual and ideological necessity of studying Classical Hollywood cinema. Yet *Underworld U.S.A.* also illustrates the developing nature of its author's critical practice and the embryonic British disciplinary context informing it. The book looks to develop not simply a working history of specific Classical Hollywood genres (film noir, the gangster film), but also elements of a transferable theoretical methodology and rationale for discussing other film genres and the overarching concept of film genre per se: 'there is a sense', McArthur argues, 'in which all Hollywood movies are genre pieces'.[13] In this, *Underworld U.S.A.* offers an early example of 'auteur-structuralism', the late-1960s/1970s attempt to combine and reconcile elements of 1960s auteurist critical approaches and the structuralist counterparts that proved prominent throughout the 1970s. For one contemporary reviewer, 'probably the most significant aspect' of the book was 'the overdue recognition by an auteur-orientated critic of the positive influence of genre [. . .] on the work of various filmmakers', while another similarly welcomed 'an interesting future for a new mixture of critical approaches, combining generic with authorial groupings'.[14] The extracts from *Underworld U.S.A.* presented here testify not only to McArthur's status as an important historian of Classical Hollywood;[15] they also illustrate elements of the evolving early-1970s milieu of British Film Studies and the long-term importance of structuralist thought within McArthur's subsequent critical career.

'Politicising Scottish Film Culture' (1976) introduces the subject matter for which, alongside his work on Classical Hollywood, McArthur is best known: the interlocking histories of Scotland's cinematic representation and the belated, late-twentieth-century emergence of an indigenous

Scottish feature cinema. The question McArthur opens this essay with –
'How might Scottish film culture be politicised?'[16] – remained pivotal
within his remarkable body of Scottish film history and criticism over
the next four decades. More generally, 'Politicising Scottish Film Culture' also demonstrates the extent to which all of McArthur's writing on
Scotland and the moving image deploys a highly distinctive (and often,
critically contentious) admixture of polemic to more standard academic
methodologies. The presence of 'Politicising Scottish Film Culture'
here also highlights important aspects of Scottish cinema history that
remain comparatively overlooked within academic scholarship. Despite
the recent emergence of significant studies of 1970s British cinema,
for example, the history of indigenous Scottish filmmaking pre-1980
remains understudied.[17]

Before study of Scotland's relationship with the moving image became
a dominant concern within McArthur's writing, '*Crossfire* and the Anglo-
American Critical Tradition' (1977) marked a final significant engagement
with Classical Hollywood cinema until two early-1990s monographs.[18]
Taking a 1947 Hollywood film which had been critically discussed primarily as a socially conscious account of post-World War II American antisemitism, the essay instead reads that text as a paradigmatic example of
film noir, thus producing a radically different (metaphysically rather than
socially focused) re-interpretation of *Crossfire*. More ambitiously yet, and
via the kind of extended close textual analysis that forms an intermittent
but consistent strain within his oeuvre, McArthur uses his microcosmic
re-reading of *Crossfire* to make a macrocosmic claim for the intellectual
and ideological value of what were by 1977 clearly emergent, politically
and theoretically radical methodological approaches (structuralism;
semiology) within Anglophone Film Studies. Such approaches, and
McArthur's individual work within them, sought to dismantle and displace
an earlier, cross-Atlantic critical consensus which, McArthur argues, was
compromised on ideological ('impatient commitment to liberal humanist
values') and formal ('faltering grasp of aesthetics'[19]) grounds alike. For
McArthur, systemic misreading of *Crossfire* – including by some of the
personnel who made it – was symptomatic of a much broader, decades-
long critical and popular cultural Anglophone dismissal of Classical
Hollywood cinema as a legitimate object of study.[20]

Although one of this volume's few pieces not explicitly concerned
with the moving image, 'Breaking the Signs: *Scotch Myths* as Cultural
Struggle' (1981), a review of a 1981 gallery exhibition of the same name
by Barbara Grigor (1944–94) and Murray Grigor, is of clear importance
for McArthur's subsequent Scottish-themed work. Encountering and

evaluating the Grigors' exhibition provided him with multiple enduring critical interests and tools.[21] If the 'political purpose' of *Scotch Myths* 'was to provoke debate about the representation of Scotland and the Scots',[22] that identified purpose on the part of others was one that McArthur's own subsequent work on Scottish film and television clearly also adopted. More specifically, the Grigors' identification of Tartanry and Kailyard as the dominant post-eighteenth-century, cross-media representational discourses within which Scottish identities and histories were constructed and circulated, both locally and globally, proved a key reference point within nearly all of McArthur's work on Scotland. The cross-media aspect ('literature, lithography, photography, the postcard, the music hall, films, television'[23]) of the Grigors' argument is an especially important influence to note. Several of this volume's essays either contextualise film and television texts through cross-references to other visual and material cultural traditions ('*Casablanca*: Where Have All the Fascists Gone?'; 'Caledonianising *Macbeth*, or How Scottish is the Scottish Play?') or take the latter as central objects of study ('The Dialectic of National Identity: The Glasgow Empire Exhibition of 1938'; 'A Dram for All Seasons').

The central argument of 'Breaking the Signs' ('the traditions of Kailyard and Tartanry have to be exposed and deconstructed and more politically progressive representations of Scotland and Scottish identities constructed, circulated and discussed'[24]) swiftly found significantly fuller expression in what is probably McArthur's most cited essay, 1982's 'Scotland and Cinema: The Iniquity of the Fathers'. The centrepiece of his edited anthology *Scotch Reels: Scotland in Cinema and Television*, 'the most influential critical and cultural analysis'[25] of Scotland's relationship with the moving image, 'Scotland and Cinema' is arguably the most important essay of Scottish film criticism written by any author to date. The first systematic critical attempt to construct a comprehensive overview of Scotland's cinematic representation, McArthur's discussion ranges from 1920s Hollywood through 1940s and 1950s British cinema to 1960s and 1970s Scottish sponsored documentary filmmaking. McArthur sets out several central positions that structured his subsequent Scottish work: the limited (and for the most part, externally created) range of representational discourses – Tartanry, Kailyard, Clydesidism – within which Scotland's cinematic image was and is constructed and circulated; the aesthetically and ideologically reactionary politics of Scotland's central film institutions, past and present; and the compromised nature of indigenous Scottish cinema considered as a whole, the symptomatic product of a historically underdeveloped national film culture that 'failed to keep a historic appointment with the discourses of Marxism and Modernism'.[26] The subject of ongoing critical re-evaluation and rejection decades on from its original publication, 'Scotland and Cinema' remains an essential starting point for students of Scottish cinema, Scotland's cinematic representation and the post-*Scotch Reels* evolution of Scottish cinema studies.[27]

'*The Maggie*' (1983) applies the totalising critical approach of 'Scotland and Cinema' to a single film, the celebrated Ealing comedy *The Maggie* (Alexander Mackendrick, 1954). Also further developing and applying aspects of McArthur's non-Scottish-themed 1970s work (such as his 1977 essay on *Crossfire*), this essay's project is a bifurcated one. A condemnatory ideological reading of Mackendrick's film ('the *locus classicus* of everything that is wrong with Scottish film culture'[28]) coexists with detailed attention to the surrounding processes of its production and contemporary popular critical reception. The latter aspect reflects McArthur's position, arrived at several years before '*The Maggie*' was written, that: 'the notion of "audience" [in academic Film Studies] ought to include theorized awareness of the social context in which particular films are received and read [. . .] the critical machinery through which responses are [constructed . . .] and their articulation'.[29] Thus, while popular processes and cultures of film reviewing constitute significant objects of scholarly enquiry within twenty-first-century Film Studies,[30] an underappreciated aspect of the work of McArthur (a practicing film journalist since the late 1960s) is its much earlier perception that 'no act of (film) criticism is innocent [. . .] a critical project is always being enacted'.[31] As a consequence, popular reviews of any given cultural text are themselves cultural texts open to critical review. Thus, extensive analysis of specific instances and general practices of popular film reviewing and related journalistic forms is a central component of not only '*The Maggie*' but many other of this volume's essays (see, for example, 'Culloden: A Pre-emptive Strike'; '*Braveheart* and the Scottish Aesthetic Dementia').[32] The same focus proves equally important within McArthur's early-2000s monograph on Mackendrick's two Scottish-themed features. Also central to that book is the idea that individual acts and wider histories of academic film criticism should themselves constitute objects, as well as instruments, of scholarly enquiry. That monograph nuances McArthur's early-1980s reading of *The Maggie* by insisting on the formal complexity and excellence of Mackendrick's directorial practice, albeit still concluding that its ultimate results remain problematic in national-representational terms.[33]

Three short mid-1980s essays reflect various aspects of McArthur's priorities during that brief period before Scottish subject matter again became a dominant focus during that decade's second half. Emerging from a BFI summer school, 'National Identities' (1984) suggests the potential transferability to other national cultural contexts of many of his early Scottish work's main arguments. The latter include the 'fundamental instability'[34] of all national identities, phenomena that are ideologically contestable and changeable precisely because they are, in the first instance, always ideologically constructed; and the central role of (often ostensibly apolitical) popular cultural media as vessels through which national identities are developed, disseminated and debated. Indeed, 'National Identities' exemplifies such transferability by focusing on metropolitan British film and television representations of WWII and reactionary mobilisations of the hegemonic myth of that historical event within the 1982 Falklands War. 'National Identities' also provides an early extended acknowledgement on McArthur's part of the work of political historian and theorist, Tom Nairn (1932–2023). Nairn's central ideas – both regarding the allegedly atypical post-1707 ideological development of Scotland specifically and the question of how Left cultural theorists ought to engage with (or even mobilise) discourses of cultural and political nationalism more generally – became obviously central reference points within McArthur's writing from here on.[35] Finally, the argument of 'National Identities' that 'TV and film constructions of the generative moments of the past need to be related quite concretely to the diverse struggles of the present'[36] represents an important staging point within McArthur's evolving thought. This position formed, for example, both the critical impetus and basis for his extensive 1990s and early-2000s analyses of *Braveheart* (Mel Gibson, 1995) as a seminal, but highly problematic, event within Scottish film and wider national cultures.[37]

Originally written for an anthology discussing the work of French literary theorist Roland Barthes (1915–80), 'TV Commercials: Moving Statues and Old Movies' (1984) applies the former's concept of intertextuality to several mid-1980s British TV commercials, demonstrating how these moving image micro-texts are constructed from, and dialogue with, other aspects and instances of popular culture past and present. 'Tele-history: *The Dragon Has Two Tongues*' (also 1984) provides a celebratory analysis of a contemporary Harlech TV series about Welsh history on account of what McArthur presents as the work's multiple formal and ideological departures from the historic norms of British television programmes about national history. '*Scotland's Story*' (1985) is a sibling piece to 'Tele-history', providing as it does a highly critical account of how a contemporaneous and comparable STV series about Scottish history presents itself as radical and forward-looking, while in fact being ensnared by regressive discourses about Scotland due to being driven in significant part by the aim of sales in North American and other diasporic broadcasting markets.

Given their respective subject matters, the mid-1980s quartet of essays described immediately above might be regarded as, to varying degrees, thematic outliers within McArthur's oeuvre. But they in fact exhibit and suggest various signature aspects of the latter's importance. All four pieces display, for example, marked sceptical interest in the cultural, economic and ideological prominence, within 1980s British society, of what 'Tele-history' terms 'the recycling and marketing of the past'.[38] In participating within 1980s and early-1990s British Film Studies and Cultural Studies' collective turn towards discussion and theorisation of contemporary 'Heritage' cultures,[39] these essays demonstrate the ongoing significance of their author's work as a suggestive historical catalyst and/or symptomatic exemplification of wider evolutionary shifts shaping the British variants of the academic disciplines within which McArthur has worked. A closely related reason for including these essays in this volume is that they constitute the only period – apart, arguably, from a comparably brief one in the mid-to-late 1970s – within McArthur's career during which television, rather than cinema, formed his main object of study.[40] When assessing the scale of McArthur's influence over modern Scottish Cultural Studies, it is relevant to note that, a few important individual exceptions aside, study of post-WWII Scottish culture has mostly overlooked the significance or impact of television.[41] Scottish cinema, in sharp contrast, forms the subject of no fewer than seven monograph-length studies during the twenty-first century's first two decades alone.[42] Such marked disparity suggests the extent to which McArthur's Scottish work has enabled subsequent scholars of modern Scottish culture, even where their ideas have disagreed (sometimes markedly) with his.

Most of the 1970s and early-to-mid-1980s essays discussed so far in this volume's introduction are united by a deep interest in diverse processes and methods of history-writing, academic and otherwise. 'The Dialectic of National Identity: The Glasgow Empire Exhibition of 1938' (1986) inaugurated an important, closely related sub-strand within McArthur's work from that date on. That sub-strand comprises detailed case study accounts, informed by extensive primary as well as secondary research, of particular historical events, cultural institutions and longer-term discursive processes, usually (but not always) Scottish-themed. 'The Dialectic of National Identity', for example, discusses the 1938 Glasgow Empire Exhibition and its contemporary press construction and representation. McArthur's career-long, Annales School-influenced conception of history as processual as well as event-driven is reflected in this essay's location of the 1938 Glasgow Exhibition within a wider European imperial tradition of international exhibitions between the mid-1800s and mid-1900s.

The essay also establishes the internal tension within the 1938 Exhibition between its nostalgic construction of 'Scotland' as rural utopia and the event's more forward-looking economic and industrial ambitions, as expressed in the modernist aesthetic of much of its specially constructed architecture.

'The New Scottish Cinema?' (1988) is a transcript of an invited lecture delivered at the Glasgow Film Theatre's Desperately Seeking Cinema event of May 1988. Explicitly geared towards the needs of a general rather than academic audience, the lecture describes the conditions which attended and determined what McArthur understands to be the most celebrated collective movements in cinema history, such as German Expressionism and Italian Neorealism, bemoans such movements' relative lack of influence within Scottish film culture past and present, and offers speculative explanations for both such absence and Scotland's failure to produce an internationally visible, but nationally specific cinematic movement-cum-moment of its own. This hitherto inaccessible work also provides, arguably, McArthur's most rhetorically distilled and readily accessible summary of how he understands his own film critical formation and identity within the wider British Film Studies field. That identity attempts to cross-pollinate the formalist study of cinematic *mise-en-scène* associated with the journal *Movie* (1962–2000) with many of the more theoretically orientated, politically radical methodologies developed within the journal *Screen* (1969–).[43]

Two of this book's earlier essays, '*Pickup on South Street*' and 'Scotland and Cinema: The Iniquity of the Fathers', have their roots in the Edinburgh International Film Festival's highly distinctive and innovative position within late-1960s to early-1980s Anglophone film culture as a bridgehead between film academic and industrial communities and a sponsor of new academic scholarship. 'The Rises and Falls of the Edinburgh International Film Festival' (1990) acknowledges this fact within what was perhaps the first critical attempt to produce an extended historical overview of the Festival.[44] Tracing EIFF's frequently shifting trajectory from its founding in 1947 until 1989, McArthur argues that the institution was most influential at moments (the late 1940s; the early 1970s) when it publicly committed to a clear, and left-of-centre, politics of film culture. Another example of the historical case study sub-strand that 'The Dialectic of National Identity' introduced into McArthur's practice, 'The Rises and Falls' arguably also prefigured the escalating centrality, within much of his 1990s and 2000s Scottish-themed work, of an institutional turn that had already been highly visible within his earliest writings in that area. In this, McArthur had possibly reached a similar conclusion to that drawn by John Caughie, also writing about Scottish film history within the same volume in which 'The Rises and Falls' originally appeared: 'representation' as practice and concept involves balancing both a 'figurative sense [. . .] of image and identity' and an 'institutional sense [. . .] of proportionality, representativeness and participation'.[45] Finally, and although it lies mostly beyond this volume's scope, it is worth noting that McArthur also regularly intervened in Scottish film institutional debates via a range of popular press publications from the mid-1970s onwards.[46]

Returning to the cross-media interests of an earlier work such as 'Breaking the Signs' and applying these within a historical case study of the type that increasingly attracted his attention during subsequent decades, 'A Dram for All Seasons: The Diverse Identities of Scotch' (1991) explores the history of mass media advertising of Scotch whisky. Confounding the potential assumption that such advertising will invariably have been cast within hegemonic Scottish representational discourses such as Tartanry and Kailyard, this essay's extensive discussion of primary visual source materials establishes instead its notable intertextual and ideological diversity. In addition to instances of Tartanry and Kailyard, the primary materials McArthur discusses draw on many other discourses and tropes, including canonical British literary and historical figures, whisky's evolving class-based connotations and its material and symbolic presence in various international locations. This essay's central conclusions represent a suggestive response to those sceptical readings of McArthur's Scottish moving image-themed work which see the latter's methodology and analysis ('a desire for clean, discernible categories [. . .] organis[ing] the heterogeneity of representation'[47]) as overly reductive and inflexible in its privileging of macrocosmic structural-historical traditions of representation over the microcosmic inflections or rejections of those by individual films and filmmakers. Without wishing to dismiss such concerns out of hand, 'A Dram for All Seasons' is of interest due to its illustration of the possibility of applying the *Scotch Reels* ideas and method in nuanced and caveated ways.

'Scottish Culture: A Reply to David McCrone' (1993) continues and further confirms the above-noted institutional turn within much of McArthur's 1990s and 2000s Scottish work. In a dialogic response to the critique of *Scotch Reels* made by another seminal work of modern Scottish Cultural Studies, the sociologist David McCrone's 1992 monograph, *Understanding Scotland: The Sociology of a Stateless Nation*,[48] McArthur distils in advance the governing methodology and rationale for a significant portion of his next decade or so of publication. He does so by calling into (rhetorical) question, 'the extent to which one can conduct an argument about Scottish culture without discussing the central arts institutions of that culture'.[49] 'Scottish Culture' can also be taken to exemplify the institutional turn driving much of McArthur's post-1990 academic writing in another way, in that the essay understands and discusses modern Scottish Cultural Studies as itself being an institutional formation.[50] That institution was one within which McArthur felt his ideas had become increasingly contested by the early 1990s. As a consequence, he occasionally sought to take the contemporary state of Scottish Cultural Studies as a dedicated object of enquiry in itself. One of this volume's final essays, 'Bring Furrit the Tartan-Necks! Nationalist Intellectuals and Scottish Popular Culture' is the most explicit example of this.

McArthur's sense of his previous work's evolving status within Scottish Cultural Studies by the early 1990s possibly explains the final main significance of 'Scottish Culture' for and within his wider oeuvre. This essay offers the first mention (one reiterated and further developed in subsequent essays) of McArthur's major retrospective augmentation of the *Scotch Reels* thesis, namely, his theory of 'the Scottish Discursive Unconscious'. Attempting to respond to critiques of that thesis which saw it as overly dismissive of the importance of individual creative agency and diversity within Scottish cultural production, McArthur's provisional formulation of the Scottish Discursive Unconscious's long-term existence, nature and influence proposes that 'it might be suggested that we tend to be written by the dominant Scottish narratives [of identity and representation] rather than ourselves writing narratives about Scotland'.[51] His most extensive and explicit elaboration of that theory perhaps came within the 1996 essay, 'The Scottish Discursive Unconscious'. There, McArthur proposes that the phenomenon's 'disabling effects' within Scottish cultural and political life stem from 'its capacity to cause Scots (and those who make images and narratives of Scotland) to turn their faces away from the modern world and scratch the scabs of the Scottish past'.[52]

Two 1993–94 essays, 'In Praise of a Poor Cinema' and 'The Cultural Necessity of a Poor Celtic Cinema', should be read in tandem: the latter develops at greater length within a peer-reviewed academic context ideas the former set out in more polemical form in a specialist film magazine article. While a significant degree of overlap inevitably applies across the two works, both are reproduced here as illustrative evidence of a prominent scholar's working process in developing and resolving particular critical ideas and positions. Reproducing both also works as a useful indication of an aspect of McArthur's practice that lies beyond this book's scope, namely, journalism's significance, since the late 1960s, as a popular platform through which he has regularly initiated, rehearsed and/or further disseminated aspects of his academic writing, 'contriv[ing]', in the words of one reviewer of a 1982 anthology of McArthur's 1970s film journalism, 'to discuss sophisticated and difficult concepts in language [. . .] accessible to any reader'.[53] 'In Praise of a Poor Cinema' is a polemic traducing of the early-1990s policies of the main Scottish cultural institutions responsible for funding indigenous film production. McArthur bemoans those institutions' conservative commitment to what he describes as a quasi-Hollywood aesthetic and industrial production model. Against the latter, he argues for a national cinema of micro-budgets and avant-garde aesthetic strategies. A more conventionally academic evolution of 'In Praise', 'The Cultural Necessity of a Poor Celtic Cinema' elaborates further on McArthur's working concept of 'Poor Cinema': a micro-budget, industrially sustainable and culturally sustaining aesthetic, commercial and ideological model for future feature film production in both Scotland and the other small British and Irish nations. For McArthur, the central film professional and political dilemma facing indigenously-based Celtic filmmakers past and present is that: 'the more your films are consciously aimed at an international market, the more their conditions of intelligibility will be bound up with regressive discourses about your own culture'.[54] He presents 'Poor Cinema' as a potential escape route from that bind.[55]

The short essay 'Wake for a Glasgow Culture Hero' (1993) celebrates both *A Wake for Bud Neill*, Murray Grigor's 1993 television documentary about the eponymous Glasgow newspaper cartoonist (1911–70), and the vitality and legacy of Neill's signature creation, the late-1940s/early-1950s cartoon-strip character, Lobey Dosser. Brief though it is, this essay connects to and further highlights many of McArthur's career-long critical interests, including: his deep interest in, and knowledge of, transnational cultural interactions between twentieth-century Scotland and the United States; his politically informed belief in the academic and cultural importance of 'low' cultural forms and traditions; and his assessment of Murray Grigor as one of Scottish film culture's most significant, but also critically and institutionally neglected, creative figures – the latter theme, for example, is one McArthur returns to within two of this book's final essays ('*Scotch Myths*, Scottish Film Culture and the Suppression of Ludic Modernism'; 'Vanished or Banished? Murray Grigor as Absent Scots Auteur').

One of this book's most ambitious essays in terms of the disciplinary diversity and cumulative scale of its primary and secondary research, 'Culloden: A Pre-emptive Strike' (1994) aims 'to re-historicise sentimental Jacobitism in general and the Culloden memorial in particular'.[56] Extrapolating from a wide-ranging survey of numerous post-1746 memorialisations of Culloden as historical event, physical site and evolving ideological myth, McArthur proposes 'the inescapable fact that there is no "natural", essentialist way of describing the events and people of 1745–46; there are only diverse "fictions" which might be constructed around them'.[57] This essay's chosen subject matter, methodology and main conclusions indicate the extent to which McArthur's Scottish work attempts radical reinterpretations of, and interventions within, modern Scottish history and culture generally, as opposed to modern Scottish film history and culture exclusively. As a result, it is of potential cross-disciplinary interest and relevance. 'Culloden', for example, contextualises evolving domestic interpretations of, and attitudes towards, the eponymous historical event within a much wider international history of public memorialising practices and artefacts. As a result, an essay written in the mid-1990s speaks to early-2020s debates around the complex ideological significance of memorial statuary associated with British imperial histories and identities.

This volume's shortest essay, '*Casablanca*: Where Have All the Fascists Gone?' (1995), suggests the value of including ostensibly 'minor' works within an anthologising overview of an individual critic's practice. Approached literally, this essay summarises the distinctive status of *Casablanca* (Michael Curtiz, 1942) as one of Classical Hollywood's most intertextually fecund films. Reiterating his marked interest in 'low' visual and material cultural traditions and artefacts, McArthur shows the extent to which *Casablanca* is quoted and reshaped within contexts that extend far beyond the moving image.[58] Seen instead as a symptomatic staging post within its author's evolving practice, however, '*Casablanca*' is of note because it starts to rehearse certain positions and preoccupations that went on to shape several of McArthur's most important 2000s essays. Recalling the position of 'Scottish Culture: A Reply to David McCrone' that academic disciplines and their internal debates themselves constitute institutional formations urgently requiring analysis, '*Casablanca*' argues that 'over a period of fifty years politics has been evacuated'[59] from *Casablanca*'s popular profile and reception. Elsewhere in his later work, McArthur perceives analogous, but far more broadly applicable, late-twentieth-century repressions of particular politicised approaches to moving image studies (most especially, ones predicated on the importance of socioeconomic class). An essay like 'The Critics Who Knew Too Little: Hitchcock and the Absent Class Paradigm' (2000), for example, takes that perception as both its critical impetus and central object of enquiry.

The volume's longest essay, 'Chinese Boxes and Russian Dolls: Tracking the Elusive Cinematic City' (1997), is a magisterial historical overview of cinematic representations of specific cities and also of 'the city' as an overarching discursive concept. For McArthur, any cinematic representation of urban locations and experiences, no matter what national cultural context it relates to or emanates from, is always textual and discursive, rather than neutral and objective. Specific cities and the wider concept of 'the city' are floating signifier[s], and their dominant meanings are potentially subject to change according to the discursive location and objective of any given act of cinematic representation: 'cities in discourse have no absolute and fixed meaning, but only a succession of temporary, positional ones'.[60] In this, 'Chinese Boxes' suggests the extent to which the concept of discourse assumed an explicit centrality within much of McArthur's post-1990 work analogous to that of the concept of genre within much of his 1970s output. More generally, this essay exemplifies a range of career-long critical interests and methods: a predominant (though far from exclusive) knowledge of and fascination with Anglophone national cinemas (Classical Hollywood and post-Hollywood; Scotland/UK); a concern to illuminate and interrogate the historical nature and consequences of 'Hollywood's post-WWI dominance in the cinematic representation of world space';[61] and extensive use of structuralist theory (in this essay, a binary opposition between city and country) as a tool through which to conduct close textual analysis of individual films and film movements.

'Artists and Philistines: The Irish and Scottish Film Milieux' (1998) extends McArthur's early-1990s interest in setting Scotland within a wider Celtic film cultural and historical context. It does so by providing a comparative account of mid-to-late-1990s Scottish and Irish institutional landscapes for indigenous film production.[62] Despite being written in the immediate aftermath of a remarkable and unlooked-for mid-1990s quantum expansion of local production levels and international profile for both nations' cinemas, 'Artists and Philistines' reiterates the extremely pessimistic terms of McArthur's 1980s and early-1990s evaluations of contemporary Scottish film institutional policies and priorities. This essay's significance within its author's wider oeuvre relates to two main considerations. Firstly, comparing Scottish cinema with its Irish counterpart provides McArthur with an additional justification for his long-term adherence to Tom Nairn's Marxist synthesis of post-1707 Scottish history, culture and identity in the latter's *The Break-Up of Britain: Crisis and Neo-Nationalism* (1977).[63] McArthur concludes that the 'Irish film milieu of the mid-to-late 1990s [. . .] dialectically engaged with Hollywood, [while] the [Scottish equivalent] surrendered to it'.[64] He explains this putative phenomenon by referencing a Nairn-derived theory of 'the very different historical experiences of the Scots and the Irish'[65] vis-à-vis their respective nations' relationships with the post-1707 British state and the wider development of modern European political nationalisms.

Secondly, identification of the production (spanning both countries) of *Braveheart* as a significant film cultural and industrial event within Scotland and Ireland alike laid the ground for McArthur's subsequent work (another 1998 essay republished here and a 2003 monograph) on *Braveheart* as film text and wider popular cultural phenomenon.[66]

The essay mentioned directly above is '*Braveheart* and the Scottish Aesthetic Dementia' (1998). Despite viewing that film as aesthetically vulgar and politically neo-fascist, McArthur nonetheless takes care to locate it within multiple explanatory contexts, including: the (sometimes overlapping) Hollywood genres of historical epic and biopic; cinematic representations of the European medieval period; the troubling ideological worldview of the film's screenwriter, Randall Wallace; and the film's popular reception and intertextual exploitation with mid-to-late-1990s Scotland. Exemplifying the argument above that McArthur conceives his work on Scottish film and television specifically as an explicitly politicised intervention within contemporary Scottish culture more generally, he argues that *Braveheart* 'needs to be discussed [. . .] as a classical narrative film engaging with the border country between history and myth, and as an event in Scottish culture. In the last analysis the two are connected'.[67] The same bifurcated approach characterises his related monograph, *Brigadoon, Braveheart and the Scots: Distortions of Scotland in Hollywood Cinema*.[68]

As noted above, television, Scottish-themed or otherwise, has formed an intermittent secondary preoccupation within McArthur's writing. His last intervention to date within Television Studies is 'The Exquisite Corpse of R(abelais) C(opernicus) Nesbitt' (1998), an extended (con)textual analysis of the long-running BBC Scotland sitcom, *Rab C. Nesbitt* (1988–2014). 'The Exquisite Corpse' is a kind of companion piece to '*Braveheart* and the Scottish Aesthetic Dementia'. McArthur proposes that, like *Braveheart*, *Rab C. Nesbitt* attained something approaching the status of 'event' within and across multiple aspects of Scottish culture, albeit he views it to be as aesthetically innovative and politically progressive as Mel Gibson's film is the opposite. Such innovation on the text's part provokes innovation in the method of the critic studying it. McArthur's suggestive attempts to contextualise and analyse *Rab C. Nesbitt* with reference to quotidian and literary linguistic cultures of vernacular Scots and to historic traditions of Scottish stage and screen acting have comparatively few, if any, antecedents or counterparts elsewhere in his oeuvre.

'*Mise-en-scène* Degree Zero: Jean-Pierre Melville's *Le Samouraï*' (2000) constitutes a re-engagement with the interlocking mid-twentieth-century French cinematic and intellectual milieus that (primarily through the writings published in *Cahiers du cinéma*) shaped both McArthur's emergent critical practice and the comparably embryonic British Film Studies tradition of the 1960s and 1970s.⁶⁹ One of the relatively few occasions where non-Anglophone subject matter becomes McArthur's central focus, this essay is one of several in this book that demonstrates not simply the identity, but also the potential transferability, of his critical method and central ideas. A critic fascinated by early-twentieth-century American cinema and popular culture takes here as his subject a French filmmaker (Jean-Pierre Melville [1917–73]) who was at least equally so. McArthur's long-term interest in popular cinema's symbiotic relationship with national identity discourses is clearly present, notwithstanding this essay's Francophone focus. A detailed, auteurist-inflected textual analysis of Melville's directorial aesthetic (McArthur terms the latter the 'cinema of process'⁷⁰) and recurring thematic concerns concludes that these were determined by, and symptomatic of, the filmmaker's personal experience of French society's complex and traumatic experience of WWII.⁷¹

As noted above, 'The Critics Who Knew Too Little: Hitchcock and the Absent Class Paradigm' (2000) exemplifies that sub-strand within McArthur's oeuvre that explores any given external object of study less as a self-sufficient end and more as a strategic vehicle through which to evaluate and critique ideas and methods that enjoy prominent or hegemonic status within a given academic disciplinary formation at a given point in time. Within such work, McArthur looks for ways to simultaneously use and whet various methodological blades. That fact constitutes another way in which and reason why his writing is of enduring scholarly interest: it offers compelling illustrative insight – sometimes symptomatic, sometimes self-consciously analytic, sometimes a mix of both – into the historical evolution of diverse aspects of Anglophone Film Studies. Indeed, the attempted overarching terms of such insight are visible within McArthur's work as early on as the mid-1970s. In, for example, a 1975 *Screen* essay on the television series *Days of Hope* (BBC, 1975), he opens his argument by identifying both the text he analyses and the agenda of the publication commissioning that analysis from him as equally important objects of study: 'I really want to write [. . . a] piece which, as well as posing *Days of Hope* as problematic, poses *Screen* [. . .] as equally problematic'.⁷² Returning to 'The Critics Who Knew Too Little', the disciplinary history that McArthur perceives and interrogates within this essay is one in which Hitchcock criticism (and, by implication, late-twentieth-/early-twenty-first-century Anglophone Film Studies more broadly), has come to be dominated by psychoanalytic feminism at the expense of the class dimension. Emphasising the lower-middle nature of Hitchcock's own class formation, McArthur argues that 'the key concept in any attempt to find such an identity at play in cinematic *mise-en-scène* would be [. . .] scopophobia – a fear of being looked at'.[73] He illustrates the presence of scopophobic images and scenarios across a notably wide range of Hitchcock's British and American films before concluding with the hope that his analysis will influence not only Hitchcock criticism specifically, but also 'help restore the category of class to the Film Studies lexicon'[74] more generally.

'Caledonianising *Macbeth*, or, How Scottish is the Scottish Play?' (2001) exemplifies a different, but equally important, sub-strand of McArthur's work, namely, his already-noted creation of extended historical case studies of specific popular cultural events, artefacts and processes. This essay's case study is the eighteenth-to-late-twentieth-century tradition of stage and screen adaptations of William Shakespeare (*c*.1564–1616)'s *Macbeth* (*c*.1606). After an extended summarisation of the play's pre-cinematic life, McArthur analyses three cinematic adaptations of it, two critically celebrated, one not: the 1948 version by Orson Welles (1915–85), the 1971 version by Roman Polanski and the 1996 version by British low-budget production house, Cromwell Films. The evaluative framework linking discussion of the sizeable canon of *Macbeth* adaptions, cinematic or otherwise, that McArthur covers involves the extent to which each was 'caledonianised' in terms of acting style, costume design, scenography, location, and so on. McArthur proposes that it is impossible to engage with *Macbeth* the unitary drama without also engaging with '*Macbeth*' the open-ended discourse – a reminder of the latter concept's pivotal position within his oeuvre.

Another 2001 essay, 'Two Steps Forward, One Step Back: Cultural Struggle in the British Film Institute', exemplifies yet another above-noted central sub-strand of McArthur's criticism: its deep interest in film institutional formations, histories and politics. Both a personal and primary source-driven account, 'Two Steps Forward' discusses its writer's experience of working in both the BFI's Education Department and, subsequently, the Institute's senior management team between the late 1960s and early 1980s. This subject matter dictates that, like many of this book's other essays, 'Two Steps Forward' illuminates important aspects of the historical evolution of British film culture and of the British Film Studies tradition.[75] Taking the concept of 'cultural struggle'[76] as its organising rubric, this essay pursues both a specific and a general goal. The former involves an illustrative insistence on the historic importance of the BFI Education Department and its affiliates in the evolution and entrenchment of Film Studies within British higher education and wider film culture. The latter involves an implicitly transferable demonstration that all public film institutions are actual or potential sites of cultural struggle and potential change. The use of the BFI's late-1960s to early-1980s history in order to propose this argument can be contextualised with reference to McArthur's regularly expressed disappointment regarding what he saw as the regressive (and/or repressed) political identities of a range of Scottish and British film institutions during the 1990s and early 2000s.[77]

Returning to the concept of the Scottish Discursive Unconscious that he first proposed and developed across several 1990s essays republished in this book, 'Transatlantic Scots, Their Interlocutors and the Scottish Discursive Unconscious' (2005) represents a significant extension of that concept's application within McArthur's work. Where earlier essays predominantly focus on domestic examples of the phenomenon at work, 'Transatlantic Scots' instead takes diasporic counterparts as its main object of enquiry. It explores the extent to which the Scottish Discursive Unconscious suffuses the actions, utterances and beliefs of successive generations of Scots (and more particularly, their descendants) who emigrated to the United States and Canada from the eighteenth century on. From his geographically transplanted critical focus, McArthur concludes that the Scottish Discursive Unconscious has little, if any, difficulty in operating across national borders: 'one is confronted by the same restricted range of images, tones, rhetorical tropes and ideological tendencies, often within utterances promulgated decades (and sometimes even a century or more) apart'.[78] The essay concludes by outlining a series of research proposals for understanding how this historical phenomenon came about.

Two of this book's most recent essays, '*Scotch Myths*, Scottish Film Culture and the Suppression of Ludic Modernism' (2009) and 'Vanished or Banished? Murray Grigor as Absent Scots Auteur' (2015), return to concerns first explored much earlier in McArthur's career. Although the polymathic artist and filmmaker Murray Grigor constituted a talismanic exemplar within McArthur's writing about Scotland as far back as 1981's 'Breaking the Signs', the 2009 essay argues of Grigor's sole feature film, *Scotch Myths* (1982), that: 'until now a film constituting one of the key reference points in [the debates which traversed Scottish film culture in the 1970s and 1980s] has had no adequate description, far less analysis';[79] the essay then attempts to rectify that lack. In addition, an accompanying history of Grigor's difficulties in producing, then preserving *Scotch Myths* leads to an early-2000s polemic reiteration of McArthur's much-quoted early-1980s evaluation of Scottish film culture as an entity diminished and disabled by collective avoidance, primarily on local film institutions' part, of a historically and culturally necessary engagement with the discourses of Modernism. The subsequent Grigor-focused essay 'Vanished or Banished?' outlines a fuller, auteurist-inflected account of Grigor's moving image oeuvre, most of it sponsored short films and television documentaries. McArthur argues that 'the most egregious lacuna in Scottish cinema'[80] relates to a structural absence of indigenous feature films that interrogate Scottish history in aesthetically and ideologically progressive ways. He speculates that Grigor might have pre-empted such an absence, had he been better supported by Scotland's main film funding institutions between the 1970s and early 2000s.

'Bring Furrit the Tartan-Necks! Nationalist Intellectuals and Scottish Popular Culture' (2009) offers perhaps the entire book's most vivid (not least because polemically inflected) exemplification of McArthur's desire to work with, as well as within, the academic disciplinary formations that shaped – and, in turn, have been shaped by – his critical thought and practice, taking their specialised histories and evolving identities as essential objects of study in their own right. This essay charts and criticises what it views as the parallel intellectual and ideological journeys of two of modern Scottish Cultural Studies' most ambitious and influential thinkers: literary historian and theorist, Cairns Craig and political historian and theorist, Tom Nairn. McArthur undertakes close reading of elements of the late-1990s and early-2000s work of both, and accompanying, albeit briefer, commentary on several other significant Scottish Cultural Studies scholars active during the same period.[81] From this, he asserts the existence of a regressive post-devolution consensus within significant sections of contemporary Scottish Cultural Studies. McArthur proposes that this latter-day received wisdom diverges markedly from the domestic intellectual milieu within which his own critical engagement with Scottish culture, history and identity emerged several decades before. Specifically, he complains that much early-twenty-first-century Scottish Cultural Studies publication activity is increasingly aligned with the political project of Scottish Independence. This is so, McArthur argues, in ways that predispose Independence-supporting scholars to misinterpret, or even caricature, the work of peers who adopt different political stances. For McArthur, the late-1990s/early-2000s work of many Independence-supporting scholars displays a contradictory relationship with Scottish popular culture and cultural history: rhetorical celebration of the latter is dependent on a calibrated lack of comprehensively sustained and open-minded intellectual engagement with it – a determination, conscious or otherwise, to not know (or not know more than is strictly necessary) of what one speaks.

On one hand, this book is a highly specific endeavour: it explores and, hopefully, extends the legacy of one individual film critical oeuvre. That project, however, is perhaps also part of a broader contemporary turn towards the curation, conservation and celebration of pioneering voices within British and wider Anglophone Film Studies as those traditions enter (depending on one's personal reading of history) their seventh decade. Analogous anthologising responses to the work of several of McArthur's significant generational peers have begun to emerge and scope exists for many more, whether conceived within or beyond classical academic publishing formats.[82] Given the nature of this book's project, it feels appropriate to leave its introduction's last significant word to the volume's subject himself. Reflecting on the identity and evolution of his own critical method, McArthur has described and rationalised it thus:

> [A] characteristic Marxist *modus operandi* of revealing ideology and discourse in particular films, hopefully with some degree of historical and cinematic awareness as well [. . .] the narrative processes of (particularly Hollywood) cinema [are] massively present on screen and [also] need[] to be addressed and perhaps interrogated about their ideological and discursive implications. Also there [is] the equally massive presence of the institutions of cinema and [. . .] how they le[ave] their traces on screen. Such a critical practice [. . .] I would designate Marxist formalist [. . .] if it needs a maxim it is this: always look outward to history, economics, institutions, ideology and discourse but, equally, always look inwards to the narrative and technical protocols of cinema itself.[83]

The following essays showcase that method and its lifelong evolutionary journey via important individual acts of application, reiteration and refinement. In this, the book aims to support its reader in thinking through the work of Colin McArthur in a dual sense: not simply acknowledging and analysing that work's historical significance for Film Studies and Scottish Cultural Studies, but also adopting and adapting its ideas for ongoing use within future scholarship in those and other disciplinary fields.

Notes

1. For a useful overview of the overlapping histories of the British variant of Film Studies and the academic study of British Cinema as a sub-field within Anglophone Film Studies more broadly, see John Hill, 'Revisiting British Film Studies', *Journal of British Cinema and Television* 7, no. 2 (2010), 299–310. For McArthur's summarising gloss on both the development of Anglophone Film Studies during his professional lifetime and his sense of his own critical identity's location within that process, see the unpaginated preface of his most recent monograph, *Along the Great Divide: High Art, Mass Art and Classic Hollywood Narrative* (London: Independent Publication, 2020).
2. McArthur's monograph publications to date are: *Underworld U.S.A.* (London: Secker & Warburg for the British Film Institute, 1972); *Television and History* (London: British Film Institute Educational Advisory Service, 1978); *Dialectic! Left Film Criticism from* Tribune (London: Key

Texts, 1982); *The Big Heat* (London: British Film Institute, 1992); *The Casablanca File* (London: Half Brick Images, 1992); Brigadoon, Braveheart *and the Scots: Distortions of Scotland in Hollywood Cinema* (London: I.B. Tauris, 2003); Whisky Galore! *and* The Maggie (London: I.B. Tauris, 2003); *Along the Great Divide*.

3. For McArthur's early-career work on Polish cinema, see: Colin McArthur, 'Polanski', *Sight and Sound* 38, no. 1 (Winter 1968), 14–17; Colin McArthur, '*Everything for Sale*', *Sight and Sound* 38, no. 3 (Summer 1969), 139–41; Colin McArthur, ed., *Andrzej Wajda: Polish Cinema – A BFI Education Department Dossier* (London: First Media Press, 1970).
4. Colin McArthur, '*Ashes and Diamonds*', in McArthur, *Cinema, Culture, Scotland: Selected Essays*, ed. Jonathan Murray (Edinburgh: Edinburgh University Press, 2023), 32.
5. See, for example, Charles Barr, 'Rethinking Film History: Bazin's Impact in England', *Paragraph* 36, no. 1 (2013), 133–52; Laura Mulvey and Peter Wollen, 'From Cinephilia to Film Studies', in *Inventing Film Studies*, ed. Lee Grieveson (Duke University Press, 2008), 217–34.
6. See, for example, Jim Kitses, *Horizons West* (London: Thames & Hudson, 1969).
7. Stuart Hall and Paddy Whannel, *The Popular Arts* (London: Hutchinson, 1964), 15.
8. Colin McArthur, 'Two Steps Forward, One Step Back: Cultural Struggle in the British Film Institute', in *Cinema, Culture, Scotland*, ed. Murray, 429.
9. Colin McArthur, '*Pickup on South Street*', in *Cinema, Culture, Scotland*, ed. Murray, 47.
10. See, for example, the other essays in the edited collection within which '*Pickup on South Street*' was originally published: Peter Wollen and David Will, eds, *Samuel Fuller* (Edinburgh: Edinburgh Film Festival '69/Scottish International Review, 1969).
11. McArthur, '*Pickup on South Street*', 48.
12. Indeed, McArthur also published a Fuller-focused chapter from *Underworld U.S.A.* as a standalone trailer for the subsequent monograph: see Colin McArthur, 'Samuel Fuller's Gangster Films', *Screen* 10, no. 6 (1969), 93–101.
13. Colin McArthur, 'Extract from *Underworld U.S.A.*', in McArthur, *Cinema, Culture, Scotland*, ed. Murray, 52.
14. Mark Bergman, '*Underworld U.S.A.* by Colin McArthur', *The Velvet Light Trap*, no. 9 (1973), 55; Michael Budd, 'Jim Kitses, *Horizons West* and Colin McArthur, *Underworld U.S.A.*', *Cinema Journal* 13, no. 1 (Fall 1973), 52. For a trenchant contemporary rejection of McArthur's early-1970s critical position and method and the wider intellectual formation from which it emerged, see Robin Wood, 'In Defense of Art', *Film Comment* 11, no. 4 (1975), 44–51. For an accessible summarising introduction to the late-1960s/early-1970s hybridisation of genre- and structuralism-based methods, see Robert Stam, *Film Theory: An Introduction* (Oxford: Blackwell, 2000), 123–30.

15. For a recent example of McArthur's ongoing accepted status in this regard, see J. E. Smyth, 'The Stuff That Dreams Are Made Of: The Dark History Behind *The Maltese Falcon* and the Birth of Film Noir', *Cineaste* 46, no. 4 (Fall 2021), 4–9; 78.
16. Colin McArthur, 'Politicising Scottish Film Culture', in McArthur, *Cinema, Culture, Scotland*, ed. Murray, 69.
17. For accounts of various aspects of the pre-1980 period, see: Colin McArthur, 'Scotland and Cinema: The Iniquity of the Fathers', in *Scotch Reels: Scotland in Cinema and Television*, ed. Colin McArthur (London: British Film Institute, 1982), 40–69, and republished in the present volume; Sarah Neely and Alan Riach, 'Demons in the Machine: Experimental Film, Poetry and Modernism in Twentieth-Century Scotland', in *Scottish Cinema Now*, eds Jonathan Murray, Fidelma Farley and Rod Stoneman (Newcastle: Cambridge Scholars Publishing, 2009), 1–19; Duncan Petrie, 'Planting the Seeds of Ambition: Scottish Film in the 1960s', in *The Scottish Sixties: Reading, Rebellion, Revolution?*, eds Eleanor Bell and Linda Gunn (Amsterdam: Rodopi, 2013), 243–60; Jonathan Murray, *Discomfort and Joy: The Cinema of Bill Forsyth* (Oxford: Peter Lang, 2011), 9–37.
18. McArthur, *The Big Heat*; McArthur, *The Casablanca File*.
19. Colin McArthur, '*Crossfire* and the Anglo-American Critical Tradition', in *Cinema, Culture, Scotland*, ed. Murray, 81.
20. For a contemporaneous attempt to use analysis of *Crossfire* as a vehicle through which to survey the methodological and ideological evolution of Anglophone Film Studies, see Keith Kelly and Clay Steinman, '*Crossfire*: A Dialectical Attack', *Film Reader*, no. 3 (1978), 106–27.
21. The dedication of McArthur's 2003 monograph Brigadoon, Braveheart *and the Scots* cites the Grigors as part of a small group of intellectuals 'who lit the way' (p. xi) for his own critical approach and ideas regarding Scottish culture and identity.
22. Colin McArthur, 'Breaking the Signs: *Scotch Myths* as Cultural Struggle', in *Cinema, Culture, Scotland*, ed. Murray, 85.
23. Ibid., 87.
24. Ibid., 93.
25. Duncan Petrie, *Screening Scotland* (London: British Film Institute, 2000), 2.
26. McArthur, 'Scotland and Cinema', in *Cinema, Culture, Scotland*, ed. Murray, 117. For by far the most extensive and informative account of the wider intellectual and institutional contexts from which the 1982 *Scotch Reels* event at that year's Edinburgh International Film Festival emerged and helped deliver McArthur's edited anthology of the same name, see David Will, 'Edinburgh', *Framework*, no. 20 (1983), 49–53.
27. For significant individual critical responses to the *Scotch Reels* thesis, see: John Caughie, 'Representing Scotland: New Questions for Scottish Cinema', in *From Limelight to Satellite: A Scottish Film Book*, ed. Eddie Dick (London/Glasgow: British Film Institute/Scottish Film Council, 1990), 13–30; Pam Cook, *Fashioning the Nation: Costume and Identity in British Cinema* (London:

British Film Institute, 1996), 24–7; Cairns Craig, *Out of History: Narrative Paradigms in Scottish and English Culture* (Edinburgh: Polygon, 1996), 82–118; Jeffrey Richards, *Films and British National Identity: From Dickens to* Dad's Army (Manchester: Manchester University Press, 1997), 175–211; Petrie, *Screening Scotland*, 5–8. For broader overviews of the historical evolution of academic discussion of Scottish cinema and the changing status of the *Scotch Reels* thesis within this, see: Jonathan Murray, 'Straw or Wicker? Traditions of Scottish Film Criticism and *The Wicker Man*', in *Constructing* The Wicker Man*: Film and Cultural Studies Perspectives*, eds Jonathan Murray et al. (Dumfries: University of Glasgow Crichton Publications, 2005), 11–36; Jonathan Murray, 'Trainspotter's Delight: Issues and Themes in Scottish Film Criticism', in *A Companion to British and Irish Cinema*, ed. John Hill (Hoboken, NJ: Wiley-Blackwell, 2019), 490–509.

28. Colin McArthur, '*The Maggie*', in *Cinema, Culture, Scotland*, ed. Murray, 121.
29. Colin McArthur, '*Dreams and Dead-Ends: The American Gangster/Crime Film* by Jack Shadoian; *Born to Lose: The Gangster Film in America* by Eugene Rosow', *Cineaste* 9, no. 3 (Spring 1979), 61.
30. See, for example, Mattias Frey and Cecilia Sayad, eds, *Film Criticism in the Digital Age* (Brunswick, NJ: Rutgers University Press, 2015); David Bordwell, *The Rhapsodes: How 1940s Critics Changed American Film Culture* (Chicago: University of Chicago Press, 2016).
31. McArthur, Whisky Galore! *and* The Maggie, 3.
32. For an illustrative example of McArthur's thought on both the professional practice and academic study of film criticism, see Colin McArthur, 'British Film Reviewing, a Complaint', *Screen* 26, no. 1 (1985), 79–85.
33. McArthur would undertake a very similar critical journey regarding his view of *Brigadoon* (Vincente Minnelli, 1954), another cinematic representation of Scotland routinely cited as totemic (albeit so for all the wrong reasons) within many writings associated with or emerging directly from the original *Scotch Reels* project. See Colin McArthur, Brigadoon, Braveheart *and the Scots*, 5.
34. Colin McArthur, 'National Identities', in *Cinema, Culture, Scotland*, ed. Murray, 137.
35. The key text in this regard is Tom Nairn, *The Break-Up of Britain: Crisis and Neo-Nationalism* (London: New Left Books, 1977).
36. McArthur, 'National Identities', 136.
37. See Colin McArthur, '*Braveheart* and the Scottish Aesthetic Dementia', in *Cinema, Culture, Scotland*, ed. Murray, 331–48; McArthur, Brigadoon, Braveheart *and the Scots*.
38. Colin McArthur, 'Tele-history: *The Dragon Has Two Tongues*', in *Cinema, Culture, Scotland*, ed. Murray, 143.
39. See, for example, Patrick Wright, *On Living in an Old Country* (London: Verso, 1985); Robert Hewison, *The Heritage Industry: Britain in a Climate of Decline* (London: Methuen, 1987); John Corner and Sylvia Harvey,

eds, *Enterprise and Heritage: Crosscurrents of National Culture* (London: Routledge, 1991). For a contemporaneous discussion of *The Dragon Has Two Tongues* influenced by McArthur's 1970s work on television, see Aled Jones, 'Making Television History', *Screen* 26, no. 6 (November/December 1985), 65–9.
40. See Colin McArthur, '*Days of Hope*', *Screen* 16, no. 4 (1975), 139–44; McArthur, *Television and History*.
41. Perhaps the most significant exceptions in this regard are: Duncan Petrie, *Contemporary Scottish Fictions: Film, Television and the Novel* (Edinburgh: Edinburgh University Press, 2004); Neil Blain and David Hutchison, eds, *The Media in Scotland* (Edinburgh: Edinburgh University Press, 2008).
42. See: Petrie, *Screening Scotland*; Petrie, *Contemporary Scottish Fictions*; David Martin-Jones, *Scotland: Global Cinema* (Edinburgh: Edinburgh University Press, 2009); Murray, *Discomfort and Joy*; Christopher Meir, *Scottish Cinema: Texts and Contexts* (Manchester: Manchester University Press, 2015); Jonathan Murray, *The New Scottish Cinema* (London: I.B. Tauris, 2015); Bob Nowlan and Zach Finch, eds, *Directory of World Cinema: Scotland* (Bristol: Intellect Press, 2015).
43. For more detail on the respective histories and legacies of *Movie* and *Screen* within British Film Studies and further afield, see John Gibbs, 'Interviews: Ian Cameron, V. F. Perkins, Charles Barr, Alan Lovell', *Movie: A Journal of Film Criticism*, no. 8 (2019), 38–71; Annette Kuhn, '*Screen* and screen theorizing today', *Screen* 50, no. 1 (Spring 2009), 1–12.
44. For subsequent accounts of the Festival's history, see Forsyth Hardy, *Slightly Mad and Full of Dangers: The Story of the Edinburgh Film Festival* (Edinburgh: The Ramsay Head Press, 1992); Matthew Lloyd, *How the Movie Brats Took Over Edinburgh: The Impact of Cinephilia on the Edinburgh International Film Festival, 1968–1980* (St Andrews: St Andrews Film Studies, 2010); Peter Stanfield, 'Notes Toward a History of the Edinburgh International Film Festival, 1969–77', *Film International* 6, no. 4 (2008), 62–71.
45. Caughie, 'New Questions', 13–14.
46. See, for example, Colin McArthur, 'How to spend £80,000 on filmmaking', *Glasgow Herald*, 13 July 1982, 4; McArthur, 'In Praise of a Poor Cinema', in *Cinema, Culture, Scotland*, ed. Murray, 219–28.
47. Caughie, 'New Questions', 19.
48. David McCrone, *Understanding Scotland: The Sociology of a Stateless Nation* (London: Routledge, 1992).
49. McArthur, 'Scottish Culture: A Reply to David McCrone', in *Cinema, Culture, Scotland*, ed. Murray, 211.
50. For a closely related critical discussion, see Michael Gardiner, *Modern Scottish Culture* (Edinburgh: Edinburgh University Press, 2005).
51. McArthur, 'Scottish Culture', 212.
52. Colin McArthur, 'The Scottish Discursive Unconscious', in *Cinema, Culture, Scotland*, ed. Murray, 280. For subsequent critical attempts to apply or

further explore McArthur's theory, see: Jennifer Oates, '*Brigadoon*: Lerner and Loewe's Scotland', *Studies in Musical Theatre* 3, no. 1 (2009), 91–9; Marilyn Reizbaum, 'They Know Where They're Going: Landscape and Place in Scottish Cinema', in *Scottish Cinema Now*, eds Murray et al. (Newcastle: Cambridge Scholars Publishing, 2009), 72–87.
53. Stuart Hood, 'Showing us how to read the signs', *Tribune*, 10 December 1982, 11. For an illustrative sample both of McArthur's film journalism and its consistent importance as a component part of his practice at all stages of his career, see Colin McArthur, 'Sam Peckinpah's West', *Sight and Sound* 36, no. 4 (Autumn 1967), 180–3; Colin McArthur, '*The Switchboard Operator*', *Monthly Film Bulletin* 36, no. 420 (1969), 189–90; McArthur, *Dialectic!*; Colin McArthur, 'Cinema needed to represent truly the Scottish people', *Glasgow Herald*, 11 November 1982, 8; Colin McArthur, 'Masters of the Screen', *New Statesman & Society*, 15 July 1988, 49; Colin McArthur, '*Braveheart*', *Sight and Sound* 5, no. 9 (September 1995), 45; Colin McArthur, 'Out, out damned Scot?', *New Statesman*, 18 October 1999, 43–4.
54. Colin McArthur, 'The Cultural Necessity of a Poor Celtic Cinema', in *Cinema, Culture, Scotland*, ed. Murray, 242.
55. For Irish perspectives on the arguments McArthur outlines in these essays, see: Jerry White, 'The Films of Bob Quinn: Towards an Irish Third Cinema', *Cineaction*, no. 37 (1995), 3–10; Ruth Barton, 'If You Want to Stay Here, You'll Have to Move On', *Film Ireland*, no. 85 (2002), 26–7. For Scottish film institutional perspectives on the arguments, see Allan Shiach, 'Cheap and Cheerless', *Sight and Sound* 3, no. 9 (September 1993), 64; John Brown, 'Poor Scots', *Sight and Sound* 3, no. 10 (October 1993), 64; Eddie Dick, 'Poor Wee Scottish Cinema?', *Scottish Film*, no. 10 (1994), 19–23; see also Duncan Petrie, 'The new Scottish cinema', in *Cinema and Nation*, eds Mette Hjort and Scott MacKenzie (London: Routledge, 2000), 162–6.
56. Colin McArthur, 'Culloden: A Pre-emptive Strike', in *Cinema, Culture, Scotland*, ed. Murray, 262.
57. Ibid., 250.
58. For a longer, not least because intensively visually illustrated, version of this essay's argument, see McArthur, *The* Casablanca *File*; for an evaluation of McArthur's overarching argument across both book and essay, see Suzanne Moore, 'Remember This', *Sight and Sound* 3, no. 5 (May 1993), 42.
59. Colin McArthur, '*Casablanca*: Where Have All the Fascists Gone?', in *Cinema, Culture, Scotland*, ed. Murray, 274.
60. Colin McArthur, 'Chinese Boxes and Russian Dolls: Tracking the Elusive Cinematic City', in *Cinema, Culture, Scotland*, ed. Murray, 290.
61. Ibid., 305.
62. For related comparative critical accounts of historical periods either side of the one McArthur covers within this essay, see: Jonathan Murray, 'Convents or Cowboys? Millennial Scottish and Irish Cinemas and *The Magdalene Sisters*', in *National Cinemas and Beyond: Studies in Irish Film 1*, eds John Hill

and Kevin Rockett (Dublin: Four Courts, 2004), 149–60; Jonathan Murray, 'Sibling rivalry? Contemporary Scottish and Irish cinemas', in *Ireland and Scotland: Culture and Society, 1707–2000*, eds Liam McIlvanney and Ray Ryan (Dublin: Four Courts, 2005), 144–63.
63. Nairn, *The Break-Up of Britain*.
64. Colin McArthur, 'Artists and Philistines: The Irish and Scottish Film Milieux', in *Cinema, Culture, Scotland*, ed. Murray, 328.
65. Ibid.
66. McArthur, '*Braveheart* and the Scottish Aesthetic Dementia'; McArthur, Brigadoon, Braveheart *and the Scots*.
67. McArthur, '*Braveheart* and the Scottish Aesthetic Dementia', 331.
68. For a thought-provoking review of that book, see Michael Coyne, 'Colin McArthur, Brigadoon, Braveheart *and the Scots: Distortions of Scotland in Hollywood Cinema*', *Journal of British Cinema and Television* 1, no. 2 (2004), 312–15; for an extended critical response to McArthur's arguments about *Braveheart* (as originally expressed in his 1995 *Sight and Sound* review of the film), see Tim Edensor, 'Reading *Braveheart*: Representing and Contesting Scottish Identity', *Scottish Affairs* 21, no. 1 (1997), 135–58.
69. Indeed, the work of Jean-Pierre Melville formed the subject of a dedicated chapter within McArthur's 1972 monograph, *Underworld U.S.A.*
70. Colin McArthur, '*Mise-en-scène* Degree Zero', in *Cinema, Culture, Scotland*, ed. Murray, 373.
71. For subsequent uses of and responses to McArthur's work on Melville, see: Tim Palmer, 'Jean-Pierre Melville and 1970s French film style', *Studies in French Cinema* 2, no. 3 (2002), 135–45; Ginette Vincendeau, 'French film noir', in *European film noir*, ed. Andrew Spicer (Manchester: Manchester University Press, 2019), 23–54.
72. McArthur, '*Days of Hope*', 139.
73. Colin McArthur, 'The Critics Who Knew Too Little: Hitchcock and the Absent Class Paradigm', in *Cinema, Culture, Scotland*, ed. Murray, 393.
74. Ibid., 399.
75. For a companion piece to this essay, see Colin McArthur, 'Implementing Cultural Policy: The Case of the BFI Distribution Library', *Cinema Journal* 47, no. 4 (Summer 2008), 147–52; 163 and also the wider dossier of articles on various aspects of the BFI's history published within the same issue of that journal. See also Geoffrey Nowell-Smith, 'The 1970 crisis at the BFI and its aftermath', *Screen* 47, no. 4 (Winter 2006), 453–59.
76. Colin McArthur, 'Two Steps Forward, One Step Back: Cultural Struggle in the British Film Institute', in *Cinema, Culture, Scotland*, ed. Murray, 427.
77. See, for example, Colin McArthur, 'Warning: beware a narrow focus on the wide screen', *The Independent*, 14 August 1997, available at https://www.independent.co.uk/voices/warning-beware-a-narrow-focus-on-the-wide-screen-1245523.html [accessed 8 March 2023].

78. Colin McArthur, 'Transatlantic Scots, Their Interlocutors and the Scottish Discursive Unconscious', in *Cinema, Culture, Scotland*, ed. Murray, 450.
79. Colin McArthur, '*Scotch Myths*, Scottish Film Culture and the Suppression of Ludic Modernism', in *Cinema, Culture, Scotland*, ed. Murray, 469.
80. Colin McArthur, 'Vanished or Banished? Murray Grigor as Absent Scots Auteur', in *Cinema, Culture, Scotland*, ed. Murray, 511.
81. For a methodologically similar counter-reading of McArthur's work and its allegedly symptomatic historical status by one of the critics McArthur discusses within this essay, see David Goldie, 'Don't Take the High Road: Tartanry and Its Critics', in *From Tartan to Tartanry: Scottish History, Culture and Myth*, ed. Ian Brown (Edinburgh: Edinburgh University Press, 2010), 232–45.
82. See, for example, Glyn Davis and Jaap Kooijman, eds. *The Richard Dyer Reader* (London: Bloomsbury, 2023); Oliver Fuke and Nicolas Helm-Grovas, *Art at the Frontier of Film Theory* (2019), more information about which is available at https://www.bbk.ac.uk/research/centres/peltz-gallery/next-exhibition [accessed 9 March 2023].
83. McArthur, *Along the Great Divide*, unpaginated preface.

CHAPTER 1

*Ashes and Diamonds**

Ashes and Diamonds (Andrzej Wajda, 1958) is set in Poland on 7–8 May 1945, the last day of war and the first of peace. This period of transition is one in which, the German occupying forces having been driven out, the Red Army is supervising the setting-up of communist central and local government. The communiques blaring from the public loudspeakers talk of victory, peace and a glorious future, but in ironic counterpoint to this, Poles have begun to slaughter each other. Certain right-wing elements in the resistance, the army and the aristocracy are attempting to undermine and change the orientation of the new communist government. These elements, seeking to make their presence felt, detail two young ex-resistance fighters, Andrzej (Adam Pawlikowski) and Maciek (Zbigniew Cybulski), to kill Szczuka (Waclaw Zastrzezynski), the new secretary of the local Communist Party, and his assistant, Podgorski (Adolf Chronicki). Andrzej and Maciek kill the wrong men and have to remain in the area for another chance. Maciek signs in at the same hotel as Szczuka and becomes involved with Krystyna (Ewa Krzyzewska), a barmaid at the hotel, to such a degree that he changes his mind about killing Szczuka. However, Andrzej convinces him that he should go through with it. Maciek kills Szczuka, but is himself killed while running away from some soldiers whom he encounters while attempting to escape.

The film opens with Andrzej and Maciek waiting to ambush and kill Szczuka. Wajda's handling of the opening sequence underlines the contrasts between peace and war, life and death and past and present which form the mainspring of the film. From the opening image of a church tower with a cross on top, suggesting peace and goodwill, the camera tilts downwards to pick up Andrzej and Maciek lying on a bank and enjoying a beautiful summer day. The singing of birds is loud on the soundtrack and

---

* Originally published in *Screen Education* (Mar/Apr 1966), 28–31.

a child with flowers for the altar comes to ask Andrzej to open the church door for her. At that point Drewnowski (Bogumil Kobiela), secretary to the local communist mayor but also in the pay of the right-wing group, warns them that a jeep is approaching. The series of images of peace, life and growth is shattered when Maciek rolls over to reveal two sub-machine guns. The thunderclap of violence which follows is one of the most harrowing acts in the whole of cinema.

The savagery of the scene in question is introduced by a sudden change of filmic technique. The earlier slow tilts and cuts with little movement within the frame give way to a swift tracking shot in which Maciek, with sub-machine gun poised aloft, runs down an embankment to fire at the oncoming jeep. The swiftness of the tracking and Maciek's movement within the frame combine to give a sense of urgency which is almost tangible. The horror of the violence is closely related to its spectacular nature: the careering jeep, the driver thrown clear of it, that man's feverish attempts to pound open the door of the church for sanctuary and, most of all, his clothing bursting into flame as Maciek's bullets cut through him. It is an ironic comment on the misdirected violence which is tearing Poland apart that the dead men are not Szczuka and Podgorski, but two workers from the local cement factory.

Ashes and Diamonds is a film of ironies and contrasts, not the least of which is that between the old, pre-war aristocratic and the new, post-war communist Poland. The characters who represent both eras are linked symbolically in kinship – Szczuka, for example, is married to the sister of Madame Staniewicz (Halina Kwiatkowska), who is the wife of an army colonel. She has brought up Szczuka's son Marek (Jerzy Jogalla), who is now a right-wing terrorist, and the Major (Jerzy Adamczak), leader of the right-wing group, shelters in her home. Marek and Maciek are presented as being so similar, even in name, that when the latter shoots Szczuka we see it as an act of patricide, a ghastly symbol of civil strife. Wajda underlines this inference when the dying Szczuka staggers forward into his assassin's arms and they embrace briefly before the old man falls. Elsewhere, the old order and the new are comparably linked in a magnificent set piece of almost unbearable sadness in which characters from the left wing join hands with those from the right and all dance into the dawn to the cracked strains of a Chopin polonaise. The import of this striking sequence is somewhat ambivalent. It may mean that this noble nation, torn by civil strife, can look forward only to a future in which the frivolous aristocracy of the past, represented by Madame Staniewicz and her set, and the new, opportunist communist elite, represented by Minister-designate Swiecki (Aleksander Sewruk), will debauch Poland.

Figure 1.1 Maciek, having shot Szczuka, catches his falling body in a 'filial' embrace.

This feeling of hopelessness is reinforced by the dead, glassy-eyed expressions of the dancers.

If there is any element of hope within this sequence, it lies in the fact that the characters dance united into another day while the porter of the Monopole Hotel unfurls the Polish flag. This raises the question of whether the overall statement of the film contains any element of hope. In the 1948 novel by Jerzy Andrzejewski (1909–83) on which the film is based, there is a feeling, even in the most terrible moments of violence and death, that life, symbolised by birds, trees, flowers and grass, is still going on. Similarly, the film begins and ends with terrible acts of violence, but the horrifying death-twitches of Maciek – in which his final foetal position suggests violence and suffering for unborn generations – are relieved by one brief shot of birds in flight. Some critics have suggested that the animals are scavengers hovering over the rubbish dump on which Maciek dies and thereby add to the hopelessness of the scene, but, alternatively, the creatures may instead echo the theme of the affirmation of life present in Andrzejewski's novel.

While all characters in *Ashes and Diamonds* are not presented with equal compassion, none is presented completely without sympathy. Swiecki and his cronies are shown as men on the make and the Staniewicz set is presented as frivolous and reactionary, but in a passive way, foolish rather than dangerous. Slomka (Zbigniew Skowronski), the manager of the Monopole

Hotel, is a lecher and a bootlicker but he is not wholly unkind, and one feels sorry for Drewnowski, the cynical opportunist and passive accomplice to murder, when he is rejected by both sides. Much of the sympathy for Drewnowski derives from the superb playing of Bogumil Kobiela (1931–69), whose portrayal of drunkenness is as convincing as any other on film. However, the film's most sympathetic figures are Szczuka and Maciek. Szczuka is presented as a tired old man who has sacrificed his life to a political idea and lost track of his wife and son in the process. Maciek is presented as a confused boy who has learned violence in the resistance and knows no other way of life. The two characters are shown in thematically parallel scenes in which each talks nostalgically of former times and lost comrades. Maciek's potential as a human being is seen in his boyishness – as when he teases Krystyna by moving the vodka glasses and compares his nose to Andrzej's to see which is straighter – and in the tenderness of his love scenes with her. The virtue of loyalty is his undoing, for with his love for Krystyna he gains some insight into what life should be like. He kills Szczuka out of loyalty to Andrzej, but fails to test this loyalty against a wider framework of moral reference. Asked to kill in the sewers of Warsaw, Maciek obeys blindly: the dark glasses he wears symbolise his moral blindness in the context of the film.

No critique of *Ashes and Diamonds* could wholly do justice to the superb technique which Wajda deploys to highlight relationships and underline the central politico-social statement of the film. With masterly economy he states and restates relationships by means of such technical devices as deep focus photography and editing. At one point Andrzej telephones his superior officer, the Major, who is at the home of Madame Staniewicz, to tell him that the attempt on Szczuka's life has failed. Andrzej is the dominant image in the right foreground of the frame and Maciek stands in its left, slightly in the background. As Andrzej speaks, Szczuka and Podgorski, the men he has tried to kill and is now talking about to the Major, enter the centre of the frame in the far background. When the telephone rings at the other end of the line, that event forms the audience's introduction to the Staniewicz household. A lesser filmmaker would simply have shown a close-up of the telephone ringing, but Wajda's visual accompaniment to that sound is a shot of a painting of Colonel Staniewicz in full uniform standing beside his white horse; the camera then tilts downwards to pick up a maid polishing his sabre. Thus, using simple technical devices, Wajda locates the Staniewicz milieu within the regressive Polish military tradition. At another point, Wajda cuts from the figure of Szczuka to an open window through which tanks can be seen rolling past and martial songs can be heard. The audience, expecting still to be in Szczuka's room, is surprised to see the figure of the Major move into frame and look out the window. The relationship of the two men is perfectly stated in the images of the rumbling tanks and martial songs. After the arrest of Marek and before the disclosure that he is Szczuka's son, Wajda cuts from Marek's interrogation at the police station to Szczuka at the Monopole Hotel, indicating the existence of a relationship which will later be made explicit. Similarly, when Maciek pulls the sheet from the dead men in the church and stands horrified before this reminder of his guilt, Wajda cuts to Szczuka and thereby forewarns us of Szczuka's subsequent death at Maciek's hands. Moreover, the sheet which covers the dead men is white. In this way, Wajda reminds his audience of Maciek's actions earlier in the film when, after he has been shot, Maciek clutches his bleeding stomach through a white sheet and is surrounded by a chorus of others billowing round him.

Wajda's film is dense with such symbols which continually remind the audience of the characters' past or future. The white horse in the painting of Colonel Staniewicz emerges as a symbol of the old, reactionary Poland and, fittingly, a white horse is also seen in the baroque setting of the Monopole Hotel. When Drewnowski has been sacked from his job as secretary to the mayor, he lurches drunkenly to the back door of the hotel, throws it open and reveals the white horse in the yard. This sight is symbolically apt since, newly spurned by communist officialdom, Drewnowski now believes that his future lies with a divided Poland's right-wing elements. The same horse trots into frame during the separate scene in which Maciek leaves Krystyna after outlining to her, besides the accusing figure of the hanging Christ, his desire for a new life free from violence. The horse attempts to eat the flowers Krystyna has given Maciek, an intrusion of reactionary values into their tender relationship. In ways and at moments such as these, Wajda skilfully intimates a sense of underlying unease by incorporating elements of violence within even the film's gentlest moments. As he lays his head in Krystyna's lap, Maciek's hand gropes around the floor for the bullet he has dropped, and as he walks the streets with his arm round her the lovers pass two squads of soldiers, one of which sings a martial song.

The particular quality of Wajda's artistic vision has been described as baroque, romantic, heroic in virtually all the UK press reviews of his films. All of these epithets are in some sense just, but his artistic vision is uniquely that of a filmmaker, in that he sees ideas in visual and dramatic terms. The most effective demonstration of this within *Ashes and Diamonds* is to compare a situation from Andrzejewski's source novel with the corresponding situation in Wajda's film. In the novel, Maciek and Andrzej engage in a long talk about dead comrades within the surroundings of the bar of the Monopole Hotel. Wajda transforms what in the novel is a fairly flat, nostalgic exchange into a series of striking visual images. In the film, Andrzej does not respond to Maciek's nostalgic prompting, so the latter goes to the top of the bar and slides five glasses of vodka down to Andrzej. As he lights three of them, Andrzej raps out the names of three now-dead former comrades. The power of this image is subtle and ambivalent. The flaming glasses, burning like destroyed tanks, suggest death, but they also suggest the eternal flame of remembrance. This is the subtle power which, coupled with its compassion, makes *Ashes and Diamonds* one of the greatest films ever made.

CHAPTER 2

The Roots of the Western[*][†]

Cinema audiences would sense that the description of the Western as 'Le cinéma américain par excellence'[1] is apt, but the quintessentially American qualities of the genre have never been defined in a manner satisfactory to historians, sociologists and film critics. Doubtless it reflects, as sociologists say, American admiration for rugged individualism and yearning for primitive innocence. To say so, however, takes no account of developments within the genre and the degree to which the sub-structure of ideas becomes part of the fabric of one Western while remaining on the level of plot in another. To sort out such complexities is the job of the film critic and the first part of that task, at least, has been competently done, less in the standard work in English, *The Western: From Silents to Cinerama* by Fenin and Everson,[2] than in two French works, 'The Evolution of the Western' by André Bazin (1918–58) and *La grande aventure du western* by Jean-Louis Rieupeyrout (1923–92).[3] However, Bazin is quite perfunctory in the way he relates the Western to American society, suggesting casually that the increased stature of the genre in the period 1937–40 might have been due to increased awareness of national identity in the pre-WWII Roosevelt era. Even Rieupeyrout, having traced the origins of the genre to dime novels, rodeos and Wild West shows, does not deal with the main social ideas in the Western and, more especially, to what degree they have become part of the respective statements made by some films while remaining dormant in others. This essay is an attempt to confront these

---

[*] Originally published in *Cinema* (October 1969), 11–13.
[†] This essay, originally written decades ago, refers to what would nowadays be referred to as 'Native American' as 'Indian'. Being adamantly opposed to the retrospective rewriting of historical texts for ideological reasons, I have left my original usage intact within this republished version of the text. In doing so, I also want to acknowledge the fact that, in using the term 'Indian' when I first wrote this essay, I lived within the dominant discourse in which Native Americans were so problematically designated.

questions. Its method is to take two closely interrelated factors, American responses to the West and American responses to Industrialism, and to relate these to several Western films. In doing so, this essay attempts to define, firstly, how the main social ideas of the Western are implicit within the two factors and, secondly, to indicate illustrative instances where one or other of them seems particularly integral to this or that individual Western film.

The most crucial document in such an investigation is Henry Nash Smith (1906–86)'s *Virgin Land: The American West as Symbol and Myth*,[4] which examines the growth of American attitudes to the West's successive frontiers and to those who peopled these, the complex (and often conflicting) delineations of the West and the westerners in literature, and the impact of the various myths of the West on American life. Nash Smith argues that of the two main attitudes to the West which emerged within American society, by far the most potent was that which saw the West as Garden:

> With each surge of westward movement a new community came into being. These communities devoted themselves not to marching onward but to cultivating the earth. They plowed the virgin land and put in crops, and the great Interior Valley was transformed into a garden: for the imagination, the Garden of the World. The image of this vast and constantly growing agricultural society in the interior of the continent became one of the dominant symbols of nineteenth-century American society – a collective representation, a poetic idea (as [Alexis de] Tocqueville [1805–59] noted in the early 1830s) that defined the promise of American life. The master symbol of the garden embraced a cluster of metaphors expressing fecundity, growth, increase and blissful labor in the earth, all centring about the heroic figure of the idealized frontier farmer armed with that supreme agrarian weapon, the sacred plow.[5]

Nash Smith discerns the image of the garden in the writings of such eighteenth-century Americans as Lewis Evans (*c*.1700–56), Nathaniel Ames (1708–64), Philip Freneau (1752–1832) and Hugh Brackenridge (1748–1816), all most certainly under the influence of Rousseau (1712–78), Montesquieu (1689–1755) and the Physiocrats, and the materials for the agrarian theory underlying the myth of the West as Garden in the post-1750 writings of Benjamin Franklin (1706–90).

The agrarian ideal is also an important aspect of the most influential nineteenth-century statement about the West, Frederick Jackson Turner (1861–1932)'s 1893 essay, 'The Significance of the Frontier in American History'. Turner's main thesis was that 'the existence of an area of free land, its continuous recession, and the advance of American settlement westward explain American development'.[6] The dominant schools of American historical thinking at the time that Turner wrote were those that interpreted

American development in terms of either the slavery issue or the growth of English institutions in the United States. The Turner thesis quickly displaced both those approaches as the basis for all orthodox history teaching about the United States, and was not seriously questioned until the mid-twentieth century. It was clearly therefore influential during the early decades of both the cinema's and the Western genre's development.

Indeed, so strong is the agrarian ideal in the early- and mid-century Western that in any clash between homesteaders and cattlemen – *Shane* (George Stevens, 1953) is a good example – the former are almost invariably presented more sympathetically. Possibly only in *Man Without a Star* (King Vidor, 1955), with its insistence on the harm done to cattle by barbed wire, is the balance redressed. Occasionally, the agrarian ideal becomes even more than a conditioned response in the Western and achieves something close to mystical affirmation. Possibly the earliest such statement is *The Covered Wagon* (James Cruze, 1923). As noted above, Nash Smith speaks of 'the supreme agrarian weapon, the sacred plow'. The latter is a mystical symbol in *The Covered Wagon*. The film's intertitles speak of the Oregon-bound pioneers as 'the men of the plow', and at the work's beginning there are two carefully composed shots in which the plow dominates the frame. In the first of these the pioneers, before setting out, are grouped round a plow and one of them (in the intertitles) speaks of longing to plunge his plow into the rich Oregon soil. In the similarly composed second shot, a group of Indians stand round a plow and one calls it the weapon which will kill the buffalo.

Such an innocently unambiguous paean to the agrarian ideal would be impossible in the contemporary American cinema. Indeed, the last such statement was possibly *The Westerner* (William Wyler, 1940), in which tilling of the soil achieves religious endorsement as the homesteaders kneel and pray before the harvest and the camera composes a hymn to the glories of the maize. The most consistent cinematic statement of the agrarian ideal has been in the work of John Ford (1894–1973), but it has been more an underlying assumption than a major motif celebrated on the screen within Ford's oeuvre. Ford does indeed rejoice in the hay-making images in *Drums Along the Mohawk* (1940), but even here it is clear that his major interest is in the sense of community evolving in an agrarian society, an interest most strikingly obvious in the church dedication sequence of *My Darling Clementine* (1946).

Post-WWII Westerns have been preoccupied with themes other than the agrarian ideal: most notably, the place of the Indian in the West, the ageing gunfighter's problems of adjustment to encroaching modernity, and the examination of contemporary societal obsessions within the pre-existing framework of the genre. Such films have, understandably, been less affirmative than the Westerns of the twenties and thirties, but endorsement of the agrarian ideal has not disappeared nor become wholly nostalgic. The aspirations of Budd Boetticher (1916–2001)'s amiable badmen are towards the small homestead, although the action of his films is remote from any kind of social organisation. Jesse James (Robert Wagner), in *The True Story of Jesse James* (Nicholas Ray, 1957), is retiring to the homestead when he is shot and the scene of Steve Judd (Joel McCrea)'s peaceful death in *Guns in the Afternoon* (Sam Peckinpah, 1962) (also known as *Ride the High Country*) is the bountiful Knudsen homestead from which the only incongruous element, the Calvinist Knudsen (R. G. Armstrong), has been removed.

Of course, American history, and by extension its treatment within the Western, is too complex to admit of any simple and singular set of attitudes to the West and its people. There are several Westerns, such as *The Man from Laramie* (Anthony Mann, 1955), in which the figure of the homesteader does not appear and the narrative and structural conflict is between greater and lesser cattlemen or between cattlemen and sheepmen. It could well be argued that films of this type are similar to homesteader films in that they invariably sympathise with the weaker party, the small cattlemen or sheep-farmers against the cattle baron. Nevertheless, whatever veneration is accorded the agrarian homesteader in the Western, accumulated impressions of the genre place the man on horseback – as cowboy in *Red River* (Howard Hawks, 1948) or as gunfighter in *Shane* – at its dramatic centre. The homesteaders played by Van Heflin (1908–71) in *Shane* and *3.10 to Yuma* (Delmer Daves, 1957) lack heroic dimension (in the traditional terms of the genre) because of their closeness to the soil.

The dominant image of trans-frontier America in the Western might therefore be the West as Garden or the West as Pasture. However, Nash Smith discerns a further image of the West in nineteenth-century literature:

> In the decade following the Civil War the impetus of the westward movement and the implied pledge of the victorious Republican party to develop the West were uncontrollable forces urging the agricultural frontier onward. On the level of the imagination it was therefore necessary that the settlers' battle with drought and dust and wind and grasshoppers should be supported by the westward expansion of the myth of the garden. In order to establish itself in the vast new area of the plains, however, the myth of the garden had to confront and overcome another myth of exactly opposed meaning, although of inferior strength – the myth of the Great American Desert.[7]

The image of the Great American Desert becomes part of William A. Wellman (1896–1975)'s view of the West in *The Ox-Bow Incident* (1943) and *Yellow Sky* (1948) and John Ford's disgruntled older officers swelter out their disciplinary banishment to the desert in *Fort Apache* (1948). But, perhaps the Great American Desert's importance to the Western genre derives from the nineteenth-century view of the arid West as the natural refuge of Indians and, by extension, of all outlaws. The agrarian ideal, with its roots in Rousseau's thought, defined civilisation as evolving from the agricultural life, so the migratory Indians – often compared in nineteenth-century writings to Tartars and Bedouin – were, by reason of their socioeconomic organisation, outside the pale of civilised society and the area in which they moved was regarded as fit only for outlaws. It is as a milieu within which men outside civilised, agrarian society resolve their tensions, both personal and social, that the Western has used the myth of the Great American Desert, as in *Riders of Death Valley* (Ford Beebe and Ray Taylor, 1941), *The Last Wagon* (Delmer Daves, 1956), *The Law and Jake Wade* (John Sturges, 1958) and the Boetticher cycle.

If America's response to the West was therefore complex, its initial response to Industrialism was less so. Men such as Franklin and Thomas Jefferson (1743–1826) hailed the coming of the machine as contemporary evidence of mankind's progress, and while not oblivious to the evils of European factory organisation, they were confident that the New World environment would purify the system. The warnings uttered by Friedrich Schiller (1759–1805), Thomas Carlyle (1795–1881) and, later, Karl Marx (1818–83), on the damage done by technology to human lives, did not go unheard in eighteenth- and nineteenth-century America, but were swamped by the visible evidence of progress, the popular rhetoric of Tench Coxe (1755–1824) and Daniel Webster (1782–1852), and the tributes of Ralph Waldo Emerson (1803–82) and Walt Whitman (1819–92). The aspect of technology which most caught the popular mind, and that was most used by artists as the symbol of progress, was the railroad. But even within ostensible eulogies to the new machines, there were symptomatic signs of misgivings. These were sometimes implied in the imagery used to describe trains, 'dragons of mightier power with iron muscles that never tire, breathing smoke and flame through their blackened lungs, feeding upon wood and water'.[8]

Explicit hatred of the machine, or at least an ambivalent response to it, is characteristic of men of letters. It has taken a particularly poignant form in American literature due to the obvious incompatibility of technology and the agrarian/pastoral ideal. Serious writers – like F. Scott Fitzgerald (1896–1940) in *The Great Gatsby* (1925) – have tried to celebrate the richness of technological progress while retaining the promise of the garden myth, so it is scarcely surprising that the popular cinema has also tried to have it both ways. But the Western, by its very nature, must veer to the side of the agrarian and pastoral ideal that found its main political expression in the ideology of Agrarian Populism. The other side of the coin regarding that discourse's commitment to the land and the archetypal figure of the 'little man' was a suspicion and hatred of big business and, implicitly, Industrialism:

> There are but two sides in the conflict that is being waged in this country today. On the one side are the allied hosts of monopolies, the money power, great trusts and railroad corporations who seek the exactment of laws to benefit them and impoverish the people. On the other are the farmers, laborers, merchants, and all other people who produce wealth and bear the burdens of taxation.[9]

The two principal symbols for this anathema in the Western are the railroad and, less ambiguously, the mining of gold and silver. As in American literature, there are interesting tensions between the optimistic celebration of the railroads in *The Iron Horse* (John Ford, 1924) and, more particularly, *Union Pacific* (Cecil B. DeMille, 1939) and the results that accrue from them. Much is made in both films of the historical importance and epic endeavour of building the railroad – the ceremony of driving home the last rivet, for example – but in the DeMille film particularly, the railroad brings to the West a scabrous rabble of gamblers, prostitutes, land speculators and con men, while the men who actually build the railroad live in squalor and violence along its sides. The railroad subsequently reappeared in the Western at a crucial period of its later development. Since the tendency of genre cinema is to work in cycles, the ripples from *High Noon* (Fred Zinnemann, 1952) were discernible in *3.10 to Yuma* and *Last Train from Gun Hill* (John Sturges, 1959). In all three films the railroad would appear to be a mere plot device to replace the earlier cliché of the stagecoach, but its function goes deeper than this. In all three films the inevitability of the train's leaving or arriving on time is stressed, as though it were quite beyond the influence of local agencies. A stagecoach can be conceived of as being delayed; a train, never. The trains in these films represent the only element within the narrative situation that the main protagonists cannot control. These 1950s railroad Westerns are therefore significant, in that they lead up to the direct confrontation between the Westerner and that figure's technological environment in a handful of revisionist Westerns in the sixties. The image of the railroad has always, however, been a somewhat ambivalent one. This is best summed up in the response of Nicholas Ray (1911–79)'s schizoid version of Jesse James in *The True Story of Jesse James*: as soured homesteader-turned-bandit, he robs trains; as bourgeois businessman, he rides in them. Traditionally in the Western, the visual relationship between train and horseman has involved the chasing, overtaking and boarding of the former by the latter. However, in two more recent Westerns, *The Professionals* (Richard Brooks, 1966) and *The Wild Bunch* (Sam Peckinpah, 1969), that process is reversed: in a race between horsemen and train, the former are left trailing. The triumph of technology is complete.

Elsewhere, mining is a more general symbol in the Western for the evils of Industrialism. 'Where there's gold there's stealin', and where there's stealin', there's killin'', says a character in *The Far Country* (Anthony Mann, 1954), and the mining camp in *Guns in the Afternoon* is, in one of its character's words, 'a sinkhole of depravity' that director Sam Peckinpah (1925–84) deliberately presents in Dantean terms. The mining camp sequence has been the most praised element within this film, critics using words such as 'Expressionist' and 'Surrealist' to define its impact. Peckinpah, however, regards this sequence as wholly realistic, perhaps testifying to the characteristic American revulsion to Industrialism as the destroyer of the agrarian ideal.

The tension inherent in the disparity between the agrarian ideal and the reality of commercial/industrial America was bound to make itself apparent at some stage in the Western's development. It might have manifested itself as an explicit treatment of populist unrest or even of the rigours of the West in Depression-era America, but, as it happened, most modern early-1960s Westerns have been set in contemporary America and the prevailing mood has been one of nostalgia. At least four films of that type incorporate elements of the tension between the old order and the new: *The Misfits* (John Huston, 1961), *Hud* (Martin Ritt, 1963), *Lonely Are the Brave* (David Miller, 1962) and *Guns in the Afternoon*. In neither *Hud* nor *Guns in the Afternoon* is the clash between the agrarian ideal and the real America central: Martin Ritt (1914–90)'s main theme is the necessity of moral choice and Sam Peckinpah's, the question of personal identity. The writing and direction of *The Misfits* are out of alignment; screenwriter Arthur Miller (1915–2005)'s main interest is fairly clearly in the psychology of the characters, especially the girl, but director John Huston (1906–87) seems to have responded to the tension between the old West and the new. Interestingly, the weight of nostalgia in both *The Misfits* and *Lonely Are the Brave* shifted from the figure of the idealised yeoman farmer mentioned by Nash Smith to that of the (cinematically, more acceptable) figure of the itinerant cowboy. Much of the force of *The Misfits* derives from the visual contrasts between, on the one hand, images of traditional figures such as the itinerant cowboy and the mustangs and, on the other, images of the twentieth century such as aeroplanes and automobiles. It is on this visual level that *Lonely Are the Brave* succeeds most strikingly.

Figures 2.1 and 2.2 Agrarianism versus Industrialism. The wagon train divides and the 'holy plow' is discarded.

Lead character Jack Burns (Kirk Douglas) and his horse Whisky could fit into a classical Western, but throughout the film they share the frame with jet planes, helicopters and automobiles until, finally, they are destroyed by an articulated lorry. The film is, however, too heavily symbolic: the articulated lorry contains an arch-symbol of contemporary America, flush toilets, and the driver suffers from a major twentieth-century ailment, dyspepsia.

It seems fitting, however, that the single Western film which most unambiguously endorses the agrarian ideal, *The Covered Wagon*, should contain one of the cinema screen's most graphic attacks on Industrialism. The film's intertitles inform viewers that one of the most formidable hazards facing the character of Wingate (Charles Stanton Ogle), the leader of the wagon train, is greed arising from the California gold strike of 1849. Several pioneers opt to dig gold in California rather than plow land in Oregon. In a visual composition symbolically resonant with the importance and irrevocability of that choice, the wagon train divides, one part going north and the other south, while visible in the foreground lie the discarded plows of those who have forsaken the agrarian ideal. These shots from a silent Western summarise a major split in the American psyche.

Notes

1. Jean-Louis Rieupeyrout, *Le Western, ou, Le cinéma américain par excellence* (Paris: Éditions du Cerf, 1953).
2. George N. Fenin and William K. Everson, *The Western: From Silents to Cinerama* (New York: Bonanza Books, 1962).

3. André Bazin, 'Evolution du Western', in *Cahiers du cinéma*, no. 54 (December 1955); Jean-Louis Rieupeyrout, *La grande aventure du western: du Far West à Hollywood, 1894–1963* (Paris: Éditions du Cerf, 1964).
4. Henry Nash Smith, *Virgin Land: The American West as Symbol and Myth* (Cambridge, MA: Harvard University Press, 1950).
5. Ibid., 138.
6. Frederick Jackson Turner, 'The Significance of the Frontier in American History', https://nationalhumanitiescenter.org/pds/gilded/empire/text1/turner.pdf [accessed 20 July 2022].
7. Nash Smith, *Virgin Land*, 202.
8. Quoted in Leo Marx, *The Machine in The Garden: Technology and the Pastoral Ideal in America* (Oxford: Oxford University Press, 1964), 207.
9. Populist manifesto quoted in Richard Hofstadter, *The Age of Reform: From Bryan to F.D.R.* (London: Jonathan Cape, 1962), 64–5.

CHAPTER 3

*Pickup on South Street**

Richard Hofstadter (1916–70), in his 1964 essay 'The Paranoid Style in American Politics',[1] traces the recurrent fear of conspiracy which dominated the thinking of certain minority political groups in the United States from the Anti-Masonic movement of the 1820s and 1830s to the Black Muslims and White Citizens of the 1960s. That fear has recurred in forms as disparate as Nativism and Anti-Catholicism, certain elements of the Anti-Slavery Movement, Anti-Mormonism, the Manicheanism of particular Greenback and Populist writers, and anxieties regarding a munitions makers' conspiracy during World War I. The early 1950s, the period in which *Pickup on South Street* (Samuel Fuller, 1953) appeared, provided two significant examples of this recurrent American impulse: the hysterical Anti-communism associated with the name of Senator Joseph McCarthy (1908–57), and the (possibly more reasonable) allegations, associated with the name of Senator Estes Kefauver (1903–63), of the existence of a nationwide, Mafia-controlled crime cartel. Both of these fears of the period relate, in different ways, to Samuel Fuller (1912–97) and *Pickup*.

In Dwight Taylor (1903–86)'s original story for Fuller's film, the plot revolves round drug trafficking. The politicisation of that original story material comes with Fuller's adaptation of it, in which the revised plot involves microfilm which communists are trying to smuggle out of the United States. Contemporary British reviewers, ignorant of Fuller's wider work, saw this as the only level of politicisation within *Pickup* and dismissed the film as a McCarthyite tract. And yet, *Pickup* is, politically speaking, perfectly consistent with what we know of Fuller both as artist and man. On one level, the political impetus Fuller gave to *Pickup*'s plot is consistent with his romantic nationalism which, in the climate of the early fifties, could scarcely fail to view communists as the enemies of

---

*Originally published in *Samuel Fuller*, eds Peter Wollen and David Will (Edinburgh: Edinburgh Film Festival '69/Scottish International Review, 1969), 28–31.

America. On another level, the politicisation seeps some way into the fabric of the film so that, as in earlier Fuller films such as *The Steel Helmet* (1951) and *Fixed Bayonets!* (1951), America is seen once more defended by outcasts from American society. In *Pickup*'s case, that defence is provided by the petty criminals of the New York underworld, and the most virulent attacks on communism come from Moe (Thelma Ritter) and Candy (Jean Peters), characters who are no more capable of understanding the ideological debate between communism and capitalism than are Fuller's mercenary soldiers in his earlier war movies. Moe ('Some people peddle apples, lumber, lamb chops. I peddle information') is willing to sell the film's hero, Skip McCoy (Richard Widmark), to the police and to Candy, but not to the communists. That distinction arises not out of any awareness of the nature of communism, but out of an irrational commitment to an American society in which Moe has no stake: 'What do I know about commies? Nuthin'. I know one thing: I just don't like 'em'. If *Pickup* is indeed, as alleged by some, no more than a McCarthyite tract, then Fuller has chosen strange mouthpieces for his message. Skip, an archetypal Fullerian loner, 'shifty as smoke' and 'living in out of the way places', can with justice ask incredulously of the police, 'Are you waving the flag at me?' and dismiss the appeals of the FBI as 'patriotic eyewash'. Throughout

Figure 3.1 Nationalism in the *mise-en-scène*. Skip's final confrontation with Joey shot against a recruiting poster for the US Army.

the film, he stands apart from both American society and the communists in its midst, playing, as another character puts it, both ends against the middle. When Skip finally decides to bring down the communists, it is not out of an abstract conception of loyalty to America, but – similar to the character of Tolly Devlin (Cliff Robertson) in Fuller's later film, *Underworld U.S.A.* (1961) – in pursuit of personal vengeance (in Skip's case, for the beating and shooting of Candy).

Pickup is, therefore, a political film in the sense that it emanates from its author's intense nationalism and connects with the recurrent theme in Fuller's work of the demands of nationality, an authorial preoccupation which attains its purest expression in *Run of the Arrow* (1957). More fundamentally, however, *Pickup* bears the imprint of another facet of Fuller's sensibility and previous professional experience, that of the crime reporter and the writer of pulp novels like *Burn, Baby, Burn!* (1935). For, on a visual level, *Pickup* is a gangster film: the work's explicitly political elements are elaborated almost wholly within its dialogue, a fact which explains why the film could be called in France, *Le Port de la drogue*. The starring presence of Richard Widmark (1914–2008), whose psychotic persona dominates the post-WWII gangster film (*Kiss of Death* [Henry Hathaway, 1947], *The Street with No Name* [William Keighley, 1948], *Night and the City* [Jules Dassin, 1950]), helps to place *Pickup* within the gangster genre, as does the conception of the character of Candy. The 'floozie' look adopted by actor Jean Peters (1926–2000) for her playing of the role places her within the performative tradition of peers Marie Windsor (1919–2000) and Lizabeth Scott (1921–2015) in countless forties and fifties gangster movies and thrillers, although it should also be noted that Fuller has a recurring thematic interest in the figure of the prostitute as an outcast from normal society (see, for example, *House of Bamboo* [1955], *Underworld U.S.A.* and *The Naked Kiss* [1964]).

The milieux within which *Pickup*'s action takes place – urban streets, waterfront shacks, precinct stations and lavish apartments – also place the film solidly within the gangster genre. Moreover, it can also be identified as a fifties gangster movie primarily by the representation of the communist organisation that drives its plot. The real-life allegations of Senator Kefauver and the disclosures of Burton Turkus (1903–82) of the existence of a nationwide murder organisation combined to produce the dominant theme of the fifties gangster movie: the power of 'the syndicate' (see, for example, *The Turning Point* [William Dieterle, 1952], *The Big Heat* [Fritz Lang, 1953], *The Brothers Rico* [Phil Karlson, 1957]). The communist organisation in *Pickup* is conceived in syndical terms, having a chain of command stretching back to 'headquarters', a security wing and a characteristic operational strategy of the 'hit' (very much like the criminal organisation at the heart of a contemporaneous gangster film such as *New York Confidential* [Russell Rouse, 1955]). Thus, the character of Joey (Richard Kiley) is given a pistol with which to kill Skip. The figures in the communist organisation are, with one exception, iconographically indistinguishable from the corresponding figures in other gangster movies: Joey, for example, is conceived and played as a hood. Only the figure of Joey's immediate superior is treated by the film in a way that suggests the latter might be part of a politically committed movement. One suspects that his tweeds and cigarette holder are Fuller's visual shorthand for that character's origins in the bourgeois intelligentsia. In addition, certain key incidents in *Pickup* derive their force partly from their having grown out of the conventions of the gangster film. Among these are the killing of Moe and the chase and capture of Joey. The death of Moe is in some sense a set-piece of the film. Her tired entry to her apartment, the playing of the record 'Ma'm'selle', her discovery of Joey's presence and his fatal shot coinciding with the ending of the record all recall analogous death scenes in other gangster films of the mid-century period, such as *Brute Force* (Jules Dassin, 1947) and *Phantom Lady* (Robert Siodmak, 1944). The subsequent chase and capture of Joey also has resonances with various gangster movies from the thirties to the fifties.

As the gritty authenticity of *Pickup*'s script (full of subcultural colloquialisms such as buzz, cannon, grifter and muffin) indicates, Fuller's prior experience as a crime reporter gives a heightened sense of definition to the film's depiction of its small-time New York underworld setting. The latter is a bleak, but strongly cohesive world aware of its own apartness from mainstream society but also conscious that the bounds between criminality and respectability are precarious. As Skip bitterly asks at one point, 'How did you become a pickpocket? How did you become what you are? Things happen, that's how.' The structuring terms of this world are concretised by Fuller in the image of a launch on the river at midnight bearing Moe's body (by then referred to only as 'number eleven') to a pauper's grave in Potter's Field where New York's impoverished were buried. The connection between the bleak underworld of *Pickup* and the political structure of the contemporary America to which its characters give their unreasoning loyalty is not one that Sam Fuller perceives. Because he fails to make the connection, however, is no good reason for undervaluing the power and personality of his work.

Note

1. Richard Hofstadter, 'The Paranoid Style in American Politics', *Harper's Magazine* (November 1964), https://harpers.org/archive/1964/11/the-paranoid-style-in-american-politics/ [accessed 21 July 2022].

CHAPTER 4

Extract from *Underworld U.S.A.**

Author's note: *Underworld U.S.A.* was written at a moment of transition in British film culture. Auteurism was still dominant, though, if not totally called in question, inflected to take account of other determinations on cinematic meaning, most notably, genre. It is therefore a 'broken-backed' book, the first four chapters written from a genre perspective, the succeeding nine devoted to directors who produced distinguished work in the gangster film and film noir: Fritz Lang (1890–1976), John Huston (1906–87), Jules Dassin (1911–2008), Robert Siodmak (1900–73), Elia Kazan (1909–2003), Nicholas Ray (1911–79), Samuel Fuller (1912–97), Don Siegel (1912–91) and Jean-Pierre Melville (1917–73). The extract reproduced here consists of the book's first two chapters, the first arguing for the centrality of genre in Hollywood cinema, the second describing the recurrent overlapping iconography of the gangster film and film noir, plus a summary of the two succeeding genre chapters.

Chapter 1: Genre

In order to reach the reality of American cinema one must first confront the notion of Hollywood. If an audience, even (or perhaps especially) an educated and sophisticated one, were asked what Hollywood means to them, their replies would very likely include the words 'glossy', 'glamorous' and 'escapist'. They would probably offer the polar opposition that Hollywood movies equal 'entertainment', European movies equal 'art'; with the addition that discussion of Hollywood should therefore be the province of the sociologist rather than the film critic. This view is held most widely in the United States itself. It is still difficult to find an educated American who

---

*Originally published in Colin McArthur, *Underworld U.S.A.* (London: Secker & Warburg in association with the British Film Institute, 1972): chapters 1 ('Genre') and 2 ('Iconography'), 11–33.

takes Hollywood movies seriously. American undergraduates rush to see the latest Godard or Bergman, but if they go to see American movies at all it is usually in the spirit of viewing a lovable piece of kitsch, like the young Vassar girl in a recent novel who went to the Museum of Modern Art to take in a Bogart retrospective.

The reasons for this kind of educated response to Hollywood are not hard to trace. The most articulate literary writing about Hollywood, the fiction of F. Scott Fitzgerald (1896–1940), Nathanael West (1903–40), Norman Mailer (1923–2007), Gavin Lambert (1924–2005) and others, stresses the grotesque philistinism of the place, and there is a constant lament about how the art of the writer/intellectual is prostituted. Other cinema movements within America have reacted against what they believed to be the problematic form or content of Hollywood movies: thus the low-budget 'realism' movement of the mid-fifties, based on New York television personnel, believed itself to be handling social issues in a more significant way than Hollywood, and the New York Underground Cinema imagined that, by rejecting the technical excellence of Hollywood and confronting experience unmediated by narrative, it was producing more personal and vital cinema.

This rejection of Hollywood and its values, though understandable and even laudable, has led to a wider rejection of American movies which is neither. When one discusses literature or painting and, up to a point, drama, one can place the artist, their work and their audience in a very direct relationship. However, no such direct relationship with their work and their audience exists for the director working in Hollywood. There are at work several modifiers of meaning, factors which complicate these relationships. The most obvious are the star system and the subject of this book, genre – both, of course, partly explicable in terms of the overpoweringly commercial basis of Hollywood production. From the beginning, with very few exceptions, American movies have been controlled by businessmen. Lewis Jacobs (1904–97), in his *The Rise of the American Film*,[1] tells how movies were used by penny arcade owners and vaudeville managers to turn a quick buck. When the growing film companies from 1910 onwards forsook the banks of the Hudson River and moved to California, it was less in search of a particular quality of light than to escape the murderous patent wars back East; and the added incentive of California was less the quality of its landscapes than the proximity of the Mexican border over which bootleg cameras could be lugged. The subsequent development of Hollywood production may have changed in form, but not in its fundamental nature. If a company produces movies that no one goes to see, it will go out of business; if a producer is consistently associated with films that do not show a profit, they will cease to produce; and if a director habitually turns out commercial flops, they will cease to get assignments. The great mavericks of Hollywood, like Erich von Stroheim (1885–1957), were artists who could not work within their budgets and bring their movies in on time.

These are all facts about Hollywood, but one should beware of making hasty deductions from them. Working from these facts, Anglo-American critics of the American Cinema have traditionally evolved two critical syllogisms as follows:

(i) All commodities produced for a mass market are shoddy and inferior.
Hollywood movies are produced for a mass market.
Hollywood movies are shoddy and inferior.

This could be called the F. R. Leavis (1895–1978) syllogism.

(ii) All great works of art are concerned with man in his social context.
Few Hollywood films are concerned with man in his social context.
Few Hollywood films are great works of art.

This could be called the Paul Rotha (1907–84) syllogism.

The first has led to neglect of and contempt for American movies among the notoriously over-literary Anglo-American intelligentsia; the second, to such weird critical judgements as, for example, that the John Ford (1894–1973) of *The Grapes of Wrath* (1940) is to be preferred to the John Ford of *My Darling Clementine* (1946) or, more generally, to the elevation of directors making overtly 'social' films at the expense of those working within more stylised, and often commercially orientated, genres.

Needless to say, the relationship between Hollywood's commercial structure and the meaning of Hollywood movies is more complex than either of these syllogisms suggests, and the influence of commerce has not been wholly or, arguably, even mainly for the worse. Simply as one example of the wealth of industry making possible the realisation of artistic vision, consider the area of technical development – deep focus photography, advances in sound recording, colour, widescreen and so on. Also, while a reasonable critic must condemn the notorious Hollywood practice of producers interfering with directors' work, he or she must also accept the possibility that particular such acts of interference may have benefited particular films. Nicholas Ray (1911–79) has described the front office interference with his plans for the making of *The True Story of Jesse James* (1957):

> My preliminary production scheme was to do the whole film on stage as a legend, with people coming in and out of areas of light, making it a period study of the

behaviour of young people and the effects of war on the behaviour of young people, but doing it as if it were all a ballad. It meant never doing anything for realism, putting the realistic, but not the real, within a stylistic form to make a unified piece of work. This idea was accepted at one time during the preparation and again they got afraid of it and so the result was, I think, a very ordinary film.[2]

If we look at the film as it now exists, particularly the magnificent Northfields raid sequence, we are compelled, in this instance, to thank God for the front office.

The emergence of genres in the American cinema belongs, up to a point, to the commercial nature of Hollywood production. There is a sense in which all Hollywood movies are genre pieces, there being in Hollywood a built-in impulse to reproduce a successful formula. Thus it is possible to classify Hollywood movies as sentimental comedies, social exposés, location-based thrillers, and so on. But there are two genres which have been especially important in the development of Hollywood: the Western and the gangster film/thriller. Each of these genres has developed its own recurrent iconography and its own themes against which individual artists have counterpointed their personal vision: sometimes following closely the contours of the genres (as in the case of John Ford or Sam Peckinpah [1925–84]); sometimes finding in the non-naturalistic qualities of the genres a way of making their baroque sensibilities seem 'normal', or at least accessible, to a wide audience (as in the case of Anthony Mann [1906–67] or Arthur Penn [1922–2010]).[3]

Also, the Western and the gangster film/thriller have a special relationship with American society. Both deal with critical phases of American history. It could be said that these genres represent America talking to itself about, in the case of the Western, its agrarian past and, in the case of the gangster film/thriller, its urban technological present. To amplify and illustrate this contention, there is a fairly consistent attitude in Westerns to, for example, homesteading and the tillers of the soil. Where these elements are present they are almost invariably depicted sympathetically (for example, *Shane* [George Stevens, 1953], the films of John Ford), and sometimes with overtones of divine ordination (*The Covered Wagon* [James Cruze, 1923], *The Westerner* [William Wyler, 1940]). This recurring cinematic depiction is a modern restatement of a traditional attitude to the West and to the figure of the frontier farmer in American culture. That longer-term attitude's growth is traced historically by Henry Nash Smith (1906–86) in his *Virgin Land: The American West as Symbol and Myth*:

> With each surge of westward movement a new community came into being. These communities devoted themselves not to marching onward but to cultivating the

earth. They plowed the virgin land and put in crops, and the great Interior Valley was transformed into a garden: for the imagination, the Garden of the World. The image of this vast and constantly growing agricultural society in the interior of the continent became one of the dominant symbols of nineteenth-century American Society – a collective representation, a poetic idea (as [Alexis de] Tocqueville [1805–59] noted in the early 1830s) that defined the promise of American life. The master symbol of the garden embraced a cluster of metaphors expressing fecundity, growth, increase and blissful labor in the earth, all centring about the heroic figure of the idealized frontier farmer with that supreme agrarian weapon, the sacred plow.[4]

Conversely, the Western incorporates sometimes ambivalent attitudes to industrialisation, the latter usually manifested as gold or silver mining and the railroad. Thus Ford and Cecil B. DeMille (1881–1959), in *The Iron Horse* (1924) and *Union Pacific* (1939) respectively, explicitly celebrate the building of the transcontinental railways, but each also shows that the railroad brought to the West widespread sexual exploitation, gambling, land speculation and assorted con men. The principal symbolic vehicle for the expression of this anti-industrialist attitude in the Western is the mining industry, as in *Bend of the River* (Anthony Mann, 1952), *The Far Country* (Anthony Mann, 1954) and *Guns in the Afternoon/Ride the High Country* (Sam Peckinpah, 1962). These are only two of the many, sometimes contradictory, attitudes found in the Western, all of which may also of course accommodate responses to contemporary events. Thus, *Broken Arrow* (Delmer Daves, 1950) was among the first of many Westerns to make reference to racial prejudice, while *High Noon* (Fred Zinnemann, 1952) and *Johnny Guitar* (Nicholas Ray, 1954) were both, in some senses, reactions to McCarthyism.

Despite these important considerations, there has been a curious reluctance among film critics to confront the notion of genre, the most usual reason offered being that genres are collections of neutral conventions which the director either animates or not, according to their qualities as author. If they are Nicholas Ray, they transcend the genre; if they are Edward Dmytryk (1908–99), they make just another Western. This widespread film critical position seems at odds with the importance placed on genre by both filmmakers and audiences. Several filmmakers, for instance, Howard Hawks (1896–1977) and Richard Brooks (1912–92), have taken conscious decisions to make Westerns at particular points in their careers, and there is good evidence for believing that, on the whole, the most coherent and personal work of John Ford, Anthony Mann and Budd Boetticher (1916–2001) has been within that genre. In addition, audiences seem to know exactly what they are getting from a Western or a gangster film/ thriller even if they do not make this knowledge articulate. The responses of filmmakers and audiences to the genres seem to offer a good prima facie case for believing that the latter are animating rather than neutral phenomena, that they carry intrinsic charges of meaning independent of whatever is brought to them by particular directors. To make a guess, it would seem possible that while the filmmaker may respond primarily to the genres' archetypal qualities, the audience responds to their historical qualities. To put it another way, our response to the Western may be coloured by our response to the epic quality of the historical opening of the West. Similarly, our response to the gangster film may be coloured by our response to the violence and excitement of American cities and urban cultures, especially in the Prohibition period. Moreover, and to complete the circle, our ideas about both these historical phenomena are very likely primarily derived from the cinema itself.

Resistance to the idea of the usefulness of genre as an element in critical debate has come from two quarters. The first of these comprises critics practising an exclusive application of the auteur theory who are deflected from paying particular attention to genre by the internal logic of their critical method. If the purpose of that method is to reveal the structuring hand of a director (or possibly, writer) in a number of films, then other considerations naturally recede. The second quarter of resistance to the idea of the animating power of genre is, more surprisingly, among some of those critics seeking a general semiology of the cinema. More surprisingly, because genre, with its obvious analogies with a sign system, an agreed code between filmmaker and audience, would seem on the face of it a fruitful starting point for investigating the semiology of the cinema.[5]

The best writers on the Western, André Bazin (1918–58), Jean Wagner, Jean-Louis Rieupeyrout (1923–92), and Alan Lovell (1935–2021), all discuss the genre primarily in thematic terms. Thus Lovell, talking about the elements that came together to make the classical Western, proposes the plot elements of hero, heroine, villain and action in early Westerns, the epic theme as in *The Covered Wagon*, and the revenge theme as in *My Darling Clementine*.[6] Similarly, the best writing about the gangster film/thriller, like Raymond Borde (1920–2004) and Etienne Chaumeton's *Panorama du film noir américain*,[7] is expressed primarily in thematic terms. Even if Borde and Chaumeton's book displays great sensitivity to the formal properties of the genre, as does Robert Warshow (1917–55)'s 1948 essay, 'The Gangster as Tragic Hero',[8] ultimately such critical writing is more concerned with sociocultural than formal questions. Is there an alternative method of writing about genre which will bring it more clearly within the province of semiology? The answer to this question would seem to lie in the nature of the relationship between genre and audience; in the fact that the audience seems to assimilate genre cinema with ease and has a set of expectations in relation to it.

A possible historical analogy for that suggestive phenomenon is the relationship between medieval and renaissance humankind and their art. It seems certain that an ordinary French person of the thirteenth century could 'read' Chartres Cathedral and that a seventeenth-century Venetian could 'read' Francesco Maffei (1605–60)'s painting of Judith of Bethulia which, according to Erwin Panofsky (1892–1968), we would be liable to confuse with contemporary paintings of Salome.[9] In both cases, a contemporary audience understood the iconography of the works in question, the meaning within their respective cultures of the objects depicted. It would seem appropriate to recall Christian Metz (1931–93)'s suggestion that one of the two valid areas of study for the semiologist of the cinema is iconography, and to point out that the example he quotes from Rieupeyrout, good and bad cowboys in white and black shirts respectively, is drawn from the conventions of genre cinema. To describe its iconography specifically would seem, therefore, the most convenient starting place for a comprehensive critical description of the gangster film/thriller.

Chapter 2: Iconography

In *Little Caesar* (Mervyn LeRoy, 1931), a police lieutenant and two of his men visit a nightclub run by gangsters. All three wear large hats and heavy coats, are grim and sardonic, and stand in triangular formation, the lieutenant at the front, his two men flanking him in the rear. The audience knows immediately what to expect of these characters by their physical attributes, dress and deportment. The audience knows, too, by the physical disposition of the figures, which is dominant and which is subordinate. In *The Harder They Fall* (Mark Robson, 1956), a racketeer and two of his men go to a rendezvous in downtown New York. As they wait for the door of the building to be opened, they take up the same formation as the figures in the earlier film, giving the same information to the audience by the same means. The fact that the trio of characters are, in the first case, policemen and, in the second case, racketeers is an interesting ambiguity which will be examined later. In *On the Waterfront* (Elia Kazan, 1954) and in *Tony Rome* (Gordon Douglas, 1967), there are carefully mounted scenes in which the central figure is walking down a dark and deserted street and an automobile drives swiftly towards him. In each case, the audience, drawing on accumulated experiences of the gangster/thriller genre, realises that the moving vehicle will be used as a murder weapon against the hero. Both these paired examples indicate the continuity, over several decades, of patterns of visual imagery, of recurrent objects, and of figures in dynamic compositional relationships within the gangster/thriller genre. These repeated patterns might be called the iconography of the genre in question, for they distinguish and differentiate it visually from other types of film and are the means whereby primary definitions of it are made.

The gangster/thriller genre's recurrent patterns of iconographic imagery can be usefully divided into three categories: those surrounding the physical presence, attributes and dress of actors and the characters they play; those emanating from the milieux within which characters operate; and those connected with the technology at characters' disposal. Among Hollywood leading men, Edward G. Robinson (1893–1973) and James Cagney (1899–1986) dominate the gangster films of the thirties; Humphrey Bogart (1899–1957) the thrillers and Richard Widmark (1914–2008) the gangster films of the forties; and, though not in such a clear-cut way, Richard Conte (1910–75) has a good claim to this role in the gangster films of the fifties. In addition to these major icons of the genre, there are other players of the second rank, such as George Bancroft (1882–1956), Barton Maclane (1902–69), Joe Sawyer (1906–82), Paul Kelly (1899–1956), Bob Steele (1907–88), Ted de Corsia (1903–73), Charles McGraw (1914–80) and Jack Lambert (1920–2002), to name only a few, who have become inseparably associated with the gangster film/thriller. The American cinema has traditionally achieved its effects with the utmost directness, and never more so than in the casting of gangster films and thrillers. Actors such as Cagney, Robinson and Bogart seem to gather within themselves the qualities of the genres they appear in, so that the violence, suffering and angst of the films is restated in their faces, physical presence, movement and speech. By the curious alchemy of the cinema, each successive appearance in a given genre further solidifies the actor's screen persona until they no longer play a role but assimilate it to the collective entity made up of their own body, personality and past screen roles. For instance, the beat-up face, tired eyes and rasping voice by which we identify Humphrey Bogart are, in part, selections we have made from his roles as Sam Spade, Philip Marlowe and others.

It is not only the actors playing the roles who recur within the gangster/thriller genre, but also the roles themselves. This and other genres become definable as such by repetition until fairly fixed conventions are established. This phenomenon is particularly apparent in the spectrum of recurring characters within the gangster film/thriller: racketeers with brains who rise to the top, gangsters without who remain as hoods, gangsters' women, stool pigeons, cops and bent cops, crusading district attorneys and legal mouthpieces for the Mob, private eyes and heroes forced by circumstances to be such, nightclub owners and their sadistic strong-arm men, and the countless secondary figures on this dark world's fringes, newspapermen, pool room and gymnasium owners, newsvendors and so on. The audience's interpretation of these roles may develop over time. For instance, James Cagney's particular physical dynamism was widely interpreted, in the gangster films of the thirties, as necessary ruthlessness in getting to the top, but in the gangster films he made in the post-WWII period, especially *White Heat* (Raoul Walsh, 1949) and *Kiss Tomorrow Goodbye* (Gordon Douglas, 1950), this same quality was instead widely interpreted as psychotic. A touchstone of normality is usually present within the genre's ensemble of recurring roles, often centred on the figure of the gangster's mother. This is apparent in the earliest examples of the genre such as *Little Caesar*, *The Public Enemy* (William A. Wellman, 1931) and *Scarface* (Howard Hawks, 1932); it is present vestigially in *The Big Heat* (Fritz Lang, 1953) and achieves almost pristine restatement in *The Brothers Rico* (Phil Karlson, 1957).

But the stock figures in the gangster film/thriller proclaim themselves not only by their physical attributes and roles but also by their dress. The peculiar squareness of their hatted and coated figures is an extension of their physical presence, a visual shorthand for their violent potential. Clothes have always been important in the gangster film, not only as carriers of iconographic meaning but also as objects which mark the gangster's increasing status within any given gangster film/thriller's narrative arc. Scenes in tailors' shops are frequent occurrences (*The Public Enemy*, *Al Capone* [Richard Wilson, 1959]), and both the characters of Rico (Edward G. Robinson) in *Little Caesar* and Tony Camonte (Paul Muni) in *Scarface* invite comments on their clothes ('How do you like it? Expensive, huh?'). Alec Styles (Richard Widmark), the gangleader in *The Street with No Name* (William Keighley, 1948), tells a new member of his gang, 'Buy yourself a closetful of clothes: I like my boys to look sharp.' Characters in *Baby Face Nelson* (Don Siegel, 1957) ('Get rid of that gunny-sack') and *Murder, Inc.* (Burt Balaban and Stuart Rosenberg, 1960) ('Burn that tent you're wearing') are instructed to change their clothes as a mark of their rising status, and Tolly Devlin (Cliff Robertson)'s ascent within the syndicate in *Underworld U.S.A.* (Samuel Fuller, 1961) is marked by syndicate boss Gela (Paul Dubov)'s comments on his clothes.

Following *The Naked City* (Jules Dassin, 1948), several gangster films and thrillers appeared carrying the word 'city' in their titles: *Dark City* (William Dieterle, 1950), *Cry of the City* (Robert Siodmak, 1948), *City Across the River* (Maxwell Shane, 1948), *While the City Sleeps* (Fritz Lang,

1956), *The Sleeping City* (George Sherman, 1950), *The Captive City* (Robert Wise, 1952), and so on. Alongside these came other films featuring the word 'street' in their titles: *The Street with No Name*, *Race Street* (Edwin L. Marin, 1948), *Side Street* (Anthony Mann, 1950), *Down Three Dark Streets* (Arnold Laven, 1954), *The Naked Street* (Maxwell Shane, 1955), not to mention *Where the Sidewalk Ends* (Otto Preminger, 1950) and *The Asphalt Jungle* (John Huston, 1950). This development simply made explicit what had always been an important element of the gangster film/thriller, the urban milieu.[10] As Robert Warshow wrote in 1948:

> The gangster is the man of the city, with the city's language and knowledge, with its queer and dishonest skills and its terrible daring, carrying his life in his hands like a placard, like a club [. . .] for the gangster there is only the city; he must inhabit it in order to personify it: not the real city, but that dangerous and sad city of the imagination which is so much more important, which is the modern world.[11]

Thus the city milieu serves both as a background for the activities of the gangster and the hero of the thriller and as a kind of Expressionist extension of the violence and brutality of their world. The sub-milieux of the gangster film/thriller are, in fact, recurrent selections from real city locales: dark streets, dingy rooming houses and office blocks, bars, nightclubs, penthouse apartments, precinct stations and, especially in the thriller, luxurious mansions. These sub-milieux, charged with the tension of the violence and mystery enacted within them, are most often seen at night, lit by feeble street lights or more garish neon, such as the Cook's Tours sign, 'The World is Yours', in *Scarface*, or the flickering signs which cast threatening shadows and half-disclose mysterious visitors in the offices of Sam Spade (*The Maltese Falcon* [John Huston, 1941]) and Philip Marlowe (*Murder, My Sweet/Farewell, My Lovely* [Edward Dmytryk, 1944]). Fritz Lang, in his German film *Metropolis* (1927), created a huge city embodying his Expressionist fantasies. When he subsequently came to America, he had no need to recreate that fantastical city: it already existed.

Being modern men of the city, the gangster and the hero of the thriller have at their disposal its complex technology, in particular, the firearms, automobiles and telephones which are recurrent images of the gangster/thriller genre. It is fitting that the Western hero, moving balletically through his archaic world, should bear graceful weapons such as the Winchester rifle and the Colt pistol. The weaponry of the gangster film/thriller is much more squat and ugly: the Police 38 Special Revolver, which forms the title image of *Kiss of Death* (Henry Hathaway, 1947) and the opening image of *The Big Heat*; the Luger; the sawn-off shotgun; the submachine gun which becomes an object of veneration in *Scarface* and *Machine-Gun Kelly* (Roger Corman, 1958). Andrew Sinclair (1935–2013), in his book *Prohibition: The Era of Excess*, describes the role of the automobile in the Prohibition/repeal debate:

> The armour-plated cars with windows of bullet-proof glass, the murders implicit in Hymie Weiss [1898–1926]'s phrase 'to take for a ride', the sedans of tommy-gunners spraying the streets of gangland, all created a satanic mythology of the automobile which bid fair to rival the demonism of the saloon. The car was an instrument of death in the hands of the crook and drunk, and prohibition was held to have spawned both of them.[12]

The automobile is a major icon in the gangster film/thriller. It has a twofold function in the gangster film. Firstly, it is the means whereby the protagonist carries out his 'work' (Tom [James Cagney] in *The Public Enemy*, awaiting orders from Nails Nathan [Leslie Fenton], stands beside his car like a member of the crew of a Panzer about to go into action). Secondly, it becomes, like the gangster's changing clothes, a visible token of his success. Eventually, however, the automobile also becomes the symbol of his unbridled aggressiveness, and it therefore seems perfectly logical that cars should be used regularly as a lethal instrument in both thrillers and gangster films (see *The Dark Corner* [Henry Hathaway, 1946], *Underworld U.S.A.*, *The Moving Target/Harper* [Jack Smight, 1966] and others).[13] So powerful a symbol of the gangster's presence has the automobile become that characters may respond with fear to the presence of an automobile without seeing the men within it (see *Kiss of Death*, *The Garment Jungle* [Vincent Sherman, 1957], *Assignment to Kill* [Sheldon Reynolds, 1968] and others). The telephone has also, on occasion, been used as a murder weapon in the gangster film/thriller and this, too, seems logical. The physical environment, an Expressionist representation of the violent potential in the genres, becomes the instrument of violence. More often, however, telephones are used to intimidate the weak, as in the threatening calls to Mrs Renata (Gia Scala) in *The Garment Jungle* and to Mrs Bannion (Jocelyn Brando) in *The Big Heat*.

It is, of course, an artificial exercise to discuss the gangster/thriller genre's individual iconographic elements in isolation when, in practice, they exist in dynamic relationship with each other within the fabric of particular films. Now and then, several iconographical elements combine in singular purity and there are found the sequences most characteristic of the genre. For instance, the opening sequence of *The Harder They Fall*, showing several figures (Bogart, racketeers and others) entering cars and hurtling through the empty New York streets to an early-morning rendezvous, evokes brilliantly the ugliness of the urban milieu and the ruthlessness of the racketeers before disclosing the squalid operation they are embarked upon. Similarly, the sequence in *Little Caesar* when Tony (William Collier Jr.), the gang's driver, is shot down on the steps of the church by Rico from a speeding car, brings dynamically together several of the genre's key iconographical elements. The same elements are interestingly used in the French gangster film *Le deuxième souffle* (Jean-Pierre Melville, 1966), in which the trademark of the central character is to shoot his victims inside a car which he himself drives. Perhaps the iconography of the gangster film is presented most strikingly (and, incidentally, the genre's non-realistic quality most clearly exemplified) in the characteristic montage sequences of thirties gangster films. In such sequences, the outbreak of gang war is chronicled and, at these points, the films prise themselves free from their inhibiting narrative structures and present the pure imagery of aggression: speeding cars, screaming tyres, figures blasting each other with revolvers and submachine guns. A freeze-frame from such a sequence would look like a Pop Art poster representation of the essence of the gangster film.

Figure 4.1 Recurrent trope of the genre: the gangster lies dead in the street in *Odds Against Tomorrow*.

But to define the gangster film/thriller solely by its iconography is to suggest that the genre is static and unchanging – that the gangster film of the thirties is indistinguishable from that of the fifties, or the forties thriller from its counterpart of the sixties. In fact, both thrillers and gangster films, especially the latter, are in constant flux, adding a new thematic dimension here, a new moral emphasis there.

Author's note: The third chapter of *Underworld U.S.A.*, headed 'Development', traverses the successive phases of the gangster film/thriller, beginning with films like *Little Caesar*, *The Public Enemy* and *Scarface*, within which the characteristic themes like Prohibition and 'look' (speeding cars, bullets ripping into shop fronts and, as the book says, 'perhaps the most rigid convention – the gangster lying dead in the street'[14]) are already in evidence. The genre's second phase came about largely on account of pressure from bodies such as the Production Code Administration (the American film industry's self-censorship mechanism) and the Catholic Legion of Decency, both constituted in 1934. Denunciatory prologues were added to the classic films of the genre's first phase and when the second phase emerged with '*G' Men* (William Keighley, 1935), the genre's central figures were no longer gangsters but government agents, though often played by the same actors (for example, James Cagney) who previously played gangsters in the first phase. As the book suggests, these second-phase films were 'iconographically indistinguishable'[15] from those of the first phase. The next discernible phase of the genre arrived in the late 1930s with *Angels with Dirty Faces* (Michael Curtiz, 1938), which, with its inclusion of juvenile street gangs like the Dead End Kids and the effect of social deprivation on them, implicitly posed a social theory of crime. It is this third phase that introduced the trope of the gangster being contrasted with a childhood friend who has grown up to be a 'respectable' figure such as a priest, lawyer or policeman, thereby contradicting the implicit social theory of crime.

While the gangster film did not disappear in the transition to the 1940s, it is overshadowed by the emergence of the film noir with such films as *The Maltese Falcon* which:

> [connected with] the tradition going back to *Little Caesar* in two ways. Iconographically it is closely linked to the gangster film: the action is played out in urban milieux of dark streets, seedy office blocks and luxury apartments; the technological icons [. . .] are evident; and the human icons [Humphrey Bogart, Barton McLane and Ward Bond (1903–60) in the case of *The Maltese Falcon*] are, in dress and deportment, conventional figures of the gangster movie.[16]

What distinguishes the film noir (apart from the central figure being, typically, a private investigator) are 'its sense of human isolation and awareness of evil',[17] the enigma posed about the motivations of the film noir woman and the form's ritualised and refined violence.

The gangster film returned in the post-WWII period in two forms. One dealt with semi-rural bank robbers like John Dillinger (1903–34) who (unlike the central figures in earlier phases who were predominantly southern European and Catholic) were of northern European Protestant stock. The other came to be known as the 'semi-documentary' or 'location thriller' and was characterised by non-studio settings, 'real-life' stories, the deployment of new technologies of crime detection and an authoritative voiceover commentary on the action. Many examples of this form had, as a background to the titles, an official dossier indicating that the story had come 'from the files of'. The semi-documentary is indissolubly linked with Louis de Rochemont (1899–1978), the co-creator of the documentary series, *The March of Time* (1935–51), who brought many of the techniques of that series to the new fictional form. From the 1940s into the 1950s there were several brief sub-cycles of films bearing the marks of both the gangster film and the film noir: several heist movies (*Criss Cross* [Robert Siodmak, 1949], *The Asphalt Jungle*, *The Killing* [Stanley Kubrick, 1956]); the brief return of James Cagney to gangster roles (*White Heat*, *Kiss Tomorrow Goodbye*); and a short cycle based on the pulp novels of Mickey Spillane (1918–2006) (*I, the Jury* [Harry Essex, 1953], *Kiss Me Deadly* [Robert Aldrich, 1955]). However, the film that marks the thematic watershed between the 1940s and the 1950s is *Murder, Inc.* As the book indicates:

> It bears many of the marks of the semi-documentary – based on actual events, location photography, emphasis on the mechanics of investigation, large numbers of unknown players – but it also sounds for the first time the dominant note of the fifties gangster film, the existence of a nation-wide crime organisation.[18]

Many of the most distinguished examples of the gangster/thriller genre partake of this theme (*The Big Heat*, *Underworld U.S.A.*). At the same time, Hollywood seemed to have become aware that it had a genre heritage when it embarked upon an extended cycle of 'retro' gangster movies, many of them biopics of notorious inter-war criminals (*Machine-Gun Kelly*, *Al Capone*, *The Rise and Fall of Legs Diamond* [Budd Boetticher, 1960]). Somewhat later, the film noir received a similar treatment, but instead of setting the films in the past (that would come much later with *Chinatown* [Roman Polanski, 1974]) they were produced in colour and, instead of being set primarily in the city, were often set in locales such as Florida. As the book puts it:

All these films are aware that they are working within the forties thriller/film noir tradition and that is their principal failing: the sour elements and the sexual aberrance are handled extremely heavily (*Gunn* [Blake Edwards, 1967] excepted). The audience is no longer allowed to deduce from the hero's physical presence that he is world-weary, cynical, hard-bitten and poor; it must see him remove last night's coffee grounds from the wastepaper basket (*The Moving Target/Harper*) or earn a few dollars by acting as correspondent in a divorce case (*P.J./New Face in Hell* [John Guillermin, 1968]).[19]

The book's fourth chapter, entitled 'Background', attempts to explain how the gangster movie/thriller came to be as it was by the time of the book's publication, not by aesthetic analysis or by exploring the internal dynamics of the Hollywood industry, but by reference to developments within the wider American society. Thus, the centrality of Italian names in gangster movies is explained not in terms of Italian predisposition to criminality, but by the patterns of late-nineteenth- and early-twentieth-century immigration into America whereby earlier waves took over certain social and institutional sectors as did, for example, the Irish in relation to urban politics. To quote the sociologist Daniel Bell (1919–2011), crime, for Italian immigrants, offered 'a queer ladder of social mobility'.[20] The patterns of crime in the gangster movie followed closely the contours of crime in the wider society. The repeal of the Volstead Act in 1933, for example, ended Prohibition both off and on the screen. Denied income from the supply of illegal liquor, criminals sought other sources of money such as labour racketeering (*Racket Busters* [Lloyd Bacon, 1938]) in the late 1930s and control of the racing wire and the numbers racket (*Force of Evil* [Abraham Polonsky, 1948]) in the 1940s. The 'G' Man-type movies of the mid-1930s were greatly enhanced by the founding in 1935 of the Federal Bureau of Investigation and the gift of its founder director, J. Edgar Hoover (1895–1972), for public relations. Also, the emergence of socially conscious gangster movies such as *Dead End* (William Wyler, 1937) in the late 1930s may have been connected to the political left turn of American society at the time and even the development of the discipline of sociology, most notably, through figures such as Robert Park (1864–1944) and Jane Addams (1860–1935) at the University of Chicago.

More generally still, some critics have attempted to relate the gangster movie to the fundamental values of American society. Robert Warshow suggests that, 'the gangster is the "no" to the great American "yes" which is stamped so big over our official culture and yet has so little to do with the way we really feel about our lives'.[21] One cannot, however, make such one-to-one connections between the film noir and American society. Noir's emergence may relate to the reverse side of the same coin that generated more socially conscious attitudes in the 1930s: the sense of unease caused by the Wall Street Crash of 1929 and the Great Depression that followed it, the rise of Fascism in Europe, and the consequent overall sense that what appeared to be the solid ground of the 1920s was now moving underfoot. As the book puts it:

> It seems reasonable to suggest that this uncertainty is paralleled in the general mood of malaise, the loneliness and angst and the lack of clarity about the characters' motives in the [noir] thriller. It seems reasonable, too, to suggest that the noir thriller's continuance into the post-war period was stimulated by the uncertainty of the Cold War, that [the genre's] misogyny was connected with the heightened desirability and concomitant suspicion of women back home experienced by men at war, and that its obvious cruelty was related to a society to whom the horrors of Auschwitz and Hiroshima and other atrocities of the Second World War had just been revealed. Where *Angels with Dirty Faces* represents a statement of general concern about the social origins of crime, *The Dark Corner* is a cry of loneliness and despair in a sick world.[22]

However, what has become clear via the research of other scholars since the book was written is how misleading it may be to make generalisations about certain cinematic genres directly affecting the 'mood' of a culture at any given point in time. With regard to the 1940s film noir, for example, although individual examples of the form performed quite well at the box office, in terms of overall commercial performance noir was surpassed by other genres such as musicals, sentimental comedies, biblical epics and Disney animation films. The top box office films for each year from 1945 to 1950 were: *The Bells of St Mary's* (Leo McCarey, 1945); *Song of the South* (Wilfred Jackson, 1946); *Miracle on 34th Street* (George Seaton, 1947); *The Snake Pit* (Anatole Litvak, 1948); *Samson and Delilah* (Cecil B. DeMille, 1949); *Cinderella* (Clyde Geronimi, Wilfred Jackson, Hamilton Luske, 1950).[23] *The Snake Pit* is the only one of these works that could be remotely bracketed with the film noir and it belongs more with those films of the time that explored problems in contemporary American society, in this case the operation of mental institutions. That said, as my essay on *Crossfire* (Edward Dmytryk, 1947) reproduced elsewhere in the present volume demonstrates, if a particular set of stylistic tropes are in the air at any given historical moment, almost any genre of the period in question may deploy those tropes: for instance, *Pursued* (Raoul Walsh, 1947) has often been called a noir Western on account of its deploying characteristic tropes of the film noir such as the flashback structure and the Freudian theme.

As already mentioned in the discussion above of *Murder, Inc.* and the syndicate cycle that emanated from it, the central factor in American

EXTRACT FROM *UNDERWORLD U.S.A.* 65

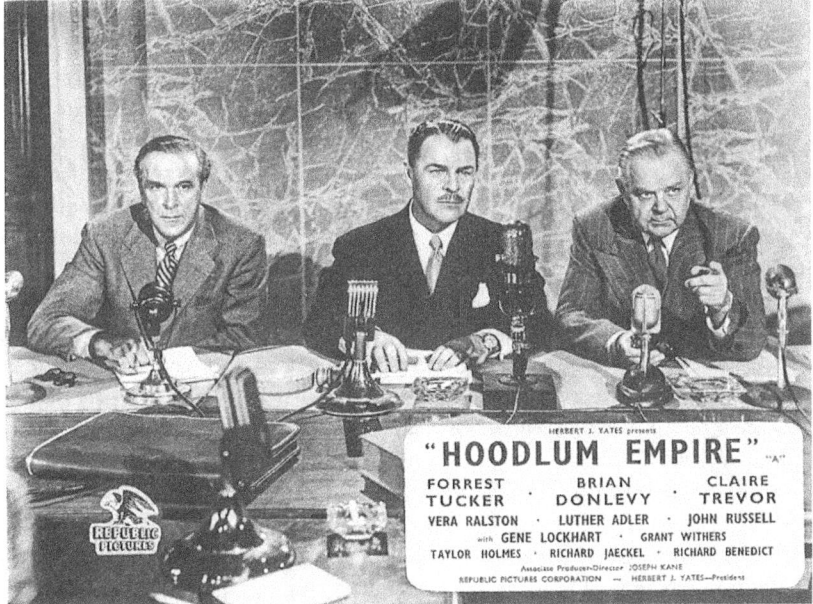

Figure 4.2 The influence of the Kefauver Committee on the gangster film: *Hoodlum Empire*; the character of Senator Stephens (centre) in the 'Kefauver' role.

society which impinged on the gangster movie in the 1950s and into the 1960s was the 1951 Senate Committee to Investigate Organized Crime in Interstate Commerce (often referred to as the Kefauver committee after its chairman, Senator Estes Kefauver [1903–63]), subsequent to which American crime in the cinema was increasingly depicted as being analogous to the operations of large business corporations. This cycle may possibly have had an effect on influential and popular later American screen works such as *The Godfather* trilogy (Francis Ford Coppola, 1972; 1974; 1990), *Goodfellas* (Martin Scorsese, 1990) and *The Sopranos* (Various, 1999–2007).

Notes

1. Lewis Jacobs, *The Rise of the American Film: A Critical History* (New York: Harcourt, Brace and Company, 1939).
2. Adriano Apra, Barry Boys, Ian Cameron, Jose Luis Guarner, Paul Mayersberg and Victor F. Perkins, 'An Interview with Nicholas Ray', *Movie*, no. 9 (1963), 21.
3. It is not only on the level of the individual director that genre acts as a catalyst between artist and audience, but also on the level of avant-garde ideas. For

example, the American cinema has absorbed elements of both Expressionism and Surrealism, habitually embedding both in genre movies. It is interesting, for instance, to compare *Un Chien Andalou* (Luis Buñuel, 1928) and *Fear in the Night* (Maxwell Shane, 1947). The first would, very likely, be unwatchable for, and largely incomprehensible to, a popular audience; the second was made in Hollywood and played with moderate success in commercial cinemas in the United States and Britain. Yet to a very great extent they both carry precisely similar imagery (razors, sharp-pointed objects) and are about the same things (dreams, relationships between fathers and sons). Also, when Buñuel had the grandfather in *Diary of a Chambermaid* (1964) call all the servant girls by the same name, this was hailed as an original directorial strategy indicating the quality of the old man's social and sexual relationships. However, no critic recalled that the device had been used to precisely the same effect in a modest little forties Hollywood thriller, *Nocturne* (Edwin L. Marin, 1946).

4. Henry Nash Smith, *Virgin Land: The American West as Symbol and Myth* (Cambridge, MA: Harvard University Press, 1950), 138.
5. In the British context the critics associated with the journal *Movie* (1962–2000) represented the former constituency; the publication of Peter Wollen (1938–2019)'s *Signs and Meaning in the Cinema* (London: Secker & Warburg in association with the British Film Institute, 1969) heralded the emergence of the latter.
6. Alan Lovell, *The Western* (London: Society for Education in Film and Television, n.d.).
7. Raymond Borde and Etienne Chaumeton, *Panorama du film noir américain, 1941–1953* (Paris: Éditions de Minuit, 1955).
8. Robert Warshow, 'The Gangster as Tragic Hero', in *The Gangster Film Reader*, eds Alain Silver and James Ursini (Pompton Plains, NJ: Limelight Editions, 2007), 11–16.
9. Erwin Panofsky, *Studies in Iconology: Humanistic Themes in the Art of the Renaissance* (New York: Harper and Row, 1965), 12–13.
10. There is within the gangster film a sub-genre beginning with *Dillinger* (Max Nosseck, 1945) and culminating in *Bonnie and Clyde* (Arthur Penn, 1967), in which the action does not take place in the city, but in the small towns of the rural Midwest. Even within the gangster films of the thirties ('*G' Men* [William Keighley, 1935], for instance), the conventions allowed the city milieu to be forsaken for a final shoot-up at the gangsters' mountain hideout. Thrillers of the 1960s and early 1970s have tended to move from the city to more exotic locales such as Florida and the Californian coast.
11. Warshow, 'The Gangster as Tragic Hero', 13.
12. Andrew Sinclair, *Prohibition: The Era of Excess* (Boston, MA: Little, Brown, and Co., 1962), 318.
13. The menace of the automobile is not, of course, confined to the gangster film and thriller. Cars are used as blunt instruments in, for example, the black comedy, *It's a Mad, Mad, Mad, Mad World* (Stanley Kramer, 1963).

14. Colin McArthur, *Underworld U.S.A.* (London: Secker & Warburg in association with the British Film Institute, 1972), 35.
15. Ibid., 38.
16. Ibid., 41.
17. Ibid., 41.
18. Ibid., 53.
19. Ibid., 56.
20. Daniel Bell, 'Crime, a Queer Ladder of Social Mobility', in *Racial and Ethnic Relations: Selected Readings*, ed. Bernard E. Segal (New York: Crowell, 1966), 177–83.
21. Robert Warshow, 'Movie Chronicle: The Westerner', in *Film Theory and Criticism: Introductory Readings*, eds Gerald Mast and Marshall Cohen (New York and London: Oxford University Press, 1974), 402.
22. McArthur, *Underworld U.S.A.*, 67.
23. Mike Chopra-Gant, *Hollywood Genres and Postwar America: Masculinity, Family and Nation in Popular Films and Film Noir* (London and New York: I.B. Tauris, 2006), 18.

CHAPTER 5

Politicising Scottish Film Culture*

The original brief I was given for this piece was: 'four thousand words on the possibility of political cinema in Scotland'. Having been landed in London by the backwash of that inexorable wave of history which, in earlier generations, beached our compatriots on the shores of Canada and New Zealand, I feel it would be presumptuous to attempt to fulfil that particular brief. It is best engaged with by the film workers who earn their bread in Scotland.

However, since I too am a film worker – as bureaucrat with the British Film Institute and as journalist with *Tribune* – my reflections on a closely related question might have some relevance, especially at this particular historical conjuncture when Scotland could be on the verge of radical political-cum-economic change.

The question is: How might Scottish film culture be politicised?

That question in its turn needs re-posing, for it is evident that Scottish film culture – or, more accurately, its discrete sections – has been highly politicised in the past. The problem has been the nature of the politics in question. Take Scottish filmmaking as example. On one hand, Scottish film workers have presented a picture of individualist effort which would gladden the heart of Margaret Thatcher (1925–2013) and which, theoretically at any rate, should have produced a great variety of films of very diverse aesthetic and, therefore, political tendencies. On the other, however, these same film workers were forced to compete with each other for limited funds disbursed by a few key Scottish institutions of patronage, the powerful voices of which, historically, have been extremely reactionary. Small wonder, then, that Scottish films critical of established aesthetic forms, cultural attitudes and political arrangements have been the exception rather than the rule.

---

* Originally published in *New Edinburgh Review* 34, no. 2 (1976), 8–10.

It was no accident that, at its Film Bang held in Glasgow last January,[1] the Scottish filmmaking community should have concentrated on this predicament above all else as the particular cross it has had to bear. It is to be hoped that the momentum towards democratic organisation generated at Film Bang can be sustained and the strength flowing from it used to readjust that inheritance.

However, important as the issue of organising filmmakers is (with its hoped-for pressure on the institutions of patronage), it is part only of the problem of politicising (that is, radicalising) Scottish film culture.

Note, it is film culture we are talking about, not just filmmaking. The problem must be posed holistically, that is, Scottish film culture has got to be grasped in its totality: its filmmakers, to be sure; its institutions (Films of Scotland, the Scottish Film Council, the Edinburgh International Film Festival, the Scottish branch of the Association of Cinematograph, Television and Allied Technicians [ACTT]); BBC Scotland and Scottish Television (STV), both with regard to the extent to which those television broadcasters use indigenous product and the terms in which they use and comment upon it; the Scottish film society movement and Regional Film Theatres; the courses in film in Scottish universities, colleges and schools; the critical commentary on film in the Scottish press and in journals such as this. All of these groups, mechanisms, institutions and impulses taken together constitute Scottish film culture. The whole must be analysed, interrogated and acted upon in a coordinated way.

Historical comparisons might be illuminating. Many of what have come to be regarded as key moments in film history have been associated with actual or potential radical social and political change: Russia in the decade or so after 1917; Germany in the Weimar period; Britain in the thirties; Italy in the forties; and France in the late fifties and early sixties.

If Scotland is on the verge of such change then it is proper that its film workers should study these historical parallels and apply what can be applied to the specificity of the Scottish situation in the light of the particular tasks history will require of them.

But, such study would reveal elements un-characteristic of Scottish film culture as it is presently constituted. Bearing in mind that I do not have access to the Scottish scene on a day-to-day basis and may therefore have a very partial view, I am struck by its fragmentation (the same is true, of course, of the British film scene, but that's another story). Small though the Scottish filmmaking community is – about sixteen production companies and sixty workers – it does not seem to have any discernible relationship or regular dialogue with the other components of Scottish film culture, or – with one or two notable exceptions – they with each other.

Figures like Sergei Eisenstein (1898–1948), Vsevolod Pudovkin (1893–1953) and Dziga Vertov (1896–1954) in post-revolutionary Russia ranged over aspects of film culture: film theory; film criticism; film production; film exhibition; film teaching. John Grierson (1898–1972), Paul Rotha (1907–84) and others in thirties Britain, while differing markedly from the Russians in principles and practice, showed something approaching the same wide range of interests and application. So too did, for example, Cesare Zavattini (1902–89) and others in post-WWII Italy, and Jean-Luc Godard (1930–2022) and others in fifties and sixties France.

The example is clear for Scottish film workers. Filmmakers, already on the way to organisation for economic reasons, must engage with the aesthetic-cum-political dimensions of their collectivism. Polemics and manifestoes must be issued, reactionary institutions and aesthetic forms proscribed. Scottish critics, teachers and exhibitors must accept that they have a special obligation to enter into dialogue with Scottish filmmakers regarding the important task of writing the history of the Scottish cinema, drawing the map of the present situation and posing new directions. The latter consideration is particularly crucial at this moment of history, for there will be no lack of corrupt and mystification-inducing images of the Scottish experience being produced by those having the greatest degree of ideological control of the media in Scotland. These images require to be exposed and alternative models constructed.

Concretely, this implies a great deal of attention being paid by Scottish film workers to the ideological analysis of specifically Scottish films and television programmes and the production of alternatives which, in themselves, offer a conscious critique of the dominant aesthetic forms and social/political/cultural assumptions encountered within the films and programmes thus analysed. Public or quasi-public mechanisms through which this work might be progressed already exist in the Edinburgh International Film Festival; the Scottish Regional Film Theatres in Glasgow, Edinburgh, Stirling, Kirkcaldy and Inverness; and the Scottish film society movement.

It is in the historic nature of the British filmic and televisual experience that the notion of politicisation is automatically associated with realist and naturalist aesthetic forms. There are many reasons for this: a too-ready acceptance of the binary opposition, Art versus Entertainment; a profound suspicion of Hollywood as 'dream factory' and, in consequence, of highly stylised aesthetic forms; the widespread belief (which needs investigation) that the most self-consciously political of British filmmakers (for example, Grierson and the thirties documentarians; the Free Cinema people of the fifties; Ken Loach and Tony Garnett [1936–2020]) have been exclusively concerned with realist and/or naturalist forms; and, most centrally of all, the pernicious belief that the world is comprehensible simply by looking at it (film and television are often spoken of as 'windows on the world') rather than by the application of a conceptual structure.

When I call for the politicisation of Scottish film culture, I emphatically do not hope for the widespread production and valorisation of the kind of documentary work we see on our television screens week after week. On the contrary, an important dimension of politicising aesthetics will be to challenge the innate conservatism of such realist/naturalist forms. Much of the theoretical ground work for this has already been done, most notably by the Edinburgh International Film Festival in its Douglas Sirk (1897–1987) and Bertolt Brecht (1898–1956) events, and by the journal of film theory, *Screen*.[2] The Scottish film community must take greater account of this theoretical work than has seemed thus far to be the case. At Film Bang, a prominent Scottish filmmaker spoke contemptuously from the platform to the effect that he had no wish to be involved in making 'Italian horror films'. This hostility to highly stylised forms – quite widespread in certain areas of British, and therefore Scottish, film culture – as being incompatible with contemporary political and social relevance needs to be reviewed and was, indeed, effectively countered in the Douglas Sirk season at Edinburgh and in the accompanying booklet.

The politicising of Scottish film culture implies film workers posing a relationship between the filmic aspects of their lives and the political aspects of their lives. This is, of course, expressed centrally in their collective organisation, but also in their practices as filmmakers, teachers and critics. In this latter respect, the notion of ideology is key.

Jean-Louis Comolli (1941–2022) and Paul Narboni, writing in *Cahiers du cinéma* (October/November 1969),[3] suggest that ideology – crudely speaking, that which is regarded as obvious and natural in any given society in any given historical epoch – may be discussed in relation to the cinema in seven ways. I have tried, where I am able, to exemplify these ways by reference to specifically Scottish films or television programmes:

(a) Those films or programmes which are imbued through and through with the dominant ideologies of Scotland and Scottishness, for example, *The White Heather Club* (BBC Scotland, 1958–68), *Sutherland's Law* (BBC Scotland, 1973–76), *Songs of Scotland* (BBC Scotland, 1973–79), *John Macnab* (BBC Scotland, 1976).

(b) Those films or programmes which attack the dominant ideologies on two levels, that of subject matter and that of the way in which 'reality'

is depicted, for example, *The Cheviot, the Stag and the Black, Black Oil* (John Mackenzie, 1974).
(c) Those films or programmes which are not directly political but which become so through the way they are filmed.
(d) Those films or programmes which have an explicit political content but which do not effectively criticise the ideological system in which they are embedded because they unquestioningly adopt its language and imagery, for example, *Willie Rough* (BBC Scotland, 1976), certain episodes of *The View from Daniel Pike* (BBC Scotland, 1971–73).
(e) Those films or programmes which seem at first sight to belong firmly within dominant ideologies, but which turn out to do so only in an ambiguous manner; these films or programmes throw up obstacles in the way of the ideologies, causing them to swerve and get off course, causing the films to crack apart at the seams, for example, *The Caledonian Account* (Brian Crumlish, 1976)
(f) Films of the *cinéma vérité* type which suffer from the illusion that, having got rid of dramaturgy, construction, emphasis on formal beauty, and so on, reality will yield itself up; for example, any piece of community video you care to name.
(g) Concrete films, that is, those films which give an active role to the plastic material of film and by so doing challenge that aspect of the dominant ideology which is concerned to render invisible the fact that process and work are involved in filmmaking.

Such a framework is useful for all film workers (makers, critics and teachers) in that it offers ideology as the key link between politics and aesthetics and poses problems about what film workers' own collective and individual interventions and practices should be. Clearly category (b) is the most progressive and it is in this category that, to my knowledge, the most forceful filmic interventions into the current political conjuncture in Scotland have occurred. However, the nature of the existing control structure of the media in Scotland renders it least likely that films in this category will be produced except as odd exceptions. Category (e), therefore, becomes potentially of very great practical political importance. The *Cahiers* writers suggest that the process of dismantling dominant ideology from within which occurs in films of this category is largely not by the conscious wish of the filmmakers involved, but rather a by-product of their integrity and clarity as artists. While this point must be taken, it is possible also to conceive of filmmakers quite consciously wishing to undermine dominant cinematic forms and also, therefore, the dominant ideologies within which they are working. For example, *The Caledonian*

Account – the Scottish example I cited of this category – substantially and consciously undermines the dreary travelogue of the Scottish Highlands which constituted its generic origin.

But having begun to talk to each other – and the preceding section on ideology offers a framework within which dialogue might take place – the various groups of Scottish film workers must also talk to other groups (or at least, the progressive elements within them) outside the film community. The traditional intellectual isolation of the British film community is legendary. British film theory over the past decade has benefited enormously from dialogue with other disciplines, most notably, linguistics, anthropology and sociology. My hunch would be that in the light of its emergent tasks, Scottish film culture will need particularly to make relationships with radical Scottish historians, sociologists and students of Scottish culture.

There is every likelihood that, in the next decade, Scotland will once more be a separate nation. A radicalised Scottish film culture could make an important contribution to defining the terms in which this is so.

Notes

1. Film Bang, held on 22–23 January 1976, was the first coming together of the (then) dozen or so independent Scottish film production companies, plus two key invitees from London, Colin Young (1927–2021), Director of the National Film and Television School, and Alan Sapper (1931–2006), General Secretary of the Association of Cinematograph, Television and Allied Technicians (ACTT), the union of film and television technicians. Among the issues discussed were the low volume of work in Scotland, the concentration of patronage in Films of Scotland (1954–82), the (non-) role of the Scottish Film Council (1934–97) in indigenous film production, the allocation of contracts to non-Scottish companies, the absence of indigenous feature film production and the lack of interest of BBC Scotland and Scottish Television (STV) in the indigenous filmmaking sector. For a fuller account of the event see Colin McArthur, 'Building a Scottish Film Culture' (1976), in Colin McArthur, *Dialectic! Left Film Criticism from* Tribune (London: Key Texts, 1982), 64–5.
2. The Sirk (1972) and Brecht (1975) events were part of an EIFF programme sustained under successive Festival Directors Murray Grigor, Lynda Myles and Jim Hickey, which ran from 1969 until the 1980s. The characteristic event format was a retrospective of the designated subject's films, a series of related seminars and a book of supporting essays. The programme began with a relatively orthodox auteurist retrospective of the films of Sam Fuller (1912–97), a strategy which did not disappear but which, subsequently, ran alongside later theme-based events and publications such as *Edinburgh '76 Magazine:*

Psychoanalysis/Cinema/Avant-Garde and *Edinburgh '77 Magazine: History/ Production/Memory*. The Sirk and Brecht events explored politicised cinema by way of two different strategies, the Sirk event seeking to reveal the tensions and fractures in American society within the apparently orthodox films of its subject, and the Brecht event by examining the oppositional aesthetics of films thought to be inspired by Brechtian principles.

3. Jean-Louis Comolli and Jean Narboni, 'Cinema/Ideology/Criticism', in *Screen Reader 1: Cinema/Ideology/Politics*, ed. John Ellis (London: Society for Education in Film and Television, 1977), 12–35.

CHAPTER 6

Crossfire and the Anglo-American Critical Tradition*

The standard works of film history and criticism in English (that is, those books whereby the cinema has been most usually represented on British and American library shelves) all, in one way or another, put Hollywood down.[1] They do so from one or other of two premises: that Hollywood is a factory and you don't get art out of factories; or that Hollywood movies are escapist and fail to confront real situations. But, so a closely associated overarching argument runs, Hollywood from time to time redeems itself by producing the odd work which, like a European art movie, is formally perfect (such as *Citizen Kane* [Orson Welles, 1941]), or which, more importantly in the Anglo-American critical tradition, is socially conscious. One movie is cited so often in this latter context that it becomes the touchstone of the socially conscious Hollywood film. That movie is *Crossfire* (Edward Dmytryk, 1947). Thus, Paul Rotha (1907–84) argues,

> To produce a good fiction film today is often a matter of luck, or the stern insistence of a director having the guts and faith to stick by his intentions. When I see a *Crossfire* [. . .] I give thanks to someone, somewhere who has broken through the defences.

and he concludes that, 'Despite all the opportunities of post-war human experience, Britain has yet to make a film that will measure up to the contemporary significance of a *Crossfire*', a film 'which dealt with the dynamite theme of antisemitism with more honesty and fearlessness than any other Hollywood film'.[2] Similarly, Arthur Knight (1916–91) proposes that:

> concern for the values of democracy was projected into the years immediately following the war in a series of films notable not only for their liberal sentiments but for their intelligent and courageous appraisal of the problems of the post-war world [. . .] anti-Semitism was openly and thoughtfully discussed in *Crossfire*.[3]

---

*Originally published in *Film Form* 1, no. 2 (1977), 23–32.

What is striking about the way the Anglo-American critical tradition describes *Crossfire* is, firstly, that the film's meaning is assumed to be unproblematic and transparent (that is, the film is unambiguously about a social problem, antisemitism); and, secondly, that the film's otherness, its difference from the normal run of Hollywood movies of the period, is insisted upon. This essay challenges both these assertions.

It is true that, unlike most murder-themed Hollywood films of the time, the killer's motive in *Crossfire* is racial hatred, and it is also true that the film contains a key scene in which a police captain delivers a homily against religious and racial prejudice. The realisation of the scenes depicting such attitudes takes up a very small proportion of *Crossfire*'s running time, but their implied centrality dominates the standard account of the film offered by Anglo-American critics. The problem which these critics evade is whether the remainder of the film (for example, the investigative structure of its narrative, its use of flashbacks, its lighting scheme and associated tonal mood, the playing, conception and realisation of other central narrative incidents) in fact endorses or in some sense cuts across, or even defuses, an explicitly social reading.

The argument concerning *Crossfire*'s otherness, the extent to which it represents a radical departure from other Hollywood films being produced at about the same time, cannot be sustained by the evidence. *Crossfire* is first and foremost a *film policier* with the attendant structure and much of the iconography of that form.[4] A crime is committed and an investigation begun by a police captain. The action passes through the *policier*'s recurrent milieux (a luxury apartment, a seedy rooming house, bars and clip joints, a precinct station). The narrative outcome is archetypal: the killer is shot down in the street. The fact that many of the film's protagonists are returned military servicemen in uniform has perhaps induced Anglo-American critics to see *Crossfire* as being apart from the main currents of Hollywood genre cinema of the period, but the motif of returned servicemen is, in fact, not unusual in other Hollywood crime movies of the time (see, for example, *The Blue Dahlia* [George Marshall, 1946], *Dead Reckoning* [John Cromwell, 1947], *Cry Danger* [Robert Parrish, 1951]).

Crossfire is also, pre-eminently, a film noir and it is this fact which throws most doubt on the social reading offered by many Anglo-American critics.[5] The film noir is definable partly in thematic and partly in stylistic terms, but what seems incontestable is that the meanings spoken by the genre are less social, relating to the problems (such as antisemitism) of a particular society, and more metaphysical, having to do with angst and loneliness as essential elements of the human condition. The latter

Figure 6.1 The opening image of *Crossfire*: an anti-Semite murders a Jew. Film noir or 'social problem' film?

are substantially the meanings spoken by *Crossfire*. In such a reading, the killing of a Jewish character becomes less a correctable aberration within American society than a characteristic symptom of the dark and monstrous world constructed by film noir. As such, that murder functions primarily as a pessimistic metaphor of the human condition.

There is ample evidence that *Crossfire* functions not (as many within the Anglo-American critical tradition would have it) as an optimistic analysis and proposed correction of a social problem, but as a bleak and pessimistic film noir. The opening image of the film, for example, is of two grotesque shadows wrestling viciously on a wall, caught in the glare of a low-slung, or perhaps overturned, lamp – a peculiar opening image for a film ostensibly analysing a social problem, but one perfectly consistent with the film noir of the time. Acts of violence are presented in a similar way in, for example, *The Set-Up* (Robert Wise, 1949) and *Phantom Lady* (Robert Siodmak, 1944) and arguably have their origin in German Expressionist films of the twenties such as *Nosferatu* (F. W. Murnau, 1922), films which could scarcely be claimed to constitute a realist and socially conscious cinematic tradition.[6] The opening image of *Crossfire* accurately reflects the overall mood and look of the subsequent film. There are no more than three daylight scenes thereafter, the rest being shrouded in a darkness that, as befits a film noir, is broken only by harsh shafts of light in which the protagonists are trapped like frightened rabbits in a car's headlights (see especially the scene in which the killer murders his erstwhile friend).

Structurally, *Crossfire* is quite complex; untypically so, one would have thought, of a film ostensibly concerned with a specific social problem. The flashback and its closely associated form, the dream sequence, are dominant strategies of the film noir, allowing an anguished raking over of time and memory. The flashback is central to *Crossfire*, sometimes in stylistically grotesque (as in Mitchell [George Cooper]'s retelling of his drunken experience in Samuels [Sam Levene]'s flat) and sometimes even untrue forms (as in the killer's account of what happened in the victim's apartment). In each case, however, such sequences confirm the anti-realist aesthetic and metaphysical meaning of *Crossfire* as opposed to the realist aesthetic and social meaning widely asserted within the Anglo-American critical tradition.

Many Anglo-American critics reading the film lay great stress on the scene in which the police captain describes how his grandfather was murdered just for being an Irishman and a Catholic and how much prejudice poisons society.[7] Such readings reflect that critical school's characteristic privileging of analysis of scripted dialogue over that of visual image and composition. However, if *Crossfire* is read as a film noir, then that particular scene recedes, becoming stylistically aberrant and thematically insignificant. Correspondingly, other exchanges of dialogue – which have no significance in a social reading – seem central to the meaning of the film. Two such conversations are (a) those between the characters of Mitchell and Samuels when they first meet in a bar, and (b) between Mitchell and the man he meets in a girl's apartment:

(a)
Samuels: It's a funny thing, isn't it?
Mitchell: Very funny.
Samuels: It's worse at night, isn't it? I think maybe it's suddenly not having a lot of enemies to hate anymore. Maybe it's because for four years we've been focusing our mind on (*picks up a peanut*) one little peanut. The 'win the war' peanut. Get it over: eat that peanut (*eats the peanut*). All at once, no peanut. Now we start looking at each other again. We don't know what we're supposed to do, we don't know what's supposed to happen. We're too used to fighting, but we just don't know what to fight. You can feel the tension in the air. A whole lot of fight and hate that doesn't know where to go. A guy like you maybe starts hating himself. Well, maybe one of these days we'll learn to shift gears; maybe we'll stop hating and start liking things again.

(b)
Mitchell: Who are you?
Man: I'm a man who's waiting for her. That alright?
Mitchell: Yeah.
Man: Coffee?
Mitchell: Sure.
Man: I'm her husband. I was a soldier, but I conked out (*taps his heart*). You're wondering about this set-up, aren't you?
Mitchell: Yeah, I guess I am.
Man: Well, ask her, then. She was a tramp when I met her. I didn't know it then, but I knew it before we were married. That's one of the reasons I enlisted, to get away from her. But I couldn't wait to get out and get back to her. But when I did, she didn't want me. Funny, isn't it? But I still want her. I still love her.
(*The man breaks off and walks away, then turns towards Mitchell again*)
Man: You know what I just told you? It was a lie, I'm not her husband. I met her, the same as you did, at the joint. I can't keep away from her. I want to marry her, but she won't have me.
Mitchell: Is that so?
Man: Do you believe that? That's a lie too. I don't love her. She makes good money, though. You got any money on you?
Mitchell: No.
Man: She makes good money sometimes. Hey, do you suppose I could be a soldier? Maybe I could in the regular Army. Make a good rating and make some dough by the next war.
Mitchell: Why not?
Man: Why not? Because I don't want to. What would I want to be a soldier for? (*Sits down and moves restlessly in the seat*) Aagh! I don't know what I want to do.

Far from expressing an optimistic commitment to exposing, then correcting a specific social problem (as Anglo-American critics like Rotha and Knight characterise *Crossfire*) these conversations reflect the existentially pessimistic world of the film noir, one in which the sense of brooding violence is almost tangible, and nothing, least of all the characters and the words they speak, is unambiguous.

My thesis is that many writers belonging to what I have called the Anglo-American critical tradition have – through their impatient commitment to liberal humanist values, their contempt for the great bulk of Hollywood cinema, and their faltering grasp of aesthetics – seriously misread the meaning of *Crossfire* and (possibly) of many other Hollywood films. This represents a serious situation for film culture because works such as Rotha's *The Film Till Now* and Knight's *The Liveliest Art* exercise a disproportionate influence over popular conceptions of film history.

I have tried to demonstrate that certain critics have misread a particular film to the extent that they do not seem to have been in the least conscious of the film's generic qualities, its narrative strategies, its lighting schemes and, more importantly, how all these features generate meanings which have to be understood if the film is to be decoded.[8] However, in the case of *Crossfire* these critics' misreading is just the tip of a monstrous iceberg of falsification which extends not only to the general public but – and this is the truly alarming thing – to the makers of *Crossfire* themselves.

Crossfire was the occasion of a furious debate when it appeared. A serious contribution to that debate, and a typical one in setting out the terrain over which it ranged, is Elliot Cohen (1899–1959)'s 'The Film Drama as a Social Force', which appeared as an open letter to moviemakers in *Commentary*, a journal sponsored by the American Jewish Committee.[9] Cohen, like the writers of the Anglo-American critical tradition, assumes that *Crossfire* is first and foremost about the social problem of antisemitism. He attacks the film for its lack of sociological understanding of antisemitism, expresses the fear that it will incite rather than quell anti-Jewish feeling, and counsels filmmakers to in future draw on sociological research in the construction of their movies and on content analysis in the reading of past movies, in order to assess their effects on the audience.[10] Clearly, Cohen is entirely immersed in liberal humanist conceptions of art, with a consequent attachment to a realist/naturalist aesthetic, and in American conceptions of social science, with their emphasis on effects studies and their almost total blindness to the existence (never mind the meaning) of aesthetic structures.

That said, however, on several occasions Cohen is quite perceptive about certain aesthetic features of *Crossfire*, arguing that: 'If a film is to reach the millions, it must be made attractive to the millions: therefore *Crossfire* is a murder melodrama in which the master detective solves the crime', and that: '*Crossfire* is no cops-and-robbers story: from the start it projects you into the involved and unhealthy atmosphere of the "hard-boiled" detective thriller (Hammett–Chandler: Bogart–Alan Ladd) in which violence and intrigue have acquired a new, sadistic dimension'.[11] But, for Cohen, such aesthetic features are unproblematic, transparent and in no way determinate of meaning. For Cohen, they do not require disciplined investigation, including the posing of relationships between aesthetic forms and social structures; they are features to be brushed aside in order to engage with the 'real' meaning of the film. Cohen, an educated member of the general public, reads *Crossfire* not as a highly conventionalised formal and fictional structure, but as a series of events which might have been happening in the street outside his window: that is, he reads this film in the way most films are read and talked about generally and in popular manifestations of film culture such as newspaper reviewing.

Public debate about *Crossfire* was conducted broadly in the terms set out in Cohen's piece, that is, the nature and extent of antisemitism in America and whether the film would be likely to help mitigate or incite that prejudice (compare this to the directly analogous debate in the British press about *Straw Dogs* [Sam Peckinpah, 1971] and *A Clockwork Orange* [Stanley Kubrick, 1971] and whether they condemn or incite violence). Inevitably, the makers of *Crossfire* were drawn into the discussion, but what is truly alarming is the extent to which they accept the terms of the debate as set out by figures like Cohen. Adrian Scott (1911–72), the producer of *Crossfire*, wrote a lengthy essay in the journal *Screenwriter*, which is substantially a discussion of the question, 'Can films help to eradicate antisemitism?' and an adumbration of a production programme, with the backing of the best psychological and sociological research, with this end in view.[12] So completely does Scott surrender to the debate as critics like Cohen, Knight and Rotha have constituted it, that he, at one point, seems to defend *Crossfire* as a realist/naturalist document: 'Monty, the anti-Semite in *Crossfire*, exists. This very night he is roaming the streets of Queens, N.Y. looking for a Jew to beat up.'[13] On the evidence of his essay, Scott, himself a screenwriter who, as producer, may have been quite deeply involved in the construction of the script and in the shooting of *Crossfire*, seems to share the view that the structure, style and aesthetic strategies of *Crossfire* are irrelevant to the film's meaning.

One is forced to the alarming conclusion that, both for filmmakers and audiences, the processes for the production and understanding of meaning within cinema have been naturalised to the degree that they are no longer (if, indeed, they ever were) grasped on a conscious level. If, as I have tried to demonstrate, this is true for an anti-realist film such as *Crossfire*, how much more true must it be for the naturalist fare which dominates television?

Notes

1. See, for example, Paul Rotha, *The Film Till Now: A Survey of World Cinema*, revised edition (London: Vision Press, 1967); Roger Manvell, *Film*, revised edition (London: Penguin, 1950); Lewis Jacobs, *The Rise of the American Film: A Critical History* (New York: The Teachers College Press, 1968); Arthur Knight, *The Liveliest Art: A Panoramic History of the Movies* (New York: New American Library, 1957); Penelope Houston, *The Contemporary Cinema, 1945–63* (London: Penguin, 1963). There is, of course, a countertradition in English which (like its principal mentor, *Cahiers du cinéma*) places Hollywood at the centre of critical interest. This tradition runs from the journal *Movie* and the writings of Andrew Sarris (1928–2012) into the journals *Monogram*, *Film Comment* and *The Velvet Light Trap*.

2. Rotha, *The Film Till Now*, 20; 37; 503.
3. Knight, *The Liveliest Art*, 265.
4. For the importance of the *film policier* in Hollywood in the forties, see Colin McArthur, *Underworld U.S.A.* (London: Secker & Warburg for the British Film Institute, 1972).
5. For a thesis of the interpenetration of the film noir, *film policier*, gangster movie and thriller in the forties, see Ibid.
6. Siegfried Kracauer (1889–1966)'s *From Caligari to Hitler: A Psychological History of the German Film* (Princeton, NJ: Princeton University Press, 1947) does, of course, argue that the German Expressionist films of the twenties (among others) constitute a prophetic account of the rise of Nazism in Weimar Germany. However, his argument is that the films were social 'symptoms' in the Freudian sense and require to be deciphered by the critic/analyst. In no sense could the films be construed as engaging explicitly with social questions, the kind of activity valorised by Rotha, Knight and other writers of the Anglo-American critical tradition.
7. See, for example, Anon, 'Films of the Week', *The Sunday Times*, 4 January 1948, no page ref; John Ross, 'Murder with a difference', *Daily Worker*, 3 January 1948, no page ref; Anon, '*Crossfire*', *Monthly Film Bulletin* 15, no. 169 (January 1948), 4.
8. In using the word 'decoded' I am implicitly employing a semiological model of the cinema. The validity or otherwise of that model is not relevant to the thesis I am putting forward in this essay, but the implication of the model can be followed up in the essays contained in *Screen* 14, nos 1–2 (Spring/Summer 1973).
9. Elliot Cohen, 'Letter to the Movie-Makers: The Film Drama as a Social Force', *Commentary*, no. 4 (August 1947), https://www.commentary.org/articles/elliotecohen/letter-to-the-movie-makersthe-film-drama-as-a-social-force/ [accessed 27 July 2022].
10. For an account of this tradition see Bernard Berelson, *Content Analysis in Communication Research* (Glencoe, IL: Free Press, 1952).
11. Cohen, 'Letter to the Movie-Makers'.
12. Adrian Scott, 'Some of My Worst Friends', *Screen Writer*, 3 (October 1947), http://www.gutenberg-e.org/langdon/pdfs/c5-2-some-of-my-worst-friends.pdf [accessed 27 July 2022].
13. Ibid.

CHAPTER 7

Breaking the Signs: *Scotch Myths* as Cultural Struggle*

The pun in the title of Barbara (1944–94) and Murray Grigors' *Scotch Myths* exhibition indicates the wit and sense of fun with which it was mounted.[1] However, this should not obscure the fact that the exhibition constitutes a major political intervention in Scottish affairs, albeit across the terrain of ideology. Its political purpose was to provoke debate about the representation of Scotland and the Scots and the first effects of this have already been seen in the *Bulletin of Scottish Politics* issue which includes two separate reviews of the exhibition itself and four other contributions which address the same problem the exhibition poses.[2] The purpose of this article is to give some indication of the strategy of the exhibition and to point to some of the ways it needs to be followed up so that the issue of ideological representation remains firmly on the agenda in Scottish political debate.

Lindsay Paterson's review of the exhibition is the more supportive, in that it recognises that the key issue posed is to what extent certain representations of Scotland and the Scots have become (and remain) dominant at the level of popular consciousness. Paterson agrees with the Grigors that the central traditions to be exposed and countered are Tartanry and Kailyard, particularly the former. The other, less supportive, review by P. H. Scott makes the argument that these traditions have less current political force than an earlier myth:

> In crude and blunt terms, this is the view that Scotland before 1707 was backward, bloody and barbarous: that it was saved by the Union, which is seen as an enlightened act of statesmanship, and that thereafter economic progress and civilisation flowed benignly northwards from England.[3]

Whatever objective historical truth might underlie Scott's position, it betrays a certain blindness as to how ideology works, in the Scottish

---

*Originally published in *Cencrastus*, no. 7 (Winter 1981/82), 21–5.

context, as a multifaceted system of images and categories of thought into which Scots of the last century and a half have been – to use Louis Althusser (1918–90)'s term – interpellated, set in place as social actors, their consciousness being defined within the limits of the capitalist system.[4] As it happens, the process is well illustrated in the account given by Andrew Noble of the young Robert Louis Stevenson (1850–94)'s attempts to respond to questions about his native land while in Germany. Noble quotes a letter Stevenson wrote to his mother:

> And thence, as I find always the case, to the most ghastly romancing about the Scottish scenery and manners, the Highland dress and everything national and local I could lay my hands upon. There is one thing that burthens me a good deal in my patriotic garrulage, and that is the black ignorance in which I grope about everything [. . .] I am generally glad enough to fall back again [. . .] upon Burns, toddy and the Highlands.[5]

In short, what Stevenson described himself as 'fall[ing] back upon' is Kailyard (or in this case, its main historical antecedent) and Tartanry. Stevenson's problem haunts us to this very day. Interpellated within an armature of discourses, of which Tartanry and Kailyard are the most important at the level of popular consciousness, we and our hearers in other lands can find no alternative, meaningful discourses within which to construct Scotland and our own Scottish identity or identities. *Scotch Myths* represents a crucial step in the re-creation, and more importantly, the circulation of alternative discourses and the despatching of them out of the academy and into popular consciousness.

One of the major achievements of the exhibition is to demonstrate both the scale and the systemic quality of the Kailyard/Tartanry interpellation. Many of us will have had the experience of recoiling, half-amused, half-aghast, from Princes Street souvenir shops, but the characteristic term we tend to use to describe what we find there, kitsch, is a politically defective one, formulated in the academy and functioning in an elitist discourse which pivots on the bourgeois notion of taste and makes the wrong kinds of distinctions between high art and popular art.[6] The detritus of Tartanry/Kailyard found in Princes Street souvenir shops has to be addressed within a discourse which is more politically aware. Such a discourse constructs these objects not as indices of taste (a category which divides the cultural haves from the have-nots), but as part of a complex sign system which has ideological force and is congenial to the maintenance of, in the Scottish context, regressive political positions and institutions. The gallery context of *Scotch Myths* immediately puts the objects on display in an interrogatory framework in a way that their presence in souvenir shops does not. Similarly, the exhibition catalogue explicitly poses the correct questions and reinserts the objects into a history spanning the mid-eighteenth century to the present day: James Macpherson (1736–96), Ossianism; European Romanticism; Walter Scott (1771–1832); the appropriation of Scott and Scotland by Europe and America; the internal re-appropriation by Scotland itself of earlier external appropriations, via the emergence of Kailyard; Scottish militarism in the context of nineteenth-century colonial wars, both World Wars and beyond; the dissemination of the ensemble of images and categories of thought within successive practices and technologies – literature, lithography, photography, the postcard, the music hall, films, television. It is one thing to see the imagery of Tartanry/Kailyard in its so-called natural habitats of the souvenir shop or the wall of a Scottish home; it is quite another thing to see it reproduced on the labels on orange crates from California. Scottish comic postcards landing from time to time on one's doormat are simply amusing, but when such objects are laid out in serried ranks and classified thematically, their role as signs in an ideological sign system becomes clearer. Such a strategy reveals the dominant motifs within which the Scot is constructed in ideological terms: parsimony; drunkenness; and sexual mystery and perhaps potency – What's under the kilt? Similarly, the awesome historical and ideological scale and suffocating pervasiveness of Tartanry/Kailyard is well conveyed in the diverse heraldic, clan-based type of postcard.

The fragmented, naturalised way we usually experience the sign system of Tartanry/Kailyard tends to conceal from us its systemic quality, the interrelatedness of its elements. Having had two centuries to develop, it now constitutes a durable and confidently dominant system. The representation of one part of it can dredge up into consciousness the system as a whole and, of course, also the complex articulation of certain attitudes to history, to nationhood and to political decisions in the here and now which it is the system's objective function to serve. The system renders dominant certain elements and combinations of elements and excludes others. This phenomenon can be illustrated with reference to the development of representations of the Scottish landscape within the Tartanry tradition.[7] Clearly, the conception of 'the view' had developed from the mid-eighteenth-century notion of the picturesque. As Scotland in the course of the late eighteenth and early nineteenth centuries was constructed as the Romantic domain par excellence, Scottish Highland scenery itself became a semiotic system signalling clusters of moods and feelings central to European Romanticism. Both in subject matter and style, a line can be drawn which links the great landscape artist of nineteenth-century

Figure 7.1 From 'Here be dragons' to the picturesque: from the late eighteenth century on, the Scottish Highland landscape became a fit subject for artists and tourists.

German Romanticism, Caspar David Friedrich (1774–1840), to Horatio McCulloch (1805–67), Edwin Landseer (1802–73) and other British artists who rendered the Highlands in a Romantic rhetoric, through to the postcard paintings of, say, Edgar Longstaffe (1852–1933).

Even when the medium is photography rather than paint, as is nowadays more commonly the case, photographers are drawn unerringly by the semiotic resonances of Scottish Highland scenery and very often attempt to render in their own medium the effects of Romantic easel painting. Compare, for instance, the relatively recent photograph, *Sunset over Skye, from Morar* (widely circulated as a postcard and quite characteristic of Scottish postcard photography) with the Caspar David Friedrich painting, *Moonrise over the Sea* (1822). A recurrent feature of Friedrich's work was the presence within the frame of figures contemplating the wonder of Nature. British Romantic painters, and their photographic descendants, tended to leave only the representation of Nature itself within the frame. So strong and diffuse had the tradition of contemplating Nature become that Friedrich's figure of the contemplator could be excluded, becoming thereby the absent, though implicit, viewer of the painting/photograph. The *Sunset over Skye* postcard is in certain respects regressive in this regard, having reinserted the figures of the contemplators into the landscape within the frame. Quite often the photograph (and indeed, the painting) which seeks to recapitulate the painterly qualities of Romanticism carries also a verbal signifier which operates in the same register. A postcard titled *The Misty Isle of Skye* does precisely this, as well as recapitulating photographically several of the recurring icons (mountains, sea, mist, torrent) and styles of Romantic easel painting. These icons, along with the loch, constitute the core ensemble of representations of Highland Scotland. A different ensemble prevails in, for instance, German Romantic representations of romantic scenery, in which mountains and snow are foregrounded (as in the German mountain films of the twenties and thirties).

The Tartanry/Kailyard ensemble permits and foregrounds only certain types of flora, fauna and humankind, the privileged icons being thistles, heather, stags, Highland Cattle, Scottish Terriers, tartaned figures (often with military connotations) and a handful of historical figures, among whom Robert Burns (1759–96) and Walter Scott are pre-eminent. The systemic nature of the ensemble, the inter-relatedness of the parts, is shown by their mutually supportive presence in many contexts. The semiotic resonances of the Scottish view may be supported by lesser or greater reliance on the clanship motif and by the addition of other icons until the view itself as icon recedes and the flora and tartan begin to carry the main message of the tradition. The confident hegemony of the tradition is expressed in those instances where, in a process of condensation and displacement, the complex ideological message of Tartanry/Kailyard is spoken by a single visual icon of the ensemble.

There is a sense in which the *Scotch Myths* exhibition has been too successful for its own good. So overwhelming has been its demonstration of the pervasiveness and systemic nature of Tartanry/Kailyard that serious public comment (as in contemporaneous Scottish press responses) has concentrated almost exclusively on that aspect and neglected those elements in the exhibition which offer alternatives to Tartanry/Kailyard or suggest ways in which the dominant tradition can be deconstructed. In one of the most explicitly editorialising sections of the exhibition, the Grigors set a number of postcard representations of Scottish militarism, whether expressed in a Romantic or more documentary rhetoric, against black-and-white blow-ups of certain well-known photographs expressing the carnage of the First World War. The implicit political tendency of this juxtaposition may be pacifist and therefore mistaken (the correct political alternative to Scottish militarism is the formation of people's militias and the rendering accountable of standing forces, not widespread disarmament). Nevertheless, the juxtaposition itself points to one of the ways in which Tartanry/Kailyard representations can be deconstructed, that is, through forms of photographic practice which stress photomontage. This is well represented in Britain at the present time, primarily in Peter Kennard's photomontage works on, among other things, Britain's nuclear role. As it happens, one of these works deconstructs a Scottish postcard view very effectively.

Also, we need to re-examine the categories within which we describe representations of Scotland and the Scots. We tend to neglect the systemic nature of these representations and rely on the dubious notion of stereotype,[8] which fragments the system into a series of disparate, unconnected one-offs and appeals for comparisons to be made between people in the real world and characters in fictions on the basis of the truth of representation. Such an approach tends to distract from the infinitely more important kind of analysis that perceives fictional characters as articulations of positions within ideological discourses and therefore concentrates on those discourses as a whole and the place of the characters within them.

The essence of myth and ideology is their inability to incorporate contradiction. Myth and ideology operate by obliterating the contradictions of the real world and making humankind whole at the level of the imagination. The function of exploring contradiction, psychological if not social, is largely fulfilled by High Art. However, no society riven with contradictions can tolerate the circulation of false myths and ideologies without at the same time ensuring that deflations of these achieve some circulation.

Such a process, which is a necessary one for allowing a society to cope with its own felt stresses, is invariably achieved through humour. If we abandon the notion of 'stereotype' and reinsert the notion of 'system of representation', or 'discourse', then the component parts of that system/discourse can be viewed in relationship with each other. Thus, just as American society, in its crazy comedies, gave the lie to the security of American maleness expressed in genres such as the Western, the gangster movie and the thriller, so can the Scottish comic postcard be read as deconstructing the figure of the handsome, warlike Highlander, and as such can be seen as progressive. For example, the silent strength of the Scot of the imagination can be deconstructed via comic depiction of the aggressive bonhomie and bombast of the professional Scotsman, ever conscious of the strength of his handshake and his superiority over the effete English. A strong, if indefinite, connotation of the Scotsman as constructed in Romantic rhetoric is his sexual potency. Many comic postcards, in a stream of jokes about what the kilt signifies and what might be beneath it, interrogate this myth. However, the raising of arguments of this kind requires the continuity of contexts of discussion, of which more presently.

Postcard publishing, like other sectors of the economy, was characterised by great diversity in its heyday, the four decades linking the nineteenth and twentieth centuries. After this time, many firms went to the wall and there emerged the few giants who today dominate the market. The effect of this has been to ensure the economic survival of the producers of the most regressive representations of Scotland and the Scots and the disappearance of the kinds of cards which could be construed as progressive in the Scottish context. The latter are quite well represented in the *Scotch Myths* exhibition, although they have elicited very little public comment. There are two groups of cards which are particularly important in this regard. The postcard artist Cynicus (Martin Anderson [1854–1932]) produced a wide range of work, some of it on Scottish themes and some not. His non-Scottish work is explicitly socialist with a strong tinge of misanthropy, and much of his specifically Scottish work is progressive in the sense that it takes venerable Scottish institutions and maxims and gives them new and subversive inflections. The rampant Scottish lion is rendered a creature swollen with smug pride and complacency; the motto of Scotland, far from being a proud and defiant cry, becomes a slogan in the hands of a prickly and crabbit wee nyaff; the 'auld hunder' ceases to be a central psalm in the Presbyterian canon and becomes instead a description of the cadres of the Unco Guid; and the question 'Where has Scotia found her fame?' is answered by showing a Holy Willie, his eyes raised sanctimoniously to Heaven while bearing a bottle of whisky on a weighty bible.[9]

Figure 7.2 Cynicus deconstructs the iconic Scottish symbol and motto.

It is extremely unusual in the Scottish context to find any comic postcard which does not depict kilted or bonneted figures. The *Scotch Myths* exhibition, however, included a sub-genre of the comic postcard which eschews such figures and holds out the promise of a more realistic commentary on aspects of Scottish urban working-class life. Characteristically, and as in popular art generally, the processes of work, the means whereby people actually earn their living, are to all intents and purposes repressed in the postcard form. Thus, even this sub-genre's more realistic rendering of urban working-class life lights on the working-class family at leisure, and, specifically, on the institution of the seaside holiday. These postcards were produced by the Glasgow publishers The Art Publishing Company and appeared under several rubrics familiar in (particularly) Glasgow working-class parlance: *Doon the Watter* (the trip from Glasgow down the Clyde coast); *The Fresh Air Fortnight* (originally a parish-based scheme for getting some sea air into the lungs of poor Glasgow children); and *In the Good Old Summertime*. These cards are extremely refreshing in the Scottish context in being entirely innocent of kilts, heather, bagpipes and the other penumbra of the debased Tartanry/Kailyard tradition. Instead, they show working-class figures negotiating the hassles of moving the family to the seaside and coping with the problems they meet there. They adopt a very familiar Glaswegian tone: humour in adversity. In the world of this sub-genre hansom cabs fall apart, spilling passengers and luggage onto the street, or the family goes into a many-layered sandwich as the tram car starts too quickly; the process of getting the family from the booking office onto the train, then to the boat becomes an obstacle race in which children fall out of carriage windows or off the boat, and the actual stay 'doon the watter' is beset by grasping landladies, verminous sheets and unremitting rain. The function of these postcards vis-à-vis other postcard constructions of Scotland and the Scots is analogous to that of the comedy of Billy Connolly set against that of Harry Lauder (1870–1950) – the latter, incidentally, another figure that the *Scotch Myths* exhibition exposes.

This essay began by stressing the political importance of ideological representations and raised the question of how the momentum of *Scotch Myths* is to be maintained as a dimension of current political struggles in Scotland. Clearly, the traditions of Kailyard and Tartanry have to be exposed and deconstructed and more politically progressive representations of Scotland and Scottish identities constructed, circulated and discussed. It is partly a question of individual artists engaging with and countering the regressive traditions but, more centrally, it should involve progressive Scottish political groups having a clearer conception of cultural struggle and finding the funds and mechanisms to engage in it. The struggle has to be carried on across the whole range of the arts or, as they are better called, the sign media.[10] In any social formation at any particular moment the whole range of sign media are articulated together in a sort of leapfrog relationship, the one borrowing motifs from the other and recoding them into its own system. Some of the concrete tasks to be undertaken would include the creation of Scottish photomontage practices; the retrieval and recirculation of the progressive images of Cynicus, The Art Publishing Company and others; pressing for the inclusion of courses on the semiotics of Scotland in educational institutions; organising dialogue with key Scottish sign institutions (for example, BBC Scotland, Scottish Television [STV], the Scottish Film Council, Films of Scotland, the Scottish Arts Council) regarding the extent to which their policies are congenial or inimical to the maintenance of Tartanry/Kailyard's cultural and ideological dominance in Scotland.

The struggle continues.

Notes

1. There was at the time of the exhibition a widely perceived phenomenon of the failed devolution referendum of 1979 resulting in directly political struggle reforming itself on the terrain of Scottish culture. Before this, however, the

Grigors had already pursued a profound interest in Scottish culture and history. The subject of Murray Grigor's first two ventures into filmmaking was the Scots architect and artist Charles Rennie Mackintosh (1868–1928) and Scottish themes would recur regularly in his work (for example, his 1977 film, *The Hammer and the Thistle* on the Scots poet Hugh MacDiarmid [1892–1978]). This interest drove the Grigors to begin collecting examples of popular signifiers of Scottishness such as might be found in tourist souvenir shops. This would culminate in their mounting, in 1981, of the *Scotch Myths* exhibition, first at the Crawford Arts Centre in St Andrews and then at that year's Edinburgh Festival.

2. James Hunter, 'Year of the Émigré', *Bulletin of Scottish Politics*, no. 2 (Spring 1981), 56–62; P. H. Scott, '*Scotch Myths* – 1', *Bulletin of Scottish Politics*, no. 2 (Spring 1981), 62–6; Lindsay Patterson, '*Scotch Myths* – 2', *Bulletin of Scottish Politics*, no. 2 (Spring 1981), 67–71; Andrew Noble, 'MacChismo in Retrospect', *Bulletin of Scottish Politics*, no. 2 (Spring 1981), 72–81; Alice McKeown, '*Ecosse*, by Christian Civardi: review', *Bulletin of Scottish Politics*, no. 2 (Spring 1981), 82–4; Neal Ascherson, '*Schottland*, by Peter Sager: review', *Bulletin of Scottish Politics*, no. 2 (Spring 1981), 84–6.

3. Scott, '*Scotch Myths* – 1', 64.

4. Louis Althusser, critical of the crudity of the traditional Marxist view of the relationship between society's socioeconomic base and its civil society superstructure, formulated, in his 1969 essay, 'Ideology and Ideological State Apparatuses: Notes Towards an Investigation', the distinction between Repressive State Apparatuses (the government, the military and the police) and Ideological State Apparatuses (the churches, the educational system, cultural institutions). He saw the ISAs as the sites within which assent to the capitalist system was elicited, the process of *interpellation* being the key mechanism bringing this about.

5. Quoted in Noble, 'MacChismo in Retrospect', 72.

6. A German word meaning 'trash', kitsch was formulated by German art historians in the mid-nineteenth century to distinguish 'serious' art from the 'inferior' versions increasingly appearing with the emergence of mass markets. To some extent, with the onset of postmodernism and the waning of the High Art/Mass Art distinction, the term has been re-theorised to deal more sympathetically with some versions of kitsch (see, for example, Celeste Olalquiaga, *The Artificial Kingdom: A Treasury of the Kitsch Experience* [London: Pantheon Books Inc., 1998]), although the disdainful original meaning of the term remains strong.

7. Although the political tendencies of Tartanry and Kailyard are regressive and in consequence their imagery operates easily in union, a more detailed discussion than is possible here would require to separate out the two strands and the extent to which they deploy distinct rhetorics.

8. Although the concept of stereotype seems to have had a productive life in the literature of sociology and social psychology, I am wary of its deployment in

relation to media fictions for the reasons outlined in the main text of this essay. For a fuller discussion of the issue, see note (1) to my essay 'Scotland and Cinema: The Iniquity of the Fathers' (reproduced elsewhere in the present volume) and, for a very full discussion of stereotyping, particularly relating to race, see Stuart Hall, 'The Spectacle of the "Other"', in *Representation: Cultural Representations and Signifying Practices*, ed. Stuart Hall (London: SAGE Publications, 1997), 223–79.

9. For readers unfamiliar with the Scots tongue, a 'crabbit wee nyyaff' means an 'ill-tempered little nonentity'; the 'Auld Hunder' means the 'Old Hundredth'; 'Unco Guid' means 'excessively righteous'; "Holy Willie' is a description of a religious hypocrite.

10. The presence of the phrase 'sign media' in this essay reflects the fact of the latter having been written during a period characterised by the increasing presence of structuralism in discourse about the arts and other social practices. Specifically, the phrase refers to the inheritance of the nineteenth-century Swiss linguist Ferdinand de Saussure (1857–1913), whose formulation of languages as sign systems would become influential, under the term semiotics, across the entire range of communications, including cinema and, as here, popular Scottish artefacts.

CHAPTER 8

Scotland and Cinema: The Iniquity of the Fathers*

> Visiting the iniquity of the fathers upon the children and upon the children's children unto the third and to the fourth generation. (Exodus 34:7)

The place, Texas; the time, that indeterminate period between the ending of the Civil War and the closing of the frontier which all moviegoers recognise as the span of the Western. The characteristic iconography and narrative form of that genre begin to unfold onscreen: dusty terrain and isolated homestead; an attack by Mexican bandits with sombreros slung round their necks; the ride to the rescue by the seven sons of the homestead. But perhaps there is something out of the way about this family; something rarely seen in the Western. One of the retreating bandits says, 'I'd rather fight a tribe of Apaches'; the sons of the family are querulous and argue about whisky; one of them is excessively religious; the womenfolk are hospitable to a fault. The homestead's walls are hung with tartan, eighteenth-century pistols and claymores. The older menfolk wear kilts and bonnets and there is even a running gag about thriftiness. The family is, indeed, constructed within an armature of what are popularly, but misleadingly, called stereotypes of the Scots but which ought more accurately to be called 'discursive positions'[1] relating to Scotland.

What is most startling of all, however, is that the film is called *7 pistole per i MacGregor* (*Seven Guns for the MacGregors*) (Franco Giraldi, 1966): it belongs to the so-called Spaghetti Western cycle of the sixties and seventies. An Italo-Spanish co-production, it was written by four Italians, was directed by another, and has a cast made up primarily of Italians and Spaniards. These facts are noted not to sneer at Italian Westerns nor to impugn the legitimacy of one society representing another in its art, but to demonstrate that the melange of images, characters and motifs

---

* Originally published in *Scotch Reels: Scotland in Cinema and Television*, ed. Colin McArthur (London: British Film Institute, 1982), 40–69.

Figure 8.1 Italy absorbs the Scottish Discursive Unconscious: *7 pistole per i MacGregor*.

constituting Tartanry and Kailyard is not only the framework within which Scots largely construct themselves but is also the grid within which other cultures construct the Scots.

The reasons why Italian cinema in the mid-sixties comes to construct Scotland and the Scots within the categories evident in *Seven Guns for the MacGregors* are complex and, historically, far-reaching. The generative cause was, of course, that massive act of 'symbolic appropriation'[2] in the eighteenth century whereby rationalist, scientific Europe defined its own identity by fashioning the identity of the peoples on its periphery (and those it encountered in colonial conquest) in terms of a set of binary oppositions to the qualities it most celebrated in itself. In true dialectical style, this had the effect of hatching, within Europe, the complex set of identifications with its own constructed alter ego retrospectively described as Romanticism.[3] Within this process, Scotland was ripe, geographically and historically speaking, to become the Romantic domain par excellence which, with the advent of James Macpherson (1736–96)'s *Ossian* (1761–63) and Sir Walter Scott (1771–1832), duly happened. Thereafter, the causes relate to the appropriation, within Italian Romanticism, of Scott's novels and their widespread adaptation into plays and operas in the nineteenth century; the popular perception of Scotland through travel books and, later, through photographic and fashion magazines; and, not least, Italian access to filmic representations of Scotland and the Scots produced inside the UK itself and in other cultures. In most of these, the dominant discourses were Tartanry, Kailyard, or hybrids of the two. This hybridisation of the two discourses is very important. Axiomatically, it could be asserted that representations of Scotland and the Scots offer tartan exteriors and Kailyard mores.

From the silent cinema onwards there have been representations of Scotland and the Scots on the screen. The history of these representations remains to be written, and would have to take account of documentary as well as fictional cinema, but it is a fairly safe bet that the traditions of Tartanry and Kailyard, and hybrids of the two, would loom large. With regard only to the narrative fiction film, it is significant that one of the earliest such films was *Bonnie Prince Charlie* (Charles Calvert, 1923), the well-known story of which sounds again the elegiac note of the *Ossian* cycle. *The Young Lochinvar* (W. P. Kellino, 1923) was already articulating for the cinema the discourse which can usefully be called Baronialism, whereby much of the Tartanry dimension of cinema is carried. As well as offering the pictorialism of Scottish scenery, Baronialism offers a site, the dark Scottish castle, within which certain kinds of specifically 'Scottish' stories – principally hinging on treachery and the betrayal of hospitality – can be played out.

The Kailyard dimension in cinema is carried in the early days by adaptations of the most popular Kailyard novels such as *Beside the Bonnie Brier Bush* (Donald Crisp, 1921) and *The Lilac Sunbonnet* (Sidney Morgan, 1922). A concern to define the essential 'Scottishness' of Kailyard should not obscure the extent to which it forms part of the corpus of popular sentimental literature of the late nineteenth and early twentieth centuries. It is this literature, and the more hardboiled literature which succeeded it in popular taste in the post-WWI period, which the cinema has consistently fed on and, in return, has nourished. A concern therefore with popular sentimental forms is evident right from the beginnings of cinema (the films of D. W. Griffith [1875–1948] provide the best-known examples). The immense popular success of the Kailyard novels in the UK and the USA ensured that they would rapidly become cinema fodder. This joined with other internationally important sentimental Scottish material of the time (most notably the songs and stage routines of Harry Lauder [1870–1950]) to ensure that 'Scottishness' was signified from very early on in the cinema. Like the novels themselves, the films based on them are primarily machines for producing tears and, to a certain extent, wry laughter. The decline of sentimental forms in popular taste (or their sophistication and toughening in such cinematic genres as the woman's picture) has meant that later versions of cinematic Kailyard have increasingly foregrounded the comic aspects.

The operation of classical Kailyard in the cinema is best exemplified by *The Little Minister* (Richard Wallace, 1934), the last of three film adaptations of J. M. Barrie (1860–1937)'s 1891 novel of the same name. To emphasise its relatedness to other popular sentimental impulses in early cinema, the film's tear-producing mechanisms are primarily centred on elderly mothers and children, the two elderly mothers being played by actresses (Mary Gordon [1882–1963] and Beryl Mercer [1882–1939]) who fulfilled similar roles in other forms – the latter was James Cagney (1899–1986)'s mother in *The Public Enemy* (William A. Wellman, 1931).[4] Some indication of the emotional register in which *The Little Minister* functions can be got from the playing and the dialogue of Mary Gordon on her imminent removal to the poorhouse: 'Oh mither, mither, you little thocht when you bore me that I would come to this'. The signifying of 'Scottishness' in *The Little Minister* is conveyed in the marked Stage Scots of most of the players, in the fey quality of the playing, in the dress and décor (Baronial in Lord Rintoul's castle, rustic elsewhere) and, very centrally, in the music, involving at various times, popular songs or airs such as 'Loch Lomond', 'The Campbells are Coming', 'Comin' Thro' the Rye', 'The Bluebells of Scotland' and a pastiche Scottish air specially written for the film, 'Scotch Love'. As in the original novel, potentially disruptive elements in the film – the weavers' riot against increased charges for materials, the sending in of the military to quell them, and the ostracising of the local constable – are either heavily recuperated or rendered comic. To have dealt adequately with these elements the film would have had to crack itself apart, to pull back into history a community that the very form of Kailyard had rendered history-less.

Pre-war films like *Bonnie Prince Charlie*, *The Young Lochinvar*, *Beside the Bonnie Brier Bush* and *The Little Minister* articulated into cinema the discourses of Tartanry and Kailyard, the roots of the former going back to the eighteenth century and those of the latter to the nineteenth century. From these roots the discourses entered various forms and artefacts: poems, novels, operas, paintings, prints, photographs, postcards, shortbread tins and soft furnishings as well as films and, later, television programmes. Since there were simply no alternative traditions of representation with comparable power, the tendency was for any film dealing with Scotland, or having a Scot as a character, to be pulled strongly towards the armature of images, characters and stories making up Tartanry and Kailyard. Thus, that armature was exploited in several films of the thirties, both British and American, dealing with Scottish soldiers on the North-west Frontier of India: *The Drum* (Zoltan Korda, 1938), *Gunga Din* (George Stevens, 1939), *Wee Willie Winkie* (John Ford, 1937), *Bonnie Scotland* (James W. Horne, 1935). The armature was flexible enough to include anti-Kailyard elements (much as George Douglas Brown [1869–1902]'s 1901 novel, *The House with the Green Shutters* was written in opposition to, and therefore defined itself within, Kailyard). In this respect the predominantly Baronial construction of Scotland in *The 39 Steps* (Alfred Hitchcock, 1935) could include the darkly Calvinist figure of John Laurie (1897–1980)'s cotter and a post-war film like *The Hasty Heart* (Vincent Sherman, 1949), although set in the Far East, could construct its whole *raison d'être* round the archetypal querulousness of the Scot.

In the decade and a half following World War II, however, there emerged the remarkable series of representations of Scotland which constitute the definitive modern statements of Tartanry and Kailyard in the cinema. Since the days of Alexander Korda (1893–1956) in the thirties, the Holy Grail which the British film industry had sought (and had failed to find) was penetration of the American market. Its consistent strategy for achieving this was the making of costly costume dramas such as *The Private Life of Henry VIII* (Alexander Korda, 1933), *Rembrandt* (Alexander Korda, 1936) and, abortively, *I, Claudius* (Josef von Sternberg, 1937) under Korda in the thirties, and the Gainsborough pictures such as *The Man in Grey* (Leslie Arliss, 1943) and *The Wicked Lady* (Leslie Arliss, 1945) in the forties. It was within this strategy (which ironically has proved successful in the context of television with *The Forsyte Saga* [BBC, 1967], *Upstairs, Downstairs* [London Weekend Television, 1971–75], and *Edward and Mrs Simpson* [Thames Television, 1978]) that the first of the two major Romantic constructions of Scotland was produced – *Bonnie Prince Charlie* (Anthony Kimmins, 1948). The second, *Rob Roy: The Highland Rogue* (Harold French, 1953) was a production of the Disney Company, whose sentimental conception of cinema on several occasions found expression in Scottish whimsy (for example, *Kidnapped* [Robert Stevenson, 1960], *Greyfriars Bobby* [Don Chaffey, 1961] and *The Three Lives of Thomasina* [Don Chaffey, 1964]), which, needless to say, allowed free passage to Tartanry and Kailyard. Every frame of these two films recapitulates the visual style of easel-painting representations of the Scotland constructed in the European imagination in the late eighteenth and early nineteenth centuries and the characters and actions relate to the same Ossianic tradition: warlike heroes; wan maidens; wise, white-haired patriarchs; blind seers and treacherous enemies. The cinematic apotheosis of this tradition is both articulated and deconstructed in the

American film *Brigadoon* (Vincente Minnelli, 1954). At one level it takes the Romantic representation of Scotland as a given, but at another level, that of the working through of the personal obsession of its director, Vincente Minnelli (1903–86), with the question of illusion and reality, this representation is revealed as the dream par excellence, as a fiction created to escape from the urban horrors of the twentieth century. No British feature film has the progressive force of *Brigadoon* in this regard.

Like *Bonnie Prince Charlie* and *Rob Roy*, the cluster of comedy films which emerged in the late forties and in the fifties, for example, *Whisky Galore!* (Alexander Mackendrick, 1949), *Laxdale Hall* (John Eldridge, 1953), *The Maggie* (Alexander Mackendrick, 1953) and *Rockets Galore!* (Michael Relph, 1958), while offering a representation of Scotland and the Scots, were meaningful along another axis: this time, a British social axis. Not all of these films emerged from Ealing Studios, but all had about them the feel of the Ealing ethos discernible across a wide range of that studio's films. Central to this was a detestation of modernity as it related to the city and to the power of capital (though the films are by no stretch of the imagination pro-socialist; rather, they are pro-feudal) and particularly to the power of central government bureaucracy. Set against these ills, the films construct a set of contrary human values invested in a range of lovable rural eccentrics and non-conformists. Their narratives are constructed in terms of the modern world (represented by English soldiers, an American tycoon, English MPs and Glasgow poachers) getting its comeuppance at the hands of the shrewd and canny Highland Scots. *The Maggie*, directed by a Scot, Alexander Mackendrick (1912–93), represents Scotland at its most self-lacerating. Precisely at the historical moment, the early fifties, when the massive penetration of American capital into Scotland was gathering pace, *The Maggie* actually sets the two halves of the contradiction – American entrepreneur and Scottish workers – in opposition to each other, but with almost wilful perversity, has the Scots win hands down. In true Kailyard style, what is not achievable at the level of political struggle is attainable in the delirious Scots imagination. Having given the powerful Americans their comeuppance, there was no stopping the breast-beating Scots. In 1955, with *Geordie* (Frank Launder), they showed the world that, by having the kilted titular figure win the hammer event at the 1956 Melbourne Olympics, whatever historical processes might be doing to Scotland, it was still (in a phrase attributed to Ally Macleod [1931–2004]), 'the best wee nation ever God put breath in'.

The objective function of popular cinema is very often to paper over the cracks in society, to mask contradictions. This has been a particularly urgent task for British cinema in its representations of Scotland as the clear benefits to Scotland of being a junior partner in imperial exploitation give way to the disabilities of being tied to a post-imperial geriatric with undiminished ambition for maintaining great power status. The ideological manoeuvre whereby this contradiction is masked is most clearly evident in *Rockets Galore!*, which, characteristically, reserves its most carefully mounted scenes for images of the Scots lamenting the putative loss of their island with dignity and – unlike the actuality of these things – draws back from the brink of evicting the people by giving them the canny ruse of painting some seagulls pink and having the island declared a bird sanctuary. With a nod, a wink and a dram, the Scots once more triumph at the level of the imagination while in the real world their country gets pulled out from under them.

In certain respects these films draw on the Romantic tradition of hills, lochs and sea and contain generic elements (for example, the rounding off of the narrative with a ceilidh) which link them to, say, *Rob Roy: The Highland Rogue*. These films, particularly *Laxdale Hall* and *Geordie*, are in a very precise sense politically reactionary in that they restore and sanctify the quasi-feudal social structure of rural Scotland. Like so many other representations of Scotland and the Scots, they are culturally reactionary as well in offering for audience endorsement and identification a range of figures and situations which offer no guidance to the solution of the problems of the modern world which some of the films themselves pose. They have in addition had a limiting effect on a whole generation of Scottish players, only the more outstanding of whom have been able to break free of this pernicious inheritance and function within other cinematic traditions.

There have been a limited number of attempts to make feature-length fiction films representing Scotland and the Scots from a standpoint more appropriate to the twentieth century. One such attempt to construct Scotland within a discourse other than Tartanry/Kailyard, *Floodtide* (Frederick Wilson, 1949), was based on a novel, and also co-scripted, by the harshest Scottish critic of Kailyard, George Blake (1893–1961). In his book *Barrie and the Kailyard School* (1951) he writes:

> What impression of Scottish life and character have non-Scottish readers got from the Scottish novelists? The various answers to this question are all surprising and mostly fantastic. Most people know that modern, workaday Scotland is as far from being a paradise for clansmen in kilts, with heather trimmings and stags at eve, as it is from being a pantomime land of comedians, in which haggis, haddocks, bagpipes, whisky and an ill-tempered God affect in their various ways the souls of its pawky inhabitants. The daily newspaper reading of the most self-centred Cockney should have convinced him by now that Scotland is, in its most urgent aspect, a highly

industrialised country, a sort of British Ruhr, with a great productivity of 'heavy' goods – coal, ships, steel – square mile upon square mile of slum, a passionate public interest in professional football and in the hazards of distant English racecourses, a lot of dog-racing tracks, and a rapidly decreasing respect for the authority of the Parish Minister. The fact is that the Industrial Revolution knocked the old Scotland sideways, with a violence in both the process and the consequences un-exampled. A strange series of historical accidents brought it about that a certain amount of native genius, and certain natural supplies of raw materials, turned the Clyde Valley almost overnight into a Black Country.[5]

Almost inevitably, therefore, *Floodtide* seeks to define the meaning of Scotland in relation to the Clyde. The impulse behind this was extremely progressive – the film opens with a dedication to Clydeside workers – and it must always be recalled how ordinary Glaswegians were thrilled at the time of the film's release to see their own milieu up there on the screen (Imagine! *Barrowland*!), to see aspects of their own lives depicted and to hear for the first time the cadences of Glasgow speech coming from the sound system of a public cinema. This dimension of the film – and it is perhaps the aspect which wears best – is carried primarily in the figure of Tim Brogan, played by Jimmy Logan (1928–2001), a popular Glasgow music hall comic. This image of the Clyde as the bustling nerve centre of a modern nation was to beckon successive generations of Scottish filmmakers with progressive instincts. The consistent problem has been the ideological framework within which the Clyde has been perceived, the celebration of its people rather than the analysis of their situation and the formal means of representation – in later decades, Griersonian documentary and, in the case of *Floodtide*, classical realist narrative. These are not, in the final analysis, separate questions: the form of classical realist narrative allows for the shaping of stories about individual psychology and interpersonal relationships and is conducive to a celebratory, mythologising tone. At the same time, that form also inhibits the entry of more analytic concepts and discourses and is not conducive to a reflective tone. However, the two sides of the problem are analytically separable.

Following through the ideological dimension first, *Floodtide* opens with an attempt to appropriate the meaning of the Clyde from one discourse to another, from country to city, from farming to shipbuilding. The opening frames of the narrative might indeed have come from a Tartanry/Kailyard film with a cart rolling towards a rustic cottage set in the hills on the Firth of Clyde. But very quickly oppositions are set up: the central figure, David Shields (Gordon Jackson), encouraged by his uncle who is a foreman in the shipyard, wants to build ships while his father wants him to remain and farm the land. The father is associated with all the regressive discourses

George Blake traduces: 'There's been a Shields in Glentoran since the time of Bonnie Prince Charlie' and '[the city is] a Sodom and Gomorrah, all noise and hammers and temptation'. However, David's uncle (being a freemason and therefore adept at ideological manoeuvre) manages to conflate the apparently incompatible discourses of father and son ('the sea's as old as the hills and a good ship's as wonderful a work of God as a Blackface ewe') and secure David's move to the Glasgow shipyard. Although the film does, of course, show shipbuilding as a socioeconomic process, its celebratory tone seeks to raise Clyde shipbuilding to a mystical level as evidence of the worth of the men who make the ships. This is done mainly through the central device by which classical narrative cinema signifies mystical possession: the look. Throughout the film there are scenes in which David stands with a faraway look in his eyes and contemplates the Clyde, a half-built hull, or a model ship in a glass case in the Kelvingrove Museum. From time to time also, the shipyard workers are presented in ways reminiscent of the Stakhanovite art of the Soviet Union, primarily through the framing of the figures. This is particularly marked in the scene of the final launching of the ship David has helped design.

Figures 8.2 and 8.3 The River Clyde functions in two discourses within *Floodtide*: the Scotland of beautiful hills and lochs and the Scotland of bustling industry.

Progressive though *Floodtide*'s impulses are, its perspective on the process of shipbuilding is consensualist: everyone from the chairman of the company to the workers on the shop floor is pulling together for the greater glory of shipbuilding and the Clyde. The shallowness of this dimension of the film has been bitterly exposed by history. In order to function mystically and consensually, two discourses prevalent in the actuality of the Clyde had to be evacuated from the text of the film – the class discourse and the sectarian discourse. The latter surfaces very briefly in the disclosure that David's uncle is going to a masonic lodge meeting. But for the film to have pursued this further into the structure of power conferred in the shipyard – particularly at foreman level – by organised sectarian allegiance, would have opened fissures which would have cracked *Floodtide*'s preferred mystical, consensual discourse apart.

The discourse of class – and, specifically, that discourse being set in motion then being repressed and evacuated – is more interesting in *Floodtide* and is perhaps best discussed in the context of the other problematic aspect of the film: the fact that it seeks to be progressive within the framework of classical realist narrative. The master structure of this narrative form – stability, followed by disruption, followed by restoration of new stability – and the attendant features of conflict, apparent resolution, reversal and final resolution, are carried both in David's progress from the shop floor to the drawing office and in his progress from the girl he meets at Barrowland to his union with the shipyard boss's daughter. Both of these movements fit easily within the form of classical realist narrative as practised up until the time of the film's making in the late forties. However, these developments of David's professional and personal trajectories are so nakedly class-based that they seriously trouble this ostensibly progressive film, which then has to find ways of masking their implications. It is interesting to see the film struggling with itself in this regard. It is clear that it is much more sympathetic to the jovial, bantering milieu of Mrs McTavish (Molly Weir)'s house, where David originally has lodgings with Tim, than to the tight-lipped, petit-bourgeois milieu of Mrs McCrae (Grace Gavin)'s house, where David is required to lodge after he leaves the shop floor and enters the drawing office. Similarly, the film lights on the absurdity of his having to wear a bowler hat in his new elevated job. However, to have pursued this awareness would have threatened the ideological project of the film: to valorise the men of the Clyde irrespective of class. The class tensions are dissolved in the ideology of the film, in which it is made clear that David, though on the way up, 'doesn't forget his friends'.

It is in order to clear the decks for David to marry the boss's daughter that *Floodtide* has to do the greatest violence to the psychological realism of the classical narrative form. In order to reactivate the drama and the reversals demanded by that form, Judy (Elizabeth Sellars), the working-class girl David meets at Barrowland, having vanished from the narrative action, is reintroduced in order to trouble David's relationship with the boss's daughter. Earlier in the film, Judy is constructed as a warm-hearted girl who makes the running in the brief relationship between her and David. But later in the film, and to mask the class basis of David's rejection of her, Judy is constructed as a slatternly virago who goes for the boss's daughter with a broken bottle. In Tim Brogan's words, Judy is ultimately constructed as 'a right bad yin'. The final ideological leap of *Floodtide* is to contrive a separation between David and the boss's daughter so that they can subsequently be reunited, on the day of the launching of the first ship he has designed, on a hill overlooking the Firth of Clyde. In this final scene the Clyde is made to function in two discourses simultaneously: the Scotland of beautiful hills and lochs and the Scotland of dynamic industrial activity. *Floodtide*, with the best of intentions, deploys inadequate ideological and formal strategies for dealing with the material reality of Scottish industrial life. This is a failure which would be recapitulated when indigenous Scots filmmakers come to grapple with the same problem in subsequent decades.

Another progressive attempt to deal with the perceived reality of Scottish experience is *The Brave Don't Cry* (Philip Leacock, 1952), one of the films made by Group 3 (1951–55), John Grierson (1898–1972)'s venture into feature film production. There is a considerable degree of pleasure, given the dire history of the representation of Scotland and the Scots in the cinema, to see an almost exclusively Scottish cast deployed on the screen to signify impulses other than Scottishness of the Romantic or Kailyard variety. Indeed, it is a poignant experience to watch *The Brave Don't Cry* from a distance of thirty years and witness Scots actors functioning with great sensitivity and restraint within the tradition of European naturalism. In succeeding years these same actors were to be denied the cinematic conditions within which to display these qualities, because they were instead forced to function within the discourse of Kailyard and in cinematic production structures fashioned outside Scotland. The case of Jameson Clark (1907–84) well illustrates this point. Known to cinematic posterity primarily as the head-scratching, comic Highland policeman of modern Kailyard exercises such as *Whisky Galore!* and *Rockets Galore!*, Clark as the mine doctor in *The Brave Don't Cry* delivers the kind of controlled and subtle performance which, up to that point, had never been seen in the cinematic signifying of Scotland.

The Brave Don't Cry operates within the tradition of classic naturalistic narrative cinema of a relatively homogeneous kind; for instance, it does not display the bizarre but interesting mix of documentary naturalism and family melodrama of *Mandy* (Alexander Mackendrick, 1952), a film close to it in time. This is not to say, however, that it is a wholly coherent and discursively trouble-free film. The locus of the film's discursive problems is the figure of actor, John Gregson (1919–75). At one level, both in the role he plays and in his status as a star in the British cinema of the fifties, Gregson represents the traces in the film text of an absent discourse which nevertheless troubles and deforms *The Brave Don't Cry*. It is no secret, as Forsyth Hardy (1910–94) has indicated,[6] that relationships between Group 3 and the British commercial film industry were less than cordial, the Group constantly having to negotiate the form of its projects in relation to the real or perceived demands of that industry. Gregson's presence – he was then a rising star of the Rank Organisation and was specifically imported on loan from Rank for commercial reasons – troubles the film deeply. This is evident in the violence his entry visits on the form of the narrative. Gregson, playing the character of a mine inspector, enters late, without satisfactory explanation, and the overall psychological realism of the film is ruptured by having him voluntarily join the trapped miners and occupy the dramatic centre of their struggle to get free from the mine. The Gregson figure is also the site of another disturbance in the film, this time an ideological one. Given the film's ideological project of celebrating the courage and dignity of the miners, issues of ownership, control and management of the mine, key questions, it might be thought, in the presentation of a mine disaster, are virtually repressed. But the introduction of the Gregson figure (he is a member of management) reactivates this issue only to then collapse it within the humanistic and classless project of the film. This is a problem which will reappear in Grierson's later, documentary-based projects in Scotland and is, indeed, the besetting problem of ostensibly politically progressive attempts to deal with Scottish life.

Forsyth Hardy has argued spiritedly and lucidly on behalf of the achievement of Films of Scotland (1954–82), which for two decades after its formation in 1954 constituted the almost exclusive channel through which indigenous Scottish film production flowed and the determining structure on the practice of several generations of Scottish filmmakers.[7] The conjuncture within which Films of Scotland emerged is spelled out by Hardy, the key elements being: the withdrawal of government money for civil service-based film production in Scotland; the presence of a well-connected and energetic ex-civil servant (Hardy himself) whose own cultural formation was strongly determined by Griersonian documentary; and the entrée to commercial cinema screens facilitated by Sir Alexander King (1888–1973), the Chairman of Films of Scotland.[8] There is no reason whatsoever to dissent from Forsyth Hardy's conclusion that Films of Scotland's remit 'to promote, stimulate and encourage the production of Scottish films of national interest'[9] was reasonably carried out over the twenty years and 150 films of his tenure as its Director, and indeed in the years succeeding this.

However, if the argument proceeds from different premises, Films of Scotland can be shown to have given, in many of its films, new and monstrous life to the regressive discourses of Tartanry and Kailyard; to have encouraged alternatives to these discourses which were politically inappropriate; and, by its institutional dominance within Scottish film production, to have pre-empted the emergence of alternative production structures which might have dealt more adequately with Scottish history, politics and contemporary life. Several questions require to be posed of Films of Scotland's activity and legacy. To what extent did the very remit of projecting life and achievement imply a political and aesthetic practice which eschewed the problematic and the contradictory in favour of the celebratory and, indeed, the incantatory? To what extent did the making of films under the sponsorship of powerful establishment bodies such as business concerns, banks and the National Trust confirm these tendencies and propel Scottish filmmakers headlong into the gaping jaws of Tartanry and Kailyard? And, to what extent did the dominance of the documentary stance within Films of Scotland's output inhibit the growth of an indigenous fiction cinema? The answers to these questions are by no means straightforward nor should the questions themselves be laid exclusively at the door of Films of Scotland. The policies, public profiles and levels of activity of other film cultural agencies in Scotland (for example, the Scottish Film Council [1934–97], the Scottish Arts Council [1967–2010] and the Scottish Federation of Film Societies [1934–c.1967]) are part of the picture too. However, Films of Scotland's long-term dominance over filmmaking in Scotland makes it appropriate that these questions be directed there first.

The evidence on which judgements can be made (virtually the total output of Films of Scotland) is to be found in the Scottish Central Film Library in Glasgow.[10] A complete analysis of that output would involve a massive research task which this essay cannot encompass. It is reasonable, however, to pose about this body of films the question with which this essay has been centrally concerned: What discourses have informed representations of Scotland and the Scots on the screen? Given the awesome power and international omnipresence of Tartanry and Kailyard, it is scarcely surprising that much of the output of Films of Scotland should be deeply marked by those discourses. Put another way, the hegemonic discourses about Scotland within which Scots, including Scottish filmmakers, are interpellated and set in place as social actors, provide a severely limited set of representations of the country and its people. It is not an issue of Scottish filmmakers' talent or lack of it – pound for pound, they are no better or worse than those of any other country. But they have two particular disabilities. Firstly, the dominant filmic representations of their country have been articulated elsewhere. Secondly, the indigenous Scottish institutions which exist to foster film culture have never articulated as a priority the helping of Scottish filmmakers towards the discourses which would effectively counter the dominant ones. Put another way, these institutions have never attempted to analyse the problem of Scottish culture and construct film policies to help remedy this problem. The encouragement of individual talent in filmmaking and the celebration of individual films are poor substitutes for such policies.

It comes as no surprise, therefore, to find the 'Tartan Monster'[11] (the phrase is Tom Nairn [1932–2023]'s) stalking the pages of the Films of Scotland catalogue. Some of the very titles chill the spine: *A Song for Prince Charlie* (Anvil Films, 1958); *Edinburgh Tattoo* (Campbell Harper Films, 1958); *By Lochaber I Will Go* (David Paltenghi, 1960); *A Touch of Scotland* (Hans Nieter, 1964); *The Tartans of Scotland* (Austin Campbell, 1966); *The Black Watch* (Mark Littlewood, 1971); *Cock o' the North* (Don-Mor Films, 1972); *Come Away In* (Laurence Henson, 1973). These and many more give free passage to, and take absolutely no critical distance from, Tartanry and Kailyard.

From among these films it would be possible to construct, Frankenstein's monster-like, the Ur-Tartan Documentary. That creation would open, accompanied by the sound of a clarsach or a plaintive Scottish violin tune, on a panorama of lochs and bens, preferably in autumn since lament is the dominant tone of the form. Against this Landseerian background (the more gross versions actually include a kilted, claymore-bearing Highlander) the commentary begins to unfold. The choice of narrator is crucial. The voice must call up the cluster of motifs characteristic of the genre: beauty, sadness, dignity, loss. Such a voice is that of Duncan Macintyre (1907–73), a frequent narrator in Films of Scotland productions and owner of a voice reminiscent of the late actor Duncan Macrae (1905–67) in one of his Highland screen roles. The film's visual, verbal and musical rhetorics are sustained throughout and frequently close on the image of a loch at sunset (indeed, one notorious, actually produced film closes with the spectacle of clinking glasses of a Scottish liqueur held, in belaced hands, against the sky). The following extracts from the actual commentaries of Films of Scotland-sponsored works indicate both the subject matter and tone of the Ur-Tartan Documentary genre: 'In the dance Scottish soldiers find a way of expressing their joy and pride in their calling and their country'; 'In Skye the past has a habit of coming alive now'; '[The battlefield of Culloden] moves the Scottish heart today as much as it did Rabbie Burns'; 'Honour the name of it; drink to the fame of it: the tartan!'; 'The honour, the glory, and the romance of the Scots'; 'Love of his native land and its romantic tradition'; 'With a kind of inward joy he looked on the Eildon Hills. He had indeed come home'; '[On] that

battleground of dreadful memory the sorrow of defeat is here recorded';
'[The statue of Flora MacDonald] searching in vain for the lost Jacobite
cause'; 'Here, on the edge of the Atlantic, everything seems to stand still';
'Soon more clansmen came; a trickle, a tumble, a cataract'; 'Scottish hearts
were high as the young prince marched through the Lowlands'; 'The River
Esk ran with blood and the English soldiers scattered like sheep'.

Dire as this dimension of its output is, Films of Scotland is not monolithic. Other discourses about Scotland are evident within its catalogue. Indeed, as Forsyth Hardy makes clear, both he and Grierson (in terms of some of the latter's Group 3 projects) were extremely critical of Tartanry/ Kailyard and throughout their careers sought to create representations of Scotland and the Scots more in keeping with the contemporary world.[12] The discourse which emerged from this impulse constructed Scotland as a bustling, thrusting, modern industrial nation and its people, rural as well as urban, not as hopeless dreamers crying into their whisky over the failure of the '45, but as strong, practical souls drawing strength from the land and from the past, yet more than able to cope with the affairs of the modern world. We might therefore name the discourse in question, 'Scotland on the Move'.

Such is the power of traditions of representation over the impulses of individual filmmakers that many Scottish ones, including some of the most talented, oscillate between the available discourses according to the projects they are working on at any given time. But the best work of some of the more talented is to be found within the discourse associated with Grierson and Hardy. The 'Scotland on the Move' discourse first emerged in the brief Films of Scotland venture of 1938. It can be illustrated with reference to the Films of Scotland-sponsored documentary short, *They Made the Land* (Mary Field, 1938). Although the film is about Scotland, its stylistic points of reference are the British documentary films of the thirties and the Soviet cinema of the twenties. It is frankly instructional, concerned with the details of processes such as draining peat bogs; but in common with British documentary films of the time, it also displays its interest in poetry within the rhetoric of its images and its voiceover commentary. When the latter refers to the 'strong, handsome women' who helped work the land, the camera frames them from below and against the sky in the manner of Soviet cinema. Similarly, the clipped, Anglicised commentary – there were no Scottish production units operating in this form of cinema in the thirties – refers to Scottish trees having 'strong roots defying the tempest' and frequently deploys the rhetorical trope of repetition which sets it apart from the more literal forms of documentary: 'the wind blew over the crops in the new-laid fields [. . .] the wind blew over the crops and knocked them down'. With the subsequent re-emergence of Films of Scotland in 1954, this 'Scotland on the Move' discourse loomed very large indeed and is to be found in many of the titles in the Films of Scotland catalogue: for example, *From Glasgow Green to Bendigo* (Robert Irvine, 1958); *Seawards the Great Ships* (Hilary Harris, 1960); *County on the Move* (Laurence Henson, 1966); *The Tay Road Bridge* (Henry Cooper, 1967); *Livingston: A Town for the Lothians* (IFA [Scotland] Ltd., 1970); and *Cumbernauld: Town for Tomorrow* (Robin Crichton, 1971). It was this discourse which received Grierson's personal imprimatur (he wrote the treatments for several of the films constructed within it) and which attracted some of the most talented of the indigenous Scottish filmmakers.

It is convenient to discuss the modern version of the 'Scotland on the Move' discourse in relation to the work of two such filmmakers, Laurence Henson and Eddie McConnell (1936–2016), because their work demonstrates both its possibilities and also its limitations. When they work together Henson usually directs and McConnell acts as cinematographer but McConnell is a filmmaker in his own right, in which role (for example, *A Kind of Seeing: The Colour of Scotland* [1967]) he seems strongly drawn to formalism and pictorialism. Indeed, *A Kind of Seeing* illustrates objectively that traditions of representation – in this case, of the Scottish landscape – can have an overwhelming and deformative effect on even the strongest individual talent and pull the latter's work into the maw of Tartanry. The joint work of Henson and McConnell is best illustrated by *Heart of Scotland* (Laurence Henson, 1961) and *The Big Mill* (Laurence Henson, 1963). The former, from a treatment by John Grierson, is about the Carse of Stirling and offers a sophisticated and well-achieved example of the 'Scotland on the Move' discourse. In many respects the work of Henson and McConnell is the apotheosis of Griersonian discourses of documentary, with its bringing beauty to bear on socioeconomic processes. Introducing one of their films on television, Grierson said: 'Documentary suggests public reports and social problems. I see it as a visual art which can convey a sense of beauty above the ordinary world'. *Heart of Scotland* moves across the Carse of Stirling and seeks to weld together elements as disparate as the battlefield of Bannockburn and the oil refinery at Grangemouth. It achieves this melding through a rhetoric of poeticisation and abstraction which is carried in the film's rich visual style, its literary commentary and its modern, abstract music. The continuity it seeks to make between the past and the present is essentially a mystical one of strength passing from the land to the people and to modern, industrial processes. The achievements of the modern 'Scotland on the Move' discourse – particularly in the hands of Henson and McConnell – are evident enough:

great pictorial beauty and a sense of social continuity and unity. Yet, its principal limitation is equally evident: a failure to accommodate analysis and contradiction.

That failure is more historically apparent in another Films of Scotland film based on a treatment by John Grierson: *Seawards the Great Ships*. The film's mythologising of the processes and personnel of the Clyde shipyards, the elementalism and gigantism of its visual and verbal imagery ('mighty', 'titanic', 'the welder is king', 'rigidity that will withstand pounding oceans') is reminiscent of the Stakhanovite art of the Soviet Union, but seems shabby and hollow in the light of what has become of the Upper Clyde shipyards in the two decades after the film was made. Starkly in retrospect, the breast-beating and tub-thumping of *Seawards the Great Ships* offers no comfort to Clydeside workers or guidance as to the historical processes which have put them out of work. That is the central failure of the Griersonian 'Scotland on the Move' discourse.

Tartanry/Kailyard and 'Scotland on the Move' in Films of Scotland films operate relatively independently of each other, with occasional transitions ('we are a people with traditions, but [. . .]') from one discursive mode to another within particular films. While most Scots can see right through the empty posturings of Tartanry and Kailyard, the absence of a tough, popularly based and analytic indigenous cinematic tradition has meant that the 'Scotland on the Move' discourse has largely filled that vacuum, especially for the Left. However, at its most pernicious, as in *Seawards the Great Ships*, it simply replaces the older discourses as the cue which sets the tartan snake uncoiling in the stomach.

A tiny minority of the Films of Scotland canon constitute far and away the most interesting films which have emerged under its auspices. These are the films which do not allow free passage to the discourses of Tartanry/Kailyard and 'Scotland on the Move' but which turn them back on themselves, render them problematic, subvert them. These films are: *The Caledonian Account* (Brian Crumlish, 1976),[13] and *Mackintosh* (1968) and *Clydescope* (1974) by Murray Grigor.

The Caledonian Account, on the face of it, sets up a range of expectations as horrendous as those of the Ur-Tartan Documentary. Sponsored by a cruise company, its narrative action is a sail down the Caledonian Canal and part of its interest is that it delivers on these expectations. However, the audience is set back on its heels to learn that the passengers on this cruise are Sir Walter Scott and Thomas Telford (1757–1834), the builder of the Caledonian Canal. A rubric at the beginning of the film sets up the practical/romantic opposition which will be played out between the two in the course of the film, as each seeks to impose his construction of Scotland on the other. This is signalled in the opening shot of the film as Sir Walter rides towards the camera mouthing: 'Breathes there the man with soul so dead / Who never to himself has said / This is my own, my native land?' The two men proceed to construct passing features encountered during their shared journey within their separate discourses. Thus, a mill which for Telford provides work for the populace becomes, for Scott, his own private Loch Ness monster; the owner of Glengarry Castle is, for Scott, the jewel among the Highland chiefs who welcomed George IV to Edinburgh in 1822 but, for Telford, is the man who resisted the building of the Caledonian Canal; and a Forestry Commission grove represents, for Telford, the putting back of something into an exploited landscape while, for Scott, it means the end of wildness and the beginning of regimentation. The film ends on a shot of the cruise vessel, named, ironically enough, *The Jacobite*, apparently located within an idyllic Highland scene. The camera pulls back, however, to reveal an industrial plant in the foreground.

The choice of Charles Rennie Mackintosh (1868–1928) as a subject by Murray Grigor is a polemical statement in itself. More than any other Scottish filmmaker, Grigor has sought consciously to interrogate the cultural inheritance which Scotland offers and to bring to that inheritance a modernist sensibility which stresses play, paradox and contradiction. He has done so in work on Scottish themes made outside Scotland (for example, the film *The Hammer and the Thistle* [Granada Television, 1977] on Hugh MacDiarmid [1892–1978], which Grigor co-directed with Gus Macdonald); in *Scotch Myths* (1981), the exhibition he co-mounted with his wife, Barbara (1944–94), and which was a massive exposure and deconstruction of Tartanry/Kailyard; and in the work he did as Director of the Edinburgh International Film Festival (Grigor is one of the few Scottish filmmakers to have shown an interest in film history, criticism and theory), where he was responsible for the extension of the Festival's traditionally central concern with documentary towards more stylised, fiction-based discourses, particularly those of Hollywood. Important also, in this context, was his inauguration at the Festival of an explicitly critical event and an associated publication which, in succeeding years, were to become key sites for the introduction of new ideas about the cinema not only to Scotland but the whole of the UK. The cool, elegant *Mackintosh* is part homage to a kindred artist and part exploration of the dialectic between tradition and modernism at the centre of Mackintosh's work.

It is entirely appropriate that Grigor should also have worked on two occasions with Billy Connolly, the Glasgow comic who has the capacity (as yet unrealised) to be a major subversive, and therefore progressive, force in Scottish cultural life. One of these occasions was the making of a Films of Scotland film, *Clydescope* (there is a strong Joycean flavour in everything Grigor does, but particularly in the titles of his projects). As a project, *Clydescope* is a veritable field of elephant traps for a Scottish artist. Sponsored by the Clyde Tourist Association, it follows Connolly on a trip from the upper reaches of the Clyde down through Glasgow to Loch Lomond and the Clyde coast. The major elephant trap (the one with the spikes at the bottom) is the Ur-Tartan Documentary discourse within which the scenic beauty and couthy folk of the Clyde might have been celebrated. *Clydescope* dodges this, and most of the other traps, neatly: indeed, the film on occasion fills them in. Far from the confident certainty of the Ur-Tartan Documentary's discourse, *Clydescope* begins with a series of puzzles and paradoxes. Connolly is stopped in the upper reaches of the Clyde by a passing motorist looking for Egypt. The puzzled Connolly confesses to knowing of a Moscow in the area, but not of an Egypt (the joke's apparent obscurity is cashed later in the film by the discovery of the town of Alexandria on Loch Lomondside). The sense of paradox that characterises the film's opening is continued in the discovery that the source of the Clyde contains 'little towns with names like Biggar' and the landmark the film chooses to foreground is not a scenic view but the Metropolitan Photographic Studio, a site where changes of personality and historical role might be purchased (indicated by Connolly's getting done up in Victorian army uniform).

In *Clydescope*, the city of Glasgow can be introduced by a coat of arms designed in the style of Charles Rennie Mackintosh, a sail down the Clyde can be merry and celebratory without being maudlin, and the Tartanry and Stakhanovite views of the Clyde are eschewed for the formally complex imagery of the Edwardian glasswork of the roof of Wemyss Bay rail station. However, *Clydescope*'s *coup de grâce* to the discourse of Tartanry is to take on and defeat Loch Lomond. This shrine of Tartanry (and also Kailyard), represented on scores of postcards, shortbread tins and table mats, and celebrated in popular song and in the Ur-Tartan Documentary, is evacuated from *Clydescope* while, on the film's soundtrack, the song 'Loch Lomond' is sonorously played on what sounds like a ship's foghorn as the ship, *The Maid of the Loch*, cruises into frame.

In considering the Films of Scotland corpus, it remains to assess its major intervention in the field of narrative fiction, *The Duna Bull* (Laurence Henson, 1972). The motives for this which Forsyth Hardy has outlined are admirable: to extend the experience of Scots filmmakers into cinematic forms previously denied them in the Scottish context (although a few had gained such experience elsewhere through bodies like the Children's Film Foundation).[14] A recurrent argument of this essay is that where powerful existing traditions of representation, or discourses, exist (as is the case with Scotland), even talented artists will find it extremely difficult to create representations outside the frameworks of those traditions. This is writ large with regard to *The Duna Bull*. An account of its storyline immediately begins to ring bells regarding the discourse within which it has been constructed. Duna, a remote Hebridean island, loses its only bull and applies for another to the Department of Agriculture (the film's sponsor) in Edinburgh. An initially hostile young official sent to investigate the request is won over by the strength of the case and the charms of the local schoolteacher. The discursive antecedents of *The Duna Bull* are, quite evidently, films like *Laxdale Hall*, *The Maggie*, *Whisky Galore!* and *Rockets Galore!*: the modern Kailyard discourse in which canny and couthy Highlanders get the better of (and in this case, win over) uncomprehending or hostile (and usually bureaucratic) forces from outside. This is confirmed in the casting and playing of the film and in its *mise-en-scène* (for instance, comic music pointing up responses in particular scenes). From this point of view, *The Duna Bull* advances Scottish film culture not one whit.

As this essay is being written a newspaper announces that Bill Forsyth's next project will be a big-budget, international film.[15] One's spirits rise: here is a gifted Scottish filmmaker whose two feature films to date, *That Sinking Feeling* (1979) and *Gregory's Girl* (1980), have decidedly eschewed Tartanry/Kailyard and deployed discourses which are not maudlin, but which relate to aspects of the lived experience of contemporary Scots. However, as one reads on a cold chill begins to come over the heart: the story will be set in the Highlands; it will be about the impact of offshore oil; and Burt Lancaster (1913–94) will play the president of a multinational oil company. One tries to blot out memories of *The Maggie*, but they will not go away. As the elephant traps begin to open, it is fervently hoped that Bill Forsyth can sidestep them.

This essay has argued that the discourses within which Scotland and the Scots have been represented in films have been wholly inadequate for dealing with the historical and contemporary reality of Scotland. Some of these filmic discourses – for example, the Tartanry of both versions of *Bonnie Prince Charlie* or of *Rob Roy: The Highland Rogue* and the Kailyardry of *The Little Minister* or *Whisky Galore!* – Scots filmmakers have been powerless to oppose, since the discourses were deployed within production structures fashioned outside Scotland. Nevertheless, the discourses had a pernicious two-fold effect. On one hand, they defined the cinematic terrain within which several generations of Scots actors could function, setting a limited range of roles and foregrounding particular modes of acting. This has had a cruelly stunting effect on Scots actors which, in terms of the growth of individual talents, could only be remedied by working outside Scotland and within different, non-Scottish discourses. On the other, the dominance of Tartanry/Kailyard has also entailed that when indigenous Scottish filmmakers came to make their own films, these powerful existing traditions of representation beckoned them, Circe-like, and lured more than a few onto the rocks. However, even when indigenous Scots filmmakers were able to produce a discourse which sloughed off Tartanry/Kailyard and attempted to come to grips with the reality of contemporary Scotland – as was the case with the adaptation of the Griersonian impulse, the 'Scotland on the Move' discourse – such developments allowed talents to develop and produced formally attractive works, but proved hopelessly inadequate for dealing both with the meaning of Scottish history and the complex socio-political condition of contemporary Scotland. Clearly, some blame for this must lie with Scots filmmakers themselves. With very few exceptions they have shown little interest in equipping themselves politically and artistically for the stern tasks to hand. The annual gathering of Scots filmmakers, Film Bang, for instance, has never addressed these problems nor come remotely close to the formulation of collective socio-aesthetic statements such as filmmakers produced in the Soviet Union of the twenties, in post-WWII Italy, and even in England in the thirties. Rather, Film Bang has seemed like a recurrent peevish cry for the resources which would lift the filmmakers, as individuals, into the stratosphere of international film production.

However, the Scottish failure has not been one primarily of individual will; it has been the failure of institutions to create the conditions for the development of more politically and artistically relevant discourses. Put in epigrammatic terms, institutions like the Scottish Film Council, the Scottish Federation of Film Societies, Films of Scotland and, more recently, the Scottish Arts Council, have failed to keep a historic appointment with the discourses of Marxism and modernism, the conjunction which has dynamised analogous institutions in other cultures. The single Scottish institution which has made this engagement to any degree, the Edinburgh International Film Festival, is the only one with any reputation in international film culture.

Needless to say, the call for a Scottish institutional engagement with the discourses of Marxism and modernism is not a plea that the institutions swallow these discourses whole and periodically regurgitate them: that would not only be intellectually deadening, but would be a wholly inappropriate role for publicly funded bodies in a pluralist society. Such bodies must have due regard for the diversity of views in the constituencies they serve, while at the same time ensuring that processes of debate and renewal occur. There is little evidence of these processes in Scottish film culture. Just as it was appropriate to raise the question of the adequacy of indigenous Scottish film production in the first instance with Films of Scotland, so too is it appropriate to raise matters concerning the general health of Scottish film culture with the Scottish Film Council – the body charged with its encouragement in Scotland. The institutional failure to engage critically with recent thinking about the cinema and society has meant that Scotland has produced no equivalents of Hans-Jürgen Syberberg's, Bernardo Bertolucci (1941–2018)'s, Theo Angelopoulos (1935–2012)'s, Santiago Álvarez (1919–98)'s and Phil Mulloy's treatments of their respective national histories; no equivalents of Jean-Luc Godard (1930–2022)'s, Nagisa Ōshima (1932–2013)'s or Dušan Makavejev (1932–2019)'s anatomising of the sexual mores of the societies in which they live; no equivalents of the sustained reflection on the processes of cinema evident in the work of Michael Snow (1928–2023) and Jean-Marie Straub (1933–2022)/Danièle Huillet (1936–2006); and – most damagingly of all – no equivalents of the accounts of women's experience to be found in the work of Chantal Akerman (1955–2015), Yvonne Rainer and Peter Wollen (1938–2019)/Laura Mulvey.

That is the extent of the institutional failure of Scottish film culture.

Notes

1. Before readers start reaching for their guns at what might seem wilful linguistic exoticism on my part, let me openly discuss a problem posed in the writing of this essay. Re-reading the draft, I recoiled at the heavy recurrence of the word 'discourse' and its affiliates (for example, 'discursive antecedents') and started scratching out these words and finding substitutes. That is, half-consciously on my part, the literary ideology of 'good style' – that cluster of practices (such as not repeating the same word too often) designed to produce the illusion of effortlessness, elegance and force in the writing and ease in the reading – came into play. Readers will no doubt perceive the traces of this ideology remaining in the text, but – quite apart from the important principle of resisting the idea of the transparency of language – I felt it necessary to resist the impulse to continue excising the word 'discourse', because of its centrality as a concept in the essay. This is best illustrated in relation to the decision to favour 'discursive positions' over 'stereotypes' (although the same argument could be deployed with regard to the essay's recurrent use of the word 'construct'). 'Stereotype' tends to get used only with regard to one aspect of the production of fictions, the

construction of character. It immediately sets up a comparison between the character as constructed in the fiction and people in the 'real' world on a one-to-one basis. For instance, it is often argued that certain races or genders are presented 'stereotypically' and that the problem is easily dealt with by presenting them 'realistically', the underlying assumption being that the fictions of the cinema or television or literature reflect or capture the world as perceived by the senses in a direct, unmediated way. To choose the phrase 'discursive positions' over 'stereotypes' is to reject this whole conception of the relationship between fictions and the 'real' world. To describe a character in a fiction as a 'discursive position' is to suggest that 'his/her' development and movement are determined not primarily by reference to the world outside the fiction but to the organising discourses within which the fiction is constructed – this is the classic structuralist position. For instance, it is argued in this essay that the actions of one of the characters in *Floodtide* (Frederick Wilson, 1949) are determined by the needs of two of the key shaping discourses of the film (the formal discourse of classical narrative and the ideological discourse of masking the class basis of the hero's choices) rather than by questions of how the character would behave in 'real' life. This factor alone – the insistence that all the elements of the fiction are part of a system and cannot be referred piecemeal to the 'real' world outside the fiction – would be grounds enough for preferring 'discursive positions' to 'stereotypes', but to remain at this point would be formalist, and would give no indication of the function of the fiction in the 'real' world. The essay poses the view that the objective function of fictions is to set audiences in place with regard to the 'real' world; to construct ways of looking at the world so that it appears natural and unproblematic from those points of view. What the essay is about, therefore, is how a certain limited number of discourses have been deployed in the cinema to construct Scotland and the Scots and to give the impression that no other constructions are possible.
2. See Malcolm Chapman, *The Gaelic Vision in Scottish Culture* (London: Croom Helm, 1978).
3. The theoretical and historical dimensions of Romanticism are discussed in, respectively, Meyer Howard Abrams, *The Mirror and the Lamp: Romantic Theory and the Critical Tradition* (London: Oxford University Press, 1953) and Carmen Casaliggi and Porscha Fermanis, *Romanticism: A Literary and Cultural History* (London: Routledge, 2016).
4. This indication of the kind of role assigned to women in Kailyard (similar domestically based roles are evident in Tartanry as well) raises the question of the strongly patriarchal nature of these discourses. This is not just a question of the representation of women on the screen, it is a feature of Scottish film culture as a whole (for example, the dearth of women filmmakers and of women prominently placed in indigenous film cultural institutions). The lack of a separate essay on this question in the *Scotch Reels* volume is perhaps a symptom of the very backwardness its authors seek to define.

5. George Blake, *Barrie and the Kailyard School* (London: Arthur Barker, 1951), 8.
6. John Caughie and Colin McArthur, 'An Interview with Forsyth Hardy', in *Scotch Reels: Scotland in Cinema and Television*, ed. Colin McArthur (London: British Film Institute, 1982), 81.
7. Ibid., 90.
8. Ibid., 88.
9. The quotation is from the Films of Scotland Committee's original 1955 Memorandum and Articles of Association. That document is available in the John Grierson Archive, University of Stirling, reference no. H.2.1.2.
10. This was the case at the original time of writing in 1982. As of 2022, these films can now be accessed, almost all online, through the National Library of Scotland's Moving Image Archive: https://movingimage.nls.uk [accessed 10 August 2022].
11. Tom Nairn, *The Break-Up of Britain: Crisis and Neo-Nationalism* (London: New Left Books, 1977), 162.
12. Caughie and McArthur, 'An Interview with Forsyth Hardy', 75; 80–1.
13. Although *The Caledonian Account* bears all the marks of being a Films of Scotland film – it was sponsored by Jacobite Cruises and the Highlands and Islands Development Board – it is not technically such, having been produced independently of that organisation.
14. See Caughie and McArthur, 'An Interview with Forsyth Hardy'.
15. This project was made and released subsequently as *Local Hero* (1983).

CHAPTER 9

*The Maggie**

> I rushed to the mirror. At the sight that met my eyes, my blood was changed to something exquisitely thin and icy. Yes, I had gone to bed Henry Jekyll, I had awakened Edward Hyde. How was this to be explained? I asked myself; and then, with another bound of terror – how was it to be remedied?
>
> R. L. Stevenson, *The Strange Case of Dr Jekyll and Mr Hyde* (1886)

In 1982, in the context of a historical survey of the way Scotland and the Scots have been portrayed in the cinema, I wrote:

> *The Maggie* [Alexander Mackendrick, 1954] represents Scotland at its most self-lacerative. Precisely at the moment, the early fifties, when the massive penetration of American capital into Scotland was gathering pace, *The Maggie* actually sets the two halves of the contradiction – American entrepreneur and Scottish workers – in opposition to each other, but with almost wilful perversity the film has the Scots win hands down. In true Kailyard style, what is not achievable at the level of political struggle is attainable in the delirious Scots imagination.[1]

Since that time my mind has been haunted by the phenomenon of *The Maggie* – not just the film itself, but the processes of its production and consumption within Scotland – as the *locus classicus* of everything that is wrong with Scottish film culture. This essay, then, is in some sense the 'talking cure' which, with any luck, will exorcise the demon.

For those who have yet to see the film, a plot summary from a contemporary review might be useful:

> *The Maggie* is a comedy from Ealing about a dilapidated, flat-bottomed steamboat, one of the 'puffers' trading in Scottish waters, which by a combination of accident and cunning has been entrusted with a valuable cargo. The owner of the cargo, an American businessman, discovering that his goods are in a ship condemned as unseaworthy, supposes that it is a simple matter to have them transferred. The rest of the film is about his battle against the stratagems of a crew determined to finish the job.[2]

---

* Originally published in *Cencrastus*, no. 12 (Spring 1983), 10–14.

The Moment of *The Maggie*

The Maggie was shot in Scotland in the summer of 1953 and released (in Scotland as elsewhere) in February 1954. I was at the time about halfway through my two years of National Service in the British Army. In common with others of my class origins and age, I had entered it with no great enthusiasm but, at the same time, with never a thought that such joining of the colours was anything other than natural. One occasionally got distorted glimpses through the popular press of individual Scots being arrested for refusing to serve with the British Army (Hugh MacDiarmid [1892–1978]'s son was, or was to become, one such). So secure and timeless did the Act of Union then seem that Scottish Nationalists could be – and indeed, were – constructed in the Scottish press simply as loonies who blew up pillar boxes.

But no matter how politically stable things appeared in those comfortable years, the long erosion of the Scottish economy was well under way. In a process that began in the fifties, by 1969 the amount of United States investment per head in Scotland was second only to that in Canada and virtually double that for the United Kingdom as a whole.[3] That debilitating process, which is visible now in the cold statistics, was contemporaneously experienced then, especially at the level of working-class life, as an exciting influx of rich, stylish Americans who made the headlines in the local press. With all the symptoms retrospectively readable as inferiorism, we thought Americans very special people and Hollywood stars, godlike. Imagine! Paul Douglas (1907–59) in Glasgow![4]

Simply at the industrial level, the making of *The Maggie* in Scotland related to the economic process outlined above. As far as these things are known, it was financed by English capital, that is, by Ealing Studios, and it gave a lot of work to a range of Scottish actors associated at the time with the Citizen's Theatre in Glasgow. However, the really massive chunks of the salary bill will have gone to the producer, director and screenwriter, none of whom were resident in Scotland, and most particularly, to the American star Paul Douglas who, *Variety* said at the time, gave the film 'marquee value' in the United States. The facts are not known, but it is possible that Douglas received a percentage of the box office takings rather than a flat fee, a fiscal device which would take even larger slices of the film's earnings out of the UK. It can readily be seen that the making of *The Maggie* in Scotland was analogous to any other foreign-based capitalist enterprise: the crumbs went to the locals and the cake went elsewhere.

How, then, was the making of *The Maggie* perceived in Scotland in the summer of 1953? The only record of that local response lies in the news features in the Scottish press at the time. Here are extracts from three:

Tommy Kearin's [sic] desk at St Margaret's School, Kinning Park, Glasgow was empty yesterday. Tommy, tousle-haired and 14, was off to Crinan, Argyllshire filming with American star Paul Douglas as the cabin boy in Sir Michael Balcon [1896–1977]'s new Scottish film about a Clyde puffer. And Tommy was in his element even though his mother from Kellas Street, Govan was there to keep an eye on him and even though a haircut was necessary for his role.

If you thought you saw an American film star strolling along Gordon Street today you were probably right. And if you thought you saw a movie camera lens poking out through the window of a closed car you were probably right again. And if you think you see the same thing again tomorrow you will still be very near the mark. The film star was Paul Douglas and the camera one of those from Ealing Studios which have been filming *Highland Fling* [an ultimately unused working title for the film] on the isle of Islay for the past five or six weeks.

Hollywood's Paul Douglas is back again in London. He has completed his Scottish location scenes for Sir Michael Balcon's *Highland Fling*. Scotland gave him a wet farewell. His last scene was, ironically, the first of his Scottish sequences to be seen in the film. It showed him arriving at a Glasgow hotel. He had only a few feet to go from a car to the hotel entrance. But it was far enough to get him thoroughly wet. It began raining the moment the camera was set up. It got steadily worse. And Paul completed his Scottish filming in a torrential downpour, to the accompaniment of distant thunder. The coat that actor Hubert Gregg [1914–2004] was wearing got wet too. But the coat didn't belong to him. At the last moment it was realised that he had the wrong type of coat with him, and then someone spotted that a visiting journalist, who had gone along to watch the filming, had exactly the right coat. The journalist agreed to lend it to the actor. The scene completed, he reminded the filmmakers that they had borrowed his coat. There was a moment's embarrassment. 'We'd like to keep it for a time,' he was told. 'You see, Hubert Gregg's some more scenes to do. We need your coat for continuity purposes.' It was the last he saw of it for a couple of days![5]

Without using a sledgehammer to crack a nut, we should note the lack, on the Scottish scene, of any kind of popular journalistic discourse capable of formulating questions about the relations of production on *The Maggie* and, even more remotely, the linking of that question to issues of filmic representation and the economic condition of Scotland at the time. This lack was to be writ large the following year, when the film opened in Scotland and the reviews began to appear.

There is a continuing problem posed by the absence of a popular film journalism which gets beyond the pervasive impressionism and mark-awarding of current practice to deal, in a lucid and accessible way, with issues such as the representation of particular groups and classes and how that representation relates to processes of cinematic narrative.[6] Thus, reviews of *The Maggie* from Britain and the United States all regard the film exclusively as a piece of entertainment and are concerned to assess it as such. There are, of course, wide variations in the insightfulness and sensitivity of the various reviewers, but their projects are identical. Here is an extract from one of the more serious reviews, by Karel Reisz (1926–2002), who would himself become an accomplished filmmaker:

> The *Maggie*, a picaresque little adventure comedy, derives most of its humour from the character of the islanders. The script, like William Rose [1914–87]'s earlier one for *Genevieve* [Henry Cornelius, 1953], is rich in incident: the obstacles which [Captain] MacTaggart contrives to prevent the American from removing his cargo become more and more ingenious, and, in spite of the extravagance of some of the escapades, progress with a sort of relentless logic. Only towards the end does the story run out of predicaments and switch to a not altogether successful passage of pathos. The director's observation of the islanders, affectionate, ironic, and quite free from patronage, brings them to life with a fresh and sometimes touching humour. They are never allowed to go out of character for the sake of a joke – as they sometimes did in *Whisky Galore!* [1949] – and the fun is all the more acceptable for it. The portrait of the American is less successful; the idea of the busy city man finding release in the example of the simple fisher-folk is treated half-heartedly, as though the director were a little shy of it. Paul Douglas plays the American with his gruff, teddy-bear charm, but it is a rather blurred performance which does not develop. The sub-plot concerning his strained relations with his wife is, in any case, weakly sketched in and uncertainly established. The direction is for the most part pleasantly discursive, yet retains a quick and flexible pace. Alex Mackenzie [1885–1965] plays MacTaggart with unobtrusive skill, and [director Alexander] Mackendrick [1912–93] has obtained a beautifully tough and sensitive performance from the boy, Tommy Kearins. One among a number of good minor performances is immediately striking: Fiona Clyne [1927–2021] plays her single, rather awkwardly written scene with sincerity and just the right suggestion of latent temperament.[7]

Reisz here exemplifies the voice of the putative movie industry professional, making judgements about the writing, the directing, the playing and the overall realisation of the film. Absent from his critical discourse, however, is any explicit addressing of the question: How are Scotland and the Scots represented? Nevertheless, buried in Reisz's review there is evidence of a position being taken on this question: the Scottish characters are 'simple fisher folk' whom the director 'brings to life' in a way that is 'affectionate, ironic and quite free from patronage'. That is, the critic (and, on his say-so, the director) is constructing the Scots in terms not dissimilar to the way nineteenth-century European ethnologists constructed the so-called primitive peoples of the world beyond Europe. But Reisz, and the wider industry-orientated discourse of film reviewing that he exemplifies on this occasion, is unaware that the construction is indeed such; for him it is an objective and neutral observation – that is the way the Scots really are. Now, it is the essence of ideology that what has been historically constructed appears natural and timeless. As far as Reisz – and, it will be argued, Alexander Mackendrick, the film's director – are concerned, the tradition of Kailyard, the dominant discourse of *The Maggie*, is not a system of representation traceable in history but merely 'the way things are' in Scotland.

The reviews of *The Maggie* which appeared in the Scottish press function within the same kind of critical discourse as the reviews of Reisz and others elsewhere: the film is a piece of entertainment to be awarded marks in terms of the professional and technical achievement of its personnel. However, the Scots reviewers, accustomed to confronting cinematic representations of their country and people fashioned in production centres outside of Scotland, have developed some sense of movies as offering discursively loaded images of the place. Thus:

> Here indeed is a fine picture, capturing the spirit of the West of Scotland and showing the world that men north of the border don't run around in kilts waving claymores all the time.

> What England thinks of this film is no concern of mine here. But I will tip it as a winner in Scotland. We are not depicted as so often we are depicted, as dour and dopey.

> *The Maggie* differs from most of the other Scottish films in that it was written direct for the screen. It is important that, in addition to the inevitable adaptations of novels and plays, there should be some films which spring direct from the life of the country. Otherwise the camera is deprived of its function as an observer and recorder, and becomes merely the servant of another medium.[8]

All these Scottish reviewers are agreed: *The Maggie* offers a sympathetic portrayal of the Scots. The *Glasgow Evening News* ecstatically serialised the film's story, lavishly illustrated with stills from the film, in a dozen parts.

Looked at from the perspective of 1983, questions surge to mind. Was there no voice raised in protest? Did no one pose the contrast between the contemporary economic processes at work on Scotland and what *The Maggie* was actually saying about the Scots? Did no one perceive that, like the turnaround in the relationship between blacks and white settlers in Africa, they (the oppressors) had the land and we were left with the Bible?

Traditions of Representation and Symbolic Appropriation

Part of the problem clearly lies in what the above consensus, outside of the Scottish press, agrees to be an appropriate popular critical discourse with regard to film. In stressing the separateness and autonomy of particular films and defining the central purpose of the critical act to be the assessment of the extent to which the individual film is realised as entertainment or art, this critical consensus forbids entry to a different conception. The latter would instead stress the continuity and dominance, within the film industry and the individual films that it produces, of particular modes of representation, their role as ideology and their relationship to politico-economic questions.

In bringing to bear on *The Maggie* such an alternative conception, the task is made considerably easier by the existence of a masterly book which, regrettably, seems not to be well known in Scotland, but which provides for us an account of the process and the categories within which Scotland and the Scots have been constructed in European history. Its author, Malcolm Chapman, describes a process which he calls 'symbolic appropriation'.[9] The discourse within which Scottish Celts have been described, and therefore constructed, has been in the hands of non-Celts and has been deployed by the latter as much to define themselves and their own respective national/cultural heritages as to define the Celts and theirs. Thus, for Chapman,

> The [eighteenth-century] Ossianic controversy promoted a picture of the Celt as natural, emotional, naive, and a failure in the rough and tumble of the modern world. This Celt soon began to occupy a place in European history [and so were constructed] the qualities that were going to dominate future debate – sentimentality, impressionality [sic], femininity and, in perhaps the most quoted phrase in the history of Celtic studies, a readiness to 'react against the despotism of fact'.[10]

One of the more chilling revelations of Chapman's book is the extent to which Scots (and particularly Gaels) come to live within the mental universe fashioned in this tradition and define their own identities accordingly.

Table 9.1 Celt/Anglo-Saxon

Celt	Anglo-Saxon
Scottish	American
Dreaming	Practicality
Tradition	Modernity
Slowness	Speed
Sea-travel	Air-travel
Unmarried	Married
Intuition	Rationality
Whisky	Vichy water
Community	Individuality
Old	New
Kindness	Ruthlessness

This phenomenon, whereby the disadvantaged define themselves within frameworks fashioned by the advantaged is a feature of diverse forms of colonialism and imperialism and has been pointed to by, among others, Frantz Fanon (1925–61), Anthony Wilden (1935–2019) and Edward Said (1935–2003).[11] This, in some measure, may explain the self-recognition and self-congratulation expressed by Scots with regard to *The Maggie* as it sails within the above constellation of oppositions.

But the delight many Scots (and cinemagoers in general) take in *The Maggie* is occasioned not only by its ostensibly flattering (but in reality demeaning) representation of Scotland, but by the particular operation of the film text itself.

The Pleasure of the Text and the Ideological Project

Going back briefly to the reviews of *The Maggie*, and while being concerned to demonstrate the absence of certain discourses there, one also has to concede that many of them have a sharp sense of the specific cinematic pleasures offered by the film. The performances are, from a technical point of view, very good indeed and Alexander Mackendrick is certainly among the more complex and interesting directors in the Ealing Studios stable.[12] What is particularly impressive about the film is the structure and pacing of its humiliation of Paul Douglas's character, Calvin B. Marshall, at the hands of Captain MacTaggart (Alex Mackenzie) and the crew of the *Maggie* and its rebuilding of him within the so-called Celtic values of Scotland. With extreme skill, this whole process, in encapsulated form, is visited on the secondary character of Pusey (Hubert Gregg), Marshall's English assistant, before being vented on Marshall himself. Outflanked partly by his own stupidity and partly by MacTaggart's eye for the main chance, Pusey, in casting, dress, and in Hubert Gregg's performance an exemplification of the archetypal English chinless wonder, is inveigled into a poaching expedition being carried out by the *Maggie*'s crew and ends up in jail while they sail on with Marshall's cargo.

When the same figurative dismemberment process is then visited on Marshall himself, it is within a carefully escalating series of scenes. From being a secure figure ensconced behind an executive desk in a tall modern office building (the physical massiveness of Paul Douglas is important here), Marshall is lured, by Pusey's failure to retrieve his cargo, onto the native terrain of the *Maggie*'s crew and begins to be taken apart. The escalatory aspect of this is crucial. From relatively minor setbacks like being outguessed by MacTaggart as to the *Maggie*'s destination and having to pay an enormous taxi fare to reach the port the puffer really makes for,

Marshall begins to be put down by the film's *mise-en-scène* in two key sequences. Once on board the *Maggie* and with it speeding through a clear sea, Marshall is contemptuous of MacTaggart's prediction that fog will engulf and slow down the boat, a prediction the film clearly attributes to MacTaggart's Celtic intuition. The image of Marshall looking ahead into the clear path and snorting 'Fog!' is immediately followed by a cut to him in precisely the same camera set-up peering through dense fog. Similarly, when the *Maggie* is beached at low tide, Marshall strides off across the sands to a distant village, calling to the reluctant MacTaggart to join him as the walk will do him good. This is followed immediately by a scene in which MacTaggart strolls into their destination while Marshall, clutching his sore feet, limps into frame behind him.

While the process of Marshall's humiliation is well under way by this stage in the narrative, the film really turns the knife in that wound during two astonishing sequences which provide evidence both for the criticism of anti-Americanism which the film attracted in the United States and also for the cogent claims made by Charles Barr regarding the complexity and darkness of Mackendrick's sensibility. Marshall appears to have got the upper hand on MacTaggart, has had his cargo unloaded from the *Maggie*, and has arranged to have it picked up off a soon-to-be-demolished pier. In an action set in motion – as is so often the case in *The Maggie* – by the Wee Boy (Tommy Kearins), MacTaggart allows his boat to rise under the pier with the tide and break the pier apart, thereby ensuring that only the *Maggie* can get close enough to shore to uplift the cargo. What is unhinging about this scene is the violence of the humiliation visited upon Marshall as he dances with rage on the pier, falls through the splintering boards, and ends up literally prostrated in front of MacTaggart. It might have been thought that the film, having brought Marshall to heel in this way, would at that point have begun the process of reconstructing him within so-called Celtic values, but one final twist of the knife is given which, in its cinematic realisation, verges on the sadistic. The cargo once more on board, MacTaggart resumes the journey with a catatonic Marshall standing in the middle of the deck. Suddenly, Marshall stares as a pig runs in front of him. This is followed by other livestock and human beings whom, it emerges, MacTaggart has decided to take across the water to a ceilidh. Marshall becomes more and more bemused as he is introduced to everyone and the scene ends with the hatch bursting open and a physically massive woman erupting like Frankenstein's monster from the swamp onto the deck and lowering over Marshall, on whose face there is an expression of what can only be described as terror.

It is at this point that the film proceeds to rebuild the shattered Marshall. This is skilfully achieved by several means. Marshall changes from his executive suit and overcoat into a seaman's jersey and trousers, becoming thereby indistinguishable from the rest of the crew (he also quite explicitly functions as one of them later in the film). Also, the series of telephone calls to his wife whereby Marshall remains in touch with his former life is ended when she hangs up on him. He is now alone and ready for entry into the absolutely pivotal ideological sequence of the centenarian's birthday party and ceilidh. This sequence is structurally central in that it marks Marshall's entry to and acceptance of the purported Celtic world, so the *mise-en-scène* stresses this threshold quality. But, given the scene has great ideological resonance, that world's asserted nature requires to be recapitulated and expressed in a highly condensed form. The Celtic world of the centenarian's birthday party is constructed to evoke a high sense of strangeness and remoteness in the audience. This effect is achieved through low-key lighting, the sight and sound of a bard speaking in Gaelic, the attendant sense of watching an ancient and mysterious ceremony, and, crucially, the fact of the centenarian being blind. This last element dredges up Ossianic connections between motifs of age, blindness, and wisdom.

The sequence's threshold quality is also stressed by having Marshall hear the sounds of the party while on board the puffer and then wander up to the house where the party is held, half curious, half holding himself apart. Appropriately, he is led into the ceremony by MacTaggart, the man who has broken and humiliated him in his former life. The uncertainty of Marshall's acceptance is brilliantly conveyed in the device of having him, through an interpreter, make to the centenarian (who speaks only Gaelic) the observation that the first hundred years are the worst. The centenarian's puzzled, blind stare, and Marshall and the assembled company's hanging on his response, gives way to the old man's wheezing laughter as he grasps the joke and Marshall's entry is assured. The party breaks into a dance and Marshall's final envelopment in the Celtic world is achieved by an image so startling as to be delirious. In a subjective shot from Marshall's point of view, a beautiful girl, Sheena (Fiona Clyne), in every sense the 'Spirit of Scotland' as constructed within European Romanticism, advances on him with arms outstretched and leads him into the dance. Not for the first or last time – Alfred Hitchcock (1899–1980)'s construction of communist societies in *Torn Curtain* (1966) and *Topaz* (1969) is another striking example – the delivery of considerable cinematic pleasure masks the peddling of dubious ideology.

Figures 9.1 and 9.2 Sheena, the Spirit of Scotland, advances with open arms and leads Marshall into the dance.

Perhaps more than anything in *The Maggie*, the 'Spirit of Scotland' image is troubling, particularly for those concerned with the way women are represented in films about Scotland. In Ouainé Bain's apt phrase, the 'fey, winsome lass'[13] who consummates Marshall's entry into the film's Celtic world offers one of the two ultimately limiting images of women which dominate Scottish culture (the other being the Ma Broon figure who holds the home together) and forbid entry to it of images of women which accord more with the needs of contemporary Scottish women. The conversation which follows between Marshall and the girl – in a scene in which the way she is lit and the playing of the actress reinforce the 'Spirit of Scotland' conception of the character – is troubling on precisely this point, the girl defining her life solely in terms of which kind of man she will become spouse to. The conversation also encapsulates the choice history has defined for the Celt:

> Sheena: The one in the window is Donald Macdougall. He's a fisherman. The one in the door is Ian McCullough. He owns the store by the pier. The question is: Which should I marry?
> Marshall: Well, how are you going to choose?
> Sheena: Oh, everyone says that Ian should be the one because he owns the store and already he is planning to buy another on Colonsay. People say that Ian McCullough will be a great man one day, but I think it will be the other one I will be taking.
> Marshall: Why?
> Sheena: Oh, it's simply that even although he's away with his brothers so much, he'll have more time for me. He'll not be so interested in what he's trying to do, or where he's going to, because he'll just be fishing. And when he's come home from the fishing, there'll just be me. And when we're very old, we'll have only what we've been able to make together for ourselves, and I think perhaps that is all we'll need.

Having experienced such an epiphany, Marshall can never be the same again. Against all his previous frugal Anglo-Saxon virtues and his training as a businessman, he orders his cargo to be jettisoned to save the boat from sinking. The Scots reign supreme in the realm of the imagination, smiling tearfully over the *Maggie* while, in the real world, remorseless economic forces shift the ground under their feet.

Conclusion

What we witness, in the production and consumption of *The Maggie* in 1953–54, is a society with no native tradition of seriously interrogating popular art caving under an ideological onslaught to the grotesque extent of mistaking the grapeshot for manna. 'Come on,' I hear you say, 'all that happened thirty years ago in a very different conjuncture. We've got a highly sophisticated and progressive political nationalism nowadays, and the women's movement, and we know our Gramsci, our Althusser and our Foucault.'

However, at the original time of writing of this essay, I had in front of me a cutting from *The Scotsman* of 12 May 1982. There was a photograph of a familiar figure writing something in a book with two young and obviously delighted girls looking on. The caption read:

> Burt Lancaster [1913–94], the American actor who is in the Fort William area shooting *Local Hero* [Bill Forsyth, 1983] signs autograph books for Caol sisters Anne and Mary Jane MacDonald. The film, produced by David Puttnam and directed by Bill Forsyth, tells the story of a Texas oilman who wants to buy a small village for oil development but has a change of heart.[14]

Notes

1. Colin McArthur, 'Scotland and Cinema: The Iniquity of the Fathers', in *Scotch Reels: Scotland in Cinema and Television*, ed. Colin McArthur (London: British Film Institute, 1982), 47–8, and also reproduced elsewhere in the present volume.
2. Anon, *The Sunday Times*, 28 February 1954, no page ref.
3. See, for example, Scottish Council Research Institute, *US Investment in Scotland* (Edinburgh: SCRI, 1974), 1.
4. The concept of 'inferiorism' is usually credited to Frantz Fanon (1925–61). While the idea circulates extensively in his work, particularly in *Black Skin, White Masks* (1952), the precise term probably does not. Fanon developed the idea in relation to the situation of people of colour under colonialism whereby they were not simply oppressed politically and economically but psychologically as well, the worldview of the oppressors colonising their

psyches. That idea has circulated also within Scotland as has the associated term, which is perhaps best known by way of the 1989 book by Craig Beveridge and Ronald Turnbull, *The Eclipse of Scottish Culture: Inferiorism and the Intellectuals* (Edinburgh: Polygon, 1989).
5. Anon, *Scottish Daily Express*, 12 May 1953, no page ref.; Anon, *Glasgow Evening Times*, 17 July 1953, no page ref.; Anon, *Edinburgh Evening Dispatch*, 30 July 1953, no page ref.
6. For a fuller discussion of this question and an attempt to pose an alternative, see Colin McArthur, *Dialectic! Left Film Criticism from* Tribune (London: Key Texts, 1982).
7. Karel Reisz, '*The Maggie*', *Sight and Sound* 23, no. 4 (April–June 1954), 199–200.
8. Anon, *Glasgow Evening News*, 4 February 1954, no page ref.; Anon, *Glasgow Evening Citizen*, 29 March 1954, no page ref.; Anon, *The Weekly Scotsman*, 5 March 1954, no page ref.
9. Malcolm Chapman, *The Gaelic Vision in Scottish Culture* (London: Croom Helm, 1978), 28.
10. Ibid., 82.
11. Frantz Fanon, *Black Skin, White Masks* (New York: Grove Press, 1968); Anthony Wilden, *The Imaginary Canadian* (Vancouver: Pulp Press, 1979); Edward Said, *Orientalism* (London: Routledge & Kegan Paul, 1978).
12. For a discussion of the nature of that complexity and interest see Charles Barr, *Ealing Studios* (London: Cameron and Tayleur, 1977). It is interesting that Barr, far and away the most accomplished critic to have engaged with *The Maggie*, does not perceive (or, at any rate, does not raise) the problem of its representation of the Scots. Ideology engulfs us all, irrespective of ability.
13. The quotation is from a presentation Bain gave at the *Scotch Reels* three-day discussion event held at the 1982 Edinburgh International Film Festival. See Colin McArthur, '*Scotch Reels* and After', *Cencrastus*, no. 11 (New Year 1983), 2–3; Douglas Bain, Ouainé Bain and Gillian Skirrow, 'Woman, Women and Scotland: *Scotch Reels* and Political Perspectives', *Cencrastus*, no. 11 (New Year 1983), 3–6.
14. My thinking about *The Maggie* benefited greatly from conversations with Ouainé Bain, John Caughie and Gillian Skirrow and the originally published essay itself saw the light of day more speedily through the research and secretarial help of Joy Wong.

CHAPTER 10

National Identities*

There is a strand of continental European historiography that is much concerned with historical time or, more precisely, with the articulation of different 'times' in specific historical moments.[1] The decision to hold a summer school entitled 'National Fictions: Struggles over the Meaning of World War II' emerged out of just such an articulation of temporalities.[2] More specifically, that decision emerged from the coming together of two phenomena. Firstly, the process, extending over some years, whereby nationalism ceased to be a scare fetish of the Left and began to be addressed in its historical dimension, and, secondly, the altogether more brief paroxysm of the South Atlantic War of 1982, in which conceptions of nationality shaped by key generative moments of the national past loomed so large.

The process of the (British) Left's coming to terms with nationalism can be followed through at a theoretical level by reference to certain key texts. The central one of these (which was studied at the summer school) is Tom Nairn (1932–2023)'s *The Break-Up of Britain*, a work deeply shaped by Nairn's own situation as a Scot perceiving the forces at work in his own country in the seventies.[3] Alongside that book's recognition of the historical necessity of nationalism, it also to some extent displays a continuing distaste for that same ideological phenomenon (and, indeed, this forms the basis of the critique of Nairn's position now emerging in Scotland). Succeeding important works seem progressively more sympathetic to nationalism. Ernesto Laclau's *Politics and Ideology in Marxist Theory*,[4] along with the useful works responding to it,[5] paved the way for the crucially important articulation of the idea of the 'national-popular' with the idea of 'hegemony' derived from Antonio Gramsci (1891–1937).[6] The figurative cleansing of nationalism within contemporary Left theoretical

---

* Originally published in *National Fictions: World War Two in British Films and Television*, ed. Geoff Hurd (London: British Film Institute, 1984), 54–6.

writing would appear to be complete in Benedict Anderson (1936–2015)'s *Imagined Communities*, which locates nationalism not within the armature of modern political -isms, but as secular heir to the great religious systems of previous epochs.[7]

This ongoing debate, therefore, became articulated with the explosive event of the South Atlantic War, when the Left and liberal opinion more generally experienced what could only be described as a deep sense of shock at the massive resurgence of a regressive definition of British national identity. That definition misconstrued Britain's role in the modern world by repressing the facts that the UK is a post-colonial power, a mediocre economic performer, a multi-racial society, and a society moving further and further away from the consensus expressed in the Westminster Parliament and in associated instruments of government such as the BBC. It repressed also the internal struggles attendant on this changed geopolitical role of the UK.

The central historical experience in the refurbished and regressive national identity associated with the South Atlantic War was the Second World War and the overarching rhetoric of its enunciation was Churchillian. The Thatcherite/Churchillian rhetoric pointed to by Graham Dawson and Bob West has its absurd dimension, and there were whole sectors of British life which were completely untouched by 'Falklands fever'.[8] For instance, an instructive comparison might be made between the British popular music ethos of the Second World War and that of the South Atlantic War. Simon Frith has indicated the indifference of British pop to the war in the South Atlantic, but memory suggests the complicity of British popular music with the prevailing rhetoric of the Second World War ('There'll be bluebirds over / The white cliffs of Dover').[9] However, the hold of the Thatcherite rhetoric over the bulk of the popular press was no less alarming for being predictable. Only time will tell whether it is a rhetoric that can sustain a workable definition of national identity in the continuing class/gender/race struggles of the contemporary UK, or whether it was usable only in the very specific conjuncture of the South Atlantic War, with its enabling ingredients of: response to military aggression; involvement of a quasi-English population; an undemocratic, militaristic enemy; and the conflict's status as a distant war, reminiscent of the colonial wars of the late nineteenth century, which did not touch the material lives of the population of the UK.

The 'National Fictions' summer school revealed that in order to make the Second World War earn its pivotal place in the Thatcherite rhetoric, it had to be constructed in a particular way. That construction is 'the finest hour' of the British people, unified and unsullied by internal contradictions and differences of any kind. It is a construction frequently endorsed by popular cinema and television in the decades since the War, but also one substantially eroded by serious historical research, by certain aspects of popular memory, by several wartime films and by some television programmes of recent years. The particular competing construction of the Second World War which had to be repressed in order for 'the finest hour' construction to function is that of the Second World War as 'the people's war', as an anti-fascist struggle. As Graham Dawson and Bob West indicate, the idea of 'Dunkirk' has been processed through diverse popular discourses so that the actual event's contradictory features – on one hand, bad military planning, military reverse, considerable resentment among the participants, and, on the other, considerable personal heroism – have been smoothed out to foreground the latter only.[10] The film *Dunkirk* (Leslie Norman, 1958), for instance, plays verbally with some of these elements, although its *mise-en-scène* massively privileges the 'finest hour' discourse and the film resolves any possible contradictions by invoking the mythical construct of Churchill (1874–1965).

Looking at war films of the fifties and sixties such as *Dunkirk* or, more particularly, *The Cruel Sea* (Charles Frend, 1952), *The Colditz Story* (Guy Hamilton, 1955) and *The Dam Busters* (Michael Anderson, 1955), reveals that the pass had been sold, so to speak, as early as this period. That is, a regressive construction of the Second World War was already being offered which repressed the 'people's war' construction and presented the War as a series of heroic actions performed in the main by middle-class, white men supported by compliant other ranks, and with women functioning as waiting sweethearts or mothers. In retrospect, this can be seen as contributory to the 'common-sense' construction of the War which was animated to such devastating effect some three decades later during the South Atlantic War. There is a lesson to be learned here which will hopefully shape future film and television research and practice.

The lesson to be learned was to some extent taken by some of the more recent television material viewed at the summer school. Under the influence of Angus Calder (1942–2008)'s book *The People's War*,[11] several TV plays – most notably David Hare's *Licking Hitler* (BBC, 1978), Ian McEwan's *The Imitation Game* (BBC, 1980) and David Pirie's *Rainy Day Women* (BBC, 1984) – offered constructions of the War informed by feminist perspectives, but were much criticised by women on account of the plays' failure to conceive of women other than as victims, as many women's contributions to the summer school's seminars made clear.

If the problem is posed as what kinds of films and television programmes need to be made and what kinds of film-cultural activity (research, writing, film distribution, film exhibition) undertaken to ensure that the British past cannot be unambiguously mobilised by the Right, the answer must focus on those historical moments which form the linchpins of rightist ideology in the present. The South Atlantic War has revealed the potency of the Second World War in this regard and there is some indication that the period of the two post-war Labour governments (1945–51) could be equally potent, in that it is largely from this historical experience that the Right culls its demons regarding the oppressive bureaucracy and joyless austerity of socialism. From this point of view, events like the 'National Fictions' summer school and TV plays such as *Licking Hitler*, *The Imitation Game* and *Rainy Day Women* are crucial ideological interventions in the here and now, active resistances to rightist hegemony of common-sense constructions of the past.

The problem needs to be posed more sharply than this, however. TV and film constructions of the generative moments of the past need to be related quite concretely to the diverse struggles of the present. It is interesting that the most talked-about progressive TV reconstructions of the Second World War (the Hare, McEwan and Pirie titles referred to above) have sought to have purchase on women's struggles in the present. Necessary as such interventions are, it is equally important that the present struggles over class and race are located in generative moments such as the Second World War.

It was notable that the British 'TV spectaculars' on the South Atlantic War viewed at the summer school all but eliminated the role in that war of British blacks as individual members of the armed forces. This omission was wholly consonant with the discursive 'script' of the South Atlantic War to which these spectaculars were made, one constructed round Churchill and the Second World War. The present struggle over race in the UK also needs to be located in relation to the generative moment of the Second World War. This points to the necessity of TV programmes being made about the substantial numbers of British West Indians who entered the armed forces at the outbreak of war and the experience of indigenous blacks, also a substantial number, on the home front. Both of these groups have been accorded no place in the 'finest hour' version of the Second World War.

In many ways the most interesting group of films viewed at the 'National Fictions' summer school were those actually made and exhibited during the War itself. These works are interesting because – unlike the films about the Second World War made in succeeding periods – they could not function unambiguously as myth, but were required to undertake substantial ideological work in relation to real problems in the society at the time.

Such problems included, for instance: the drive to recruit women into the forces, as dealt with in *The Gentle Sex* (Leslie Howard and Maurice Elvey, 1943); or getting women out of the home and into the factory for the conflict's duration, as in *Millions Like Us* (Sidney Gilliat and Frank Launder, 1943); or predisposing the British people towards the Soviet Union following decades of anti-Soviet propaganda in various popular discourses, as in *The Demi-Paradise* (Anthony Asquith, 1943). In order to achieve their ideological projects, all of these films have to struggle very hard indeed and make uneasy accommodations with totally divergent ideological tendencies. *The Gentle Sex*, for instance, can be viewed very fruitfully as an attempt both to cede autonomy to its women characters and to hold them firmly within patriarchal discourse. It is crucial that films such as these are written about and programmed for repertory screening. They, with their manifest fault lines and contradictions, speak of a suppressed history of advances made and subsequently lost and point the way towards a revision of the regressive construction of British national identity offered in the South Atlantic scenario.

The 'National Fictions' summer school's retrieval of films made and shown at the time of the Second World War, those made and shown in the fifties, and the holding of both groups within the same frame of reference as TV programmes made in the eighties, testifies eloquently to the fundamental instability of national identity. The latter is a process rather than an essence, and one which has constantly to be reworked and restated precisely in order to offer identity positions from which social and political judgements are made and actions taken. But with the recognition of such fluidity comes the possibility of change. A central ideological task of the eighties is the construction of a popularly based version of British national identity which will resist mobilisation for regressive political purposes; a version of national identity which is open and flexible (though not to the point where it eschews sites and slogans for political mobilisation), and, crucially, which is oriented to the future rather than the past.

The struggle continues.

Notes

1. See, for example, Fernand Braudel, '*La Longue Durée*', *Annales* (October–December 1958), translated as 'History and the Social Sciences: The *Longue Durée*' in *Economy and Society in Early Modern Europe: Essays from* Annales, ed. Peter Burke (London: Routledge & Kegan Paul, 1972), 11–42; and, thereafter, Louis Althusser, 'The Errors of Classical Economics: Outline of a Concept of Historical Time', in Louis Althusser, Étienne Balibar, Jacques Rancière, Roger Establet and Pierre Macherey, *Reading Capital* (London:

New Left Books, 1970), 91–118; and Pierre Vilar, 'Marxist History, a History in the Making: Towards a Dialogue with Althusser', *New Left Review*, no. 80 (July/August 1973), 65–106. The concern with time enters British historiography in, for example, Perry Anderson, *Lineages of the Absolutist State* (London: New Left Books, 1974).

2. The British Film Institute Education Department summer schools were a key part of the mission of BFI Education (alongside advice-giving, the production of study materials, written and filmic, and the University of London extramural classes in Film). All of these initiatives were designed to build a cadre of film teachers throughout the UK. The summer schools were held in diverse UK cities and, as well as being run by BFI Education staff, they increasingly drew in as lecturers and seminar leaders members of the growing cadre of actual or aspiring film teachers. Their topics followed closely the changing emphases in contemporary film culture and the particular school referred to within this essay was one of the first to deal with film in relation to current discussions within the wider society, in this case nationalism and ideology.

3. Tom Nairn, *The Break-Up of Britain: Crisis and Neo-Nationalism* (London: New Left Books, 1977).

4. Ernesto Laclau, *Politics and Ideology in Marxist Theory: Capitalism, Fascism, Populism* (London: New Left Books, 1977).

5. See, for example, Stuart Hall, 'Popular-Democratic vs. Authoritarian Populism: Two ways of taking democracy seriously', in *Marxism and Democracy*, ed. Alan Hunt (London: Lawrence & Wishart, 1980), 157–85.

6. The term 'national-popular' recurs throughout Gramsci's writings, in which it has both a political and cultural meaning. In a national-popular movement one of the fundamental classes (bourgeoisie or urban proletariat in Gramsci's time) gathers round itself other classes and class fragments and, exercising hegemony over them, bids for control of state power. National-popular culture deals with popular preoccupations and appeals to popular audiences. The concept of hegemony is also omnipresent in Gramsci's work, although shifting its meaning as his thinking developed. Its final form, which enthused and directed the work of Marxists in the 1980s, stressed the leadership of one class over the others primarily by means of consent rather than coercion, the dominant class having persuaded the others to accept its view of the world.

7. Benedict Anderson, *Imagined Communities: Reflections on the Origin and Spread of Nationalism* (London: Verso Books, 1983).

8. Graham Dawson and Bob West, 'Our Finest Hour? The Popular Memory of World War II and the Struggle over National Identity', in *National Fictions: World War Two in British Films and Television*, ed. Geoff Hurd (London: BFI Publishing, 1984), 8–13.

9. Simon Frith, 'Post-Punk Blues', *Marxism Today* (March 1983), 18–21.

10. Dawson and West, 'Our Finest Hour?'

11. Angus Calder, *The People's War: Britain 1939–1945* (London: Pantheon Books, 1969).

CHAPTER 11

TV Commercials: Moving Statues and Old Movies*

'I like the adverts; it's the programmes I can't stand.' This famous riposte constitutes, in some respects, a defensible position. A case could be made, though it would not be a very significant critical activity, for the relative merits of television commercials over the programmes that interrupt them. Certainly, in terms of production values, many commercials display flagrantly the fact that they have had ten times as much money spent on them, and the discipline of working within a one- to three-minute format can have the effect of sharpening narrative skill and honing wit.

Insofar as television commercials have been discussed critically, it has been in terms such as these, apart from the very necessary ideological critique laid on them by, among others, the women's movement and public bodies influenced by it. By and large, however, television commercials have been conceived of as 'other' among television's output, as separable from programmes and discussable in different terms, even within those critical stances which adopt a 'flow' model of the evening's viewing.[1] Substantial work has been done on, for example, news and current affairs, soap opera and sitcom television programmes, with regard to their overall shape, the working practices of their personnel, their ideological tendencies and their relationship to the institutional framework out of which they come. Such an approach, of course, requires programmes like *News at Ten*, *Panorama*, *Coronation Street* and *It Ain't Half Hot, Mum* (BBC, 1973–81) to be conceived not as separate, autonomous objects, but instead seen generically – as having formalised structures and relationships and being subject to transformations connected to events within both television and film practice and wider society. Analogous critical work on television commercials would have to begin by pointing to the similarities, not the differences, between one commercial and another.

---

* Originally published in *Television Mythologies: Stars, Shows and Signs*, ed. Len Masterman (London: Comedia, 1984), 63–6.

Over the several months in 1984 during which the original version of this essay was written, two motifs seemed particularly novel, striking and recurrent within television commercials. One of these motifs was the statue which moves. The first commercial to include this was for biscuits: statues in a fountain become animated in response to the degree of enjoyment experienced by figures seated by the fountain as the latter eat the biscuits in question. This was followed by a commercial for a torch battery, in which two policemen in Trafalgar Square are struck dumb by the statue of Nelson alighting from its column. This particular realisation of the moving statue motif, related to quite another television phenomenon, was reprised on the cover of *Radio Times*, indicating that cultural practices (in this case, the making of television commercials and the design of magazines) do not exist in a vacuum but interact with each other, reworking the same motifs. Several other television commercials also deployed the moving statue motif and, by a happy chance, a more recent example included both this and the other most novel, striking and recurrent motif with television commercials of the months during which this essay was originally written, namely, reference to, and/or the cutting in of footage from, old movies.

Two such commercials for British Telecom, for example, referred to films, one to *Tarzan the Ape Man* (W. S. Van Dyke, 1932) and the other to *The Hunchback of Notre Dame* (William Dieterle, 1939). In the latter, a figure made up like Quasimodo (or, more accurately, like Charles Laughton [1899–1962] playing Quasimodo) receives a telephone call from Esmerelda and shares his delight with an animated gargoyle on the roof of Notre-Dame Cathedral. It is difficult to be certain, but this particular commercial may have used, for its crowd scenes, intercut footage from the thirties film to which it refers. If so, this would link it to several such intercuttings in (mainly) television commercials of the mid-1980s period during which this essay was written. A commercial for the Kelly Girl secretarial agency, for example, intercut footage shot in the here-and-now with material from the German silent film *Metropolis* (Fritz Lang, 1927) – a film also appropriated in the rock band Queen's video promo for their 1984 single, 'Radio Ga Ga'. However, the most systematic such use of earlier films was in a series of commercials for Holsten lager, in which new footage of the comedian and actor Griff Rhys Jones was intercut with footage of Humphrey Bogart (1899–1957), James Cagney (1899–1986), George Raft (1901–80) and John Wayne (1907–79) from movies of the thirties and forties in which they appeared, to make coherent mini-narratives.

What, then, is the meaning of these two recurring motifs in mid-1980s television commercials? It might be useful at this stage to introduce a concept formulated and used within French structuralist and post-structuralist literary theory of that same period, the concept of intertextuality; defined crudely, the idea of works of art and discourses feeding off and dissolving into each other.[2] The concept was fashioned to deal with two problems. The first is the widely held view that the producer of a piece of creative work (whether poet, novelist, sculptor or film director) is in some sense wholly the originating source of that work. The concomitant practice is then to explain the work primarily by reference to the artist's personal qualities and background. The French structuralist and post-structuralist theoretical tradition, however, is concerned instead with the extent to which the institutions of language and literature and their specific forms predate their deployment by particular artists. The latter, therefore, can no more be said to 'invent' their works than the speaker of a particular language can be said to invent that language. Challengingly, it has been asserted that texts produce authors rather than authors, texts.[3]

The second problem the concept of intertextuality was fashioned to deal with is the widely held predisposition to assume that any given creative work's most pertinent relationships are with the 'real' world to which it refers, a predisposition particularly deeply grounded with regard to photographic practices such as cinema and television. Intertextuality, on the contrary, asserts that a more pertinent relationship exists between any given work and the other works in the wider system or genre (for example, the picaresque novel, the film noir, the television soap opera) to which it belongs. Indeed, one of the suggestions associated with intertextuality as a concept is that a reader's ability to understand a particular form is dependent upon their exposure to previous examples of it. For example, a particular kind of music above a film's opening credits and an opening image of a dark, rain-soaked street will set in train a range of expectations in the viewer as to what will follow (and those expectations will also have in part been aroused by the way in which the film has been publicised).

Clearly, the lager commercials referred to above are intertexts in a very fundamental way: they cut together footage of different decades. However, the commercials with the moving statue motif are also intertexts in the sense that they quote from earlier commercials (and, as will be suggested, films). The deployment of a concept such as intertextuality over the terrain of television commercials (a process which would, doubtless, cause their makers to raise their eyebrows) yields precisely the same benefits as its deployment on more serious cultural forms. That is to say, it points to the fact that commercials are not simply separate and autonomous objects spinning out of the talent and imagination of their makers but that, perhaps more pertinently, they exist in relationship with each other, as phenomena shaped within shared cultural determinants.

What some of these determinants are might be speculated upon quite concretely with regard to the moving statue and old movie motifs visible within mid-1980s television commercials. About eighteen months prior to their initial appearance, the film *The Draughtsman's Contract* (Peter Greenaway, 1982) opened in London to considerable critical acclaim from the broadsheet press and had a long run in a London art house. Among its motifs (formally inventive or flashy, according to one's personal view of what constitutes excellence in the cinema) was a statue which not only moved, but urinated. Almost contemporaneous with this was the opening of the American movie *Dead Men Don't Wear Plaid* (Carl Reiner, 1982), a send-up of the American crime movie and a work which intercut footage from earlier movies produced within that generic tradition into its narrative. Both films achieved a kind of cult status, being appropriated by the camp sensibility, by which is meant a sensibility which appropriates art in a hermetically sealed kind of way, to produce meanings and pleasures which have no point of purchase on the wider social and political life of society. Speculatively, the camp sensibility would seem to be very prevalent among the personnel and institutions which make up the world of television commercials. It is a sensibility uniquely well fashioned for the job is it required to do and the interests that it for the most part serves.

Notes

1. The concept of 'flow' in relation to watching television was introduced by Raymond Williams (1921–88) in his 1974 book *Television: Technology and Cultural Form* (London: Fontana), in which he stressed the difference between television viewing and reading a book or watching a film in that television programmes flowed into each other to make up what each channel presents as an evening's viewing, as, for example, when the end credits of one programme are interrupted in order to make way for the channel to announce which programme is up next.
2. The term 'intertextuality' was coined by the Bulgarian-French writer Julia Kristeva in two early essays, 'Word, Dialogue and Novel' (1966) and 'The Bounded Text' (1966–7). The former piece is available in *The Kristeva Reader*, ed. Toril Moi (New York: Columbia University Press, 1986), 34–61.
3. See, for example, Roland Barthes, 'The Death of the Author' in Barthes, *Image, Music, Text*, ed. and trans. Steven Heath (London: Fontana, 1977), 142–8; Michel Foucault, 'Authorship: What is an Author?', *Screen* 20, no. 1 (Spring 1979), 13–34.

CHAPTER 12

Tele-history: *The Dragon Has Two Tongues**

History is omnipresent in British culture: public statuary; street names; museums; so-called great houses open to the public; commemorative ceremonies like those for D-Day, VJ and VE Days; the various ceremonies surrounding the monarchy and other institutions. All of these (and more) offer constructions of the past. This, of course, is true of every society, but one has a strong subjective impression that the phenomenon is particularly deep-rooted and multifaceted in Britain. As our imperial role recedes and our old manufacturing industries decline, there is one industry in which we are still pre-eminent: the recycling and marketing of the past.

Needless to say, this massive national investment in the past is not value-free: it serves certain ideological interests in the present. This is not to say that there is a general conspiracy among the more conservative forces in our society to ensure that the past is constructed in terms congenial to their ideological interests. Rather, the most common and freely available discourses about the past, the discourses most of us live within and regard as the obvious, natural, common-sense accounts of history, are in general more congenial to centre-right rather than left-wing interests.

With regard to television, this process is discernible in the early-sixties development of the first great archival compendium tele-series, *The Great War* (BBC, 1964), and, somewhat later, the historical drama series, *Upstairs, Downstairs* (London Weekend Television, 1971–75). The process of recycling the past takes place both on factual and fictional fronts, although, to make clear what is actually involved, it is better to think in terms of, and consequently refer to, 'fictions in the documentary mode' and 'fictions in the dramatic mode'. This does not mean that any of these series, or the personnel involved in them, are

---

*Originally published in *Cencrastus*, no. 21 (Summer 1985), 40–2.

calculatedly setting out to falsify history. Rather, it is that terms such as these make more explicit the essentially constructed nature of television, whether documentary or drama, and undermine the widely held notion (particularly with regard to documentary forms) that television offers 'a window on the world'.

The most important question to be asked of tele-history in any of its documentary and dramatic modes is what conception of history and historiography does it subscribe to: What categories does it use to explain the past? With historical drama, the overwhelming category around which series are structured is that of the Great Man (or, occasionally, Woman). This is particularly evident in the titles of drama series of this type (*Edward the Seventh* [ATV, 1975], *Edward and Mrs Simpson* [Thames Television, 1978], *Churchill and the Generals* [BBC, 1979] and so on). But closer scrutiny of documentary series reveals that, despite their titles (such as *The British Empire* [BBC, 1972], *Civilisation* [BBC, 1969], *Destination America* [BBC, 1972] and so on), they too are often structured round the lives of individuals. This has the effect of explaining history in terms of the actions of (particularly so-called great) men and women and forbidding entry to other analytical categories (such as class, race, gender and institution) by which the past might be constructed in different terms. The same conception is at work in those documentary series dealing with events in living memory. Here, the most favoured mechanism is individual testimony, again suggesting the massive purchase of individuals in the making of history (as opposed to the much more nuanced idea of their shaping it through their class, gender, racial or institutional positions). Such an emphasis on the individual as an untrammelled force in history is clearly homologous with ethical and political discourses which stress individualism as the key to success and the cornerstone of society.

Put baldly, the dominant conception of history and historiography in television is the bourgeois conception. The latter possesses features additional to its wholesale investment in the idea of the centrality of the individual. Such additional features include: a belief in the uniqueness of historical events and a consequent lack of any disposition to seek connections among them; an absence of concern with the roles of classes and institutions; a belief in progress; a commitment to linearity; and the belief that if connections must be sought between disparate events, then the best basis for this is contemporaneousness. More than anything, however, the bourgeois conception of history has difficulty in coping with the notion of contradiction. In terms of television programmes about history, this difficulty reveals itself in the impulse to construct everything into a seamless web. This is achieved in television historical drama through the procedures of classical narrative. In fictions in the documentary mode, it is achieved primarily through the mechanism of the narrator. In such series as *Civilisation*, *The Ascent of Man* (BBC, 1973), *Destination America* and *The Age of Uncertainty* (BBC, 1977), attention is actively called to the presence of their narrators (respectively, Kenneth Clark [1903–83], Jacob Bronowski [1908–74], Alastair Cooke [1908–2004] and J. K. Galbraith [1908–2006]) on account of their eminence. Such series are indeed often called 'personal histories'. It is worth noting, however, that it was not until the advent of Channel 4 that an explicitly Marxist historian, Basil Davidson (1914–2010) with *Africa: A Voyage of Discovery with Basil Davidson* (Channel 4 Television, 1984), wrote and presented a television series on history. In this context absence speaks as eloquently as presence, and it might be worth asking why such distinguished Left historians as Eric Hobsbawm (1917–2012), E. P. Thompson (1924–93), Christopher Hill (1912–2003) and Raymond Williams (1921–88) were never invited by the broadcasting institutions to write and present tele-history series.

Crucial as such onscreen presenter-cum-narrators like Clark, Bronowski, Cooke and Galbraith are in knitting the seamless web and repressing (or at least containing) contradiction, the process is more insidiously achieved through the characteristic narrational device of the disembodied voiceover. What we might term (after Pierre Macherey) that voiceover's 'absent presence' is powerful precisely because it is less accountable in the absence of the narrator's visible physical presence within the work. Most usually, the device has supplied the cement to homogenise whatever disparate or contradictory tendencies the documentary material being treated within any given work of this type might have had. At a certain point in the development of tele-history this omnipresent voice was that of white, middle-class, southern England, the 'natural' accent and tone for constructing the world. Thus, *The Great War* was narrated by Sir Michael Redgrave (1908–85); *The World at War* (Thames Television, 1973–74) by Lord Olivier (1907–89); *The British Empire* by Robert Hardy (1925–2017); and so on.[1] It was precisely the growing recognition that Standard English was not a natural, but a socially constructed and, therefore, ideological category which caused cracks to appear in the white, male, middle-class, southern English hegemony over tele-history narration. This was so most scandalously in Thames Television's series on Ireland, *The Troubles* (1981), being narrated by a woman, albeit one with a southern English, middle-class accent. However, and while necessary, gender shifts in this regard do not guarantee progressive positions within works of tele-history, as is demonstrated in Scottish Television (STV)'s recent execrable series, *Scotland's Story* (1984), which had the voiceover narration shared by a man and a woman.

The foregoing discussion attempts to demonstrate the existence of a certain dominant tradition in British tele-history, one which is uncongenial to radical, left-wing views of history and society. The discussion culminated with the question of who speaks and who is permitted to speak history on television, since this is the most accessible starting point for dealing with the television series which, thus far, has most radically transgressed the dominant British tradition of fictions in the documentary mode. The series in question is Harlech Television's *The Dragon Has Two Tongues* (1985).[2]

The Dragon is outstanding among tele-history programmes in its refusal of the dominant tradition, achieved in part through its insistence (in the first pre-credits frames of the series) that historiography involves debate about the nature of the past. The series begins in an oaken, book-lined university hall with Wynford Vaughan Thomas (1908–87), the distinguished broadcaster, journalist and series co-writer/presenter, addressing a group of students. He relates his going up to Oxford in 1927 and the response of his tutor when he announced the wish to study history: 'What is history? Divine gossip about the past among gentlemen. Have another glass of port.' But even as Vaughan Thomas is speaking, another voice is rising on the soundtrack. This heralds another pre-credits scene, one involving the other co-writer/presenter of the series, Gwyn Williams (1925–95), the eminent Welsh Marxist historian. This second scene's milieu (a political street meeting) could not be further from the port-bibbing repose of Vaughan Thomas's anecdote, nor could Williams's words be further from Vaughan Thomas's: 'History is more than appears in a book. History is the buckle that bites your back. History is the sweat hanging above your eyes. History is the fear growing in your belly.' The dialectical nature of these pre-credits scenes is reprised in the images which constitute the credits sequence of the series, most obviously in the frame being shared at one point by two images: a static one of the investiture of the Prince of Wales, and the other a frenzy of movement in which the police struggle with a crowd (the context suggests a pro-Welsh language demonstration).

It is important, however, to indicate the extent to which *The Dragon* partakes of the dominant tradition of tele-history as well as where it departs from it. Both writers/presenters are 'personalities', and, indeed, of a rather similar type: warm, ebullient, liking the feel and sound of words; and the pre-credits sequence discussed above is a classic 'hook' in the dominant narrative tradition. As such, even though the sequence presents different views of the nature of history, it is non-analytic, and its prime function is dramatic. It is the sequences immediately following the credits which more coolly present the fundamentally opposed conceptions of history held by Vaughan Thomas and Williams, and the dialectical nature of *The Dragon* as a whole is signalled in the title of the first episode, 'Where to Begin?' Vaughan Thomas is seen scrambling over the rocks on the Welsh coast and coming upon a cave with a skeleton more than 17,500 years old; Williams, meanwhile, is seen going down a coal pit which has been converted into a museum. Vaughan Thomas talks of the start of a long journey which 'will bring Welsh history to vivid life', that is, he poses the classic bourgeois view of history as story, as linear development. As well as taking a much shorter view (1,500 years) as to when it was appropriate to start using the term 'Welsh', Williams gives a sharp rejoinder to the idea of narrative, linear history:

> History isn't something you can bring to life, because history isn't a story, it's an enquiry [. . .] the past is chaos. We in the present make sense of the past by manufacturing a history out of it. We do that by putting questions to it and the questions you put depend on who you are, what you are and when you are. We don't ask the same questions as our grandparents. A collier won't ask the same questions as a merchant banker, a wife as a husband, a Welsh speaker as an English speaker.

Vaughan Thomas's view is that history is there and will virtually tell its own story, while Williams's is that it has to be constructed and that the nature of that construction has political implications.

In the same opening speech, Williams declares that political commitment and challenges the view of history as uninterrupted linear development:

> To my mind, the questions we need to put are the ones that serve the majority, the ordinary working men and women of Wales who throughout the 1,500 years have carried the rest on their backs, their generally bent and exploited backs [. . .] We have been around for 1,500 years but our history has been an endless history of brutal ruptures [. . .] and with every break the Welsh people have been transformed [. . .] the Welsh people have lived in a permanent state of emergency.

It is to the series's credit that it does not simply set Vaughan Thomas up to be taken apart by Williams. The former makes counter-arguments against the latter as when, standing by the ancient Arthur's Stone, he responds directly to Williams's position and, in so doing, reveals the essentially mystical basis of his own:

> Welsh history as a permanent state of emergency? Wales constantly reinventing itself? That's not the way I see it. This is Arthur's Stone [. . .] I stroke the rugged rock and feel I am directly in touch with the people who set it up 2,500 years ago BC. And as I stand here, don't talk to me about the lack of continuity in Welsh history.

Though Vaughan Thomas, as a decent man of liberal and democratic convictions, would be aghast to hear it said, this utterance is perilously close to 'blood and soil' conceptions of history.

The shape of *The Dragon*'s opening episode, with its posing of the question of whether history is story or discourse, is crucial to the series as a whole. Its importance as a departure point from dominant conceptions of tele-history justifies its being examined in some depth: the seriousness of the series is beyond question. What also needs to be communicated, however, is its *élan* and, indeed, courage, in knowing when and how to lighten its tone. This is achieved in the opening episode by having Gwyn Williams arrive by helicopter and the previously separated monologues of the two presenters become a bantering, affectionate, but deadly serious argument about when Wales and the Welsh might appropriately be called by these names: Vaughan Thomas stresses the pre-Celtic, and Williams, the Roman period. These head-to-head confrontations between the co-writer/presenters with which each episode closes are important sites for the raising of key historiographical problems as the series unfolds.

That *The Dragon* is so fundamentally transgressive of the dominant form of British tele-history very much relates to the track record of its producer/director, Colin Thomas. Thomas is comparatively rare among television professionals in having an extremely un-hermetic relationship with the world outside television. Even more unusually, he has some acquaintance with the debates about the media which occur in academia and academic publishing. In particular, this has given him a strong sense of the constructed nature of television, that the medium is a form of discourse rather than 'a window on the world'. This is as evident in his earlier television film *Freeborn John* (1980), which brings the techniques of television current affairs programmes to bear on an incident in seventeenth-century English history (rather as does *Culloden* [Peter Watkins, 1964]). Similarly, the closing credits of *The Dragon*'s first episode show the production crew actually at work on the series, thereby saying to the viewer: 'This, too, is discourse; this, too, has a point of view which requires judgements to be made on it.' Such an awareness is all too rare among the wider community of television professionals.

The dialectic set up in *The Dragon*'s opening episode is continued throughout the series, with interesting disagreements occurring between the two presenters about, among other things, the extent to which there was an authentic Welsh identity and autonomy in the Romano-British period and, in a particularly interesting episode dealing with eighteenth-century Wales, an argument about the appropriate terminology for dealing with the role of the gentry in this period. This episode is rich in local realisations of the two fundamentally opposed conceptions of history respectively espoused by the presenters. Vaughan Thomas discusses the Welsh parsonry and unerringly focuses on the life of a particular individual, Griffiths Jones (1684–1761). Williams consistently talks about the historical role of particular classes, the percentage of the population they made up, and how they connected with emergent European movements of the time. However, it is the verbal exchange between the two regarding whether the gentry be judged in moral terms (Vaughan Thomas's accusation against Williams) or as a material, historical force (reminiscent of the exchange in an earlier episode about whether it is permissible to use modern concepts like colonialism to deal with Owain Glyndŵr ($c.1354$–$c.1415$)'s early-fifteenth-century war of independence against the English) which exemplifies the most remarkable features of the series. There is a cluster of issues raised in exchanges such as this (for example, the distinction between Marxism and vulgar Marxism; whether to be Marxist necessarily means being determinist; the distinction between ethical and politico-historical judgement) which simply have not been raised elsewhere in popular British tele-history.

The historiographical and ideological oppositions set up in *The Dragon*'s early episodes are replayed across the entire span of Welsh history as the series unfolds. Vaughan Thomas opts for ideas of stability, slow development, and the lack of revolutionary potential in Wales, illustrating his argument with charming anecdotes about peoples and places. Williams, on the other hand, stresses ideas of social upheaval, rupture and contradiction, deploying dates, data, tables, price fluctuations (the whole armature of empirical historiography) and citing individual persons primarily as representatives of the social classes emerging in turmoil in modern Wales. The ideological positions inherent in the two co-writer/presenters' differing views of history are reflected in the things they are seen to do during the series (for example, Vaughan Thomas on horseback in the grounds of a great house; Williams participating in the Welsh branch of the early-1980s People's March for Jobs).

The Dragon marks a significant advance in tele-history. It cleverly takes the dominant British tradition, retains much of it (including some questionable aspects such as the fetishisation of place) as a known form that helps guarantee access to a wide audience, but inflects and, indeed, cracks it apart to pose history and historiography as problematic questions. As such, this series deserves wide exposure and careful study.

Notes

1. The fact that these figures are all actors associated with highly stylised and rhetorical stage roles indicates that these series were signalling both their profundity and their status as 'art', but that is a separate question which need not be explored here.
2. A similar rupturing of the tradition as it applied to 'fictions in the dramatic mode' was achieved by *The Cheviot, the Stag, and the Black, Black Oil* (John Mackenzie, 1974).

CHAPTER 13

Scotland's Story*

Structuralism, lately freshening the air of many venerable institutions and discourses, has been fruitfully deployed in what Thomas Carlyle (1795–1881) once termed the 'dismal science', economics. The opposition core/periphery has been used to demonstrate the structural relationship between the wealth of the First World and the poverty of the Third.[1] Like all productive oppositions, core/periphery signifies a relationship and not an essential condition. Thus, in one version, Scotland may be seen as part of the developed world, but in another version with a somewhat longer timespan, that country (like all the Celtic margins of the British Isles) may instead be seen in a peripheral relationship with the Anglo-Saxon core of England.

The core/periphery opposition fashioned within economic discourse is now being applied to questions of culture and ideology with dramatic results. The power of the core region does not lie simply in the disposition of its periphery or peripheries' economic and political affairs. It also lies in the core's control over the institutions and practices of discourse production, such as the mass media, which contribute to the ordering of what goes on inside the heads of the peoples of the periphery or peripheries. Thus it is that (certainly over the last 250 years, and arguably for much longer) the identity of the Scots has been defined elsewhere than in Scotland. The new social type, *homo oeconomicus*, initially coming to ascendancy in the eighteenth-century dynamic core societies of England and France, was defined by the ideologues and artists of those societies within the mode of Romanticism, and by means of a process of structural opposition.[2] Those core societal ideologues and artists created an Other (let us call the latter *homo celticus*, although similar identities were assigned to other so-called primitive peoples throughout the world) who was all the things that *homo oeconomicus* was not:

---

*Originally published in *Framework*, no. 26–7 (1985), 64–74.

Table 13.1 *Homo Oeconomicus/Homo Celticus*

Homo Oeconomicus	Homo Celticus
Urban	Rural
Civilised	Wild
Rational	Emotional
Barbered	Unbarbered
Astute	Innocent
Ambitious	Shiftless
Masculine	Feminine

Oppressed peoples the world over know this discourse to their bitter cost. It may take an overtly hostile form (the 'savage' mode) or an apparently benign one (the 'poetic' mode), but it matters little. What is important is that the Celtic Other (or African, or Polynesian, and so on) is allocated their place and constructed within a discourse enunciated elsewhere. The historic rise to hegemony of this discourse has had truly Orwellian consequences: oppressed peripheral societies have increasingly lived their lives and thought their thoughts within categories proposed by their core oppressors, and have taken on identities which represent the fears, dreams and repressions of those who have the whip hand over them. The process is well described in the writings of, among others, Frantz Fanon (1925–61) and Edward Said (1935–2003) and, with regard to the Scots, in the best and most neglected book of the last decade about Scotland, Malcolm Chapman's *The Gaelic Vision in Scottish Culture*.[3]

One of the reasons for this discourse's continuing hegemony is its comprehensiveness, its suffusing of virtually every aspect of social life and its colonisation of every available mode of representation. Consequently, local realisations of the general core/periphery discourse offer identities not only for specific national groups, but for the very terrains they inhabit. Scotland, for instance, despite being primarily an industrial nation, four-fifths of whose population live in cities, is constructed in literature, easel painting, films, television programmes, popular song, travel brochures and postcards as a timeless land of mountains, mists, torrents and ghostly castles, either beautiful or threatening, and its people as savage/dignified inhabitants of the appropriate terrain.[4] Bill Forsyth's film *Local Hero* (1983) is simply the most recent and best-known example of a tradition which has blighted Scottish life for a very long time. Clearly, other discourses about Scotland circulate. Indeed, the ever-present imperative of economic development gives rise to discourses which pose a more modern identity for Scotland and the Scots, one which enters into collision with the older, hegemonic identity constructed within the core/periphery opposition.[5]

There is, then, no act of representing Scotland which is not formulated either within or in reaction to the hegemonic discourse, whether the relationship is recognised or not by the creators of and/or audiences for such acts. A twenty-four-part television series, written by a Scot and produced by a Scottish broadcaster, Scottish Television (STV), is therefore an extremely important event. The crucial question is the extent to which this series contests, or simply acts as a conduit for, the hegemonic view of Scotland.

Scotland's Story (1984) believes itself to be progressive. Its publicity handouts promise a radical dismantling of the hegemonic view of the nation and its history:

> Some might call it controversial and nationalistic. But it is not romantic. The Scots were not being romantic when they massacred each other at Glencoe, when they suffered the ravages of the Highland Clearances, when they struggled to make a new life for themselves over the four corners of the earth.
> (writer/producer Tom Steel [1943–2007] in the STV press release for *Scotland's Story*).

> It is very gritty history. There's a lot about dissent, destruction and treachery and very little about braw, bricht moonlicht nichts. To put it another way, the skeletons of Scottish history will be coming out of the cupboard but the haggis and sporran will be kept firmly under lock and key.
> (director Les Wilson in the STV press release for *Scotland's Story*)

These utterances show an awareness of the power of the hegemonic discourse, but far from undermining it, *Scotland's Story*, often unconsciously, endorses it. The essence of the hegemonic discourse is to construct the Celt as a figure incompatible with the modern, bourgeois, capitalist world. The twisted vestiges of this identity are evident in the statements above, with their stress on hardness, opposition and departure. The inherited discourse which presents itself for modern Scots to define themselves within is, above all, an elegiac discourse, a modality shared (for similar, though not identical, historical reasons) with their fellow Celts, the Irish. Elegy is writ large over vast tracts of *Scotland's Story*. If a single recurring image defines the series, it is that of a desolate winter landscape with the wind whistling plaintively across. This image has figured in episodes as disparate as those dealing with Scotland in Roman times, the 1745 Jacobite Rebellion, the Highland Clearances, and the role of the Scots in the British Empire. Elegiac discourses are evident in other aspects of the pictorial style of the series, for example, in the décor and lighting of scenes of historical reconstruction, and in the playing of the actors portraying historical figures within these. Elegiac discourses can occur in an urban as well as a rural context, as the episode 'Made in Scotland', substantially about the decline of traditional Scottish industries, shows. They can also occur in a modern as well as a historical context, as the episode 'A Generation Lost', mainly about the impact of the First World War on Scotland, indicates. Almost every episode of the series defines a particular historical period with one major idea and crams in various other aspects of that period. 'A Generation Lost', for example, also deals with the rise of urban working-class politics, but the overall framing idea is, as the title suggests, the loss of Scottish servicemen in the First World War. This is underlined by the episode beginning and ending with a Remembrance Day ceremony at the Scottish National War Memorial in Edinburgh, and by the usual end credits music being replaced with the bagpipe lament, *The Flowers o' the Forest*. H. V. Morton (1892–1979), that inveterate perpetuator of regressive myths about Scotland, wrote about that same war memorial over fifty years ago:

> I think the Cenotaph in London and the National Shrine in Edinburgh are the most remarkable symbols in existence of the temperamental difference between the two nations. One is Saxon and inarticulate; the other is Celtic and articulate. Grief locks the English heart, but it opens the Scottish. The Celt has a genius for the glorification of sorrow. All his sweetest songs are sad; all his finest music is sad; all his greatest poetry springs from tragedy. That is why Scotland has built the greatest war memorial in the world. *The Flowers o' the Forest* have all turned to stone.[6]

It would be difficult to find a more perfect example, even down to the structural opposition between Saxon and Celt, of that hegemonic discourse which, the Scots having learned to live within it, leads them to self-indulgence, not to say self-laceration. Albeit in a form rather more restrained than that of the unspeakable Morton, *Scotland's Story* refurbishes the same armature of the elegiac discourse, that curse of Scottish art and life, which is such a politically disabling factor in the present.

In an important sense, irrespective of what the makers of *Scotland's Story* think they are doing, the series is being written within dominant discourses about Scotland inherited from the past. The reverse side of the Scottish elegiac mode's coin is a certain assertiveness about the importance of Scotland, relative to its size, within the development of the modern world. This discourse is evident in a current television commercial which goes through a long list of discoveries, reveals they were made in Scotland, and urges firms to 'locate' there. The 'Great

Scots' motif recurrent in Scottish journalism and publishing is evident throughout *Scotland's Story*. Its presence is at its most grotesque in the episode entitled 'The Scots Empire', which is a turgid catalogue of how individual Scots played major roles in creating the British Empire. Such a focus on the phenomenon of imperialism is not only distorting, but also offensive as a way of dealing with that question in the late twentieth century. As elsewhere in the series, the attitude of the episode in question to its historical subject is revealed not only in the repeated references to 'natives' in the voiceover commentary, but in the episode's visual style. This is particularly so in the footage used as visual backing to an account of David Livingstone (1813–73)'s missionary activities. That footage is of an African tribal dance at night, full of images of dancing shadows, fire and bobbing masks – in short, that armature of images within which Africa is constructed as 'the dark continent', a source of mystery and terror to the white man, and, incidentally, a construction which Basil Davidson (1914–2010)'s contemporaneous television series, *Africa* (Channel 4 Television, 1984) has been at pains to expose and refute.

This ideological (and, in the final analysis, political) regressiveness is central to *Scotland's Story*. Connecting with the dominant elegiac mode of Scottish art, the series's version of Scotland eschews genuine modernity. The reminiscences of Scottish aristocrats are reprised in the mystical land constructed by Scots-Americans. But there is another, parallel story about which the series is silent. Nothing is said about the several waves of immigration into Scotland since the mid-nineteenth century: the Italians, the Jews, the Poles and the peoples of the Indian sub-continent. Nor are there any interviews with the substantial numbers of mixed-race descendants of Scots in the (formerly British) Caribbean islands. Such concerns are inadmissible within the series, raising, as they do, questions about the closed and mystical construction of Scottish heritage on which *Scotland's Story* is predicated.

Scotland's Story, then, is written within discourses of which its makers are largely unconscious or only partially comprehend. But as well as the centuries-old discourses discussed above, *Scotland's Story* is also determined by a newer, though no less powerful discourse, that of British television history. Some years ago, in an essay on precisely this area, I wrote:

> It is reasonable to expect, therefore, that television programmes about history will [. . .] bear many of the features of th[e following] dominant conception of historical explanation [. . .] a belief in the uniqueness of the event; belief in the free will and moral responsibility of individuals; belief in the role of historical accident (or, more accurately, no search for structural explanations of events); a strong reliance on the role of testimony of individual (particularly 'great') men and women; a strong

concern with the nation state in both its political and military dimensions; belief in progress and in 'chronological monism'. Conversely, we would expect the relative subordination of features characteristic of the non-dominant (i.e., Marxist) conception of history: the central importance of modes of production; the concept of class; the historical importance of social institutions rather than the actions of individual men and women; the notion of differential temporality in one historical period and the posing of conceptual relationships among events in diverse historical periods.[7]

This statement could stand as a very precise description of *Scotland's Story*'s conception of historical explanation. The series offers substantially a pageant view of history, primarily structured round the actions of individuals, thus far (the series is still running as I write) from Calgacus (*c*. AD 50–100) to the whisky barons and shipping magnates of the nineteenth and twentieth centuries. Sometimes this can lead to grotesque reversals of the kind of historical explanation required, as in the suggestion that an international interest in Scotland at the end of the eighteenth century and throughout the nineteenth was brought about mainly by the efforts of Sir Walter Scott (1771–1832), rather than Scott functioning (albeit pre-eminently) in the discourse about Scotland enunciated in the artistic/philosophical parlours of the great core societies of England, France and, somewhat later, Germany and Italy.

An overreliance on individual testimony is another of the central mechanisms of *Scotland's Story*, the precise form of the testimony giving rise to considerable offence. In the episodes up to the Victorian period, and to some extent thereafter, such testimony has come from the descendants of the Scottish aristocracy. The programme makers' rationale for this is that the present incumbents of historic aristocratic titles are best placed to know the histories of their own families. The outcome, however, is the shady spectacle of the descendants of an exploiting class desperately seeking to exculpate their ancestors. This is most outrageously so in the case of the Campbell in charge of the 1692 Glencoe massacre, whose descendant, himself a soldier, insists on the necessity of obeying orders. A further source of offence is the impeccable English Home Counties accents of the majority of the current clan chiefs. Needless to say, the series does not interrogate its aristocratic interviewees, or seek to uncover the social processes which gave them the kind of accents they have. The content of what these interviewees say is very often trivial and anecdotal, highlighting once more *Scotland's Story*'s lack of concern with classes, institutions and structural explanations of historical events, and its failure to take account of the distinguished body of historical work, written from quite diverse political positions, which has emerged in recent years in and about Scotland.

Scotland's Story's impulse towards a 'popular' history has reinforced the pageant quality of the series. For example, the 1745 Jacobite Rebellion is a key event marking the final collapse of Catholic Absolutism in favour of Protestant Constitutionalism in Scotland. But this event and wider process are recounted using the same cast as is to be found in the countless novels and songs about the '45 which disfigure Scottish libraries and concert platforms: Charles Edward Stuart (1720–88), the Duke of Cumberland (1721–65) and Flora MacDonald (1722–90). It is this cast, of course, which allows the Scots to go on constructing the '45 within an elegiac discourse. The series believes itself to be progressive in that it is critical rather than favourable to the Stuarts, but its real commitment is more evident in the visual style of the episode dealing with the '45 and in its maintenance of entirely peripheral figures, such as Flora MacDonald, on centre stage. This is a particularly acute problem with the series, given both the regressive emotional investment Scots have in the '45 and the solid body of historical work, neglected outside the academy, on aspects of Jacobitism such as the role of sea power in the '45, the role of France, and the meaning of the '45 within the wider British polity. Both the historical evidence and, if interviewee testimony is required, the professional academic practitioners, are there to present a different construction of the '45, one which would relate it to the overall struggle between quasi-feudal absolutism and bourgeois constitutionalism stretching from the sixteenth to the twentieth centuries across Europe and its imperial peripheries.

Scotland's Story displays virtually all the negative features of British tele-history: unseen and unaccountable narrators; the tendency for historical reconstructions to become autonomous mini-dramas within individual episodes; and the deadly performative affliction which strikes actors when they don historical costume, causing them to lose all sense of the appropriate scale of television performance. In this context, the controlled playing of Bill Paterson as the late-eighteenth-century radical, Thomas Muir (1765–99) demonstrates once more that he is the finest Scottish actor of his generation.

There is, finally and damningly, an absent discourse which nevertheless leaves its traces in *Scotland's Story*. It is a mark of every British tele-history series that it foregrounds the resources of television by whisking the audience, within the same episode, from one continent to another. *Scotland's Story* is no exception to this general rule. It is within this general phenomenon that the absent discourse leaves its traces. Many viewers were puzzled that the opening sequence of the first episode in the series dealt with the Scots in North America. This motif reappeared subsequently to a disproportionate extent. The absent discourse this signifies is that of the economics of television production, within which the Holy Grail is the selling of a series in the United States. In the light of this absent discourse, certain other more bizarre features of *Scotland's Story* (for example, the heavy reliance on the testimony of incumbent clan chiefs) begin to make sense.

Scotland is currently at a political watershed. It is an open question whether it will be part of the United Kingdom at the end of this century. The position individual Scots take on this question will partly be determined by what the Scottish (and other) media say about where Scotland has come from and where it is going. It might have been hoped that a twenty-four-part series from a Scottish television company on Scottish history would have clarified problems and options. *Scotland's Story*, in its unerring attachment to regressive discourses about Scotland, signally fails to do this.

Notes

1. Most notably in Immanuel Wallerstein, *The Modern World System*, vols I and II (Cambridge, MA: Academic Press, 1974; 1980).
2. *Homo oeconomicus* is a theoretical construct which circulated in nineteenth-century economic discourse. Within it, humans were assumed to be rational, well-informed and pursuing self-interest. The term was first used by John Stuart Mill (1806–73) in an 1829–30 essay, 'On the Definition of Political Economy and on the Method of Investigation Proper to It'.
3. Frantz Fanon, *Black Skin, White Masks* (New York: Grove Press, 1968); Edward Said, *Orientalism* (London: Routledge & Kegan Paul, 1978); Malcolm Chapman, *The Gaelic Vision in Scottish Culture* (London: Croom Helm, 1978).
4. See Colin McArthur, ed., *Scotch Reels: Scotland in Cinema and Television* (London: British Film Institute, 1982). The analogous dialectical construction of Native Americans as savage/innocent and their habitat as desert/garden is explored in Henry Nash Smith, *Virgin Land: The American West as Symbol and Myth* (Cambridge, MA: Harvard University Press, 1950).
5. For an account of just such a collision see Colin McArthur, 'The Dialectic of National Identity: The 1938 Glasgow Empire Exhibition', in *Popular Culture and Social Relations*, eds Tony Bennett et al. (Milton Keynes: Open University Press, 1986), 117–34, and reproduced elsewhere within the present volume.
6. H. V. Morton, *In Search of Scotland* (London: Methuen & Co. Ltd., 1929), 54.
7. Colin McArthur, *Television and History* (London: BFI Publishing, 1978), 9.

CHAPTER 14

The Dialectic of National Identity: The Glasgow Empire Exhibition of 1938*

Tir nam Beann, Dachaidh Mo Ghaoil [Land of the mountains, my beloved home]
Inscription above the entrance to the Clachan, Glasgow
Empire Exhibition, 1938

In the summer of 1983 the Scottish Development Agency entered into a promotional exercise with Selfridges, the London department store. Over a substantial area of floor space a Scottish village was constructed, the shape of the papier mâché walls reprising Scottish rural vernacular architecture, the square containing a (by all appearances) genuine parish pump and trees, and the backdrops consisting of painted hills and castles. Attached to the walls at various places were enamelled signs, of the type common between the Wars, for products such as Wild Woodbine and Richmond Gem cigarettes, and leaning against the various trees and walls were milk churns, wagon wheels and a grocery boy's delivery bike of the kind generations born between the Wars can recall from their childhood. The names over the buildings included *Flora MacDonald's China Gifts*, *The Balmoral Shop* (crystal and glass), *The Laird's Shop* (knitwear), *The Sweetie Shop*, and *The Gamekeeper's Inn*. The interior of the latter was panelled in wood, had sheep and stags' heads on the wall, stuffed grouse and salmon in glass cases, and an old copper kettle on top of the iron stove which nestled in a homely papier mâché hearth. The only potentially discordant note was the handful of vinyl records scattered on the rough-hewn table outside the inn, but the titles of the discs were entirely in keeping with the overall milieu: *The Gathering of the Clans*, *Caledonian Heritage* and *The Crags of Tumbledown Mountain*, the latter with the pipes and drums and regimental band of the Scots Guards celebrating the regiment's exploits in the Malvinas (more popularly known as the Falklands) War.

---

*Originally published in *Popular Culture and Social Relations*, eds Tony Bennett, Colin Mercer and Janet Woollacott (Milton Keynes: Open University Press, 1986), 117–34.

The central contradiction which the Selfridges Scottish village (needless to say, unconsciously) poses is as follows. A country, four-fifths of whose population live in cities and are oriented towards industrial production (in transition, of course, from traditional coal and steel-based heavy industry towards electronic industries), is constructed – not by poets and artists, but by the central government agency concerned with national economic regeneration – in exclusively rural Highland terms. That contradiction is a complex but illustrative issue of the historical construction of national identity and the reasons why such constructions were and are necessary.

It is often assumed (perhaps most markedly in nationalist rhetorics) that national identity is an essence, a given, a timeless fact of nature, rather than the product of concrete historical forces. Tom Nairn (1932–2023) explores nationalism as a general European phenomenon of a specific historical period and comes to a very different conclusion:

> How may we describe the general outlines of nationalist development, seen as 'general historical process'? Here, by far the most important point is that nationalism is as a *whole* quite incomprehensible outside the context of that process's uneven development. The subjective point of nationalist ideology is, of course, always the suggestion that one nationality is as good as another. But the *real* point has always lain in the objective fact that, manifestly, one nationality has never been even remotely as good as, or equal to, the others which figure in its worldview. Indeed, the purpose of the subjectivity (nationalist myths) can never be anything but protest *against* the brutal fact: it is mobilisation against the unpalatable, humanly unacceptable, truth of grossly uneven development.
>
> Nationalism in general is (in Ernest Gellner [1925–75]'s words), 'a phenomenon connected not so much with industrialisation or modernisation as such, but with its uneven diffusion'. It first arose as a general fact (a determining general condition of the European body politic) after this 'uneven diffusion' had made its first huge and irreversible impact upon the historical process. That is, after the combined shocks engendered by the French Revolution, the Napoleonic conquests, the English industrial revolution, and the war between the two super-states of the day, England and France.
>
> This English–French 'dual revolution' impinged upon the rest of Europe like a tidal wave, what Gellner calls the 'tidal wave of modernisation'. Through it the advancing capitalism of the more bourgeois societies bore down upon the societies surrounding them – societies which predominantly appear until the 1790s as buried in feudal and absolutist slumber.
>
> Nationalism was one result of this rude awakening. For what did these societies – which now discovered themselves to be intolerably 'backward' – awaken into? A situation where polite Universalist visions of progress had turned into means of domination. The Universal Republic of Anacharsis Cloots [1755–94] had turned into a French empire; the spread of free commerce from which so much had been hoped was turning (as Friedrich List [1789–1846] pointed out) into the domination of English manufactures – the tyranny of the English 'City' over the European

'Country'. In short, there was a sort of imperialism built into 'development'. And it had become a prime necessity to resist *this* aspect of development.[1]

Nationalism, then, is a response to the phenomenon, much discussed in the modern world, of the core/periphery relationship, the process whereby economically strong core countries draw weaker contiguous countries (or more accurately, regions) into a satellite relationship across the entire range of the forms of social life. The core/periphery phenomenon has been extensively discussed with regard to economics and politics, but less extensively so with regard to culture and ideology.[2] With regard to economics and politics, the emphasis has been correctly on the extent to which the core regions use and benefit from those on the periphery and, to a certain extent, the area of culture and ideology can also be discussed in the same terms. However, the exploration of the opposition in relation to culture and ideology has to be much more dialectical for, in the very act of equipping themselves ideologically to be core countries and to sustain the undoubted strains of so becoming, the core countries at the same time defined the Other, the regions they themselves were not, that is, the peripheral regions.

This raises a second strand of Nairn's argument that nationalism is pre-eminently a bourgeois form and that a particular class fraction of the bourgeoisie – the intellectuals and artists – was central in the process of mobilisation of the masses that was necessary to make particular nationalisms potent politically and, in certain cases, militarily. As Nairn points out, the cultural mode within which this mobilisation took place was Romanticism.[3] It is within the categories of Romanticism that the process whereby the core and its Other, the periphery, were simultaneously defined took (and continues to take) place. The process was and is a complex one, with contradictions within and between cores and peripheries. However, the central, inescapable fact is that the point of utterance

Table 14.1   Core/Periphery

Core	Periphery
City/Town	Country
Civilisation	Barbarism
Rationality	Emotion
Individual	Community
Dressed	Undressed
Barbered	Unbarbered
Culture	Nature

of the differentiating categories, the site within which the ideological and cultural contours of the core and its Other, the periphery, were defined, lay within the core countries. Thus it was that, in the period beginning in the mid-eighteenth century, a particular kind of person and society came to be defined within the core countries, largely by posing their opposites and finding them to be located within peripheral societies. The ideological construction both of the core and the periphery can be illustrated by the above table of oppositions (Table 14.1).

This system of oppositions (which is by no means exhaustive) comes into play whenever a core culture has dealings with a peripheral one, for example, in European encounters with the South Seas in the eighteenth century and Africa in the nineteenth or, within a single set of national borders, in the relationship between immigrants of European stock in the USA and the First Nations or African Americans.

However, the same process of definition by structural opposition was at work within Europe itself as well as between Europe and other parts of the world. This was so most notably in the defining of the Celtic fringe as Other to the dynamic core societies of England and France. As Malcolm Chapman says in his exemplary book, *The Gaelic Vision in Scottish Culture*:

> Since the eighteenth century, the Celtic fringes have posed for the urban regions as a location of the wild, the natural, the creative and the insecure. We can often find it said, with warm approval, that the Celts are impetuous, natural, spiritual and naïve [. . .] Such an approval is drawing on the same system of structural oppositions as is the accusation that the Celt is violent (impetuous), animal (natural), devoid of any sense of property (spiritual), or without manners (naïve), the bracketed terms [being] synonyms of the words that precede them, that we would use to praise rather than to deride [. . .] We are dealing here with a rich verbal and metaphorical complex [. . . It is not] important to distinguish between those who find a favourable opinion of the Gael within this complex, and those who dip into it to find the materials for derision. In both cases the coherence of the statements can only be found at their point of origin, the urban intellectual discourse of the English language, and not at their point of application, the Celt, the Gael, the primitive who is ever-departing, whether his exit be made to jeers or to tears.[4]

As Chapman notes, it was part of the dialectical complexity that – as the darker side of the new core societies became more apparent – the ideological architects of the new nationalisms, the core societal intellectuals and artists, often began to identify more and more with the Other that they had themselves constructed. Apparently complimentary descriptions of the Other ('natural', 'sensitive', 'spiritual', and so on) constitute a discourse which exploited peoples the world over know to their cost. Ostensibly flattering to them, such descriptions are in reality the ideological dimension of economic and political expropriation, a discourse formulated by the oppressor within which the needs of the oppressed are allocated their place in terms congenial to the oppressor's needs and fears. One of Chapman's more chilling revelations is the extent to which Gaels (and indeed, Scots as a whole) came (and still come) to live within the mental universe fashioned by their oppressors and to define their own identities accordingly. This phenomenon is a general feature of diverse kinds of colonialism and imperialism and has been emphasised by, among others, Frantz Fanon (1925–61), Anthony Wilden (1929–2013) and Edward Said (1935–2003).[5]

The cumulative effect of such historically pervasive core/periphery discourses is to produce serious problems of identity for the oppressed and to establish traditions of representation which lay down rules by which particular races and terrains will be represented within the entire range of available discourses and sign systems.[6] This is decidedly a handicap (but, by the very nature of the phenomenon, a rarely recognised one) for indigenous artists seeking to represent their own cultures or even, at a more workaday level, for exhibition organisers seeking to construct a Scottish village in Selfridges in 1983.

However, there is a fundamental instability in the process of quasi-ventriloquism whereby the core speaks through the periphery in terms conducive to its own interests. The nature of that instability can be clarified by reference back to the Nairn/Gellner assertion that nationalism is the product of uneven economic development and the motor for mobilising social forces to achieve modernisation. Even the most so-called backward of regions is under compulsion to develop economically. At the ideological level that factor very often throws into crisis and destabilises the identity assigned to the so-called backward region or race. That identity is one assigned initially by their oppressors but subsequently (through the coming to dominance of established discourses) by the so-called backward race themselves. This moment of crisis in its diverse concrete instances is worthy of attention: quite diverse core/periphery relationships produce similar dialectics of national identity.

A recurrent site of this contradiction is the national exhibition, a mechanism evolved by core countries such as England and France to bind up the wounds of civil strife at home and celebrate their industrial or colonial triumphs. Due, however, to the compulsive nature of the developmental process, the national exhibition strategy was also adopted by peripheral countries and regions in their own striving for modernity.[7] For such a pervasive and ideologically replete mechanism (there were in excess of fifty such exhibitions in the UK alone in the period from 1890–1939), it has been remarkably under-researched. Scotland has figured quite substantially within the practice of national exhibitions, both as a nation in its own right and as a component of the wider United Kingdom and British Empire, from the Glasgow Exhibition of 1901, through the Highland and Jacobite and Scottish Home Industries Exhibitions of 1903, the Scottish National Exhibition of 1908, the Coronation Exhibition of 1911, the British Empire Exhibition of 1924, to the Empire Exhibition of 1938. The latter was held in Glasgow and, as such, was the site of multiple contradictions.[8]

Before proceeding to an examination of the 1938 Exhibition from the point of view of its negotiation of the contradiction of Scotland as a historically assigned terrain of the imagination and Scotland as a dynamic, modern industrial nation, it is necessary to reassert the complexity and instability of the concept of national identity. National identity is not an essence but a process constantly open to change and development according to the needs of any given historical moment. This is graphically illustrated by the mechanism whereby the core countries such as France and England, through their control over discourse, created the Other. The peripheral (and often, physically distant) terrains of the latter became, with the development of travel and tourism, the playgrounds within which the core countries' *homo oeconomicus* would replenish his soul. However, this mechanism proved insufficient for that figure's spiritual/ideological needs as the eighteenth- and early-nineteenth-century dream of infinite progress soured and (with the horrors of industrialisation) the landscape he himself inhabited darkened. What was required as a consequence was the creation of a spiritual/ideological Other on *homo oeconomicus*'s own terrain. For the English variant of *homo oeconomicus*, this creation involved a timeless England of the imagination, different from (though serving the same spiritual/ideological needs as) the peripheral Others fashioned by the ideologues of bourgeois nationalism across England and other core European societies. By the time of the Coronation Exhibition of 1911, for example, not only were there being constructed an Ireland and a Scotland of the imagination, but an England, too.

The 1983 Selfridges conception of Scotland as a Lowland, rural village set against a Highland backdrop is, therefore, one with 250 years of dominant discourse underpinning it. It represents an amalgam of the two hegemonic literary discourses within which Scotland has been represented: Tartanry and Kailyard. The former involves a world of Romantic grandeur, embodied initially in the works of Sir Walter Scott (1771–1832), while the latter represents 'a Scotland of parochial insularity, of poor, humble, puritanical folk living out dour lives lightened only by a dark and forbidding religious dogmatism',[9] embodied initially in the works of Sir James Matthew Barrie (1860–1937). Tartanry and Kailyard have both reproduced themselves across the entire range of available sign systems, including easel painting, photography, advertising, postcards, film and television. It is not that the organisers of the various national exhibitions in the nineteenth and twentieth centuries set out deliberately to construct Scotland in the terms embodied most recently by the Selfridges village; rather, it is that modern European history had bequeathed no alternative models of representing Scotland. It comes as no surprise, therefore, to find the village (or ruralised town) as a key motif in every national exhibition within which Scotland has been represented. However, such is the force of the dialectic between uneven economic development and the assigned identity of Scotland as 'natural' and rural, that the discourse of the village (or ruralised town) has to enter into constant collision with the competing idea of Scotland as a dynamic, thrusting, modern industrial nation. This collision can be followed through virtually every aspect of the 1938 Glasgow Empire Exhibition and the meta-discourses (guide books, special issues of local newspapers, newsreels) which surround it.[10]

To a great extent the 1938 Exhibition was conceived and developed primarily within an economic discourse. It arose as an idea within the Scottish Development Council in the summer of 1936 and the preparatory work was done by the Council's Finance and General Purposes Committee. The Council itself had been set up in 1931 to encourage industrial development and it operated throughout the early 1930s in a context of sharp debate about the chronic unemployment and social deprivation of (particularly the West of) Scotland. That social experience and those debates shaped profoundly the nature of the economic discourse within which the Exhibition was conceived and developed and were a strong determining factor on the themes (for example, public health) within which Scotland as a modern, industrial nation was presented.[11] By the time the Exhibition actually occurred, the West of Scotland, under pressure principally of naval rearmament, was emerging from the Depression, but the economic discourse of the Exhibition constantly threw glances over its shoulder to the bleak conditions within which the event was conceived. Moreover, the modern, thrusting economic discourse of nation was also compelled to constantly negotiate the other, historically hegemonic, discourse which conceived (and still conceives today) of Scotland in different terms. That dialectic is evident within particular contemporary statements about the Exhibition:

> Behind an event of this kind there must, of course, be an industrial motive [. . .] It is fairly obvious that an exhibition which contains a Palace of Engineering [. . .] two great Palaces of General Industry [. . .] a Palace of Travel, Transport and Industry, a Coal Utilisation Pavilion and an Agricultural Pavilion is comprehensive, measured

by any standard, but when there is added to that an immense number of Dominion, Colonial, and private pavilions it is clear that the whole industrial structure of the British Empire and its potentialities will be on view [...] The Highland Clachan, if not new in conception, is exceptionally well done and mirrors the environment in which lie the roots of our race, a race which thrived on hardship and which, however widely it has spread itself over the world's surface, clings to its essential characteristics.[12]

The dialectic was also evident in the layout of the Exhibition itself and in the contents of the *Glasgow Herald*'s special Exhibition issue, with articles on 'Britain's Shop Windows: The Palaces of Industry' and 'British Craftsmanship: Palace of Engineering' lying cheek by jowl with articles on 'Building the Empire: Great Part Played by Scotsmen' and several pieces on Scotland's past. The two Scottish pavilions effectively conveyed the Jekyll-and-Hyde quality of a Scottish identity caught within the dialectic of urban/modern against rural/ancient, the one pavilion concerned with the health of modern Scotland, the other containing tableaux of Scotland's past.

However, the purest expression of the Scotland of the imagination was unquestionably the Clachan as described in the *Glasgow Herald*'s account of the visit of the King and Queen to it. The account is deeply informed by the dialectic and, in the particular incident it recounts, is reminiscent of the tributes of Indian princes at a nineteenth-century imperial durbar, recalling the description of Scotland's relationship with the British state as a form of internal colonialism:[13]

> From the base of the Tower the King and Queen were taken through the country house and modern flats erected by the Scottish Committee of the Council for Art and Industry, and then they stepped out of the Exhibition's modernistic atmosphere of severely designed and gaily coloured pavilions into the homely setting of the Clachan's thatched cottages, calm lochan and stony paths.
>
> It was a memorable picture and an unusual experience for the royal couple, as it will be for thousands of visitors to the Exhibition. A piper played stirring marches and reels on the banks of the lochan, into which tumbled a laughing burn, and from some of the cottages came the gentle lilt of Gaelic singing.
>
> The Queen stopped first at the Highland post office and listened for a moment to clarsach playing in an adjacent cottage, but the most touching incident of the tour came in the St Kilda Cottage. The King and the Queen were received by 75-year-old Finlay McQueen – regarded as 'king' of St Kilda before the evacuation of the island – who greeted them with 'God bless you both and your family' in Gaelic – his only language – then he dropped on one knee to kiss the hands of their Majesties.[14]

In one of the contemporaneous visual representations of the Clachan there can be glimpsed an oddly discordant feature: looming over the Clachan is the Tower of Empire. The very essence of modernity, the latter seems to have been inspired in equal measure by Le Corbusier (1887–1965), MGM and the *Flash Gordon* serial (1936). The Clachan and the Tower of Empire are the polar points of the overarching dialectic which, in 1938, threatened (and still threatens today) to render individual Scots schizoid. That dialectic, one which encompasses the general nature of the ideological struggle between cores and peripheries, also ran through the address of welcome to the 1938 Exhibition by its President, the Earl of Elgin and Kincardine:

> Scotland as the home of the Exhibition has at once a unique privilege and a magnificent opportunity.
>   She will be 'At Home' [. . .] For her visitors from far and near she will display her manufactures and her wares; she will disclose and emphasise her opportunities for trade and commerce and she will 'discover' her heart.
>   In Bellahouston Park there will be gathered comprehensive and constructive proof of Industry, Science, Art, Engineering, Social Progress and Recreation. It will be a great meeting-place and in its widest sense a University of Empire. But the Exhibition will also be for many a stepping stone to a more intimate knowledge of Scotland's history and romance, and to a fuller enjoyment of her opportunities for sport and pleasure.[15]

By 1938, Scotland had for nearly 200 years lived within a classic peripheral identity assigned to it by the artists and ideologues of the great

Figure 14.1   Scotland as Janus. Past and future as the modernist Tate tower looms over the Clachan.

European core cultures through the mode of Romanticism and their control of the means of (intellectual) production. However, the brute fact of subsequent uneven economic development compelled the Scots to bring into collision with that historically assigned identity a new-fashioned identity more appropriate to a dynamic, modern nation. Great national moments of self-presentation, such as the Glasgow Empire Exhibition of 1938, were the occasions when the ongoing dialectic of modern/urban against rural/ancient emerged in its most public and delirious form. Such occasions therefore hold a political lesson. The process of speaking with two voices – the fissures; the uncertainties; the grating shifts of gear from one discourse to another – assert, once more, the fluid, unstable character of national identity. Such occasions proclaim that national identity is not a set of inborn, natural characteristics in a people, but the product of that people's history. With the realisation of instability comes the realisation of the possibility of change. National identity comes to be seen, therefore, not as a set of eternal, mosaic tablets, but as a terrain of struggle where, to be sure, certain regressive and politically disabling discourses may currently be dominant, but which require constant re-utterance and re-articulation to sustain that dominance. Crucially, that dominance is open to challenge by a counter-narrative offering new definitions of national identity.

Clearly such a task is massive in the Scottish context, so heavy is the weight of inherited discourse about what it means to be a Scot and to inhabit the peculiar terrain that is Scotland. As with the transformation of national identity wrought on the Scots through the discourse of Romanticism during the period between 1790–1830, the role of artists and intellectuals – the producers of discourse – in effecting and sustaining another transformation today will be central. The level of consciousness of the problem and of the task to be accomplished is not high among Scottish artists and intellectuals. Scottish cinema and television, from *Local Hero* (Bill Forsyth, 1983) to the annual Hogmanay Specials of the various television channels, are deeply complicit with the regressive discourses of Tartanry and Kailyard, while contemporary Scottish literature and the visual arts seem substantially preoccupied with the less productive, formalist aspects of cosmopolitan modernism. The most hopeful growth points on the Scottish scene are those figures and mechanisms that have identified the regressive discourses within which most of the artistic work produced in Scotland is shaped and that have made the starting point of their work the confronting and dismembering of those discourses. The filmmaker Murray Grigor in *Scotch Myths* (1982), for example, takes apart the major historical figures from James 'Ossian' Macpherson (1736–96) to

Harry Lauder (1870–1950) who have constructed Scotland in regressive terms; the printmaker and ceramicist Eric Marwick (1946–2018) pricks venerable Scottish institutions and reflects on Scotland's relationship with the outside world; and the cultural journal *Cencrastus* interrogates (somewhat unevenly) the whole spectrum of art and media practice from a Left nationalist perspective. However, these piecemeal interventions will be for naught unless the question of Scottish culture is made a central area of concern in Scottish political institutions. Scottish Left and/or nationalist political institutions have in common with similar British institutions a fundamentally depoliticised view of art. To be sure they are different from more ostensibly conservative political institutions in calling for more money for the arts, but their ideology of art is virtually indistinguishable from that of the Right: a belief in the artist as expressive fount and in works of art as discrete objects wholly explicable in terms of their creators' 'talent' or 'genius'. An arts and education policy which rejected this conception would define art rather as the site of ideology, as one of the central processes whereby individuals are encapsulated into positions from which they make a wide range of judgements about the society they live in. Such a policy, however, would require the major Scottish 'discourse' institutions – the Scottish Education Department, the National Trust for Scotland, the Scottish Arts Council (1967–2010), the Scottish Film Council (1934–97), and the Scottish universities – to address the question of Scottish culture more urgently than they currently do and in a much more debate-centred way.

Within such a policy it is just possible to imagine a Scottish National Exhibition in which the discourses of Scotland as prelapsarian Eden and as bustling capitalist nation have got, at the very least, to struggle to maintain their current dominance.

Notes

1. Tom Nairn, *The Break-Up of Britain: Crisis and Neo-Nationalism* (London: New Left Books, 1977), 96–7.
2. The politico-economic dimension is discussed most notably in Immanuel Wallerstein, *The Modern World System*, vols I and II (Cambridge, MA: Academic Press, 1974; 1980). An important exception to the absence of cultural/ideological discussion is the essay by Cairns Craig, 'Peripheries', *Cencrastus*, no. 9 (Summer 1982), 3–9. I am indebted to Cairns Craig for drawing my attention to the extensive socioeconomic literature on the core-periphery question.
3. Nairn, *The Break-Up of Britain*.

4. Malcolm Chapman, *The Gaelic Vision in Scottish Culture* (London: Croom Helm, 1978), 18.
5. Frantz Fanon, *Black Skin, White Masks* (New York: Grove Press, 1968); Anthony Wilden, *The Imaginary Canadian* (Vancouver: Pulp Press, 1979); Edward Said, *Orientalism* (London: Routledge & Kegan Paul, 1978). But see Homi K. Bhabha, 'The Other Question: The Stereotype and Colonial Discourse', *Screen* 24, no. 6 (November–December 1983), 18–36 for the complexity and instability of stereotypes.
6. For an account of how Scotland and the Scots have been and, regrettably, continue to be represented in the cinema and on television, see Colin McArthur, ed., *Scotch Reels: Scotland in Cinema and Television* (London: British Film Institute, 1982).
7. For an excellent discussion of the ideological meanings of the Paris Exhibition of 1889 ('reconciliation, rehabilitation at home, and imperial supremacy abroad'), see Debora L. Silverman, 'The 1889 Exhibition: The Crisis of Bourgeois Individualism', *Oppositions: A Journal of Ideas and Criticism in Architecture*, no. 8 (Spring 1977), 71–91.
8. The remainder of this essay deals only with one of the contradictions of the 1938 Exhibition, that relating to Scottish identity in terms of rural/ regressive against urban/modern. A full account of the Exhibition would have to discuss the articulation of these discourses with the central organising discourse of the Exhibition: imperialism.
9. See Cairns Craig, 'Myths Against History: Tartanry and Kailyard in 19th-Century Scottish Literature', in *Scotch Reels*, ed. McArthur, 7–15.
10. It is a collision which recurs thereafter in recent Scottish history. It is present in the half-dozen or so documentary films specially made for the 1938 Exhibition through Films of Scotland and in the near-thirty-year output of the post-WWII version of the same body set up in 1954. For a fuller discussion of this see Colin McArthur, 'Scotland and Cinema: The Iniquity of the Fathers', in *Scotch Reels*, ed. McArthur, 58–63, and reproduced elsewhere in the present volume.
11. See R. H. Campbell, 'The Scottish Office and the Special Areas in the 1930s', *The Historical Journal* 22, no. 1 (1979), 167–83.
12. *Glasgow Herald*, special Exhibition issue, 28 April 1938, 15; 61.
13. Michael Hechter, *Internal Colonialism: The Celtic Fringe in British National Development, 1536–1966* (London: Routledge, 1975).
14. *Glasgow Herald*, special Exhibition issue, 13–14.
15. G. F. Maine, *Scotland's Welcome* (Glasgow: Collins, 1938), 17–18.

CHAPTER 15

The New Scottish Cinema?*†

The New Scottish Cinema, *Le nouveau cinéma écossais*, *Das neue schottische Kino*, *Il nuovo cinema scozzese*, *El nuevo cine escocès*, *Novoye shotlandskoye kino*.

Sometimes I have a dream, maybe a fantasy, that the New Scottish Cinema becomes the hottest thing in international film culture. The phrase is on everyone's lips in every language on the five continents; there is no reputable film festival or cinémathèque in the world that does not run a retrospective entitled *New Scottish Cinema*; no film journal that does not carry in-depth analysis of the films constituting this startling new movement and extensive interviews with its writers, directors, producers, actors and camera-people.

Their qualities marked through exposure at film festivals, Scottish actors begin to appear in French, German, Italian, even American movies, and production executives from all over the globe start swarming into Glasgow and Edinburgh, their pockets bulging with co-production contracts. Even Scottish merchant banks sit up and take notice, and make their first tentative investments in an indigenous Scottish film industry.

Finally, the New Scottish Cinema enters the canon, taking its place alongside the great milestones of film history: Hollywood and Scandinavia before World War I; German Expressionist Cinema; Revolutionary Soviet Cinema; British Documentary of the 1930s; Italian Neorealism; French New Wave; Poland, Czechoslovakia, Cuba and Hungary in the 1950s and 1960s, and so on.

Then the dream, or fantasy, turns to reflection. Why is this not so? Why is there not a movement perceived as the New Scottish Cinema, and why

---

* Originally published in *Desperately Seeking Cinema: What Kind of Scottish Film-making Do We Want?*, ed. Kenny Mathieson (Glasgow: Glasgow Film Theatre, 1988), 7–11.
† This essay is an edited transcript of a lecture given at the Glasgow Film Theatre, 18 May 1988.

is it not being celebrated in the way I have outlined? It is not because there are no films, or because there is a lack of indigenous talent or film activity. In the last decade or so the number of people earning their living from filmmaking in Scotland has risen eight-fold.

There are, in fact, a considerable number of films of very diverse kinds: political documentary (Cormorant Films's work on housing in Edinburgh and on Nicaragua; Pelicula Films's *How To Be Celtic* [Roy Lomas and Bob Service, 1983] and *Gramsci: Everything that Concerns People* [Mike Alexander, 1987]); the very different comedies of Charles Gormley (1937–2005) (for example, *Heavenly Pursuits* [1986]) and Bill Forsyth (for example, *Comfort and Joy* [1984]); the very different political fictions of Freeway Films (*Blood Red Roses* [John McGrath, 1986]) and Jam Jar Films (*Brond* [Michael Caton-Jones, 1987]); films about the lives of artists (for example, Timothy Neat's *The Tree of Liberty* [1987] and Murray Grigor's *E.P. – Sculptor* [1987]); films about Scottish history (for example, Bill Bryden (1942–2022)'s *Ill Fares the Land* [1983], Murray Grigor again with *Scotch Myths* [1982], Ian Wyse with *Fall From Grace* [1984]). Nor is this list in any way exhaustive.

So what's missing? Why, if the films and the talent are there, is there not an entity perceived as the New Scottish Cinema and celebrated as such? Some will say immediately that the orientation (in terms of production, distribution, and/or aesthetic form) of most of the works I have cited is televisual rather than cinematic. There is a substantial point here. How many of the titles I have mentioned do not have television money – and Channel 4 money in particular – in them? This may be part of the reason for the New Scottish Cinema not being perceived as such, but it is not the whole story. For instance, I can remember the buzz that was around some years ago about something called the New German Cinema, and how, when films were shown under that rubric at festivals and/or cinémathèques, the television work of Rainer Werner Fassbinder (1945–82) and others was invariably included. Indeed, if you remember, the German television channel ZDF was constituted as one of the main auteurs of the New German Cinema, and seasons were devoted to its work.[1]

No, the tie-up with television is not a sufficient reason for the lack of recognition of the New Scottish Cinema. We have to find other reasons.

Here, I begin to think aloud and, although we must be careful about making overly simplistic comparisons, one of the questions I continually ask myself is: What particular cluster of factors existed in those societies in which, at particular moments, cinema was regenerated and definable movements began to be perceived?

Firstly, an important recurrent element seems to be profound – and, in some cases, cataclysmic – social change. This is certainly true of post-WWI Germany, post-revolutionary Russia, Britain in the 1930s, post-WWII Italy, and post-revolutionary Cuba. It is arguably true about 1950s France and 1960s Czechoslovakia, but less obviously true of Germany in the 1960s and 1970s. I pose the question: Is Scotland in any sense in an analogous situation in the late 1980s?

Secondly, and very importantly, there were, in all these societies, substantial cadres of artists and intellectuals (including filmmakers) who defined their work around the concerns of class and nation. In a very urgent sense – in some cases – their films were actively forming and consolidating new class-based and/or national identities within their societies. For very special historical reasons, which Tom Nairn (1932–2023) examines in his 1977 book, *The Break-Up of Britain*, and which relate to the constitutional identity of Scotland as part of the UK having been settled nearly a century before the appearance of nationalism in Europe, the Scottish intelligentsia, taken as a whole, have never felt the material need to engage with the issues of class and nation.[2] I pose once more the question: Is this situation changing?

There is an additional factor perhaps related to the historical absence of the Scottish intelligentsia's concern with class and nation, a factor which is present in Scotland but absent from (or perhaps, in the respective cases of nations like Cuba and Czechoslovakia, present in a different form in) the other societies which I have mentioned. This is the factor of Scotland's peripheral status, its being politically, economically and, above all, culturally incorporated within the sphere(s) of influence of stronger core societies – in Scotland's case, England and the USA.

This opposition of core/periphery is a very fruitful one and will, I think, go a long way to clarifying Scotland's cultural infirmity. It was formulated within the discipline of development studies, most notably in the work of Immanuel Wallerstein (1930–2019), to demonstrate not only the wealth of the developed world and the poverty of the Third World but, more crucially, the structural relationship between one and the other.[3] The core/periphery idea has been applied, if not always in the same terms, in the area of culture and ideology to demonstrate that not only do strong core countries (which are very often past and/or present-day imperial and colonial powers) control the economic and political life of the weaker peripheral countries, but the latter's cultural and ideological life as well.

To put the issue starkly: the inhabitants of peripheral countries may very often define their own identities primarily in terms of discourses originating elsewhere. The process has been brilliantly analysed in the works of Frantz Fanon (1925–61), Edward Said (1935–2003), and, as far as Scotland is concerned, Malcolm Chapman.[4]

This phenomenon occurred with regard to Scotland within a long and complex historical process, one beginning in the mid-eighteenth century and still operating now. Within this process, the figure of the Celt was constructed as displaying all the obverse qualities of that of the non-Celt, essential qualities that fitted the former to operate in the realm of fancy and the imagination, but not in the realm of politics and economics. Within this discourse, the Celt inhabits a magical land which has the capacity to soften, captivate, and transform the stranger.

It would take us too far from the main lines of this lecture's argument to go into more detail on this, but the operation of this process helps to explain why Alexander Mackendrick (1912–93) could make a movie like *The Maggie* in 1953 and Bill Forsyth one like *Local Hero* in 1983. It is not that Bill Forsyth lacks talent, or that *Local Hero* is not in many ways an agreeable and entertaining film, but simply that there is a problem with it in this context. I would regard this historical discourse of the Celt as a major inhibiting factor on cultural development and self-awareness in Scotland.

To come back to the main lines of the present argument, however, I was thinking aloud about these factors which were present in the various national societies in which film has been regenerated, in which distinct movements have been perceived, at different historical junctures. As well as wider precipitating factors such as fundamental local social change and indigenous cadres of artists and intellectuals addressing questions of class and nation, there was also invariably present intense argument about the intrinsic nature and social role of cinema itself. This was true of all the societies I have cited, but perhaps for us most familiarly so in the 1920s Soviet Union and 1950s France.

Such intense arguments about cinema involved denunciations of established orders, the issuing of polemics and manifestoes, the formation of avant-gardes, the starting up of small magazines, and, particularly in the post-WWII period, the obsessive re-viewing of earlier cinema as a way of nourishing the present. Although one can see an encouraging growth of interest – inside Scottish educational institutions at all levels – in the question of the representation of Scotland and the Scots in art and discourse, one would be hard put to find, in the Scottish filmmaking community taken as a whole, the kind of intense engagement with the cinema and its history such as I have pointed to the existence of within various other nations.

I also want to concentrate finally on a yet narrower question which also constitutes an apparent absence in the Scottish film scene: the absence of a concern with film style, or, as it has been called within one critical tradition, with cinematic *mise-en-scène*. Thinking aloud again, I often wonder how Scottish filmmakers talk to each other about the particular cinematic effects they are trying to achieve in their films, or what films (and from which time and place) they have in mind when they embark on their own projects. More concretely, in those Scottish educational institutions which offer courses in filmmaking, what kind of training is given, what kinds of films do Scottish drama students look at, and what kinds of learning exercises do they do as a consequence?

There is a reason, within British film culture, why a concern with the specificity of cinema, with cinematic *mise-en-scène*, is not as fully developed as it might be. That concern was most forcefully articulated in 1960s Britain within the journal *Oxford Opinion* (1956–66) and then *Movie* (1962–2000). Very much influenced by the French journal *Cahiers du cinéma* (founded in 1951), the critics grouped around these journals tended to locate cinematic excellence primarily in Hollywood, and to see the central figure in the cinema as the director. The approach received its fullest statement in Victor Perkins (1936–2016)'s *Film as Film* (terribly limited as that book was in other ways), and its great strength was its attention to the way in which images work in particular films.[5]

But almost before the *Movie* tradition had established a foothold in British cultural and academic life, it was progressively overshadowed by another journal, *Screen* (first established in 1952 as *The Film Teacher*, but relaunched as *Screen* in 1969), one quite as polemical as *Movie* had been in its earliest days, and bristling with the intellectual weaponry of Marxism, feminism, structuralism, semiotics and psychoanalysis. *Screen* critiqued *Movie* as representing a limited formalism, and traduced its leading practitioners, even though there was some re-emergence of *mise-en-scène* in *Screen*, in a much more theoretical way.[6]

The *Screen* tradition at its best displayed a real sensitivity to the way cinematic images work, and related this, in a way the *Movie* tradition never had, to wider questions of ideology and discourse, but the overall effect of *Screen*'s escalating hegemony within academic film and television studies courses in the UK was to produce a generation of students that could talk cogently about ideology in particular films, but which would be hard put to describe how particular effects were produced by, say, one kind of camera movement rather than another. Also, the *Movie* tradition seemed to me to provide a valuable basis on which the training of filmmakers and actors might proceed, but that too was stillborn.

I want to close – still following the thread of what might be lacking in Scottish film culture – by attempting to pose some kind of fruitful union between what I have described as the *Movie* tradition and the

Screen tradition respectively, between the former's passion for and awareness of the process of filmmaking and the latter's acute awareness of ideology and discourse.

If I were to be asked what is most lacking and what I would most like to see in Scottish filmmaking today, I would say the union of the kind of *mise-en-scène* which is steeped in cinematic history and gives us maximum cinematic pleasure, with a hard political analysis of Scottish history and contemporary Scotland.

I'm very impressed with the extent to which this unity has been achieved in other times and places – in some of Jean Luc Godard (1930–2022)'s work, for example; the political thrillers of Costa-Gavras; certain of Andrzej Wajda (1926–2016)'s films; most of Hans-Jürgen Syberberg's films; some of the work of Ousmane Sembène (1923–2007); certain Quebecois films, such as *The Decline of the American Empire* (Denys Arcand, 1986); and – above all in my view – the films of Theo Angelopoulos (1935–2012).

Another particularly interesting example is the work of Jean-Louis Comolli (1941–2022). A co-editor of *Cahiers du cinéma*, he was also co-author in that journal of the remarkable analysis of John Ford (1894–1973)'s film *Young Mr Lincoln* (1939), which, using the methods of structuralism and psychoanalysis, revealed the repressions and silences of that film, particularly those relating to politics and sexuality.[7] Comolli went on to become a filmmaker and his film *La Cecilia* (1975) exemplifies perfectly the unity between cinematic pleasure and hard political thinking that I would describe as the Dream Ticket of filmmaking.

La Cecilia is about a motley band – socialists, communists, libertarians, anarchists, anti-clericals, intellectuals, peasants and artisans united only in their detestation of bourgeois society – who set up a commune in Brazil in the 1880s. The film is about the recurrent dilemmas and contradictions which they – and any egalitarian enterprise – face: Should there be occupational specialisations? Should the peasants attend solely to primary food production and the carpenters build the houses? Should fences – to many, the very symbol of private property – be built to keep the animals from treading on the crops? Are the women among them comrades or wives? Should the family unit be retained in any form? Should regular hours of work be set or should people work when they feel like it? And so on.

Implicitly, one of the questions *La Cecilia* seems to be asking is: What is the appropriate cinematic style for a film that is not about individual characters and their problems as individuals, but about the contradictions people face when they try to live in an egalitarian way? In my view, Comolli is able to answer this question elegantly not only because he has thought about political issues, but because he is immersed in the history of cinema (particularly classical Hollywood, F. W. Murnau [1888–1931], Kenji Mizoguchi [1898–1956] and Max Ophüls [1902–57]), and has thought continuously about how images work.

In this talk, I have dangled before you the image of the New Scottish Cinema which might take international film culture by storm. I have tried to indicate some of the factors which have attended the emergence of historically important film movements in other times and places. And, I have zoomed in on what seems to me the crucially important question of such movements being immersed in film history, and acutely aware of how cinematic *mise-en-scène* works.

We can begin to skin the cat in various places. At some stage, we would have to address the question of what kind of institutions are required to sustain the New Scottish Cinema. Wherever we might wish to begin, I am sure we would be looking to the same ending – an indigenous Scottish film industry which will take the world by storm.

A New Scottish Cinema indeed.

Author's Selected Films and Contextualising Text

The above lecture was delivered as part of an event, *Desperately Seeking Cinema?*, held at the Glasgow Film Theatre in May 1988. Additionally, there was a panel discussion and a brief season of fiction feature films selected by the author, which are listed below together with the author's brief contextualising texts on each.

The Travelling Players (Theo Angelopoulos, 1975)
The Tragedy of the Switchboard Operator (Dušan Makavejev, 1967)
Le Cecilia (Jean-Louis Comolli, 1975)
Les Carabiniers (Jean-Luc Godard, 1963)
Johnny Guitar (Nicholas Ray, 1954)

Over the past decade or so film production in Scotland, including films for television, has advanced markedly. In 1976, Colin Young (1927–2021) was rightly deploring the fact that all the Scottish filmmakers could be brought together in one room. In 1988, it is estimated that upwards of 400 people earn their living from film production in Scotland.

Clearly, a lot of the energy fuelling this advance has gone directly into production activity itself and, because of the particular slant film production has taken in Scotland, into diverse market hustlings to secure further production funding. But film production, like every other social practice, is always embedded in a complex social formation and historical moment. That fact should be borne in mind when making cross-cultural comparisons, but when in other societies and other times film production has been re-energised (for example, in post-revolutionary Russia, 1930s Britain, post-WWII Italy, late-1950s France, early-1960s Czechoslovakia), such re-energisation was accompanied by a cluster of factors curiously absent from Scotland in the 1980s. That cluster includes: sharp public debate about the role of cinema in the wider society; the production of polemics and manifestoes; the emergence of avant-gardes; a proliferation of writings on the cinema; the reviewing, in critical discussion-based contexts, of earlier cinemas; and, not least, the association of filmmakers with political movements.

It is partly from the lack of these factors on the contemporary Scottish film cultural scene that Scottish film production, with few exceptions, arguably operates within unusually narrow confines: able but orthodox fiction feature films and documentaries. Scottish feature film production is heavily oriented towards the orthodox narrative film. This is both the inclination of those filmmakers who have ventured into the feature field and the main emphasis, if not the whole stance, of the major contemporary indigenous funding organisation, the Scottish Film Production Fund (1982–97).

The following five feature films and five documentaries offer examples, all from other national societies, of alternative ways of approaching cinema. Each film points to a lack in current Scottish film production.

The Travelling Players: We await the arrival of a Scottish filmmaker who will offer an analysis of two decades of Scottish history within a confidently deployed *mise-en-scène* which draws on forms as disparate as Hollywood cinema of the 1940s and Hungarian cinema of the 1960s and 1970s (in particular, that of Miklós Janscó [1921–2014]). Using the linking device of a travelling troupe performing a classical pastoral play, director Theo Angelopoulos offers an analysis of Greek history from the Metaxas dictatorship of the 1930s to the return of forms of democracy in the 1950s. He is particularly skilful in rendering sharp political statements within the specific resources of cinema, such as cutting and framing.

The Tragedy of the Switchboard Operator: Some years ago there was a concept, associated with Jerzy Grotowski (1933–99), of poor theatre, that is, a theatre rich in imagination but slender in resources. It is odd that the concept has not become a compelling one in Scottish film production. *The Switchboard Operator* is poor cinema par excellence. The basic narrative of a telephonist setting up house with a sanitary inspector, falling pregnant, and accidentally drowning, is fractured and richly interwoven with other discourses which analyse and comment upon the motivations of the two central figures and the mores of the society in which they live. These discourses include criminology, sexology, public health and politics. Since it is the analytic strain which is particularly absent from Scottish filmmaking, *The Switchboard Operator*, which is analytic but with an exceptionally light touch, is a particularly important model for Scottish filmmakers to reflect on.

Le Cecilia: Brazil in the 1880s: a disparate group of Italian communists and anarchists set up a commune. *La Cecilia* is rather like *The Travelling Players*, in being a genuine group film in which individual performances take second place to the exploration of the political contradictions and options facing the group, as well as evincing a knowledge of and affection for classical Hollywood cinema. Director Jean-Louis Comolli was co-editor of *Cahiers du cinéma* at the crucial moment when that journal was moving beyond a concern solely with cinema, while still responding to the cinema's singular pleasures. The sophisticated mix of political analysis and cinematic pleasure is well conveyed in *Le Cecilia*.

Les Carabiniers: Like *The Switchboard Operator*, this too is a compelling example of poor cinema in Jerzy Grotowski's terms. It offers an object lesson in how to construct a movie from diverse discourses: in this case, early cinema and the cinema of Roberto Rossellini (1906–77); archive footage; Brechtian theatre; literary quotation; and modernist music. Like all of director Jean-Luc Godard's films, it is a sustained reflection on the nature of cinema.

Johnny Guitar: In 1950s and 1960s British film culture (for example, in the journal *Movie* and later in V. F. Perkins's 1972 book, *Film as Film*) considerable attention was given to the question of cinematic *mise-en-scène* within the overall project of championing Hollywood cinema. This somewhat formalist concern with how the diverse resources of the cinema (sound, lighting, camera movement, décor, actors' performance, editing, and so on) combined to produce a specifically cinematic pleasure and meaning was overtaken in Britain by later critical positions mainly preoccupied with the operation of particular ideologies within films. However, the earlier approach has much to teach us about how cinematic effects are achieved. The films of Nicholas Ray (1911–79) were a central point of reference in 1950s and 1960s British critical discussions of *mise-en-scène*, and *Johnny Guitar* is perhaps the most turbulent and breathtaking of Ray's films in this regard. This is so particularly in its pushing of actors' performance to delirious levels and its choreographing of actors in relation to the cinematic frame. It represents a particular deployment of cinema which is thin on the ground in Scotland.

Within a conception of poor cinema, documentary filmmaking must loom large. Again, with few exceptions, the Scottish inheritance is orthodox. Documentaries as diverse as *Hell Unltd* (Helen Biggar, 1936), *Diptyque* (Walerian Borowczyk, 1967), *The Itch-scratch-itch Cycle* (Manuel De Landa, 1977), *Frozen Music* (Mick Eaton, 1983) and that reworking of the tradition of British Documentary of the 1930s, *Industrial Britain* (Roger Buck, 1980), remind us that the bounds of documentary cinema extend beyond *Panorama*.

Taken together, all the above films exemplify two qualities which I would particularly like to see within a rich and pluralist Scottish cinema: sharp analysis and optimum cinematic literacy and pleasure. Above all, however, I would like to see Scottish filmmakers embrace the notion of poor cinema, for there may well be a relationship between current Scottish cinema's film industrial aspirations and practices and its failure to deliver a politically incisive and cinematic cinema.

Notes

1. See, for example, Richard Collins and Vincent Porter, *WDR and the Arbeiterfilm: Fassbinder, Ziewer, and others* (London: British Film Institute, 1981); Thomas Elsaesser, *New German Cinema: A History* (Brunswick, NJ: Rutgers University Press, 1989).
2. Tom Nairn, *The Break-Up of Britain: Crisis and Neo-Nationalism* (London: New Left Books, 1977).
3. Immanuel Wallerstein, *The Modern World System*, vols I and II (Cambridge, MA: Academic Press, 1974; 1980).
4. Frantz Fanon, *Black Skin, White Masks* (New York: Grove Press, 1968); Edward Said, *Orientalism* (London: Routledge & Kegan Paul, 1978); Malcolm Chapman, *The Gaelic Vision in Scottish Culture* (London: Croom Helm, 1978).
5. V. F. Perkins, *Film as Film: Understanding and Judging Movies* (London: Penguin, 1972).
6. See, for example, Thierry Kunzel, 'The Treatment of Ideology in the Textual Analysis of Film', *Screen* 14, no. 3 (Autumn 1973), 44–54; Mark Nash, '*Vampyr* and the Fantastic', *Screen* 17, no. 3 (Autumn 1976), 29–67.
7. The Editors of *Cahiers du cinéma*, '*Young Mr. Lincoln* de John Ford', *Cahiers du cinéma*, no. 223 (August 1970), 29–47 and republished in English as 'John Ford's *Young Mr Lincoln*', *Screen* 13, no. 3 (Autumn 1972), 5–44.

CHAPTER 16

The Rises and Falls of the Edinburgh International Film Festival*

In diplomatic circles it is said that a newly independent nation's first acquisition is an airline and its second, a film festival. The popular idea of a film festival is that of a glittering period of two to three weeks of important films, important people in evening dress, and important awards – a magical time when the cinema and its denizens come within hem-touching distance of ordinary mortals. A film playing to near-empty houses as part of a season on Yugoslav cinema can become, within a film festival, a focus of adulation or condemnation, a source of journalistic copy, an event.

There are today in excess of 250 film festivals throughout the world, and the number is rising. Most function mainly or exclusively within the popular idea of a film festival and it is becoming more difficult, from year to year, entirely to eschew this idea. More arguably, it may not be desirable for any given festival to hold itself apart from the popular idea, but embracing it exacts a heavy price.

This has not always been so, as the history of the Edinburgh International Film Festival (EIFF) demonstrates. The impetus for its being set up in 1947 – only Venice and Cannes predate it – was not, as the tendency is nowadays, to confer prestige on the Festival's locality and to attract tourists. The thrust behind Edinburgh's creation was a passion for cinema, and more, a politics of cinema, the wish to advance the collective interest in certain cinematic forms and institutions, and to create knowledge and debate about them. The key figures in the group which set Edinburgh up were Norman Wilson (1906–87) and Forsyth Hardy (1910–94), both of whom had been active in Scottish film culture in the decade and a half prior to 1947 as film journalists, members of the Edinburgh Film Guild and, in Hardy's case, as a wartime civil servant in charge of documentary

---

* Originally published in *From Limelight to Satellite: A Scottish Film Book*, ed. Eddie Dick (London/Glasgow: British Film Institute/Scottish Film Council, 1990), 91–102.

film production in Scotland. Hardy's film column in *The Scotsman* newspaper, the journal *Cinema Quarterly*, edited by Wilson, and the exhibition activities of the Edinburgh Film Guild were important in raising film consciousness in quite diverse ways in 1930s Scotland. That generalised local passion for cinema heated up into an active politics of the medium as the decade wore on, the cutting edge of that politics being the documentary idea. Hardy, in particular, was a close friend and associate (and was later to become the official biographer) of John Grierson (1898–1972), who was at that time very effectively propagandising on behalf of the documentary idea in British government circles and realising the idea institutionally through official organisations like the Empire Marketing Board.[1] The documentary idea was further institutionalised during the Second World War at the end of which, as an idea and practice, it was riding high. Its practitioners had made a massive contribution to the war effort and British Documentary had come to be perceived as a major movement in the development of initiatives in many other countries and, arguably, as inflecting the aesthetics of narrative cinema in Italy, Poland and even the United States.[2]

It is scarcely surprising, therefore, given the orientation of figures such as Forsyth Hardy and the demonstrable importance of the ideas and practices he had championed throughout the thirties and the WWII period, that the idea of documentary should underpin the emergence of a film festival in Edinburgh. Indeed, the inaugural edition was called the First International Festival of Documentary Films, its advisory committee included such stalwarts of the British Documentary movement as Basil Wright (1907–87) and Paul Rotha (1907–84), and its programme booklet was entitled *Documentary '47*. A key feature of any film festival emerging out of a passion for cinema rather than prestige and hype is the quality of its accompanying documentation. The first Edinburgh programme booklet carried considered pieces by John Grierson and Forsyth Hardy and articles on documentary practice in Australia, Poland, Czechoslovakia, Denmark and Canada. There is even a piece by Norman Wilson on documentary in Scotland which is, in retrospect, hauntingly prophetic:

> There are no technical fireworks about Scottish documentary. The subject matter – the social problem, the question of ways and means, the organisation of resources – is regarded as more important than surface brilliance. Beyond that it is difficult to say that Scotland has evolved any distinguishable quality in its films. Perhaps that in itself is characteristically Scottish.

It is clear, even at the start of EIFF, that its organisers were beginning to expand the idea of documentary beyond simple factual short films to embrace the notion of documentary/realist aesthetics, although this was never worked out at a theoretical level. The Festival's first edition included, for example, feature films such as Roberto Rossellini (1906–77)'s *Paisan* (1946) and Georges Rouquier (1909–89)'s *Farrebique ou Les quatre saisons* (1946) and the second edition in 1948 opened with the world premiere of Robert Flaherty (1884–1951)'s *Louisiana Story* (1948) and also included Rossellini's *Germany, Year Zero* (1948). The Festival's continuing commitment to knowledge and debate about the cinema was evident not only in its programme booklet (which again included substantial essays and even more wide-ranging reports on the documentary scene throughout the world), but also in that other indicator of serious intent in a festival, a programme of public lectures and debate. The lecturers in 1948 included Basil Wright, Paul Rotha and Arthur Elton (1906–73) and the lectures dealt with 'the aims and principles of documentary'.[3] By 1950, however, there were indications that the politics of documentary, at least as far as the Festival was concerned, was running out of steam. The event was already referring to itself as the Edinburgh International Film Festival, having dropped the word 'Documentary' from its title, and while it continued to produce a programme booklet structured round documentary and show films like Luchino Visconti (1906–76)'s *La terra trema* (1948), the opening film of the 1950 edition was the fiction film *The Wooden Horse* (Jack Lee and Ian Dalrymple, 1950), a problematic choice not only in terms of its quality but also in relation to questions of documentary even in that term's widest application.

Cultural operations rarely come to a sudden stop, however. The principle of uneven development applies even in processes of decline. Thus, EIFF maintained its attempt to generate debate about cinema in, for example, its 1952 conference, 'New Directions in Documentary', and its 1953 conference, 'Television, Film and Reality', even while the films it showed and the critical documentation it produced moved ever further from the documentary idea. By 1954, even the annual Festival booklet had shed the term 'documentary' and included an article on the American feature film producer Walter Wanger (1894–1968) and one on John Huston (1906–87).[4] Symptomatically, another piece in the 1954 booklet, on film in America, begins by talking about documentary but ends up talking about *On the Waterfront* (Elia Kazan, 1954), *Riot in Cell Block 11* (Don Siegel, 1954) and *A Time Out of War* (Denis Sanders, 1954). Some of the feature films shown by the Festival over this period also indicate how far it had drifted from the discourse of documentary that had contributed to the event's creation during the previous decade: *Gate of Hell* (Teinosuke Kinugasa, 1953), *Ugetsu Monogatari* (Kenji Mizoguchi, 1953),

The Caine Mutiny (Edward Dmytryk, 1954), *Doctor at Sea* (Ralph Thomas, 1955), *East of Eden* (Elia Kazan, 1955), and *Lady and the Tramp* (Clyde Geronimi, Wilfred Jackson and Hamilton Luske, 1955). But perhaps the clearest signal that the end had come for Edinburgh's politics of cinema predicated on documentary was the title of a piece in the 1954 Festival programme booklet by John Maddison (1912–89), entitled 'Documentary is NOT Dead'.

The deceleration of Edinburgh's original, documentary-based politics of cinema was clearly bound up with the contemporaneous waning of that form in the wider cinema. Cinema audiences were in decline; television was rising, and, as a consequence, cinema was beginning to explore other formal systems, such as colour and widescreen, which, if not inherently hostile to documentary, were certainly not associated with the form; and many of documentary's ablest practitioners were moving into other fields. John Grierson himself became involved in feature film production with the British government-aided Group 3 production initiative.[5] Forsyth Hardy re-entered film production as Director of Films of Scotland in 1954, his considerable energy thereafter being directed primarily towards the raising of funds for sponsored documentary films in Scotland rather than towards Festival affairs.

The subsequent stagnation which is evident in EIFF from the mid-fifties to the mid-sixties, though flowing primarily from the lack of a policy on cinema to replace the founding, but now worn-out, documentary one, was undoubtedly exacerbated by the administrative arrangements for running the Festival during this period, which witnessed a series of short-term appointees acting as Festival Director for a year apiece. The tensions which afflicted EIFF with regard to its own identity and function at this time are well described in the report of an officer of the US State Department who had attended the 1952 Festival:

> The directors are under pressure to maintain the 'integrity', 'the character of the Festival', that is, to keep it a 'producers' festival', an open forum for 'the loving makers of movies' [. . .] They are under no less pressure from public opinion [which] asks why the film has failed to take its proper place among the Popular and Cultural Arts in the Festival of Music and Drama, why its starry-eyed devotees flock by themselves in smaller theatres instead of filling large houses with people [. . .] In other words, there is pressure to turn the 'producers' festival' into a 'public's festival' on the order of what Venice and Cannes claim to be.

This, like Norman Wilson's 1947 remarks on Scottish documentary filmmaking, offered another hauntingly prophetic formulation. There is a danger of erecting a quasi-folkloric account of EIFF whereby, after the energetic commitment to the documentary idea during the Festival's early years, everything simply switched off for a decade only to then be reborn, phoenix-like, with a passionate commitment to a new politics of film. Of course, the actuality was much less clear-cut. Although Norman Wilson was still claiming, in 1955, that, 'Edinburgh will remain the centre for Films of Reality', the aesthetic identities and strategies of films programmed at Edinburgh became ever more diverse: *Reach for the Sky* (Lewis Gilbert, 1956), *The King and I* (Walter Lang, 1956), *Lust for Life* (Vincente Minnelli, 1956), *The World of Apu* (Satyajit Ray, 1959), *Eyes Without a Face* (Georges Franju, 1960), *The Virgin Spring* (Ingmar Bergman, 1960), *The Criminal* (Joseph Losey, 1960), plus scores of short films of every conceivable aesthetic form. EIFF over this period initiated (and, it seems, discarded) two awards which it presented each year. There are references in the mid-fifties to the Selznick Awards and to *Ugetsu Monogatari* receiving the Festival's Golden Laurel in 1955, the latter award to be given to 'a film-maker whose work through the years has contributed to international goodwill and understanding'.[6] Such a formulation sounds the warning bells of decline. The cutting edge of a precise politics of cinema such as had characterised the documentary initiative is replaced by a woolly gesture which could mean anything and which would not be out of place at the crassest of commercial film festivals. The Golden Thistle Award, sponsored by Films of Scotland, appeared at the Festival in 1964 and was presented that year to King Vidor (1894–1982). Though less crass than the earlier Golden Laurel award – for instance, the Golden Thistle involved the retrospective showing of six of the awardee's films, with the implication that there might be a structuring relationship among the latter – the new award's terms of reference remained worryingly vague: 'made annually in recognition of an outstanding contribution to the Art of the Cinema'. The crucial omission was any argument as to why King Vidor was important and what the purpose was in honouring him in 1964.

Yet, to muddy the idea of a total shutdown of ideas and commitment within EIFF over this period, the very notion of running a retrospective of filmmakers' work at a film festival was, in the 1960s, quite a progressive move. Further scrutiny of the period reveals other commitments to the idea of a serious film festival, however half-baked they now seem. The 1962 press digest refers to the EIFF having instituted 'a five-year plan whose general aim is to demonstrate the links between the art of the film and the older arts'.[7] Attempts to fulfil that plan included the programming of films round the themes of Film and Literature and Film and Drama, but the ongoing process of decline in EIFF's commitment to a politics of cinema is most marked in the thin and anecdotal accompanying documentation, symptomatically now called the 'souvenir programme', which supported these initiatives. A residual seriousness was evident on other fronts, too. Annual EIFF conferences (such as 1963's 'What is a Television Film?') continued, as did some form of public lecture programme, though these came to be styled, chillingly, 'celebrity lectures'. The first of these was delivered in 1954 by Anthony Asquith (1902–68) on the theme of the relationship between actor and director, and succeeding lectures included Roger Manvell (1909–87) on 'Shakespeare to Sillitoe' (1962) and Jerzy Toeplitz (1909–95) on 'The Creative Impulse in Film-Making' (1965). Whatever the merits of what might have been said by particular lecturers, as a programme it was completely unfocussed. It comes as no surprise to find the 1966 lecture by Fons Rademakers (1920–2007) untitled. Celebrity reigns: anything goes.

Thus, while it is correct to see the period between roughly the mid-fifties to the mid-sixties as one of decline for EIFF, it should not be thought that the Festival lost completely its seriousness of intent. Its institutional arrangement of short-term directorial appointments was not conducive to the continuity and development of Festival policy and the full realisation of that policy within programming, documentation and events. But the crucial lack, following the withering of the founding documentary initiative, was the presence of a Festival Director who had a passion for cinema, a wish to advance the claims of certain cinematic forms over others, and the appetite to conduct this argument in public. It is to the credit of EIFF that it was able to put its own house in order in precisely these terms.

Murray Grigor was appointed Director of EIFF in 1967. Film festivals are complex mechanisms and (again, reflecting the law of uneven development) we do not find a new politics of cinema emerging fully formed, from the head of Zeus as it were, in that year's edition. Carol Reed (1906–76) was awarded the Golden Thistle, with no particular case being made for his receiving the award, the programme booklet contains a desultory discussion by Frederic Raphael on film censorship, and little else was produced by way of critical documentation. There is evidence of a greater attempt to impose order on the diversity of films shown by grouping them under headings such as 'A British Film School?', 'The American Eye', 'Experimental '67' and 'Film and the Arts'. Perhaps the most resonant portent of things to come, however, was the selection of Robert Aldrich (1918–83)'s *The Dirty Dozen* (1967) for EIFF's opening gala performance that year. Although historically oriented to the documentary idea and to the related notion of cinema as High Art, EIFF had not eschewed an interest in Hollywood. However, that interest tended to focus on the older, more respectable aspects of Hollywood. What was scandalous about opening the 1967 EIFF with *The Dirty Dozen* was the suggestion, implicit at that stage, that the violent underbelly of contemporary Hollywood was a source of legitimate cinematic pleasure and critical interest.[8] That portent was not realised in the 1968 EIFF which, in retrospect, had about it the feeling of a memorial service for the documentary initiative of earlier years. The main organising principle for the 1968 programme booklet is indeed 'The Documentary Idea' and John Grierson looms very large throughout. He delivered the celebrity lecture that year and the programme booklet contains a reprint of his 1933 essay, 'Documentary Symphonies' and his outline treatment for *Seawards the Great Ships* (Hilary Harris, 1961), an Oscar-winning documentary about Clydeside shipbuilding which had been produced through Films of Scotland.[9] Grierson's receiving the Golden Thistle award in 1968 further enhances the sense of closure on the relationship between EIFF and the principles and practices with which he was associated. Simultaneously, however, the more extensive critical documentation of the 1968 booklet can be read retrospectively as one of the signs of EIFF's return to a serious engagement with cinema, albeit under a new political framing.

Subsequently 1969 proved the year in which the most decisive break with the Festival's past was evident. Murray Grigor had been joined at EIFF by Lynda Myles and David Will and their collective orientation was towards a very different kind of cinema than had enthused the generation of Forsyth Hardy and Norman Wilson. The revaluation of Hollywood cinema became a central interest of younger critics such as Grigor, Myles and Will at this time.[10] Like all other cultural movements this was a complex and uneven phenomenon, but two of the strands which fed into it were the presence in the educational system of a new generation of teachers from working-class backgrounds who wished to validate rather than condemn their students' cultural choices (Stuart Hall [1932–2014] and Paddy Whannel [1922–80]'s *The Popular Arts* is a key text here[11]) and growing familiarity with, and importation into Britain of, the ideas of French film criticism through journals such as *Oxford Opinion* (1956–66) and *Movie* (1962–2000). It was within this movement, and with allies drawn from its various cadres, that Grigor, Myles and Will were to re-energise EIFF and give it once more that passion for cinema and commitment to a politics of cinema which had characterised the Festival's founding and early years.

At the particular late-sixties moment when Grigor, Myles and Will connected institutionally with this movement, two ideas about Hollywood cinema were central. The first was that precisely because Hollywood was a highly compromised milieu, in terms of commercial demands, institutional interference and the presence of powerful genre traditions such as the Western and the gangster movie, it was fruitless to try to discern the art of the Hollywood director on the basis of looking at their films piecemeal. Only on the basis of considering the whole or a substantial part of any given Hollywood director's canon might the nature of their recurring thematic and stylistic concerns be revealed.[12] Originally formulated in French film criticism as the *politique des auteurs*, this approach was subsequently anglicised as 'the auteur theory'. The second central idea about Hollywood which was current at the historical moment under discussion at this point was that a Hollywood film might be of interest as much for the way it was realised on the screen as for the ostensible seriousness of its subject matter. This opened the way for films previously dismissed or reviled to be looked at carefully. This interest in cinematic *mise-en-scène* was developed in Britain primarily by the journal *Movie*.

These two ideas came together triumphantly in the 1969 EIFF's retrospective of the films of Samuel Fuller (1912–97) with a supporting book of critical essays. The impact of the Fuller retrospective as an event, with the gregarious Fuller himself present throughout, the innovative book of essays, and the discernible influence of both book and event in the wider film culture (other books and articles on Fuller proliferating,[13] the season being taken up by the National Film Theatre in London and other film theatres elsewhere) tend to obliterate the memory of other highly significant strands within EIFF that year on student and independent films, AIP Thru Roger Corman, Kenneth Anger (1927–2023), Andy Warhol (1928–87), a graphics season and a tribute to the recently deceased young British filmmaker Michael Reeves (1943–69). In fact, this list connects well with the Fuller retrospective in its attention to the interstices of Hollywood and American independent cinema and the presence of the visceral qualities of those interstices within Reeves's films.

A powerful if uneven sense of such an identity and associated politics of cinema was subsequently evident within EIFF for the next decade or so. The most significant strands of that project were the Festival's commitment to younger Hollywood directors such as Martin Scorsese, John Carpenter and Paul Schrader; its openness to avant-gardes; its early recognition of the significance of figures such as Werner Herzog, Ousmane Sembène (1923–2007) and Hans-Jürgen Syberberg; and its close alliance with new thinking about the cinema among British critics, theoreticians and educationists. Over this period, substantial seasons and publications were produced on Roger Corman, Douglas Sirk (1897–1987), Frank Tashlin (1913–72), Raoul Walsh (1887–1980), Jacques Tourneur

(1904–77), Psychoanalysis and Cinema, and History/Popular memory.[14] The productivity of this work was immense, in particular feeding into the work of teachers of film and cultural studies, the activities of regional arts associations and regional film theatres, and the practices of the nascent British film workshop movement. The break in the above list between posing questions around the work of particular directors and around more depersonalised, theoretical questions indicates some degree of divergence between the interests of EIFF and its allies in film theory and education, although both parties remained mutually supportive. To structure retrospectives and publications round the films of Fuller, Corman, Sirk, Tashlin, Walsh and Tourneur, while scandalous to a certain kind of conservative critical thinking about the cinema, nevertheless took as given the unproblematic existence and nature of directorial authorship. Yet, it was precisely this same idea which became increasingly problematic within film theory and education, even as it became more widely current in the journalistic film culture of the broadsheet press, at that time the main conduit of news and opinion about film festivals.

It could be argued that EIFF's identity became much less clear-cut in the 1980s, although, as with earlier periods in the Festival's history, that decade can be seen as exemplifying the principle of uneven development. The strength of Edinburgh in its earliest years and during the decade from about 1969 was the Festival's sense of purpose, its clear awareness of why it did what it did and its commitment to an explicit politics of cinema and culturally productive film work. While such qualities did not wholly vanish in the eighties (for example, the EIFF-supported 1982 'Scotch Reels' season and accompanying volume had discernible influence on film studies within Scotland and beyond[15]), it is difficult to gauge the rationale for certain significant Festival decisions during this period. Why, for instance, was it considered important to mount a Joseph H. Lewis (1907–90) retrospective in 1980, or a retrospective of Japanese cinema in 1984, and where is the evidence of either of these initiatives being culturally productive in terms of new ideas, new writing or new filmmaking practices?

EIFF was reorganised in 1989, with Jim Hickey (who had been with the Festival since 1969 and had succeeded Lynda Myles as Director in 1981) relinquishing the Directorship to David Robinson, film critic of *The Times* newspaper. On the evidence of the official programme for 1989, Edinburgh's distinctiveness as a film festival with a specific politics of cinema was at a (hopefully temporary) end. That programme reads:

> We have tried to create a festival which is not elitist or exclusive, but will offer something to every sector of the community. As always, the Festival aims primarily to bring to Edinburgh the best of the past year's international cinema [. . .] The main

focus of the Festival this year, however, is on new talent. At least thirty films are by new directors. Fifteen of these have been selected for a special New Directors series; and these will compete for the Charles Chaplin New Directors' Award [...] Edinburgh is by tradition a non-competitive festival, but we are very proud to host not only this prestigious new award, but also three other prizes, destined for student filmmakers, whose work is selected for the Young Film Maker of the Year Competition [...] As well as [this] there are daily Lunchtime Animation shows, while documentary – always a special concern of Edinburgh – is highlighted in a new Eyes of the World series. A further innovation is the New British Cinema section. One of this year's two retrospectives is also British. Titled *1939 – Another Country*, it sets out to present a portrait of Britain on the eve of the Second World War [...] A second retrospective offers the complete works of Pier Paolo Pasolini [1922–75].

At both historical moments (the immediate post-WWII period and the decade or so from 1969) when Edinburgh's critical cutting edge was sharpest, there was the strongest possible sense of great issues being at stake (documentary/realist versus more stylised/escapist cinema; popular versus high art) with appropriately explicit critical discourses for advancing the arguments involved. All of this seems very far from the bland nebulousness of 1989's statements such as, 'will offer something to every sector of the community', 'the best of the past year's international cinema' and 'the main focus [...] is on new talent'. Other questions also suggest themselves. What was the rationale, other than the anniversary-related one, for the *1939 – Another Country* retrospective and where is the accompanying critical documentation which explores the issues (both cinematic and historical) that it posed? Why was Pasolini chosen as the subject of a retrospective at this particular moment and where was the accompanying critical documentation which explained that choice and explored the issues raised by it? Was it wise – given the repeated demonstration in recent years of the constructed nature of all cinema, including documentary – to entitle a documentary strand, 'Eyes of the World'? Who were the figures making up the group to choose the winner of the Charles Chaplin Award and what criteria governed their choice? There is no suggestion here of deliberate secrecy. A telephone call to David Robinson revealed that the group consisted of Krzysztof Zanussi, Percy Adlon, Susannah York (1939–2011), Jim Haynes (1933–2021), Forsyth Hardy and János Rózsa. What was at issue was the assumption that the criteria for choosing the members of the group and the winner of the award did not need to be spelled out publicly. This is an assumption at one with a critical discourse which talked about 'the best of cinema' and 'new talent', a discourse which was slippery and elusive compared with the more concrete and polemical discourses of earlier phases of EIFF.

In fairness to David Robinson, it should be said that he took over the Directorship just about a hundred days before the 1989 EIFF was about to happen, but once again the central issue lies elsewhere, specifically, in conceptions of what a film festival should be and do. When EIFF reconstituted itself in 1989 it opted, in David Robinson, for a distinguished, well-informed and well-connected film journalist capable of delivering the kind of festival which offers 'something to everyone' and which would offer a critical discourse much closer to traditional public discourse about the cinema – a festival, in fact, like all the others. In making this choice, EIFF certainly created a responsible operation which, once a year, would bring considerable pleasure to Edinburgh. What is more doubtful, however, is the extent to which EIFF recognised the fact that it had opted not to fashion for the 1990s a politics of cinema analogous to the documentary initiative of the forties and the auteurist and post-auteurist initiatives of the late sixties and seventies.

This essay has been substantially concerned with the cultural policy of EIFF up to the start of the 1990s (the original version of the essay was published in 1990). However, anyone with a passing knowledge of how film festivals operate will know the extent to which finance and administration impinge upon policy. This can be exemplified as a series of financial/administrative questions. Will EIFF's Director be given enough money to travel abroad and see what is actually being made in world cinema? Will individual filmmakers, film companies and, sometimes, national governments permit their films to come to Edinburgh? Will the chosen films arrive in time and in a form which is screenable? Will there be money available to repair the projectors if they fail? Is there enough money to cover the expenses of visiting filmmakers? Will they throw tantrums and make demands on the Festival Director's packed schedule? Will the programme booklet be ready on time? And from what sources will the money come to cover all of these considerations and requirements? Such questions have impinged on policy right from the start of EIFF, but they became acute in the 1980s as a result of changing British central government policy towards arts bodies in receipt of public funding. It was Jim Hickey's unenviable lot to have to wrestle with these problems throughout that decade. It makes no real sense, therefore, to write about cultural policy without assessing the importance, or perhaps even the determining nature, of finance and administration, and it is to be hoped that future accounts of EIFF can do this in more detail than is possible here.

At its founding in 1947, and for many years thereafter, EIFF seems to have functioned largely on the basis of voluntary labour augmented by temporary secondments from existing Scottish film cultural institutions such as the Scottish Film Council (1934–97) and Films of Scotland

(1954–82). From quite early on the Festival did have a money-raising mechanism, called the Edinburgh Film Festival Fund, into which were paid small donations, mostly from film trade bodies, which were recorded in the annual programme booklet. These donations tended, individually, to be under £30 and, even by 1962, the largest donations were £200 from the Scottish Film Council and £250 from Granada Theatres. The financing of EIFF throughout the seventies was complicated, due to its tie-up with the Festival's emergent, permanent year-round film theatre base, the Edinburgh Filmhouse, and the two institutions' consequent sharing of premises and personnel. However, the Festival entered the eighties with an income of over £50,000, about 20 per cent of which was trading income, the remainder being grants from the Scottish Film Council and the British Film Institute (BFI). Due to the peculiarities of arts funding in the United Kingdom, the latter had for a long time been a player on the Scottish film scene at the level of capital funding (revenue funding being handled by the Scottish Film Council). At about the time of EIFF's second great moment (the late sixties/early seventies), the BFI also became influential in revenue funding with regard to EIFF, partly out of general recognition of the Festival's increasing excellence, but more particularly because a faction within the BFI valued EIFF more highly than the BFI's own London Film Festival and sought to advance Edinburgh's interest accordingly.

However, as well as entering the eighties with sharply increasing income, EIFF also carried a substantial deficit. Its history over the decade from 1980 might be written as the struggle between cultural and financial considerations, and EIFF's makeup and orientation in the nineties might be understood in part as the outcome of that struggle. By 1988, Festival income had risen to over £100,000 and the institution was showing a surplus of over £18,000. The proportion of income earned at the box office had risen to nearly 40 per cent, with grants from the SFC and BFI making up the same amount. The Festival's 1988 accounts also record for the first time a figure (£6,700) described as 'sponsorship'. It seems clear that, in common with other arts bodies relying heavily on public funding during the chill Thatcherite wind of the eighties, EIFF sought (with some measure of success, it would seem) other sources of income and cost-saving. The crucial question is the extent to which the changed financial environment of the late eighties and early nineties was connected with EIFF's apparent abandonment of the polemical stance which, in its two great historical moments, earned it the right to be called the best film festival in the world.

Notes

1. Forsyth Hardy, *John Grierson: A Documentary Biography* (London: Faber & Faber, 1979).
2. For example, there was a substantial exchange of ideas, and to a limited extent personnel, between Italy's nascent Neorealist filmmakers and British documentarists in the 1930s. Alberto Cavalcanti (1897–1982) taught at the Centro Sperimentale di Cinematografia in Rome and contributed to one of the two most important Italian film periodicals of the time, *Bianco e Nero* (the other was *Cinema*); several of the writings of Paul Rotha were translated into Italian; and the Italians were reportedly particularly interested in the 'creative' use of sound by Cavalcanti and John Grierson: see L. Caminatti, 'The Role of Documentary Film in the Formation of the Neorealist Cinema', in *Global Neorealism: The Transnational History of a Film Style*, eds Saverio Giavacchini and Robert Sklar (Jackson: University Press of Mississippi, 2011), 52–67. The geographical sweep of the British documentary influence is perhaps best conveyed in film historian Nicholas Pronay's experience when standing in for Grierson on a visit to Japan. Pronay recalls the Japanese director Kon Ichikawa (1915–2008) telling him: 'Please tell Grierson-san that we are all his children here.' See Nicholas Pronay, 'John Grierson (1898–1972)', in *Grierson Awards Programme* (Peterborough: Grierson Trust, 2009), 8.
3. For further detail, see Forsyth Hardy, *Slightly Mad and Full of Dangers: The Story of the Edinburgh Film Festival* (Edinburgh: The Ramsay Head Press, 1992), 20.
4. For further detail on the Festival's early-1950s qualification of its founding focus on documentary, see Ibid., 27–37.
5. For further detail, see Simon Popple, 'Group Three – a lesson in state intervention?', *Film History* 8, no. 2 (1996), 131–42.
6. For further detail, see Hardy, *Slightly Mad and Full of Dangers*, 33–4.
7. For further detail, see Ibid., 72–94.
8. Forsyth Hardy, for example, retrospectively argued of *The Dirty Dozen*'s inclusion in the 1967 programme that 'it posed but did not give a convincing answer to the question: What is a Festival Film?' (Ibid., 92).
9. Ibid., 99.
10. For further detail, see Ibid., 95–146.
11. Stuart Hall and Paddy Whannel, *The Popular Arts* (London: Penguin, 1964).
12. Jim Hillier, ed., Cahiers du cinéma, *the 1950s: Neo-Realism, Hollywood, New Wave* (London: Routledge & Kegan Paul in association with the British Film Institute, 1985) offers translations of an excellent selection of auteurist writings from that journal which were to influence British criticism, most notably the magazine *Movie* and individual critics such as Robin Wood (1931–2009) (*Hitchcock's Films* [London: Zwemmer, 1965]; *Howard Hawks* [London: Secker & Warburg in association with the British Film Institute, 1968]) and Peter Wollen (1938–2019) (*Signs and Meaning in the Cinema*

[London: Secker & Warburg in association with the British Film Institute, 1969]).
13. Phil Hardy, *Samuel Fuller* (London: Studio Vista, 1970); Nicholas Garnham, *Samuel Fuller* (London: Secker & Warburg in association with the British Film Institute, 1972).
14. Paul Willemen and David Will, eds, *Roger Corman: The Millenic Vision* (Edinburgh: Edinburgh Film Festival '70 and *Cinema* magazine, 1970); Laura Mulvey and Jon Halliday, eds, *Douglas Sirk* (Edinburgh: Edinburgh Film Festival '72 in association with the National Film Theatre and John Player and Sons, 1972); Claire Johnson and Paul Willemen, eds, *Frank Tashlin* (Edinburgh: Edinburgh Film Festival and *Screen*, 1973); Phil Hardy, ed., *Raoul Walsh* (Edinburgh: Edinburgh Film Festival, 1974); Paul Willemen and Claire Johnston, eds, *Jacques Tourneur* (Edinburgh: Edinburgh Film Festival, 1975).
15. Colin McArthur, ed., *Scotch Reels: Scotland in Cinema and Television* (London: British Film Institute, 1982).

CHAPTER 17

A Dram for All Seasons: The Diverse Identities of Scotch*

In 1988 Arthur Bell & Sons initiated an advertising campaign on hoardings and in the colour supplements of the broadsheet press, which was of the greatest interest to students of how signs operate in society. The contents of each individual advertisement altered but the form remained constant – a kind of *trompe l'œil* realism best exemplified by a certain tradition in American painting which reached its popular apotheosis in the work of Norman Rockwell (1894–1978). Each advert depicted a shelf-cum-bookcase (and, in one case, a pinboard) carrying objects with Scottish associations: a Balmoral bonnet; antique copies of the Waverley Novels of Sir Walter Scott (1771–1832); historic golf balls of the period 1850–1905; an old Scots postcard; an antique microscope beside a copy of Sir Alexander Fleming (1881–1955)'s book on penicillin; part of the manuscript for Felix Mendelssohn (1809–47)'s *The Hebrides* overture (1830–32); tickets for a Scotland versus France rugby match; the hilt of a claymore; and so on. The single recurrent item in each advert was a bottle of Bell's *Extra Special Scotch Whisky*.

The strategy of the campaign was clear. Bell's whisky was consistently located among objects which signified, most obviously, 'Scotland', but which also signified non-nationally specific ideas such as venerable old age, tradition and a certain kind of comfortable living, thereby transferring those qualities, by association, to the whisky itself. This cluster of meanings was enhanced by the advertisements being painted rather than photographed. While rendered in a highly realistic style, the advertisements, by bearing all the signs of the process of easel painting, were located in yet another discourse (that of High Art) and thus further reinforced the campaign's central appeal to discourses of age and tradition.

---

*Originally published in *Scots on Scotch*, ed. Phillip Hills (Edinburgh: Mainstream, 1991), 87–102.

What interested students of signification about the Bell's campaign was what could be called its semiotic overkill, its piling, one on top of another, of every conceivable emblem which might signify the conjunction of 'venerable' and 'Scottish'. Redundancy, the process of offering more channels of meaning than are strictly required for any given message to be understood by its intended recipient, is a feature of most sign systems, but seldom can redundancy have been carried further than in the Bell's campaign, which corrals emblems from virtually every discourse within which Scotland and the Scots have been signified, historically speaking. Or, more accurately, the campaign pressed into service those discourses compatible with the specific semiotic conjunction, 'venerable/Scottish/comfortable'. Older and newer discourses about Scotland which might have troubled this conjunction were eschewed. The longstanding narrative of Glasgow as 'the city of dreadful night', serially rehearsed and re-rehearsed in public health and urban planning literature, novels, tabloid newspapers and, latterly, in films and television programmes, was clearly incompatible with the ideological thrust of the campaign, but so, too, was the newer narrative of Glasgow as commercially dynamic and upwardly mobile, perhaps because it lacked that element of venerable tradition so central to the campaign.[1]

So familiar has the strategy become of linking particular products to imagined histories (for example, Hovis bread and northern English working-class life) and so widespread has it become with regard to Scotch whisky specifically, that we might be forgiven for assuming that it has held sway unopposed since the marketing of Scotch whisky began: to think of whisky advertising is to think of the ensemble of images of Scotland deployed in the Bell's campaign. As this essay will show, however, the historical actuality is rather more complex. The whisky industry has in fact displayed remarkable diversity and flexibility in its marketing strategies. To be sure, particular companies at particular moments have opted for one or other Scottish discourse within their advertising. But, at other times, according to changes in the target audience or (in the argot of the trade) product placement, they have been prepared to abandon a Scottish national discourse for a wider British counterpart, or to abandon both for other discourses, most notably, that of social class.

There is a debate among historians about the vexed question of historical time. The dominant practice (certainly among historians in the English-speaking world) has been to construct the past into periods (the Ancient World, the Classical World, the Dark Ages, the Renaissance, and so on) with a tendency to view these constructs as hermetically sealed from each other. A rather more sophisticated view sees events and institutions as existing in several historical times simultaneously. For instance, the historian Pierre Vilar (1906–2003) has described the outbreak of the French Revolution in 1789 as a fusion of three separate times: a long time (the economic expansion of the eighteenth century); a medium time (the recurrent economic depressions of 1774–88); and a short time (the price crisis of 1789).[2] An analogous model of the interlacing of long, medium and short-term discourses is necessary to understand the extremely complex history of the marketing of Scotch whisky. Several discourses are often present simultaneously. In the 1988 Bell's campaign, for example, there are to be found, alongside the dominating discourses of nation and class, the discourse of High Art (via the adverts' painterly visual and intertextual references – for example, to Mendelssohn) and a Scottish variant of the biography-as-hagiography discourse (for example, 'Great Scots' such as Fleming). Five minutes in any Scottish library or bookshop will confirm the suffocating omnipresence of this hagiographic strain in our national life.

The most surprising feature of early whisky advertising, in the fifty years or so before World War I, was its diversity. It was not dominated, as might be supposed, by images of Scotland. Although such images were not absent, one has the impression that they were simply one constituent element of an extremely wide range of discourses drawn upon to sell the product. Those adverts which did deploy Scottish motifs often opted for one of two images: the Highlander, whether in his romantic or comic dimension, and Scottish soldiers in the British Army, an inflection of the romantic motif in which the supposed warlike qualities of the Scots are evoked. However, such images in early whisky advertising are in a minority. It comes as no surprise that the oldest folkloric idea about whisky, its alleged health-giving properties, is pressed into service. More surprisingly, we find whisky advertising of this period deploying images as varied as a naval ironclad, Father Christmas, Chelsea Pensioners, English law courts and Japanese prints.

The development of the mass market, and therefore of advertising, in the last third of the nineteenth century coincided with a specific opportunity for Scotch whisky to enlarge its market. Up until the 1880s brandy and gin, both of them coded as socially superior to whisky, had been the main spirits drunk by the English. The English upper classes had increasingly encountered whisky on their sojourns to the Scottish Highlands in the wake of Queen Victoria (1819–1901)'s imprimatur on the area.[3] Whisky had hitherto been seen as a robust, outdoor drink with perhaps some health-giving qualities, but it had a commercially unfortunate association with the lower orders and therefore was quite unsuitable for clubs or salons.

Figure 17.1 Contrary to popular belief, whisky's historical advertising did not always contain representations of Scotland or Scots.

The devastation of the continental brandy trade in the 1880s due to phylloxera gave Scotch whisky the opportunity to make inroads into the club and salon market. But for this to succeed two factors were necessary: at the level of physical taste, whisky's robustness had to be tempered by blending and, at the level of social taste, it had to be constructed ideologically as a proper beverage for more refined milieux. This latter construction of whisky's class discourse began to be apparent in its marketing, became an increasingly dominant motif across diverse brands, and established itself as one of the major long-term discourses associated with the product, as is apparent in the present-day Bell's campaign referred to above.

The central discourse of that campaign was, of course, that of longevity and tradition. This discourse is one that became established quite early in the history of whisky advertising. Haig had the edge on its competitors, having some claim to be the oldest whisky-maker, which was exploited in the company's marketing. For example, it celebrated 1927 as its tercentenary and its advertising in that year referred back to the way various things were done in the year 1627. Significantly, and perhaps somewhat surprisingly, the 1927 campaign did not deploy Scottish motifs. Other brands were forced to suggest their longevity by more connotative means, as in Dewar's campaign of the turn from the nineteenth to the twentieth century. This presented the firm's name chiselled in stone, with historical and even archaeological associations. Although the organising discourse of both the Haig and the Dewar's campaigns is that of Age/Tradition, there is also a formalist discourse present within both, that of repetition. In the case of the Dewar's campaign, that repetition involves the motif of stone-carving while, in the Haig case, it involves disparate events of the year 1627. Indeed, it could be said that repetition is professional marketing's formalist discourse par excellence, the recurrent identifying feature which gives the very idea of 'the marketing campaign' meaning in the first instance.

As the marketing of Scotch whisky developed, so did its deployment of a cluster of discourses signifying Scotland and indissolubly linking the advertised product to its place of origin. This became so to the extent that, faced with the Bell's campaign of 1988, we tend to think of the link it makes between whisky and Scotland as natural rather than historically constructed. The representation of Scotland and the Scots had risen in international cultural prominence and importance over two centuries, much encouraged by the *Ossian* controversy in the eighteenth century[4] and by Queen Victoria's association with the Highlands in the nineteenth. But those specific events were themselves symptoms of a long historical process, dating from the mid-eighteenth century, whereby Scotland became, for European pre-Romantics and Romantics, a delirious realm of the imagination in which the land itself, peopled by a noble race of bards, warriors and winsome lasses, exercised a magical, transformative sway over any who came there. A constructed identity was imposed on the land and people of Scotland, which to a large extent they have come to live within. The process was not dissimilar to that visited on other peripheral peoples in their encounters with European imperialism (for example, the Polynesians, the respective peoples of Africa and Arabia, and so on) as has been set out in the writings of Frantz Fanon (1925–61) and Edward Said (1935–2003).[5]

This discourse of Scotland, with its cluster of motifs and its accretions and contradictions (for example, the archetypal comic versus the archetypal romantic Scot) was deployed within every conceivable sign system (novels, paintings, operas, ballets, postcards, films, television programmes), and not least in the marketing of Scotch whisky. The Scottish discourses deployed in whisky marketing were not wholly static and repetitive. Certain images of the Scots present in early whisky advertising became less and less apparent: most notably, the parsimonious and, in particular, the drunken Scot. As the discourses of class-based 'respectability' and 'Heritage' became increasingly important in whisky advertising, these merged in that symbolic figure of the modern centaur who is Scots from the waist down and English gentleman from the waist up. He, above all, is the icon who represses and displaces his ancestral counterpart, the rumbustious drunkard, as whisky climbs the social ladder. The drunken Scot, with his cousin the miserly Scot, continued to stalk other sectors of representation, particularly the Scottish comic postcard, and over time became the demented alter ego of the refined Anglo-Scottish gentleman languidly or heartily raising his glass in innumerable whisky adverts. The shelves and pinboards of the 1988 Bell's marketing campaign assuredly do not belong to this deranged Mr Hyde. Indeed, it would be an amusing exercise to redesign the Bell's campaign in order to appeal to the drunken proletarian. Instead of a teak bookcase, a clumsily erected chipboard one; instead of two tickets for the Scotland versus France rugby game, two tickets for a Rangers versus Celtic cup tie; instead of first editions of Robert Burns (1759–96) and Walter Scott, a paperback version of Alexander McArthur (1901–47) and Herbert Kingsley Long (1890–n.d.)'s *No Mean City* (1935) and a video cassette of *Take the High Road* (Scottish Television, 1980–2003); instead of the *Fingal's Cave* overture (1832), the sheet music of Andy Stewart (1933–93)'s *A Scottish Soldier* (1965); instead of a piece of fine, antique Scottish silver, a ceramic, tartan-tammied Scotty bearing the words 'a wee gift frae Dunoon', and so on.

Although the discourses of Class, Age/Tradition and Scotland were to become entrenched and dominant as the marketing of Scotch whisky developed, another long-term discourse also came to be deployed, one which is best described as Formalism in the sense that it emerges from the structure of language and narrative itself. An early example of the formalist discourse in question is Buchanan's marketing their brand *Black & White* around the structural opposition of these colours. Discourses are rather like Chinese boxes or Russian dolls, in that one may lie housed and hidden within several others. It is clear that when the Buchanan's black and white opposition was deployed in relation to visual images of people this would abut on ideas of racism and imperialism, themselves discourses in the process of construction during the late nineteenth century. As time passed, the Buchanan's marketing opposition increasingly centred on images of the black and white Scotch Terriers which became a trademark for the brand. A similar structural opposition central to narrative, that between 'then' and 'now', 'past' and 'present', informed a Johnnie Walker campaign of the late 1940s. Although Bell's in recent years have marketed within an archetypically Scottish discourse (imbricated, of course, with other discourses such as Class), for a long time their marketing relied on the formalist device of the visual pun on the company's own name, a device also extensively deployed by Teacher's.

Whisky, in common with other products (and increasingly so in the 'Heritage' context of 1980s and early-1990s British society[6]), has often geared its marketing round particular historical figures. To restate the point that whisky's marketing has historically extended far beyond images of Scotland, it is probable that the main historical figures used have not in fact been Scots (for example, Queen Anne [1665–1714], George IV [1762–1830], William IV [1765–1837]). However, the main Scottish historical personages who have figured in the marketing of Scotch whisky are particularly interesting: Drambuie's Charles Edward Stuart (1720–88); Highland Queen's Mary, Queen of Scots (1542–87); and Chivas Regal's Robert the Bruce (1274–1329). Significantly, the dominant popular narratives of Mary and Charles Edward are associated with tragedy and loss, exemplifying the romantic pessimism, the sentimental wallowing in ill-fortune, which is such a disabling feature of so much Scottish life and art. Associated with the use of royal figures is that other discourse, common to many peripheral countries, of celebrating the so-called great men that the society in question has produced. This discourse was particularly deployed by Dewar's in their pre-World War I campaign, Famous Scots, which used reproductions of a series of portraits of figures such as Charles Edward Stuart, Sir Walter Scott, Sir Harry Lauder (1870–1950) and many others that Dewar's commissioned from contemporary artists.

It is something of a cliché that British culture is primarily literary and dramatic rather than oriented to the visual arts. This argument certainly seems to be confirmed by Scotch whisky marketing's forays into British culture. That marketing has from time to time drawn upon both British popular and high cultures. Johnnie Walker, for example, ran an extensive campaign in the pre-World War I period which was structured round English popular songs. When whisky marketing has turned to high culture, the terrain has been dominated by those literary giants of British culture, William Shakespeare (c.1564–1616) and Charles Dickens (1812–70). Dewar's, for example, ran a campaign in the 1920s around the slogan 'The spirit of . . .' illustrating such ideas as Friendship, Humour and Hope by reference to Shakespearean characters. Buchanan's ran a campaign during World War I round the characters of Dickens's novels and Justerini & Brooks used images of Dickens himself in one of their American campaigns of the 1960s. What is, of course, particularly interesting about such examples is their suggestion that Scotch whisky has often primarily deployed British rather than Scottish culture in its marketing: Dickens and Shakespeare rather than Burns and Scott, English rather than Scottish popular song. This does not mean that figures such as Burns and Scott have been entirely repressed, however. One can hear resonances of Scott in the whisky brand named *The Antiquary*, although its advertising does not make that connection explicit. However, this provides further evidence that, historically speaking, our contemporary impression that the marketing of Scotch whisky is wholly bound up with images of Scotland is probably mistaken.

As has been noted above, one of the earliest motifs in the very diverse ensemble of marketing strategies deployed by the whisky trade was the image of the Highland soldier. On closer inspection, however, this deployment was often part of a wider, non-nationally specific discourse of militarism. This was so, for example, in the colourful mid-1930s campaign run by Buchanan's, which made reference to a whole range of British Army regiments, only some of which were Scottish. However, the tradition of deploying warlike Highlanders in whisky advertising was notably continued in a campaign run by Dewar's in the United States in the early 1940s, both before and after the United States's entry into World War II. This campaign, which linked Dewar's own winning of awards at international trade fairs to battle honours won by Scottish regiments, may have represented a discreet linking of contemporaneous commercial, militaristic and patriotic imperatives.

This essay has suggested that the discourses of Age/Tradition, Formalism and Scotland constitute the deep-seated and recurrent long-term discourses within which Scotch whisky has been marketed, and that a range of secondary, medium- and short-term discourses have also entered the field. One of the most powerful such discourses at play within British society, particularly in the period 1880–1945, was that of Imperialism. Marketing strategies for whisky were less prone to deploy this discourse during that period than were those for many other products (for example, tobacco, rubber) the raw materials for which originated in the (then) colonies of the British Empire. It would be gratifying, if rather wishful, to think that Scotch whisky's reluctance to play the imperialist card during the late nineteenth and early twentieth centuries was due to the industry's recognition of Scotland's status as, arguably, an internal colony within the British state.[7] However, the Scotch whisky industry and its barons were more than complicit with that state and its imperial pretensions. Indeed, on the occasions when the discourse of Imperialism did appear in whisky advertising it was no less inhibited than elsewhere, as in Dewar's 1920s 'Spirit of the Empire' campaign. Although other whisky brands deployed imperialist images no less aggressively, Dewar's pre-eminence in this regard is perhaps best summed up in its 1937 marketing image of John Bull raising a glass of *White Label*.

To categorise discourses as long-, medium- and short-term is a convenient analytic tool, but it has its limitations. Is, for example, Imperialism to be considered a long- or a medium-term discourse? A long-term discourse can also be strategically employed as a short-term one within a particular historical moment, as in the case of the Peter Dawson marketing campaign of 1924, which was structured round that year's Empire Exhibition at Wembley. The two World Wars unquestionably constituted short-term discourses and it is very instructive to compare the terms in which Scotch whisky was marketed during both conflicts. As befits the differences in tone in Britain's attitudes to World War I and World War II respectively, and the differing public rhetorics which flowed from these, wartime marketing campaigns for Scotch whisky were quite different from one war to the other. Johnnie Walker's jingoistic campaign of 1914–15, for example, may have been of a piece with other events in British society of that time, such as the handing out of white feathers and smashing shops with German names. It is certainly more breast-beating and xenophobic than the campaigns by the same brand and by Vat 69 during World War II. The most short-term of all discourses deployed in the marketing of Scotch whisky are those that related to yet more specific and concrete historical moments. The discourses in question cover diverse events: the Royal Jubilee of 1935 (Dewar's); the flu epidemic of 1936 (Dewar's); the World War II pact among Britain, the USA and the Soviet Union (Dewar's); the 1951 Festival of Britain (Dewar's); the 1953 Coronation (Vat 69); and the 1964 opening of the Forth Road Bridge (King George IV).

This essay has sought to examine the popular perception that the marketing of Scotch whisky is dominated by images of Scotland. While such images have been present from the start, have developed into one of the most central discourses within which Scotch whisky presents itself to the world, and may today constitute the dominant images, this has not always been so. Historically speaking, the marketing of Scotch whisky has deployed a rich variety of discourses, most of them not specific to Scotland. Where that marketing history has adopted images of Scotland, these have been highly selective, tending to the rural and the kitsch, repressing the urban and the contradictory, and invariably interpenetrated with other hegemonic discourses such as that of Class. As nationhood moves further up the agenda of world politics, this process is unlikely to be reversed.

Notes

1. For further detail, see Ian Spring, *Phantom Village: The Myth of the New Glasgow* (Edinburgh: Polygon, 1990).
2. Pierre Vilar, *A History of Gold and Money: 1450–1920* (London: New Left Books, 1976).
3. For more detail, see David Duff, ed., *Queen Victoria's Highland Journals* (Tiverton: Webb & Bower, 1983); Michael J. Stead, *Queen Victoria's Scotland* (London: Octopus, 1992).
4. James Macpherson (1736–96) published in 1760 *Fragments of Ancient Poetry Collected in the Highlands,* followed by other such 'fragments' culminating, in 1765, in a collected edition under the title *The Works of Ossian,* Ossian being the ancient Gaelic bard who ostensibly had written the material. Macpherson's claim simply to have translated the 'fragments' from the Gaelic was contested at the time and it is now believed that he wrote them himself. Much as the argument about their authenticity raged in the late eighteenth and early nineteenth centuries, far and away the most important feature of the episode was its bringing Highland Scotland to the centre of intellectual and emotional attention throughout Europe and its colonial outcrops in the New World. As anthropologist Malcolm Chapman has written, 'It was through this controversy, and through the inauthenticity of Ossian, that the Scottish Gael found his way into the European imagination' (Chapman, *The Gaelic Vision in Scottish Culture* [London: Croom Helm, 1978], 23).
5. See, for example, Frantz Fanon, *Black Skin, White Masks* (New York: Grove Press, 1968); Edward Said, *Orientalism* (London: Routledge & Kegan Paul, 1978).
6. See, for example, J. M. Fladmark, *Heritage and Identity: Shaping National Identity* (London: Routledge, 1999); Rodney Harrison, *Heritage: Critical Approaches* (London: Routledge, 2012).
7. For more detail, see Michael Hechter, *Internal Colonialism: The Celtic Fringe in British National Development* (London: Routledge, 1975).

CHAPTER 18

Scottish Culture: A Reply to David McCrone*

Originally written and published in 1993, this essay sought – and still seeks – to enter into dialogue with certain ideas proposed by the sociologist David McCrone in his 1992 monograph, *Understanding Scotland: The Sociology of a Stateless Nation*. In setting out to pursue that aim, the work of another eminent sociologist came swiftly to mind, for reasons that will become steadily more apparent as this essay's argument progresses. The second sociologist is Stuart Hall (1932–2014), who argues that:

> Cultural identities come from somewhere, have histories. But, like everything which is historical, they undergo constant transformation. Far from being eternally fixed in some essentialised past, they are subject to the continuous 'play' of history, culture and power. Far from being grounded in a mere 'recovery' of the past, which is waiting to be found, and which, when found, will secure our sense of ourselves into eternity, identities are the names we give to the different ways we are positioned by, and position ourselves within, the narratives of the past.[1]

The particular strength of McCrone's *Understanding Scotland* is to see Scotland in its specificity, but a specificity constrained, if not determined by, supranational economic and political institutions.[2] Within this framework McCrone offers sociological data and perspectives on phenomena (for example, the myth of Scottish egalitarianism; the nature of the Scottish polity; the extent to which Scotland's relationship with the British state has been one of dependence) which many of us have tended to deal with impressionistically.

One of the chapters in the book deals with Scottish culture and McCrone poses the problem thus:

> the last twenty years have seen a cultural renaissance in Scotland, in those aspects which confirm its separate identity. Yet the dominant analysis of Scottish culture

---

*Originally published in *Scottish Affairs*, no. 4 (1993), 95–106.

remains a pessimistic and negative one, based on the thesis that Scotland's culture is 'deformed' and debased by sub-cultural formations such as Tartanry and Kailyardism [. . .] While media representations of Scotland are often simplistic and distorted, the search for a pure national culture as an alternative is doomed to fail in a complex, modern, multinational world.[3]

Since several of my own writings are among those cited as constituting 'the dominant analysis', I offer this reply to David McCrone, not in the spirit of defending an entrenched position, but rather of exploring, under his intelligent prodding, some very complex cultural questions.

Throughout this essay I shall be using the term 'culture' and its affiliates in a semiotic sense, that is to say, I would regard as 'cultural' any artefact or practice which signifies. In particular, I would not regard as pertinent (to the argument of this essay) the traditional distinction between High Culture, such as certain canonical works of literature and drama, and Popular Culture, such as cinema, television and journalism.

Kailyard and Tartanry

It might be useful to begin with those elements in McCrone's argument which ought now to be conceded or, more accurately, assented to, since the writings he critiques are those of the early 1980s and things have, hopefully, moved on somewhat. McCrone argues that Kailyard and Tartanry were/are much less hegemonic over Scottish culture than has been claimed. He cites Knowles as evidence that Kailyard, in its incorporation of 'British Victorian elements [. . .] the gothic novel, the fairy tale, eighteenth-century sentimentalism, the Victorian penchant for dying and death',[4] was influential primarily outside of Scotland (in passing, I would note that I have also made the point that Kailyard was part of a wider movement of popular, sentimental forms).[5] McCrone also cites William Donaldson as evidence of a much more fissiparous nineteenth-century Scottish culture in which the influence of Kailyard within book publishing was more than tempered by the effect of the newspaper-based popular literature which, dealing with contemporary (often urban) events in un-idyllic prose, was all the things Kailyard was not.[6]

These cited works increase our understanding of both Kailyard and (until the appearance of Donaldson's book) the forgotten tradition of Scottish newspaper fiction, but the legitimacy of McCrone's mobilising them in an across-the-board critique of those writings which have stressed the influence of Kailyard is open to doubt. This is due to the somewhat abstract nature of his critique, which lumps together works setting out to do rather different things. For example, Beveridge and Turnbull, included in McCrone's critique, are themselves critical of several of the other works that McCrone additionally cites and critiques.[7] Those writers he mentions who are concerned with cultural phenomena substantially internal to Scotland and, to an important degree, with literature must answer for themselves about the extent to which his critique holds water.[8] One of the central points I have made about the historical dominance of Kailyard (and Tartanry) in cinematic representations of Scotland and the Scots is precisely that these were articulated elsewhere (Hollywood and London, mainly) and that because of the absence, with few exceptions up to the mid-1950s, of indigenous filmmaking, they were the only available cinematic models.[9] As such, they exercised a hegemony over Scottish fictional filmmaking. A different discourse, British Documentary, exercised a hegemony over Scottish factual filmmaking. These discourses are separated out for analytic reasons, for they are heavily interpenetrated in the products of Films of Scotland (1954–82), the virtually exclusive Scottish filmmaking milieu of the two decades from 1955. Thus, while McCrone can correctly cite Donaldson as evidence of an indigenous literary tradition hostile to Kailyard, that citation and accompanying argument cannot be mobilised to demonstrate the existence of an alternative cinematic tradition overlooked or downplayed by myself and other writers.

McCrone also calls into question the often-asserted hegemony of Tartanry in Scottish cultural life. Here again his position warrants assent. When my and a group of associated writers' analysis of cinematic and televisual representations of Scotland appeared in the 1982 edited volume *Scotch Reels*, we were of the view that Tartanry was irretrievably tarnished.[10] So locked was that discourse into regressive images of Scotland that it was impossible to conceive of it being deployed progressively. Subsequent events have proved this not to be the case. What we should have remembered, as good structuralists, is that images do not have intrinsic, essential, unchanging meanings.[11] Rather, their meanings are constantly remade, renegotiated in (usually) opposition to other meanings. The most convincing account of this (with regard to Tartanry) deploys concepts derived from Michel Foucault (1926–84), Jacques Derrida (1930–2004), Roland Barthes (1915–80), Jean Baudrillard (1929–2007), Erving Goffman (1922–82) and Mikhail Bakhtin (1895–1975) to demonstrate (among other things) that the Tartan Army of Scots football supporters at the 1990 World Cup in Italy reconstituted its traditional image (drunken ruffians) in direct opposition to that of English supporters in order to project an image of convivial internationalism.[12] Giulianotti defines that remaking in a table of oppositions (simplified for this article) as follows:

Table 18.1 English/Scottish

English	Scottish
Violent	Non-violent
Drunk	Merry
Chauvinistic	Pluralistic
Xenophobic	Internationalist
Serious	Playful

Strictly in the context of Italia '90, therefore, the Scots supporters defined for themselves a wholly progressive identity, and their insignia (tartan tammies and scarves, Lion Rampant and Saltire flags) became signifiers of that identity. In short, images which many of us had dismissed as the signifiers of sentimental backwardness were on this occasion transformed into markers of a modern and politically progressive consciousness.

But let's be cautious about this. There is, in the postmodernism which informs McCrone's book, something of an implication (which I will return to later) that the pick-and-mix conception of identity is not just the very condition of postmodernity, but that it also constitutes a kind of political Nirvana impervious to the horrendous -isms of the earlier cultural-historical era of Modernity. Once again, structuralism reminds us that the meanings of signs are constantly renegotiated according to their contexts. That Tartanry was (re)constructed for positive ends in Italy in 1990 is no guarantee that it will not be mobilised for regressive purposes in other contexts.

Plural Identities: A Novelty?

All that said, McCrone's conception of culture and identity is extremely attractive in the following formulation:

> Identities as well as societies can coexist. If Scots were 'Scottish' for certain purposes and 'British' for other purposes as John Mackintosh [1929–78] pointed out, then they were simply recognising the complex pluralities of modern life [. . .] similarly, being black, Glaswegian and female can all characterise one person's culture and social inheritance without one aspect of that identity being paramount (except in terms of self-identification). What is on offer in the late twentieth century is what we might call 'pick 'n' mix' identity in which we wear our identities lightly and change them according to circumstances.[13]

As an aspiration, that is fine. Indeed, it is a position close to the one I have arrived at over the past decade since *Scotch Reels* was published.

Interestingly, the main influence in this regard was not only my own life experience: Glaswegian son of a Gaelic-speaking 'Wee Free' mother and a Clydeside communist father; resident in England for nearly thirty years; married to a Trinidadian woman herself of Asian origin; father of mixed-race children who define themselves primarily as South Londoners. The influence was also the discussion about identities which has gone on in the Black British community.[14] The position has been elegantly restated by Schlesinger in the context of his insightful discussion of *Play Me Something* (Timothy Neat, 1989), a film which manages to be both Scottish and European simultaneously.[15] The position we all now seem to favour is to conceive of culture and identity as necessarily hybrid. But, as I will go on to demonstrate, that hybridity may not be wholly within the playful control of individual actors as postulated by certain postmodernisms. Rather, it is constrained by historically far-reaching discourses operating below the level of individual actors' consciousness.

However, there are several further aspects of McCrone's position which require interrogation. *Understanding Scotland* is itself a structuralist work, in that it defines its conception of Scottish culture and identity in opposition to other conceptions. In doing so it creates something of a straw man of those other positions, characterising them as seeking a pure, essentialist model of Scottish culture against which McCrone poses his hybrid conception. Once again, the others critiqued by McCrone must answer for themselves, but it would be an extremely perverse reading of *Scotch Reels* which saw it as canvassing an essentialist, unitary, unproblematic conception of Scottish culture to be counterposed against the dreaded Tartanry and Kailyard that it attacked. There are constant references throughout *Scotch Reels* to the need for a Scottish cinematic practice that is adequate to the task of dealing with the complex socio-political condition of modern Scotland. The films it cites as approaching such adequacy (for example, Brian Crumlish [1944–94]'s *The Caledonian Account* [1976] and Murray Grigor's *Mackintosh* [1968] and *Clydescope* [1974]) are to some extent themselves necessarily analytic and fissured works. Similarly, my own essay in *Scotch Reels* concludes with a list of possible models for a Scottish cinematic practice:

> Scotland has produced no equivalents of Hans-Jürgen Syberberg's, Bernardo Bertolucci [1941–2018]'s, Theo Angelopoulos [1935–2012]'s, Santiago Álvarez [1919–98]'s and Phil Mulloy's treatments of their respective national histories; no equivalents of Jean-Luc Godard [1930–2022]'s, Nagisa Ōshima [1932–2013]'s or Dušan Makavejev [1932–2019]'s anatomising of the sexual mores of the societies in which they live; no equivalents of the sustained reflection on the processes of cinema evident in the work of Michael Snow [1928–2023] and Jean-Marie

Straub [1933–2022]/Danièle Huillet [1936–2006]; and – most damagingly of all – no equivalents of the accounts of women's experience to be found in the work of Chantal Akerman [1955–2015], Yvonne Rainer and Peter Wollen [1938–2019]/ Laura Mulvey.[16]

Now, the choice of these particular filmmakers might be argued with, but citing them cannot be interpreted as calling for a unitary, seamless, national culture. On the contrary, the words which spring first to mind are 'contradictory', 'ironic' and 'self-reflexive'. Incidentally, the Scottish filmmaking scene has not improved markedly in the ten years since these words were written and the reasons for that today, as back then, are institutional (of which more below).

Cultural Institutions

There is one particularly odd feature of McCrone's chapter on Scottish culture. It is, to say the least, surprising (although perhaps a by-product of the book's postmodernist approach) that, in a work of sociology, none of the major institutions of Scottish culture are discussed. There is not even a mention of the Scottish Arts Council (1967–2010), the Scottish Film Council (1934–97) or the Scottish Film Production Fund (1982–97). Now, *Scotch Reels*'s traducing of Tartanry, Kailyard and what it called the 'Scotland on the Move' discourse (that conception of documentary filmmaking central to Films of Scotland and ultimately deriving from Griersonian documentary discourse[17]) was above all a critique of institutions. Thus:

> The Scottish failure has not been one primarily of individual will; it has been the failure of institutions to create the conditions for the development of more politically and artistically relevant discourses. Put epigrammatically, institutions like the Scottish Film Council, the Scottish Federation of Film Societies, Films of Scotland and, more recently, the Scottish Arts Council have failed to keep a historic appointment with the discourses of Marxism and modernism, the conjunction of which has dynamised analogous institutions in other cultures [. . .] Needless to say, the call for a Scottish institutional engagement with the discourses of Marxism and modernism is not a plea to swallow these discourses whole and periodically regurgitate them: that would not only be intellectually deadening, but would be a wholly inappropriate role for publicly funded bodies in a pluralist society. Such bodies must have due regard for the diversity of views in the constituencies they serve, while at the same time ensuring that processes of debate and renewal occur.[18]

As well as dealing with institutions, this passage supports the above argument about *Scotch Reels*'s call for an intrinsically debate-based national culture, rather than for a unified and homogeneous one.

These words may now seem quaint in a (temporarily?) post-Marxist and post-Modernist world.[19] However, as the lands of the Soviet periphery resound with the cries of babies thrown out with the bathwater, they are perhaps words worth remembering. The point at issue here is the extent to which one can conduct an argument about Scottish culture without discussing the central arts institutions of that culture. Since *Scotch Reels* was published the Scottish film scene has acquired another institution, the Scottish Film Production Fund, which, like the institutions pilloried in *Scotch Reels*, has failed lamentably to produce a production policy adequate to the economic and cultural specificity of Scotland.[20]

How Autonomous are Individuals?

It would seem, nevertheless, that McCrone wishes to conduct the argument solely at the level of *discourse*. So be it. Postmodernism, responding to a defect in classical Marxism, is centrally and laudably concerned with individual agency and empowerment.[21] In its crasser formulations it would evaporate determinations of any kind, leaving the human subject in a state of free play within which multiple choices of role and identity are endlessly available. Most contentiously, it would evaporate the concept of the Unconscious. McCrone does not address this question, but it is clear from his description of identity as multiple cited above that he would emphasise the idea that considerable autonomy and agency characterise individual human beings' control of identity. This argument seems particularly problematic in the context of Scottish culture, given that many of its central discourses have been articulated elsewhere over several centuries, thus producing what might be called a Scottish discursive unconscious. For instance, it seems at least possible that when he made *Local Hero* (1983), Bill Forsyth was not altogether conscious of the discourse which guided his hand: that historical narrative within which Scotland is a magical realm which transforms the incoming stranger. While that discourse was one initially articulated in the great provincial centres of Enlightenment, Pre-Romantic and Romantic Europe, it has been thoroughly ingested by Scots themselves over the subsequent two centuries through exposure to art works (defined in the widest sense) formulated under its sway.[22] The undoubted presence of this discourse in *Local Hero* might perhaps best be responded to with a question. Is it present (as I would suggest) as an unconscious tradition within which Bill Forsyth is working, or is he wholly aware of it and manipulating it for his own ends?

Elegy

If a Scottish discursive unconscious with the capacity to inhibit the free play of the 'pick 'n mix' identity McCrone is canvassing does exist, how might it operate? Consider the following two quotations from the works of the historian, John Prebble (1915–2001):

> From the green saucer of Glenaladale dipping down to Loch Shiel, Alexander Macdonald had taken one hundred and fifty men to serve in Clanranald's regiment. Within a century there was nothing there but the lone shieling of the song.

> What the red soldiers began in February 1692, sheep finished one hundred and fifty years later, and the people of John of the Heather were gone from the Valley of the Dogs.[23]

These quotations exemplify what could be called the elegiac discourse, a multifaceted narrative two tropes of which are present here: the mantra-like rolling of the names of people and places off the tongue; and closure on a symbolic image of silence, solitude and loss. The Scottish version of this discourse probably has its origins in the European appropriation of the *Ossian* poems (1761–63) of James Macpherson (1736–96). The presence of the elegiac discourse, manifestly rhetorical and fictive as it is, in Prebble's books is curious. They are, after all, works of historiography, an ostensibly rational, indeed quasi-scientific discourse which deploys the sober mechanisms of consulting original sources and weighing evidence. Hayden White (1928–2018) has demonstrated that all historiography is cast within narrative structures, but the question remains why one particular such structure, the elegiac discourse, should loom so large in Prebble's work.[24]

The answer surely is that works such as Prebble's books are about Scottish history, and that when anyone sets out to tell stories about Scotland, certain forms of narrative beckon, Circe-like, unconsciously guiding the writer's hand and setting the tone of the story. Polemically, it might be suggested that we tend to be written by the dominant Scottish narratives rather than ourselves writing narratives about Scotland. These dominant narratives vary according to the time and place within Scotland when and where any given individual story is set. For example, the dominant (and equally atavistic) narrative about twentieth-century Lowland Scotland revolves round taciturn masculinity, drink, sport and explosive violence. That narrative has its origins as much within public health and housing discourses of the nineteenth century and journalistic discourses of the interwar period of the twentieth as within more obviously artistic traditions such as the novel. A recent illustrative example of it is the film, *The Big Man* (David Leland, 1990).

When other individual stories are instead about the Scottish Highlands of the past, however, it is the elegiac discourse that comes into play almost like an automatic pilot. With absolutely predictable inevitability, for example, that discourse reared its malign head in the Scottish press coverage of the Glencoe massacre tercentenary early in 1992, its tropes surfacing not only in the written copy but in the accompanying photographs and their captions. Certain pieces, to their credit, resisted the lure of elegy and gave sober accounts of the historical circumstances surrounding the events of 1692,[25] although one of the photographs accompanying one of the articles in question is captioned, 'Glencoe in all its gloom' and that image's visual rhetoric – mist, rock, a tangled tree and, above all, *solitude* – exemplifies the commitment to moralised landscape (the emotions of the viewer being projected into what is viewed) that is so central to the elegiac discourse. A photograph in *The Scotsman* of 13 February 1992, showing a piper beside the Glencoe monument and captioned, 'Under a blood-red sky . . .' deploys similar rhetorical devices.

Another press article on the anniversary is transitional in the sense that it sets out to deal with the historical facts but gets waylaid by the elegiac narrative's awesome discursive power. The article opens: 'Glencoe. The word rings through the annals of Scottish history like a mournful gong' and closes with a quotation from the Executive Director of the Clan Donald Society:

> All this about people hearing voices and music and people talking, I put down to people coming up from the hurly burly to a lonely spot and for the first time hearing the silence. There is music and voices but not people, just the way nature has of blowing the wind and making water drip onto stone – that's the only thing you hear.[26]

The rhetoric of this verbal discourse is so close to that of the main photograph accompanying the article that part of it is used as a caption for that image.

But it is in two pieces by the journalist Brian Pendreigh that the elegiac discourse is most marked. The first concerns a visit to the present-day village of Glencoe; the second describes the actual commemoration ceremony of the massacre. The characteristic tropes of the elegiac discourse appear early in Pendreigh's account of his visit to Glencoe Village ('this is Glencoe, the village at the foot of that most dramatic of glens, where the waters run down the precipitous black rock-faces like tears of pain and shame at what happened 300 years ago'[27]) but the discourse's self-lacerative qualities are most evident in his account of the commemoration ceremony: 'The chill of highland rain numbs the flesh. The chill

Figure 18.1 Unlike the dominant discourse about Glencoe, this collage evokes laughter rather than tears. Artist: Murray Grigor.

of highland history numbs the heart. The tears on the cheek could be the work of either.'[28] Tears, indeed, are just what the elegiac discourse is objectively designed to call forth. Not historical understanding, not political mobilisation and action, but tears – if, in these postmodern times, it is not deemed heretical to suggest that a specific rhetorical strategy might elicit its intended response.

The history of how the elegiac discourse came to dominate accounts of the Gàidhealtachd has been traced by Malcolm Chapman: 'It is often difficult to avoid the impression that many Scottish intellectuals are glad the Forty-five happened, however sordid and disastrous the consequences'.[29] The same might be said of Glencoe. There comes to mind the Russian short story about the countess who, in a warm box in the theatre, sheds copious tears over a sentimental play while her coachman, waiting for her in the street, freezes to death.

A Cure?

By a profound historical irony, almost contemporaneously with that scab-scratching, self-indulgent charade at Glencoe, 2,500 people crammed the Usher Hall in Edinburgh to debate the constitutional position of contemporary Scotland. While both events were about national identity, one was open, wide-ranging and forward-looking, whereas the other was closed, narrow-minded and regressive. The Glencoe event and, more particularly, the elegiac discourse which surrounded it, constitute not just an emotionally disabling inheritance, but a politically disabling one also. There is every reason to hope that Scots are now in the process of fashioning a modern identity, however hybrid, but it has to be understood that the historically dominant narratives about Scotland can impede political advance. Those narratives must therefore be confronted, deconstructed and replaced with new ones. One of the issues in this debate is the extent to which the new can be created without first dismantling the old.

Fashioning these new narratives of the Scottish nation is every bit as important and difficult as creating new political structures for it. It will require thought as well as feeling, irreverence as well as respect. Murray Grigor, for example, once produced a collage on Glencoe: over a bleak, nineteenth-century print of the glen, he superimposed the logos of Campbell's Soup and the fast-food chain McDonald's. My hunch is that McCrone would admire Grigor's collage as much as I do, perhaps seeing it (rightly) as a light-hearted, postmodern assertion of modern Scottishness. However, I would wish to emphasise another dimension of the work in question – its deconstruction of the elegiac discourse within which Glencoe is usually encased. Such deconstruction, across the whole range of regressive Scottish discourses, is a continuing cultural, and therefore political, task. In this context, I warmly recommend the *Rab C. Nesbitt* Hogmanay Special and the particular episode of the series in which Rab and company visit Ardlui.

Returning to the relevance of this essay's opening quotation from Stuart Hall, it is clear that his argument can be read in two ways, one stressing fluidity and change and the other, continuity with the past. Clearly, and against what I see as McCrone's over-readiness to play down the effectivity of the past, I would wish to stress the second reading. Concretely, the question on which McCrone and I would disagree most sharply is how effective (and affective) discourses such as Clydesidism, Tartanry and Kailyard (and their sub-forms such as the Scottish variant of the elegiac discourse) are within contemporary Scotland. Can they be sloughed off or playfully reworked (the argument that appears to be the implication of McCrone's writings)? Or do they continue to lurk, iceberg-like, in the Scottish discursive unconscious? I fear the latter, but debating these questions in journals such as *Scottish Affairs* might help effect the 'talking cure' whereby that discursive unconscious will be understood and tamed.

Notes

1. Stuart Hall, 'Cultural Identity and Diaspora', in *Identity: Community, Culture, Difference*, ed. Jonathan Rutherford (London: Lawrence & Wishart, 1990), 225.
2. David McCrone, *Understanding Scotland: The Sociology of a Stateless Nation* (London: Routledge, 1992). A revised edition of McCrone's book (its subtitle amended to read 'The Sociology of a Nation') was published by Routledge in 2001.
3. Ibid., 13.
4. T. D. Knowles, *Ideology, Art and Commerce: Aspects of Literary Sociology in the Late Victorian Scottish Kailyard* (Gotenborg: Acta Universitatis Gothoburgensis, 1983), 64.
5. Colin McArthur, 'Scotland and Cinema: The Iniquity of the Fathers', in *Scotch Reels: Scotland in Cinema and Television*, ed. Colin McArthur (London: British Film Institute, 1982), 42, and reproduced elsewhere in the present volume.
6. William Donaldson, *Popular Literature in Victorian Scotland: Language, Fiction and the Press* (Aberdeen: Aberdeen University Press, 1986).
7. Craig Beveridge and Ronald Turnbull, *The Eclipse of Scottish Culture: Inferiorism and the Intellectuals* (Edinburgh: Polygon, 1989). Works critiqued by both McCrone and Beveridge and Turnbull include: Tom Nairn, *The Break-Up of Britain: Crisis and Neo-Nationalism* (London: New Left Books, 1977); Colin McArthur, 'Breaking the Signs: *Scotch Myths* as Cultural Struggle', *Cencrastus*, no. 7 (Winter 1981/82), 21–5, and reproduced elsewhere in the present volume.
8. For example, Beveridge and Turnbull, *The Eclipse of Scottish Culture*; Nairn, *The Break-Up of Britain*; Douglas Gifford, ed., *The History of Scottish Literature: Volume 3 (The Nineteenth Century)* (Aberdeen: Aberdeen University Press, 1988).
9. McArthur, 'Scotland and Cinema'.
10. Colin McArthur, ed., *Scotch Reels: Scotland in Cinema and Television* (London: British Film Institute, 1982).
11. Characteristically, structuralism is less interested in critical evaluation than description, but Peter Wollen, in his famous structuralist account of the films of John Ford (1894–1973) and Howard Hawks (1896–1977), uses the malleability of structuralist oppositions precisely as the basis of his valuing Ford's films over Hawks's: 'My own view is that Ford's work is much richer than that of Hawks and that this is revealed by a structural analysis; it is the richness of the shifting antinomies in Ford's work that makes him a great artist beyond being simply an undoubted auteur' (Peter Wollen, *Signs and Meaning in the Cinema* [London: Secker & Warburg in association with the British Film Institute, 1969], 102); and: 'part of the development of Ford's career has been the shift from an identity between civilised versus savage and European versus Indian to their separation and final reversal, so that in *Cheyenne Autumn* [John Ford, 1964] it is the Europeans who are savages, the victims who are heroes' [Ibid., 96]). The most obvious contrast with *Cheyenne*

Autumn is *Stagecoach* (John Ford, 1939), in which the Native Americans are savages, but the shift begins to be discerned in *Fort Apache* (John Ford, 1948).
12. Richard Giulianotti, 'Scotland's Tartan Army in Italy: The Case for the Carnivalesque', *Sociological Review* 39, no. 3 (1991), 503–27. I am grateful to Raymond Boyle for this reference.
13. McCrone, *Understanding Scotland*, 195.
14. See, for example, Rutherford, ed., *Identity: Community, Culture, Difference*.
15. Philip Schlesinger, 'Scotland, Europe and Identity', in *From Limelight to Satellite: A Scottish Film Book*, ed. Eddie Dick (London/Glasgow: BFI Publishing/Scottish Film Council, 1990), 221–32.
16. McArthur, 'Scotland and Cinema', 67–8.
17. For more on Griersonian discourse, see Alan Lovell and Jim Hillier, *Studies in Documentary* (London: Secker & Warburg for the British Film Institute, 1972); Ian Aitken, *Film and Reform: John Grierson and the Documentary Film Movement* (London: Routledge, 1990).
18. McArthur, 'Scotland and Cinema', 67.
19. See Andrew Noble, 'Bill Douglas's *Trilogy*' in *From Limelight to Satellite: A Scottish Film Book*, ed. Eddie Dick (London/Glasgow: British Film Institute/Scottish Film Council, 1990), 149 for an apoplectic response to them.
20. Colin McArthur, 'What is the Scottish Film Production Fund Up To?', *Scottish Film and Visual Arts*, no. 10 (4th quarter 1992), 20.
21. For a lucid account not only of Postmodernism's commitment to agency but also its ultimate limitations in this regard, see Matthew McManus, 'Post-Modernism, Agency and Democracy', *Philosophies* 3, no. 4 (2018), DOI: https://doi.org/10.3390/philosophies3040032 [accessed 21 August 2022].
22. See Malcolm Chapman, *The Gaelic Vision in Scottish Culture* (London: Croom Helm, 1978).
23. John Prebble, *Culloden* (London: Penguin, 1967), 315; Prebble, *Glencoe* (London: Penguin, 1968), 262–3.
24. Hayden White, *Metahistory: The Historical Imagination in Nineteenth-Century Europe* (Baltimore, MD: Johns Hopkins University Press, 1975); Hayden White, *Tropics of Discourse: Essays in Cultural Criticism* (Baltimore, MD: Johns Hopkins University Press, 1978).
25. See, for example, Magnus Linklater, 'Let it be secret and sudden', *The Scotsman*, 13 February 1992, 15; David Ross, 'Clan's chief offers olive branch as feud is declared buried', *The Herald*, 14 February 1992, 5.
26. Gillian Ferguson, 'The Ghosts of Glencoe', *Scotland on Sunday*, 12 January 1992, 27.
27. Brian Pendreigh, 'Myth and mystique in a cruel glen', *The Scotsman*, 13 February 1992, 15.
28. Brian Pendreigh, 'Rain joins tears for victims of outrage', *The Scotsman*, 14 February 1992, 3.
29. Chapman, *The Gaelic Vision in Scottish Culture*, 21.

CHAPTER 19

In Praise of a Poor Cinema*

In its 1991 *Annual Report*, the Scottish Film Production Fund (1982–97) trumpeted its institutional mission as being:

> To ensure the development of a viable, vigorous, and substantial Scottish film industry designed to attract and deploy the talents of Scottish filmmakers and to enable them to make films in their own country.

The quotation above is, of course, a fantasy which has beguiled the SFPF and its parent body, the Scottish Film Council (1934–97), since the Fund's inception in 1982. As, in these post-Marxist days, babies are being thrown out with the bathwater all over Europe, many indispensable concepts are being jettisoned. One such concept, that of uneven development, describes perfectly Scotland's relationship with diverse sectors of the UK economy, not least film production. To put it bluntly, Scotland is, on the filmmaking front, a third-world country, but this is tragically misrecognised by those holding the purse strings north of the border. There have always been signs that the SFPF and SFC were on a collision course with reality. One of the earliest officers of the Fund talked about discovering the next generation of Bill Forsyths and senior officers of the SFC, at their most delirious, have been heard to speak of 'Hollywood on the Clyde'.

When the stated policy is compared with the reality of the Fund's most recent investment, *Prague* (Ian Sellar, 1992), the gulf is stark. Apart from the fact that producer Christopher Young, producer/director Ian Sellar and one of the principal actors, Alan Cumming, are Scots, *Prague* has nothing to do with Scotland and could not be remotely construed to fulfil what might be assumed to be a central impulse of a new national cinema – the exploration of the contradictions of the society from which it comes.

---

*Originally published in *Sight and Sound* 3, no. 8 (August 1993), 30–2.

Individual filmmakers should not be blamed for using whatever production mechanisms are available to them, but the Scots involved in *Prague* were the fig leaf which allowed the project to absorb a massive proportion of the SFPF's available funds over an extended period and decorated the Europudding the film was to become. During the period when *Prague* was in development and production, the SFPF stood at about £250,000 per annum. Over two financial years it invested no less than £130,000 in *Prague*, having in previous years put an equally generous £100,000 into an earlier film, *Venus Peter* (Ian Sellar, 1989), by the same production/direction team. This tendency to put available eggs into a small number of baskets is reminiscent of central Scotland's costly dependence on a few heavy industries earlier in the twentieth century.

The precise details of the discussions between Young/Sellar and the SFPF will probably never be known, but what is clear is that Young himself would like to be making considerably cheaper films than *Prague*, at £1.95 million, turned out to be. Did the SFPF actively steer *Prague* towards inflationary mechanisms like the involvement of the BBC's Screen Two commissioning strand, which put up about £500,000 of the budget?

There are also cultural as well as economic questions to be asked of *Prague* and the SFPF's involvement with the project. For example, it seems that Young, in the letter which accompanied his original script submission, indicated that the central character might be American (rather than, as in the realised film, Scottish). Despite the fact that this would further distance the project's already tenuous connection with Scotland, the SFPF did not regard it as in any way problematic. A major insertion of French money brought *Prague*'s budget up to nearly £2 million and the project was designated a British–French co-production. In recompense, the French required that some 45 per cent of the budget be spent in France, a condition realised primarily by having the film processed at a French lab. As far as I am aware, none of *Prague*'s budget was spent in Scotland.

The main impulse of the SFPF is towards projects which will attract finance from diverse sources and consequently compete for attention on the world stage. A largely unrecognised contradiction here is that the larger the project, the less Scottish it becomes. It might be argued that the Fund's most successful area of operation has been in springboarding a handful of Scottish filmmakers into international production. It has been the Fund's practice to subsidise the graduation films of Scottish students at the National Film and Television School in Beaconsfield. One such was Michael Caton-Jones's *The Riveter* (1986). Caton-Jones is now comfortably ensconced in Los Angeles. In an interview in *The Observer*

Magazine in 1991, he remarked: 'In a way I had no roots. I had left Scotland at eighteen and drifted to the London area. Leaving for Los Angeles was no great wrench [. . .] I doubt if I'll go back to Britain.' So much for the SFPF's above-quoted policy 'to enable [Scottish filmmakers] to make films in their own country'. Caton-Jones is currently listed as director of the forthcoming *Rob Roy* (producer Peter Broughan; writer Alan Sharp [1934–2013]), which is already in receipt of development finance from the Fund.[1]

Commitment to the Mainstream

This springboarding of individual careers is joined by a complete misconception of what might constitute an appropriate production policy for Scotland's economic and cultural circumstances. There is one statistic which should be branded on the foreheads of those who call the shots in the SFPF and the SFC: of the eight British feature films analysed in the 1993 *BFI Film and Television Handbook*, the average budget was £1.8 million, and the average net revenue only £0.8 million. Presumably data of this order was available to the SFPF when it became involved with *Prague*.

The root cause of the SFPF and SFC's failure to articulate a meaningful production policy lies in their surrender to an industrial model of indigenous film production rather than in posing the question in terms of cultural need. The Fund's commitment to film as commodity is evident from the projects into which it puts the bulk of its funds and from the backgrounds of those who have recently served as part of the group which makes its funding decisions, including Roger Crittenden (NFTS); Bill Forsyth (director); Charles Gormley (1937–2005; director); Mamoun Hassan (1937–2002; producer); Liz Lochhead (writer); Bernard MacLaverty (writer); Lynda Myles (producer); Bill Paterson (actor); Iain Smith (producer); and Archie Tait (producer). Individually, these are all bright and able people but collectively, with the exception of Liz Lochhead, the orthodoxy of their recent professional filmmaking backgrounds and their commitment to mainstream (and therefore expensive) aesthetic forms is overwhelming. A costing of the projects in which they have been involved within recent years would be hardly likely to dip beneath the recent national feature production budget average of £1.8 million cited above and would most likely be considerably above it. The most glaring absence from the list is any figure who could bring in a feature film (such as Derek Jarman [1942–94]'s *Wittgenstein* [1993]) for around £300,000. The absence is not accidental. Like the SFC, the SFPF has from the outset set its face firmly against the aesthetic tradition of such films. One of the most unfortunate results of both institutions' freezing out of alternative voices is that public funders and potential private investors in Scotland are kept in the dark about film production practices which are not only more commercially viable, but more culturally necessary than the practices currently funded.

Institutions are rarely monolithic, and the current Director of the SFPF, Kate Swan, was herself the producer of *Play Me Something* (Timothy Neat, 1989), an excellent film which managed, on a budget of £375,000 and in a way *Prague* did not, to be both Scottish and European (and a great deal more) simultaneously. To underline the lack of monolithic institutional culture, the SFPF put a small amount of money into *Play Me Something*. But the promising track record of the Fund's current Director and its own occasional backing of the right horse must be set against the orthodox professional backgrounds and associated mindset of those making the funding decisions and where they have put the vast bulk of available monies.

The present board of the SFPF gives even less comfort to those looking for a low-budget cinematic aesthetic: Allan Shiach (Chairman); David Aukin (Head of Drama, Channel 4); Colin Cameron (Head of Television, BBC Scotland); Paddy Higson (independent producer); Sandy Johnson (independent television director); Margaret Matheson (independent film producer for television); Scott Meek (independent film producer for television); George Mitchell (Controller of Programmes, Grampian TV); Colin Young (1927–2021; former Director of the National Film and Television School). There is one figure in the above line-up who has recently become a key player. Under the name Allan Shiach, he is a rich and prominent businessman (Chairman of the Macallan-Glenlivet whisky operation); under the name Allan Scott, he is a successful Hollywood screenwriter, most notably in his collaborations with Nicolas Roeg (1928–2018), such as *Don't Look Now* (1973) and *Castaway* (1986). He is now Chairman of both the SFC and the SFPF.

It is possibly not accidental that following Shiach/Scott's entry into the Scottish film scene there should emerge Movie Makars, an event designed to explore the craft of classic Hollywood screenwriting and which brought Hollywood screenwriter William Goldman (1931–2018) to speak in Scotland. The discourse about classic Hollywood screenwriting is immensely interesting and has achieved considerable prominence in recent years through manuals such as Syd Field (1935–2013)'s *Screenplay* (1979) and *The Screenwriter's Workbook* (1984) and through Robert McKee's Screen Structure Course. But one of its effects is to fetishise the classic two-hour Hollywood script and forbid entry to other ways of thinking about and making cinema. As such, it dovetails perfectly with the dominant ideology of film production in Scotland.

One other recently created mechanism has given the final impetus to Scotland's headlong rush towards an industrial conception of filmmaking – the Glasgow Film Fund. The latter currently stands at £150,000 per annum, made up of contributions from the Glasgow Development Agency, Strathclyde Business Development, Glasgow City Council and the European Regional Development Fund, and will be administered by the SFPF, concentrating nearly all public funding of filmmaking in Scotland within a single tight group of individuals working to highly exclusive policy criteria. The GFF's terms of reference are frankly commercial, designed to stimulate filmmaking in the Glasgow conurbation and to pull money into the local economy. Only feature film projects with a budget of at least £500,000 are said to be eligible to apply.

Staggering Banality

Given the career profiles of those who serve on its board, it is perhaps understandable that the SFPF should lock on to an industrial model of filmmaking. It is more surprising that an ostensibly cultural body like the SFC should espouse the same values. It recently produced *The Charter for the Moving Image in Scotland* (1993), a document of staggering banality which, when not whining about the inequity of public funding of the moving image in Scotland in relation to the rest of the UK, proposes utopian structures of truly megalomaniacal proportions, such as a Scottish Screen Agency which would subsume all existing film mechanisms and concentrate funding powers in even fewer hands.[2] Symptomatically, during the period when the resounding phrases of the *Charter* were being sculpted, Scotland's only independent film studio and lab facility closed down.

All this would be serious enough, but conversations with Scottish filmmakers who have had dealings with these bodies suggest a more disturbing picture, one in which those projects most rooted in Scottish culture and most challenging to the locally dominant ideology of production are actively opposed, if not as a matter of explicit policy by these bodies, then by powerful individual voices within them. It might indeed be asserted that the most distinctively Scottish of recent films (*Silent Scream* [David Hayman, 1990], *Tickets for the Zoo* [Brian Crumlish, 1991], *Blue Black Permanent* [Margaret Tait, 1992], *As an Eilean* [Mike Alexander, 1993]) have been made because forces outside Scotland, particularly two English commissioning editors at Channel 4, Alan Fountain (1946–2016) and Rod Stoneman, have been prepared to put money into projects that figures in the Scottish film establishment would have preferred to see die. As a footnote to that establishment's judgement, the projects it has been most hostile to are the ones which have won awards at foreign festivals, such as *Silent Scream*'s notable success at the 1990 Berlin International Film Festival.

The absence of cultural analysis in the governing discourses of the SFC and the SFPF has meant that they have both been unequipped to think of alternatives to the industrial model of filmmaking, or to recognise the problems relating to national culture and identity that the industrial model might create. For instance, a recent article in the Scottish press indicated that research had revealed that German executives have an image of Scotland which leads them to think of it as a place to rest, rather than to invest, in. In short, 'dream Scotland'. To the extent that the main impulse of Scottish films is to address a wider market – a key principle of the SFPF – the dilemma such films face is how to do so without recourse to regressive discourses such as 'dream Scotland'. It might be thought, given their commitment to an industrial model of filmmaking and their rhetoric about attracting inward investment into Scotland, that the SFPF and SFC would have given some thought to how the 'dream Scotland' narrative might be dislodged from the heads of German executives and replaced by other narratives more conducive to seeing Scotland as a modern industrial nation. But there is no evidence that the SFPF and SFC are even aware of the problem.

The SFC and SFPF have had too easy a ride. Mainly because Scottish filmmaking grew out of the sponsored documentary tradition of Films of Scotland (1954–82), active between the mid-1950s and early 1980s, there have been no substantial cadres of avant-garde independents putting pressure on them analogous to that exercised on the British Film Institute in England and Wales. With a few honourable exceptions, local film journalists have shown no capacity to interrogate, as opposed to simply report, the initiatives of Scottish film institutions. This environment has reinforced the evasiveness of the SFC and SFPF and ensured that they would face no sustained pressure to articulate policy options and discuss these with their constituencies. Thus the industrial model of filmmaking simply 'emerged' in Scotland, rather as the leader of the Conservative Party used to, without any proper discussion of alternatives. What, then, is to be done?

Questions of National Identity

When the SFC and SFPF finally face up to the fact that Scottish filmmaking of a kind relevant to questions of national identity and culture must be low-budget filmmaking, they are going to have to educate themselves and their constituencies into a different set of aesthetic strategies and institutional arrangements. An obvious first step would be to strengthen the workshop sector in Scotland, the only sector (apart from a handful of independent producers) with the necessary expertise to facilitate what could be called a Poor Scottish Cinema – that is to say, poor in resources and rich in imagination. The Scottish workshops ought, in effect, to become mini-studios through which grantees from the SFPF should realise their projects.

The SFPF must also begin to recruit to its board figures who have some understanding of the aesthetics and economics of Poor Cinema. One obvious such figure is James Mackay (as it happens, a Scot from Inverness), whose production credits include Ron Peck (1948–2022)'s *What Can I Do With A Male Nude?* (1985; budget £5,000), Derek Jarman's *The Last of England* (1987; budget under £250,000) and *The Garden* (1990; budget £370,000), and John Maybury's *Man to Man* (1992; budget £155,000). Mackay's projects have consistently used Super-8 (often blown up to 35mm for cinematic release) and, increasingly, electronic imaging. Another recruit to the SFPF ought to be the man who coined the term 'electronic imaging', Colin MacLeod, a world authority on the subject working at Napier University, Edinburgh.

The SFC and the SFPF must then lead their constituencies through a process of discussion about how imaginative and culturally relevant cinema can be achieved on meagre resources. There are good examples from within Scottish film history itself, for example, Bill Douglas (1934–91)'s *Trilogy* (1972–78), the early feature films of Bill Forsyth, and certain of the films of Murray Grigor, Brian Crumlish (1944–94) and Mike Alexander. But examples should also be drawn from further afield: *La Jetée* (Chris Marker, 1962), which is wholly made up of still images, and *Night and Fog* (Alain Resnais, 1956), which is partly so; *Les Carabiniers* (Jean-Luc Godard, 1963) and *The Tragedy of the Switchboard Operator* (Dušan Makavejev, 1967), which make extensive use of pre-existing footage; *Ludwig: Requiem for a Virgin King* (Hans-Jürgen Syberberg, 1972), which instead of built sets uses blown-up transparencies as background to the action; the austere cinema of Robert Bresson (1901–99); the cinema of Derek Jarman and other English independents; Third World cinemas, particularly those of Africa and Latin America.

Getting feature production budgets below £300,000 would not only make profitability more likely for individual films, but would see many more specifically Scottish features emerging, perhaps eventually reaching the critical mass of ten features a year which the SFC is fond of canvassing.

What it would at the very least produce, however, is a pack of cards whereby the nature of a Scottish cinema, its recurrent themes and styles, might begin to be discerned. As things stand, the possibility of a nationally specific Scottish cinema (which need not preclude influences from Hollywood and elsewhere or fail to recognise the necessary hybridity of all national cultures in the modern world) is becoming increasingly remote as Scots filmmakers are forced into contortions to raise money from American and pan-European sources.

This leads naturally to the question of how critical recognition of national cinemas is generated. Festival entry and public subsidy for distribution and exhibition of individual films may not (by themselves) be the most effective or economic routes to such recognition. There is a historical lesson to be learned here. Italian Neorealism, French *Nouvelle Vague*, Brazilian *Cinema Novo* and so on were internationally recognised as nationally specific cinematic movements mainly because they were taken up and discussed in film criticism and journalism. It is not beyond the bounds of imagination that a *nouveau cinéma écossais* might be similarly constructed. As is so often the case in Scotland (as with *Gregory's Girl* [Bill Forsyth, 1980]), celebration abroad might facilitate recognition (and further funding) at home. It would be nice to think that a simple journal could be sent free of charge to every cinematheque, film festival, film magazine and Channel 4-type television network in the world. Without being a hype-based or lapdog publication, that journal's main aim would be to outline what is happening in Scottish cinema and to construct its diverse films as some kind of collectivity. There are several historical precedents for this, for example, the journals circulated by Unifrance and Film Polski (1945–52), the titles of which are simply the names of these organisations.

Tartan Shorts

This essay will be read perversely on several fronts. It will be suggested that it is intrinsically hostile to classic narrative cinema, though that can be easily discounted by the most cursory glance at the author's other critical writings (for example, his 1972 book, *Underworld U.S.A.* and his 1992 book, *The Big Heat*). It will be suggested that the concept of Poor Cinema envisages a restricted range of aesthetic forms. Quite the reverse, as the examples cited above (from the Loachian realism of *Tickets for the Zoo* to the Brechtian multi-textuality of *Les Carabiniers*) indicate. Finally, it will be suggested that this essay trashes the entrepreneurial efforts of individual Scots filmmakers. This also is not true. One can have nothing but admiration for those Scots who have fought their way through to some kind of international recognition (well, most of them), although they may have had to pay a price in terms of the relevance of their work to Scottish culture.

As this article was going to press the SFPF did two things which encapsulate all that is wrong with its policy. Firstly, it issued a press release hailing the success of the first round of short films it funds jointly with BBC Scotland. Named Tartan Shorts – appropriately enough, the project wraps itself in that most regressive of Scottish discourses, Tartanry – it provides for three ten-minute shorts to be funded each year at a cost of £30,000 per short. The SFPF press release is clear about the kind of films to be funded. They must be 'narrative shorts' and it is envisaged that grantees will 'springboard from the making of a short on to a first feature film'.

Secondly, and concurrent with the press release, two young Glasgow-based film/video-makers, Douglas Aubrey and Alan Robertson, received a letter from the SFPF informing them that their request for funding to complete their feature film had been turned down. *Work, Rest and Play* is a bitter, Kerouacian road movie in five twenty-minute parts, two of which have already been completed with £6,000 of Aubrey and Robertson's own money and the downtime of sympathetic facilities houses, independent producers and educational institutions. It is also a technological palimpsest for our time, involving video footage shot on VHS, low- and high-band U-matic, Hi8 and Betacam SP; computer graphics realised by Quantel Paintbox, Spaceword Matisse and Wavefront; and the deployment of sound samplers and digital storage systems. In short, it is a superb example of Poor Cinema.

It is scarcely credible, but at the very moment when it was passing up the chance to put £15,000 (the sum requested by Aubrey and Robertson) towards the realisation of a feature-length Scottish road movie, the SFPF was trumpeting abroad the fact that it had invested £90,000 in three ten-minute shorts. By a cruel irony, the director of one of these shorts (*Franz Kafka's It's a Wonderful Life* [1993]) is Peter Capaldi, writer of the flashily empty road movie *Soft Top Hard Shoulder* (Stefan Schwartz, 1992) which has none of the 'condition of Britain' bite of *Work, Rest and Play*.

More than ever, the creeping centralisation of film funding in Scotland needs to be reversed and the following key issue addressed: What kind of cultural and economic (in that order) policies need to be adopted by Scottish film institutions to create a (in the first instance) culturally relevant and (in the longer term) economically viable Scottish cinema? To raise such an issue implies the possibility of change in those great lumbering dinosaurs of Scottish film culture, the SFC and the SFPF. Dream on![3]

Notes

1. Caton-Jones's return to his native heath for the film in question, *Rob Roy* (1995), proved to be a one-off, his subsequent career being primarily American-based.
2. Something like this did indeed emerge with the subsequent creation of Scottish Screen (1997–2010) in 1997.
3. Critique of particular institutions' policies is a separate question from the personal qualities and professional competence of those institutions' officers. I thank Kate Swan, Director, and Ivan Mactaggart, administrator, of the SFPF, who have invariably been friendly, helpful and efficient in all my dealings with them.

CHAPTER 20

Wake for a Glasgow Culture Hero[*†]

If you lived in Glasgow between 1949 and 1955, you would have had to have been blind and deaf and monumentally lacking in humour not to have known about Lobey Dosser. Lobey, the sheriff of Calton Creek, astride his faithful two-legged mare, El Fideldo, rode the comic strip ranges of Glasgow's *Evening Times* newspaper and he and his galaxy of enemies, friends and acquaintances – the major villain Rank Bajin (and, occasionally, his wife, Ima); Lobey's brother, Dunny; the Indians, Toffy Teeth and Rubber Lugs; the rancher, Whisk E. Glaur and his daughter, Adoda; Rid Skwerr and Fairy Nuff; Han O' Gold; Watts Koakin; Stark Stairin; Roona and Nikka Boot; Fitz O'Coughin; and the Mexican bandit, Cortez Pantzonanale – became the subject of popular banter and their exploits lovingly retold in pub and school alike.

Lobey's adventures (and the life and other work of his creator, Bud Neill [1911–70]) are celebrated and explored in a film to be transmitted, later in the year, on Scottish Television (STV): Murray Grigor's *A Wake for Bud Neill* (1993). The film is a fitting culmination of a process spanning several years within which the genius and complexity of Bud Neill have been increasingly recognised. Part of that process was the erecting, by public subscription, of a statue of Lobey and Elfie (El Fideldo) in the West End of Glasgow and the tireless and loving research work of artist Ranald MacColl, who recently published five painstakingly reconstructed Lobey adventures under the title, *Lobey's the Wee Boy!*[1]

---

[*] Originally published in *Scottish Film and Visual Arts*, no. 6 (1993), 11–12.

[†] This essay, originally written decades ago, refers to what would nowadays be referred to as 'Native American' as 'Indian'. Being adamantly opposed to the retrospective rewriting of historical texts for ideological reasons, I have left my original usage intact within this republished version of the text. In doing so, I also want to acknowledge the fact that, in using the term 'Indian' when I first wrote this essay, I lived within the dominant discourse in which Native Americans were so problematically designated.

There are two reasons why it is appropriate to discuss *A Wake for Bud Neill* in *Scottish Film and Visual Arts*.[2] This journal has consistently called for an indigenous Scottish film and video industry, indigenous not only in the sense of being made in Scotland but also in being culturally rooted here. Bud Neill's work displayed this quality par excellence and Murray Grigor's film faithfully reflects it, making no concessions to that Scottish moving image lobby which argues that specifically Scottish material has to be 'toned down' for audiences outside of Scotland.

Neill's work was firmly rooted in working-class West of Scotland culture. The fact that the *Lobey* strips usually take place in the American West (although most characters speak in Glasgow dialect) is a source of comic disproportion. It also reflects that long love affair with American culture which people born in this century have pursued and to which (this is a subjective authorial view) Scots are particularly prone. The rootedness of Neill's work in working-class West of Scotland culture is reflected in its constant references to geographical locales, events and phenomena familiar to that culture: Springburn, Calton, Clydebank, Yoker, Duntocher; 'My heart was goin' like the big drum in the Govan burgh band'; 'Ther's mair dials here than there are at the Hillington clock works'. It is reflected, too, in the unsparing use of West of Scotland language and idioms: get the polis; auld buck: gie them laldy; keep the heid; feart; napper; jiggered, and so on.

That Neill was primarily addressing a working-class, West of Scotland audience is indicated by the presence within his work of the cultural references and in-jokes of that group. Adoda Glaur's husband is in the Texas Rangers and, of course, therefore appears attired in football gear; Rank Bajin, en route for Hampden, substitutes a tartan bunnet for his usual black hat; and a woman explains her shortage of money by reference to 'my man's blin' week at the yerd'. But that local West of Scotland culture, in the post-WWII period, was heavily interpenetrated with the wider British and, particularly, American cultures. Throughout Neill's work, therefore, there are constant references to UK and world political developments and to the radio programmes, pop songs and films that his readership were exposed to. Lobey phones the White House and asks for Harry [Truman]; Rank Bajin, having set up an Indian ambush for Lobey, expresses the hope that he will be 'chopped thinner than a Strachey steak', a reference to the Minister of Food in the post-WWII austerity Labour government (1945–51). The characters sing snatches of popular songs of the time such as 'Slow Boat to China', 'Buttons and Bows', and 'Ghost Riders in the Sky', refer to current film stars like Stewart Granger (1913–93) and Rita Hayworth (1918–87), and quote from popular BBC radio shows like *Dick Barton: Special Agent* (1946–51) and *Riders of the Range* (1949–53).

Precisely because it is primarily a working-class, West of Scotland audience Neill addresses, there may well be anti-bourgeois and anti-English elements present within the *Lobey* strips. Rank Bajin's national origins are obscure, but he speaks a floridly archaic form of English in which feet become 'pedal extremities' and he reads Agatha Christie (1890–1976), always a giveaway. And what are we to make of Lobey's claim that he 'would rather be scalped by Toffy Teeth than spend a day in Edinburgh'? Without himself being racist – there is evidence from his life that he was decidedly anti-racist – certain of Neill's strips deploy racist stereotypes. The images of Mexican and East European (presumably Russian) heavies fall into this category and his Little Black Sambo-ish characters, Hannibal and Annabelle McAnnibal, would nowadays be likely to attract the attention of the Commission for Racial Equality. But these are images which most working-class West of Scotland people lived within in the 1950s.

The claim of Murray Grigor's film *A Wake for Bud Neill*, and a fact increasingly recognised more widely, is that Neill was not simply a superb popular artist, but that there were elements of his art which can readily be encompassed within 'high art' traditions, the terms 'popular' and 'high' being used here in a descriptive, not evaluative, sense. Neill had been a student at the Glasgow School of Art, an institution which is (or, more accurately, the denizens of which are) generally lampooned in the *Lobey* strips. The latter contain references to Sigmund Freud (1856–1939), William Shakespeare (*c*.1564–1616), Leo Tolstoy (1828–1910) and other writers and, at one point, Rank Bajin threatens his horse with being painted by Henri Matisse (1869–1954). This draws attention to one of the two central features of Neill's work which (post)modern discourse about the arts would find most congenial. By having Bajin draw attention to the way his horse is represented on the page, Neill emphasises the self-reflexivity which runs through his work much more generally. He constantly intervenes, for example, to address the reader directly, to draw attention to his own presence as manipulator of the unfolding images, and to signal the reader's own presence within the text. Thus, a character in the Calton Creek saloon asks for 'two glesses o' lemonade, seein' as how there's a lot of wee boys readin' this strip'; Bajin is at one point described as 'slippery as a Neill; I mean, an *eel*'; and, sketching a jungle only in outline, Neill adds a note: 'Hint to young artists – jungles ain't easy'.

The second central feature of Neill's work with which (post)modern discourse about the arts is much preoccupied is the polyvalence of language, how words slip their meanings and forms, dissolving into one another to the point where meaning lacks fixity and becomes elusive. The Pawnee Indian tribe contains both a Pawnee Mary of Argyll and a Shetland Pawnee. Toffy Teeth threatens Rank Bajin that he 'will take it out of your hide, and maybe your Jekyll too'; and Lobey sings, 'All the flora and fauna is fauna Flora, but Flora isnae fauna me'. Sometimes this complex wordplay reaches an unhinged level of surreality, as when a character asks about the meaning of the word 'heinous' and is told that 'they make the baked beinous'.

This article began with the suggestion that there are two reasons why *A Wake for Bud Neill* ought to be discussed in *Scottish Film and Visual Arts*. Apart from its rootedness in Scottish culture, Grigor's film is also a prime example of Poor Cinema.[3] There is virtually only one set, a reconstruction of Sammy Dow's bar done in the style of Bud Neill by Ranald MacColl. On this set various Scots worthies, mostly of the generation that came of age during Neill's reign at the *Evening Times*, recount their favourite scenes or offer interpretations of Neill's work or life. The film does not shirk from the darker aspects of the latter, such as alcoholism and (possibly) attempted suicide. In addition, the film from time to time wittily animates aspects of the strips and intercuts footage from contemporary newsreels and from the films of W. S. Hart (1864–1946), a figure, it is said, for whom Neill had a particular affection. This multi-discourse quality is very characteristic of Murray Grigor's cinema more generally (see, for example, his 1982 feature, *Scotch Myths*), and Grigor is surely among the top three or four filmmakers cruelly undervalued by Scottish journalists.

A Wake for Bud Neill is an object lesson to those who think that meaningful cinema cannot be achieved without large budgets.

Notes

1. Ranald MacColl, ed., *Lobey's the Wee Boy!* (Edinburgh: Mainstream Press, 1992).
2. The publication in question (in which the original version of this essay first appeared) was a short-lived venture during the early 1990s; its publisher was the Glasgow-based Arts & Entertainment Publishing Ltd.
3. Poor Cinema took its name and concept from the Italian art movement *Arte Povera*, which emerged in the late 1960s and early 1970s and is usually credited with being named by the critic/curator Germano Celant (1940–2020). Using found, discarded and commonplace materials such as rags and plastics of various kinds, the movement sought to challenge the ethos and commercialisation of the art gallery as well as the gallery ethos's commitment to modernism. More distantly, the writings and practice of the Polish theatre director Jerzy Grotowski (1933–99), with his austere practice centred primarily on the actor's body, fed into the concept of Poor Cinema. In the

Scottish context, the term 'Poor Cinema' emerged in the context of a critique of the policies of the main public film funding bodies in Scotland with their emphasis on Hollywood- and/or European art cinema-style narrative feature films. A full version of the critique is contained in the author's own essays 'In Praise of a Poor Cinema' and 'The Cultural Necessity of a Poor Celtic Cinema', both reproduced elsewhere in the present volume. As a concept, Poor Cinema has affinities with similar movements such as Slow Cinema.

CHAPTER 21

The Cultural Necessity of a Poor Celtic Cinema*

There is currently something of a groundswell in favour of 'low-budget/ no-budget' filmmaking in Scotland. Simultaneously, but without prior consultation, several individuals have set in train initiatives which, in diverse ways, have addressed the question. The present writer published a piece in *Sight and Sound* magazine;[1] the former Director of the Edinburgh International Film Festival (EIFF), Jim Hickey, announced his move into film production with a series of low-budget 'exploitation' movies based on the 1960s practice of Roger Corman in the United States; and EIFF's present Director, Penny Thomson (1950–2007), included in the Festival's 1993 programme two events which broached different aspects of the question: *Visionary Tactics*, which explored both the common ground and contradictions between low-budget orthodox cinema and video art, and a series of viewings and discussions under the thematic heading, *Just Do It*. The latter was mainly concerned with the experience of contemporary American independents and particularly with that of Robert Rodriguez, whose debut feature, *El Mariachi* (1992), was reputedly made for $7,000. The processes of discussion at Edinburgh revealed that even venerable British film institutions like British Screen, up until now mainly associated with orthodox, quasi-European art cinema aesthetics and financial structures, have been attempting to devise mechanisms which would lower British feature production budgets drastically.

All of these initiatives may represent a challenge to those institutions charged with the public funding of filmmaking in Scotland, the Scottish Film Council (1934–97) and the Scottish Film Production Fund (1982–97), both of which are widely suspected of favouring relatively high-budget, orthodox narrative films intended to compete for attention

---

*Originally published in *Border Crossing: Film in Ireland, Britain and Europe*, eds John Hill, Martin McLoone and Paul Hainsworth (London/Belfast: British Film Institute/ Queen's University Institute of Irish Studies, 1994), 112–25.

on the European, if not the world stage. One says 'suspected' because both bodies operate with a certain degree of sleekitness, to use an evocative Scots word. This evasiveness is expressed in their claims to be all things to all people while demonstrably making an attempt to create an orthodox narrative cinema in Scotland their main financial commitment. Each body would proclaim its autonomy from the other, but both are chaired by the same man – under the name Allan Shiach, the Chairman of the Macallan Glenlivet whisky firm, and under the name Allan Scott, a successful screenwriter, most notably in his collaborations with Nicolas Roeg (1928–2018). Although the SFPF has assisted diverse types of film (features, documentaries, animations, shorts), its 'Guidelines for Applicants' state that 'the Fund will continue to lean towards the development, and sometimes, to the finance of narrative films'. This policy did not come about as a result of public debate in Scotland. It was the outcome purely of the taste of key figures in the SFC and, since 1982, in the SFPF, with these institutions increasingly debarring alternative voices and becoming the preserve of orthodox film industry figures and senior television executives.

The final element accelerating the Gadarene rush to film as commodity in Scotland was the setting-up in 1993 of the Glasgow Film Fund. Doubtless created through the active lobbying of the SFC and the SFPF, it currently stands at £155,000 per annum, a sum made up of contributions from the Glasgow Development Agency, Strathclyde Business Development, Glasgow City Council and the European Regional Development Fund. Unsurprisingly, the Fund will be administered by the SFPF and its criteria are frankly commercial. Only feature films with a budget of £500,000 or over may apply and its main function is to increase spending, through film production, within the local economy. The SFPF has committed the entire first year allocation of GFF's funds to only one project, *Shallow Grave* (Danny Boyle, 1994), and Glasgow City Council is already turning down applications from low-budget filmmakers they formerly might have supported, on the basis that all their film funding is now going to be channelled through the GFF. Moreover, all of this has happened within an economic discourse which has explicitly excluded the consideration of issues of representation and cultural identity, issues markedly to the forefront of many low-budget filmmakers' concerns.

It might be thought that the SFC, as an ostensibly cultural body, would have held itself at arm's length from some of these developments, but it has been an enthusiastic cheerleader for them all. It recently produced the *Charter for the Moving Image in Scotland*, an attempt to indicate what ought to be done on the various Scottish film fronts and the institutions needed to undertake those actions. Several responses to the *Charter*, not least that of the producers' association, PACT (Scotland), have criticised its discourse of advocating production – *any* kind of production – at any price. It is mentioned here to indicate the extent to which its proposals (for example, the uniting of all publicly funded film mechanisms into one single Scottish Screen Agency, which indeed came to pass with the creation of Scottish Screen [1997–2010] in 1997) are hand-in-glove with the centralising, inflationary, market-driven production ideology of the SFPF.

It was also the SFC which, along with the SFPF, in 1992 first co-mounted Movie Makars, an event designed to bring the forms of classical Hollywood screenwriting to Scotland. Its lavishly produced report indicates the style and ethos of the event and the worldview which permeates it: that document's title page carries a photograph of Allan Scott and William Goldman (1931–2018), the invited 'star' of the proceedings. The terms of the event's genesis can be gathered from the report's quasi-theological dedication to 'Allan Scott (the inspiration) who in manifest and incalculable ways provides the spirit of Movie Makars'. The bringing of Allan Shiach/Scott – with his dual discourse of business and Hollywood – into the Scottish film cultural picture would make an interesting case study. My own reading is that his arrival, probably the result of lobbying of the UK government's Scottish Office by the SFC and the SFPF, further demonstrates their capacity to misjudge what Scottish cinema actually needs, both economically and culturally.

Movie Makars can be read as an instance of contemporary British film culture's growing obsession with the concept of 'story structure'. An intrinsically interesting discourse which renders explicit the Hollywood writing practices of the past half-century, 'story structure' entered Britain by way of screenwriting handbooks such as those by Syd Field (1935–2013) and, most dramatically, through Robert McKee's much-hyped story-structure courses, now incorporated into his book *Story*.[2] The discourse's value is to spell out the elements of the classic Hollywood two-hour script; how stories are articulated, developed and resolved; how characters are given motivation; and at what point stories need to be 'turned', and so on. Its downside is that it tends to fetishise the specific form of storytelling associated with classical Hollywood cinema, to render it 'natural' and other ways of telling stories aberrant. With one stroke, it wipes off the agenda alternative ways of thinking about and making cinema. By the criteria of the 'story-structure' discourse, filmmakers such as Sergei Eisenstein (1898–1948), Roberto Rossellini (1906–71), Yasujirō Ozu (1903–63), Robert Bresson (1901–99), Jean-Luc Godard (1930–2022), Dušan Makavejev (1932–2019), Derek Jarman (1942–94) and countless others would be deemed failures.

Needless to add, Movie Makars is wholly complicit with the production ideology of the SFC and the SFPF and many of the event's participants (by invitation only) were either members or beneficiaries of the Fund.

What, then, has this increasingly market-driven institutional policy delivered to Scottish film culture? In its decade or so of existence, the SFPF has assisted about fifty projects, about one fifth of which have been feature films (although that proportion is increasing over time) and the remainder being shorts, documentaries and animation projects. Though one might wish to commend the competence (and, occasionally, the excellence) of particular SFPF-funded films, one would be hard-pressed to describe the sense in which they constitute a Scottish film movement: a historically and culturally specific grappling with the contradictions of the Scottish past and present, a set of recurrent themes and styles discernibly amounting to a collectivity. What we have, rather, is a ragbag of films which, competitively and individualistically, have clawed their way through the available Scottish, UK or pan-European funding mechanisms. There are startlingly few titles on the list which have achieved any kind of critical reputation, with, perhaps, the exceptions of *The Tree of Liberty* (Timothy Neat, 1987), *Venus Peter* (Ian Sellar, 1989), *Play Me Something* (Timothy Neat, 1989), *Silent Scream* (David Hayman, 1990) and *Tickets for the Zoo* (Brian Crumlish, 1991). Part of the problem, of course, is that there has been no systematic attempt to generate critical writing about these features or to address the extent to which they might relate to each other (of which more below).

The most serious misgivings about the SFPF's policy have been expressed over *Prague* (Ian Sellar, 1992). Out of an annual subvention of (at the time) about £250,000 per annum, the SFPF put £130,000 into *Prague* over two years. The film seems to have been a commercial failure but, even more seriously, questions are being asked about its relevance to Scottish history and culture. Virtually its only claim to be connected with Scotland (having been shot in Prague, largely with French money) is that some of its personnel – producer Christopher Young, writer/director Ian Sellar and lead actor Alan Cumming – are Scots. With its budget of £2 million made up from diverse countries and funding mechanisms, *Prague* has about it the petrified feel of a Europudding, connecting with no actually existing society except, perhaps, that of the pan-continental European art house. The case of *Prague* does not encourage a 'thumbs up' for either the SFPF's (unspoken) cultural policies or its economic ones, but the latter might be better judged over the next two years when some of its projects in development hit the screen. These are marked by some well-known names such as writer Alan Sharp (1934–2013) and directors Ken Loach, David Hayman and Michael Caton-Jones. These projects intensify the tendency for funding to be sought from diverse mechanisms: British Screen, the Glasgow Film Fund, and SCRIPT (the European Script Development Fund) loom large in the data so far released about them.

The current pervasiveness of 'market-speak' in Scottish film affairs has two noticeable effects. Firstly, it inflates budgets. This is true not only at the high end of the scale, like *Prague*, but, even more perniciously, at the bottom end as well. Two events, occurring simultaneously, illustrate this fact. Firstly, the SFPF issued a press release announcing that, in association with BBC Scotland, it had invested £90,000 in three short films: £30,000 per ten-minute short. In accordance with the SFPF's overall ideology of production, the projects supported were to be 'narrative shorts' and it is envisaged that their makers will 'springboard from the making of a short on to a first feature film'. The project is called 'Tartan Shorts', a singularly offensive title which reveals a massive ignorance, among those involved, of the regressive character of Tartanry in Scottish culture (although its defenders would contend that the title represents an ironic, postmodernist playing with that tradition). Secondly, and concurrent with the issuing of the press release, the SFPF sent out a letter to two young, Scotland-based film/videomakers, Douglas Aubrey and Alan Robertson, turning down their request for £15,000 to complete their feature-length road movie, *Work, Rest and Play* (1992). By a sharp irony, one of the recipients of the £30,000 Tartan Shorts grants was the actor Peter Capaldi, writer of the amusing but empty road movie *Soft Top Hard Shoulder* (Stefan Schwartz, 1992), which has none of the condition-of-Britain quality of *Work, Rest and Play*. Once again, the SFPF demonstrated graphically its commitment to orthodox financial structures and aesthetics – *Work, Rest and Play*, for example, makes extensive use of electronic imaging and computerised procedures.

The second effect of the pervasiveness of 'market-speak' in Scottish film affairs is that it has created a climate within which to utter the word 'culture' is to elicit pitying smiles. While the official documents of the SFC and the SFPF make ritual obeisance to the idea of 'Scottish film culture', no indications are forthcoming as to that culture's content. Reliant upon the single, ineffable concept of 'talent' to decide the validity of any given project, the SFC and SFPF as institutions do not have (although certain of their officers as individuals do) the analytic resources or categories to explain what the concept of a 'Scottish film culture' might mean or how it might relate to wider Scottish cultural or social questions. The individual projects they invest in, awarded on the basis of the 'talent' of the grantees, cannot be read by these institutions in terms other than as separate, autonomous films possessing no connection with each other or with Scottish history and contemporary culture.

The absence of a cultural discourse from the SFC or SFPF can be indicated by their failure even to perceive the problem which was thrown up recently in the research findings of a Scottish development agency. The research, conducted among a population of top German industrialists, revealed that the latter's dominant mental image of Scotland led them to conclude that the country was a good one to rest in, but not to invest in. Scottish Cultural Studies academics know immediately the historical reasons for this: Scotland's coming to the forefront of the European imagination, principally through the literary phenomena of Ossianism and Sir Walter Scott (1771–1832), in the period after 1770; the consequent construction of images of Scotland and the Scots taking place outside of Scotland and having more to do with the aims, needs, fears and fantasies of the emergent European bourgeoisie than with the self-image of the Scots; and the complex of historical factors (not least the de-politicisation of nationalism in Scotland) which caused the Scots increasingly to live within images of themselves that were enunciated elsewhere. Although the historical experience of the Scots is quite specific and cannot be conflated with that of other peoples, their representation in discourse has something in common with that of other 'subordinate' groups. The word 'subordinate' with regard to the Scots must be put in inverted commas, since it is part of their national-historical specificity that they were/are not subordinate – or not pertinently so – in economic terms. As Tom Nairn (1932–2023) has pointed out, Scotland was a well-rewarded junior partner in the British imperial enterprise.[3] The subordination of the Scots has instead been on the terrain of discourse.

It is useful to think of the process of the discursive construction of the Scot as a by-product of the European bourgeoisie's eighteenth- and nineteenth-century construction of its own identity, one formulated by creating a monstrous Other that bore all the negative features the European bourgeois (*homo oeconomicus*) did not wish to have and/or could not bear to self-acknowledge. The process can be represented as a series of binary oppositions thus:

Table 21.1 *Homo Oeconomicus/Homo Celticus*

Homo Oeconomicus	*Homo Celticus*
Urban	Rural
Civilised	Uncivilised
Barbered	Hirsute
Ambitious	Shiftless
Cultured	Natural
'Masculine'	'Feminine'

The oppositions are potentially endless. However, their point of controlling articulation and definition of identity is always *homo oeconomicus* and never *homo celticus*. The process of Othering, in all its historical and geographical diversity (*homo pacificus, homo africanus*, 'Woman') has been explored by Frantz Fanon (1925–61), Edward Said (1935–2003), Homi Bhabha and others.[4]

As well as understanding the reasons for the problem thrown up by the recent survey of German industrialists, Scots Cultural Studies academics also know what needs to be done in response: the confronting and deconstruction of the regressive, disempowering discourses within which the Scot has been constructed and the replacement of these with discourses more appropriate to a modern, industrial, multi-racial Scotland. This is also a position arrived at intuitively by certain Scottish filmmakers, for example, in *The Caledonian Account* (Brian Crumlish, 1976) and *Scotch Myths* (Murray Grigor, 1982), but such understanding has not penetrated to the SFC or SFPF. Hooked on the notion of 'talent', those institutions see no need for cultural discourse or for a filmmaking strategy which might help dislodge regressive ideas about Scotland from the heads of German industrialists, among other diverse external audiences.

Clearly, the framework of ideas within which the discursive figure of the Scot was constructed, initially over the period 1770 to 1830, subsequently became disseminated over every available sign system: literature, painting, opera, ballet, fashion, postcards and also – with increasing momentum in the twentieth century – advertising, cinema and television. The collection of essays, *Scotch Reels: Scotland in Cinema and Television*, is substantially about this historical process, in particular how the cinemas of Hollywood and Ealing have constructed the Scots, the apotheoses of these traditions being *Brigadoon* (Vincente Minnelli, 1954) and *The Maggie* (Alexander Mackendrick, 1954) respectively.[5] Clearly, an analogous process was also at work with regard to the discursive construction of Ireland. *The Maggie* and *The Quiet Man* (John Ford, 1952) are, discursively speaking, almost identical: the respective narratives of both present an incoming American being humanised and 'feminised' through his encounter with an otherworldly Celtic milieu. Needless to say, this historical process whereby particular groups are constructed within discourse as having no 'head' but only 'heart', no capacity for politics or economics, but only for 'feeling', is the ideological equivalent of the material expropriations of colonialism and imperialism. Indeed, Malcolm Chapman calls the process 'symbolic appropriation'.[6] The truly terrifying dimension of this, however, is that *homo celticus* comes to live within the discursive categories fashioned by the oppressor to the extent of casting themselves in that imposed role within the stories they make about themselves and their indigenous culture.

The *locus tragicus* of this phenomenon with regard to Scotland is *Local Hero* (Bill Forsyth, 1983). As in *The Maggie*, a hard-nosed American executive comes to Scotland (in *Local Hero*'s case, in order to set up an oil terminal) but, softened through his encounter with 'dream Scotland', opts instead for an observatory and marine life sanctuary. The main Scottish female characters he meets are called Stella (the sky) and Marina (the sea): Scotland is 'Nature'. What distinguishes *Local Hero* from *Brigadoon* and *The Maggie* is that its director, Bill Forsyth, has spent his entire life in Scotland. The chilling fact, therefore, is that, in its representation of Scotland, *Local Hero* is ideologically indistinguishable from the earlier films.[7]

It is at this point that economics and culture intersect and where the argument for the cultural necessity of what we might term 'a poor Celtic cinema' becomes most compelling. *Local Hero* was the first film of Bill Forsyth aimed at the international market. It was produced and packaged by David Puttnam precisely in those terms. So internationally ramified has the *homo celticus* discourse become in the two centuries or so since its original articulation that movies about Scotland or Ireland which are not formulated within it, or which do not exist in some readily discernible relationship with it, are likely to be quite literally unreadable to a wide international audience. To go back once more to the above-cited example of the present-day German executives: because they 'know' that Scotland is about rest and recuperation, about escape from the harsh worlds of politics and economics, about a people in touch with the 'eternal verities', to present them with different kinds of stories would seriously disorient them. It is no accident that *Local Hero* is a cult film in Germany and elsewhere. To offer an axiom to Celtic filmmakers: the more your films are consciously aimed at an international market, the more their conditions of intelligibility will be bound up with regressive discourses about your own culture.

The 'market-speak' of the SFC and SFPF – and possibly of analogous institutions in other Celtic countries – is thus a recipe for the continuing discursive entrapment of the Celtic peoples. The lack of recognition by the SFC and SFPF of any discursive problem is paralleled by the lack of awareness among most individual Celtic filmmakers that they are living within regressive discourses. This is a problem which goes beyond filmmaking to suffuse the whole of Scottish culture, so much so that the present writer has felt it necessary to fashion the concept of 'the Scottish Discursive Unconscious' to try to explain the phenomenon.[8] What seems to happen is that when Scots are required to deal with particular aspects of their own history, certain narrative forms and tones come into play unconsciously: on 'automatic pilot', so to speak. That process happens over, and

THE CULTURAL NECESSITY OF A POOR CELTIC CINEMA 243

in relation to, a range of Scottish historical 'moments', but is particularly marked with respect to the Gàidhealtachd. It was writ large, for example, at the 1992 tercentenary of the Massacre of Glencoe, during which most of the Scottish press adopted an elegiac (often emotionally self-lacerative) tone oscillating between images of solitude and loss. One shudders to imagine the emotional self-indulgence which is bound to accompany the 250th anniversary of the Jacobite Rebellion of 1745–46 in 1995, an anniversary which will incorporate that cynosure for the glorification of Scottish sorrow/sorrow as Scottish – the Battle of Culloden. One cannot but agree with Malcolm Chapman's view that, despite the suffering which it entailed, many Scots intellectuals are glad Culloden occurred.[9] A more charitable view of the flagellation Scots visit on themselves within their indigenously produced art and discourse when dealing with Glencoe, Culloden, the Highland Clearances or, to give a more contemporary example, the demise of shipbuilding on the Upper Clyde, is that they are indeed not wholly responsible for their actions. Rather, they are largely under the sway of 'the Scottish Discursive Unconscious'. Their country and its history have been constructed by voices outside Scotland, within a discourse which places *homo celticus* in a timeless, unchanging dreamworld that exists to transform the incoming stranger. That being so, what other response is possible when contemplating the reality of Scottish history and contemporary life than to mourn the land of lost content?

It is one of the delusions of the SFC and SFPF that this discursive inheritance has no purchase on the sensibilities of contemporary Scots filmmakers, and can be sloughed off in the grand march to 'Hollywood on the Clyde'. It is a dismal paradox that the more grandiose their delusions become, the higher such institutions and individuals rack up indigenous feature film production budgets; and, by thus proclaiming ever more firmly the idea of film as commodity, the more surely do they become mired in regressive discourses about their country. If they only knew it, their only salvation lies in a poor Celtic cinema. The term 'poor cinema' was suggested by the title of the 1950s Italian art movement *Arte Povera*, within which artworks were made out of the materials which were to hand and, consequently, did not need to compete with the glitzy and financially inflated world of the gallery circuit. However, its cinematic lineage goes back rather longer, certainly being discernible in the quasi-artisanal practice of the British Documentary movement of the 1930s, in post-WWII Italian Neorealism, in the French *Nouvelle Vague* and, not least, in certain Third World cinematic practices in which distinctions among filmmakers, critics and audiences might be eroded.[10] In all of these instances, however, the films made were low-budget not just for economic reasons, but in order to be able to say things which remained unsaid in more orthodox cinematic production structures and practices.

What, then, would a poor Celtic cinema look like in both economic and cultural terms? The *BFI Film and Television Handbook* of 1993 profiled eight recent British feature films. The most important information thrown up was that, while the average production budget across the eight was £1.8 million, the average box-office return was £0.8 million.[11] Basic Micawber-ish economics would suggest that, at the very least, no budget within a poor Celtic cinema should exceed £0.8 million, but economically well-founded recent British film production practices, such as that of producer James Mackay (whose productions and budgets have included *What Can I Do with a Male Nude?* [1985; production budget of £5,000], *Man to Man* [1991; production budget of £155,000] and *The Last of England* [1987; production budget of £250,000]) suggest that the absolute upper limit should be £300,000. Even this figure is large in relation to the public monies available for filmmaking in Scotland: excluding the £10 million or so allocated by the Gaelic Television Committee, which has a special linguistic aim and may not in the long term be renewable, there is currently available about £0.5 million spread over three or four mechanisms. Budgets considerably smaller than existing ones, predicated upon different aesthetic strategies, would be possible, but, as the case of *Work, Rest and Play* indicates, this is not a road the SFPF intends to go down. A demand that budgets should not exceed £300,000 (and this envisages inputs from other non-Scottish mechanisms) should be the centrepiece of the call for a poor Celtic cinema. A key consideration in awarding grants should be the degree of imagination potentially displayed by the awardee working with limited resources. This would compare well with the present long-winded system of development monies, innumerable drafts of scripts, and bloated sums being paid to a few elite personnel.

As well as drastically curtailing the size of local feature production budgets, the SFC and SFPF must develop low-cost production facilities which will enable awardees to realise their projects without recourse to costly hire facilities. Clearly the best way to achieve this is to strengthen the already existing Scottish film and video workshops so that they become enabling production houses. The Scottish workshops never attained the status and level of funding of their southern analogues such as the Birmingham Film and Video Workshop. There were complex reasons for this, not least the presence in England and Wales of substantial cadres of independent filmmakers and small production companies who, through active organisations like the Independent Filmmakers Association, got into a devastatingly effective relationship with the Association of Cinematograph, Television and Allied Technicians (1933–91), at that time the major film and television technicians' union in the UK. This relationship wielded extraordinary leverage on the British Film Institute, strengthening the hand of sympathetic figures within that organisation to produce the *Workshop Declaration* of 1982 and the series of BFI/Channel 4-funded workshops. In retrospect, they proved to be problematic creations, not least for the sense of exclusiveness generated among those fortunate to have acquired long-term production funding through attachment to one of the recognised workshops. Eventually they fell apart as funding levels and ideologies changed within the BFI and Channel 4.[12] One of the main reasons the Scots equivalents did not advance so markedly was the indifference bordering on contempt for workshops historically displayed by the SFC and SFPF.

The recent First Reels project illustrates the lack of thought given by the major Scottish film institutions to the workshops. Jointly funded by the SFC and Scottish Television, First Reels gave grants of between £100 and £2,000 in its first year to thirty applicants. The project gave no thought to how the awardees might produce their material. Predictably, they turned for help to the already resource-starved Scottish workshops and small independent production companies which, giving what help they could, made their irritation plain to the SFC. It is to be hoped that the SFC and SFPF will recognise that proper funding of the Scottish workshops is the way to ensure that a Scottish filmmaking culture evolves, and not merely the springboarding of a few individuals into international film production. At the same time, these organisations should learn from the recent historical experience of England and Wales that workshops should be enabling houses rather than production houses.

In opposition to the marked literary bias of the present funding system, in which a disproportionate weight is given to scripts, awardees within a poor Celtic cinema should be required to demonstrate their cinematic literacy in the sense of understanding the aesthetic traditions they propose working within. This will be read perversely as a requirement that awardees have an A-Level in Film Studies. Nothing of the kind! However, it might be expected of awardees that they would know what a film looked like if made by Sergei Eisenstein, Fritz Lang (1890–1976), John Ford (1894–1973), Roberto Rossellini, Yasujirō Ozu, Vincente Minnelli (1903–86), Kenneth Anger (1927–2023), Jean-Luc Godard or Michael Snow (1928–2023). My impression is that the vast majority of applicants to and beneficiaries of the various grant-giving mechanisms are not cine-literate, or not systematically so in a way that would help produce a poor Celtic cinema. The harsh economic climate of the last decade has all but eradicated the policy of retrospectives of particular directors' oeuvres in publicly subsidised film theatres and film festivals in the UK, and video availability has not wholly compensated for this. A generation of filmmakers is emerging which will have been exposed almost exclusively to classic and contemporary Hollywood movies and selected European art cinema. It is quite likely that only a minority of them will have seen a movie by Vsevolod Pudovkin (1893–1953) or Dziga Vertov (1896–1954), Norman McLaren (1914–87) or Len Lye (1901–80), Kenji Mizoguchi (1898–1956) or Nagisa Ōshima (1932–2013), Jean Vigo (1905–34) or Robert Bresson, Andrzej Wajda (1926–2016) or Wojciech Has (1925–2000), Lindsay Anderson (1923–94) or Bill Douglas (1934–1991), and so on. It would doubtless be regarded as quaint by the SFC and SFPF if it were suggested to them that they might systematically programme, document and debate those elements in the history of cinema which demonstrate the most imaginative deployment of limited resources. One has in mind films like Godard's *Les Carabiniers* (1963), Makavejev's *The Switchboard Operator* (1967) and Peter Bogdanovich (1939–2022)'s *Targets* (1968), all of which cannibalise previously existing footage. Equally imaginatively austere are those innumerable films in the cinema's history which are wholly or partly made up of still images. Chris Marker (1921–2012)'s *La Jetée* (1962) and Alain Resnais (1922–2014)'s *Nuit et Brouillard* (1956) spring to mind. Some of the early films of Hans-Jürgen Syberberg – most notably *Ludwig, Requiem for a Virgin King* (1972) – delivered an incredible richness of image by using not built sets but blown-up transparencies. On the sound front, a considerable number of the cinema's most distinguished films have used wild tracks, in whole or part, often in the voiceover mode (Bresson and Godard come to mind here). Similarly, the SFC runs the Scottish Central Film Library, which contains, among other things, the entire output of Films of Scotland (1954–82), the sponsored documentary mechanism which was the seedbed for the older generation of Scots filmmakers between the mid-1950s and early 1980s. Many of these films cry out for critical deconstruction, not least on account of the representations they offer of Scotland and the Scots.

The concept of poor cinema has already provoked howls of derision, being travestied – usually by those with a vested interest in preserving more orthodox filmmaking practices – as 'films nobody wants to see'.[13] The implication is that poor cinema must out of necessity consist of avant-garde, difficult and perhaps (to use one of the terms of the 1970s debates) 'unpleasurable' works.[14] On the contrary, poor cinema should not be prescriptive about aesthetic forms (the besetting sin of the 'anti-Hollywood/Mosfilm' position in the 1970s debates) and should certainly accommodate quite traditional narrative movies such as *Targets* and *El Mariachi*. However, it should be noted simply as a historical fact that the makers of low-budget, traditional narrative movies often see them as stepping stones to careers in the orthodox industry, as is evidenced by the alacrity with which Hollywood snapped up both Peter Bogdanovich and Robert Rodriguez.

A condition of public funding award within a poor Celtic cinema should be that any proposed film deal in some sense with the contradictions of the Celtic past and present. That is, any proposed film should display a sense of history and society and should be manifestly rooted in the society from which it comes. *Prague* is only the most recent and notorious example of the practice of funding films which could be taking place on another planet, for all the relevance they bear to their country or countries of origin. The cardinal error of bodies like the SFC and SFPF is to assume that a 'Scottish cinema' will come into being by making a series of one-off films and marketing them as such through international film festivals. There is nothing more pitiable than the sight of gaggles of film bureaucrats (regrettably, Scots now among them) hovering around the fringes of festivals such as Cannes in vain attempts to market their films. Recalling how ragbag the past decade's production by the SFPF looks, the lesson has to be learned that national cinemas or film movements do not simply happen, they are in great measure actively constructed. Movements such as (to take only post-WWII examples) Italian Neorealism, Polish cinema of the 1950s, the French *Nouvelle Vague*, Czech cinema of the 1960s and Brazilian *Cinema Novo* were perceived as such mainly because they were constructed in film criticism and journalism as constituting nationally specific collectivities – diverse within and among themselves, to be sure, but collectivities nevertheless, specific cinematic responses to complex national moments. International critical recognition then helped finance the continuing existence of these movements. If the cultural questions are properly addressed, the economic questions will take care of themselves. It is the bitter experience of (some?) of the Celtic countries that this formulation has been reversed. I await with bated breath the first critical articles, special magazine issues, cinémathèque seasons and festival retrospectives which will proclaim the arrival of *le nouveau cinéma pauvre celtique*!

Notes

1. Colin McArthur, 'In Praise of a Poor Cinema', *Sight and Sound* 3, no. 8 (August 1993), 30–2, and also reproduced elsewhere in the present volume.
2. Syd Field, *Screenplay* (New York: Dell Publishing Company, 1979); Robert McKee, *Story: Substance, Structure, Style and the Principles of Screenwriting* (London: Methuen, 1998).
3. Tom Nairn, *The Break-Up of Britain: Crisis and Neo-Nationalism* (London: New Left Books, 1977).

4. Frantz Fanon, *Black Skin, White Masks* (New York: Grove Press, 1968); Edward Said, *Orientalism* (London: Routledge & Kegan Paul, 1978); Homi K. Bhabha, ed., *Nation and Narration* (London: Routledge, 1990).
5. Colin McArthur, ed., *Scotch Reels: Scotland in Cinema and Television* (London: British Film Institute, 1982).
6. Malcolm Chapman, *The Gaelic Vision in Scottish Culture* (London: Croom Helm, 1978), 28.
7. Although widely perceived as a wholly negative assessment of *Local Hero*, my arguments were so only from the perspective of the dominant critical orientation towards 'Scottish' cinema in the 1980s, the question of how Scotland and the Scots were represented. This analytical perspective had little interest in the totality of the meaning of the film or the nature of its director's personal vision. That situation has changed substantially: see, for example, Jonathan Murray, *Discomfort and Joy: The Cinema of Bill Forsyth* (Oxford: Peter Lang, 2011) which not only advances (in its chapter on *Local Hero*) persuasive arguments on both these fronts but, in its comprehensive account of critical responses to the film, effectively charts the trajectory of Scottish film criticism over nearly three decades.
8. Colin McArthur, 'Scottish Culture: A Reply to David McCrone', *Scottish Affairs*, no. 4 (Summer 1993), 95–106, and also reproduced elsewhere in the present volume; Colin McArthur, 'The Scottish Discursive Unconscious', in *Scottish Popular Theatre and Entertainment*, eds Alasdair Cameron and Adrienne Scullion (Glasgow: Glasgow University Library Studies, 1996), 81–9, and also reproduced elsewhere in the present volume.
9. Chapman, *The Gaelic Vision in Scottish Culture*, 21.
10. Jim Pines and Paul Willemen, eds, *Questions of Third Cinema* (London: British Film Institute, 1989).
11. Anon, 'UK Film, Television and Video: Statistical Overview', in *BFI Film and Television Yearbook 1993* (London: British Film Institute, 1992), 30.
12. See, for example, Claire Holdsworth, 'The Workshop Declaration: Independents and Organised Labour', in *Other Cinemas: Politics, Culture and Experimental Films in the 1970s*, eds Laura Mulvey and Sue Clayton (London: I.B. Tauris, 2017), 307–12.
13. See, for example, Eddie Dick, 'Poor Wee Scottish Cinema?', *Scottish Film*, no. 10 (1994), 19–23.
14. During the 1970s it was part of the core position of the journal *Screen* that the classic Hollywood narrative tradition be sidelined in favour of an oppositional form of filmmaking. The latter envisaged a somewhat puritan commitment to 'unpleasure'. See, for example, Peter Wollen, 'Godard and Counter Cinema: *Vent d'Est*', *Afterimage*, no. 4 (Autumn 1972), 6–17. A classic structuralist document, this essay presents, as a series of binary oppositions, the alleged qualities of 'Hollywood/Mosfilm' and 'Godardian' counter-cinema. One of the binary oppositions Wollen proposes is 'pleasure/unpleasure'.

CHAPTER 22

Culloden: A Pre-emptive Strike*

In a previous issue of *Scottish Affairs*, in the course of engaging with David McCrone's *Understanding Scotland: The Sociology of a Stateless Nation* (1992), I identified a peculiar feature of those acts of discourse production (novels, plays, films, television programmes, paintings, history books and so on) which set out to tell stories about Scotland (whether the teller of any given such story is themselves Scots or not is irrelevant).[1] I called this feature 'the Scottish Discursive Unconscious'[2] and suggested that it operated in a way akin to automatic piloting. That is, when telling stories about Scotland narrators tend not so much to invent those narratives (or, in the case of non-fiction, lay out the facts of them) as to succumb to powerful and historically deep-seated, pre-existing narratives which shape the tone and substance of their work. The example I dealt with in depth was the discourse dealing with the Gàidhealtachd of the past and the former's tendency to fall into the elegiac mode, as exemplified most recently by Scottish press accounts of the January 1992 tercentenary commemorations of the Massacre of Glencoe.

In passing, I indicated that the same elegiac mode is characteristic of accounts of the 1745–46 Jacobite Rebellion and, in particular, of the Battle of Culloden (1746). What I might have added was that we are likely to be in for a deluge of tearful, breast-beating, elegiac paroxysms from the commemorations of these events on their 250th anniversary in 1995–96. This essay is, as its title suggests, in the way of a pre-emptive strike – an attempt to counter the tsunami of tearful remembrance around the event. The strategy is to re-historicise both the '45 and Culloden and to reinscribe these key historical events, important personnel within them, and the memorialisation of both into discourses other than the dominant elegiac one. Sometimes these alternative discourses are historically challenging,

---

*Originally published in *Scottish Affairs*, no. 9 (1994), 97–126.

and sometimes they are flamboyantly absurd (and even offensive). Always, however, they assert the inescapable fact that there is no 'natural', essentialist way of describing the events and people of 1745–46; there are only diverse 'fictions' which might be constructed around them. In asserting the fictiveness of every discursive practice I am not, needless to say, casting doubt on the professional practice of historians, sociologists, journalists or the makers of television documentaries. Within the necessarily constructed nature of all the artefacts produced within those professions there is still the crucial difference between lying and telling the truth. There is also, however, an increasing recognition, both within academia and without, of the ideological nature of professional protocols. What is currently happening is nothing less than the rapid convergence of paradigms, in the humanities and beyond, around the question of textuality.[3]

I am, of course, hardly the first theorist to emphasise and explore the complex ideological and psychological resonances of public monuments and related practices of popular and official memorialisation. In, for example, his *Five Lectures on Psychoanalysis* (1909), Sigmund Freud (1856–1939) noted that:

> Not far from London Bridge you will find a towering [. . .] column, which is simply known as 'The Monument'. It was designed as a memorial of the Great Fire [1666] [. . .] What should we think of a Londoner who shed tears before the Monument that commemorates the reduction of his beloved metropolis to ashes although it has long since risen again in far greater brilliance? [. . .] Yet every single hysteric and neurotic behaves like [this] unpractical Londoner. Not only do they remember painful experiences of the remote past, but they still cling to them emotionally, they cannot get free of the past and for its sake they neglect what is real and immediate.[4]

As Freud realised, memorials are potential sites of trouble, especially in times of violent revolution or counter-revolution or even when the memorials allude to such times. Quite recently, a memorial set up in a Renfrewshire field to commemorate the landing there in 1941 of Deputy Führer, Rudolf Hess (1894–1987), was smashed by militant anti-fascists.[5] A moment's reflection brings to mind a surge of similar incidents going back at least as far as 1789. There was extensive vandalising of the memorial statuary of the Ancien Régime at this time and a notable event of the Paris Commune of 1870 was the toppling of the Vendôme Column commemorating the achievements of Napoleon Bonaparte (1769–1821).[6] Within the time frame of the moving image, several analogous moments are imprinted on the mind: the desecration of churches in St Petersburg/Petrograd in 1917 and in Barcelona in 1936; the dynamiting of swastika-laden facades

Figure 22.1 Poster advertising an exhibition of the photomontages included in the original version of this essay. The photomontage reproduced here is entitled 'Imagined Community'.

on German buildings in 1945; the pounding with sledgehammers of statues in Budapest in 1956; statues of the Shah (1919–80) hauled from their plinths by horses in revolutionary Iran; and, most recently, television pictures of numerous statues of Vladimir Lenin (1870–1924) being smashed, toppled or hoisted from their accustomed places in the heartlands and peripheries of the Soviet imperium. One celebrated set of pictures from Bucharest showed a priest of the Orthodox Church apparently exorcising the ghost of Lenin as his shackled statue was hoisted by crane from its plinth.[7] There is apparently talk in Spain of doing away with Francisco Franco (1892–1975)'s notorious Valley of the Fallen, its massive monument built by the slave labour of those vanquished in the Spanish Civil War (1936–39). But perhaps the most interesting, and certainly the best documented, example of the memorial as site of trouble is the Vietnam Memorial in Washington DC.[8] The latter constitutes the clearest example of argument about politics and ideology masquerading as argument about aesthetics.

The plan for a single memorial to the fallen in Vietnam was set in train by an open competition in which artists were invited to submit designs anonymously. In May 1981 the judges, specialists in the field of architecture and design, announced their unanimous decision to award the $20,000 prize to a design which turned out to have been submitted by a twenty-one-year-old Chinese-American woman, Maya Lin. When the nature of that design – an austere, V-shaped wall in polished black granite bearing the names of the fallen – became public, a group of influential men, some of them Vietnam veterans, and orchestrated it is said by Ross Perot (1930–2019), mounted a campaign of abuse against the Lin project. Among their criticisms were that the monument was black and not white, that it skulked along the ground and did not soar to the heavens, and that it listed the fallen by the dates of their deaths and not alphabetically. This apparently aesthetic discourse became openly political from time to time, as when Lin's design was denounced as 'a memorial to the war at home rather than to the one in Southeast Asia' and 'a tribute to Jane Fonda'.[9] The official response to the furore was to settle on a compromise. Another memorial was commissioned from a figurative sculptor, Frederick Hart (1943–99), this time a traditional rendering of three larger-than-life GIs, one of them black, in battle dress and bearing arms with, alongside the sculpture, a fifty-foot flagpole bearing the US flag. The two memorials now coexist within sight of each other, each asserting a different way of commemorating the fallen. As Elizabeth Hess has written, 'If Lin's memorial is a tribute to Fonda, then Hart's is a tribute to John Wayne [1907–79]'.[10] What is remarkable when one reads the detail of the argument is the extent to which all the flash points of politics are in play: gender, race, class, religion (in a very general sense) and national identity. Several of them come together in the proposal made at one point by the anti-Lin faction that the Hart memorial should be set astride the V of the Lin memorial.

Given the potential for trouble round memorials, it is interesting to speculate why the Culloden memorial has moved so apparently placidly through history. The last time there was a major commemoration of Culloden was on the 200th anniversary of the battle in 1946. A local newspaper's account of the ceremony, organised by the Gaelic Society of Inverness and held at the base of the memorial cairn, speaks of up to 500 people attending the event, and details the procedures of wreath-laying, lament-playing and poetry-orating which constituted the commemoration.[11] The account offers extensive summaries of the various addresses delivered or attached to wreaths, of which the following are representative:

> Rear Admiral Lachlan D. Mackintosh CB, DSO, DSC, placed on the Cairn the Elizabeth Stewart wreath which bore the inscription in Gaelic – 'Although 200 years have gone the memory of the heroes lives' [. . .] Mr Malcolm Macinnes, honorary piper of the Gaelic Society, played the old Gaelic psalm tune 'Torwood' and at intervals during the proceedings 'The Lament for the Children', the lullaby 'The Isles are in Sorrow', 'Lochaber No More' and 'MacCrimmon's Lament' [. . .] After the Reverend Dr John Macpherson, Daviot, had offered up a prayer in Gaelic, he invited Captain Shaw to speak, remarking that it was appropriate that a Shaw should take the leading part in the ceremony, since the Shaws were an important sept of the great Clan Chattan and one of the oldest clans in the highlands [. . .] 'Today,' said Captain Shaw, 'our thoughts turn to those who fought and fell on Drumossie Moor, and whose graves are around. We are here today to honour them. Their memory shall never fade. They march in a deathless army' [. . .] 'this ground,' said Dr Galbraith, 'has passed into the care of the nation. I speak for the Gaelic Society and for all Highlanders when I say we look upon this battlefield as a sacred burial place'.[12]

Apart from the involvement of the aristocracy, the church and the military in the proceedings, the most striking feature of the commemoration and the press account given of it is the assumption of meaningful continuity between those who fell at Culloden in 1746 and those present at the 1946 ceremony, and the implication that the process of commemoration stretches back over the intervening two centuries. What is all but repressed in the events of 1946 and the description of them is the fact that the constituting of the Culloden memorial is a relatively recent event. The existing cairn was erected only in 1881, although it incorporates an inscribed stone executed in 1858 and meant for a cairn which was never built. The headstones allegedly marking the graves of the various clans were similarly erected in 1881 and the site (or, more accurately, elements of it) was designated an ancient monument as late as 1925, the same year that the Gaelic Society of Inverness raised money for the maintenance of the memorials and instituted the commemoration ceremony. It was only in 1944 that the cairn and the burial ground around it passed from private hands into the keeping of the National Trust for Scotland.[13] The process whereby Culloden Moor became constituted as a memorial is, therefore, a classic case of what has been called 'the invention of tradition'.[14] That latter process, closely intertwined with the phenomenon of nationalism, was particularly virulent in the period 1880 to 1920 but is still active today. Michael Ignatieff, in his television series and book on modern nationalism, witnessed in the new republic of Croatia a presidential guard in traditional Croatian costume carrying out intricate drill movements. Ignatieff revealed that both costumes and movements had been devised recently by a Croatian choreographer.[15]

Although 'the invention of tradition' is a still potent phenomenon and may have been most intense in the four decades spanning the transition between the nineteenth and twentieth centuries, its historical origins are much more far-reaching. It would have been inconceivable without that sense of the past created by the accelerating pace of material change in the post-Renaissance world,[16] a 'time/space compression' within which the very discipline of historiography was fashioned.[17] Located within these wider historical processes, evolving perceptions of Culloden, culminating in its mid-twentieth-century constitution as 'a sacred burial place', can be tracked along several axes. Consider, for example, the difference between the following two travellers' accounts of Culloden Moor with only sixty years between them:

> August 16. Passed over Culloden Moor, the place that North Britain owes its present prosperity to, by the victory of April 16, 1746.[18]

> The moor is as grim and shelterless a waste as vengeance could desire for an enemy's grave [. . .] It is impossible to contemplate unmoved those verdant spots, which, contrasting with the dun hue of the heather, distinctly indicate the shallow graves of the slain [. . .] The snows of upwards of seventy winters have, since the hurried entombment of the gallant dead, fallen and melted upon Culloden.[19]

If the difference between the two could be summed up in one word, that word would be Romanticism.[20] It is the dreamy and brooding Botfield, rather than the matter-of-fact Pennant, who displays the Romantic structure of feeling – laboriously and unevenly constructed over the period between 1770 and 1830 and intimately related to the wider historical processes referred to above – which would project onto Culloden Moor the viewer's feelings about what had occurred there and which would regard the construction of a Culloden memorial as an appropriate gesture. But that structure of feeling was struggling into birth in areas other than travel writing.[21] Within this process, Scotland – principally through the writings of James Macpherson (1736–96) and Sir Walter Scott (1771–1832) – came to fulfil a special role as the Romantic dream landscape par excellence, a factor perhaps not unconnected with the way succeeding generations, not least of Scots, would come to view Culloden.[22]

Throughout the nineteenth century, in an ideological manoeuvre which would be much repeated, Culloden was transmuted from being a direct threat to the Hanoverian dynasty to becoming, in some sense, part of their lineage. This process was at work as early as 1822. John Prebble (1915–2001), describing a significant example of 'the invention of tradition', namely, the pageantry devised by Sir Walter Scott to mark the visit of George IV (1762–1830) to Edinburgh in that year, writes:

> Much of the pageant to be devised by Scott would be what his occasionally irreverent son-in-law called 'Sir Walter's Celtification of Scotland'. There was the echo of an old song, an unconscious or deliberate recall of a far-away autumn when the night-fires of the clans were lit on Arthur's Seat, the wynds of the Royal Mile echoed to the wild pibroch of 'Lochiel's Gathering' and a young Prince in lace and tartan danced through the candlelight at Holyroodhouse. Some of the execrable doggerel Scott wrote for the occasion was based upon the presumption that a Jacobite King was at last enjoying his own again. He clearly wished to believe that the spiritual nature of a Stuart and therefore a Scottish monarchy, purified by exile and the blood of Culloden, had been made manifest in the fat form of the landlord of Brighton Pavilion. Since George IV was as much a Stuart as the Young Pretender had been, the suggestion was perhaps not as preposterous as it might appear. Certainly it is not a claim that the King himself would have strenuously resisted.[23]

Prebble's history-writing is the verbal equivalent of Victorian history-painting, as much incantation as explication, and executes its own ideological manoeuvre by succumbing to the very same discourse it here anatomises.[24]

Like her kinsman George IV, Queen Victoria (1819–1901) was more than willing to mask the contradictions between the eighteenth-century Stuart conception of monarchy and that of her own house. This was part of Victoria's wider 'symbolic appropriation' of the Scottish Highlands.[25] Forgetting that the Stuarts represented quasi-feudal, Catholic absolutism is even today quite common in Scotland. Victoria, travelling in the Highlands in 1873, on several occasions records the ideological conflation of Stuart and Hanover dynasties-cum-discourses in her journal:

> It was as General Ponsonby observed afterwards, a striking scene. 'There was Lochiel', as he said, 'whose great-grand-uncle had been the real moving cause of the

rising of 1745 – for without him Prince Charles would not have made the attempt – showing your Majesty (whose great-great-grandfather he had striven to dethrone) the scenes made historical by Prince Charles' wanderings. It was a scene one could not look on unmoved'. Yes, and I feel a sort of reverence in going over these scenes in this most beautiful country, which I am proud to call my own, where there was such devoted loyalty to the family of my ancestors – for Stuart blood is in my veins, and I am now their representative, and the people are as devoted and loyal to me as they were to that unhappy race.[26]

And, on witnessing Glenfinnan, where the Stuart standard was raised in 1745:

> I thought I never saw a lovelier or more romantic spot, or one which told its history so well. What a scene it must have been in 1745! And here was I, the descendant of the Stuarts and of the very king whom Prince Charles sought to overthrow, sitting and walking about, quite privately and peaceably.[27]

But this ideological conflation of the houses of Stuart and Hanover could be sustained only by repressing from memory distasteful features of the past, not least relating to Culloden. About a year before seeing Glenfinnan, Victoria recorded another trip:

> Nairn lies very prettily on the shore of the Moray Firth. We passed Culloden, and the moor where that bloody battle, the recollection which I cannot bear, was fought. The heather beautiful everywhere and now the scenery became very fine.[28]

Clearly, then, the structure of feeling about Culloden was shifting throughout the nineteenth century to the point, in 1881, when it would be generally deemed appropriate to raise a memorial cairn.

However, the unevenness of that process is striking. One might posit with confidence the idea that Sir Walter Scott, in 1822, was psychologically ready for the act of formally memorialising Culloden, but this was far from being a mental condition shared by his fellow Scots of the time. Indeed, Culloden is marked by its discursive invisibility in pre-1815 Scotland. The cumulative index of the *Inverness Courier* (the latter was named the *Inverness Journal* until 1817) carries only one entry under 'Culloden' over the period 1746–1820, referring to a brief item in 1816 about a ninety-nine-year-old local man who had participated in the battle. As would be consistent with the changing structure of feeling, there are then four entries under 'Culloden' in the period 1825–41. However, it is not until 1846, the centenary of the battle, that it could be said that local attention became firmly fixed on Culloden. The *Courier* carried an extensive description of the events surrounding the centenary, but what strikes the modern reader is the carnivalesque mood of the proceedings rather than, as has come to be expected in more modern times, the elegiac:

> The air was clear and bracing, the sun bright, and the whole country breathing of spring. The pleasantness of the season, joined to the interesting associations connected with the day, drew vast crowds of persons to the field of Culloden. Most of the teachers in town indulged their pupils with a holiday, and groups of the little wanderers might be seen in all directions spreading over the moor, or sitting by the graves of the slain, listening to tales of the battle and the positions of the rival armies as detailed by the peasantry. Others, more advanced in years, were intent on hunting rabbits: while girls were seen decorating themselves with tufts of heather and aged men and women related the exploits of their fathers or grandfathers, not a few of whom had fought and bled at Culloden. Parties in carriages, gigs and carts were frequently arriving; and altogether these could scarcely be less, in the middle of the day, than three thousand persons on the moor. The scene was highly animated and striking, presenting a vivid contrast to the usual quietude of that large, sombre tableland, the solitary scene of battle.[29]

John Bodnar, in his study of public memory formation in the United States, stresses the dialectical nature of such processes and traces the never-ending negotiation within them between what he calls the 'official' and the 'vernacular' modes of public memorialisation:

> Adherents to official and vernacular interests demonstrate conflicting obsessions. Cultural leaders orchestrate commemorative events to calm anxiety about change or political events, eliminate citizen indifference towards official concerns, promote exemplary patterns of citizen behaviour, and stress citizen duties over rights. They feel the need to do this because of social contradictions, alternative views, and indifference that perpetuate fears of societal dissolution and unregulated political behaviour. Ordinary people, on the other hand, react to the actions of leaders in a variety of ways. At times they accept the official interpretations of reality. Sometimes this can be seen when an individual declares that a son died in defence of his country or an immigrant ancestor emigrated to build a new nation. Individuals also express alternative renditions of reality when they feel a war death was needless or an immigrant ancestor moved simply to support his family. Frequently people put official agendas to unintended uses as they almost always do when they use public ritual time for recreational purposes or patriotic symbols to demand political rights.[30]

Clearly, and as per Bodnar's model, the idea of Culloden Moor as 'a sacred burial place' was not uppermost in the minds of the good burghers of Inverness on that bright spring day in 1846. Nevertheless, the uneven nature of the evolution of the Romantic structure of feeling that would eventually categorise Culloden in those terms meant that the breezy account of the festivities also contained the seeds of the later elegiac discourse and reference to the architectural form in which it would be embodied:

> The long-meditated project of erecting some memorial to the dead at Culloden was again revived and some discussion took place as to the nature of the testimonial which would be most appropriate. Mr Maxwell deprecated any Cockney cenotaph or pillar on such a field, and proposed a simple, but massive, cairn as the most touching and the most noble memorial of the nation's admiration and respect.[31]

In an offer which, if it had come to fruition, might have sparked a controversy somewhat akin to that around the Vietnam Memorial, a Mr Patric Park (1811–55) of London proposed sculpting, free of charge except for the materials, a twelve-foot-high statue of a Highlander. A design for such a statue is to be found in the Inverness Museum.

The wave of enthusiasm attending the 'rediscovery' of Culloden, so to speak, seemed to sustain itself for a number of years until, in 1849,

> The foundation stone of the Culloden monument was laid on the battlefield with masonic honours. Sir Robert Peel [1788–1850] had been asked to perform the ceremony, but declined, although he expressed appreciation of the proffered honour and had previously sent a donation of £5 to the funds. There was a procession from Inverness, led by a band of music, and including the six incorporated Trades and masonic deputations. The stone was laid by Mr William Anderson, Right Worshipful Master of St John's Operative Mason Lodge of Forres. The monument [. . .] was intended to be a gigantic cairn with flights of rustic steps leading to the top. It was hoped that tablets and memorials to clans and individuals would occupy places in it; also that a group of statuary would be placed in front.[32]

The irony of deploying masonic honours in the commemoration of an enterprise designed to restore an absolutist Catholic monarchy to the British throne seems to have been lost on the participants – another example, perhaps, of the Stuart/Hanover ideological manoeuvre discussed above. However, Murray Pittock suggests that Jacobite iconography in fact incorporated masonic elements.[33] By 1852 the project had been abandoned for lack of funds. Another cairn was begun in 1858 but it too was abandoned, although not before one Edward Power had carved for it the stone which was to be incorporated into the 1881 cairn and which remains there to this day. Its dedication reads: 'THE BATTLE OF CULLODEN was fought on this moor / 16 April 1746 / THE GRAVES OF THE GALLANT HIGHLANDERS / who fought for / SCOTLAND AND PRINCE CHARLIE are marked by the names of their clans'. The assigning of a 'Scottish' motivation to the dead Highlanders – the interpretation widely held in the popular mind nowadays – represents both a travestying of the non-nationalist, dynastic, social-systemic issues at stake in the battle and wider rebellion and the kind of retrospective appropriating of the Highlanders which was to become all too common in the twentieth century.[34]

Why, then, should 1881 be the year in which the cairn was finally built? We should not discount the 'invention of tradition' argument about the importance of the period between 1880 and 1920 in the production and proliferation of the physical tokens of actual or aspiring nationhood, such as flags, stamps, coinage, statuary, national exhibitions and so on. But this is not the whole story. As is always the case, there were complex determinations. The accelerating material processes of the Industrial Revolution and the space/time compression which gave rise to a sense of the past and to the discipline of historiography at the same time also threw into relief experiences of individual human change and mortality. Thus, the period between 1820 and 1840 saw the founding of many cemeteries in Europe and America, including Glasgow's Necropolis in 1832.[35] This process of personal memorialisation would segue into public memorialisation. Many European countries had instituted state systems of monument protection by the middle of the nineteenth century, but it was not until 1869 that the question of a national monuments policy for the UK was mooted in the House of Commons and not until 1873 that a bill was first introduced. Although bitterly contested as a potential drain on the public purse and encroachment on the rights of private property, it nevertheless put the question of collective heritage and public memorialisation on the agenda. The bill was eventually ratified by Parliament, in a much constrained form, as the Ancient Monuments Protection Act 1882 and the culmination of this 'mood' was the setting-up of three Royal Commissions on Historical Monuments, including one specifically for Scotland, in 1908. A different, but related process of social sedimentation saw the founding of the National Museum of Antiquities of Scotland in 1851, the Royal Scottish Museum in 1854, the National Gallery in 1859, the Scottish National Portrait Gallery in 1889 and the National Library of Scotland in 1925.

Another part of the mosaic which was to make up the picture, characteristic of the second half of the nineteenth century, within which the relatively new-found veneration for the Scottish past was put at the service of national (and, indeed, racial) ends, was the process whereby Saxon was analytically separated from Celt. The alleged otherness of the inhabitants of the Gàidhealtachd had never been in dispute, but the barbarian image of pre-Ossianic times was increasingly tempered, in the late eighteenth and nineteenth centuries, by the image of the Highlander as 'natural' and 'poetic'. This evolution can hardly be seen as an advance, however, since both images were articulated outside the Gàidhealtachd and served the needs, fears and fantasies of those individuals and societies that fashioned the images. Nevertheless, the discursive separation of Saxon and Celt – increasingly marked in the mid-to-late nineteenth century by figures as disparate as Matthew Arnold (1822–88) and Ernest Renan (1823–92)[36] – may have helped generate, among Highlanders and the increasing number of Lowland and diasporic Scots who identified with them, a sense of the Highland past and the impulse to commemorate it.

As the above remarks about George IV and Queen Victoria indicate, the sentimental Jacobitism which they professed ran like a snake through nineteenth-century Scottish life and is far from exhausted even today. Tom Nairn (1932–2023) has seen the overripe, not to say demented, quality of this phenomenon as stemming from its failure to be incorporated into the service of genuine nation-building, as was instead the case with analogous impulses in nineteenth-century Italy, Poland or Scandinavia.[37] Sentimental Jacobitism is traceable in every dimension of Scottish life: literature; easel painting; music; films and television programmes; right through to the marketing of whisky, shortbread and, through the mechanism of tourism, of Scotland itself. The great merit of Nairn's work has been to historicise this phenomenon, to explain it in the context of the eighteenth- and nineteenth-century rise of European nationalism and its cultural mode, Romanticism, and to ground it in the cataclysmic material changes that arose in eighteenth-century European society.

This essay's argument that the constituting of the Culloden memorial requires to be historicised – and is, indeed, explicable within the same analytical framework deployed by Nairn – might perhaps be bolstered by considering a closely related phenomenon: the constituting of Flora MacDonald (1722–90) as the Jacobite heroine par excellence. Part of the process of nation-building is the construction of national heroes and heroines. The *locus classicus* of this is the nationalist historiography of France, within which Joan of Arc (1412–31) was reconstructed to the point of canonisation in 1920.[38] Somewhat earlier, Scottish popular historiography had constructed William Wallace (1270–1305) as its hero, culminating in the erection, between 1861 and 1869, of the Wallace Monument at Stirling. This was an impulse which was to ripple outwards to the Scots diaspora, most notably in the unveiling of a Wallace statue in Ballarat, Australia in 1889.[39]

If Wallace was the hero of popular reconstructions of the Scottish past, then Flora MacDonald was the heroine. A leaflet issued in Inverness in 1868 and headed 'Flora MacDonald Memorial Fund' reads:

> From time to time, for many years, strangers visiting the Church-yard of Kilmuir, in the Island of Skye, have complained that no memorial has been placed over the

grave of Flora MacDonald. Reference is made to the fact in the last edition of James Boswell [1740–95]'s *Journal of Dr Johnson's 'Tour of the Hebrides'* . . . [1785]. The late Alexander Smith speaks feelingly on the subject in his 'Summer in Skye': many letters have appeared in the newspapers, upbraiding the descendants of Highland Jacobites for this neglect, and within the last few weeks attention has been drawn to it in the *Illustrated London News*. Flora MacDonald's grave has thus acquired a celebrity which, in its present neglected state, is, to say the least of it, undesirable; and it is evident, from the tone of the public communications on the subject, that the only thing necessary to remove this reproach from the Highlands is that someone should take a little trouble to collect subscriptions and ascertain the wishes of subscribers as to the form the Memorial should assume.[40]

The eventual outcome of the campaign was the statue erected in Inverness in 1896. Subsequent sentimental Jacobitism has it that the statue represents MacDonald, hand cupped over her eyes, watching Prince Charlie's ship disappearing over the horizon. However, a contemporary magazine account (which, significantly, opens with the words 'The canonisation of Flora MacDonald is reaching an acute stage'), describes it differently:

> The subject carries out the motto 'Air Faire (On the Watch)', and represents the heroic maiden standing with her favourite collie dog, shading her eyes with her hand, on the look-out for any possible enemies of the Prince, who is supposed to be hiding.[41]

Like the Culloden memorial, MacDonald's statue came to be represented on numerous postcards and other popular artefacts. The Florian cult, if such it can be called, grew apace, and one of its most nauseating instances is to be found in the *Transactions of the Gaelic Society of Inverness*, recording the moment in 1922 when the Society was addressed by one Dr Vardell (1860–1958), President of the Flora MacDonald College of North Carolina:

> Dr Vardell then referred to his feelings while he stood at the grave of Flora MacDonald, and said her heroism was one of the bonds that tied the great Empire across the sea to the great British Empire [. . .] He would read to them one of their college toasts which had been written by a student of the college:

> (F)air is the name of,
> (L)ovely the face of you;
> (O)ver the sea of years
> (R)each we our hands to you
> (A)sking your blessing.
> (M)ists of the drifting years
> (A)lmost would cover you:
> (C)ould we, forgetting you,
> (D)are speak of loyalty

(O)r of true courage!
(N)o! We drink now to you,
(A)ll glasses high to you,
(L)ong and right heartily
(D)rink to your memory,
Flora MacDonald.[42]

Certain social formations, most notably the Third Reich and the American South, exhibit a noxious melange of brutality and sentimentality. It is well known, of course, that sometime after the failure of the '45, Flora MacDonald and her husband emigrated (temporarily, as it was to turn out) to North Carolina, hence the name of Dr Vardell's college. As Roland Barthes (1915–80) has demonstrated, myths are able to function only so long as contradictions within them and/or to which they refer are repressed.[43] Another of Dr Vardell's 1922 remarks gives a clue to the literally unspeakable, contradictory element in the Florian myth: 'They were very Scottish (in North Carolina). The niggers [sic] didn't call a man "captain" or "boss"; they called him "Mr Mack".'[44] Flora MacDonald lived in a slave-owning community in North Carolina. It will be argued, with some justice by those wishing to preserve the Florian myth, that slave-owning in eighteenth-century North Carolina was part of day-to-day life and should not be held specifically against her. True, but rather beside the point: Flora MacDonald exists, in herself and as part of an ensemble of images which includes the Culloden memorial, within the discourse of sentimental Jacobitism. Apparently historical, that discourse exists outside of history in the domain of myth. To dredge to the surface the fact that Flora MacDonald led part of her life in a slave-owning society cracks the myth apart, forcing it to be seen within the brutal reality of the Atlantic slave trade. Also, the breast-beating rhetoric of the Florian myth, its easy deployment of terms like 'courage', 'honour' and 'dignity in adversity', begins to sound sanctimonious when looked at from this new perspective.

The purpose of this essay has been to re-historicise sentimental Jacobitism in general and the Culloden memorial in particular. It poses the question of why the memorial, unlike so many other historical monuments, has provoked so little 'trouble'. Clearly, the main reason is the general ideological assent given to sentimental Jacobitism, even by those objectively hostile to it (for example, the Freemasons of 1858) in Scotland. But the absence of trouble is due also to the relatively stable polity of the UK, within which regimes and their triumphal representations have not (in recent centuries, at any rate) been toppled and smashed, and, finally, also to the Culloden memorial's geographical remoteness within the UK. The dislodging of monuments such as the Vendôme Column and the diverse statues of Lenin, for example, occurred in populous metropoles where their symbolic import had greatest force.

However, the additional possibility that the Culloden cairn's aesthetic form has inhibited dissent should not be ruled out. As well as being the Scottish sculptural form par excellence, the cairn does not carry with it any overtones of contemporary art ideologies (for example, modern versus traditional) such as were deployed so abusively in the context of the Vietnam Memorial or, most recently, the Holocaust Museum project, also in Washington.[45] Cairn building, to the Scots, is part of everyday life, not a self-conscious 'artistic' activity. I recall as a schoolboy at Boys' Brigade camp near Crianlarich our celebrating a successful ascent of a local mountain by adding stones to the cairn on its summit. The men of Ness go each year to the island of Sula Sgeir for a supply of guga (the young of the gannet). When a man decides that he has reached an age when such a visit will be his last, he leaves a cairn on the clifftop. More recently, a number of cairns are being erected on the Isle of Lewis to commemorate the crofters' struggles of the nineteenth century. If, on the other hand, some commemorative structure other than a cairn had been erected on Culloden Moor in 1881, it would have run the risk of signalling particular politico-religious affiliations simply by the nature of its artistic form. In the Scottish context, the Gothic style tended to carry Episcopalian or Roman Catholic associations, while the Neo-Classical had Presbyterian equivalents.[46] The latter would have been particularly unsuitable for a Jacobite monument, given the Enlightenment's anti-Jacobitism, but, as has been demonstrated, myth in general and sentimental Jacobitism in particular have a remarkable capacity to mask contradictions.

The 200th anniversary of the Battle of Culloden, commemorated at the Culloden memorial in 1946 and described above, shows sentimental Jacobitism in full spate. The appeals to the past and the implied continuities with it might suggest a timelessness about the annual commemoration ceremony itself. In fact, as a quasi-official (under the auspices of the Gaelic Society of Inverness) regular event the ceremony dates only from 1925. However, by the start of the twentieth century, the Culloden memorial had become something of a tourist attraction, the most prestigious and best-documented visit probably being that of Field Marshall Earl Roberts (1832–1914), at the time Chief of the Imperial General Staff, in August 1903. Occasional wreath-laying ceremonies by individuals appear to have taken place, the most grotesque of whom is Theodore Napier (1845–1924). Like many another unhinged nationalist, Napier's origins lay outside the land which obsessed him. He was born in Australia, probably in 1845, and died there in 1924. He lived in Edinburgh from around 1893 to 1912 and was the source of much hilarity on account of his wandering around in a costume of Royal Stewart tartan. Like other local eccentrics of the time (Kirkintilloch's Petticoat Dan [1835–1913] was another), Napier was the subject of several contemporaneous postcards, one showing him, fierce and bearded, 'in the garb of old Gaul'; another as a 'Highland Chief – XVI Century'; and yet another masquerading as a Highland chief in a pageant held during the 1908 Scottish National Exhibition in Edinburgh. He seems to have been active in several nationalist stunts in the early years of the twentieth century (for example, on a Mary, Queen of Scots demonstration at Fotheringay, and as a speaker at the Bore Stone, Bannockburn). A postcard exists of Napier placing a wreath on the Culloden cairn on 16 April 1904 and his address on a previous occasion (1903), with its limping verse, breast-beating, elegiac quality, and citing of crackpot bodies whose participation he had mobilised, deserves quoting:

> Land of the loyal when the Stuart fell
> They, faithful mountains, sighed a fond farewell
> The dirge of freedom pealed along the gale
> And tears of sorrow flowed in every vale.
>
> Fellow-Scotsmen and friends. I call you friends because, though I am not of these parts, I come here regularly on my annual pilgrimage to this shrine. I feel more at home every time I come north although this scene and circumstance should make us all feel sore at heart. Before coming this year, I issued an appeal for wreaths and floral tributes and the response has been most gratifying. These tokens of our pride and sorrow include tributes from the Legitimist Jacobite League of Great Britain and Ireland; the Flora MacDonald Club of Glasgow; and the White Cockade Legitimist Club of St Ives [. . .] Why do we bring these wreaths to this cairn? It is not, as has been suggested, for the purpose of ostentatiously displaying ourselves. It is to show our regard for the men who fell in the Stuart cause. They were men in those days, not the pygmies we find around us now.[47]

The newspaper article that reported Napier's remarks goes on to record the response of those who witnessed this pantomime. To the latter's credit, they greeted it with jeers and catcalls.

It might be wondered if the incipient nationalism of any other country has reached such a pitch of comic-opera absurdity. This impulse to theatricality, the concentration on signs rather than substance, was present in the earliest pre-history of modern Scottish nationalism, as witnessed by the furore over flags and coins in the 1850s.[48] The expenditure of energy on irrelevancies was to prove a recurrent problem for Scottish nationalism. One can have nothing but sympathy for the exasperation of a pragmatic nationalist like Lewis Spence (1874–1955) following his defeat as a

National Party candidate in the North Midlothian and Peebles by-election of January 1929:

> I am all for the new nationalism, but at the moment it presents to me a maelstrom boiling and bubbling with the cross-currents of rival and frequently fantastic theories, schemes and notions, riotous with tumultuous personality and convulsive with a petulant individual predilection [...] We have people who want all Scotland to speak the Gaelic, and who hate Braid Scots, people who continue the Old Language and clatter out a gutter Scots with an English basis of syntax in the sad belief that it is the genuine article. Some hark back to the hope of a sixteenth-century Scotland regained, others suggest a national approchement [sic] with France, still others a Jacobite restoration. A certain group sees in the expulsion of all the English and the Irish in Scotland the country's only chance of survival.[49]

The most substantial study of Jacobitism's ideological force in Scottish life is by Pittock.[50] It is markedly more sympathetic to Jacobitism, and figures such as Napier, than the present essay. Pittock assembles convincing evidence of the historical complexity of Jacobitism but, more controversially, stresses its radical potential in Scottish culture past and present. A more detailed debate with Pittock's position would be out of place here, but one must, at the very least, be sceptical about an argument which adduces as evidence of that radical potential the modern-day 'execrable doggerel'[51] of the Corries' 1960s folk anthem, 'Flower of Scotland'.

By 1925 commemorative deployment around the Culloden memorial, precisely because it now had the imprimatur of 'respectable' bodies such as the Gaelic Society of Inverness, approached something close to sanity. However, as the quotations above from the 1946 commemorative event speeches indicate, the differences between figures like Captain Shaw and Theodore Napier relate to matters of comportment, tone and style rather than more substantial ones of ideology: both are firmly locked within sentimental Jacobitism. The question of why the Culloden cairn was raised in 1881, rather than earlier or later, is but one enquiry that requires to be posed. A closely related and comparably important question is why the 'officialising' of the Culloden memorial and the establishing of the annual commemoration ceremony occurred precisely in 1925. To some extent, that latter timing was the inevitable consequence of sentimental Jacobitism's growing hegemony in Scottish life or, to put it in the terms adumbrated at this essay's outset, the accelerated writhing of the Scottish Discursive Unconscious. However, events invariably have complex determinations. If there is, on one hand, the *longue durée*[52] of sentimental Jacobitism at work on the events of 1925, the shorter-term determination is undoubtedly the profound impulse to memorialisation provided by the Great War of 1914–18 on the other. Paul Fussell (1924–2012), although primarily concerned with that conflict's effect on literary sensibilities, nevertheless reveals how the experience of it seared the minds of all those who survived.[53] It was the Great War which produced those resounding images of national remembrance such as the Flanders poppy and the two minutes' silence, images and practices which have not altogether lost their emotional power even today. What has been lost, however, is the general sense in the society of being in direct contact with the events which gave rise to them:

> The British Legion sold eight million Flanders poppies in 1921, when the practice was started, and in 1926, when the depression had deepened, the figure was thirty million. On November 11 [. . .] the engines were stopped on Cunard liners and poppies sold; on a Daimler air-express flying between Manchester and London in 1922, all engines were shut off and the passengers stood to attention with bared heads as the plane glided.[54]

The Great War is not simply one of the determining factors behind the foregrounding of the Culloden commemoration in 1925; it was inscribed into that commemoration itself. The Earl of Cassillis, placing a memorial wreath on the Culloden cairn and speaking in Gaelic, said:

> Since the '45 the Gael has proved his devotion to his country in no small measure. During the last war many districts of the Highlands were depleted of able-bodied men who went to fight and die for King and country. Those men, like Macrimmon, would not return to them. Those who lay on Culloden field would not return, nor would those who died in the Great War. But they lived in hope of going to them. Their love and devotion would ever remain the pride of the Gaelic race whether in this country or scattered in many lands and divers climes.[55]

At one level, therefore, the Culloden memorial has passed out of history into myth, specifically, the lachrymosely elegiac myth of sentimental Jacobitism. At another level, however, it is profoundly in history, its temporal evolution shaped by the long, unevenly developing discourses of the nineteenth century and shorter-term counterparts associated with specific events like the Great War.

While engaging with history far less dramatically than the Vendôme Column or the statues of Lenin, the Culloden memorial is, therefore, no less historical than them. Mark Lewis speculates on how Lenin himself might have felt about what has become of his statues. He suggests that the Lenin of 1917–18 might never have approved of the erection of permanent public monuments in the first place. Lenin at that time instead called for a monumental propaganda the purpose of which was to instruct the masses at precise historical conjunctures. The proper material for statuary, therefore, should be plaster rather than marble, granite or bronze: not only was plaster cheaper, it was also impermanent.[56] Indeed, such hostility to permanent monumentality in sculpture is not new. Both the Neo-Classics and Romantics were profoundly ambivalent about this, though their particular delusion was that monumentality was possible and desirable in literature instead.[57]

The notion of the non-permanent memorial seems to be more readily acceptable in societies other than Britain. James E. Young, for example, describes Jochen and Esther Gerz's 1986 'countermonument' against fascism in Hamburg:

> To [the artists'] minds, the didactic logic of monuments, their demagogical rigidity, recalled too closely traits they associated with fascism itself. Their monument against fascism, therefore, would amount to a monument against itself: against the traditionally didactic function of monuments, against their tendency to displace the past they would have us contemplate – and finally, against the authoritarian propensity in all art that reduces viewers to passive spectators. The artists decided that theirs would be a self-abnegating monument, literally self-effacing. So when Hamburg offered them a sun-dappled park setting, they rejected it in favour of what they termed a 'normal, uglyish place'.[58]

The place in question was a dingy, working-class Hamburg suburb called Harburg with a large minority of Turkish 'guest workers'. The monument itself is in the form of a twelve-metre-high, one-metre-square pillar made of hollow aluminium and covered with a thin layer of soft, dark lead. A temporary inscription at the base – in German, French, English, Russian, Hebrew, Arabic and Turkish – reads:

> We invite the citizens of Harburg, and visitors to the town, to add their names here to ours. In doing so, we commit ourselves to remain vigilant. As more and more names cover this 12 metre tall lead column, it will gradually be lowered into the ground. One day it will have disappeared completely, and the site of the Harburg monument against fascism will be empty. In the end, it is only we ourselves who can rise up against injustice.[59]

A steel-pointed stylus, for visitors to add their names, is attached to each corner, and as the names progressively cover it the monument is lowered into a chamber in the ground the same depth as the height of the column. Young comments:

> With audacious simplicity, the countermonument thus flouts any number of cherished memorial conventions: its aim is not to console but to provoke; not to remain fixed but to change; not to be everlasting but to disappear; not to be ignored by passers-by but to demand interaction; not to remain pristine but to invite its own violation and desanctification; not to accept graciously the burden of memory but to throw it back at the town's feet. By defining itself in opposition to the

traditional memorial's task, the countermonument illustrates concisely the possibilities and limitations of all memorials everywhere. In this way, it functions as a valuable 'counterindex' to the ways time, memory and current history intersect at any memorial site.[60]

The Gerzs' strategy is not dissimilar to that of the French installation artist Christian Boltanski (1944–2021), whose work has memorialising dimensions also relating to the Holocaust. In an early-1990s *South Bank Show* television programme devoted to his work, he suggested that monuments should be made of fragile materials so that they would have to be remade over and over again and thus forestall our forgetting why they were made in the first place. It is intriguing to think of the Culloden memorial being executed in plaster on one of the wettest and windiest sites in Scotland, but the Culloden memorial is made in (to all intents and purposes) impermeable stone.

What, then, is to be done? It is an open question whether monuments should ever be vandalised, however disagreeable their implicit or accreted ideological meanings might be felt to be.[61] As President Václav Havel (1936–2011) of the Czech Republic has demonstrated in his suggestion that the Socialist Realist monuments of the past be placed in a forest and nature allowed to engulf them, there are more intelligent ways of dealing with the embodiments of discarded ideologies. Similarly, Samir al-Khalil, in his book on Saddam Hussein (1937–2006)'s sword-bearing forearms monument in Baghdad, speculates about what Iraqis should do with the monument, apart from tearing it down, after Saddam's demise.[62]

It is certainly not desirable to physically interfere with the Culloden memorial, but it can be repositioned ideologically, if only in words and pictures, in order to refuse the easy responses of sentimental Jacobitism and lachrymose elegiac discourse more generally – in short, to derail the Scottish Discursive Unconscious.

Notes

1. David McCrone, *Understanding Scotland: The Sociology of a Stateless Nation* (London: Routledge, 1992). A revised edition of McCrone's book, with the revised subtitle, 'The Sociology of a Nation', was published by Routledge in 2001. My essay referred to is: 'Scottish Culture: A Reply to David McCrone', *Scottish Affairs*, no. 4 (1993), 95–106, and also republished elsewhere in the present volume.
2. See McArthur, 'Scottish Culture', 101.
3. Notable examples include, in the field of historiography, Hayden White, *Metahistory: The Historical Imagination in Nineteenth-Century Europe* (Baltimore,

MD: Johns Hopkins University Press, 1973); in social psychology, John Shotter and Kenneth J. Gergen, eds, *Texts of Identity* (London: SAGE Publications, 1989); and in ethnography, Paul Atkinson, *The Ethnographic Imagination: Textual Constructions of Reality* (London: Routledge, 1990).
4. Sigmund Freud, *Five Lectures on Psychoanalysis* (1909), available at https://ia902907.us.archive.org/17/items/SigmundFreud/Sigmund%20Freud%20%5B1909%5D%20Five%20Lectures%20on%20Psych-Aanalysis%20%28James%20Strachey%20translation%2C%201955%29.pdf [accessed 20 March 2023].
5. A. Laing, '"Offensive" monument to Hess destroyed', *The Herald*, 19 November 1993, 1; D. Macgee, 'Memorial to Hess flight smashed', *The Scotsman*, 19 November 1993, 8.
6. Mark Lewis, 'What is to be done?', *Parachute*, no. 61 (January/February/March 1991), 28–36.
7. Ibid.
8. See, for example, Elizabeth Hess, 'A Tale of Two Memorials', *Art in America*, (April 1983), 121–6.
9. Ibid.
10. Ibid., p. 126.
11. The 19 April 1946 issue of the *Inverness Courier* contains an account of the 200th anniversary commemoration of the Battle of Culloden and a reprint of the account of the 100th anniversary commemoration from the same journal's 22 April 1846 edition.
12. *Inverness Courier*, 19 April 1946.
13. Iain Cameron Taylor, *Culloden: A guidebook to the battlefield with the story of the battle, the events leading to it and the aftermath* (Edinburgh: National Trust for Scotland, 1965).
14. See Eric Hobsbawm and Terence Ranger, eds, *The Invention of Tradition* (Cambridge: Cambridge University Press, 1983).
15. Michael Ignatieff, *Blood and Belonging: Journeys to the New Nationalism* (London: Vintage, 1994).
16. See David Harvey, *The Condition of Postmodernity: An Enquiry into the Origins of Cultural Change* (Oxford: Blackwell, 1989); Donald M. Lowe, *History of Bourgeois Perception* (Brighton: Harvester Press, 1982).
17. Ronald N. Stromberg, *European Intellectual History Since 1789*, 5th edition (Hoboken, NJ: Prentice Hall, 1990).
18. Thomas Pennant, *A Tour in Scotland 1769* (Chester: John Monk, 1771), 144.
19. B. Botfield, *Journal of a Tour Through the Highlands of Scotland During the Summer of MDCCCXXIX* (Edinburgh: Norton Hall, 1830), 174–5.
20. The theoretical and historical dimensions of Romanticism are discussed in, respectively, Meyer Howard Abrams, *The Mirror and the Lamp: Romantic Theory and the Critical Tradition* (London: Oxford University Press, 1953) and Carmen Casaliggi and Porscha Fermanis, *Romanticism: A Literary and Cultural History* (London: Routledge, 2016).

21. Andrew Hook, 'Scotland and Romanticism: The International Scene', in *The History of Scottish Literature, Vol. 2: 1660–1800*, ed. Andrew Hook (Aberdeen: Aberdeen University Press, 1987), 307–22.
22. See Malcolm Chapman, *The Gaelic Vision in Scottish Culture* (London: Croom Helm, 1978); Leah Leneman, 'A New Role for a Lost Cause: Lowland Romanticisation of the Jacobite Highlander', in *Perspectives in Scottish Social History: Essays in Honour of Rosalind Mitchison*, ed. Leah Leneman (Aberdeen: Aberdeen University Press, 1988), 107–24; Murray Pittock, *The Invention of Scotland: The Stuart Myth and the Scottish Identity, 1638 to the Present* (London: Routledge, 1991); Charles Withers, 'The Historical Creation of the Scottish Highlands', in *The Manufacture of Scottish History*, eds Ian Donnachie and Christopher Whatley (Edinburgh: Polygon, 1992), 143–56.
23. John Prebble, *The King's Jaunt: George IV in Scotland, 1822* (London: Collins, 1988), 18.
24. See McArthur, 'Scottish Culture'.
25. For more detail on the concept of 'symbolic appropriation', see Chapman, *The Gaelic Vision in Scottish Culture*.
26. Queen Victoria, *Our Life in the Highlands* (Newton Abbott: Victorian and Modern History Book Club, 1972), 112.
27. Ibid., 182.
28. Ibid., 149.
29. *Inverness Courier*, 22 April 1846 edition.
30. John Bodnar, *Remaking America: Public Memory, Commemoration and Patriotism in the Twentieth Century* (Princeton, NJ: Princeton University Press, 1992), 15.
31. *Inverness Courier*, 22 April 1846 edition.
32. *Inverness Courier*, 30 August 1849, 2.
33. Pittock, *The Invention of Scotland*.
34. See Chapman, *The Gaelic Vision in Scottish Culture*; Pittock, *The Invention of Scotland*.
35. James Stevens Curl, *The Victorian Celebration of Death* (Newton Abbott: David and Charles, 1972).
36. See Chapman, *The Gaelic Vision in Scottish Culture*; Peter J. Bowler, *The Invention of Progress: Victorians and the Past* (London: Blackwell, 1989).
37. Tom Nairn, *The Break-Up of Britain: Crisis and Neo-Nationalism* (London: New Left Books, 1977).
38. Stromberg, *European Intellectual History*.
39. H. J. Hanham, *Scottish Nationalism* (London: Faber & Faber, 1969).
40. The Fraser-Mackintosh Papers, a collection of mainly nineteenth-century family papers in the Inverness Public Library, contains a range of material relevant to the issues discussed in this essay, including the 1868 leaflet calling for donations to a Flora MacDonald memorial.
41. *The Sketch*, 22 April 1896 edition.

42. *Transactions of the Gaelic Society of Inverness*, 1922 edition, 64–5. These documents are suffused with the ideologies discussed in this essay, but clearly those entries around the annual Culloden commemoration are among the most significant.
43. See, for example, Roland Barthes, *Elements of Semiology*, trans. Annette Lavers and Colin Smith (London: Jonathan Cape, 1967); Roland Barthes, *Mythologies*, trans. Annette Lavers (London: Paladin, 1973).
44. *Transactions of the Gaelic Society of Inverness*, 1922 edition, 64–5.
45. Ken Johnson, 'Art and Memory', *Art in America*, no. 81 (November 1993), 90–9.
46. Eric Grant, 'The Sphinx in the North: Egyptian influences on landscape architecture and interior design in eighteenth- and nineteenth-century Scotland', in *The Iconography of Landscape: Essays on the Symbolic Representation, Design, and Use of Past Environments*, eds Denis E. Cosgrove and Stephen Daniels (Cambridge: Cambridge University Press, 1988), 236–53.
47. For more detail on Napier, see Murray Pittock, 'The Jacobite Cult', in *Scottish History: The Power of the Past*, eds Edward J. Cowan and Richard Findlay (Edinburgh: Edinburgh University Press, 2002), 191–208.
48. See Hanham, *Scottish Nationalism*.
49. Ibid., 154.
50. Pittock, *The Invention of Scotland*.
51. As noted earlier in this essay, the phrase is John Prebble's, a description of the kind of poetry written by Sir Walter Scott on the occasion of the 1822 visit by George IV to Edinburgh: Prebble, *The King's Jaunt*, 18.
52. The term, coined by Fernand Braudel (1902–85), means 'long time span' and characterises the approach to historiography represented by the journal *Annales d'histoire économique et sociale* which, rather than examining short-term events and their effect on populations, focussed on long-term demographic changes brought about by shifts in, for example, climate and geology. Its use in relation to sentimental Jacobitism is metaphoric since, from the point of view of the *Annales* School, this phenomenon is but the flicker of an eyelid.
53. Paul Fussell, *The Great War and Modern Memory* (Oxford: Oxford University Press, 1975).
54. L. Bayley, 'Public Monuments and the Great War' (MA diss., University of Northumbria, 1987), no page ref.
55. *Transactions of the Gaelic Society of Inverness*, 1925 edition.
56. Lewis, 'What is to be done?'
57. Anne Janowitz, *England's Ruins: Poetic Purpose and the National Landscape* (Oxford: Blackwell, 1990).
58. James E. Young, *The Texture of Memory: Holocaust Memorials and Meaning* (New Haven, CT: Yale University Press, 1993), 28.
59. Ibid., 30.
60. Ibid., 30.

61. When I wrote this piece in 1994, I had no idea that the issue of erasing monuments would return with such ferocity nearly thirty years later with statues and memorials being toppled like ninepins, from Bristol in the UK to Richmond, Virginia in the USA. The key differences between the two moments is the rise of identity politics (particularly the Black Lives Matter movement) and the increasing haplessness and spinelessness of public bodies in caving in to pressure from disparate vociferous groups, a consequence of their not understanding the nature of history and historiography. I am still of the view that memorials of any kind should never be erased. During the Cold War we saw as the very core of totalitarianism the Soviet regime's removal of the figure of Leon Trotsky (1879–1940) and others from official photographs. I am, however, in favour of the re-contextualisation of memorials as a recognition that history is never a closed book but a series of temporary ideological closures ever open to reassessment. The foregoing is an argument for the principle of not erasing memorials, but there is also a strong argument for the political pragmatism of not doing so. The great Chinese general Sun Tzu (544–496 BC), in his book *The Art of War* (*c*.500 BC), insisted on the wisdom of always leaving the enemy a bridge to retreat over. Translating this into the situation of contemporary Confederate nostalgists in the American South (and, for that matter, people of conservative views in the UK), where do they go, what action do they take when the tokens of their sense of identity are erased?
62. Samir al-Khalil, *The Monument: Art, Vulgarity and Responsibility in Iraq* (London: Andre Deutsch, 1991).

CHAPTER 23

Casablanca: Where Have All the Fascists Gone?*

When *Casablanca* (Michael Curtiz, 1942) was originally released, round about Christmas 1942, no one was in any doubt about its meaning. Warner Brothers, in a magazine advertisement late in 1942, explicitly linked the film to the Allied landings in North Africa on 11 November of that year and spoke of *Casablanca* as a 'symbol of the American way of living', that is, as a film committed to democracy. A film trade magazine of the time wrote that:

> *Casablanca* [. . .] opened Thanksgiving night under the sponsorship of France Forever and the Free French War Relief. Prior to the performance a Fighting French Delegation of Foreign Legionnaires, veterans of North African warfare, aviators recently returned from the battle fronts and leaders of the de Gaulle [1890–1970] movement paraded from the Free French Headquarters on Fifth Avenue to the theater: recruiting, souvenir and other booths were set up by the delegation.[1]

In 1942–43 it was impossible to view *Casablanca* as other than inseparably locked into the Second World War and the film's central meaning as other than the moral choice of the individual to be passive in the face of or actively resist fascism. In certain respects, the composite figure of Rick/Humphrey Bogart (1899–1957) became the emblematic anti-fascist hero of the time, initially reluctant to make a commitment but driven by human decency into an active stance against fascism. Indeed, this is the kind of role Bogart would also play in *Across the Pacific* (Vincent Sherman and John Huston, 1942), *Action in the North Atlantic* (Lloyd Bacon, 1943), *Passage to Marseille* (Michael Curtiz, 1944) and, perhaps most famously of all, *To Have and Have Not* (Howard Hawks, 1944).

In 1992, *Casablanca* was re-released. To mark its half-centenary, a special commemorative poster was issued with the figure of Rick/Bogart

---

* Originally published in *Random Access: Crisis and its Metaphors*, eds Pavel Büchler and Nikos Papastergiadis (London: Rivers Oram Press, 1995), 85–94.

at the centre of the composition as the forward point of a triangle which unites him with Ilse/Ingrid Bergman (1915–82) and Sam/Dooley Wilson (1886–1953), the black singer/piano player. The meaning is clear – *Casablanca* is a film about a love affair between Rick and Ilse, with Sam tying them together through the playing of 'As Time Goes By'. In the right lower foreground of the poster is a German military cap, the sole concession to the Second World War, and the key anti-fascist figure, Victor Laszlo/Paul Henried (1908–92), is nowhere to be seen. Over a period of fifty years politics has been evacuated from the film.

Figure 23.1 The design of this fiftieth-anniversary poster reflects the marginalisation of the Second World War in modern accounts of *Casablanca*.

How did this come about?

It is not that the film passed from memory over this period, but rather that the massive presence of quotations from, and references to, *Casablanca* in cinema and popular culture as a whole operated within strict parameters, oscillating between the ideas of cult, romance and nostalgia. This began quite soon after the original release of *Casablanca* with the appearance of the Marx Brothers movie *A Night in Casablanca* (Archie Mayo, 1946), which recognisably grows out of the earlier film and, in certain minor respects, explicitly refers to it. In particular, it retains the anti-fascist theme. *Casablanca* then seems to have vanished from cinematic consciousness for about a decade and to have resurfaced on the back of an emerging cult centred on Humphrey Bogart as an existential hero shorn of political affiliations. This is most evident, for example, in *À bout de souffle* (Jean-Luc Godard, 1960), in which the small-time crook played by Jean-Paul Belmondo (1933–2021) explicitly identifies with Bogart. Bosley Crowther (1905–81), writing about the Bogart cult in *Playboy* in 1966, dates its emergence to 1956, the year before Bogart's death, when the Brattle Theatre in Cambridge, Massachusetts ran *Beat the Devil* (John Huston, 1953) and got an unusually enthusiastic response from its mainly Harvard undergraduate audience.[2]

The screenwriter Howard Koch (1901–95) wrote in 1968 about his involvement with *Casablanca*:

> In recent years a sort of mystique has grown up among the younger generation around *Casablanca*, which probably has played more revival dates than any film and is now being prepared for the musical stage. Students tell me of 'Casablanca Clubs' in many colleges in which members are expected to attend a showing each time it is revived in their area. Some reported seeing it as many as fifteen times.[3]

Out of this, there emerged the film most obviously intertextual with *Casablanca*, *Play it Again, Sam* (Herbert Ross, 1972), written by and starring Woody Allen, with Allen, Diane Keaton and Tony Roberts in the Bogart, Bergman and Henreid roles. Concerned solely with romance and the sexual problems of the protagonists, Allen's 'homage' to *Casablanca* begins to evoke the other mode so central to the modern world – nostalgia. A piece in *Sight and Sound* in 1968 begins: 'No two ways about it, we say with comfortably complacent pessimism as we get up from an evening's television: they don't make pictures like that anymore. What we mean can be summed up in one word: *Casablanca*'.[4] However, it is a nostalgia prepared to repress politics.

From the mid-1970s the cultist and nostalgic references to *Casablanca* become delirious and omnipresent: '*Casablanca*, the aftershave that lingers on'; the British television comedy of Eric Morecambe (1926–84) and Ernie Wise (1925–99), Bobby Davro and Russ Abbott; a Eurovision Song Contest entry; the name and marketing campaigns of an Austrian brand of cigarettes; the advertising of Moroccan oranges, upmarket British newspapers and a German airline; and even a Teenage Mutant Ninja Turtles card. The title and lyrics of 'As Time Goes By' serve as the titles for books not remotely connected with the song, and function as sub-editors' headings in newspapers and magazines. The 'real' Casablanca in Morocco begins to be reconstructed to fit the tourist's image of the fictional Casablanca of the film, and the Hyatt Regency Hotel in Casablanca opens a Rick's Bar based on the décor of the bar in the film.

So dominant have the modes of cult and nostalgia become in discussions of *Casablanca* that, alongside the repression of the 'historical' dimension of anti-fascism so central to the film and its original historical moment, entry has also been forbidden to more recent political discourses. While the film's cult status and its intertextual ramifications became the subject of papers by Umberto Eco (1932–2016) and Thomas Sebeok (1920–2001), one might search the literature in vain for an analysis of *Casablanca*'s politics.[5] It is surprising that there have been no feminist readings of the film, given the extent to which Ilse would seem, prima facie, to be a pawn between Rick and Laszlo; it is curious that the substantial work, since the 1980s, on the representation of blacks in the cinema has not included an examination of the role of Sam in *Casablanca*, particularly since some of the film's dialogue is overtly racist; and, given the impact of Edward Said (1935–2003)'s work in recent years, it is striking that no analysis of the West's encounter with the Orient has been brought to bear on *Casablanca*.[6]

Re-readings of art works of the past are inevitable. As some of the more 'Frankensteinian' aspects of nationalism reassert themselves in Europe and in the rest of the world, we should perhaps remember that *Casablanca* meant something other than cult, romance and nostalgia to earlier generations. If today's audiences are wont to think of 'As Time Goes By' as the theme song of *Casablanca*, we can perhaps call to mind another of the film's several songs. Victor Laszlo, hearing the Nazi Major Strasser (Conrad Veidt) and his comrades singing 'Die Wacht am Rhein', strides over to the orchestra and orders it to play 'La Marseillaise' which, drowning out the Nazis' singing, evokes from the clientele of Rick's Bar the cry, 'Vive la France! Vive la démocratie!'

Notes

1. *Motion Picture Herald*, 28 November 1942, 58.
2. Bosley Crowther, 'The Career and the Cult', *Playboy* (June 1966), 110–11; 158; 160–2; 164–7.
3. Howard Koch, 'Notes on the Production of *Casablanca*', in *Persistence of Vision: A Collection of Film Criticism*, ed. Joseph McBride (Madison, WI: The Wisconsin Film Society Press, 1968), 93.
4. Arkadin, 'Film Clips', *Sight and Sound* 37, no. 4 (autumn 1968), 210.
5. Umberto Eco, '*Casablanca*: Cult Movies and Intertextual Collage', *SubStance* 14, no. 2 (1985), 3–12; Thomas A. Sebeok, *A Sign Is Just a Sign* (Bloomington: Indiana University Press, 1991).

6. It is perhaps best to follow the subsequent critical engagement with *Casablanca* by holding it up as a template against the major discourses relating to film and society which have continued or emerged in the four decades or so since this essay was written. A useful starting point is the special issue on *Casablanca* of the *Journal of Popular Film and Television* (27, no. 4 [2000]). Jack Nachbar's 'Nobody Ever Loved Me That Much: A *Casablanca* Bibliography' (42–5) reflects primarily the continuing interest in the biographies of the film's actors but also in the reminiscences of the 'behind the camera' personnel such as the director, Michael Curtiz (1886–1962) and (some of) the writers such as Julius Epstein (1909–2000) and Casey Robinson (1903–79); Kathy Merlock Jackson's 'Playing It Again and Again: *Casablanca*'s Impact on American Mass Media and Popular Culture' (33–41) – like my own *The* Casablanca *File* (London: Half Brick Images, 1992) – applies the theoretical concept of intertextuality to the film's presence in the culture; and Thomas Cripps's 'Sam the Piano Player: The Man Between' (16–23) reflects the increasing presence of race as an analytic category relating to film. Nachbar's other essay, 'Doing the Thinking for All of Us: *Casablanca* and the Home Front' (5–15), exemplifies the continuing interest in relating *Casablanca* (and film more generally) to the society which produced it and within which it is consumed. Beyond the special issue of the *Journal of Popular Film and Television*, the growing critical interest in narrative structure is reflected in the most widely read of the 'story-structure' books, Robert McKee's *Story: Substance, Structure, Style and the Principles of Screenwriting* (London: Methuen, 1998), within which *Casablanca* figures centrally. Gender and sexuality in *Casablanca* (from the point of view of feminist gaze theory) are addressed in Bennett Caplin, 'In the Eyes of the Beholder: Perspective in *Casablanca*' (2016), available at https://sites.williams.edu/engl117s16/author/bsc1/ [accessed 23 November 2022] and there is an extensive literature on queer readings of *Casablanca*, for example, Peter Kunze, 'Beautiful Friendship: Masculinity and Nationalism in *Casablanca*', *Studies in Popular Culture* 37, no. 1 (2014), 19–37.

CHAPTER 24

The Scottish Discursive Unconscious*

In 1953 a film was made in which a tough American executive comes to Scotland and is softened by his encounter with the land and the people to the extent that he sheds his suit, dons the garb of a fisherman and eventually sacrifices his property to save a beat-up old Clyde puffer boat. In 1983 a film was made in which a tough American executive comes to Scotland and is softened by his encounter with the land and the people to the extent that he sheds his suit, dons the garb of a fisherman and his company eventually abandons the plans it had to build an oil terminal in Scotland and instead creates an observatory and a marine life sanctuary.

The 1953 film is, of course, Alexander Mackendrick (1912–93)'s *The Maggie* and the 1983 film Bill Forsyth's *Local Hero*. Since Bill Forsyth had apparently not seen *The Maggie* before making his film, what, then, might be the explanation for the two films' similarity? Not the similarity of their respective plots, which is relatively unimportant, but the fact that they land on exactly the same ideological spot, equating Scotland and the Scots with Nature and suggesting that to encounter both is to be transformed from a materialistic into a spiritual being.

My argument is that when they came to make their films, both Mackendrick and Forsyth fell under the sway of the Scottish Discursive Unconscious, a mechanism which, potentially at least, comes into play when anyone seeks to represent Scotland and the Scots in any sign system: literature, easel painting, music, photography, advertising, journalism and, of course, film and television.

The Scottish Discursive Unconscious is a theoretical construct, invented to try to explain a phenomenon otherwise inexplicable, that is, why those seeking to tell stories about Scotland will often move into automatic pilot, so

---

*Originally published in *Scottish Popular Theatre and Entertainment*, eds Alasdair Cameron and Adrienne Scullion (Glasgow: Glasgow University Library Studies, 1996), 81–9.

to speak. The storytellers in question will have their hands guided unconsciously by one or other of several powerful, pre-existing narratives about Scotland which they may have internalised to the extent that those narratives have become 'natural' to their eyes. It has been suggested to me that a more appropriate term to describe this phenomenon might be 'Scottish Discursive Imaginary', since the word 'unconscious' suggests repression with discernible clinical symptoms in the patient. My reply is: 'Exactly!' Quite apart from the fact that the term 'unconscious' is graspable by a wide readership (the term 'imaginary' would require an unproductive detour into Lacanian psychoanalysis), its overtones of diseased misrecognition provide a perfect metaphor for the disabling effects the Scottish Discursive Unconscious has on Scottish life, its capacity to cause Scots (and those who make images and narratives of Scotland) to turn their faces away from the modern world and scratch the scabs of the Scottish past.

To try to understand the workings of the Scottish Discursive Unconscious is to peel away successive layers of discursive hegemony exercised on Scotland. Following this argument through with regard to cinema, Hollywood achieved an economic, and therefore discursive/cultural/ideological hegemony within Scotland in the decades before World War II, and a more general, post-WWII United States economic and political hegemony then saw American discursive/cultural/ideological hegemony further extended. Scots of my generation, coming of age in the early 1950s, experienced (and enjoyed) this hegemony perhaps even more than any generation before or since. Not only was the 1950s the moment of increasing American economic investment in Scotland, but the US political and military presence made itself increasingly felt and the US's cultural presence was completely hegemonic in movies, music, dress, hairstyles and so on. These contemporaneous phenomena were interpenetrated and fed off each other. This multifaceted hegemony meant that many of the major screen representations of Scotland and the Scots were from Hollywood, like the 1934 adaptation of J. M. Barrie (1860–1937)'s *The Little Minister* (Richard Wallace, 1934) through films like Laurel and Hardy's *Bonnie Scotland* (James W. Horne, 1935) to the apotheoses of Hollywood Scottishness, *Rob Roy: The Highland Rogue* (Harold French, 1953) and *Brigadoon* (Vincente Minnelli, 1954). But there was another tradition of representing Scotland and the Scots, that of the British Ealing Studios in such films as *Whisky Galore!* (Alexander Mackendrick, 1949), *The Maggie* and *Rockets Galore!* (Michael Relph, 1958). This is the tradition which connects with *Local Hero*. Although Bill Forsyth may not have seen *The Maggie*, it is said that producer David Puttnam's conception of *Local Hero* was that of a modern Ealing comedy.

Two things are worth noting about these apparently different traditions of representing Scotland and the Scots. Firstly, both construct Scotland as the natural 'Other' to materialistic modernism. This has been spelled out above with regard to the Ealing tradition of *The Maggie* and *Local Hero* but it is equally true of *Brigadoon*, which involves a New York advertising man on a visit to Scotland falling in love with a Scots faery woman and eventually joining her in the timeless Highland village of Brigadoon to live for eternity in a never-never land. The binary opposition Scotland = Nature / America = Culture is thematically apparent, but one of the reasons *Brigadoon* is more interesting than many other cinematic representations of Scotland is that this very theme, the tension between drab reality and artistic utopianism, is central to director Vincente Minnelli (1903–86)'s oeuvre as a whole, most notably in *The Bad and the Beautiful* (1952) and *On a Clear Day You Can See Forever* (1970). That centrality gives the theme's physical realisation in the *mise-en-scène* of *Brigadoon* great force and energy. For instance, there is a justifiably famous cut when the American, having taken a sad farewell of the faery woman in Scotland, is transported back to New York. The gentle emotions and music of the Scottish scene cuts to a vertiginous overhead view of New York's skyscrapers accompanied by sudden, blaring, cacophonous, modern brass music. The scene that follows, set in a crowded and noisy New York cocktail bar, has the American listening to his New York fiancée's chattering, which fades out from time to time to be replaced by the musical themes of the Scots village as he drifts into reverie.

The other element which joins the apparently diverse 'Scottish' discourses of Hollywood and Ealing is that they were both articulated outside of Scotland itself. But neither Hollywood nor Ealing invented the discourses within which they constructed Scotland and the Scots. They deployed already existing discourses. The key question is: Where and when did such discourses arise? This question is addressed in a brilliant but neglected book by Malcolm Chapman which will inform much that follows.[1] No class rises to hegemony without appropriate descriptions, explanations and justifications of itself as a class. A long process of ideological construction, spanning several centuries from the late medieval to the Renaissance periods, finally delivered classical bourgeois man. The process probably began in the philosophical and juridical discourses of the medieval Italian universities and its central category was 'the individual'. This extended process of ideological construction came to its fullness in Enlightenment Europe, producing an ideal social type who might be called *homo oeconomicus*. However, groups tend to define themselves dialectically by fashioning a monstrous Other who bears all the features they themselves do not have (and/or do not wish to acknowledge themselves as having). *Homo oeconomicus*, therefore, was in significant part created by fashioning an Other who might be called *homo celticus*. The dialectical nature of the process and its governing binary opposition can be shown thus:

Table 24.1 *Homo Oeconomicus/ Homo Celticus*

Homo Oeconomicus	Homo Celticus
Urban	Rural
Civilised	Uncivilised
Rational	Emotional
Individualist	Communitarian
Elegantly attired	Roughly garbed
Barbered	Hirsute
Cultured	Natural
Ambitious	Shiftless
Masculine (in gender and sensibility)	Feminine (in sensibility)

The list of oppositions is endless. The dynamic core societies of Europe, in the post-Renaissance period, created all kinds of monstrous Others in their encounters across the globe, a process described by (among others) Frantz Fanon (1925–61) and Edward Said (1935–2003).[2] Malcolm Chapman refers to this process as 'symbolic appropriation'[3] whereby the strong core societies took not only the material goods of those they encountered on their peripheries, but took hold of their identities as well. The truly chilling possibility is that *homo celticus*, denied discursive power over their own representation, a character in somebody else's story, will come to think and live within the terms proposed by *homo oeconomicus*. Something like this occurred, I believe, with regard to Scotland and was a major factor in producing the Scottish Discursive Unconscious. By the end of the nineteenth century, the discourse which constructed *homo celticus* in the above terms had become hegemonic across every available sign system: novels, ballets, operas, paintings, postcards, advertisements and, into the twentieth century, film and television.

About a decade ago, this framework of ideas was deployed in *Scotch Reels*, a book of essays that was an account of the discourses which had shaped cinematic and televisual representations of Scotland and the Scots.[4] Partly because of its polemical force, and partly because it was the only serious intervention in the field, *Scotch Reels* achieved the paradoxical status of being detested within certain filmic milieux in Scotland while becoming the orthodoxy in Scottish education by, for example, significantly affecting film and media studies syllabuses from secondary through to higher education.

Up until now there has been no serious debate about *Scotch Reels*'s central claims and categories, but that is changing. For example, David McCrone's 1992 book, *Understanding Scotland: The Sociology of a Stateless Nation* contained a chapter on Scottish cultural identity.[5] McCrone identifies what he describes as the dominant tradition of Scottish cultural analysis and criticises it for seeing Scottish culture as inherently tarnished and deformed by its peculiar history (the absence of a politicised nationalist intelligentsia, the emigration of intellectuals, and so on). Along with *Scotch Reels*, McCrone includes within this tradition Tom Nairn (1932–2023)'s *The Break-Up of Britain* (1977), Craig Beveridge and Ronald Turnbull's *The Eclipse of Scottish Culture: Inferiorism and the Intellectuals* (1989) and the journal *Cencrastus* (1979–2006).[6] McCrone challenges the view of certain works within this tradition that Scottish culture has been dominated by Tartanry and Kailyard, pointing to other scholarship which reveals other popular impulses at work.[7] He also makes the substantial point that discourses are never passively consumed; rather, they are negotiated, that is to say, people bend discourses to their own uses rather than simply swallowing them whole. McCrone's final indictment of what he sees as the dominant tradition of modern Scottish Cultural Studies is that it in effect poses Scottish culture as an essence rather than a process. But, McCrone argues, there is in fact no such thing as an essential culture in the modern world (if, indeed, there ever was): hybridity is the very condition of modernity. McCrone's position has a postmodernist thrust, in its implication that Scots (or any other) cultural identity can be lightly worn, can be conceived as a pick-and-mix identity involving any number of disparate traditions and impulses. There is undoubtedly much truth in this. It is impossible to conceive of cultural identity in the modern world without some measure of hybridity. That said, where I would part company with McCrone is in the extent to which he elides those unconscious elements that are work in the creation of cultural identity – specifically, I would contend, the Scottish Discursive Unconscious.

I have tried to indicate where the historical origins of the Scottish Discursive Unconscious might lie and its historic operation in relation to cinema. To have any substantial critical use, however, the concept must be applicable more generally to Scottish culture and to image-making (verbal as well as visual) relating to Scotland. To take but one illustrative example, John Prebble (1915–2001) has made a popular reputation as a historian of

Scotland. The following are quotations from two of his books, *Culloden* (1961) and *Glencoe* (1966) respectively:

> From the green saucer of Glenaladale dipping down to Loch Shiel, Alexander MacDonald had taken one hundred and fifty men to serve in Clanranald's regiment. Within a century there was nothing there but the lone shieling of the song.

> What the red soldiers began in February 1692, sheep finished one hundred and fifty years later, and the people of John of the Heather were gone from the Valley of the Dogs.[8]

These quotations exemplify what could be called the elegiac discourse of Scotland, Scottishness and the Scots, a multifaceted narrative two tropes of which are present here: the rolling of the names of people and places, mantra-like, off the tongue, and the closing on an image of silence, solitude and loss. That discourse's Scottish version (it doubtless exists in other cultures) probably has its origins in the European appropriation of James Macpherson (1736–96)'s *Ossian* poems (1761–63) and may even have seeped more directly into Lowland Scottish culture and the cultures of the Gaelic diaspora. The presence of the elegiac discourse, floridly rhetorical and fictive as it is, in Prebble's books is curious, for they are works of historiography, an ostensibly rational, indeed quasi-scientific discourse which deploys the sober procedures of consulting original sources and weighing evidence. The cultural historian Hayden White (1928–2018) has demonstrated that all historiography is cast within narrative structures, but the question remains why one particular such structure, the elegiac discourse, should loom so large in Prebble's work.[9]

The answer, surely, is that books such as *Culloden* and *Glencoe* are about Scottish history and that when anyone sets out to tell stories about Scotland, the Scottish Discursive Unconscious comes into play. Certain forms of narrative beckon, Circe-like, unconsciously guiding the writer's hand and setting the tone of their story. Polemically, it might be suggested that we tend to be written by the dominant Scottish narratives rather than ourselves writing narratives about Scotland. These dominant narratives, local realisations of the Scottish Discursive Unconscious, vary according to the time and place within Scotland when and where any given Scottish story is set. For example, the dominant (and equally atavistic) narrative about twentieth-century Lowland Scotland revolves round taciturn masculinity, drink, sport and explosive violence, a narrative that has its origins as much within reports on public health and housing and journalistic discourses of the nineteenth and twentieth centuries as within more obviously 'artistic' sites such as the novel. These impulses were exemplified most recently in the film *The Big Man* (David Leland, 1990), but they are also evident in the 1970s and 1980s television plays of Peter McDougall, whatever other admirable qualities those may have.[10] When the story is about Scottish Gaeldom, it instead spins into the orbit of the elegiac discourse as though fitted with a homing device. It can vitiate works of real quality like Bill Bryden (1942–2022)'s television film *Ill Fares the Land* (1983) about the 1930s end of the settlement on St Kilda and, predictably, it reared its malign head in Scottish press coverage of the Glencoe massacre's tercentenary in 1992, its tropes surfacing not only in the written copy but in the accompanying photographs and their captions. The elegiac discourse reached its most delirious in two pieces in *The Scotsman*, the first about a visit to the present-day village of Glencoe, the second describing the actual commemoration ceremony:

> This is Glencoe, the village at the foot of that most dramatic of glens, where the waters run down the precipitous black rock-faces like tears of pain and shame at what happened 300 years ago.
>
> The chill of highland rain numbs the flesh. The chill of highland history numbs the heart. The tears on the cheek could be the work of either.[11]

The history of how this discourse came to dominate accounts of the Gàidhealtachd is traced by Malcolm Chapman, who writes: 'it is often difficult to avoid the impression that many Scottish intellectuals are glad the 'Forty-five happened, however sordid and disastrous the consequences'.[12] The same might be said of the Glencoe event of 1692. The discourse surrounding the tercentenary is reminiscent of the Russian short story about the countess who, in a warm box in the theatre, weeps copious tears over a melodrama while her coachman, waiting for her in the street, freezes to death. The elegiac discourse is about national self-dramatisation and emotional indulgence. If, as I have suggested, it largely erupts from the Scottish Discursive Unconscious, it is a severe hindrance to the production of forms of Scottish art and public discourse relevant to the late twentieth century.

The discussion above of the elegiac discourse began with the works of John Prebble, who is English-Canadian. It is clear, therefore, that the Scottish Discursive Unconscious is not confined solely to Scots but is liable to affect anyone setting out to tell stories about or make images of Scotland. Two more examples relating to Glencoe indicate the weed-like efflorescence of the phenomenon, the first from Bertrand Russell (1872–1970)'s *Autobiography* (1951–69) and the second from Alistair MacLean (1922–87)'s novel, *When Eight Bells Toll* (1967):

> We drove home to St Fillans through the gloomy valley of Glencoe, as dark and dreadful as if the massacre had just taken place.[13]

> Many places have evil reputations. Few, at first seeing, live up to those reputations. But there are a few. In Scotland, the Pass of Glencoe, the scene of the infamous massacre, is one of them.[14]

I earlier suggested that there is a dominant historical narrative about Lowland Scotland, particularly Glasgow, which stresses its darkness, poverty, drunkenness, sectarianism and male violence. The historical construction of this narrative can also be tracked. Accounts of Glasgow in the eighteenth century in fact stressed the quality of the city's air and ambience and the other urban settlement it was most often compared with was Oxford. Clearly, the area which was to become the Glasgow conurbation altered radically under the onslaught of industrialisation and, by the end of the nineteenth century, the city was being constructed in discourse as a very different place from that of a century earlier. The new narrative might be called 'Glasgow as City of Dreadful Night' and the stages of its articulation would include: nineteenth-century public and charity reports on health and housing; Thomas Annan (1829–87)'s photographs of Glasgow slums; twentieth-century inter-war journalistic accounts of gang warfare in Glasgow; through to novels like H. Kingsley Long (1890–n.d.) and Alexander McArthur (1901–47)'s *No Mean City* (1935). There is a tendency to separate off popular art and discourse such as tabloid journalism from High Art. For example, the poetry of Hugh MacDiarmid (1892–1978) tends to be viewed as the original, untrammelled vision of the artist in tension with certain traditional Scottish and international modernist literary forms, and not as a form of social discourse connected with his ordinary fellow countrymen and women. However, suppose the template of the burgeoning discourse of Glasgow as City of Dreadful Night is put over, say, MacDiarmid's acerbically despairing 1962 poem 'Glasgow', which laments that 'stupidity' is the only thing that truly lives within the city: it might be that MacDiarmid, when he came to write this poem, was 'spoken through' as well as speaking, was in effect as much under the thrall of the Scottish Discursive Unconscious as his humbler fellow Scots.

If there is such a thing as the Scottish Discursive Unconscious this has several implications, not least for art production in Scotland. If conscious attempts to remould cultural identities are constantly menaced by the Scottish Discursive Unconscious's iceberg-like lurking under so much discourse relating to Scotland, then Scottish artists and critics have a deal of work to do in exposing its workings. Looked at from this point of view, the work of certain artists whose work foregrounds the moods and icons of the Scottish Discursive Unconscious assumes added importance – artists such as filmmaker Murray Grigor and photographer Calum Colvin. The process of bringing the operations of the Scottish Discursive Unconscious to light should be seen as the 'talking cure' which will clear the ground for the creation and dissemination of conscious discursive strategies relevant to the modern world.[15]

Notes

1. Malcolm Chapman, *The Gaelic Vision in Scottish Culture* (London: Croom Helm, 1978).
2. See, for example, Frantz Fanon, *Black Skin, White Masks* (New York: Grove Press, 1968); Edward Said, *Orientalism* (London: Routledge & Kegan Paul, 1978); Edward Said, *Culture and Imperialism* (London: Chatto & Windus, 1993).
3. Chapman, *The Gaelic Vision in Scottish Culture*, 28.
4. Colin McArthur, ed., *Scotch Reels: Scotland in Cinema and Television* (London: British Film Institute, 1982).
5. David McCrone, *Understanding Scotland: The Sociology of a Stateless Nation* (London: Routledge, 1992).
6. Tom Nairn, *The Break-Up of Britain: Crisis and Neo-Nationalism* (London: New Left Books, 1977); Craig Beveridge and Ronald Turnbull, *The Eclipse of Scottish Culture: Inferiorism and the Intellectuals* (Edinburgh: Polygon, 1989).
7. See, for example, William Donaldson, *Popular Literature in Victorian Scotland: Language, Fiction and the Press* (Aberdeen: Aberdeen University Press, 1986).
8. John Prebble, *Culloden* (London: Penguin, 1967), 315; Prebble, *Glencoe* (London: Penguin, 1968), 262–3.
9. Hayden White, *Metahistory: The Historical Imagination in Nineteenth-Century Europe* (Baltimore, MD: Johns Hopkins University Press, 1975); Hayden White, *Tropics of Discourse: Essays in Cultural Criticism* (Baltimore, MD: Johns Hopkins University Press, 1978).
10. For a discussion of some of McDougall's work, see Jonathan Murray, 'Scotch Missed: *Play for Today* and Scotland', *Journal of British Cinema and Television* 19, no. 2 (2022), 194–216.
11. Brian Pendreigh, 'Myth and mystique in a cruel glen', *The Scotsman*, 13 February 1992, 15; Brian Pendreigh, 'Rain joins tears for victims of outrage', *The Scotsman*, 14 February 1992, 3.
12. Chapman, *The Gaelic Vision in Scottish Culture*, 21.
13. Bertrand Russell, *Autobiography* (London: Routledge, 1998), 561.
14. Alistair MacLean, *When Eight Bells Toll* (London: Harper Collins, 2020), 130.
15. This paper was originally delivered as a contribution to a Scottish Popular Theatre and Entertainment event at the University of Glasgow. I was, at the time, preparing a reply to David McCrone's 1992 book, *Understanding Scotland: The Sociology of a Stateless Nation* for the journal *Scottish Affairs*, so some of the material (particularly relating to Glencoe and the elegiac discourse) overlaps between one piece and the other.

CHAPTER 25

Chinese Boxes and Russian Dolls: Tracking the Elusive Cinematic City*

Alasdair Gray (1934–2019)'s 1981 novel, *Lanark* contains the following much-quoted passage:

> 'Glasgow is a magnificent city', said Thaw [. . .] 'Think of Florence, Paris, London, New York. Nobody visiting them for the first time is a stranger, because he's already visited them in paintings, novels, history books and films. But if a city hasn't been used by an artist not even the inhabitants live there imaginatively.'[1]

Thaw is both right and wrong. He is right to emphasise art as a key domain within which sense of place is articulated, but wrong to limit this process solely to artists. Gray implicitly recognises this by including history books in Thaw's list, but this is undermined once more by his insisting that the artist is the sole operational figure in the process. The key missing concept is, of course, discourse, a concept which, as well as including works of art, would also encompass more obviously 'factual' productions such as official reports, newspaper accounts, photographs, anecdotes and jokes.[2] This is not to argue that there are no pertinent differences between works of art and these other sites, but simply that they might all be considered under the rubric of discourse. From this point of view, and as Thaw puts it, Glasgow has a substantial discursive presence which has been influential in determining popular attitudes to that city and shaping subsequent narratives about it.

It is perhaps surprising that in eighteenth-century travellers' accounts Glasgow is most often compared with Oxford for the beauty of its prospect and the excellence of its ambience. It was post-Industrial Revolution accounts of the city that began to articulate the 'Glasgow discourse' which was to become hegemonic. Initially signalled in urban planning and public

---

*Originally published in *The Cinematic City*, ed. David B. Clarke (London: Routledge, 1997), 19–45.

health reports of the nineteenth century, this discourse was powerfully accelerated by tabloid journalistic accounts of gang warfare in interwar Glasgow and by folkloric embellishments of these. The result was (and, arguably, still is) that a monstrous Ur-Narrative comes into play when anyone (not least, it should be said, Glaswegians themselves) seeks to describe or deal imaginatively with that city. In this archetypal narrative, Glasgow is the City of Dreadful Night with the worst slums in Europe, its citizens living out lives which are nasty, brutish and short. The milieu of Glasgow is so stark, so the narrative runs, that it breeds a particular social type, the Hard Man, a figure whose universe is bounded by football, heavy drinking and (often sectarian) violence. This image of Glasgow, which beckons, Circe-like, to any who would speak or write of that city, is one of men celebrating, coming to terms with or (rarely) transcending their bleak milieu. An order of marginalisation, if not exclusion, is served on women. Mothers or lovers of the hard-eyed men who stalk this world, they are allowed no space to articulate their own sense of what it means to be a woman in Glasgow. So all-embracing is this narrative that it can provide the underlying *langue* for the jocular act of *parole* in which a male Glaswegian announces in Edinburgh (the Athens of the North) that he himself is from 'the Sparta of the North'. One wonders how active the narrative was in producing the (perhaps apocryphal) medical statistic that the unhealthiest man in Britain is likely to be a middle-aged, bachelor barman who smokes and lives in Glasgow.

Like many hegemonies, however, the hegemonic Glasgow narrative is fragile and contested. Other narratives about Glasgow circulate: Glasgow as the centre of 'the Red Clyde', the region where communist revolution in the British and Irish Islands was thought most likely; Glasgow as the warm, open-hearted city that welcomes all comers (the implicit contrast here is with cold, thin-lipped Edinburgh); and the most recent arrival: Glasgow as City of Culture. This latter narrative is distinguished from the earlier ones by the substantial presence of public relations consultants within its making, initially under the early-1980s rubric 'Glasgow's Miles Better', a marketing slogan which implicitly refers to the hegemonic discourse that it seeks to supersede: Glasgow as City of Dreadful Night.[3]

What the example of Glasgow indicates is that cities (and, indeed, all urban spaces and even 'natural' landscapes) are always already immersed in narrative: constantly moving social and ideological chess pieces in the game of defining and redefining utopias and dystopias. It should come as no surprise, therefore, that cities in discourse have no absolute and fixed meaning, but only a succession of temporary, positional ones. As the opposition Edinburgh/Athens – Glasgow/Sparta shows, to cite one half of the dualism is to invoke the other, even if the other is not explicitly mentioned. The high ideological valency of the discursive city and its volatility of meaning has meant that it has been diversely mobilised within the great transitions of history: the rural to the urban; the agrarian to the industrial; and, most significantly of all, the feudal to the capitalist.[4] This lack of fixedness of meaning cannot be overstressed. Within those great historical oppositions which shaped the modern world a whole range of spaces can be identified: wildernesses; pastoral landscapes; agrarian landscapes; villages; rural towns; suburbs; inner cities; metropolises. Several diverse binary oppositions from among this list may be deployed to signify the discursive positions characteristically taken within the great historical debates. Thus, in one version, the wilderness may be set against all urban spaces as a sign of moral worth, while in another version the small town might be valorised at the expense of the inner city. In considering the question of cities in films, one therefore has to be alert to such changing valencies and to the possibility that while in certain film texts a structural opposition to the city may be present, in other texts such an opposition may be only implicit or even wholly absent.

It has been suggested that in American silent cinema, roughly pre-1930, cities were used as random backdrops for action, the implication being that the city milieu in these films carried little or no ideological charge and that the films said nothing in particular about cities.[5] This argument is perhaps tenable if applied only to such films as Keystone Cops and Harold Lloyd (1893–1971) comedies, but alongside such works were other films in which contemporaneous debates around the transition to modernity, and the place of the city within these, resonated profoundly. Such debates could not have been more starkly stated, for example, than in the opening of *Lights of New York* (Bryan Foy, 1928). The first shot of a rural townscape is accompanied by the intertitle 'Main Street. Forty-five minutes from Broadway – but a thousand miles away'; a later shot of the city carries the intertitle 'Broadway. Forty-five minutes from Main Street – but a *million* miles away'. This stark opposition is played out dramatically in the film. The country/city opposition, with the former figured as Arcadia and the latter as Sodom, furnishes the key structural opposition in *Sunrise: A Song of Two Humans* (F. W. Murnau, 1927). That film's plot is very basic: a woman from the city comes to the country and destabilises the marriage of a country couple. The master opposition of country/city is so deeply woven into *Sunrise*'s fabric that a whole series of sub-oppositions can be laid out which contrast the figure of the city girl with that of the country girl:

Table 25.1 City Girl/Country Girl

City Girl	Country Girl
Dark, short hair	Long, blonde hair
Short dress	Long dress
Smoking	Non-smoking
Makeup	No makeup
Unmarried	Married
Undomesticated	Domesticated
Erotic	Chaste

So deeply grounded in American culture is the country/city opposition that it surfaces in the least expected places. For instance, in *The Barkleys of Broadway* (Charles Walters, 1949), the central players, Fred Astaire (1899–1987) and Ginger Rogers (1911–95), decked out in sports clothes, disembark enthusiastically from a train for a weekend in the country. However, they have dragged along their unwilling friend, Oscar Levant (1906–72) – in life and art a quintessentially urban neurotic – still dressed in his city clothes. As Levant is frogmarched along a country lane by Astaire and Rogers, the three of them launch into 'A Weekend in the Country', a call-and-response song which starkly states and restates the country/city opposition. Astaire and Rogers sing the praises of the country, and Levant those of the city:

> Astaire: With golf and tennis round you and no cares to hound you.
> Rogers: When Mother Nature beckons, who can decline?
> Levant: Till Mother Nature vetoes the bees and mosquitoes, Mother Nature is no mother of mine.
> Astaire and Rogers: From Saturday night to Monday morn there's always joy ahead.
> Levant: From Saturday night to Monday morn I wish that I was dead.
> Astaire and Rogers: A weekend in the country will never let you down.
> Levant: You'll pardon my effont'ry, but I'd rather spend it in town.

In *Sunrise*'s narrative the country/city opposition is played out largely in the country, with one brief visit to the city. In that of *Mr. Deeds Goes to Town* (Frank Capra, 1936), however, the same opposition is played out in the city. The film's titular central character, a simple, down-to-earth resident of a small town in rural Vermont, inherits $20 million and is precipitated into a millionaire's city life. When he attempts to give the money away, in the form of agricultural smallholdings, to Depression-hit American working men, the slick city lawyers administering his inheritance attempt to have him declared insane. As Sam Rohdie (1939–2015) has pointed out, this simple plot situation allows a whole series of oppositions to be set up.[6]

Figure 25.1 City versus Country in *The Barkleys of Broadway*. Fred Astaire and Ginger Rogers drag Oscar Levant for a weekend in the country.

To illustrate the shifting valencies of the spatial categories referred to above, the master opposition in *Mr. Deeds Goes to Town* is not, as in *Sunrise*, that of country versus city, but rather, small town versus metropolis. Like those shifting master antinomies, the sub-oppositions too begin to shift and turn in the course of the film, as in the slick lawyers' version of insanity being undermined by the film's version:

Table 25.2 Metropolis/Small Town

Metropolis	Small Town
Words	Deeds
Hypocrisy	Honesty
Cash relations	Human relations
Opera	Brass band
High art	Popular art
Individual	Community
Culture	Nature
Wit	Fun
Excess	Modesty
Sane (mad)	Mad (sane)

It was not accidental that the interwar period in America should throw up films such as *Sunrise* and *Mr. Deeds Goes to Town*. They represent America talking to itself about the great national transition to modernity which, like everything else in that society, was severely telescoped. If Oscar Wilde (1854–1900)'s observation that the United States was the only society to have passed from barbarism to decadence without the intervening stage of civilisation overstates the case, the following statistics indicate the rapidity of the transition:

> In 1810 over 90 per cent of the US population was classified as rural, many were self-sufficient farmers. Even as late as 1880 the farm population was 44 per cent of the total population. One hundred years later this figure had dropped to under 3 per cent.[7]

It was in the interwar period, however, that the United States could truly be said to have become an urban society in terms of demography and organised political power. Rural America, as expressed in Prohibition, Christian fundamentalism and nativist organisations such as the Ku Klux Klan, went down fighting tooth and nail, licking its wounds until the later moment, during the 1980s and beyond, when it would reconstitute its alliances and once more attempt to remake America in its own image. That the so-called moral majority was able to do this with some degree of success during that period may be partly explained by the survival and enhancement within American life of anti-urban, pro-small town/agrarian/pastoral/wilderness ideologies, even (or perhaps, especially) among city dwellers.

The valorisation of the small town and its values is a consistent theme in the films of Frank Capra (1897–1991), the director of *Mr. Deeds Goes to Town*, even if, as in *It's a Wonderful Life* (1946), Capra's defence sometimes has to invoke desperate fantasies. A similar celebration of the small town is at work in the Andy Hardy film cycle of the mid-1930s to mid-1950s and in other films of the period, such as *Meet Me in St. Louis* (Vincente Minnelli, 1944). As has already been stressed above, all discursive spaces have volatile valencies: the same space can be (and often is) deployed to signify quite incompatible ideological positions. Thus, the small town in Hollywood cinema, as well as signifying all that is supposedly good in America, has also been made to stand as an icon of bigotry, small-mindedness and explosive violence, as in *Fury* (Fritz Lang, 1936), *Intruder in the Dust* (Clarence Brown, 1949), *Bad Day at Black Rock* (John Sturges, 1955), *Easy Rider* (Dennis Hopper, 1969) and, deliriously, *Blue Velvet* (David Lynch, 1986).[8] In fact, those two traditions of representation continue to exist side by side: despite (or perhaps because of) increasing demographic evidence of the growth of cities, the small town continues to function in American cinema as a balm to hurt minds and bodies.

This is strikingly so, for example, in the film *Sleeping with the Enemy* (Joseph Rubin, 1991). As is so often the case, the small town here operates as the binary antinomy not of the city itself but, more precisely, of 'city values'. The lead character, physically and emotionally abused by her Wall St commodities broker husband, fakes her own drowning and moves from their chilly, modernist Cape Cod house to a small Midwest town where she forms a relationship with a drama teacher. Interestingly, the bleak Cape Cod beaches are, along with the abusive husband's New York skyscraper office, the structural opposite of the warm, homely Midwest town. In other discourses, of course, the sea coast could instead be made to signify positive qualities in opposition to the city, as in *Local Hero* (Bill Forsyth, 1983). As with *Sunrise* and *Mr. Deeds Goes to Town*, the master antinomy of city–Cape Cod versus Midwest small town is supported by innumerable sub-antinomies as follows:

Table 25.3   City–Cape Cod/Midwest Town

City–Cape Cod	Midwest Town
Concrete/Steel/Glass	Wood
Commodities broker	Humanities teacher
Haute cuisine	Apple pie
Haute couture	Laura Ashley dress
Sand	Garden
Hector Berlioz	Van Morrison
Moustache	Beard
Suit	Jeans

When the lead character first arrives by bus in the Midwest town, her face shows palpable joy as, from her viewpoint, the camera picks up the townspeople going about their everyday activities. The entry of individual characters to a new milieu – in *Sleeping with the Enemy*'s case, from (putative) city to small town, but in other films often a rural figure entering a city – is frequently when oppositional ideologies are most sharply posed, as, for example, in the entry of Clint Eastwood's western sheriff to New York in *Coogan's Bluff* (Don Siegel, 1968), Jon Voight's cowboy hustler entering the same city in *Midnight Cowboy* (John Schlesinger, 1969) and Kirk Douglas (1916–2020)'s wandering cowboy entering Duke City in *Lonely Are the Brave* (David Miller, 1962). There is a similar entrance to

New York, this time by ferry across the Hudson River, in a much earlier Hollywood film about the city and modernity, *The Crowd* (King Vidor, 1928). In fact, *The Crowd* sends out conflicting signals about the city. On the central protagonist's entry to the city, a montage of urban scenes – milling crowds, bumper-to-bumper automobiles and aerial views of houses packed together – culminates in a series of vertiginous shots up the face of skyscrapers and into a massive open-plan insurance office where hundreds of workers, including the central protagonist (with his own assigned number), sit in serried ranks of identical desks. Alongside this powerful visual statement of the city's impersonality, however, the urban milieu is also represented as a site of romance, excitement and enjoyment, as in scenes depicting a ride through the New York streets in an open-top bus and a visit to Coney Island. Though there are repeated intertitle references to 'the crowd' (the film is silent), the work does not sustain the Expressionist visual style of its introduction to the city. Moreover, various scenes set away from the city – the opening sequence set in a small town, a honeymoon at Niagara Falls, and a seaside family picnic – are not constructed as ideological opposites to the city, as is the case in *Sunrise*. Niagara Falls, for example, functions within *The Crowd* as an image of sexual passion, as it was to do later, more feverishly, in *Niagara* (Henry Hathaway, 1953). The driving ideology of *The Crowd* is that of American popular novelist Horatio Alger (1832–99): making it and getting a lucky break.

Coincidentally, two figures associated with the Hollywood representations of the city discussed immediately above – the actor Gary Cooper (1901–61) from *Mr. Deeds Goes to Town* and the director King Vidor (1894–1982) from *The Crowd* – came together in 1949 to make a film which cannot be ignored in any discussion of the cinematic city: *The Fountainhead*. Adapted by Ayn Rand (1905–82) from her own 1943 novel of the same name, *The Fountainhead* is about the struggles of an architect (based, it is said, on Frank Lloyd Wright [1867–1959]) to have his work accepted in the teeth of philistine opposition. Locatable in a cycle of anti-communist films which Hollywood produced in the late 1940s and early 1950s, *The Fountainhead* is a product of the wilder shores of the American Right. Although it fitted perfectly into the hysteria and paranoia of the Cold War, the novel itself had been drafted in the late 1930s when its particular target had been F. D. Roosevelt (1882–1945)'s New Deal (1933–39). *The Fountainhead*'s cinematically breathtaking, but ultimately demented, melange of anti-intellectualism, anti-collectivism, sadomasochism, barely repressed homoeroticism, architectural gigantism and pathological individualism makes the description 'crypto-fascist' not unreasonable, if the phrase is understood as indicating a psychological disposition rather than an organised political movement. The image of the city offered in this *triomphe de la ville* is of a series of towering, Le Corbusier-ian skyscrapers produced as an act of will by their creator and existing in no relationship whatever with the society around them. *The Fountainhead* demonstrates that, as with the Italian Futurist art movement, modernism is as easily mobilised by the political Right as by the Left. The reference to Italian Futurism here is not entirely fortuitous. Although certain of *The Fountainhead*'s images fleetingly suggest the films of Leni Riefenstahl (1902– 2003), the image at the end of the film of Cooper's architect character, clad in black, hands on hips and legs apart, standing atop the highest skyscraper in New York (which, of course, he has built), is particularly evocative of the fascist *squadrista* as represented in interwar Italian graphics, including some works by Futurists.

However, *The Fountainhead* is also aesthetically and politically explicable within the trajectory of American modernism. One of the New Deal's central maxims, 'Getting America back to work', extended into the area of art production. The particular mechanism that put American artists back to work was the Works Progress Administration (1935–43) which, by 1936, was employing over 6,000 artists, each drawing $28.32 a week for producing work commissioned by the government. The particularly favoured form of such work was mural paintings in post offices and other public buildings. Often the murals depicted significant episodes in local or national history and were executed in a broadly realist (and, therefore, implicitly anti-modernist) style. It was quite logical, therefore, for Ayn Rand, in attacking New Deal-ism, also to attack its 'official' aesthetic and to valorise its opposite, High Modernism. Moreover, Rand's endorsement of modernism from the extreme Right was supported by contemporaneous changes in the American art world that took their impulse from quite another political quarter. Throughout the 1940s an important turn towards High Modernism was taking place within American art. Indeed, it has been said that at this time the centre of gravity of global modern art moved from Paris to New York.[9] This was to come to full flowering, at the level of art practice, in the 1950s Abstract Expressionist movement in which the central figures were Jackson Pollock (1912–56), Willem de Kooning (1904–97) and Mark Rothko (1903–70). That movement's ideological underpinning was provided principally by two critics, Clement Greenberg (1909–1994) and Harold Rosenberg (1906–78). Greenberg, in particular, had been active on the Left in the 1930s but seems to have become disillusioned after events such as the Moscow treason trials (1936–38). It would seem that, in the field of American art, anti-Stalinism mutated into Trotskyism and then into 'art for art's sake'. Although figures such as Greenberg and Rosenberg retained something of the rhetoric of the 1930s Left, their writings increasingly stressed that the act of artistic creation was for its own sake and that of its creator, sentiments recurrently voiced by Howard Roark, the architect character in *The Fountainhead*. Thus it was that, through a complex set of over-determinations, art production in late-1940s America became prised away from social meaning and defined primarily as self-expression. As such, art became open to mobilisation within American Cold War rhetoric, a process that achieved its most unhinged statement in *The Fountainhead*. However, it has been pointed out that there is a profound contradiction at the heart of *The Fountainhead* both as novel and as film.[10] Despite trumpeting the virtues of High Modernism and sneering at the art of the past, *The Fountainhead*, in both its literary and cinematic forms, displays all the features of the classic narrative structure of the Victorian novel.

Such was the overwhelming psychological effect of modernity, and within it the oppressiveness of the city, that even filmmakers relatively unconcerned with the milieux in which their films were set were affected by it. For example, Alfred Hitchcock (1899–1980) offers, in the opening sequences of *Shadow of a Doubt* (1943), an intriguing glimpse of what might have been had he become self-consciously preoccupied with the transition to modernity rather than simply living within it. Very much like the celebrated opening of his *Psycho* (1960), *Shadow of a Doubt* begins with a series of increasingly narrowing cityscapes until the film enters the room of its central protagonist, Uncle Charlie (Joseph Cotton). The rundown nature of Hitchcock's city – foreshadowing the image of the city as urban wasteland so central to the American cinema of the 1980s and 1990s – is rendered even more strange by the oblique angle of some of the camera set-ups; the strange music on the soundtrack, including an off-key version of the *Merry Widow* waltz; and by the fact that the police are closing in on Uncle Charlie, a modern Bluebeard who disposes of rich widows. The bleak cityscape is immediately succeeded by the place to which Uncle Charlie goes to lie low for a while. Santa Rosa, California is the archetypal American small town with, instead of detectives closing in for the kill, a genial middle-aged traffic cop and, instead of the sinister, off-key strains of Franz Lehár (1870–1948), the kind of soundtrack music that signifies normal, placid, small-town America. In some respects the introduction to Santa Rosa in *Shadow of a Doubt* foreshadows the central character's entry to the Midwest town in *Sleeping with the Enemy*. However, having set up the city/small town opposition, Hitchcock does not follow it through. Instead, he moves swiftly to his own recurrent obsessions: the transference of identity and the transference of guilt that goes with the secret knowledge of murder having been committed.

Turning to other mid-century cinematic genres, film critics are generally agreed that the gangster film and its generic affiliates such as the film noir and the *film policier* occupy a special place in the representation of the city. This insight is, for example, at the core of the first serious critical account of the gangster genre:

> The gangster is the man of the city, with the city's language and knowledge, with its queer and dishonest skills and its terrible daring, carrying his life in his hands like a placard, like a club [. . .] for the gangster there is only the city; he must inhabit it in order to personify it: not the real city, but the dangerous and sad city of the imagination which is so much more important, which is the modern world.[11]

Robert Sklar (1936–2011) subsequently widened that argument beyond the gangster film and its generic affiliates to suggest that the cinema was the structure-in-dominance among the various sociocultural and ideological determinations which produced a particular American social type, the City Boy:

> The City Boy was a product of performance, genre and ideology transmuted into popular entertainment. He did not so much mirror social life, if contemporary observers are to be believed, as create a model for life to imitate him. Arising from the teeming ethnic polyglot of the modern industrial city, especially New York, he began playing a central social role with the more or less simultaneous occurrence, in the late 1920s, of talking pictures and the Great Depression. His rise to prominence alongside the cowboy as a major figure in the representation of American manhood seemed to suggest important changes in concepts of male behavior – of individualism in relation to social constraint, of sexuality, romance and family life.[12]

It is no accident that the particular 'City Boys' whom Sklar discusses, James Cagney (1899–1986), Humphrey Bogart (1899–1957) and John Garfield (1913–52), were key players in the gangster film and its generic affiliates. Although the gangster film's antecedents have been traced to times well before 1930, it was in that year that the film appeared which is generally conceded to be the first fully recognisable gangster film: *Little Caesar* (Mervyn LeRoy, 1931).[13] Making explicit what was to remain implicit in most other gangster films, *Little Caesar* dramatises the tension between the old, agrarian European societies from which the gangsters sprang and the heartless, wide-open world of the American city in which they make their way. This tension is particularly acutely embodied in the figure of one gang member. Seduced on the one hand by the money and easy life of the city but drawn, on the other, to his Italian-speaking mother, home and church, this figure, in a scene which was to become archetypal of the genre, is shot dead in the street from a moving car as he mounts the steps of the church to confess his involvement with crime.

As many critics have pointed out, so central is the city as a presence within the gangster film, the film noir and the *film policier* that it and its milieux very often figure in the titles of such films: *Big City Blues* (Mervyn LeRoy, 1932); *Scarlet Street* (Fritz Lang, 1945); *The Street with No Name* (William Keighley, 1948); *Cry of the City* (Robert Siodmak, 1948); *The Naked City* (Jules Dassin, 1948); *City Across the River* (Maxwell Shane, 1949); *Dark City* (William Dieterle, 1950); *Night and the City* (Jules Dassin, 1950); *Where the Sidewalk Ends* (Otto Preminger, 1950); *The Asphalt Jungle* (John Huston, 1950); *Down Three Dark Streets* (Arnold Laven, 1954); *The Naked Street* (Maxwell Shane, 1955); *While the City Sleeps* (Fritz Lang, 1956); and so on.[14] Aside from a sub-genre of films about (often) Midwestern, Depression-era criminals, from *High Sierra* (Raoul Walsh, 1941) to *Bonnie and Clyde* (Arthur Penn, 1967), the action of the gangster film is played out within a circumscribed set of urban milieux: dark streets; dingy rooming houses and office blocks; bars and nightclubs; precinct stations; and luxury penthouses. As mentioned above, a recurrent motif of the genre is the gangster being shot down in the street or, memorably in *Underworld U.S.A.* (Samuel Fuller, 1961), being shot elsewhere and crawling into an alley to die.

To discuss the gangster film in detail and at length is, perhaps, to exemplify one of postmodernism's most self-congratulatory features, namely, the evaporation of the traditional distinction between High and Mass Art.[15] Clearly, this has had a beneficial effect to the extent that any act of discourse production, no matter how 'lowly', is grist to the mill of serious analysis. However, there are two less useful outcomes associated with the same feature: firstly, a refusal to recognise as pertinent the substantial rhetorical differences between High Art and Mass Art and, secondly, a purblind ignorance regarding the extent to which those two areas have been historically interpenetrated, not least in Hollywood cinema. For example, one of the great Modernist (and therefore High Art) responses to the city was Paul Citroën (1896–1983)'s photomontage *Metropolis* (1923). Citroën's work conveys a vertiginous sense of 'cityness', capturing both the sense of the city's oppressiveness and its breathtaking excitement as felt by at least part of the population of Weimar Germany. While it is often remembered that an analogous form of cinematic montage was practised and extensively theorised in the Soviet Union during the 1920s, it is usually overlooked that, from the 1930s, Hollywood cinema practised its own form of montage. Equally overlooked are the facts that this Hollywood form was doubtlessly influenced by what was going on in the Soviet cinema, and that it posed no problems of readability for a contemporary mass audience. The characteristic Hollywood montage sequence is very short and comprises several visual and sonic images superimposed upon each other by way of dissolves. Often signifying in condensed and accelerated form the passage of time and space, such sequences frequently deployed images of fluttering calendar pages, train wheels, place names and newspaper headlines. While the gangster film was by no means the only site for such Hollywood montage practice, the outbreak of gang warfare and its extension over time, or a gang's reign of terror extended over physical urban space, would often be signified by a montage sequence. What is important from the point of view of representations of the city is that the presence of such a moment, usually made up of speeding automobiles, blasting machine guns and newspaper headlines, within a gangster film (that of '*G*' *Men* [William Keighley, 1936] is a good example) offers a condensation of the idea of 'cityness'. Indeed, a freeze-frame from such a sequence, taken from the heart of a piece of Mass Art, would not be dissimilar to certain High Art photomontages of the same period, such as those of Paul Citroën.

If, after *Little Caesar*, the country/city antinomy tended to recede and the city remain as the Expressionist milieu which shaped characters' lives, it was to re-emerge from time to time, as in *On Dangerous Ground* (Nicholas Ray, 1951) and *Witness* (Peter Weir, 1985). In both films city police officers are forced to go into the country, but the two films' respective handlings of the country/city opposition are very different. In *Witness*, while violent acts occur in the city it is not represented as inherently evil, but the country – in the shape of an agrarian Amish community – is constructed as sentimentally Arcadian. A much more profound film than *Witness*, *On Dangerous Ground*'s explosively violent policeman lead character is empty and alienated because of the city and what his job there requires him to do. His journey to the country becomes a spiritual quest which ends up in a kind of redemption. The country in *On Dangerous Ground* is no prelapsarian Eden. It is a pitiless midwinter wilderness inhabited by figures capable of ferocious acts of violence, but the policeman is nevertheless humanised and transformed by confronting the violence within himself. The philosophical (and, indeed, theological) underpinning of *On Dangerous Ground* becomes explicit from time to time. A fugitive boy is represented in terms of animal imagery and the boy's blind sister, with whom the policeman forms a tenuous relationship, is called Mary Walden, a name which invokes the American naturalist Henry David Thoreau (1817–62) and locates the film right at the heart of century-spanning American debates about past and present, ruralism and urbanism, agrarianism and industrialism, and individuality and community.

As might be expected, the worsening condition of 'real' inner cities in the late twentieth century was paralleled by cinematic representations of the city as a desolate battleground traversed by human monsters on the very margins of sanity. Such a view is signalled in films such as *Death Wish* (Michael Winner, 1974), *Taxi Driver* (Martin Scorsese, 1976) and *Hard Core* (Paul Schrader, 1979) and has been accurately described by Frederic Jameson as 'a new Third World space within the First World city'.[16] This dystopian city has been realised most potently in certain of the films of John Carpenter, particularly *Assault on Precinct 13* (1976), *Escape from New York* (1981) and *Big Trouble in Little China* (1986). In *Escape from New York* the dystopian view of the city is taken to its imaginative extreme when, within a narrative set only fifteen years ahead of the film's production date, Manhattan has become a hermetically sealed prison colony for America's most violent inmates. It is not coincidental that Carpenter is also the co-translator of *Report from the Besieged City and Other Poems*.[17] In some respects associated with the Carpenter-ian view of the city as desolate battleground, but in other respects dissimilar, are two other late-twentieth-century perspectives on the city. These might be called the comic book view and the postmodern view. Both further loosen the hinges which have held cinematic representations of the city in some contact with 'real' cities. The comic book view is exemplified by *Batman* (Tim Burton, 1989) and *Dick Tracy* (Warren Beatty, 1990). Signalling the complete collapse of time and space in cinematic representation, the postmodern city has been realised most forcefully in the work of Ridley Scott, its fullest expression being *Blade Runner* (1982). The shrill, postmodern city of *Blade Runner* – all concrete, glass and neon and its cosmopolitan denizens indistinguishable from the manufactured replicants who move among them – bears some resemblance to the actual Japanese city of Osaka, which forms the main setting of Scott's 1989 film, *Black Rain*. Peter Wollen (1938–2019) conflates the comic book city and the postmodern city perspectives, seeing both, with some justice, as depicting 'the post-Fordist city of deindustrialisation, casual and freelance employment, large-scale immigration, the privatisation of welfare, and social polarisation'.[18]

Such traditions of cinematic representation of the city are perhaps symptomatic reflections of the wider fact that the dominant ideologies of American life valorise the country over the city. Where, then, in American cinema are sympathetic representations of the city to be found?[19] When, in a 1930s gangster movie, a city criminal holed up in the country says, 'I don't like the country. The crickets make me nervous', and when, in *Sweet Smell of Success* (Alexander Mackendrick, 1957), a megalomaniac newspaper columnist looks around the New York streets and says, 'I love this dirty old town', the city can hardly be said to have sympathetic mouthpieces. Less reprehensible enthusiasm for the city within American cinema is discernible principally in two areas. One is the American film musical. Although there are to be found from time to time downbeat and even sinister elements within that tradition, the Hollywood musical is usually maniacally upbeat. Richard Dyer, for example, has talked about the Hollywood musical's 'utopian sensibility' and analysed its workings through five categories: energy, abundance, intensity, transparency and community.[20] All of these categories, wherever they are deployed, are liable to produce congenial milieux. The Hollywood musical sometimes creates rural utopias, as in *Oklahoma!* (Fred Zinnemann, 1955) and *Carousel* (Henry King, 1956), and one of the screen's most venomous representations of the city is in *Brigadoon* (Vincente Minnelli, 1954), where the movement from the titular faery village to New York is accomplished by one of the great transitions in the history of cinema. The tranquillity of Brigadoon gives way to a vertiginous view of the New York skyline accompanied, on the soundtrack, by harsh, discordant, modernist brass music. However, the Hollywood musical is also the site of many of the most affirmative representations of the city. This is evident in the abstractly signified 'cityness' of certain sets in the backstage musicals of *42nd Street* (Lloyd Bacon, 1933), backdrops for intense expressions of *joie de vivre*, but most triumphantly of all in *On the Town* (Gene Kelly and Stanley Donen, 1949). As Dyer describes it: 'what makes *On the Town* interesting is that its utopia is a well-known modern city. The film starts as an escape – from the confines of navy life into the freedom of New York.'[21] Again and again in the Hollywood musical 'real' cities are transformed into utopian spaces: Rio de Janeiro in *Flying Down to Rio* (Thornton Freeland, 1933); Paris in *An American in Paris* (Vincente Minnelli, 1951), *Funny Face* (Stanley Donen, 1957) and *Gigi* (Vincente Minnelli, 1958). The bleak, rain-soaked streets of the film noir become, in a musical like *Singin' in the Rain* (Gene Kelly and Stanley Donen, 1952), the site for delirious outpourings of happiness and joy in living.

The other major site for an affirmative view of the city within American cinema is the work of Woody Allen, whose films could be described collectively as a continuing love affair with New York.[22] So central is that city to Allen's life and art that one critical work is called simply *Woody Allen: New Yorker* and yet another includes a chapter on the urban geography of three of his films.[23] Allen's celebration of New York is at its warmest and most intense in the opening sequence of *Manhattan* (1979). Justly famous for its monochrome beauty, that sequence deploys – to the accompaniment of George Gershwin (1898–1937)'s *Rhapsody in Blue* (1924) – several images of New York, including the city skyline, the Empire State Building, the Brooklyn Bridge and Central Park. Attempting to find an appropriate narrative voice, the off-screen narrator makes several references to the city: the fact that New York exists for him 'in black and white and pulsated to the great tunes of George Gershwin'; that 'New York meant beautiful women and street-smart guys who seemed to know all the angles'; and that 'New York was his town and always would be'. The narrator of *Manhattan* is here traversing the same terrain as the novelist Alasdair Gray's character Thaw quoted at the beginning of this essay.

Clearly, then, Hollywood cinema consistently takes 'real' American cities such as New York – the 'real' being in inverted commas because those cities are already functioning discursively – and reinscribes them into discourse once more: predominantly, those discourses about the quality of the 'natural' and the built world through which meaning has been imposed on the cultural, economic and social transition to modernity. But, as the above references to *An American in Paris*, *Funny Face* and *Gigi* indicate, it is not only American cities which have been so 'discursified'. Roughly speaking since the end of the Second World War, Hollywood has operated both an economic and aesthetic hegemony over world cinema.[24] For instance, of all films shown in British cinemas in 1992, 85.8 per cent were in every sense Hollywood films and a further 4.6 per cent were Hollywood-financed though made in Britain.[25] Although the figures differ from one national culture to another throughout the world, the broad argument about Hollywood dominance holds good. The ideological outcome of this dominance is that many national cultures, where they are not wholly dependent on Hollywood movies for cinematic representations of themselves, are certainly faced with a situation in which Hollywood movies offer the most popular and dominant representations.

With regard to the cinematic representation of geographical space, both urban and non-urban, diverse national audiences' sense of such space is overwhelmingly derived from Hollywood films. The problem is that since the point of utterance of such representations is American, they reflect an American perception of the wider world. In short, Hollywood has created a series of Others which in no sense relate to the self-definition of diverse other places and peoples: rather, that series projects the needs, fears, fantasies and representations of particular American ideologies. It is necessary to de-individualise this question. It cannot be said that Hollywood movies simply promote the worldviews of those individuals who make the movies. For instance, despite the substantial presence of people of Jewish origin in powerful positions in Hollywood, Hollywood cinema's ethnic and ideological norms have consistently been WASP, although this may have been changing from the very late twentieth century onwards.[26] With regard solely to the representation of cities, there must hardly be a major world city which (to inflect Thaw's argument quoted at this essay's outset) is not known primarily by way of Hollywood. Like Robert Warshow (1917–55)'s above-quoted gangster city, these too are cities of the imagination, heavily imbricated with America's sense of the Other and characteristically introduced by a globally familiar local landmark (for example, the Eiffel Tower, the Colosseum, the Brandenburg Gate, Big Ben) and a few bars of 'ethnically' signifying music. Thus, for example, *An American in Paris* constructs that city primarily as the centre of world art and as a fountain of inspiration for American artists; *Funny Face* sees Paris as the locus of a comic, and probably bogus, intellectualism; *Three Coins in the Fountain* (Jean Negulesco, 1954) and *The Roman Spring of Mrs. Stone* (José Quintero, 1961) suggest that Rome is primarily a source of romance between American tourists and impecunious Italian aristocrats; the Berlin of *Cabaret* (Bob Fosse, 1972) is shaped within the dominant narrative of Weimar decadence (also the historic point of view of National Socialism, incidentally); and the Moscow of *Telefon* (Don Siegel, 1977), suffused with Cold War ideology, is dark, cold and menacing.

While taking note of Hollywood's post-WWII dominance in the cinematic representation of world space, it should not be suggested that Hollywood is the point of origin of all of the discourses within which all world spaces and places are constructed. The cinematic representation of London is instructive in this regard. There is, in the film *Ziegfeld Follies* (various, 1945), a dance number entitled 'Limehouse Blues'. Set in an indeterminate, pre-WWII London, it shows a bleak, fog-ridden Thamesscape populated primarily by Chinese but also by stalwart Bobbies, Bill Sykes-type ruffians, pawky and cheerful Pearly Kings and Queens, and bizarre down-and-outs. Where does this representation of London, in a 1940s Hollywood movie, come from? There is a specific cinematic reference point, *Broken Blossoms* (D. W. Griffith, 1919), but this simply pushes the question back by a generation. It is quite likely that the 'London discourse' informing both *Broken Blossoms* and *Ziegfeld Follies* is a composite derived from travellers' accounts of London, the novels of Charles Dickens (1812–70) (particularly *Bleak House* [1852–53]), the Sherlock Holmes stories of Sir Arthur Conan Doyle (1859–1930) and press accounts of the Jack the Ripper murders (1888). The same discourse (or, more accurately, part of the bricolage making it up) underpins the American popular song 'A Foggy Day in London Town'. Certainly, this construction of London (or diverse aspects of it) is evident in many Hollywood-based or -financed movies, such as *The Dark Eyes of London* (Walter Summers, 1939), *Gaslight* (George Cukor, 1944), *Hangover Square* (John Brahm, 1945), *The Verdict* (Don Siegel, 1946), *Night and the City* and, in a more upbeat form, *Mary*

Poppins (Robert Stevenson, 1964). Although the London of *Ziegfeld Follies* is in colour, the colour is mostly very muted. The 'London discourse' shaping the above films may have found the harsh black and white of the classic film noir a more congenial form of expression, hence the clustering of these titles around the 1940s.

However, the London example also demonstrates that it is never a question of a discursive view of any particular geographical space giving way to a more 'realistic' view. There is only ever the possibility of other discourses arising to compete with existing ones. Put another way, realism is itself a discourse, a convention of representation which might perhaps be better described as 'the realist effect'. Thus, there have been several 'London discourses' over and above the one discussed briefly above. Offering a more detailed discussion of the cinematic representation of London than is possible here, Anthony Sutcliffe (1942–2011) suggests that a new cinematic discourse relating to London emerged through the work of those figures from the 1930s British Documentary movement who were drafted into making propaganda films (always a feature of that movement) about the Second World War.[27] The orientation of this new 'London discourse' is summed up in the title of one such film, *London Can Take It!* (Humphrey Jennings and Harry Watt, 1940), which mobilises particular London landmarks, such as the dome of St Paul's, and Ralph Vaughan Williams (1872–1958)'s *London Symphony* (1936) to create a narrative about a proud city enduring under the bombardment of the Luftwaffe. This more upbeat discourse mutated in the post-WWII period into active 'boosterism' of place as the wartime documentary movement opened out into the making of more diverse, sometimes commercially sponsored, films dealing, among other things, with post-war planning and tourism.[28] However, to talk about a specifically urban discourse is to extrapolate from the 'discursive bundle' which makes up any particular film. To do full justice to the complexity of *London Can Take It!*, that film would have to be related to the curious melding of Surrealism and Englishness which informs the entire oeuvre of its co-maker, Humphrey Jennings (1907–50).[29] Nevertheless, the wartime documentaries' less fog-ridden London images, which carried over into post-war, London-based feature films such as *Waterloo Road* (Sidney Gilliat, 1945) and *The Blue Lamp* (Basil Dearden, 1950), marked a development in the cinematic representation of London. So, too, did the all-pervading 1960s discourse of 'Swinging London' traceable across journalism, advertising, fashion, gossip and anecdote. Energetic, colourful, demotic and, ultimately, totally superficial, that discourse is perhaps best signalled in *Blow-Up* (Michelangelo Antonioni, 1966). If, however, as Homi Bhabha suggests, 'the historical and cultural experience of the western metropolis cannot now be fictionalised without the marginal, oblique gaze of its postcolonial migrant populations cutting across the imaginative metropolitan geography of territory and community, tradition and culture',[30] then this fact will increasingly register within present-day cinematic representations of London. It has already done so most notably in *My Beautiful Laundrette* (Stephen Frears, 1985), while at the same time also signalling the presence in British culture (albeit in a less deranged form) of the dystopian view of the city as urban battlefield that was so markedly present in late-twentieth-century American cinema. Peter Wollen, for example, reads British films such as *Sammy and Rosie Get Laid* (Stephen Frears, 1987), *The Last of England* (Derek Jarman, 1987), *The Cook, the Thief, His Wife and Her Lover* (Peter Greenaway, 1989) and the London sequences of *Brazil* (Terry Gilliam, 1985) as lucidly anti-Thatcherite and, as such, connecting with the economic, social and political forces that shaped the contemporaneous cinematic representation of American cities as urban wastelands.[31]

Although Hollywood's economic, psychological and aesthetic global dominance requires that this cinema's negotiating of the great historical transition to modernity be privileged in any discussion of cinematic representations of the city, the same transition was also being negotiated in other national cinemas – initially, those of Europe but, eventually and as a result of uneven development, those of Third World countries as well. Much recent scholarly work has been preoccupied with the changes in perception which have attended the transition to modernity. It has been suggested that:

> A series of sweeping changes in technology and culture created distinctive new modes of thinking about and experiencing time and space. Technological innovations including the telephone, wireless telegraph, x-ray, cinema, bicycle, automobile and airplane established the material foundation for this reorientation; independent developments such as the stream of consciousness novel, psychoanalysis, Cubism and the theory of relativity shaped consciousness directly.[32]

David Harvey's phrase 'space-time compression'[33] elegantly subsumes both the material and psycho-aesthetic dimensions of the process of transition to modernity, which was nowhere more self-consciously confronted with regard to the city and cinema than in Weimar Germany. The cluster 'modernity/city/cinema' was addressed rhetorically by Walter Benjamin (1892–1940) and Siegfried Kracauer (1899–1966) and practically by a diverse range of modernist-orientated German filmmakers.[34] Just as the weighty presence of the city forced itself into the very titles of many early-twentieth-century Hollywood films, so, too, in Weimar Germany was there a series of 'street films', including *The Street* (Karl Grune, 1923), *The Joyless Street* (G. W. Pabst, 1925) and *Tragedy of the Street* (Bruno Rahn, 1927). The psychological weight of the city was given monstrously Expressionist form in *Metropolis* (Fritz Lang, 1927), but perhaps the most interesting Weimar film (from the point of view of signifying the new sense of urban space) is *Berlin, Symphony of a Great City* (Walter Ruttmann, 1927). The latter is abstract and modernist in several ways: its lack of formal plot; its lack of interest in the human beings who inhabit the city; its formal construction on the basis of musical theory; and its linkages through the formal characteristics of the images (for example, cutting or dissolving between objects of the same shape). However, its reception in Weimar Germany indicates the extent to which – despite its virtually complete repression of the city's structural Other, the country – it was perceived as an intervention in that very debate about the country and the city which had so informed American cinema of the same period:

> As *the* metropolis of Weimar Germany, Berlin was the focus of both desire and anxiety in relation to modernization much commented upon by contemporaneous social theorists of the left and right. One should not be so awestruck today by the cultural brilliance of the avant-garde, for whom the cosmopolitan atmosphere of Berlin represented the best impulses of Weimar Germany, to forget that for a broad spectrum of anti-modernist and folkish Germans, Berlin and all it stood for was the devil incarnate. Berlin became a crystallization point of resentment against industrialization, capitalism, democracy and the cultural influence of the West following Germany's defeat in World War I. Anti-modernists penned the term 'asphalt culture' to refer to the lack of genuine culture and social values promoted by urban life. The term connoted a loss of direct contact with the soil and the ethical life, an agrarianist ideology attributed to it, as well as the rootlessness (artificiality) of urban life. During the 1920s, the position was also explicitly tied to a critique directed against the democratic government of the Republic and its 'soulless' culture, nowhere more materially manifest than in Berlin. Wilhelm Stapel [1882–1954], a folkish writer and editor of *Deutsches Volkstum* [1919–38] phrased the debate being waged in Weimar Germany as one between the German landscape and the city. 'The spirit (*Geist*) of the German Folk rebels against the spirit of Berlin. Today's battle cry must be "The resistance of the landscape against Berlin".'[35]

Berlin, Symphony of a Great City was mobilised by both sides of this debate: as an affirmation of the diversity and excitement of modernity and the city, and as a reflection of the city as Sodom. What is most interesting about the above quotation, however, is its revelation that the same discourses about country and city are condensed, in different cultures, into specific national ideologies which circulate within, or are mobilised in response to, particular films. Thus, in the United States, discussion of *Mr. Deeds Goes to Town* is usually 'cashed' in terms of agrarian populism, while in Weimar Germany such discussion might be 'cashed' in terms of proto-Nazism. Without suggesting that the work of F. W. Murnau (1888–1931) displays any such tendency, it is perhaps worth noting that the maker of *Sunrise* – that arch-condemnation of the city – had a distinguished career in Weimar Germany before going to the United States.

In some respects, *Berlin, Symphony of a Great City* can be seen as the archetype of the 'city symphonies' and many other modernist cinematic responses to modernity which were appearing in many societies during the interwar period. Other notable examples are *Manhatta* (Charles Sheeler and Paul Strand, 1921) in the United States, *Rien que les heures* (Alberto Cavalcanti, 1926) in France and *Man with a Movie Camera* (Dziga Vertov, 1929) in the Soviet Union. There was even, for almost the whole of the twentieth century's first three decades, a Neapolitan city cinema which, unusually, dealt primarily with women's lives.[36] The phenomenon reached as far afield as Japan which, very much under the influence of German film culture, had its own 'street films' and, in 1929, a 'city symphony', *Tokai kokyogaku* (Kenji Mizoguchi, 1929). The impulse found its way even into the interstices of mainstream film culture: the 'tenement symphony' in the Marx Brothers film *The Big Store* (Charles Reisner, 1941) may represent an attenuated instance.

As the twentieth century progressed, the great ongoing historical debate about the relative virtues of the country and city would be replayed in the films of many European and non-European societies in the face of the inexorable drift of peasants into cities throughout the world. *Rocco and His Brothers* (Luchino Visconti, 1960), for example, begins with the death of a peasant farmer in southern Italy and the movement of his family to the northern industrial city of Milan. Much of the strange power of *Los Olvidados* (Luis Buñuel, 1950), set in Mexico City, comes from the clash between the bizarre rituals and beliefs of the incoming peasantry and those of the more cynical, materialistic sub-proletariat of the city. A similar tension is apparent within British cinema in a film such as *Floodtide* (Frederick Wilson, 1949) which, through its celebration of Clydeside shipbuilding, is heavily imbricated with the country/city opposition. The film begins in the country with the explicit rejection of farming by the central protagonist in order to pursue a career in shipbuilding in Glasgow. It has been a recurrent theme of this essay that the dualisms within discourse are fundamentally unstable and capable of being mobilised into incompatible ideologies. Such is the case in *Floodtide*, within which the River Clyde is made to function in two contradictory discourses relating to Scotland: the Scotland of dynamic, industrial activity and the Scotland of beautiful hills, lochs and rivers.[37] In the nearly contemporary

The Gorbals Story (David MacKane, 1950), the Clyde's ideological meaning shifts yet again to become the dividing line between working-class and middle-class Glasgow.[38]

As evidence of the extent to which modernisation and urbanisation increasingly provoked psycho-aesthetic responses throughout the Third World as the twentieth century approached its close, the Taiwanese film *Homecoming* (Yim Ho, 1984) deals with two friends separated in childhood: one has gone from mainland China to Hong Kong and become a publisher, while the other has remained in a mainland village and become a schoolteacher. The former is subject to the problems characteristic of city dwellers throughout the world: fragile economic status, disintegrating family and shattered relationships. It is through her reconnection to a mythic, agrarian China that she is able to come to terms with the drawbacks of the materially oriented city life of Hong Kong. *Homecoming* is quite subtle in its negotiation of the country/city opposition and is, of course, filtered through specific Chinese ideologies (for example, those relating to family and ancestors) and complicated by the fact that the People's Republic of China, in the post-Mao (1893–1976) period, embarked upon a specific policy of modernisation, an inhibition on unambiguous endorsement of the country side of the country/city opposition. Such a policy has no bearing on those Asiatic societies which have no relationship with mainland China. The South Korean film *The Oldest Son* (Lee Doo-Yong, 1985), for example, has been described as '[allegorising] the rural–urban opposition in stark, moralistic terms'.[39]

This essay has argued that there are few more useful structures than the historically far-reaching country/city opposition for understanding the way in which cities have been represented on film. It also has to be recognised, however, that this strategy proposes an extra-cinematic determination of the process. In the last analysis, this is entirely proper because films appropriate and recycle discourses at large in the world outside cinema and ideologies current in specific societies. That said, there is much truth in the view that art is made from other art rather than from 'reality'. As many a filmmaker will testify, the impulse to make a particular film may come as much from exposure to other films as to the events happening around the filmmaker in question. In talking about the representation of cities in cinema, therefore, one has to confront the inflection given to such representations, in the post-WWII period, by the massive international influence of Italian Neorealism on films made at that time. Neorealism, like any other artistic movement, incorporated the most diverse temperaments and practices – at one extreme, the austere de-dramatisation of Roberto Rossellini (1906–77), as in *Paisan* (1946), and, at the other, the sonorous melodrama of Vittorio De Sica (1901–74), as in *Bicycle Thieves* (1948). But some of the elements that various films dubbed Neorealist had in common were location-based rather than studio shooting, use of non-actors and the tracing of the impact of social (and sometimes metaphysical) forces on the most vulnerable members of society (for example, women, children, unemployed workers). Such films were seen and greatly admired by critics and cineastes throughout the world and their influence is discernible in every national cinema in the decade or so following the Second World War. To illustrate the critical problem in question, a recurrent image in three post-war films from diverse societies is of children moving through the ruins of war-torn cities. However, underneath the identical visual look of these films quite different things are going on. *Five Boys From Barska Street* (Aleksander Ford, 1954) is concerned with the implacable working of social and historical forces on the lives of its titular five boys; *Germany, Year Zero* (Roberto Rossellini, 1948) is more interested in the corruption of childhood by Nazism's legacy; and *Hue and Cry* (Charles Crichton, 1947) is simply an engaging English comedy. Clearly, despite the diversity of their ideological projects and Italian Neorealism's manifest influence on their overall look and foregrounding of child protagonists, all of these films offer images of the war-torn fabric of their respective contemporary urban milieux and, as such, create new images of Warsaw, Berlin and London respectively.

When people respond to cinematic representations of the spaces they inhabit in the 'real' world with pleasurable recognition, this should not be dismissed with academic arguments about our incapacity to know the world except through discourse. Yet at the same time, the act of filming any space is clearly an act of discourse production, one prey to complex elision, condensation and repression, and as dependent on previous acts of discourse production as on relationships with the 'real' world.

This is a tension we must simply live with.

Notes

1. Alasdair Gray, *Lanark: A Life in Four Books* (Edinburgh: Polygon, 1981), 243.
2. Discourse is a term with a wide range of meanings from 'a conversation between two people' to 'a complete system in which meaning is assigned to all the elements within it'. The term is particularly central to the work of the French philosopher Michel Foucault (1926–84), who stressed the extent to which power was exercised through language or, put another way, how language constitutes (rather than describes) the phenomena it purports to describe, most often to the benefit of powerful groups within society although oppositional discourse may emanate from other groups. Foucault's writings

could be said to describe how diverse social phenomena have been historically constituted in language, and thereby rendered discursive: madness in *Madness and Civilisation* (1961); modern medicine in *The Birth of the Clinic* (1963); intellectual activity itself in *The Archaeology of Knowledge* (1969); the application of the law in *Discipline and Punish* (1975); and sexuality in *The History of Sexuality* (1976–84). A concrete example of discourse in action might be how the idea of withdrawal of labour or striking is constituted in different discourses. Those whose interests are threatened by a strike might talk about 'the country being held to ransom' by the strikers while possible beneficiaries of the strike might talk about 'a last resort to protect the living standard of working people'. The concept of discourse is central to several of the essays in the present volume (for example, 'A Dram for All Seasons: The Diverse Identities of Scotch' and 'Transatlantic Scots, Their Interlocutors and the Scottish Discursive Unconscious'), usually in describing how Scotland and the Scots are constituted by a limited number of tropes.

3. See Ian Spring, *Phantom Village: The Myth of the New Glasgow* (Edinburgh: Polygon, 1990).
4. In a classic case of throwing the baby out with the bathwater, some postmodernisms – seeking to deconstruct the binary oppositions so dear to structuralism on account of (among other things) their alleged privileging of one half of the dualism (for example, Man/Woman, Nature/Culture) – have abandoned binarism entirely. This is to discard one of the most useful critical tools for dealing with (particularly popular) culture. This essay's strategy is to retain binarism but to insist on the instability of meaning on both sides of any dualism, on their capacity to signify even incompatible positions in different discursive situations. For example, 'small town' in *Mr. Deeds Goes to Town* and *Sleeping with the Enemy* signifies quite the reverse of what it signifies in *Easy Rider* and *Blue Velvet* and 'city' likewise in *Sunrise* and *On the Town*. To reassert classical structuralist binarism, in each case the meaning of 'small town' or 'city' derives from what it has been set against in the particular discursive context.
5. See Larry Ford, 'Sunshine and shadow: lighting and colour in the depiction of cities on film', in *Place, Power, Situation, and Spectacle: A Geography of Film*, eds Stuart C. Aitken and Leo E. Zonn (Lanham, MD: Rowman & Littlefield, 1994), 119–36. The central emphasis in this essay is on Hollywood cinema and the cinema of Weimar Germany. This is so due to the forcefulness of representations of the city in these cinemas. In a pleasing homology, very likely connected with this fact, the history of discourse about the city has been categorised (see, for example, Richard Sennett, ed., *Classical Essays in the Culture of Cities* [Englewood Cliffs, NJ: Prentice-Hall, 1969]) into a German school, represented primarily by figures such as Max Weber (1864–1920), Georg Simmel (1858–1918) and Oswald Spengler (1880–1936), and an American (Chicago) school represented by Robert Park (1864–1944), Louis Wirth (1897–1952) and Ernest Burgess (1886–1966). There is some

overlap between the two schools, possibly due to the fact that Park had been Simmel's student at the University of Heidelberg before the First World War. What the two schools had in common was a perception of the effect of cities on individuals in the sense of fragmenting lives into different compartments and relationships as opposed to the seamless continuity of pre-urban living. However, it is not academic works themselves which enter general consciousness, but journalistic commentaries and popular appropriations of them. At the risk of considerable oversimplification, it might be said that Weimar Germany tended to appropriate the Spenglerian view of the city as oppressive and alienating while America appropriated Park's ideas, particularly the suggestion that the city offered the promise of human growth and the possibility of non-conformity. Such emphases were to some extent incorporated into these societies' cinematic representation of cities. For instance, it is tempting to see the popularisation of the Chicago school's ideas underlying that cycle within the gangster film which, in the mid-1930s, offered a social theory of crime. The best-known films of that cycle were *Dead End* (William Wyler, 1937) and *Angels with Dirty Faces* (Michael Curtiz, 1938), both of which register the significant presence of the city.

6. Sam Rohdie, 'Totems and movies', unpublished seminar paper (London: British Film Institute Education Department, 1969).
7. John Rennie Short, *Imagined Country: Society, Culture and Environment* (London: Routledge, 1991), 104.
8. P. Roffman and B. Simpson, 'The small town in American cinema', in *A Political Companion to American Film*, ed. Gary Crowdus (New York: Lakeview Press, 1994), 395–402.
9. Serge Guilbaut, *How New York Stole the Idea of Modern Art: Abstract Expressionism, Freedom, and the Cold War* (Chicago: University of Chicago Press, 1983).
10. See Julian Petley, 'The Architect as Übermensch', in *Picture This: Media Representations of Visual Art and Artists*, ed. P. Hayward (London: John Libbey, 1988), 115–25; John A. Walker, *Art and Artists on Screen* (Manchester: Manchester University Press, 1993).
11. Robert Warshow, *The Immediate Experience: Movies, Comics, Theatre & Other Aspects of Popular Culture* (New York: Doubleday, 1962), 131.
12. Robert Sklar, *City Boys: Cagney, Bogart, Garfield* (Princeton NJ: Princeton University Press, 1992), xii.
13. See Marc Vernet, 'Film noir on the edge of doom', in *Shades of Noir*, ed. Joan Copjec (London: Verso, 1993), 1–31.
14. See, for example, Colin McArthur, *Underworld U.S.A.* (London: Secker & Warburg for the British Film Institute, 1972); Jack Shadoian, *Dreams and Dead Ends: The American Gangster/Crime Film* (Cambridge, MA: MIT Press, 1977); Eugene Rosow, *Born to Lose: The Gangster Film in America* (New York: Oxford University Press, 1978); Foster Hirsch, *Film Noir: The Dark Side of the Screen* (New York: Da Capo Press, 1981).

15. When I first published this essay in 1997, I noted at this point that the history of the High Art/Mass Art opposition, its centrality in certain Hollywood movies – *Shall We Dance?* (Mark Sandrich, 1937), *Sullivan's Travels* (Preston Sturges, 1941), *Do You Love Me?* (Gregory Ratoff, 1946), *Three Daring Daughters* (Fred M. Wilcox, 1948), *The Band Wagon* (Vincente Minnelli, 1953) – and its eventual collapsing by postmodernism deserved a book in its own right, that such a study would range across all the arts, and, as in the example given here of montage vis-à-vis Hollywood cinema, that it would have to take account of the historical interpenetration of the two modes, as in the involvement of classical *virtuosi* with popular musical forms. I subsequently attempted to write precisely the kind of book I described: Colin McArthur, *Along the Great Divide: High Art, Mass Art and Classic Hollywood Narrative* (London: Independent Publication, 2020). In many respects an archetypal figure in this postmodernist conflating of modes is the classical violinist Nigel Kennedy. His ear studs, spiky hair, creatively tailored dress suit and loud bow tie, 'estuary' accent, passion for Aston Villa football club, tendency to introduce his rendering of Vivaldi as 'a bit of Viv', and dropping of the 'communing with the Infinite' demeanour in favour of a laughing photograph on his record sleeves, is anathema to an older generation of classical music lovers. While much of Kennedy's style may be a cynical commercial attempt to cross over and incorporate a further sector of the paying public, there is probably an important shift of sensibility taking place as well.
16. Frederic Jameson, 'Remapping Taipei', in *New Chinese Cinemas: Forms, Identities, Politics*, eds Nick Browne et al. (Cambridge: Cambridge University Press, 1994), 148.
17. Zbigniew Herbert, *Report from the Besieged City and Other Poems*, trans. John and Bogdana Carpenter (New York: Ecco Press, 1985).
18. Peter Wollen, 'Delirious projections', *Sight and Sound* 2, no. 3 (July 1992), 26.
19. While note (4) above enters a plea for the retention of binarism, it is appropriate here to sound a note of caution. The discussion of cinematic representations of the city has been structured thus far under the broad opposition negative/ affirmative. The note of caution is about the extent to which any discourse says anything about the 'real' space it signifies as opposed to the moral/ ideological frameworks within which the enunciators of the discourse live. This problem is explored at length with regard to the literary representation of geographical space by Leo Marx, 'The Puzzle of Antiurbanism in Classic American Literature', in *Cities of the Mind: Images and Themes of the City in the Social Sciences*, eds Lloyd Rodwin and Robert H. Hollister (New York/ London: Plenum, 1984), 163–80. However, a distinction may have to be made between literary and photographic/cinematic discourse because of the iconic dimension, in the Peircian sense (see Charles S. Peirce, *Semiotic and Significs* [Bloomington: Indiana University Press, 1977]) of the latter, due to the existential connection between what is set before the camera and what appears on the resultant film. A concrete example of this is the evident sense

of recognition and pleasure we display when confronted with photographs of ourselves, those we know and the spaces we inhabit. This pleasure exists in tension with another response, the sense of otherness produced by mechanical features of the photographic apparatus and the photochemical features of the film stock, as when the latter picks up and foregrounds a red cushion cover we have hardly noticed in the pro-filmic event (that is, the situation photographed). When we remark that the thing which stands out most in the photograph is the red cushion cover, we are recognising, implicitly at least, one dimension of photography's complex discursivity.

20. Richard Dyer, 'Entertainment and Utopia', *Movie*, no. 24 (Spring 1977), 2–13.
21. Ibid., 12.
22. New York's centrality in both affirmative and negative representations of the city is recognised in A. Barbera et al., eds, *New York, New York: La Citta, il Mito, il Cinema* (Torino: MACE, 1986), which includes: a filmography of about 500 films set in New York; an account of the recurrence in these films of particular sites (for example, Broadway, Central Park, Greenwich Village, the Empire State Building, Harlem); and extracts from interviews with diverse film directors who have made observations about the city. P. Hillairet et al., eds, *Paris vu par le cinema d'avant-garde: 1923–1983* (Paris: Paris Experimental, 1985) offers an analogous account of the representation of Paris in cinema; G. P. Brunetta and A. Costa, eds, *La Citta Che Sale: Cinema Avanguardie, Immaginario Urbano* (Trento: Manfrini Editori, 1990) discusses the more general representation of cities in film; F. Niney, ed., *Visions Urbaines: Villes d'Europe à L'Ecran* (Paris: Centre Georges Pompidou, 1994) discusses the cinematic representation of 'real' cities such as Paris, Berlin, London, Rome and Prague as well as such cities of the imagination as 'Tativille' – the urban space constructed in the films of Jacques Tati (1907–82).
23. Graham McCann, *Woody Allen: New Yorker* (Cambridge: Polity Press, 1990); Stephen J. Spignesi, *The Woody Allen Companion* (Kansas City, MO: Andrews and McMeel, 1992).
24. See, for example, John Ellis, *Visible Fictions: Cinema, Television, Video* (London: Routledge & Kegan Paul, 1982); Kristin Thompson, *Exporting Entertainment: America in the World Film Market, 1907–1934* (London: British Film Institute, 1985).
25. David Leafe and Terry Illott, eds, *The BFI Film and Television Handbook 1994* (London: British Film Institute, 1993).
26. See, for example, Lester D. Friedman, ed., *Unspeakable Images: Ethnicity and the American Cinema* (Urbana: University of Illinois Press, 1991).
27. Anthony Sutcliffe, 'The metropolis in the cinema', in *Metropolis 1890–1940*, ed. Anthony Sutcliffe (London: Mansell, 1984), 147–71.
28. John R. Gold and Stephen V. Ward, '"We're going to do it right this time": Cinematic representations of urban planning and the British New Towns, 1939–1951', in *Place, Power, Situation, and Spectacle*, eds Aitken and Zonn, 229–58.

29. Julian Petley, 'Realism and the problem of documentary', in *BFI Distribution Library Catalogue*, ed. Julian Petley (London: British Film Institute, 1978), 3–27.
30. Quoted in J. Donald, 'The city as text', in *The Social and Cultural Forms of Modernity: Understanding Modern Societies*, eds Kenneth Thompson et al. (Cambridge: Polity Press, 1992), 455.
31. Wollen, 'Delirious Projections'.
32. Quoted in Wolfgang Natter, 'The City as Cinematic Space: Modernism and Place in *Berlin, Symphony of a City*', in *Place, Power, Situation, and Spectacle*, eds Aitken and Zoon, 224–5.
33. David Harvey, *The Condition of Postmodernity: An Enquiry into the Origins of Cultural Change* (Oxford: Blackwell, 1989).
34. Walter Benjamin, *Illuminations* (New York: Schocken Books, 1969); Siegfried Kracauer, *From Caligari to Hitler: A Psychological History of the German Film* (Princeton, NJ: Princeton University Press, 1947).
35. Natter, 'The City as Cinematic Space', 214–15.
36. Giuliana Bruno, *Streetwalking on a Ruined Map: Cultural Theory and the City Films of Elvira Notari* (Princeton, NJ: Princeton University Press, 1992).
37. See Colin McArthur, 'Scotland and Cinema: The Iniquity of the Fathers', in *Scotch Reels: Scotland in Cinema and Television*, ed. Colin McArthur (London: British Film Institute, 1982), 40–69, and also republished elsewhere in the present volume.
38. John Hill, '"Scotland doesna mean much tae Glesca": Some notes on *The Gorbals Story*', in *Scotch Reels*, ed. McArthur, 100–11.
39. Rob Wilson, 'Melodramas of Korean national identity', in *Colonialism and Nationalism in Asian Cinema*, ed. Wimal Dissanayake (Bloomington: Indiana University Press, 1994), 102.

CHAPTER 26

Artists and Philistines: The Irish and Scottish Film Milieux*

Introduction

Ireland and Scotland are often spoken of as Celtic countries, but that common description tends to obscure the fact that they have had radically different relationships with the British state. In the case of Scotland that relationship has been one of compromise and union, the nature of the Scottish polity having been settled in 1707, almost a century before the arrival of nationalism on the historical stage with the French Revolution of 1789. By this latter time Scotland had become a well-rewarded junior partner in the United Kingdom, a highly profitable enterprise which was becoming the world's most economically advanced state through its eighteenth-century agrarian and industrial revolutions and its amassing of imperial booty, particularly in the nineteenth century. As Tom Nairn (1932–2023) has demonstrated, the historical role of nationalism was to allow the bourgeoisies of powerful and soon-to-be powerful European states such as France, Germany and Italy to mobilise the masses, throw off feudal overlordship (often of foreign dynasties) and emerge as competitors to the United Kingdom within the intense economic and imperial struggles of the modern world.[1] In order to facilitate this transition, the intelligentsias of these emergent states had to fashion appropriate nationalist ideologies which would make national mobilisation possible. Hence, the turn to indigenous languages, folklore and peasant dress, all expressed through Romanticism, the cultural mode of nationalism.[2]

Scotland was not immune to these developments, but since their role in France, Germany, Italy and Poland was to provide the ideological ammunition to further political (and sometimes military) advance, there was no obvious use for them in Scotland, given that its polity and economy

---

* Originally published in *Journal for the Study of British Cultures* 5, no. 2 (1998), 143–53.

had already been defined in 1707. As a consequence, the characteristic tropes of romantic nationalism were, in the Scottish context, diverted into non-political and non-military (in the sense of nationalist struggle) channels. This produced a peculiarly demented, introverted and sentimental romanticism which, since it could not focus on the future, oriented itself obsessively to the past.[3] To the extent that this introverted nationalism found a contemporary role, it was in the service of British imperialism within which Scottish administrators and soldiers were disproportionately prominent. This fact is invariably recognised in films about, for example, British India, whether British (*The Drum* [Zoltan Korda, 1938]), or American (*Wee Willie Winkie* [John Ford, 1937] and *Gunga Din* [George Stevens, 1939]). A perfect metaphor for the historical relationship between Scotland and the British state circulated in the film *Mrs Brown* (John Madden, 1997), which deals with the curious emotional involvement of Queen Victoria (1819–1901) with her Scottish servant, John Brown (1826–83). Brown's apparent irreverence and autonomy conceals a deeper servitude, rather in the way that the licensed insolence of so-called 'house niggers' in films about the pre-Civil War American South masks the real cruelty and injustice of slavery.

There is no such record of co-option and compromise in the historical relationship between Ireland and the British state, which has, at least since the reign of Elizabeth I (1533–1603), been marked by discrimination, repression and violence. The very fact that there are now two communities sharing the land mass that is Ireland – Protestants committed to the United Kingdom in the north and Catholic nationalists with their own republic in the south and also comprising a substantial minority in the north – is a dimension of this oppressive relationship, the northern Protestants largely having been planted as *Pieds-Noirs* from Scotland in the seventeenth century. Unlike that of Scotland, therefore, Irish nationalism has much in common with European nationalisms in having both a political and military dimension. The effect of this has been to politicise culture much more explicitly than in Scotland. As Luke Gibbons observes:

> All culture is, of course, political, but in Ireland historically it acquired a particularly abrasive power, preventing the deflection of creative energies into a rarefied aesthetic or 'imaginary' realm entirely removed from the exigencies of everyday life. To engage in cultural activity in circumstances where one's culture was being effaced or obliterated, was to make a political statement.[4]

As argued above, such a politicising of culture did not occur in Scotland. To the extent that culture was politicised in the Scottish context, the operative discourses were socialism and communism rather than nationalism, at least in the period up to 1979, the date of the first (failed) referendum on Scottish devolution. The difference in Ireland and Scotland's respective historical experiences with regard to the British state could be called the hidden foundation which has determined the distinctive character of culture, including film, in these two 'Celtic' countries. The process of determination is not always immediately apparent, but becomes visible through close examination of Irish and Scottish cultural institutions, their governing cultural discourses and the orientation and calibre of the personnel appointed to staff them. The process of analysis might usefully begin with an event which occurred recently in Scotland.

The Roots of a Scandal

In January 1997 a scandal broke in the pages of *Scotland on Sunday*, a Scottish weekly broadsheet newspaper. Bill Forsyth, then the most internationally prominent of Scottish filmmakers, resigned from the Scottish Film Production Fund (1982–97), at that time the premier body for dispensing public subsidy for filmmaking in Scotland, calling in question its procedures for allocating grants. The core of Forsyth's allegations, which were undoubtedly true, was that the Fund functioned as a cosy club, with its committee members – most of them Scots film directors and producers – handing out grants of up to £1 million to each other, sometimes, it was alleged, on the basis of a few telephone calls without the committee actually meeting. Following Forsyth's resignation and disclosures, several other filmmakers weighed in with criticisms of the Fund. Although it was morally correct for Forsyth to have resigned and made public the 'you scratch my back, I'll scratch yours' attitude of SFPF committee members and the total lack of proper procedures and public accountability, it was a pity that he formulated the issue, and that the press reported it, as solely a question of finance and administration. The issue went much deeper, connecting with what I have described above as 'the hidden foundation' of Scottish culture and its effect on how the highest political officials in Scotland define their role and that of Scottish cultural institutions.

The question might be posed thus: Why is it that the moment substantial funds were injected into the system (via revenue channelled from the recently created UK National Lottery) the SFPF should start coming apart at the seams, its officers and committee members lashing out at each other, while the Republic of Ireland's analogous film institution, operating in almost identical financial circumstances, should go from strength to strength? The answer lies in the diametrically opposed policies set in train by Ireland and Scotland's respective government ministers and implemented by their officers, particularly relating to the balance between culture and commerce. Until the 1997 British General Election, in which every Conservative MP in Scotland lost their seat, the relevant Scottish minister had been Michael Forsyth. An acolyte of Margaret Thatcher (1925–2013), he had for many years followed his mentor's hard-nosed policies in letting the arts in Scotland more or less fend for themselves, aside from a small subsidy which it would have been politically counter-productive to remove. If any single event could be said to have changed his mind, it was the luring of *Braveheart* (Mel Gibson, 1995) from Scotland to the Republic of Ireland with the incentives of tax concessions and the promise of 6,000 Irish Army reserves to act as film extras. Notoriously philistine in his attitude to the arts (a particular badge of honour within the Conservative Party), Forsyth was not slow to perceive the economic benefits culture of Gibson's type might bring to Scotland. Whether catalyst or symptom, the *Braveheart* affair was contemporaneous with Forsyth's becoming more publicly 'Scottish'. Formerly one of the most vociferous defenders of the historic policy of submerging Scottish identity within that of the United Kingdom, he took to wearing Highland dress at official functions (his wearing of the kilt at *Braveheart*'s premiere in Stirling elicited howls of derision from the assembled crowds). He also convinced then-Prime Minister John Major that the return of the Stone of Scone (folklorically regarded as the traditional Scottish coronation stone and looted by English monarch Edward I [1239–1307] in 1296) to Scotland would help convince Scottish voters that the Conservative Party cared about Scottish culture and history. Cynical observers were of the opinion that Forsyth's newfound Scots identity was not unconnected with the fact that he held his parliamentary seat with a slender majority over the Scottish National Party.

With specific regard to film, the outcome of Forsyth's conversion was the commissioning of a report, *Scotland on Screen*, on the future of the film and television industries in Scotland and the subsequent implementation of its main proposals.[5] The latter included the setting-up of a new umbrella organisation, Scottish Screen (1997–2010), through the amalgamation of four existing film bodies, some of which had a cultural and educational orientation and others an industrial bent. At the same time, public subsidy for film was substantially enhanced. Forsyth's public statements on film were few and sparse, but one in particular is most revealing about how he viewed the future of film in Scotland. Prior to a preview of the film *Loch Ness* (John Henderson, 1996) for American tourism executives in New York, Forsyth addressed the invitees. Having stressed that the new measures he had put in place were designed to make Scotland an even more attractive location for foreign filmmakers and to develop an indigenous film industry, he made the following chilling statement: 'I will also be looking to [Scottish Screen] to free up some of its existing resources to reflect the more commercial rather than cultural emphasis which is now important.'[6] The key point about Forsyth's conception of film in Scotland is his separation of commerce and culture and the Gadarene pursuit of the former at the latter's expense. That policy had already been gestating within Scottish Screen's predecessor, the SFPF, and led to disastrous consequences, such as the Bill Forsyth allegations.

Michael Forsyth's Irish counterpart at the time was Michael D. Higgins, who was also to lose his ministerial portfolio when the coalition government of which his party was the senior partner lost power in 1997. As Minister for Culture and the Gaeltacht, Higgins posed a startling contrast to Michael Forsyth. A sociologist and poet before entering the Irish parliament, Higgins was far from reticent about pronouncing on film in Ireland, and his utterances have been as different from Forsyth's as night from day. In an extended conversation between Higgins and the distinguished cultural critic Stuart Hall (1932–2014), Higgins, in reply to a question Hall posed about the cultures of small nations in the face of transnational capitalism and globalisation, argued:

> The issue is very serious. In many ways we're talking about the last great colonisation, the colonisation of the imagination. And the choice is stark, I would say a choice between a monopolised, global, leisure empire or a diversity of cultures [. . .] The choice is whether we will have a democratic theory of culture or a non-democratic consumerism. I believe in a political model that can, in fact, negotiate the future of cultural diversity while accepting the market as a mechanism of exchange. But what is crucial [. . .] is that to accept the hegemony of the market will be disastrous. It will lead [. . .] in film to a formula that will more and more come from North America. I haven't an argument about North American film, only to say that it is surely wrong that all the images of the world would come from one place.[7]

It is not that Higgins was neglectful of commercial matters: it was he who initiated the tax structures which made 1990s Ireland such an attractive location for foreign film capital. But unlike Michael Forsyth and (as will be seen) the officers Forsyth put in place to oversee publicly funded filmmaking in Scotland, Higgins refused to let the market wholly dictate his policy. That this is so relates only partly to the fact that Higgins is an intellectual and Forsyth a philistine. It relates more profoundly to the above-noted 'hidden foundation' of modern Irish and Scottish cultures: given the nature of the Irish historical experience, culture cannot be divorced from questions of national identity and, therefore, politics.

To what extent, then, did these starkly dissimilar ministerial statements set the tone for the film milieux of their respective countries at the twentieth century's close? This issue is far from straightforward. It may be that Forsythian attitudes had been in place in Scotland for many years, cumulatively downgrading film as culture in favour of film as commerce. Such a reading is possible when considering the rise to hegemony in 1990s Scottish film affairs of Allan Shiach, whisky magnate and Hollywood screenwriter, former Chair of the Scottish Film Council (1934–97) and the SFPF and the first Chair of Scottish Screen. Certainly, the following extract from his 1996 BAFTA Scotland lecture gives pause for thought:

> Why does Hollywood succeed while we in Britain are only on the margin? How can we redress the situation and what ought we to be doing to achieve this aim? I offer six points. (1) (2) (3) (4) and (5): Hollywood makes movies that worldwide audiences want to see. (6): Hollywood makes movies that worldwide audiences want to see.[8]

The tone and discourse flowing down from ministerial level profoundly affects the kind of appointments made to national public film bodies. If Allan Shiach's track record as a Hollywood screenwriter may not already have impressed Michael Forsyth, his part-ownership of the Macallan Scotch whisky company certainly would, hence Shiach posed no problem as Scottish Screen's first Chair. This orientation was carried over into the appointment of that infant organisation's first Chief Executive, John Archer, a senior television manager, and had a knock-on effect on policy formation and execution to the point where word got around that only films which were quasi-Hollywoodean and market-oriented would receive support, thus further determining the kinds of projects Scots filmmakers spent their time developing.

It is instructive in this regard to compare mid-1990s annual reports from the SFPF (prior to its incorporation within Scottish Screen) and the Irish Film Board (IFB). There is one mention of the word 'culture' in the introduction to the SFPF's 1996 *Annual Report*, written by its Director, Eddie Dick, a simple assertion that the diverse mechanisms set up by the Fund had been 'successful in entrepreneurial and cultural terms.'[9] The word order of that statement is as significant as its sparseness. By contrast, the introduction to the IFB's 1995 *Annual Report*, written by its Director, Rod Stoneman, is suffused with references to the Board's cultural as well as commercial aims. At one point Stoneman refers to Eurimages, a European Union screen industries initiative provoked by the dominance of the United States in the audio-visual field also noted in the Michael D. Higgins quote above:

> Eurimages provides a pan-European perspective indicating the way in which dynamic and consolidated Irish cinema(s) can play a role in the vigorous development of European film. The project is overdue in terms of the serious penetration

and domination of our screens by American product. It is time to recognise the important differences of cultural approach and mode of production and play to our strengths, throwing out the fantasy, especially persistent in English-language cinema, of competing with Hollywood on its own ground. Whatever the illustrious histories of various European cinemas, the future does not lie in attempting to make inadequate imitations of large-scale industrial product from America. The plural range of films, of very different budgets, genres and aesthetics, being produced in Ireland at this time is a contribution to this wider project. They can also participate as a catalyst at a time of rapid social and cultural change in this country.[10]

Two points need to be stressed about this passage. It explicitly rejects the quasi-Hollywood type of film which was widely suspected to be the agenda of the SFPF and Scottish Screen and which is clearly signalled in the remarks by Allan Shiach quoted above. Secondly, it specifically poses a catalytic role for the IFB's films within the highly contested social formation of the contemporary Irish Republic. This is a clear signal that the mid-1990s Board expected the films that it funded, or some of them at least, to engage with the great debates in Irish society, such as the Catholic Church's role in the state, divorce and abortion, and how the Republic should position itself with regard to events in Ulster.

The cultural policy followed by the IFB, the clarity of its criteria relating to how its funded films function within Ireland itself, as well as the calibre of its officers and panellists, permitted it to advance steadily. Insofar as there was dissent from IFB policy, it came largely from those whose applications for funding were unsuccessful. Otherwise, there seems to have been at least tacit recognition of the IFB's seriousness, efficiency and integrity. Mention of the SFPF, in contrast, elicited nothing but anger and contempt and it was significant that Scottish Screen's early public statements offered reassurances only on the question of administrative procedures: its policy framework and its perception of its place within Scottish culture remain unchanged from those of the outgoing SFPF. For the historical reasons outlined at the start of this essay, the IFB would not be permitted by its constituency to embark on policies which were irrelevant to Irish culture and, ultimately, politics. In Scotland, however, a different historical inheritance has meant that there was (and still is) no substantial constituency of, for example, journalists and intellectuals demanding that public film bodies in Scotland work to policies which relate to Scottish history and culture.

The Effect on Scottish and Irish Films

During the early 1990s, the present writer, a Scot resident in London, attempted (without, it has to be said, much success) to provoke the kind of debate which might lead to production of films more analytic of

Scottish history and contemporary culture.[11] The rubric under which this was attempted was 'Poor Cinema', a cinema meagre in resources but rich in imagination which would shun large budgets and the necessity of capturing large audiences and which would challenge the traditional way of telling stories in the classic Hollywood cinema. It can be said quite unambiguously that Scottish film institutions have never offered any kind of consistent support for such a cinema and, as will be seen presently, both the corresponding Irish institutions and their personnel were, up until at least the mid-1990s, much more favourably disposed to it.

The diverse funding criteria – some aesthetic, some social, some linguistic, some commercial – of the institutions supporting filmmaking in Scotland, and the fact that budgets may be made up of contributions from more than one institution, make it difficult to construct an argument which applies to all of them equally. However, certain tendencies in mid- to-late-1990s Scottish filmmaking may be discerned. Significant public institutions of the period, such as the Glasgow Film Fund and Scottish Screen Locations, existed simply to lure film companies to make films in their geographical catchment areas: there was and is hardly a Scottish region or city which does not now have such film offices. The Gaelic Television Committee's funding criteria of the period were primarily linguistic and social in nature: to sustain the Gaelic language in Scotland through investment in film and television production in that language. The SFPF had both commercial and (albeit vague) aesthetic criteria, but what is most interesting is the tendency of its funding decisions. The SFPF's future direction (as part of the wider Scottish Screen) was already signalled by its substantial investment in the script development of *Rob Roy* (Michael Caton-Jones, 1995), a mainline Hollywood production starring Liam Neeson and Jessica Lange.

Unquestionably the most progressive institution making a funding input into filmmaking in 1990s Scotland, however, was Channel 4, a British-wide terrestrial television channel with (at that period) a specifically defined responsibility to serve minority interests. It was no accident that Rod Stoneman held successive roles as (first) Deputy Commissioning Editor for Independent Film at Channel 4 and (latterly) Director of the Irish Film Board during the 1990s. Channel 4's independent film commissioning strand was the principal source of funding for the two Scottish films which come closest to realising the definition of 'Poor Cinema' outlined above. *Scotch Myths* (Murray Grigor, 1982) was a witty, yet profoundly serious interrogation of the role of certain key historical figures in the construction of the dominant myths and narratives about Scotland. It is common knowledge that this insightful and stylish work was received coldly by the apparatchiks of the SFPF, and director Murray Grigor subsequently received no encouragement and little financial support from them. He all but quit Scotland and became primarily engaged instead in making elegant documentary films about architecture and diverse historical art movements for Channel 4 and American public broadcasting. The other important Scottish 'Poor' cinematic work primarily funded by Channel 4 (and also including some funding from the SFPF) was *Play Me Something* (Timothy Neat, 1989). This film is described, in an insightful analysis, as follows:

> *Play Me Something* [. . .] not only deals with the question of cultural and political identities in different settings, but has also been critically received (in line with its makers' intentions) as being both 'European' and 'Scottish' [. . .] Directed from a script co-written with the well-known art critic and historian John Berger [1926–2017] [. . .] the central theme is the role of story-telling within a given cultural group . . . Translated to another level of analysis, we are talking about the communal transmission and modification of culture.[12]

By the mid-to-late 1990s, it had become most unlikely that films like either *Scotch Myths* or *Play Me Something* would receive any encouragement, far less funding, from Scottish Screen, so heavily commercial had its funding criteria become by that point. Astonishingly, there were, for example, no written criteria for its script development programme, which had instead to be deduced from the criteria it published for applicants for production finance to the Scottish Arts Council National Lottery Fund, for whom Scottish Screen acted as advisor. These criteria were:

> The general public must benefit substantially from the project, which must be of high quality in both artistic content and execution.
> Lottery funding must produce significant improvements or new developments which would not otherwise have taken place.
> There must be a demonstrable demand for what is proposed.
> There must be an element of partnership funding.
> The project must be financially viable.
> There must be evidence of effective management of the project.
> Every aspect of the project must adhere to Equal Opportunities principles.[13]

These were criteria applicable to all approaches to the Lottery Fund, film- and non-film-based, but there were three additional criteria specific to film-based approaches:

> The project must show creativity and originality.
> There must be a realistic distribution/marketing plan.
> In the case of productions which are intended to realise a profit, the probability of achieving this should be demonstrated.[14]

To the extent that there were any references to culture within these criteria, they were of such a level of generality ('creativity and originality') as to allow the funders to back anything they deemed to be appropriate. Again astonishingly, there seems to have been no public debate about the absence of criteria for script development and the effective lack of cultural criteria in the Lottery principles. The Scottish film community seemed to have become bemused by the international success of two films, *Braveheart* and *Trainspotting* (Danny Boyle, 1996), the former partly and the latter wholly made in Scotland. It is questionable – despite the fact that both provoked sharp disagreement – whether either engendered productive debate about Scottish history or contemporary culture. What felt certain at the time, however, was that *Trainspotting*, with its nihilistic portrayal of a young, drug-ridden underclass, would provide a template to which many young Scots filmmakers would then work in the years immediately following.[15] In short, there was, in the mid-to-late 1990s, nothing in Scottish history, or Scottish cultural institutions, which compelled Scottish filmmakers to produce work which engaged with Scottish politics and history.

The situation was substantially different in Ireland during the period in question. As was the case with Scotland, Ireland attracted the interest of Hollywood. However, the 'Irish' projects which followed in the wake of the Oscar successes of *My Left Foot* (Jim Sheridan, 1989), *The Field* (Jim Sheridan, 1990), *The Commitments* (Alan Parker, 1991), *The Crying Game* (Neil Jordan, 1992) and *In the Name of the Father* (Jim Sheridan, 1993) in large measure managed, albeit in different ways and to different degrees, to retain a historical and political seriousness. And when *Michael Collins* (Neil Jordan, 1996) is contrasted with *Braveheart*, the former's manifest seriousness and the latter's vulgar absurdities are writ large. That is to say, even when making a film at the heart of the Hollywood system, as Neil Jordan did with *Michael Collins*, the nature of the Irish historical experience, the closeness to the surface of Irish public life of political questions and the sophistication of politico-cultural debate in the Irish film community forced Jordan, quite apart from his own personal intellectual and artistic ability, to make a film which was politically mature. Moreover, that level of seriousness is discernible throughout the Irish filmmaking system to an extent that is not so in Scotland. At the low-budget end of the Irish system, from *Lament for Arthur Leary* (Bob Quinn, 1975) and *Poitín* (Bob Quinn, 1977), through *Our Boys* (Cathal Black, 1981), *Traveller* (Joe Comerford, 1981), *Reefer and the Model* (Joe Comerford, 1988) and *High Boot Benny* (Joe Comerford, 1993), to *Maeve* (Pat Murphy, 1981), *Anne Devlin* (Pat Murphy, 1984) and *Hush-a-Bye Baby* (Margo Harkin, 1990), there was, up until at very least the early

1990s, a level of engagement with crucial local historical and contemporary public issues which was far in advance of that of Scots filmmakers. The fact that two female filmmakers are cited in the above list testifies to the fact that the stakes are altogether higher for Irish women in relation to the policies of the Irish state and the Catholic Church on issues such as divorce, birth control and abortion. In an outstanding account of late-twentieth-century Irish filmmaking, Martin McLoone outlines the terrain which the above films collectively traversed:

> An interrogation of the rural mythology which underpinned cultural nationalism and is encapsulated in the use of landscape;
> A new concern to represent urban experience which was largely submerged and ignored by this rural mythology;
> A consequent desire to reveal the social and political failures of modern Ireland;
> An interrogation of religion in Ireland, especially in relation to education and sexuality;
> An interrogation of Irish history and Irish tradition, especially the manner in which these have been used to construct notions of identity;
> The question of women in Ireland, especially in relation to nationalist rhetoric, Catholic teaching and imagery, and the discourse around women's bodies;
> The question of Northern Ireland, political violence and the disputed notions of identity which form the crux of the conflict;
> Overall, an assessment of the discourse of Irish nationalism and its continuing dominance over political and social discourse in Ireland, and especially its relationship to progress and modernisation.[16]

Conclusion

The piece from which the above quotation comes is titled 'National Cinema and Cultural Identity: Ireland and Europe' and is much preoccupied with how national cinemas throughout the world position themselves in relation to the hegemony of Hollywood. McLoone is aware that simply to oppose Hollywood films and call for some kind of essential purity within any national cinema is wholly unrealistic, since Hollywood films have become part of the popular culture of virtually every national society on the planet. Indeed, as McLoone points out, it was in fact Hollywood films which offered images of a more modern and liberated society to an Ireland which, certainly up until the 1960s, was priest-ridden and oppressive. The strategy, as McLoone correctly understands, is to engage in some kind of dialectic with Hollywood, as has been fruitfully done in France (in particular, in the films of Jean-Pierre Melville [1917–73]) and in Germany (especially in the films of Wim Wenders) without wholly surrendering to Hollywood values, aesthetic forms and American-led international capitalism.[17] It is on this front particularly that the differences between the Scottish and Irish film milieux of the mid-to-late 1990s were most acute. Where the latter dialectically engaged with Hollywood, the former surrendered to it. This was a position ultimately determined by the very different historical experiences of the Scots and the Irish, as outlined at this essay's outset.

Notes

1. Tom Nairn, *The Break-Up of Britain: Crisis and Neo-Nationalism* (London: New Left Books, 1977).
2. The theoretical and historical dimensions of Romanticism are discussed in, respectively, Meyer Howard Abrams, *The Mirror and the Lamp: Romantic Theory and the Critical Tradition* (London: Oxford University Press, 1953) and Carmen Casaliggi and Porscha Fermanis, *Romanticism: A Literary and Cultural History* (London: Routledge, 2016).
3. See Colin McArthur, 'Culloden: A Pre-emptive Strike', *Scottish Affairs*, no. 9 (1994), 97–126, and also republished elsewhere in the present volume.
4. Luke Gibbons, *Transformations in Irish Culture* (Cork: Cork University Press, 1996), 8.
5. Hydra Associates, *Scotland on Screen: The Development of the Film and Television Industry in Scotland* (Glasgow: Scott Stern Associates, 1996).
6. Scottish Office Information Directorate, 'News Release: A New Era for Scotland on Screen' (Edinburgh: The Scottish Office, 1996), 1.
7. 'Cinema in Ireland: Panel Discussion' (London: National Film Theatre, 1995), 4.
8. Allan Shiach, 'Celebrity Lecture' (Glasgow: BAFTA Scotland, 1996), 5.
9. Eddie Dick, 'Introduction', in *Scottish Film Production Fund Annual Report 1996* (Glasgow: Scottish Film Production Fund, 1996), 3.
10. Rod Stoneman, 'Introduction', in *Irish Film Board Annual Report 1995* (Galway: Irish Film Board, 1995), 5.
11. See Colin McArthur, ed., *Scotch Reels: Scotland in Cinema and Television* (London: British Film Institute, 1982); Colin McArthur, 'In Praise of a Poor Cinema', *Sight and Sound* 3, no. 8 (August 1993), 30–2, and also republished elsewhere in the present volume; Colin McArthur, 'Culloden'; Colin McArthur, 'The Cultural Necessity of a Poor Celtic Cinema', in *Border Crossing: Film in Ireland, Britain and Europe*, eds John Hill, Martin McLoone and Paul Hainsworth (London/Belfast: British Film Institute/Queen's University Institute of Irish Studies, 1994), 112–25, and also republished elsewhere in the present volume.
12. Philip Schlesinger, 'Scotland, Europe and Identity', in *From Limelight to Satellite: A Scottish Film Book*, ed. Eddie Dick (London/Glasgow: British Film Institute and the Scottish Film Council, 1990), 228.

13. *Scottish Screen Information Pack* (Glasgow: Scottish Screen, 1997), no page ref.
14. Ibid.
15. That prediction was, in fact, not borne out by the subsequent evidence. Although Scots filmmakers may have envied and wished to emulate *Trainspotting*'s commercial success, it was not on them that the film proved most influential. It was certain UK film funding operations, most notably Channel 4, which poured money into indigenous Scottish film production in the expectation (or, at least, the hope) of generating commercially successful films from within Scotland, often to the chagrin of local filmmakers chafing under the strings attached to such funding (see Jonathan Murray, *The New Scottish Cinema* [London: I.B. Tauris, 2015], 56).
16. Martin McLoone, 'National Cinema and Cultural Identity: Ireland and Europe', in *Border Crossing: Film in Ireland, Britain and Europe*, eds Hill, McLoone and Hainsworth, 157.
17. The emergence of the New German Cinema in the 1970s offers an interesting model for countries seeking to develop an indigenous film industry. Whatever their difficulties within Germany itself, the post-Oberhausen generation of German filmmakers offers the optimum trajectory of a wholly diverse film culture: some, like Werner Schroeter (1945–2010), Herbert Achternbusch (1938–2022) and, perhaps, Alexander Kluge making films which primarily addressed domestic German questions and did not 'travel' well; Wim Wenders, Werner Herzog, Hans-Jürgen Syberberg and Rainer Werner Fassbinder (1945–82) functioning primarily within international art cinema (although their films are profoundly German); and Volker Schlöndorff and (particularly) Wolfgang Petersen (1941–2022) embracing mainline, Hollywoodean production (see Eric Rentschler, ed., *West German Filmmakers on Film: Visions and Voices* [New York/London: Holmes & Meier, 1988]; Thomas Elsaesser, *New German Cinema: A History* [New Brunswick, NJ: Rutgers University Press, 1989]). Clearly, Irish filmmaking is beginning to approach this diverse model while the Scots are increasingly seeking to define themselves solely on the Hollywoodean example.

CHAPTER 27

Braveheart and the Scottish Aesthetic Dementia*

Braveheart (Mel Gibson, 1995) needs to be discussed in two quite separate ways: as a classical narrative film engaging with the border country between history and myth, and as an event in Scottish culture. In the last analysis the two are connected.

First, the question of historiography and popular narrative film. Let us put together a composite figure: a historian, preferably of Scotland; better still, a medievalist. They are in the best position to point out *Braveheart*'s widely derided historical inaccuracies: the unlikelihood that William Wallace (1270–1305) and his army would have worn kilts and sported tartan of any kind (they were Lowlanders, not Highlanders) or woad (a feature of the Picts who had inhabited Scotland about a millennium earlier); that Wallace might have bedded and impregnated Isabelle (1295–1358), the French princess married to the future Edward II (1284–1327), since there is no evidence that they ever met and the princess delivered her first child several years after Wallace's death; and that English and Scots nobles would have been accoutred differently (in the film the former wear metal and fine cloth and the latter, leather and rough homespun) since both groups were of Anglo-Norman origin, had attained broadly the same level of material development, inhabited the same European code of chivalry and, very often, held lands in both England and Scotland. All of these inaccuracies are verifiable by reference to historical works on late-medieval Scotland.

A more difficult problem concerning *Braveheart*'s historical veracity relates to the film's omissions of verified historical facts that might detract from its ideological construction of Wallace as implacable opponent, such as his overtures to Edward I (1239–1307) seeking less severe

---

*Originally published in *Screening the Past: Film and the Representation of History*, ed. Tony Barta (London: Praeger, 1998), 167–87.

treatment after Edward's defeat of Wallace at the Battle of Falkirk (1298). Ranald Nicholson suggests that Wallace may have made such overtures early in 1304; J. G. Bellamy is more definite, speaking of Wallace as being willing to 'submit to [Edward's] honest peace without surrendering into his hands, body or head'.[1] Such a fact is quite literally unspeakable within the ideological universe *Braveheart* constructs: the film's populist nationalism has something in common with Trotskyist conceptions of the working class as ever ready to rise spontaneously and secure the communist revolution.[2] This repression of facts uncongenial to the work's ideological project is a feature of much historical fiction, most notably, the work that arguably inaugurated the genre in general and historical fiction about Scotland in particular: Sir Walter Scott (1771–1832)'s *Waverley* (1814).[3]

To return to our medievalist: having made these points about historical inaccuracy and omission, they are quite likely to adopt a position far at variance from that which they would take faced with a written document containing the same errors. None of this matters, they are liable to say, because *Braveheart* is 'a ripping yarn, a thundering good tale', implying that the film ought to be outside the protocols of historiography. Our historian's stance is, of course, explicable by reference to deep-seated ideologies regarding popular cultural forms such as cinema. Seeing cinema as irretrievably tarnished by one strand of its origins, that of mass entertainment, and therefore fundamentally Other from the serious, elite business of academic historiography, they would simply be expressing the High Art position in the High Art/Mass Art debate which has riven European culture (and its colonial affiliates) certainly since the onset of industrialisation and the development of mass markets, and arguably before that.[4] Such a position might be understandable, if not entirely excusable, in a medievalist who, after all, is not obliged by their calling to take a professional interest in debates about the origins and development of mass cultural forms. The same attitude, however, is wholly inexcusable within the writings of journalists professionally concerned with cinema. But the 'it is historically inaccurate, but what the hell' attitude is to be found in a very high proportion of reviews of *Braveheart*, albeit seldom expressed with such haughty disdain as in Scottish journalist Alan Taylor's explanation of why he was not going to bother even seeing the film:

> What I find most wearisome [. . .] is the bellyaching of those who are upset over the film's lack of historical accuracy [. . .] What do they expect? This is Hollywood, not a BBC documentary, and it's best to remember that everything is a sacrificial lamb to the demands of studio moguls and box office returns.[5]

Taylor expresses a knee-jerk anti-Hollywood prejudice rather than exploring a very real problem. The question of *Braveheart*'s historical inaccuracies and omissions is far from unimportant. But to note them and then celebrate the film or, conversely, to note them and traduce the film on that account, is to close off discussion of a crucial question. The latter involves the interface between cinema and historiography, of what it means for cinematic institutions of our own time to represent cultures distant in time and space. With regard to *Braveheart*, the issue needs to be reformulated in order to enquire what determinants existed in the film's production process that required it to countenance historical inaccuracies and omissions of the kinds noted above. This enquiry must involve engaging with the Hollywood (or, more accurately, post-Hollywood) milieu, but in a much more cautious and nuanced way than Taylor's blanket condemnation. Exploration of the question requires reference to economics, aesthetics and ideology, and to their interrelationship. While still holding *Braveheart* within an evaluative framework relevant to historiography, the question might be posed: If this film constitutes historical evidence, what is it evidence of? The work's widely acknowledged historical lapses suggest that the last thing it might be evidence of is the actuality of late-medieval Scotland.[6] However, *Braveheart* does constitute historical evidence of two things: firstly, of a certain (post-Hollywood) classical narrative, genre filmmaking, and, secondly, of the curious melding of two modern discourses. One of the latter relates to the construction, or narrativising, of the medieval world, and the other to the constructing, or narrativising, of Scotland.

To describe *Braveheart* as a post-Hollywood work is not to make a point crucial to its status as a historical film. It is simply to observe that this film was set up as a commercial project through the route characteristic of the period following the demise of the major Hollywood studios as production mechanisms around (roughly speaking) the early 1960s. That said, the winding down of the considerable resources the classical Hollywood-era studios devoted to historical research in their heyday may contribute to the historical lapses of some post-Hollywood productions. *Braveheart* was put together as an independent packaging exercise built primarily round a bankable star, Mel Gibson, and a workable script, all the elements being developed and financed by independent production companies (Gibson's own company, Icon productions, and the Ladd Company). The finished film was released by one of the major Hollywood studios, Twentieth Century Fox, in its modern role of distributor rather than producer. However, to describe *Braveheart* as a classical (post-) Hollywood *narrative* film is to begin to engage more directly with the reasons for its historical inaccuracies and omissions. Although at 178 minutes *Braveheart* is half as long again as the characteristic late-twentieth-century narrative fiction film, it displays all the necessary components of that form: a situation of dramatic stasis (medieval Scotland, prone to dynastic squabbling and threats from England); an inciting incident (the murder of Wallace's wife); a central individual protagonist (Wallace) and antagonist (Edward I); protagonist's motivations that are both internal/psychological (revenge for his wife's death) and external/social (emancipation of his country); a series of struggles, gains and reversals; and a return to a new dramatic stasis after the protagonist's triumph, literal or symbolic. The triumph is symbolic in Wallace's case: *Braveheart* constructs him as the sacrificial John the Baptist who paves the way for Robert the Bruce (1274–1329)'s Christ.[7] Such a narrative schema implies a progressivist conception of history.

As well as being a classical narrative film *Braveheart* is also a genre film, although it is not altogether certain to which genre it belongs, another factor which might help explain its tenuous relationship with historical accuracy. On the one hand, it might be seen as an epic involving a quasi-mythical figure. The various film versions of the Robin Hood story fall into this category, as does *El Cid* (Anthony Mann, 1961). All such films set their shadowy heroes alongside actually existing historical personages. On the other hand, *Braveheart* might instead (or also) be seen as an historical bio/pic, a genre present since early in the cinema's development but which solidified into an important Hollywood genre in the late 1930s, particularly with Warner Brothers's series of biographies of important historical figures such as Benito Juárez (1806–72), President of Mexico, and Paul Ehrlich (1854–1915), the discoverer of Salvarsan.[8] Whether *Braveheart* is epic, bio/pic, or both, it delivers the three things required of both genres if they are composited: spectacle, heterosexual love (often, though not necessarily, involving the central protagonist), and an ideological framework congenial to the film's primary consumers, the global mass cinema audience.[9] Clearly, these three requirements overlap with the overarching requirements of any (post-) Hollywood classical narrative feature film. Spectacle is, of course, primarily delivered in *Braveheart*'s battle scenes (a feature many reviewers, including some not well disposed to the film overall, commented favourably on). But the generic necessity to deliver spectacle connects with one dimension of the film's historical inaccuracy, namely, its tendency to undermine the geographically and historically key distinction between the Scottish Highlands and Lowlands and between Highlanders and Lowlanders, although the dominant post-1770 discourses within which Scotland has been constructed also give powerful impetus to

Figure 27.1 Romanticism and Caspar David Friedrich in *Braveheart*: Wallace atop a mountain.

the erroneous view that Scotland is primarily a rural, Highland society (of which more presently). Clearly, the generic requirement of delivering heterosexual love (along with the more formal requirement of minimising the number of central characters within the narrative) explains the historical inaccuracies relating to Princess Isabelle.

In celebrating heterosexual love (and, in *Braveheart*'s case, traducing homosexual love), the epic, the historical bio/pic, and, indeed, all Hollywood genres advance an ideological framework congenial to the great bulk of the popular audience.[10] But they also advance a congenial ideological framework in a more general political sense. *Juarez* (William Dieterle, 1939), for example, accomplished its ideological project of valorising Benito Juárez by consistently identifying him with Abraham Lincoln (1809–65), having lead actor Paul Muni (1895–1967) dress in the same funereal clothes as the American president instead of Mexican garb, and by having photographs of Lincoln on the walls of Juarez's rooms.[11] One of the mechanisms whereby an epic or historical bio/pic is rendered ideologically congenial to a popular audience is by linking the central protagonist to one single, oft-reiterated word that evokes a favourable audience response. For example, in *Rob Roy* (Michael Caton-Jones, 1995), another excursion into Scottish history, that word is 'honour' (a singularly inappropriate choice, given what historians know about the actual activities of

Rob Roy).[12] In *Braveheart*, the word is 'freedom'. This fact in turn connects with another sense in which *Braveheart* is historically adrift. It constructs Wallace as a kind of modern nationalist guerrilla leader in a period half a millennium before the appearance of nationalism on the historical stage as a concept under which disparate classes and interests might be mobilised within a putative nation state. As Tom Nairn (1932–2023) and others have argued, modern nationalism is the consequence of the uneven economic development produced by the English agricultural and industrial revolutions of the eighteenth century, the banner under which the bourgeoisies of France, Germany, Italy and elsewhere mobilised the forces within their own geographical areas to catch up with Britain.[13] The reverse consequence of *Braveheart* being anachronistically marked by modern nationalism is that the film feels no need to engage with the ideological structures of the late medieval period, most notably, feudalism, the Church and the chivalric code. Of course, it is prepared to press into service limited aspects of feudalism that can be made to function within the film's modern ideological framework. This is true particularly of *jus primae noctis*, the feudal right of the lord to one night of sexual access, before her husband, to a newly married tenant.

Braveheart assumes, and expects its audience to assume, that *jus primae noctis* was an unambiguous act of sexual tyranny.[14] In this respect it contrasts interestingly with *The War Lord* (Franklin J. Schaffner, 1965), which, although a classical narrative movie in the same tradition as *Braveheart*, was constructed round a medieval lord's refusal to return a bride to her spouse after his exercise of *jus primae noctis*. Clearly, *The War Lord* expected its audience to see the lord's refusal, and the bride's connivance in it, as the triumph of 'modern' love over feudal convention. Nevertheless, with a subtlety altogether absent from *Braveheart*, *The War Lord* attempts to get inside the medieval mind by presenting the lord's tenants' outrage, not at his having deflowered the bride but at his refusal to return her to her husband. The motivation of Liam Neeson's Rob Roy in the 1995 film of that name is also constructed partly in relation to the sexual abuse of his wife, as though modern filmmakers have difficulty in conceiving lead protagonist motivations that do not involve sexuality (but see above regarding the requirement of classical Hollywood narrative movies to deliver heterosexual love). A rare example of a film which, while dealing with sexuality, attempts to represent the otherness of the medieval world is *Blanche* (Walerian Borowczyk, 1971). It does this partly by using distancing devices such as medieval music played on medieval instruments and incorporated diegetically into the film with medieval modes of musical presentation, and a visual style based on the flat, non-perspectival look and range of colours of medieval painting. *Braveheart*, by contrast, has a lush, non-diegetic, romantic score based on vaguely Celtic motifs which, as it happens, sound more Irish than Scottish – perhaps appropriately so, given the production was lured to Ireland from Scotland by promises of tax incentives and Irish Army reservists as extras. Significantly, *Blanche* is usually categorised and presented as an art house rather than a mass entertainment movie.[15]

Certainty about how to represent the past recedes the further back you go. The convention is that late Victorians are stiff and hypocritical at home and languidly supercilious in their imperial setting; Regency figures (and possibly early Victorians) are jolly and Dickensian; and eighteenth-century figures are sexually rumbustious. Prior to that, however, certain 'Dark Ages' tropes predominate: darkness; religiosity and/or mysticism; grinding poverty and filth; physical deformity and disfiguring disease; and, above all, unrestrained and unspeakable cruelty. These are the dominant tropes of *Braveheart*. This cinematic discourse of Dark Ageism can be tracked through *The Private Life of Henry VIII* (Alexander Korda, 1933), in which Charles Laughton (1899–1962)'s messy eating and wife-beheadings are key tropes; *Day of Wrath* (Carl Dreyer, 1943); *The Seventh Seal* (Ingmar Bergman, 1957) and *The Virgin Spring* (Ingmar Bergman, 1960); and *The Vikings* (Richard Fleischer, 1958) to *The Name of the Rose* (Jean-Jacques Annaud, 1986). Day explores brilliantly how *Monty Python and the Holy Grail* (Terry Gilliam and Terry Jones, 1975) simultaneously presents and deconstructs this discourse, implicitly posing the question: How can we, in the modern world, adequately represent the Middle Ages?[16] Chris Peachment traverses some of the same terrain in a witty and accessible journalistic way.[17] Cinematic Dark Ageism suffuses *Braveheart*, particularly its battle scenes, which are all gore, pierced eyes and genitals, cloven skulls, severed limbs and awful screams.[18] It is present, too, in the morbid explicitness of Wallace's execution and the malignant leprosy of Robert the Bruce's father.

However, dominant as Dark Ageism is in the construction of *Braveheart*, it is alloyed from time to time with another powerful discourse within which Scotland is constructed: Tartanry. This discourse has many facets, not all of which *Braveheart* mobilises. It emerged during the Neo-Classical period in the wake of James Macpherson (1736–96)'s alleged translations (but in fact, inventions) of fragments of Gaelic poetry about ancient heroes such as Ossian and Fingal, and received periodic boosts through subsequent phenomena such as Sir Walter Scott's writings and Queen Victoria (1819–1901)'s imprimatur being conferred on the Highlands, not least through her residence at Balmoral. The cumulative effect of the Tartanry discourse was to construct Scotland, in the eyes of pre-Romantic and Romantic Europe, as a magical landscape of hills and mists peopled by fierce warriors and wan maidens living close to Nature, a realm with the power to transform strangers and teach them to dream. This discourse was, as Malcolm Chapman and others have pointed out, an act of 'symbolic appropriation'[19] by pre-Romantic and Romantic ideologues who constructed Scotland in terms of the dreams, fears, fantasies and repressions of their own societies, just as they were to do with the South Seas, Orient and Africa.[20] Tartanry was subsequently to dominate every form of signification relating to Scotland: novels, plays, music, operas, ballets, easel painting, photography, advertising, right down to film and television in the present day.[21] So hegemonic did Tartanry become in the representation of Scotland that anyone seeking to speak about the country was drawn, Circe-like, to that discourse, its pernicious tropes guiding the hands of artists and intellectuals of all kinds, including, most grievously, Scots themselves. It is Tartanry, therefore, that requires *Braveheart*'s Scottish characters to wear tartan, though the historical evidence is that they did not, and to be seen in mountainous terrain although theirs was primarily a Lowland struggle. *Braveheart*'s aesthetic might be described as debased Romanticism, if one conceives (as Tom Nairn and others have done) of Romanticism as the cultural mode of nationalism.

This is not to say that a Romantic aesthetic cannot deliver serious analytic screen history. *The Leopard* (Luchino Visconti, 1963) triumphantly demonstrates this. Its lush musical score, based on the late music of Anton Bruckner (1824–96), Gustav Mahler (1860–1911) and Giuseppe Verdi (1813–1901), and its visual style, based on Romantic painting, are entirely appropriate to the film's theme, an analysis of the situation of an aristocratic Sicilian family at a moment of historical change in Risorgimento Italy. *Braveheart*'s debased Romanticism is unstiffened by *The Leopard*'s kind of precise historical analysis; the latter film is a Realist work in the Lukacsian sense of the term, its characters incarnating the social and political contradictions of their time.[22] *Braveheart*'s Romanticism is closer to the popular meaning of the term, suggesting something very far removed from reality, dealing with heightened emotions and displaying a certain vulgar pictorialism. The latter quality is evident throughout the film, but is most gross in the scenes involving Wallace and the two women in his life, his wife, Murron (Catherine McCormack), and his lover, Princess Isabelle (Sophie Marceau). The full realisation of this vulgar pictorialism depends upon the orchestration of every dimension of *mise-en-scène* at key moments: acting, lighting, music, use of slow motion, and the like. The obverse of this sentimentality is the savagery of the battle scenes and the way Wallace's execution is mounted.

Any argument about *Braveheart*'s aesthetic insensitivity cannot be conducted in generalities: it must get down to the specific *mise-en-scène* of particular moments within the film. But the resultant argument will often be about the extent to which the film unerringly opts for aesthetic strategies that are, so to speak, 'off the shelf': clichés emerging from the filmmakers working on automatic pilot rather than thinking carefully about the scene in question. Neal Ascherson, one of the writers cited in this essay's second half, refers to a particular scene in which the child Wallace, standing by his father's grave, is handed a thistle flower by the child Murron. The present essay's argument about *Braveheart*'s aesthetic crassness would raise questions about the casting of the child players (particularly the boy playing Wallace, who looks like a tearful, fetching urchin from a Joan Eardley [1921–63] painting); about the performances the director has asked the children to deliver; about the colour and focusing of the shots; and, above all, about the music track accompanying them. *Braveheart*'s *mise-en-scène* seeks to bludgeon the audience's emotional response. The same kind of analysis can be applied to the scene of Wallace's execution. To show a close-up of a bench covered with sacking and then to draw back that material to reveal the ghastly array of implements to be used in Wallace's hanging, drawing, castration, beheading and quartering is to indulge in torture porn. One of the paradoxes of film reviewing is that tabloid reviews, albeit for the most part retellings of the plot and superficial expressions of the reviewer's taste, sometimes cut to the heart of shallow pretentiousness in film acting and direction in a way that ostensibly more serious broadsheet reviews may not. Such was the case with one such piece, which described the above scene with the children as 'more of a Bird's Eye advert than serious drama'.[23]

Narratives about certain societies – the Antebellum American South and Nazi Germany spring to mind – seem particularly prone to a melange of savagery and sentimentality, and narratives about Scotland show something of the same tendency. In *Braveheart* this noxious mix is occasionally offset by other elements, most notably, Mel Gibson's playing of Wallace with some humour, a feature of his roles more generally. The extent to which this is so may be judged by imagining how Charlton Heston (1923–2008), another leading man associated with cinematic epics for a substantial part of his career and an actor not given to self-mockery, might have played the role. This, of course, cuts two ways. There are moments in *Braveheart* when Gibson's repertoire of signs (particularly, ironic movements of his eyes) recalls his earlier roles in the *Lethal Weapon* (1987–98) and *Mad Max* (1979–85) film cycles, posing the legitimate question of that repertoire's appropriateness for signifying a late-medieval warrior within the film's own illusionist aesthetic, a key element of which is that things look (superficially, at least) authentic.

No such ambiguities, however, mitigate the thoroughly debased Romanticism of Randall Wallace's novelisation of his own screenplay for *Braveheart*.[24] To adapt Oscar Wilde (1854–1900)'s remarks on Charles Dickens (1812–70)'s account of the death of Little Nell in *The Old Curiosity Shop* (1841), one must have a heart of stone to read Wallace's *Braveheart* novel without laughing. Usefully, however, this piece of sub-Barbara Cartland (1901–2000) pulp literature indicates the extent to which the devil's brew of savagery and sentimentality is present in the cinematic *Braveheart*'s writing as well as its direction. The quality of Wallace's writing may be gleaned from the following extracts, the first from the scene in which Wallace and Robert the Bruce meet for the first time, the second from the scene of the first encounter between Wallace and Princess Isabelle:

> Wallace stood with his feet planted as wide as his shoulders, and for a man with shoulders so broad, the posture could have looked bullying. But his face contained none of the surly arrogance of the brute. He was handsome, strikingly so; manly, calm and self-contained – young Bruce could see why tough men like the Highlanders [sic] would follow this man into battle. It was a face women would like, with softness in the pale green eyes and light playing in the blondish hair. His chin was up, his mouth set, his eyes still. And young Robert the Bruce knew that before him stood a man who never had nor never would subjugate himself to any other man [. . .]

> [A]nd while the princess reminded William Wallace of everything he had loved and lost, he haunted her with everything she wanted and had never found. Tall, powerful, commanding, his shoulders thick, his hair wild, his eyes soft, even pained. A man facing the hatred of the world's most powerful king; a man who had won great battles and commanded armies, yet who looked as if he could spur his horse away right now and ride away from adoration and glory and never miss any of it. She had never seen a man like this. She had never known such a one existed.[25]

What Randall Wallace's novelisation offers that the film does not is a prologue and epilogue outlining his own take on the story of William Wallace. The epilogue, in particular, is remarkable for its melange of authorial hubris; mystical, quasi-blood-and-soil ideology; and a staggeringly vulgar and sentimental sensibility. In the following extract, Randall Wallace describes returning to the Smithfield area of London where William Wallace met his end:

> I wanted to visit that sanctuary [a church on the site] again to find a private place away from the crowded street, where people passed neither knowing or caring about the long-dead Scot remembered on the plaque or the American who stopped before it, gazing up at it with tears in his eyes.

> The church was closed that day. So I stood in the arched shelter of its entryway, beside its graveyard. I had meant to pray inside the church, but where I now found

myself seemed no less fine a place for prayer. So I thanked God for my family and friends and for my calling as a storyteller. And I thanked God for William Wallace. I wondered if William Wallace was just as glad I had come upon his story. And then something strange happened. I can't say that I saw him; it may be an overstatement to say that I felt his presence. But I felt that I could talk to him there. I thanked him personally. I told him I had no idea if we were related by blood, but I had come to feel a kinship with him and felt that somehow I was meant to be there, seven hundred years after he was, to tell his story. I told him there were few promises I could make him as to what would become of this telling of his tale, but I could make him the same one I had made to God and to myself; I would do my best to convey the truth as I saw it to those around me.[26]

In Randall Wallace's universe, even a piece of ostensible authorial reportage takes on the character of a Romantic trope: the swearing of an oath to a departed 'ancestor'.

The key question that arises from all of the above, however, is how the ludicrously debased Romanticism of Randall Wallace's writing and Mel Gibson's direction should provoke such a powerful response within Scotland. The indices of *Braveheart* as 'event' in Scottish culture are diverse. A useful starting point is the decision of the film's producers to mount its European premiere in Stirling, a medium-sized Scottish town somewhat to the north of, and equidistant from, Edinburgh and Glasgow, but deemed appropriate for the premiere since it was close to the site of Wallace's victory over the English at the Battle of Stirling Bridge in 1297 and also of the Wallace Monument, raised in the 1860s as part of the culture of nationalism's 'invention of tradition', a phenomenon ably described in the book of essays of that title.[27] The extent to which the producers' awareness of the Scottish nationalist/separatist ideology of their film was also a factor in the siting of their premiere in Stirling is an open question. It was a factor about which they (and particularly, Mel Gibson) were somewhat coy when the Scottish National Party (SNP) appropriated *Braveheart* as a whole into its party rhetoric and specific images from the film into its party literature (of which more presently). Most societies are to some extent dazzled by the idea of Hollywood, and particularly by the opportunity to see Hollywood stars in the flesh. It is a mark of Scotland's provincialism that it has regularly feted (in the form of breathless national and local media coverage) those Hollywood stars who have come there and, what is worse, celebrated those films which have constructed Scotland within regressive discourses.[28] This long-term dazzlement was, with regard to *Braveheart*, most evident in the local newspaper, the *Stirling Observer*, which announced delightedly on the front page of its 2 August 1995 edition that the film's European premiere would be in Stirling. Subsequent issues reported the arrangements for the premiere and, in a variation on a regular feature of the paper, ran a competition offering as prizes tickets to it. The culmination of the *Stirling Observer*'s coverage came with a special *Braveheart* Souvenir Issue of 6 September 1995, which carried four pages of stories and pictures about the premiere, the stars and the great and the good attending it, and the ecstatic response of the local people who waited for up to eight hours in pouring rain to catch a glimpse of the visiting notables. Such was the local demand for this issue that the relevant four pages were reproduced in the issue of 8 September. The Scottish national tabloid press was no less ecstatic, the *Daily Record* of 4 September 1995 quoting a Stirling Old Age Pensioner: 'I've lived here all my life and I've never seen anything like this. Stirling has become the centre of the world.' It was left to an English broadsheet, *The Guardian*, to describe the premiere in altogether more sardonic terms.[29]

Another index of the extent to which *Braveheart* became an event in Scottish culture was the film's intertextuality, its capacity to be referred to, quoted from and analogised in sites far removed from cinema. It became a fruitful source for political and other press cartoons; one newspaper talked of a snooker player as 'Braveheart of the green baize'; a travel feature on walking in Scotland was titled 'For the Brave Hearted'; a staff recruitment advertisement by Scottish Enterprise was headed 'William Wallaces wanted'; a football match report referred to East Fife manager Steve Archibald as 'Brave Arch!'; and (a sure sign of intertextual status) the British television comedy programme *French and Saunders* (BBC, 1987–2005) included a sketch which satirised both *Rob Roy* and *Braveheart*. The latter was accurate in sending up both films' heavily macho ethos and *Braveheart*'s aesthetic grossness. *Braveheart* is not unique with regard to intertextuality: certain films, most notably, *Casablanca* (Michael Curtiz, 1942), are profusely intertextual.[30] The point made here, however, relates to *Braveheart*'s fecund intertextuality in the specifically Scottish context, the first film since *Local Hero* (Bill Forsyth, 1983) to function in this way and an indicator of its status as event in Scottish culture.

The third index of *Braveheart*'s status in this regard is its above-noted appropriation by the Scottish National Party. The UK Conservative government's Secretary of State for Scotland, Michael Forsyth (who also happened to then be the MP for Stirling), and his parliamentary shadow, Labour MP George Robertson, both attended the Stirling premiere and made half-hearted attempts to square their own parties' unionist politics with the film's clear independence message, but everyone knew that there was no way they could construct the Wallace of *Braveheart* as anything other than separatist.[31] As well as the film's deployment within SNP campaigning literature, it also figured substantially in the address of the Party's National Convenor, SNP MP Alex Salmond, at the 1995

SNP annual conference a few weeks after the Stirling premiere. Indeed, the entire opening section of Salmond's address was structured round the film and is worth quoting in detail:

> A funny thing happened to me on the way to the *Braveheart* Premier [sic]. There was the hero draped in tartan just waiting to be cheered by the thousands lining the streets as he entered the cinema. And what happened? Well first he got booed in. Three hours later he was booed out. For this wasn't the Hollywood hero but the local hero – not Mel but Michael, the Secretary of State Against Scotland – the man whom Lady Thatcher once described in her memoirs as a 'Young Lochinvar'. They [Michael Forsyth and George Robertson] were certainly having trouble explaining away the message. Michael said that Wallace was a fighter for Scottish 'interests'. George said he fought for Scottish 'identity'. Notice this difficulty with the 'I' word.
> The one word they didn't want to mention was INDEPENDENCE which is what Wallace was actually fighting for.
> The *Braveheart* screenwriter Randall Wallace tells of how he talked to some local youngsters in the shadow of the Wallace monument. They knew it was called the Wallace monument but couldn't tell him anything about the man it commemorated.
> The story of Wallace should and does inspire us, but the story of the youngsters who had never heard of Wallace should make us pause and ponder.
> We should be ashamed that it has taken Hollywood to give so many Scots back our history.
> And George and Michael should also be worried because now, as anyone who knows the story and has seen the film will know, the real villains are not the English but the establishment leadership of Scotland who bought and sold their country for personal advancement.[32]

Salmond then went on to deal with more substantial issues of policy, but the ideological capital of the film's bringing the shadowy historical figure of Wallace back to public attention was cashed once more in the final words of his address: 'We can say with Wallace – head and heart – the one word which encapsulates all our hopes – Freedom, Freedom, Freedom.'[33]

This essay began by suggesting that, in the final analysis, there is a connection between *Braveheart* as aesthetic object and *Braveheart* as event in Scottish culture. To be more concrete, there is a connection between the film's debased Romanticism, its post-1789 populist nationalism and xenophobia, and the way it has been appropriated by individuals and institutions in Scotland. The eminently knowledgeable Scots journalist Neal Ascherson, who understands better than most nationalism's universality, virtual inevitability and appalling dangers within the modern world, wrote about *Braveheart*'s seductive populism in an article about heroes, popular and official:

> Seeking heroes, I went the other day to see *Braveheart*. As an account of the real William Wallace, or of late 13th-century Scotland, it is a joke. The list of cultural howlers and historical distortions rolls on for ever. As in the similar *Rob Roy*, the

English feature as degenerate, upper-class sadists [. . .] you go to scoff [. . .] and yet there are moments when this shilling schlocker takes you unawares. One strong-minded, progressive friend found herself in tears. Another Scottish colleague reacted with a furious attack on the film for reducing his country's struggles to crude anti-English racism. Both went to the film certain they were immune to its allure – but neither was. They saw a child give a flower to a boy standing at his murdered father's grave, and the flower was a thistle. They heard a man speak easily of his country's 'freedom' without seeking a lesser word. Suddenly, they were undone. Wallace is a real hero, which means that he lives on in the shadows at the back of people's heads.[34]

Ascherson's point about *Braveheart*'s seductiveness was repeated, with a much diminished sense of the film's dangers or aesthetic affront, by his fellow Scottish journalist Brian Pendreigh:

Braveheart provides one of Scotland's great heroes with a monument as impressive in its own way as the one outside Stirling. But, more than that, it provides the Scots with a powerful creation myth which will surely help to focus our national sense of identity.[35]

And the Scottish actor James Cosmo, who plays Wallace's right-hand man in the film, was reported in the *Stirling Observer* as 'bursting with pride'. It is as if an aesthetic dementia had gripped the Scots, rendering them blind to the empty populism, slavering xenophobia and sheer stylistic vulgarity of *Braveheart*. Dismaying enough in individuals, it is decidedly sinister when a national political party aligns itself with such a truly appalling film. One of the *Stirling Observer*'s parting shots on the topic of the *Braveheart* premiere was a photograph of a kilted Mel Gibson in a prominent position on the front page of its 8 September 1995 issue under the headline 'It's Mel Mania!' At the bottom of the same page, under the headline '"Anti-English" alert', was an item about local police looking for information concerning leaflets and graffiti canvassing the sentiment 'English Go Home'. The *Stirling Observer* made no connection between the two items, although a film more calculated to encourage the sentiments the leaflets and graffiti expressed could not be imagined. One would heartily wish that *Braveheart*, to quote Leon Trotsky (1879–1940), 'will be swept into the garbage heap of history'. One's fear, however, is that, available for domestic viewing, it will play to packed buses of Scottish soccer and rugby supporters en route to matches against England, whipping them into a frenzy of xenophobia.

Afterword

This afterword was written some months after the above essay. In the intervening period *Braveheart*'s delirious intertextuality had continued apace, culminating in the discursive '*Braveheart*-isation' of the Scotland versus

England soccer match during the June Euro '96 tournament. Throughout the latter one could scarcely open a newspaper or listen to a sports broadcast without hearing the Scots team described as 'bravehearts' and, indeed, this was the trope deployed on the cover of the Scottish edition of *Radio Times* concurrent with the competition. However, *Braveheart*'s discursive visibility also had a curious effect on the rhetorical construction of the England team, particularly in the English tabloid press. This could be described as the 'medieval-isation' of England. It was as if the tabloids, aware of the heroic construction of the Scots in terms of the figure(s) of William Wallace/Mel Gibson, sought to construct the English in analogous terms. This resulted in extensive referencing of the English team as 'lionhearts' and – an English central hero on the scale of Wallace being a requirement in this narrative – the accoutring of star player Paul Gascoigne in the masquerade of Henry V (1386–1422).

However, I am happy to report that – despite the waving of life-size cut-outs of Mel Gibson at the game – the dire foreboding about the effects of *Braveheart* on the Scots fans with which I ended the above essay proved unwarranted. No doubt there were complex reasons for this, including the excellent spirit within which the competition was played and better stadium facilities, stewarding and police intelligence. However, I would like to think that Richard Giulianotti's intriguing theory also had something to do with it. His argument, based on the evidence of the 1990 football World Cup in Italy, is that the Scots fans, popularly known as the Tartan Army, now construct their identity dialogically in relation to the identity of the English national team's fans. The latter had arrived in Italy in 1990 with a well-earned reputation for xenophobia, moroseness and violence. Wishing not to be associated with this, Giulianotti argues, the Scots constructed themselves as internationalist, convivial and placid. The most important part of his argument is that the Scots fans projected this new identity (their own historical one had itself been rather alarming) through the same range of icons (including tartan scarves, kilts and Saltire and Lion Rampant flags) as before.[36] By suggesting that these icons are empty vessels waiting to be filled with either progressive or regressive identities, Giulianotti calls into question the position of those writers (the present one included) who see such icons as irretrievably tarnished by the previous uses to which they have been put and the historic range of attitudes associated with them.[37]

Notes

1. Ranald Nicholson, *Scotland: The Later Middle Ages* (Edinburgh: Oliver & Boyd, 1974); J. G. Bellamy, *The Law of Treason in England in the Late Middle Ages* (Cambridge: Cambridge University Press, 1970), 33.

2. As will become clear, this chapter is not a crude attack on historical films, in particular those made within the Hollywood tradition. At the same time, historical films should not be let off the hook of historical veracity because they are dramatic reconstructions. After all, academic works of historiography are themselves acts of reconstruction, albeit using a different rhetoric from that of narrative fiction. The distinction False Invention/True Invention has been illuminatingly discussed in Robert A. Rosenstone, *Visions of the Past: The Challenge of Film to Our Idea of History* (Cambridge, MA: Harvard University Press, 1995).
3. In a novel devoted to the 1745 Jacobite Rising, it is astonishing that the Battle of Culloden (1746) should be, to all intents and purposes, repressed. However, the repression does facilitate the novel's pro-unionist closure. See Claire Lamont, '*Waverley* and the Battle of Culloden', in *History and the Novel*, ed. Angus Easson (Cambridge: D. S. Brewer, 1991), 14; 26.
4. James Naremore and Patrick Brantlinger, eds, *Modernity and Mass Culture* (Bloomington: Indiana University Press, 1991).
5. Alan Taylor, 'Tinseltown history', *The Scotsman*, 4 September 1995, 12.
6. Many historians and students of film, operating from diverse theoretical positions, would regard this as a foregone conclusion. Pierre Sorlin stresses the inevitability of historical films being about the time and place in which they were produced and not the time and place of the events they represent: Pierre Sorlin, *The Film in History: Restaging the Past* (Oxford: Basil Blackwell, 1980). David Day talks about the impossibility of grasping 'the Medieval Other': David Day, 'Monty Python and the Medieval Order', in *Cinema Arthuriana: Essays on Arthurian Film*, ed. Kevin J. Harty (New York/London: Garland, 1991), 83–92; Robert Rosenstone, under the influence of postmodernist attempts to eclipse history, canvasses a form of historical film that is self-referential, palpably as much about its own take on the past as the past itself: Robert Rosenstone, *Visions of the Past*.
7. A detailed account of the operation of classical Hollywood narrative and how it privileges individual and not collective solutions to problems can be found in David Bordwell and Kristin Thompson, *Film Art: An Introduction* (New York: Knopf, 1986).
8. George F. Custen, *Bio/Pics: How Hollywood Constructed Public History* (New Brunswick, NJ: Rutgers University Press, 1992).
9. See Leger Grindon, *Shadows on the Past: Studies in the Historical Fiction Film* (Philadelphia: Temple University Press, 1994). Grindon writes interestingly about romance and spectacle in historical films, in particular, about spectacle as bearer of their trans-individual, historical elements.
10. GLAAD (Gay and Lesbian Alliance Against Defamation) demonstrated against *Braveheart* at its opening in nine American cities on account of its construction of Edward I's son and his gay lover.
11. Grindon, *Shadows on the Past*, 12.
12. It is well established among historians that Rob Roy was, among other things, what would today be called a stool pigeon, acting as an informant for the

Hanoverian government against his erstwhile Jacobite comrades. See James Allardyce, ed., *Historical Papers Relating to the Jacobite Period, 1699–1750* (Aberdeen: New Spalding Club, 1895); Allan I. Macinnes, *Clans, Commerce and the House of Stuart* (East Linton: Tuckwell Press, 1996).
13. Tom Nairn, *The Break-Up of Britain: Crisis and Neo-Nationalism* (London: New Left Books, 1977).
14. It is widely assumed that *jus primae noctis* actually existed in medieval Europe, but a search of the historiographical work relating to the period reveals a curious absence of the concept. The idea is dealt with in the *Encyclopaedia Britannica* under the heading '*droit de seigneur*': 'The evidence of its existence in Europe is almost all indirect, involving records of redemption dues paid by the vassal to avoid enforcement. A considerable number of feudal rights related to the vassal's marriage, particularly the lord's right to select a bride for his vassal, but these were almost invariably redeemed by a money payment or 'avail' [. . .] it seems likely that the *droit du seigneur* amounted, in effect, only to another tax of this sort' (*Encyclopaedia Britannica*, 15th edition [1973], 670).
15. Steve Neale, 'Art Cinema as Institution', *Screen* 22, no. 1 (1981), 11–39.
16. Day, 'Monty Python and the Medieval Order'.
17. Chris Peachment, 'All you need is mud', *The Independent*, 7 September 1995, 8.
18. *Braveheart*'s representation of violence seems to have set new standards. It is reported that the producers of *The Bruce* (David McWhinnie and Bob Carruthers, 1996), yet another foray into Scottish history, ordered its battle scenes to be reshot since the first version did not reach the level of gore achieved in *Braveheart*. See M. McBain, 'Bruce has his bloody encore', *Scotland on Sunday*, 14 January 1995, 1.
19. Malcolm Chapman, *The Gaelic Vision in Scottish Culture* (London: Croom Helm: 1978), 28.
20. Chapman, *The Gaelic Vision in Scottish Culture*; Frantz Fanon, *Black Skin, White Masks* (New York: Grove Press, 1968).
21. Colin McArthur, ed., *Scotch Reels: Scotland in Cinema and Television* (London: British Film Institute, 1982).
22. György Lukács (1885–1971), philosopher, literary critic and political activist, formulated in works such as *The Historical Novel* (1937) a sophisticated, antimodernist theory of literary realism. This was too hastily discounted by the modernist Left in its elevation of Bertolt Brecht (1898–1956), with whom Lukács had a stinging debate in the interwar period. See Theodor Adorno, Walter Benjamin, Ernst Bloch, Bertolt Brecht, and Georg Lukács, *Aesthetics and Politics* (London: Verso, 1980).
23. Simon Rose, 'Mel of a super hero', *Daily Mirror*, 7 September 1995, 3.
24. Randall Wallace, *Braveheart* (London: Signet/Penguin Books, 1995).
25. Ibid., 146–7; 163.
26. Ibid., 276–7.
27. Eric Hobsbawm and Terence Ranger, eds, *The Invention of Tradition* (Cambridge: Cambridge University Press, 1983).

28. *Brigadoon* (Vincente Minnelli, 1954), *The Maggie* (Alexander Mackendrick, 1954) and *Local Hero* (Bill Forsyth, 1983) have in their respective times been rapturously welcomed in Scotland. *Brigadoon* (arguably one of the more complex films on the question of the representation of Scotland) in particular drives Scots intellectuals to distraction. It is repeatedly cited as the very nadir of mawkish Tartanry.
29. Erlend Clouston, 'Little Mel Walks Tall in Adulation of Scots Fans', *The Guardian*, 4 September 1995, 2.
30. Colin McArthur, *The* Casablanca *File* (London: Half Brick Images, 1992).
31. Arnold Kemp, 'Battling Over *Braveheart*', *The Guardian*, 11 September 1995, 13.
32. SNP News Release (1995).
33. Ibid.
34. Neal Ascherson, 'Now is the time for official heroes to come to the aid of the party', *The Independent on Sunday*, 24 September 1995, 20. Ascherson's call for a proper place to be accorded to popular national heroes echoes that of Raphael Samuel, 'The people with stars in their eyes', *The Guardian*, 23 September 1995, 27. Both essays are considered Left responses to the remarks of Nicholas Tate, Chief Executive of the School Curriculum and Assessment Authority, who had argued for the resuscitation of British national heroes/heroines such as Alfred the Great (848–99) and Horatio Nelson (1758–1805) so that children might once again become proud of their national past. Tate's was an intervention from the Right into the essentially political struggle over the national curriculum's content. For the extent to which the struggle over the meaning of the past is characteristic of all advanced capitalist countries concerned about their 'place in the world', see Frank Füredi, *Mythical Past, Elusive Future: History and Society in an Anxious Age* (London: Pluto Press, 1992).
35. Brian Pendreigh, 'Gibson turns Wallace into Mad Mac', *The Scotsman*, 4 September 1995, 4.
36. Richard Giulianotti, 'Scotland's Tartan Army in Italy: The Case for the Carnivalesque', *Sociological Review* 39, no. 3 (1991), 503–27.
37. This essay's arguments were first rehearsed at two events, one at the University of Aberdeen, the other at the University of Glasgow. With regard to the former, I express my thanks to the chair of the panel discussion, Professor Allan I. Macinnes; to my co-panellists, Dr Grant Simpson and Dr Peter Murray; and to the committee of the Aberdeen University Historical Society, Dawn Bailey, Alison Cathcart, Rosie Fell, and Karen Jillings. With regard to the second event, I thank Dr Irene Maver and Dr David Limond of the Department of Scottish History. The essay is dedicated to the memory of Barbara Grigor (1944–94), who, with her husband Murray, did so much to contest regressive accounts of Scottish history and culture.

CHAPTER 28

The Exquisite Corpse of Rab(elais) C(opernicus) Nesbitt*

In the Beginning was the Word

The following discussion of BBC Scotland's networked television sitcom *Rab C. Nesbitt* (1988–2014) demonstrates the acuity of the literary theorist and historian Cairns Craig's ambitious synthesising perception that:

> What happened in Scotland in the 1960s and the 1970s and what laid the foundation for the enormous creative achievements of the 1980s was the liberation of the voice. The Scottish voice declared its independence [. . .] The liberation of the voice was at first an acceptance of and an assertion of the vernacular [. . .] But the real liberation of the voice came not from the assertion of the rights of the vernacular itself, but from the assertion of the right to move without boundaries between the vernacular and standard English, between the demotic and the literary.[1]

For exactly the far-reaching reasons Craig outlines, *Rab C. Nesbitt*, despite eliciting praise from most English television reviewers and achieving some sort of cult status, also provoked a strong sense of Otherness from the same sources. Their collective response emphasises the series's linguistic difficulty for non-Scots. Thus:

> Apart from the impenetrability of the Govan Glasgow accents, given the operatic level of violence and caricature on which *Rab C. Nesbitt* is pitched, subtitles would be helpful to English speakers.[2]

> Many viewers still complain that they can't understand a word of the broad dialect and need subtitles.[3]

> Virtually incomprehensible to anyone born south of Berwick-upon-Tweed.[4]

---

* Originally published in *Dissident Voices: The Politics of Television and Cultural Change*, ed. Mike Wayne (London: Pluto Press, 1998), 107–26.

> There are problems with the show for Southerners [. . .] Heaven knows what the Ceefax subtitler manages to make of lines which often seem to have the phonetic structure 'Ochty baster nachty blooin'.[5]

> [S]urely the filthiest and most disgusting character on television, I am convinced that [Rab] is broadcast in England only because the censors cannot understand his Gorbals accent.[6]

One reviewer even provided a glossary of 'Rabspeak': '*Stoating*: most agreeable; *To rip the pish oot o'*: to take a rise out of; *A ran dan night*: a hugely enjoyable evening'.[7]

In general, metropolitan press observations about the linguistic difficulty of *Rab C. Nesbitt* are good-humoured enough. But, as in jokes about 'wogs', 'niggers' and 'paddies', the underlying discourse of power may be revealed in all its imperial arrogance and viciousness in other linguistic situations relating to Scotland. Take, for example, Booker Prize judge Rabbi Julia Neuberger's public dissociation of herself from the decision, of the panel on which she served, to award the 1994 Prize to Glasgow writer James Kelman's novel, *How late it was, how late* (1994). Neuberger described herself as 'implacably opposed to the book. It is not a book which is publicly accessible'.[8]

Kelman himself describes the experience (a common one for Scots as for other peripheral peoples) of being on the sharp end of this Standard English imperium, of seeking vainly within English literature for any adequate representation of the inner life of Glaswegians like himself:

> How do you recognise a Glaswegian in English literature? [. . . H]e's the cut-out figure who wields a razor-blade, gets morocolous drunk and never has a single, solitary 'thought' in his entire life. He beats his wife and beats his kids and beats his next door neighbour. And another striking thing: everybody from a Glaswegian or working-class background, everybody in fact from any regional part of Britain – none of them knew how to talk! [. . .] Unlike the nice stalwart upper-class English hero [. . .] whose words on the page were always absolutely splendidly proper and pure and pristinely accurate whether in dialogue or without [. . .] Most interesting of all, for myself as a writer, the narrative belonged to them and them alone. They owned it. The place where thought and spiritual life exists.[9]

When Kelman talks of 'the narrative belonging to them and them alone', he echoes Frantz Fanon (1925–61) and Edward Said (1935–2003)'s accounts of how imperial power expropriates not only the material life of the colonised, but their mental life as well, causing them to think of their own identities within categories fashioned by their oppressors.[10] The Scots are perhaps particularly schizophrenic in this respect. At a material level, they are a First World people, the beneficiaries of being what

Tom Nairn (1932–2023) has described as the junior partners in a highly profitable imperial enterprise.[11] Inside their heads, however, Scots are (or have been) a Third World people, their identities shaped by images and discourses (English literature, Hollywood movies) articulated elsewhere but lived within by Scots themselves.[12] As the quotation at this essay's head suggests, it has been the profound political as well as artistic achievement of novelists such as James Kelman and Irvine Welsh, and poets such as Edwin Morgan (1920–2010), Tom Leonard (1944–2018) and Liz Lochhead, to have fashioned a distinctively Scottish voice, one homologous with Scots' interior life and experience of the world.

This is a claim I would make also for *Rab C. Nesbitt*. Indeed, I see the emergence and consolidation of the series during the early 1990s as being part of the 'revolution of the word' Colin MacCabe discerns in the context of Ireland and James Joyce (1882–1941) and entirely in line with the process described by Cairns Craig above.[13] This is so even though the mix of internationalist modernism and 'parochial' vernacular differs in these two examples. What is often not grasped by outsiders is that Scotland is a tri-lingual society comprising Gaelic, English and Scots: it is part of the imperialism of Standard English that it regards Scots as an inferior version of itself rather than as a separate language, a fate suffered by diverse creoles and pidgins throughout the colonised world. The language spoken by *Rab C. Nesbitt*'s central characters, particularly Rab (Gregor Fisher) himself, is that of working-class Glasgow, a vernacular variant of Standard English heavily laced with Scots words such as *jaicket* (jacket), *wean* (child), *merrit* (married), *shilpit* (puny), *feart* (afraid), *keech* (shit) and *glaikit* (stupid).

In 1969 the French film journal *Cahiers du cinéma*, exploring the relationship between films and ideology, offered a seven-category classification which was to become very influential in 1970s British film theory.[14] Far and away the greatest interest was stimulated by category (e): those films which at first sight appear wholly within dominant ideology but which, in fact, dismantle (or at least, critique) it from within by the nature of their 'writing'. By the latter term, *Cahiers* meant primarily cinematic *mise-en-scène*. This classification has, in postmodern times, fallen from favour – seen as being irretrievably bound up with the Marxist grand narrative and therefore too monolithic to account for the diversity of meanings films generate in their passage from production to consumption. Nevertheless, another of the *Cahiers* categories can, if stretched somewhat, offer a useful model for how *Rab C. Nesbitt* is operating ideologically within the faultlines between metropolitan British and Scottish cultures and between the metropolitan BBC and BBC Scotland. *Cahiers* defined its category (c) as those films in which 'the content is not explicitly political, but in some way becomes so by the criticism practiced on it through its form'.[15] This formulation seems very close to what *Rab C. Nesbitt* does by foregrounding the Scottish vernacular voice, although (as we shall see) the series also becomes increasingly political in the more direct sense. In order to heighten the 'vernacularism' of the central characters – Rab, Cotter (Tony Roper), Mary (Elaine C. Smith) and Ella (Barbara Rafferty); Rab and Mary's two sons, Gash (Andrew Fairlie) and Burney (Eric Cullen); and Rab's friends Andra (Brian Pettifer) and Dodie (Iain McColl) – the series operates non-naturalistically. Many authority figures (even working-class ones such as policemen, Department of Social Security clerks, social workers, shopkeepers and licensees) often speak with rather posh, Received Pronunciation-based Scottish accents. The nature of the Word is *Rab C. Nesbitt*'s central political terrain.

The vernacular turn, in any culture, carries with it certain dangers, most notably the adopting of a whining, nostalgic, sentimental and self-congratulatory 'here's tae us, wha's like us' tone. *Rab C. Nesbitt* substantially avoids this, primarily on account of its corrosively satirical stance, often towards those very institutions that more nostalgic vernaculars celebrate. The series's virtues in this regard are, for example, writ large when compared with two other prominent late-twentieth-century examples of the turn to the Scots vernacular, the poetry of Adam McNaughtan and the plays and television films of Bill Bryden (1942–2022). In one McNaughtan poem the poet reflects on the changes which have come about in his native city: 'Oh where is the Glasgow where I used to stey / The white wally closes done up wi' pipe cley / Where you knew every neighbour frae first floor tae third / And to keep your door locked was considered absurd'.[16] Ian Spring has accurately described McNaughtan's work as '"stairheid" nostalgia par excellence'.[17] Bill Bryden, a native of Port Glasgow, achieved a well-deserved international reputation as a theatre director. A brilliant theatrical technician and *metteur-en-scène*, his exploitation of the resources of theatre and, in particular, his movement of large ensembles through theatrical space was often breathtaking. However, as a writer, his turn to the Scots vernacular in plays and TV films such as *Willie Rough* (1972), *Benny Lynch* (1974), *Ill Fares the Land* (1983), *The Ship* (1990) and *The Big Picnic* (1994) revealed a sensibility suffused with a coarsely sentimental populism. This may reflect the power, within the Scottish vernacular tradition, of one particular strand of Victorian sentimental literature, namely, the Kailyard School, the best-known exemplar of which is J. M. Barrie (1860–1937). Although the extent of Kailyard's power within Scottish culture is contested,[18] a 'worst case scenario' argument would be that it has irretrievably damaged the sensibilities of several generations of Scottish writers. However, in consequence of the tough-mindedness of *Rab C. Nesbitt*'s key creative personnel (writer Ian Pattison and producer/director Colin Gilbert), the series may possibly have body-swerved urban Kailyard and connected instead with certain older, more scabrous traditions of Scots vernacular explored below.

Is There Such a Thing as Scottish Screen Acting?

Clearly, *Rab C. Nesbitt* marks a significant advance for the local vernacular on Scottish and (due to the series being networked, British) television. There is a sense, therefore, in which the question above is redundant. Manifestly, Scottish actors, deploying vernacular voices, throng Scottish screens and are also significantly present in British television and beyond. An actor like Richard Wilson, although born in the West of Scotland, has built his reputation mainly by playing within Received Pronunciation. But others, such as Bill Paterson, Robbie Coltrane (1950–2022) and, above all, Sean Connery (1930–2020), have tended to 'Scotticise' any roles they have played (though this is less true of Coltrane, who is particularly adept at accents). So, the answer to the above question, if confined solely to questions of voice, is assuredly 'Yes'. It is less certain, however, that the same affirmative answer would be given if the question were posed in relation to gesture and body language. There is a dearth of scholarly work in this area, so the following argument should be regarded as impressionistic and provisional.

James Naremore, to the extent that he discusses acting and ethnicity, does so primarily in relation to voice.[19] I first began thinking about the 'problem' of Scottish screen acting while watching newsreel footage of the Upper Clyde Shipbuilders' 'work-in' of 1972: in an inspirational act of working-class industrial tactics, the workforce, threatened with the closure of their yard, occupied it. The charismatic workers' leader, Jimmy Reid (1932–2010), famously addressed the workers, urging them to behave with dignity and self-discipline and proposing a series of prohibitions on certain kinds of behaviour. Expressed with his superb sense of public rhetoric, Reid couched his speech within the recurring trope, 'There will be no [. . .]'. When he reached his ultimate prohibition ('There will be no bevvying'), Reid, as he hit the operative word, threw his torso forward and moved his head slightly to right and left in a piece of body language as distinctive to the West of Scotland as the dismissive hand gesture deployed by a New York Jew telling you, 'I don't want any of that stuff'. Such geographically rooted pieces of body language seem to have been 'ironed out' of Scots actors' screen performances. While much more work would have to be done to confirm or refute this, my sense is that Scots actors who, like Connery, appear to maintain a Scots vernacular in their performances do so solely at the level of voice. Gesturally speaking, their performances have become subsumed within the classic, naturalistic screen acting style so heavily influenced by Stanislavskian ideas filtered through the practice of Lee Strasberg (1901–82) and the Actors Studio. To the extent that geographically and culturally rooted gesture and body language survive into Scots screen actors' performances, my impression is that they were, in the 1990s at least, to be found principally in *Rab C. Nesbitt*. For example, in the episode in which he takes his pet canary out for a walk on a lead, Rab, exclaiming 'Go on, ya beauty!', kicks his leg across his body in a very specific piece of West of Scotland body language. The series asserts and brings to public view not only the West of Scotland vernacular voice, but the West of Scotland vernacular style as well.

This celebration of *Rab C. Nesbitt*'s foregrounding of vernacular voice, gesture and body language as important political as well as aesthetic advances should not be misread as an all-out call for parochialism and naturalism on Scottish screens. Powerful forces at work in Scottish moving image culture seek to deracinate screen representations coming out of Scotland so that they become more assimilable by the world audiovisual market, which basically means the American one.[20] The chimera that such forces chase is films which, like *Four Weddings and a Funeral* (Mike Newell, 1994), make a financial killing in the American market. The discussion over the extent to which *Trainspotting* (Danny Boyle, 1996) required redubbing for its American release doubtless encouraged these forces to advocate such commercially motivated self-censorship at the production stage, rather as one prominent British producer, contemplating a film about the 1932–33 'Bodyline' tour of Australia by the English cricket team, instructed the screenwriter not to have players getting out Leg Before Wicket (LBW), as this would not be understood by the Americans. Happy to go along with Hollywood's historical and continuing hegemony, such forces have a reductive, impoverishing effect on Scottish screen acting, one which a series such as *Rab C. Nesbitt* to some extent counteracts by setting down markers of the possible. Those forces in Scottish moving image culture choke off a rich source of performativity by turning their backs on the Scottish vernacular, seeking to elide a 'natural' process of development of the national moving image culture before it has even arrived. Think of the incredibly expressive boost given to American cinema by the 1930s arrival of the ethnic/proletarian screen acting styles of James Cagney (1899–1986), Humphrey Bogart (1899–1957) and

John Garfield (1913–52).²¹ In short, Scottish cinema and television need to go through a period in which mimetic theories of acting are stressed and the country's vernacular resources of voice, gesture and movement are exploited.

That said, acting as mimesis should not be fetishised. It has been correctly argued that the dominance of the Strasbergian version of Konstantin Stanislavski (1863–1938)'s method has had a profoundly impoverishing effect on American acting.²² There are other traditions from which Scottish acting can learn much and which, it has to be recognised, are designed precisely to deracinate and universalise the acting process. The post-Poor Theatre work of Jerzy Grotowski (1933–99) is a case in point, with his discussion of the extent to which hunters in every culture in every continent adopt the same posture and body movement.²³ However, the particular conjuncture in Scotland, both in terms of its body politic and its screen industries' level of development, requires that acting as mimesis be foregrounded. No better example of this exists than *Rab C. Nesbitt*.

Where Extremes Meet

Alongside English reviewers' preoccupation with *Rab C. Nesbitt*'s linguistic difficulty, there is another curious feature about their accounts of the series: their recurring description of Rab himself as 'philosopher': 'a lone drunken philosopher raging briefly and incoherently into the ether';²⁴ 'the ranting, Glaswegian street philosopher';²⁵ 'philosopher, drunk and general Glaswegian bauchle'.²⁶ On the face of it, 'philosopher' is a strange description and not one which has been applied to those other great television sitcom ranter characters, Alf Garnett (*Til Death Us Do Part* [BBC, 1965–75]) and Victor Meldrew (*One Foot in the Grave* [BBC, 1990–2000]). However, the reviewers may be onto something more than they know. As Cairns Craig has observed in another context:

> To the extent that much of Scottish middle-class society models itself on English values, distinctively Scottish culture has more affinity with the working classes than English culture [. . . T]o the extent that the element of the middle classes who are active in Scottish culture are professionals – legal, religious, educational – the tonality of Scottish culture is much more abstract and philosophical than in England. Scotland has retained links with the traditions of European intellectual debate in a way that England, locked into a conception of philosophy as description rather than criticism, has not [. . .] Scottish writers are both more working-class and more philosophical than is normal in English culture.²⁷

Such an inheritance has meant that what T. S. Eliot (1888–1965) called the 'dissociation of sensibility',²⁸ that dire separation of thought from feeling which Eliot purported to find in post-Metaphysical Poetry English literature, never took hold north of the border and there remained in Scottish culture a peculiar, perhaps unique, melding of the most disparate elements from what might be called High Culture and (often the most scurrilous) Low Culture. This mixture is well conveyed, for example, in Hugh MacDiarmid (1892–1978)'s 1935 poem 'Glasgow 1960', despite the fact that he was being ironic and thought of Glasgow as a cultural wilderness. The poem's narrator has returned to Glasgow 'after long exile' and is amazed to find buses and trams packed with people heading towards Ibrox stadium on their way to a philosophical debate rather than to watch football. Meanwhile, the news boys shout the headlines, 'Special! Turkish Poet's Abstruse New Song [. . .] / and, holy snakes, / I saw the edition sell like hot cakes'.[29]

The mix of the vernacular and the abstruse or, more generally, of High Culture and Low Culture, is central to *Rab C. Nesbitt*, very often within Rab's monologues and asides to camera. Rab's description of himself as 'Govan's Renaissance Man', of his children as 'the fruit of my loins', and of Govan humour as 'the Laughter of Cruelty', and his references to MacDiarmid's 'A Drunk Man Looks at the Thistle' (1926), T. S. Eliot's formulation of 'birth, copulation and death',[30] Aleister Crowley (1875–1947) and 'wee Frankie Kafka' (1883–1924) have worried certain reviewers.[31] Misreading the series as a wholly naturalistic sitcom, they complain that such High Art allusions would be beyond the frame of reference of such as Rab. They are more comfortable with the Low Culture side of the equation, as in Mary's observation to Rab that 'I wouldnae rattle a stick in a shite pail for you', or the likelihood that, should you have a cup of tea at the Nesbitts', you are liable to be served 'an impetigo scab for a biscuit'. *Rab C. Nesbitt*'s undissociated sensibility is beautifully conveyed in Rab's description of his son Gash as 'seventeen-year-old and so anal retentive he's still shitting rusks'.

This conjoining of the entire spectrum of human experience and cultural reference is evident in much 'serious' Scottish writing, for example, the poetry of Edwin Morgan or the novels of William McIlvanney (1936–2015). But, as with *Rab C. Nesbitt*, an undissociated sensibility is present also in Scottish popular cultural forms, most notably in the work of the 1940s/1950s Glasgow newspaper cartoonist Bud Neill (1911–70), which, as well as covering a similar vernacular linguistic range to *Rab C. Nesbitt*, also makes extensive reference to a diverse range of totemic High Cultural thinkers and artists.[32] This phenomenon extends backwards in Scottish history to Robert Burns (1759–96) and beyond. Burns, still popularly thought of as, in Henry Mackenzie (1745–1831)'s words, 'this Heaven-taught ploughman',[33] a kind of eighteenth-century noble savage, was in fact extremely well educated in philosophy, science and the humanities.[34] Even Rab's much-commented-upon verbal aggression might be linked with the ancient Scottish rhetorical form of flyting as described by Edwin Morgan:

> Fantasy, catalogues, and a far more grotesque pullulation of images characterise the extreme and peculiarly Scottish kind of satire called the flyting [. . .] a contest in virtuosity of vituperation, [it] has some antecedents or analogues in other poetic traditions, including especially Gaelic tradition, and in part at least it may be regarded as a ritualised, aestheticised survival of the belief in bardic power, anciently shown in superstitious conviction that an enemy could be 'rhymed to death'. Something of this dark power remains in the Scottish flytings yet the fact that the abuse has been ritualised has not removed, but rather heightened the unease, the sense of nightmare which the performance produces in us.[35]

'Virtuosity of vituperation' and 'abuse [. . .] ritualised' could stand as highly appropriate rubrics for *Rab C. Nesbitt* generally, achieving glorious local realisation in, for example, the moment when Cotter, returned after a night on the 'ran-dan', has his testicles seized by Ella. As he writhes in her vice-like grip, she warns him about his future conduct and the dire consequences of his backsliding: 'You'd better hope there's somebody oot there wi' a bollock donor card, pal, for you're gonny need it.'

However, the holding together of High Culture and Low Culture is, to some extent, at odds with another powerful current in Scottish life. Edwin Morgan has observed that:

> In a country where life tended to be harder, and people poorer, than in England, uppishness and pretentiousness were ready targets for mockery, and the well-known and not always very amiable Scottish 'reductive idiom' makes its appearance, lying in wait to bring down every climbing hypocrisy and puncture every vain aspiration [. . .] How far does this bespeak some worry about the national psyche, the national identity?[36]

Successful Scots, particularly those who have achieved acceptance furth of Scotland (Billy Connolly would be a good example), constantly complain about the tendency of their fellow Scots to take them down a peg. Alexander Scott (1920–89), in his 1972 poem 'Scotched', deals with a wide variety of Scots institutions in a series of brief verses. His verse headed 'Scotch Equality' reads: 'Kaa the feet frae / Thon big bastard'.[37] The dichotomy between the two traditions – the undissociated sensibility which regards as perfectly proper the holding together of the scurrilous and the abstruse, High Culture and Low Culture, and Morgan's 'reductive idiom' which says woe betide anyone who gets above themselves – breeds a peculiar sensibility among Scots intellectuals of working-class origin. That sensibility proclaims its commitment to ideas and 'High' culture while at the same time ironically disclaiming that commitment. This hedging of bets is, ultimately, a sign of nervousness about appearing 'uppity' towards or within the milieu from which one has come. It is a leitmotif running through the work of numerous Scots 'organic' intellectuals (Antonio Gramsci [1891–1937] termed as 'organic' those intellectuals who emerged as leaders of their own [usually, working] class and remained committed to the interests of that class). It is present, for example, in Liz Lochhead's poem 'Inter-City' when she (or the work's female narrator), menaced by hard-swearing oil rig workers on a train, speaks of 'the artsy-fartsy magazine I'm not even pretending to read'; in singer and cultural critic Pat Kane's remark, in an interview with Elaine C. Smith (who plays Rab's wife, Mary), that 'once we agree on the minimum moral substance of *Nesbitt* [. . .] we get down to pontification about its "meaning"';[38] in the suggestion of a Glasgow academic, recounted by Angus Calder (1942–2008), that the Glasgow version of Gramsci's concept of 'hegemony' might be 'Hey, Jimmy';[39] and not least in the account of Ian Pattison, writer of *Rab C. Nesbitt*, of moving, as a child, from industrial Govan to greener Johnstone:

> There was a thing that Alasdair Gray once said which I'll paraphrase badly – that Glasgow's skies are very grey, but that there's a hint of another colour out there somewhere. And that was Johnstone: the other colour. We had a bit of wasteland across from our new house. I felt as if I could have written Dvorak's 'New World' Symphony at that time. I thought, 'Fuck! All this space!'[40]

Glasgow's Miles Better

In 1982 a local advertising agency was commissioned by Glasgow City Council to devise a campaign aimed at improving the city's image. The resulting slogan was 'Glasgow's Miles Better'. If anyone had thought to ask the question 'Better than what?' the answer would have been: 'than the historical image of Glasgow constructed in discourse over more than a century – Glasgow as City of Dreadful Night'. In the eighteenth century Glasgow was much praised for the quality of its air and the beauty of its ambience, the city with which it was most often compared being Oxford. It was after industrialisation that the city's image altered, the change traceable through public health and housing reports, the emergent practice of photography, interwar newspaper accounts of gang warfare and the appearance of key novels such as *No Mean City* (1935).[41] The image of Glasgow as a bleak, tenement-dotted landscape inhabited by taciturn, hard-eyed men whose lives were bounded by football, heavy drinking and explosive (sometimes sectarian) violence, often with cut-throat razors, was to become an Ur-Narrative which beckoned any who would speak, write or make visual images of Glasgow. Jeremy Isaacs, addressing a conference in Edinburgh – the Athens of the North – amused his audience by telling them that he himself was from Glasgow, the Sparta of the North. I have written elsewhere about the Scottish Discursive Unconscious, that ensemble of Ur-Narratives and discourses (Highland Scotland as elegy would be another component) which operates deterministically on representations of Scotland in official reports, through acts of historiography, to easel painting, imaginative literature, drama, postcards, newspaper and magazine features, photographs, films and television programmes and advertising.[42] So powerful that even the Scots themselves live within it, this ensemble forces Scotland, including Glasgow, 'out of history', to use Cairns Craig's term, with the concomitant failure of (or, at best, difficulty for) Scots artists to imagine the real landscapes they live within as having any transcendent meaning, any meaning that relates to a tradition, to history.[43] This phenomenon is well expressed in a much-quoted passage from Alasdair Gray (1934–2019)'s novel *Lanark* (1981):

> 'Glasgow is a magnificent city', said MacAlpin. 'Why do we hardly ever notice that?' 'Because nobody ever imagines living here,' said Thaw [. . .] 'think of Florence, Paris, London, New York. Nobody visiting them for the first time is a stranger because he's already visited them in paintings, novels, history books and films. But if a city hasn't been used by an artist not even the inhabitants live there imaginatively.'[44]

Gray puts too much emphasis on the conscious constructions of artists. He might also have included ostensibly 'documentary' discourses such as social reports, photographs and television documentaries, but his point is well taken.

Clearly the 'City of Dreadful Night' discourse and the 'Glasgow's Miles Better' discourse, with its tropes of art galleries, shopping malls and haute cuisine, are in contradiction – deliberately so, since the latter was evolved to contest the former. So intense is the struggle between competing conceptions of the city that any film, novel, play or television programme about Glasgow gets sucked into the controversy and judged in terms of its 'good' or 'bad' image of the city. Such has been the case par excellence with *Rab C. Nesbitt*, which has been both traduced and lauded in readers' letters to the Scottish press, ferociously attacked by a Glasgow councillor and the subject of a complaint (not upheld) to the Broadcasting Complaints Commission. The discursive construction of Glasgow was a topic at an annual conference of the Royal Geographical Society held in the city in the 1990s and *Rab C. Nesbitt*'s centrality as a point of reference in the debate was marked by Ian Pattison's being invited to the conference. The issue of the city's discursive representation had, indeed, also been a factor in actor Gregor Fisher's early reservations about the character of Rab and is even alluded to within the series itself during one of Rab's rants:

> See us scum, us keech? We're havin' a bloody hard time aff the shortbread set [. . .] You know *[adopts posh voice]*, 'Oh, look, look at that! It's stereotypes like him that give Glasgow a bad name. Give us Van Gogh'. Aaagh! Bloody Van Gogh! The best o' it is, see that Van Gogh? He was a bigger heidbanger than me. See if I met Van Gogh in the lavvy o' the Two Ways? I would dae a U-turn in case he chibbed me wi' his palette knife.

The rant in question is also, of course, a good example of the series's (and wider Scottish culture's) melding of High and Low Cultures referred to above.

Unquestionably, *Rab C. Nesbitt* deals with the same lumpen proletarian fragment of society as those other representations of the West of Scotland – including the television plays of Peter McDougall or the novels of William McIlvanney – most often cited when the 'bad' image of the Glasgow conurbation is discussed. As a frequent user of this kind of ideological analysis, I have to admit that it is a blunt weapon, good for broad discursive strokes but less effective when dealing with nuances and questions of quality within particular artefacts. As will have been clear from this essay's opening section on the linguistic aspects of *Rab C. Nesbitt*, I regard the series as extremely progressive on that front, a move into the terrain of popular television of those attempts by more 'serious' artists, the poets and novelists, to speak with an authentically Scottish voice and slough off the tyranny of Received Pronunciation.[45] Developing the point made above – that it is not simply the fact that *Rab C. Nesbitt* deals with a lumpen proletarian milieu, but how the series handles that milieu that is important – I want now to look in greater detail at two episodes in the series which show *Rab C. Nesbitt* at its best, artistically and ideologically.

Class and Nation in *Rab C. Nesbitt*

There are, dotted throughout *Rab C. Nesbitt*, multiple indications that Rab, his family and friends belong to an urban underclass: their repeated self-denigrations as 'shite' and 'scum'; constant references to the DSS and provident cheques; repeated expressions of disbelief by judges, policemen and assorted members of the middle classes about the way Rab and his friends conduct their lives ('Until something turns black and drops off, they don't like to bother the doctor in Govan'); repeated spells in prison and brushes with the law ('It's a long time since I got oot a caur withoot a blanket ower ma heid'); and, on one occasion, the taking into care of Rab's children. However, the question of class is sometimes given a more political (in the widest sense of that term) turn, as when Rab, watching some kids playing in the street, observes:

> Look at them, eh? The classic look of the eternal British underclass. Faces like clenched fists, eyes like the ringholes in spanners. We made them that way, you know. Nice and picturesque for the Sunday supplements so as the middle class could have a piquant seasoning of armchair pity over their breakfast croissant.

However, class has never been more corrosively represented than in the episode entitled 'Lesson' (1992), in which Rab returns in flashback to his schooldays. Having just emerged from a spell in prison, and stumbling drunkenly past his old school, Rab concludes one of his monologues to camera with the words: 'Schooldays are the happiest days of your life. The happiest days of your life! What a lot of shite I talk! The happiest days of your life if you happen to be a sado-masochist.' We see exactly what Rab means in the flashback. As played by the morosely estimable Scots actor James Cosmo, Rab's teacher is an upwardly mobile ('a semi in Clarkston') sadist with a withering contempt for his charges, whom he keeps in order with frequent applications of his lochgelly, a length of thick, hard leather named after the Fife town where it is manufactured. His attitude can be gleaned from his addresses to the class:

> You all know my philosophy. Children should be seen and not heard [. . . *looks menacingly at Rab* . . .] and 'free dinner' children shouldn't be seen at all. [*Having belted Rab,*] Merely looking at you people is an affront to my sensibilities. But I'm paid to teach you and teach you I will. I will teach you respect. I will teach you the most important lesson people of your class can learn. Keep your head below the parapet and you won't get hurt. Work! Work hard and some of you may rise to the mediocre.

Such darkly accomplished writing and playing may seem odd in what is, after all, a situation comedy. But one of the benefits of writer Ian Pattison, producer/director Colin Gilbert and the excellent ensemble cast having worked together over several series (and, indeed, previously on *Naked Video* [BBC Scotland, 1986–91]) is that they are able to take chances and extend the artistic and emotional range of particular episodes.[46] 'Lesson' is particularly rich in this regard. As well as delivering the series's most sombre representation of class, it is remarkable in two further respects: its extending of Rab's emotional life and the richness of its *mise-en-scène*. The point of the drunken monologue with which Rab re-enters his childhood in flashback is to illustrate his realisation that he has 'merrit the wrang wummin'.

The flashback reunites him with his childhood sweetheart, Isabel (Susan Nisbet). Several features of the *mise-en-scène* are worthy of note. Gregor Fisher's playing of the child Rab, at one level humorously grotesque, is also as inventive as the analogous playing of children by adult actors in Dennis Potter (1935–94)'s *Blue Remembered Hills* (BBC, 1979). Television usually suffers in comparison with cinema in the poverty of its *mise-en-scène*, its tendency to rely on static shot/counter-shot set-ups closely following the verbal exchanges of the actors. However, one of the exceptional features of the TV crime series *Hill Street Blues* (NBC, 1981–87) and, more recently, of *ER* (NBC, 1994–2009), was the mobility of their cameras, which picked up and left diverse groups of actors within the same continuous shot. Something of the same thoughtfulness regarding style and narrative economy is evident in 'Lesson'. One series of shots/counter-shots shows Rab and Isabel exchanging looks, he in the body of the class, she at the blackboard. One such shot, from Rab's point of view, is interrupted when the teacher enters left of frame, runs his basilisk eye along the line of Isabel's gaze and lights on Rab. What this suggests, on the part of Colin Gilbert as director, is an attempt to go beyond the standard stylistics of television sitcom and thereby heighten dramatic effect. A similar thoughtfulness about the dramatic use of televisual space occurs at the end of 'Lesson', when Rab returns to his temporary lodging with Cotter (both have been evicted by their wives) and finds him in bed with a woman who turns out to be Isabel's sister. In a scene unusual for its emotional poignancy, she informs Rab that Isabel is dead. But the way the scene is realised is also unusual. Rab, facing the other two characters, is in the left foreground, the woman in the mid-ground, and Cotter in the background. When she gives Rab the news of Isabel's death, Rab turns away from them, and towards the camera, to hide his grief, but the three figures, in the three planes of the shot, remain visible with their different responses. Both thematically and stylistically, 'Lesson' rises above the characteristically mundane level of TV sitcom to reach something close to serious television drama.

'Country' (1992) has none of the sombreness of 'Lesson' or, indeed, its inventive *mise-en-scène*. It remains at the level of the broad, not to say gross, comedy of the series as a whole, but it nonetheless says serious things about Scottish national identity. Having first demonstrated their dubious patriotism – they have slogans such as 'Bonnie Scotland' and 'Scotland Forever' tattooed on diverse parts of their anatomy but are vague about the exact geographical location of Loch Lomond – Rab, Mary, the kids, Cotter and Ella weekend at a cottage on Loch Lomondside. Stretching the idea of the Highlands somewhat, the episode indulges in some traditional Lowland jokes at the expense of Highlanders, referring to them as 'teuchters' and 'anguses' and suggesting that their sexual preferences extend to dogs and sheep. It takes passing swipes at the religious and political sanctimoniousness of certain Scottish rock bands; at the Anglicisation of the Highlands; at those climbers and hikers wearing boots 'that cost as much as a three-piece suit'; and at Scots who ape American ways. 'Country' directs its most venomous outbursts, however, at two targets: the use of Scotland as a nuclear dumping ground and tearful, breast-beating assertions of Scottishness.

The attack against the former is carried out primarily within a long monologue by Rab as he searches for the lost Cotter, a monologue delivered, with appropriate irony, against a backdrop of heather-clad hills and photogenic Highland sunsets:

> These are my mountains, eh? Keep the bloody things if ye want them. They're nuthin' but lids for nuclear dumps anyway. I mean, you can just see the equation in the Westminster nappers, can't ye? The Jocks! The Jocks! Hauf their industry's deid on its feet, but they'll have to pay for their giros some way. Why don't we just get a lot o' nuclear keech and dump it in their front rooms, eh? The bonny purple heather! The ****ing stuff glows in the dark.

The squawk of a moorhen, doubtless applied strategically in post-production, renders inaudible the profane word before 'stuff'. Continuing his rant, Rab repeatedly jumps up and down on the camouflaged roof of a nuclear bunker: 'That's for Dounreay! And that's for Hunterston! And that's for 9–3 at Wembley in 1961.' Rab then wanders off, muttering, 'Well, that's Scottish history avenged.'

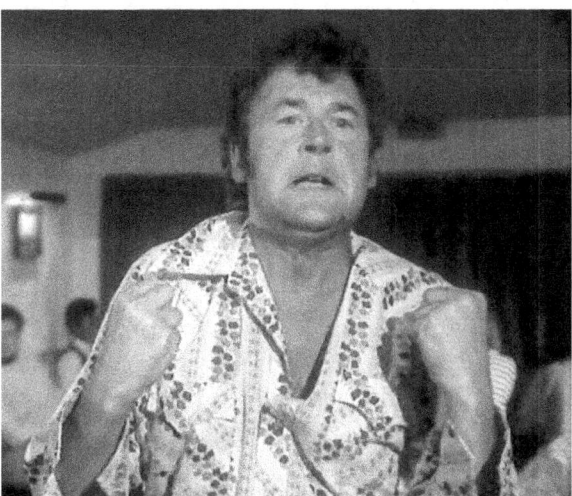

Figure 28.1 'Ich bin ein sheep-shagger!' *Rab C. Nesbitt*'s Cotter, moved to tears on hearing 'Flower of Scotland', expresses solidarity with Highland Scots.

The episode's de(con)struction of the kind of misty-eyed Scottish patriotism that eulogises kilts, lochs and mountains and sobs into its whisky over battles lost centuries ago is carried out primarily within a drunken monologue by Cotter at a ceilidh which he and Rab attend in grotesquely ill-fitting kilts. Elia Kazan (1909–2003) has talked about 'the Anatolian smile', that submissive grin Armenians wore in encounters with their Turkish overlords.[47] The Glasgow equivalent is a kind of nasal whine which proclaims to the world its owner's sense of himself as the scum of the earth. Tony Roper, the actor who plays Cotter, deploys this magnificently. Lurching drunkenly among the dancers at the ceilidh, he ends up beside Rab:

> I've fun' ma spiritual hame, here among the anguses, Rab. See the anguses, they're oor brothers. *[Cotter hears the ceilidh band strike up 'Flower of Scotland' and starts to weep]* 'Floor o' Scotland', Rab. That's oor anthem. Come on, let's hear it for the teuchtars! A struggle on your soil is a struggle on mine. *[Poses dramatically]* Ich bin ein sheep-shagger!

Appropriately, Rab's advice to Cotter is to 'stop makin' an arse of yersel'. It is, indeed, appropriate that *Rab C. Nesbitt*'s satirising of this kind of patriotism should light on 'Flower of Scotland', a song of petrifying banality, both musically and lyrically. That this 'execrable doggerel' (a phrase used by John Prebble [1915–2001] about some of Sir Walter Scott [1771–1832]'s poetry[48]) should be, according to opinion polls, the favoured anthem for an independent Scotland is, to some Scots, argument enough against the idea of Scotland as a separate state. Rab's final statement on the national question is one many Scots would assent to: 'See when you come doon tae it? Your country's like your own fizzer, intit? It might be a pock-marked, drink-ridden eyesore, but you're stuck with it. So you may as well try and love it'.

A Structuring Absence?

Any cultural critic who encountered structuralism in the 1970s would probably agree that one of its enduring legacies is the importance it attaches to absences from, as well as presences within, texts and discourses. The idea of structuring absence is one which, present in the respective works of Louis Althusser (1918–90), Roland Barthes (1915–80) and Pierre Macherey, was carried over into film criticism in the famous analysis of *Young Mr. Lincoln* (John Ford, 1939) by the editors of *Cahiers du cinéma*, in which they demonstrate that, in order to fulfil its ideological project of presenting Lincoln as a mythical figure free of contradictions, the film has to repress known elements about his politics.[49] Macherey's view in relation to the ideological functioning of texts that 'in order to say anything, there are other things which must not be said',[50] suggests, when applied to *Rab C. Nesbitt*, that the 'structuring absence' of the series is sectarian allegiance.

In order to indicate the extent to which consciousness of sectarian difference is part of the warp and woof of the 'real' social milieu *Rab C. Nesbitt* represents, let me be autobiographical for a moment about my own Glasgow upbringing. Although my immediate family stood at some distance from religious bigotry – my father, a communist, expressed nothing but withering contempt for Orangeism and freemasonry and my mother, although several of her brothers were freemasons, regarded people who went on Orange marches as not altogether 'respectable' – we had a keen sense of ourselves as Protestant working-class and of Catholics as Other. When I was in my mid-teens and starting to go out on dates, my mother would not pose directly the question uttered in more rabidly Protestant homes, 'What foot does she kick with?' (a 'left-footer' being one of the local terms for a Catholic). Rather, she would pose coded questions: 'What's her name?' 'What school did she go to?' On occasion I would wind my mother up by telling her, 'Her name is Teresa Kelly and she went to St Bonaventure's', whereupon my mother would blanch, put her hands to her head and say 'Oh, my God!' Such domestic interactions reflected the fact that our social milieu was suffused with awareness of and jokes about sectarian affiliation. There were jokes about Catholic mothers who would not feed their children orange juice and Protestant men who refused to obey the little green man on the pedestrian crossing. In Glasgow dance halls of the 1940s and 1950s, a time when 'modern' dances like the Waltz and the Quickstep were interspersed with 'old-time' dances, one of the latter, the Veleta, involved dancers kicking one leg out (rather like Rab does in the example cited above). In certain halls the Protestants would shout 'Willie Waddell' (the name of a Glasgow Rangers football player) as they kicked, while the Catholics shouted 'Charlie Tully' (a Glasgow Celtic player). On a recent conference visit to Glasgow, I went to play putting with several delegates, one of whom was of Glasgow-Irish ancestry and a vociferous Celtic supporter. Collecting the differently coloured golf balls, I made great play of giving him the orange one. The point about this story is that the joke would have been meaningless – as indeed it was to the non-Scots in the company – without our mutual awareness of the historically deep-seated and pervasive sectarian narrative of Lowland Scotland.

On the face of it, therefore, that narrative's absence from *Rab C. Nesbitt* is inexplicable. The central protagonists' surnames, Nesbitt and Cotter, suggest that they are Protestant, as does the absence of Catholic iconography from their homes and from the classroom in 'Lesson'. On the few occasions Rab has had recourse to the clergy, for example, in the episode titled 'Ethics' (1992), they are dressed like Protestant clergymen. On the other hand, in the same episode Rab attempts what is clearly a confession within a confessional. Nor can the absence of the sectarian narrative from *Rab C. Nesbitt* specifically be explained by its absence from Scottish television comedy more generally. Robbie Coltrane played the Protestant bigot Mason Boyne in *Naked Video*, the series within which the character of Rab was born and to which Ian Pattison contributed, and *Only an Excuse?* (BBC Scotland, 1993–2020) has explored the close connection between sectarianism and football in Scotland. Significantly, apart from the reference in 'Country' to the Scottish national team's 9–3 defeat by England at Wembley in 1961, there have been few or no further references to Scottish football in the series. Could it be that religion, so closely tied up with football in Lowland Scotland, is precisely a structuring absence, one which is quite literally unspeakable and which, if filled, would deform the series by constantly reminding viewers that, even in this blackest of black comedies, sectarianism (as events in Ulster over the last few decades have proved) is no laughing matter? In other words, could it be that *Rab C. Nesbitt* could not function in precisely the way it does, implicitly addressing a unified working class and its sympathisers in other classes, if the sectarian discourse were to be uttered?

Conclusion

We now turn in conclusion to the somewhat odd title of this essay.

Robert B. Ray is blisteringly critical about the way film, and more generally cultural, criticism is practised.[51] He seeks to find new ways of writing – and, indeed, new knowledge – by recourse to the avant-garde, most particularly Surrealism, which he sees as a kind of workshop of ideas and methods which might help free critical writing from its current malaise. He refers to the famous Surrealist game of Exquisite Corpse, in which four players, each unbeknownst to the others, write down their assigned parts of speech, two players assigned nouns and two, adjectives. The result is invariably a bizarre, collectively produced metaphor which reveals the new and unexpected combinations residing in language itself and releasable by automatic writing. I cannot claim that the writing in this chapter is very far removed from academic orthodoxy. Nevertheless, I hope the title moves in the direction indicated by Ray. Its 'exquisite corpse' points to the marvellously innovative linguistic dimension of *Rab C. Nesbitt*, at times verging on the surreal. It is widely assumed that Rab's full name is Robert, but I have chosen to think that it might be Rabelais, a name wholly in accord with the series's humorous (and frequently scatological) irreverence. As far as I am aware, the precise meaning of Rab's middle initial 'C.' has never been revealed. I have chosen to think that it might stand for Copernicus, a name appropriate to a figure who is ultimately as philosophically serious as he is funny. Let's hear it for *Rab C. Nesbitt!*[52]

Notes

1. Cairns Craig, *Out of History: Narrative Paradigms in Scottish and British Culture* (Edinburgh: Polygon, 1996), 193–4.
2. T. Patrick, 'Alien Life Forms', *The Times*, 5 May 1992, 3.
3. J. Kupferman, *Daily Mail*, 30 January 1993, 37.
4. M. Berkmann, 'Scot with a taste of Porridge', *Daily Mail*, 23 May 1992, 42.
5. V. Lewis-Smith, 'Hail the King of Giro Valley', *Evening Standard*, 19 November 1993, 43.
6. Anon, 'A lout for our times', *Daily Telegraph*, 15 May 1992, 19.
7. S. McKay, 'Holding court with the Laird o' Giro Valley', *Mail on Sunday*, 24 May 1992, 22.
8. Quoted in Andrew O'Hagan, 'The Scottish write to be different', *The Guardian*, 13 October 1994, 22.
9. James Kelman, *Some Recent Attacks: Essays Cultural and Political* (Stirling: AK Press, 1992), 82.
10. Frantz Fanon, *Black Skin, White Masks* (New York: Grove Press, 1968); Edward Said, *Orientalism* (London: Routledge & Kegan Paul, 1978).
11. Tom Nairn, *The Break-Up of Britain: Crisis and Neo-Nationalism* (London: New Left Books, 1977).
12. See Malcolm Chapman, *The Gaelic Vision in Scottish Culture* (London: Croom Helm, 1978); Colin McArthur, ed., *Scotch Reels: Scotland in Cinema and Television* (London: British Film Institute, 1982); Colin McArthur, 'The Dialectic of National Identity: The Glasgow Empire Exhibition of 1938', in *Popular Culture and Social Relations*, eds Tony Bennett et al. (Milton Keynes: Open University Press, 1986), 117–34, and republished elsewhere in the present volume.
13. Colin MacCabe, *James Joyce and the Revolution of the Word* (Basingstoke: Macmillan, 1979).
14. Jean-Louis Comolli and Jean Narboni, 'Cinema/Ideology/Criticism', in *Screen Reader 1: Cinema/Ideology/Politics*, ed. John Ellis (London: Society for Education in Film and Television, 1977), 12–35.
15. Ibid., 16.
16. Quoted in Ian Spring, *Phantom Village: The Myth of the New Glasgow* (Edinburgh: Polygon, 1990), 32.

17. Ibid., 32.
18. See, for example, William Donaldson, *Popular Literature in Victorian Scotland: Language, Fiction and the Press* (Aberdeen: Aberdeen University Press, 1986).
19. James Naremore, *Acting in the Cinema* (Berkeley/Los Angeles: University of California Press, 1988).
20. Colin McArthur, 'The Cultural Necessity of a Poor Celtic Cinema', in *Border Crossing: Film in Ireland, Britain and Europe*, eds John Hill, Martin McLoone and Paul Hainsworth (London/Belfast: British Film Institute/Queen's University Institute of Irish Studies, 1994), 112–25, and also republished elsewhere in the present volume.
21. Robert Sklar, *City Boys: Cagney, Bogart, Garfield* (Princeton, NJ: Princeton University Press, 1992).
22. Richard Hornby, *The End of Acting: A Radical View* (New York: Applause Books, 1992).
23. Jerzy Grotowski, 'Tu es le fils de quelqu'un', *The Drama Review* 31, no. 3 (Autumn 1987), 30–41.
24. Lewis-Smith, 'Hail the King of Giro Valley'.
25. Berkmann, 'Scot with a taste of Porridge'.
26. G. Bowditch, 'StringalongaRab', *The Times*, 13 November 1995, 6.
27. Cairns Craig, 'Introduction', in *The History of Scottish Literature, Vol. 4: Twentieth Century*, ed. Cairns Craig (Aberdeen: Aberdeen University Press, 1987), 3.
28. T. S. Eliot, 'The Metaphysical Poets', in T. S. Eliot, *Selected Essays* (London: Faber & Faber, 1922), 287.
29. Hugh MacDiarmid, 'Glasgow, 1960', in Hugh MacDiarmid, *Complete Poems: Volume II* (Manchester: Carcanet Press Ltd, 1994), 1039.
30. T. S. Eliot, *Sweeney Agonistes: Fragments of an Aristophanic Melodrama* (London: Faber & Faber, 1932), 24.
31. See Pat Kane, 'Rabbery with menaces', *The Guardian*, 5 January 1996, II: 7.
32. See Colin McArthur, 'Wake for a Glasgow Culture Hero', *Scottish Film and Visual Arts*, no. 6 (1993), 11–12, and also republished elsewhere in the present volume; Ranald McColl, ed., *Lobey's the Wee Boy! The Collected Lobey Dosser* (Edinburgh: Mainstream, 1992).
33. Henry Mackenzie, 'Extraordinary account of ROBERT BURNS, the Ayrshire Ploughman; with extracts from his Poems', *The Lounger*, no. 97, 9 December 1786, 272.
34. Kenneth Simpson, ed., *Burns Now* (Edinburgh: Canongate, 1994).
35. Edwin Morgan, ed., *Scottish Satirical Verse: An Anthology* (Manchester: Carcanet, 1980), xviii.
36. Ibid., xi.
37. Ibid., 164.
38. Pat Kane, 'Class Act', *The Guardian*, 20 November 1993, 27.
39. Angus Calder, *Revolving Culture: Notes from the Scottish Republic* (London: I.B. Tauris, 1995), 240.

40. Kane, 'Class Act', 26.
41. Alexander McArthur and H. Kingsley Long, *No Mean City: A Story of the Glasgow Slums* (London: Longmans, Green and Company, 1935).
42. See McArthur, 'The Cultural Necessity of a Poor Celtic Cinema'; Colin McArthur, 'Culloden: A Pre-emptive Strike', *Scottish Affairs*, no. 9 (Autumn 1994), 97–126, and also republished elsewhere in the present volume.
43. Craig, *Out of History*.
44. Alasdair Gray, *Lanark: A Life in Four Books* (Edinburgh: Polygon, 1981), 243.
45. To speak of any kind of identity (and, perhaps especially, national identity) as 'authentic' needs some qualification. Much recent writing on the question (see, for example, David McCrone, *Understanding Scotland: The Sociology of a Stateless Nation* [London: Routledge, 1992] and Pam Cook, *Fashioning the Nation: Costume and Identity in British Cinema* [London: British Film Institute, 1996]) insists upon the hybridic, impure, provisional nature of all identities. As an ultimate position this can be assented to, but such arguments seem to me to take inadequate account of the dialectical nature of concrete identities, which are rarely in a state of rapid slippage whereby they are, so to speak, 'open to all comers'. More characteristically, identities are formed in the crucible of struggle, usually with a powerful core identity which fashions the identities of the materially weaker groups on its periphery. One such core/periphery relationship is that of England (or perhaps better, the United Kingdom) and Scotland, bearing in mind that in other relationships (the UK vis-à-vis the USA, or Scotland vis-à-vis the Third World), the core can become a periphery and vice versa. A victory, however fluid and provisional, for the periphery over the core, such as I have argued to be the case with regard to *Rab C. Nesbitt*, is ground enough for the application of the term 'authentic'. However, to suggest that the language and style of *Rab C. Nesbitt* is authentic is not to preclude the series's hybridity. Indeed, the whole discussion of the melding of High and Low Culture is just one example of its 'impurity'. A similar argument could be developed with regard to the presence of American elements in the series, a striking feature of Glasgow working-class life as of so many other milieux. The particular 'enemy' underlying this discussion is the position that would seek to promote the idea of a fixed, essential, unchanging national identity which is exclusive of outsiders. There are too many groups making this kind of argument in Scotland. The case of the former Yugoslavia should be an object lesson as to where this argument leads.
46. *Naked Video*, replayed from time to time on cable television, is a useful source of evidence as to how the characters in *Rab C. Nesbitt* have developed. The most remarkable transformation is in the character of Cotter, whom Tony Roper played in *Naked Video* without the distinctive whine and tendency to overreach himself intellectually that are the hallmarks of his performance in *Rab C. Nesbitt*.
47. *The Anatolian Smile* was the British title of Kazan's 1963 film *America, America*, which he wrote, produced and directed.

48. John Prebble, *The King's Jaunt: George IV in Scotland, August 1822* (London: Collins, 1988), 18.
49. Louis Althusser, Étienne Balibar, Jacques Rancière, Roger Establet and Pierre Macherey, *Reading Capital* (London: New Left Books, 1970); Roland Barthes, *S/Z* (London: Jonathan Cape, 1975); Pierre Macherey, *A Theory of Literary Production* (London: Routledge & Kegan Paul, 1978); A collective text by the Editors of *Cahiers du Cinéma*, 'John Ford's *Young Mr. Lincoln*', in *Screen Reader 1: Cinema/Ideology/Politics*, ed. John Ellis, 113–52.
50. Macherey, *A Theory of Literary Production*, 85.
51. Robert B. Ray, *The Avant-Garde Finds Andy Hardy* (Cambridge, MA: Harvard University Press, 1995).
52. Many thanks to Ian Mowat of Glasgow Caledonian University for sharing with me his encyclopaedic knowledge of Scottish radio and television comedy and for supplying materials relevant to *Rab C. Nesbitt*.

CHAPTER 29

Mise-en-scène Degree Zero: Jean-Pierre Melville's *Le Samouraï**

Melville: Surrealism/Existentialism/Americanophilia

Attempting to define the particular kind of noir sensibility which emerged in post-WWII Paris, James Naremore lights on the figure of Boris Vian (AKA 'Vernon Sullivan') (1920–59).[1] Several facets of Vian connect with filmmaker Jean-Pierre Melville (1917–73): the adoption of an American pseudonym (Melville was born Jean-Pierre Grumbach); a deep involvement with American culture (in Vian's case, jazz; in Melville's, primarily cinema); the capacity to oscillate between, and perhaps to meld, high culture and mass culture; and a personal association with both the contemporary movements of Surrealism and Existentialism.

Indeed, this last point illustrates the extent to which the interpellative discourses open to the post-WWII Parisian intelligentsia were dominated by Surrealism and Existentialism. Both movements partook of American culture, it being probable that the Surrealists were particularly taken with American cinema and the Existentialists with American literature. André Breton (1896–1966)'s favourite film was *Peter Ibbetson* (Henry Hathaway, 1935) and James Naremore has demonstrated[2] that, although the term 'noir' had to some extent been applied by the French to their own pre-WWII cinema, the application of the term 'film noir' to certain American films in post-WWII Paris by critics such as Raymond Borde (1920–2004) and Etienne Chaumeton came from within Surrealist circles.[3] If Surrealist-inspired Borde and Chaumeton saw in the American film noir all that was 'oneiric, bizarre, erotic, ambivalent, and cruel',[4] the Existentialists drew other lessons from the novels of Dashiell Hammett (1894–1961), Raymond Chandler (1888–1959) and James M. Cain (1892–1977), 'pulp'

---

* Originally published in *French Film: Texts and Contexts*, eds Susan Hayward and Ginette Vincendeau (London: Routledge, 2000), 189–201.

writers whom they bracketed with 'serious' novelists like Ernest Hemingway (1899–1961), William Faulkner (1897–1962) and John Dos Passos (1896–1970). The Existentialists were entranced by a particular kind of American hero driven to action in a meaningless universe.

Jean-Pierre Melville was very close to being of the generation of Jean-Paul Sartre (1905–80) and, apart from a brief brush with Surrealism through his association with Jean Cocteau (1889–1963) in the making of *Les Enfants terribles* (Melville, 1950), the philosophical basis of Melville's work was to remain throughout his life Americanophile Existentialism or, perhaps more accurately, Americanophilia later bolstered by Existentialism before it became fully politically committed. This is particularly true of his great gangster trilogy: *Le Doulos* (1962), *Le deuxième souffle* (1966) and *Le Samouraï* (1967). The rubrics which introduce these films resonate with the sense of ontological solitude central to Existentialism. In the case of *Le Doulos*, the rubric is: 'One must choose [. . .] to die or to lie' (which may be a quotation from Louis-Ferdinand Céline [1894–1961]) and with *Le deuxième souffle* it is: 'At birth man is offered only one choice – the choice of his death. But if this choice is governed by distaste for his own existence, his life will never have been more than meaningless.' In the case of *Le Samouraï*, the rubric is ostensibly a quotation from Inazō Nitobe (1862–1933)'s *Bushido: The Soul of Japan* (1899), but was in fact written by Melville himself: 'There is no greater solitude than that of the Samouraï, unless perhaps it be that of the tiger in the jungle'. With their recurrent vocabulary of solitude, choice and death and their underlying theme of the necessity of integrity (of, in Sartrean terms, avoiding 'bad faith'), these rubrics might be passages from a Sartre novel of the 1930s or 1940s. As will be demonstrated, the same Existentialist concerns are realised in a recurrent range of haunting images within Melville's films, culminating in the austere beauty of *Le Samouraï*.

Melville's philosophical and political attitudes seem to have become 'frozen' as a result of his experience of the outbreak of the Second World War. A communist in the 1930s, he was, by his own account, overcome with a profound sense of national shame over France's surrender in 1940. He indeed spoke of contemplating suicide for the only time in his life at that moment.[5] His politics remained frozen around wartime anti-fascism and his post-war life was marked by a retreat into an apparently 'pure' cinephilia, although his films remained profoundly Existentialist and, as will be argued, deeply shaped by the experience of the surrender and the subsequent Resistance.

Taking his philosophical position very largely from Existentialism and his politics from wartime anti-fascism, Melville's Americanophilia, like that of the Surrealists, centred very largely on cinema. A cursory look at the noir-ish quality of his oeuvre would suggest that the defining cinematic moment for Melville was the delirious post-war reconnection with American films, with critical attention focusing particularly on five films of the 1940s: *The Maltese Falcon* (John Huston, 1941); *Double Indemnity* (Billy Wilder, 1944); *Laura* (Otto Preminger, 1944); *Murder, My Sweet* (Edward Dmytryk, 1944); and *The Lost Weekend* (Billy Wilder, 1945). This is, however, to some extent misleading. Although Melville's love affair with American cinema was to continue well into the post-war period – he is on record as saying that *The Asphalt Jungle* (John Huston, 1950) is the greatest film ever made[6] – he had already acquired a deep love and encyclopaedic knowledge of pre-war American cinema.

Melville's Americanophilia, however, also goes beyond cinema into a kind of mystical relationship with America itself. Several interviews reveal a kind of ecstatic response to the American landscape.[7] Melville's mystical Americanophilia is strongly present in his *L'aîné des Ferchaux* (1963), most particularly in the hypnotic car rides through New York and New Orleans and in the 'pilgrimage' to the house in which Frank Sinatra (1915–98) was born. More generally, the intensity with which Melville experienced both America and its cinema helps explain why – at a conscious level at any rate – they, rather than contemporary France or French culture, seem to be the major shaping influences on his work.

Melville and the 'Cinema of Process'

In his long interview with Melville, Rui Nogueira recalls a description of him as 'the Francis Ponge [1899–1988] of cinema',[8] Ponge being a Surrealist-influenced poet noted for his detailed descriptions of objects. To indicate the extent to which Sartrean Existentialism hovered over all intellectual and artistic endeavour in post-war Paris, Ponge's poetic preoccupations clearly also connect with one strand of Existentialism, namely, that sense of the brute facticity of objects in the real world. Melville, understanding how Ponge's poetry comes out of this tradition, correctly links it to the *nouveau roman* which, despite its practitioners' critiques of Sartre, was very much concerned with the same phenomenon.[9]

With due allowance for the differences between the Existentialists and the *nouveau romanciers*, clearly they both insisted on the materiality of the real world. Melville also addressed this question in relation to cinema by evolving what might be called a 'cinema of process', one which went some way to honouring the integrity of actions by allowing them to happen in a way significantly closer to real time than was the case in fictive (and particularly, Hollywood) cinema. If one film should be singled out as influential on Melville's evolving style in this regard, it is probably *Le Trou* (Jacques Becker, 1960) (although *Du rififi chez les hommes* [Jules Dassin, 1955] may also have been important). Strikingly similar, thematically speaking, to Melville's own work (it is about loyalty and betrayal among convicts in a prison cell), it is at the level of its handling of narrative action in relation to real time that *Le Trou* connects with the literary and philosophical concerns current in France at that time and inaugurates the 'cinema of process'. What this means can best be illustrated by one particular scene. Putting the escape plan at the heart of the film's narrative into effect, one of the convict central characters detaches the iron leg from his bed and begins to strike the raw concrete of his cell. In a 'normal' Hollywood prison picture there would then have been a cutaway to the men in the cell and a return to the floor when the hole had been made. Becker's camera, on the contrary, remains remorselessly fixed on the concrete floor as the iron hits it again and again and again until, after multiple blows, it slowly begins to chip and crumble. It is only after this lengthy action, carried on within one unbroken shot, that Becker permits himself a dissolve to the completed hole.

The 'cinema of process' is a recurrent feature of Melville's work, particularly in his gangster movies, but two illustrative examples will suffice. The enigma which drives the plot of *Le Doulos* is whether Silien (Jean-Paul Belmondo) has betrayed his friend Faugel (Serge Reggiani). The answer is given in an intricately plotted sequence, described in detail by Murray Smith, in which Silien manufactures the evidence which will reveal his loyalty.[10] This sequence, cinema of process par excellence, centres on virtually wordless attention to physical actions. The twist in the tail is that by the time Faugel learns of Silien's loyalty, his contract killer is already in place at Silien's house waiting for him. The film ends, in typically Melvillian style, with everyone dead.

The second illustrative example of Melville's 'cinema of process' comes from *Le deuxième souffle*. One of the most intriguing figures in that film is Orloff (Pierre Zimmer). In many respects Orloff is a dry run for the later figure of Jef Costello (Alain Delon) in *Le Samouraï*. As with so many of Melville's films, *Le deuxième souffle*'s action turns on the possibility of betrayal by one of the gang members. Orloff and Antoine (Denis Manuel) have developed a mutual antipathy. When the film's hero, Gu (Lino Ventura), is captured and made to seem as if he has betrayed the rest of the gang, Orloff arranges a rendezvous with Antoine and two others. Sometime before the meeting, Orloff goes to the scene of it and systematically explores the room for places he might conceal a weapon. Melville, in a superb example of the 'cinema of process', follows Orloff's extended casing of the room, finally showing him concealing a gun (which he ascertains he can reach with a quick upward movement) on a shelf by the window. Satisfied that he can now control the meeting to come, he leaves. Melville then shows Antoine going to the room after Orloff, casing it in his own terms and finding the gun Orloff has planted. When the meeting takes place and Orloff takes up his position by the window, the audience expectation is that at some point he will reach for the gun he has planted, find it gone and be killed by Antoine. Orloff does not do this, however. Ignoring the shelf, he takes a gun from his overcoat and is thus able to dictate the meeting's terms. By not reaching for the gun Antoine has removed, Orloff reveals that his calculations have included the realisation that Antoine, professional that he is, will have gone to the rendezvous and discovered the weapon. By thus taking a trope much favoured by both Existentialists and *nouveau romanciers* – that is, the detailed artistic perusal of physical actions and objects – Melville, so to speak, thickens the soup of his film's atmosphere and plot. He raises the valency of the process, by locating it within the intensely professional *amour-propre* of the characters and the intricacy of his own narrative plotting. More than anything in Melville's work, it is his 'cinema of process' which makes him both an auteur and an entertainer, a mainline filmic craftsman and an artist of profound seriousness.

Melville and the Resistance: The Return of the Repressed

Rui Nogueira's 1971 book *Melville on Melville* includes two photographs juxtaposed on the same page. One shows Lino Ventura as Gu Minda, the gangster from *Le deuxième souffle*, and the other Lino Ventura as Philippe Gerbier, the Resistance fighter from *L'Armée des ombres* (Jean-Pierre Melville, 1969). There is a curious similarity between the photographs. What explanation can there be for an image from a gangster movie and an image from a film about the Resistance being virtually identical? Could it be that, throughout his several gangster films, Melville has indeed been obliquely addressing the Resistance?

Susan Hayward has talked about the 'unsignifiability'[11] of the WWII period in post-war French cinema. In contrast to the lack of historical consensus with regard to the respective cinemas of Vichy and occupied France, Hayward points to the consensus among film historians vis-à-vis French films about the period made after the war, namely, that the reality of the Nazi occupation was left unspoken until *Le Chagrin et la Pitié* (Marcel Ophuls, 1969) and that 'the sacrosanct image of the Resistance was untouched until Jean-Pierre Melville's *L'Armée des ombres*'.[12] Hayward explains this primarily in terms of the immediate post-war need for national unity repressing the messy contradictoriness of the Resistance.

The issue of public evasion of the war years and their psycho-social legacy in post-war France has been most fully addressed by Henry Rousso, who uses psycho-medical terminology such as 'syndrome', 'repression' and 'neurosis' to explore the phenomenon.[13] More recently, Sylvie Lindeperg has suggested that, among other things, attention to certain post-war French comedies might provoke a revision of the established view that the reality of the occupation was not adequately dealt with.[14] In essence, Melville had been able to address the Resistance directly in 1949 with *Le Silence de la mer* and again, after an intervening period of twenty-two years, with *L'Armée des ombres*, on both occasions securing the approval of some at least of the *résistants*.

An active member of the Resistance himself for two years before joining de Gaulle (1890–1970)'s Free French forces in London, Melville was in his early twenties when these events took place. France's surrender, the Nazi occupation, the betrayal of Vichy, and the subsequent Resistance were the key formative political influences on Melville's generation. What became, then, of the repressed of Melville's Resistance during the two decades of tacitly agreed silence from 1949? It seems reasonable to speculate that it returned in the displaced form of the obsessive preoccupation with comradeship, integrity and betrayal in his gangster films, particularly *Le Doulos* and *Le deuxième souffle*.

Just as Melville's Existentialism is discernible in his *mise-en-scène* (the recurrent images of figures alone in empty rooms or walking deserted corridors and streets), so too is the question of solidarity worked into the fabric of *Le deuxième souffle*'s *mise-en-scène*. There are recurrent images of (primarily) men embracing, gently touching and gazing at each other. Although this account mobilises that ensemble of touches and gazes as evidence of a concern with solidarity and, arguably, with the (repressed) Resistance, the ensemble also gives a powerful homoerotic charge to *Le deuxième soufflé*, one which is present also in *Le Doulos* and, in particular, *L'aîné des Ferchaux*. The other side of the coin related to *Le deuxième souffle*'s concern with loyalty and solidarity is the film's detestation of betrayal. When Gu is tricked by the police into revealing Paul Ricci (Raymond Pellegrin)'s participation in the armoured car robbery and the lie of his betrayal is circulated to the press, Gu's response is to slash his wrists. It is not unreasonable, in this context, to recall the young Melville's contemplating suicide at the moment of France's wartime surrender.

This central concern with loyalty and betrayal appears to wane in *Le Samouraï*, which is an altogether more bleak and austere film than the other two entries in Melville's gangster trilogy although it certainly connects with them in other ways. However, at least one critic has suggested that a concern with truth and lies, appearance and reality, unites all three films.[15] To be speculative, through re-workings of the gangster movie the repressed tropes of the Resistance might have forced their way on to French screens during a post-war period in which they were tacitly discouraged.

Melville and *Le Samouraï*

It is now time to gather together the general arguments made thus far about Melville's work and life – ideas about the centrality of Existentialism and Americanophilia, the 'cinema of process' and the (repressed) Resistance – and assess their applicability to *Le Samouraï*. The film can usefully be divided into three parts. The opening section covers the introduction to Jef Costello, his theft of a car, construction of an alibi in advance of deploying it, and carrying out of a contract killing. In the middle section Jef is hauled in with other suspects to take part in an identity parade. The final section shows him pursued both by the police and the figures who originally contracted him, culminating in his being shot by the police. Each section is in itself an extended example of the 'cinema of process', and within each there are individual scenes which are themselves local realisations of the same. The other strands of Melville's cinematic universe – the Existentialism, the Americanophilia, the (repressed) Resistance – are woven into the fabric of the film's overall structure.

The opening section of *Le Samouraï* is breathtaking in its boldness – barely a word is spoken for the first ten minutes of the film – and its austerity. It begins at night, with Jef lying on his bed in a darkened room, the only sound, apart from the ambient noise of passing traffic, being the chirping of a canary. As the credits cease and plaintive music rises, Melville deploys a curious technical procedure, a simultaneous track back and zoom forward, but in a staggered, stop-go way, which has a profoundly disturbing effect on the spectator. Melville has spoken of this as a signal to the audience of Jef's schizophrenia, but such psychologising of the character is not illuminating. Jef is readable primarily as the Existentialist Melvillian hero taken to his furthest point. This is partly achieved by the lengths Melville went to in order to drain any vestiges of colour from this opening scene, despite the film being in colour. Apparently, Melville replaced banknotes, a cigarette packet and the label of a bottle of mineral water with black-and-white photocopies of the originals in order that there would be no splash of any colour in the scene.[16] The scene's muted décor, stillness and (by the standards of Hollywood narrative cinema) inordinate length combine to produce an overwhelming sense of solitude. This sense is reinforced by the (on the face of it, narratively redundant) scenes of Jef walking alone in streets and corridors and standing alone in areas of cinematic space unrelieved by any furnishings. Most of all, however, it is Alain Delon's astonishing performance which defines Jef as the Melvillian hero par excellence. Several of Melville's other heroes are solitary and relatively wordless – for example, Silien and Faugel in *Le Doulos* and Gu and Orloff in *Le deuxième souffle*. Indeed, as already mentioned, Orloff looks in retrospect like a dry run for the figure of Jef, although the former's solitude is softened by the respect and affection of other gangsters. Jef Costello, incarnated in the hard-eyed impassivity of Alain Delon, is metaphysically alone.

At a conscious level it is clear that Melville's films are made out of cinema rather than out of 'life'. This is evident in the extent to which he deploys within his work the same iconography as classic American gangster films: cars, guns, telephones, rain-soaked nocturnal streets, Art Deco nightclubs in which progressive jazz is played and women dance with top hats, canes and long cigarette-holders, and the particular shape made on the screen by a certain kind of hat and raincoat. The latter is ritualised to an incredible degree in *Le Samouraï*, with the camera lingering over Jef's enrobing before the mirror each time he leaves his apartment, complete with the characteristic running of his fingers over the hat brim which Delon appropriated from Melville himself. To illustrate the extent to which *Le Samouraï* connects iconographically with American gangster movies of the 1930s and 1940s, simply compare its look with that of American gangster movies contemporaneous with it – apart, of course, from such historical reconstructions as *Bonnie and Clyde* (Arthur Penn, 1967). Films such as *Gunn* (Blake Edwards, 1967) and *Point Blank* (John Boorman, 1967) are suffused with light, exploit the entire range of the colour spectrum, and both their hoodlums and their investigators, in line with changing fashions in American life, are without hats or overcoats.

Additionally, Melville's Americanophilia may make itself felt in the actual structure of his films. Although they are extremely 'French' in their philosophical underpinning, tone and the (by Hollywood standards) inordinate length of certain scenes and sequences, their narratives (despite their often intricate plotting) are very direct, much like those of Hollywood movies, and are constructed round protagonists' actions rather than states of mind, a position more readily associated with Hollywood popular cinema than European art cinema, where the watchwords are likely to be social concern and/or intellectual seriousness. *Le Samouraï*, despite its philosophical bleakness and stylistic austerity, delivers many of the traditional pleasures of action in line with classical Hollywood gangster movies. Indeed, measured against the three-act structure which is at the centre of what might be called 'story-structure discourse',[17] *Le Samouraï* conforms very closely to the Hollywood narrative paradigm.

It has been suggested above that Melville's gangster movies, with their obsessive returning to issues of comradeship and betrayal, might be read as displaced renderings of the French wartime experience. Such an argument is well evidenced by *Le Doulos* and *Le deuxième souffle*. Superficially, it seems to fit less easily with *Le Samouraï*, since the male solidarity and detestation of betrayal so evident in the earlier films is entirely absent from the latter. However, on closer inspection it can be seen that questions of loyalty and betrayal have not vanished from *Le Samouraï*: rather, they have been ceded to the two women in the film, Jef's girlfriend, Jeanne (Nathalie Delon), and the nightclub pianist, Valérie (Cathy Rosier), on whose account Jef in effect commits suicide. Jeanne's devotion to Jef is dog-like, to the extent of being prepared to lose her sugar daddy, Wiener (Michel Boisrond), and risk the threat of the vice squad in order to maintain Jef's alibi which she knows to be false. While it is not entirely clear in the film itself, Melville has described Jef as having fallen in love with Valérie and thereby, for the first time, having become vulnerable. She is clearly the lover of the gang boss, Olivier Rey (Jean-Pierre Posier), who has given Jef the initial contract to kill the nightclub owner. Jef finds out about their relationship and, concluding that the second contract he is given (to kill Valérie) is part of an elaborate plan to lure him back to the club (a plan he believes she is party to), points an empty gun at her and is shot by the police. The critic seeking to locate this act – suicide in the face of betrayal – in relation to Melville's displaced (and perhaps not altogether conscious) handling of his wartime experience, might again link this to Gu's attempted suicide in *Le deuxième souffle* and to Melville's own response to France's wartime surrender.

As mentioned above, the three sections, or 'acts', of *Le Samouraï* can themselves be seen as extended examples of the 'cinema of process' and there are to be found within each local realisations of this concept equal to anything else in Melville's oeuvre. When Jef leaves his apartment for the first time in the film, for example, there occurs the scene in Melville's work most reminiscent of that in Becker's *Le Trou* where the 'real' time of breaking a hole in a prison cell floor is to a large extent allowed to be seen unblinkingly on screen. In a busy Parisian street, Jef enters a car he

 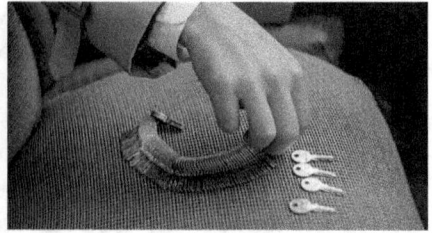

Figures 29.1 and 29.2 Jean-Pierre Melville's Cinema of Process: Jef, stealing a car, searches for a compatible ignition key in *Le Samouraï*.

wants to steal. In an analogous Hollywood movie the thief would tinker with the wiring and quickly jump-start the car (this is indeed the way it happens in the ostensible American remake of *Le Samouraï*, *The Driver* [Walter Hill, 1978]). In Melville's film, however, Jef sits impassively in the driver's seat, takes out a ring carrying about a hundred ignition keys, and slowly and deliberately begins to try each one in sequence. He succeeds with the fifth key.

In a later example of the 'cinema of process' from *Le Samouraï*'s third section – the police placing a bug in Jef's room – Melville has the police enter Jef's place by an exactly similar procedure involving a large ring of diverse house keys, a characteristically Melvillian conflation of the respective moral universes of police and criminals. Many other sequences in *Le Samouraï* might be discussed in terms of the 'cinema of process'. Jef's intricate construction of a two-part alibi in advance of his fulfilling the first contract killing (which, like the sequence from *Le Doulos* discussed in detail above, is a process that the audience only understands retrospectively) is one such sequence. So, too, is the masterly scene within the second section in which Weiner unwittingly backs up Jef's alibi by recreating the composite figure he saw in the foyer of Jeanne's building: Jef's face; Jef's hat, worn by another figure in the identity parade; and Jef's coat, worn by yet another figure included in it. The term 'cinema of process' might also be applied to Jef's bandaging of his wounded arm and the celebrated chase through the Paris Métro with Jef being picked up and lost by a succession of plainclothes policemen while the Inspector (François Périer) follows the chase, Mabuse-like, on a giant illuminated map of the Métro system.

Melville's work, to the chagrin of many critics and on his own recurrent insistence, is hermetically sealed, has no direct purchase on the 'real' world and is ultimately (in its conscious dimensions at any rate) about 'cinema' rather than 'reality'. These facts are brought sharply home by the figure within *Le Samouraï* of Valérie, who is black. Melville did not demur when Rui Nogueira suggested that she represents Death, which Jef is so manifestly seeking.[18] In common with the film's other characters, nothing is revealed about her background and motivation. Although she is black, there is a certain ambiguity about her territorial origins and, indeed, her ethnicity (similarly beautiful, non-white women hover round the edges of both *L'aîné des Ferchaux* and *Le deuxième souffle*). Valérie could be of African, West Indian or Asian origins. The point is that *Le Samouraï* offers nothing about her that would encourage a social or political reading of the film. True to Melville's stated policy, at the conscious level of its construction *Le Samouraï* is an exercise in the sophisticated reworking of American generic forms. However, as the argument of this essay makes clear, this does not preclude it from serving unconsciously as a vehicle for Melville's deepest philosophical and political values.

Melville and the Critics

Jacques Zimmer and Chantal de Béchade argue that 'the long love affair between Jean-Pierre Melville and the critics, which saw a honeymoon, quarrels, fierce discords and reconciliations, ended in irredeemable divorce'.[19] They regard *L'aîné des Ferchaux* as the film which marked Melville's entry into the critical pantheon of French auteurs, but in the four-year gap between that film and *Le deuxième souffle* his critical reputation had begun to unravel, producing an extraordinary effect of critical polarisation. On the one hand, *Le deuxième souffle* provoked an ecstatic essay by Gilles Jacob in which he ranked it alongside *Le Trou*, 'that jewel in the firmament of the *film policier*'.[20] On the other hand, the extent to which *Cahiers* abandoned Melville is starkly conveyed in the critical responses to *Le deuxième souffle* in 'Le Conseil des dix', a long-standing feature in the journal whereby a rotating panel of ten critics (several associated with *Cahiers*) offered a consumer guide to the month's releases by awarding each film from four stars to one or by consigning a film literally to a black-ball category designated as '*inutile de se déranger*', which translates colloquially as 'don't put yourself out [to see this]'. Of the ten critics voting in the December 1966 'Conseil', two gave the film the four star 'masterpiece' rating, but the four *Cahiers* critics on the panel (Jacques Bontemps, Michel Delahaye [1929–2016], André Fiéschi [1942–2009] and Jean Narboni) all gave it the black ball.[21] A year later, Narboni would go on to give *Le Samouraï* a brief, largely dismissive review.[22]

Like most Melville films, then, *Le Samouraï* divided the critics, producing some of the most crassly blinkered responses to his work. However,

Jacques Zimmer's evaluation of the film, in its insistence not only on *Le Samouraï*'s stylistic excellence but on its moral seriousness, provides a fitting epitaph both for the film and for Jean-Pierre Melville's work more generally: '*Le Samouraï* is a Picasso canvas: three strokes of vivid simplicity, fifty years of work, a hundred sketches, and a masterly talent. It is the culmination of doggedness, style [. . .] and morality'.[23] As Melville increasingly becomes a point of reference for contemporary makers of film noirs in diverse cultures (Quentin Tarantino and John Woo are two recently identified disciples[24]) and as, within France, questions of film culture and ideology become more and more divergent, there are signs that Melville's cinematic excellence is coming to be appreciated more unanimously in his own country. Two simultaneous events signalled this emergent consensus. The November 1996 issue of *Cahiers du cinéma* contained an extensive reassessment of Melville's work under the appropriate title 'Le deuxième souffle de Melville' and alongside this, the Cinémathèque Française ran an extensive Melville retrospective.[25] His rightful place in the pantheon has at last been assured.

Notes

1. James Naremore, 'American Film Noir: The History of an Idea', *Film Quarterly* 49, no. 2 (Winter 1996), 14.
2. Ibid., 18.
3. Raymond Borde and Etienne Chaumeton, *Panorama du film noir américain, 1941–1953* (Paris: Éditions de Minuit, 1955).
4. Naremore, 'American Film Noir', 19.
5. Rui Nogueira, ed., *Melville on Melville* (London: Secker & Warburg for the British Film Institute, 1971), 159.
6. Ibid., 67.
7. See Eric Breitbart, 'An Interview with Jean-Pierre Melville', *Film Culture*, no. 35 (1964/5), 15–19; Rui Nogueira and François Truchaud, 'A Samurai in Paris', *Sight and Sound* 37, no. 3 (Summer 1968), 119–23.
8. Nogueira, *Melville on Melville*, 54.
9. Active from the mid-1950s, the group known as the *nouveau romanciers* (which included Alain Robbe-Grillet [1922–2008], Natalie Sarraute [1900–99], Marguerite Duras [1914–96] and Michel Butor [1926–2016]) shared a rejection of the forms of the naturalistic novel (for example, clearly drawn characters and a lucid narrative with a beginning, middle and end), replacing them with the ad hoc complexity of the individual consciousness and a detailed description of the everyday world.
10. Murray Smith, *Engaging Characters: Fiction, Emotion, and the Cinema* (Oxford: Clarendon Press, 1995), 216–23.
11. Susan Hayward, *French National Cinema* (London: Routledge, 1993), 189.

12. Ibid., 189.
13. Henry Rousso, *The Vichy Syndrome: History in France since 1944*, trans. Arthur Goldhammer (Cambridge, MA: Harvard University Press, 1991).
14. Sylvie Lindeperg, *Les écrans de l'ombre: La seconde guerre mondiale dans le cinéma français (1944–1969)* (Paris: CNRS Éditions, 1997).
15. Robin Buss, *The French Through Their Films* (New York: Ungar, 1988), 143–4.
16. Nogueira, *Melville on Melville*, 130.
17. Syd Field, *Screenplay* (New York: Dell Paperbacks, 1978).
18. Nogueira, *Melville on Melville*, 130.
19. Jacques Zimmer and Chantal de Béchade, *Jean-Pierre Melville* (Paris: Edilig, 1983), 111.
20. *Cinema 66*, no. III (December 1966), 89.
21. Various, 'Le Conseil des dix', *Cahiers du cinéma*, no. 185 (December 1966), no page ref. but adjacent to 8.
22. *Cahiers du cinéma*, no. 196 (December 1967), 72.
23. Zimmer and Béchade, *Jean-Pierre Melville*, 109.
24. Ginette Vincendeau, *Jean-Pierre Melville: An American in Paris* (London: British Film Institute, 2003), 1.
25. Thierry Jousse and and Serge Toubiana, 'Le deuxième souffle de Melville', *Cahiers du cinéma*, no. 507 (November 1996), 63.

CHAPTER 30

The Critics Who Knew Too Little: Hitchcock and the Absent Class Paradigm*

Introduction: Why Hitchcock?

Aside from the convention that artists' centenaries are good moments for reassessing their work, several factors combined to give this essay its particular orientation. Designing a course on Alfred Hitchcock (1899–1980) during the late 1990s, I was obliged to address the question of what might constitute an appropriate critical discourse at that historical moment. On the one hand, I had noted the marked contemporary turn towards British film history in academic Film Studies in the UK and beyond and wished to connect with that movement.[1] On the other hand, and not least, I had also become increasingly uneasy about the unseemly haste with which the category of class had been evacuated from political and cultural discourse in general and from Film Studies in particular.[2]

To mount a dedicated course on a named director might seem rather old-fashioned, but the Film Studies cat can be skinned in any number of ways and I retain an enormous personal investment in the pleasure to be derived from certain directorial signatures, not least Hitchcock's. That said, the trajectory of film theory over the last three decades of the twentieth century made (and still today makes) it problematic simply to erect a descriptive/celebratory course on any filmmaker. Greatly influenced by Robert E. Kapsis, my syllabus therefore took the form of examining the successive critical paradigms which had been brought to bear on Hitchcock's films: the early 'master of suspense' paradigm; the auteurist (in its French, British and North American variants and its structuralist and narratological inflections); the feminist/psychoanalytic; and, most recently, the gay/lesbian/queer.[3] Needless to say, those paradigms do not succeed each other in any neat, hermetically sealed way, but are heavily interpenetrated. At the time of designing my course, there were also some

---

*Originally published in *Film Studies*, no. 2 (2000), 15–28.

stirrings towards Hitchcock among reader reception critics, but not yet a paradigm.[4] The most curious absences from this list were, of course, race and class: those missing paradigms became an additional topic of the course and, in the case of class, this essay's central focus.

The increasing attention paid to British cinema is one of the more encouraging aspects of academic Film Studies (although the price being paid is an excess of unwarrantable critical claims on behalf of particular filmmakers and fact-grubbing on their behalf – a price, it should be said, that my own generation also paid in its auteurist enthusiasm for Hollywood). Alan Lovell (1935–2021), in a pleasing rhetorical manoeuvre, entitled a late-1990s essay 'British Cinema: The Known Cinema?', a reference to his own earlier paper, 'British Cinema: The Unknown Cinema'.[5] The profusion of late-twentieth- and early-twenty-first-century writing on British cinema confirms the validity of Lovell's later title. However, a crucial question immediately arose in the late 1990s. Within what critical paradigms was this reappropriation of British cinema to be accomplished? If we take a long perspective it can be seen that Hitchcock had to some extent already figured in the scholarly turn to British cinema. The *politique* of Tom Ryall's path-breaking book, *Alfred Hitchcock and the British Cinema* is exemplary: to reinsert Hitchcock into the British film cultural and industrial milieu.[6] Given its orientation, Ryall's book is much more concerned with institutional rather than textual questions, but he points to another dimension of the reappropriation which is highly textual, that associated with a mid-1980s collection of essays edited by Charles Barr, *All Our Yesterdays*,[7] which is 'broadly antirealist and pro- a cinema of fantasy'.[8] Ryall quotes Barr on Hitchcock's British films:

> These films [. . .] are rich in precisely those elements which make Hitchcock important to a new and productive school of structuralist and psychoanalytic criticism. The same elements that have drawn Laura Mulvey and Raymond Bellour into detailed analyses of, for instance, *Notorious* [1946] and *North by Northwest* [1959] [. . .] are strikingly present in the British films [. . .] Some of the silent films are, already, powerful Oedipal stories with sophisticated narrative structures [. . .] Increasingly, Hitchcock makes a point of showing us characters asleep or otherwise unconscious [. . .] as if to convey all the more strongly the oneiric, subjective logic of the action.[9]

This 'anti-realist' bent is most succinctly discernible in Julian Petley's concept of 'the lost continent',[10] a domain of British cinema seething with libidinal energy – all the more demented for being constrained within English reserve – encompassing figures such as Hitchcock and Michael Powell (1905–90) and Emeric Pressburger (1902–88) and British genres such as Gainsborough melodramas and Hammer horror films. While recognising the critical sophistication of this rereading of British cinema history, I would wish to pause on the decided flight from realism and note, particularly in the above quotation from Barr, a certain imperialism associated with the feminist/psychoanalytic paradigm and its tendency to homogenise critical discourse round questions of gender and sexuality. This essay attempts to engage with that paradigm on its own terrain, so to speak: that of looking and being looked at, but while also reinserting the category of class into the analytical process. Above all, it is the wish to retain this category, so cursorily jettisoned in recent discourse, which fuels the following discussion.

Class: The Vanishing Category

Indicating the frightening ease with which class had been pushed off the academic agenda by the 1990s, David James reports that at the 1989 gathering of the major American organisation of film and television scholars, the Task Force on Race and Class voted to dissolve and reconstitute itself as the Task Force on Race.[11] James's invaluable account of how this particular evacuation of class related to the politics of American higher education, the lacunae in classical Marxist theorisations of class, and the contemporary imperialism of psychoanalytic feminism in American Film Studies needs to be supplemented by a more detailed socio-historical explanation, such as that of Patrick Joyce.[12] Joyce speaks of the paradox of class being abandoned as an explanatory category precisely when economic life was in its greatest turmoil since the 1930s: the shift from production to consumption; the simultaneous rise of globalism and localism; the dispersive effect of new technologies; sharpened redefinitions of the concept of the self; and the rise of identity politics. As Joyce tartly observes, however, the only identity not registered within the latter is that of class.[13] It might be added that the demise of the Soviet Union in 1991 and the attendant perception that the western democracies had 'won' the Cold War was the final nail in the coffin of class as an explanatory concept. While it is entirely understandable that feminism might wish to dislodge class in favour of gender, it was particularly galling that class should be evacuated from its own heartland, Marxism. Characteristically, this evacuation did not take the form of an outright abandonment of class, but rather of a drift towards other determinations, most usually gender.[14]

In addition to these complexly interwoven extra-filmic factors, there were (and are) specific filmic elements inhibiting the development of a class-based Hitchcockian critical paradigm. The most substantial pre-auteurist British critical engagements with Hitchcock – those of John Grierson (1898–1972) in the 1930s and Lindsay Anderson (1923–94) in the 1940s – were mounted from a social-democratic rather than a Marxist perspective and (though this is to simplify their positions somewhat) from a concern with 'content' rather than 'form', to use terms which are not wholly adequate. Thus, Grierson, writing in 1930:

> Hitchcock is the only English director who can put the English poor on the screen with any verisimilitude [. . .] Will Hitchcock take counsel from Arnold Bennett [1867–1931], and give us a film of the Potteries or of Manchester, or of Middlesborough – with the personals in their proper places and the life of a community instead of a benighted lady at stake.[15]

Anderson, writing in 1949 about a group of Hitchcock's British films, described them as gaining 'a particular excitement from their concern with ordinary people (or ordinary-looking people) who are plunged into extraordinary happenings'.[16] Grierson and Anderson shared a profound distrust of cinematic artifice, a consequent suspicion of Hollywood and a commitment to a social realist aesthetic which would put the lives of 'ordinary people' on screen. Grierson's advice to Hitchcock elicits Julian Petley's derision as 'the most off-beam prescription in the history of film criticism',[17] understandably so from Petley's 'lost continent' perspective on British cinema history. I have to agree that Hitchcock taking Grierson's advice might have denied us the excellence of his American films. But I also wish to pause and concur with Grierson and Anderson that the cinematic exclusion, marginalisation or stereotypical representation of particular socioeconomic groups is an important issue.

The earliest 'master of suspense' critical paradigm was, as the name suggests, primarily concerned with the mechanics of Hitchcock's films. The French auteurists chose to stress religion rather than class.[18] And, even if Robin Wood (1931–2009)'s book *Hitchcock's Films Revisited* had not been part of the British auteurist sub-paradigm virtually founded on a distaste for British cinema, it was precisely class questions which most repelled Wood when he contemplated British Hitchcock, as he was to confess when (in his book's revised 1989 edition) he recanted his earlier dismissal of the British period.[19]

As Tom Ryall has pointed out, Hitchcock's career might have developed in different directions – towards European art cinema, or even a version of documentary in which the (petty) bourgeoisie rather than the proletariat might have been the subject. At one point Hitchcock even seemed ready to adopt the mantle of cine-laureate of the middle classes.[20]

Anderson appreciated Hitchcock's capacity to render the middle classes on screen but, like Grierson, what he really hankered after was a more nuanced delineation of the proletariat. Whichever class Grierson and Anderson wanted to see on screen, their remarks on Hitchcock are posed primarily at the level of film content. Erecting a class paradigm in relation to Hitchcock's films must also involve a consideration of their formal elements. A prior step, however, is to probe more fully than previous critics have felt necessary into Hitchcock's class formation, since Donald Spoto (1941–2023), for example, bases his understanding of Hitchcock's films partly on his assumptions about how the figures in Hitchcock's class milieu would behave.

Hitchcock and the English Petty Bourgeoisie

Donald Spoto's biography of Hitchcock is not sensitive to the nuances of the British class system, sometimes describing the Hitchcock family as Cockney, and therefore working-class, and at other times suggesting they were middle-class.[21] Ryall is more sure-footed on Hitchcock's class origins, but since his project is to reinsert Hitchcock into British culture, he is more interested in the wider filmic context of interwar Britain. By the time Hitchcock was born in 1899, his father, William (1862–1914), owned a greengrocer's shop and was therefore, in more accurate sociological terms than Spoto offers, petty bourgeois. In 1899 the English middle classes in general, and the petty bourgeoisie in particular, were under threat, squeezed between the traditional power of the haute bourgeoisie and the increasingly enfranchised proletariat.[22] Since William Hitchcock's business interests had, by the time of his death in 1914, extended to a fishery in Limehouse, he belonged precisely to the class fraction most threatened by new legislation such as: the Workmen's Compensation Act (1897), which made employers responsible for injuries sustained in the workplace; the Trades Disputes Act (1906), which gave trade unions immunity from legal action by employers for damage incurred as a result of industrial action; and by the generally redistributive tax policies of the Liberal government of 1906–14. This perceived onslaught on middle-class interests led, in 1906, to the formation of the Middle Class Defence League, comprising businessmen, self-employed workers and shopkeepers and some sympathetic Conservative and Liberal MPs. The same sense of middle-class oppression gave rise to the Anti-Socialist Alliance and the United Kingdom Property Owners Association. Spoto does not tell us whether William Hitchcock was a member of any of these organisations, whether he was a typical or atypical petty bourgeois, or whether the prevailing sense of his class being under siege significantly affected the young Alfred's psychic formation. The earliest photograph of Hitchcock that Spoto includes, taken about 1907, elicits no comment from him, despite its curious features. In that image, William Hitchcock is dressed in the uniform of what appears to be a Territorial Army regiment and Alfred, about eight years old and astride a pony, wears an identical miniature version of the uniform. Although it was not uncommon throughout Europe at this time to dress children in military (most usually naval) uniform, taken as a whole the photograph suggests that William was an orthodox enough patriot to have joined the TA and to have inculcated some of the same values in his son, values likely to have been typical of the Edwardian petty bourgeoisie.

The British petty bourgeoisie is relatively unstudied in comparison to those of other European countries, so it is not easy to draw a psychological profile of that class fraction in the period of Hitchcock's formative years. Nevertheless, some work has been done on an analogous fraction of the middle class, white-collar clerks, the fastest-growing occupational group in British society during the period 1850–1910 and, incidentally, that within which Hitchcock found his first employment. Since our concern here is with the typical psychic makeup of the class fraction in which Hitchcock was born and raised, Ian Bradley's remarks on white-collar clerks may be pertinent:

> The first handbook for clerks published in 1878 listed the qualities they required as 'patience, perseverance, cheerfulness, and perhaps more than any other quality, a humble distrust of self and a deferential respect for the judgment of others'. It went on to add that the model clerk should be 'quiet and unassuming' in his clothing.[23]

This latter point brings to mind Spoto's account of Hitchcock's wardrobe: 'six identical dark suits [. . .] six identical pairs of shoes, ten identical ties, and fifteen identical shirts and pairs of socks'.[24] Without wishing to canvass an exclusively class-based theory of psychic determination, I note Spoto's account of how Hitchcock's 'natural quietness and youthful eagerness'[25] commended themselves to his employers in his first clerking job, and also Spoto's account of Hitchcock's energetic application in his first full-time job in the film industry.[26]

There are several teleologies at play in Spoto's biography, several predetermined narratives to which Hitchcock is made to conform. One of these is that the characteristics of the mature man should be discernible in his early life. Predicated as Spoto's work is on a teleology which culminates in the great works of Hitchcock's later Hollywood years, he is at a loss to explain his young subject's diligence in lowly work that sat apart, Spoto implies, from Hitchcock's fully formed artistic ambitions.

From the class-based analytical perspective I am offering here, however, the Hitchcock that emerges from Spoto's account could be read as a kind of Uriah Heep figure, humble and eager to please, the very embodiment of the above-quoted contemporary injunctions to white-collar clerks. Clearly Hitchcock was a figure of immense artistic potential, but that is not at all incompatible with his inhabiting the primary identity of petty bourgeois clerk at this early stage of his life.

The central teleology in Spoto's biography, however, is the Freudian. As a consequence, he went out of his way to research accounts of Hitchcock's mother, Emma Jane (1864–1942), and Alfred's relationship with her (as opposed to his relative indifference to the father). It is easy to see how the following passage might be readable into Hitchcock's films:

> Each evening [. . .] Alfred was made to answer her detailed questions about the business of the day [. . .] 'I always remember the evening confession,' he recalled fifty years later [. . .] It tells us something about the degree of their psychological intimacy, although there seems something overwhelming about it, something too intimate, a devotion exacted by a mother whose interest in her son's life imprisons rather than frees, investigates rather than encourages – and inculcates guilt of a scrupulous and neurotic kind.[27]

Beyond the basic data of his lineage, occupation, poor health and early death, Hitchcock's father is a shadowy presence within Spoto's work. Virtually the only other comment on him is to relay the notorious 'locking in the cell' story with the observation that, if it is true, it reveals in William Hitchcock 'an oddly cruel streak'.[28] Spoto's gloss reinforces the Oedipal trajectory of his narrative. Unlike his spare treatment of William, for example, Spoto sought out an eyewitness account of Emma Jane:

> According to a cousin, Emma Hitchcock was 'a smartly dressed woman, very quietly spoken and with an aristocratic manner. She was very meticulous when preparing a meal, at which she was very good. She would not venture out of her room unless neatly, perfectly dressed, and she quietly conducted her affairs in a dignified manner.'[29]

Spoto does not comment on the specifics of this description. Rather, he uses it to put some measure of flesh and blood round his contiguous references to Emma Jane's 'doting affection' and her compulsion that Alfred 'satisfy her whims'.[30] That is to say, Spoto locates his description of Emma Jane Hitchcock within his own teleological narrative, one which comes to horrifying fruition in *Psycho* (Alfred Hitchcock, 1960). Without wholly discounting this reading, I would wish to situate the above description of Emma Jane within the framework of English petty bourgeois life in the early post-Victorian period and suggest that, shorn of Spoto's Oedipal glosses, what the description yields is a sense of social typicality rather than extraordinary monstrous otherness.

Unless, therefore, the Hitchcocks were markedly untypical of the English petty bourgeoisie of the time, they are likely to have inculcated in young Alfred the qualities of respectability, restraint, diligence, deference to social superiors, coolness to inferiors and a certain sense of their class being under threat. This does not seem wildly out of kilter with what we know about Hitchcock. Also relevant here is one other feature of the petty bourgeoisie of the time – its capacity for getting things wrong socially – succinctly captured in the following poem by Hilaire Belloc (1870–1953):

> The Rich arrived in pairs
> And also in Rolls Royces.
> They talked of their affairs
> In loud and strident voices.
> The Poor arrived in Fords
> Whose features they resembled;
> They laughed to see so many Lords
> And Ladies all assembled.
> The People in Between
> Looked underdone and harassed
> And out of place and mean
> And horribly embarrassed.[31]

The early-twentieth-century English petty bourgeois response to constantly being 'on edge' is summarised by François Bédarida (1926–2001):

> Their reaction [. . .] was a wide adoption of various kinds of conformity: political – hence their unfailing support for the Conservative Party between the wars; social – the cult of respectability was a fetish; moral – adherence to a puritanical strictness of behaviour; religious – assiduous attendance at an Anglican church or Nonconformist chapel. Even more than in 1914 they made desperate and absurd efforts to ape their betters, in their houses, furnishings, dress, reading habits and general way of life, and to be recognised by them, without ever succeeding.[32]

With the obvious substitution of Catholicism, it seems not unreasonable to assume that this is close to the kind of world into which the young Alfred was interpellated. However, this speculation in itself offers little insight into how Hitchcock's films work. My criticism of Grierson's and Anderson's remarks on Hitchcock was that they took no account of his films' formal features. The great richness of the auteurist and the feminist/psychoanalytic paradigms is what they reveal about the workings of Hitchcock's films as films. The feminist/psychoanalytic paradigm's project of seeking to reveal the trans-individual, familial and societal structures of patriarchy manifesting themselves in Hitchcock's *mise-en-scène* is intriguing. The key question this essay poses is whether there is another trans-individual, societal structure at play in Hitchcock's *mise-en-scène*, but this time one generated by class rather than patriarchy.

Petty Bourgeois Scopophobia and H. M. Bateman

The key concept in the feminist/psychoanalytic paradigm is scopophilia – the fascination of looking.[33] Given the terms of early-twentieth-century English petty bourgeois identity outlined above, the key concept in any attempt to find such an identity at play in cinematic *mise-en-scène* would be rather scopophobia – a fear of being looked at. Such a mechanism is discernible in the work of some British artists, including Hitchcock. However, in order to demonstrate that it is not peculiar to Hitchcock, but is rather a product of his class formation, I will trace the recurrence of scopophobia in the work of the cartoonist and illustrator, H. M. Bateman (1887–1970). Allowing for certain differences between them – Bateman was born in 1887, Hitchcock in 1899; Bateman, born in Australia, returned to England as an infant, while Hitchcock spent his early years in a London suburb; unlike Hitchcock, with his gargantuan inertness, Bateman was a keen sportsman; Hitchcock was a glutton, Bateman was abstemious; Bateman, unlike Hitchcock, came from a family with no strong religious affiliations – there is a marked correlation in other important aspects of their lives. Like Hitchcock, Bateman was brought up in a petty bourgeois milieu (his father was a small businessman) and in a London suburb. Bateman's official biography was written by a family member, Anthony Anderson, and is therefore more reticent than Spoto's of Hitchcock.[34] In particular, Anderson's book does not have an explicitly Oedipal narrative. It is all the more interesting, then, that Anderson's account of Bateman's mother, shorn of Spoto's Freudian innuendoes, should so closely parallel the latter's account of Emma Jane Hitchcock. Bateman's mother emerges as a distant and forbidding woman who eventually moved in with her son and his wife and, according to Anderson, 'bent her son's will to her own'.[35] Anderson's description of Bateman as shy, introspective and hypochondriac applies also to Hitchcock, as does Bateman's customary stance toward the world – that of the observer, a figure slightly on the edge of things.[36]

Both Hitchcock and Bateman passed from petty bourgeois meagreness to considerable wealth, becoming extremely retentive of their material assets in the process. Moreover, both men were sexually inexperienced before they married and their relationships with their spouses became increasingly tense as they grew older. Like Hitchcock, Bateman often put an image of himself into his drawings and it seems clear that their particular expressions of petty bourgeois angst sometimes translated into similar images. Spoto links the locking in the cell story to the recurring theme of guilt in Hitchcock's films.[37] Bateman's cartoons *The Guest Who Filled his Fountain Pen with Hotel Ink* (1916) and *The False Income Tax Return and Its Rectification* (1917) are interesting both for their theme of guilt and for their proto-cinematic style, being, in essence, cinematic storyboards. Spoto gives innumerable examples of a macabre streak in Hitchcock.[38] This too was present in Bateman: Anderson tells of his using his own blood, spilled while participating in the bouts of sparring he so much enjoyed, to draw pictures.[39] Bateman's Hitchcockian tendency to appear in his own cartoons sometimes took a macabre turn, as in *The Man Who Would Not Share the Fire* (1921), within which a demented Bateman takes an axe to the vexatious titular figure. Spoto and many other critics have drawn attention to the Hitchcockian theme of monstrous horror lurking just under the surface of 'normal' life and 'ordinary' people. This theme is also particularly evident in two cartoons Bateman executed during World War I, *The Recruit Who Took to It Kindly* and *It's the Same Man* (both 1917).

To cap the Bateman/Hitchcock correlation, both men in their later years put considerable effort into constructing themselves not simply as popular entertainers but as 'serious artists'.[40] However, the main evidence for associating Bateman with petty bourgeois scopophobia is his long series of cartoons and advertisements, mainly from the 1920s and 1930s, known as *The Man Who . . .* series (a pleasing echo of Hitchcock's *The Man Who Knew Too Much* [1934 and 1956]). As described by Anderson, each piece revolves round a figure who has become the centre of unwelcome attention through a social gaffe.[41] The deployment of the concept of scopophilia within the feminist/psychoanalytic paradigm brought with it a repertoire of terms associated with vision, notably, look, gaze and glance. To deploy the concept of scopophobia requires a somewhat different vocabulary, one in which the key term would be stare (and its structural opposite, a haughty aversion of the eyes from the offender). Both mechanisms are at play in Bateman's *The Man Who Threw a Snowball at St Moritz* (1926), *The Man Who Coughed at the Bridge Tournament* (1931), *The Man Who Arrived at the Country Club with a Mixed Bag* (1934) and *The Woman Who Said She Had Never Heard of the New World Gas Cooker* (1939). Taken together, such works represent the forays of the wretchedly aspiring English petty bourgeois into the world of the upper middle class and the dreadful payoff when individual petty bourgeois social climbers are unmasked. Seldom has the viciousness of the British class system been represented with such ferocity.

Petty Bourgeois Scopophobia and Hitchcock

The feminist/psychoanalytic paradigm has so thoroughly appropriated Hitchcock's films (often delivering dazzling critical insights) that it has inhibited questions about the extent to which it may have simultaneously homogenised analysis of processes of looking round issues of gender and sexuality.[42] Such gender-based looking is unquestionably there, both within the films themselves (in the looking of the male characters and the being-looked-at state of the female ones) and in the relationship between spectators and screen. My suggestion is, however, that not all looks within Hitchcock's films relate to gender and sexuality. Several instead relate primarily to class (needless to say, often articulated along with the gendered look) and insisting on this fact helps reinsert Hitchcock back into British culture. To recall the extent to which Hitchcock was marked by his petty bourgeois interpellation may not radically change the way we read his films. It should, however, remind us that his British films in particular come out of a highly class-structured and class-conscious social formation and are likely to bear the traces of this, even if only in their interstices.

For example, Hitchcock's famous obsession with blonde, fair-skinned heroines predates his translation to Hollywood and may have class-based (and, indeed, racial) implications. Certain of his films resonate with class tensions (particularly *Rebecca* [1940], *The Paradine Case* [1947], *Under Capricorn* [1949] and *Frenzy* [1972]) and Scotty (James Stewart)'s (re)transformation of Judy (Kim Novak) into Madeleine (also Kim Novak) in *Vertigo* (1958) has a class as well as a sexual dimension.[43] If we accept the idea of the continuing resonance of Hitchcock's having been interpellated as a petty bourgeois, it is tempting to read the auction scene in *North by Northwest* – in which Thornhill (Cary Grant) makes a mockery of the bidding in order to have the police summoned – as a comic catharsis of the petty bourgeois terror of making an exhibition of oneself. Certain Hitchcock sequences strongly recall the Bateman cartoons, notably Flusky (Joseph Cotton)'s entrance to the Governor's ball in *Under Capricorn* and Hetty (Ingrid Bergman)'s mortified exit, and Father Logan (Montgomery Clift)'s emerging from the courtroom into the withering stares of the bystanders in *I Confess* (1953) – a displacement, perhaps, of Hitchcock's petty bourgeois sense of outraged convention onto a scene which has invariably been talked about in religious terms. Thinking about class should also send us back to the scene in *The Paradine Case* in which Mrs Paradine (Alida Valli) is brought into court. The looks exchanged between her and the spectators carry both class and ethnic charges, since she is both a false haute bourgeois and foreign. And there are further Batemanesque displacements, as in the malevolent staring at Manny Balestrero (Henry Fonda) in the insurance office in *The Wrong Man* (1956).

Yet another such displacement may be at play in a justly famous scene which has tended to be read, in the 'master of suspense' paradigm, as an exemplary 'Hitchcock touch' and, in the auteurist paradigm, as a dry run for the scene in *Marnie* (1964) in which Strutt (Martin Gabel) enters the Rutland home and recognises Marnie (Tippi Hedren). The scene is, of course, the mobile crane shot towards the end of *Young and Innocent* (1937), which ends in a close-up on the face of the murderous 'blinking man'. If, rather than raiding Hitchcock's British films for what they might tell us about his 'mature' Hollywood pictures, we instead attempt to situate them in British culture, another reading of the scene might be suggested. Stephen Shafer provides statistical evidence of significant class interaction in British films made between 1929 and 1939. For example, in 1934 over 20 per cent included the theme of class consciousness or elitism.[44] An intriguing aspect of this was the number of films in which characters pretend to belong to another class. The *Young and Innocent* scene is constructed partly round this phenomenon. The runaway, middle-class hero has earlier pretended to be working class and in the 'blinking man' scene, the tramp who can recognise the latter as the murderer changes his rags for the posh outfit which will permit his entry to the upmarket hotel. The drama in the scene arises from the psychic collapse of the 'blinking man' – disguised as the drummer in a blackface band – as his being recognised becomes inevitable. It is the idea of being looked at which induces his psychic collapse, during which – like other Hitchcockian scopophobes – he attempts to conceal his face with his hand.

No one should write about this scene from *Young and Innocent* without relating it to that other great lacuna in Hitchcock criticism – race. The fact that the band is blackface is one of the few moments in Hitchcock's work when the repressed issue of race is glimpsed. The manner of Hitchcock's representation of the band suggests that he was entirely complicit with the attitude to race dominant in British (popular) culture at the time.[45] Anyone seeking to explore issues of race extensively with regard to Hitchcock's work will have to plough the hard furrow of reading for absences.[46]

Reading Hitchcock's films with class questions in mind may also bring back into focus some of his films which other critical paradigms have passed over in virtual silence. *Mr. & Mrs. Smith* (1941), although centrally about '(re)creating the couple',[47] nevertheless is structured at certain moments in unambiguously class-based terms and within a scopophobic *mise-en-scène*. The Smiths, having returned to a restaurant with romantic associations, are dismayed to find it has gone downmarket. Their response to a group of gawping urchins looks and sounds like a Bateman cartoon as they turn their icy class stare on the children and Mr Smith (Robert Montgomery) says, 'Just outstare them. That'll make them embarrassed.' However, there is another instance of scopophobia in the same film which, even though it appears within a comedy, is almost as unsettling as the scene from *Young and Innocent* discussed above. Smith, hoping to make his estranged wife (Carole Lombard) jealous, arranges to meet an acquaintance and his two women friends in a posh restaurant that he knows his wife will be attending. To his horror, the two women turn out to be 'floozies' and he has to endure his wife's searching stare as he sits with them. Like the 'blinking man', his scopophobia causes him to cover his face. Just as re-scrutiny of *Young and Innocent* reveals, additionally, the repressed issue of race, so too does a re-examination of *Mr. and Mrs. Smith* reveal a barely concealed homoerotic subtext.

Some critical paradigms regard the break between Hitchcock's British and American films as significant, often raiding the former for the light they can throw on the latter. It would be an oversimplification to suggest that class issues are paramount in the British films and then cease to matter in the American ones. Just as Freudians and Lacanians would claim that Hitchcock's Oedipal formation resonates in both filmic sets, it also seems not unreasonable to suggest that his class formation might similarly resonate. Class issues are readily understandable by American audiences. Anyone who doubts that a subtle ensemble of class distinctions exists in American society – despite myths to the contrary – should read Paul Fussell's *Class: Style and Status in the U.S.A.* (1984).[48] Fussell notes that it was in America that perhaps the best-known modern guide to social behaviour, *Emily Post's Etiquette* (1955), was published.[49]

Above all, the retrieval of class as a critical category might modify the tendency of (particularly American) critics to read Hitchcock's British films not as complex texts emerging from a particular society at a particular historical moment, but in teleological terms as already-programmed chrysalises out of which the resplendent butterflies of the late Hollywood films will eventually flutter.[50] Recent criticism, partly in reaction against the tyranny of 'spectatorialism' – of seeing the text as constructing the spectator – has become interested once more in what real, historically situated audiences do with films as opposed to what is ostensibly done to them by films. Janet

Staiger, for instance, traverses readings of *Rear Window* (1954) on the way to outlining what a 'historical materialist reception study'[51] of the film might look like. Staiger suggests that the first stage would be to consider what reading strategies were likely to have been available to 1950s audiences. She demonstrates that the (albeit limited) range of contemporary reviews of the film that she considers appealed to four major discourses: psychoanalysis, authorship, the generic conventions of Hollywood cinema, and current social issues. Concretely, the first tended to appeal to *Rear Window*'s 'Peeping Tom' elements and how these structure the narrative; the second, to Hitchcock's technique; the third, to assignment of the film to one or another contemporary film genre; and the fourth, to the contemporary situation of city dwellers. An obvious absence from contemporary reading strategies was feminism, which did not (re)emerge as an influential critical discourse until the 1960s. However, there was another reading strategy prevalent in the 1950s that tended to divide cinemagoers into levels of aesthetic preference ('highbrow', 'middlebrow', 'lowbrow') and which may have affected audience responses. Staiger demonstrates that, in one case, a combination of a particular reviewer's sense of himself as 'highbrow' and his gender caused him to respond in contradictory terms to *Rear Window*. Writing for a 'highbrow' publication, he dismissed the film while, as a 'normal' male, he found the only tolerable thing about it to be Grace Kelly (1929–82). Strictly speaking, since he wrote for an upper-class readership and presumably belonged to that class, this reviewer should have welcomed the film for its sympathetic representation of that class by way of the Grace Kelly character. The fact that this was not so indicates that contradictions may abound in the response of individual spectators, tending to throw neat analytical categories like 'dominant ideology' – which are relatively easy to demonstrate at a textual level – into disarray. Staiger talks briefly about the class differences between *Rear Window*'s central couple being repressed only to reappear as ostensible personality differences.

It is possible to extrapolate from Staiger's discussion of the complexity of historical reception studies some general thoughts on class as the latter relates to the 'reading' rather than the 'writing' of Hitchcock's films. A clue is offered by the observations of a Scottish cinema owner writing in 1937 and referred to by Tom Ryall. It seems that at this time British film exhibitors regarded British films as suitable for the middle-class elements in their audiences, especially on the south coast of England, but that the same films posed problems for the working-class elements. To quote Ryall:

> A Scottish cinema operator suggested that 'British films' was a misnomer as the domestic industry, in fact, produced 'English films in a particularly parochial sense'

and that these were 'more foreign to his audience than the products of Hollywood, over 6000 miles away'.[52]

This observation (which, in terms of Staiger's classification, may involve both class and ethnic subjectivities) accords exactly with my own experience of viewing British films as a working-class Scot during the 1950s.

Conclusion

The point of this essay is not to dislodge the feminist/psychoanalytic paradigm from its well-earned dominant place in relation to Hitchcock studies. It is, rather, to bolster the complexity that paradigm aspires to by indicating another form of psychic structuration, one based on class, which intertwines with the Oedipal. A central limitation of cine-psychoanalysis is its tendency to essentialism, its impulse not only to homogenise the interpellations of, say, a mid-nineteenth-century Viennese of the haute bourgeoisie, a turn-of-the-century petty bourgeois Londoner, and a blue-collar New Yorker born in World War II, but to regard these interpellations as all but complete in early infancy. The addition of the class determination outlined above would help deliver a genuinely non-unified subject, help reinsert Hitchcock back into British culture and, not least, help restore the category of class to the Film Studies lexicon.

Notes

1. See, for example, Charles Barr, ed., *All Our Yesterdays: Ninety Years of British Cinema* (London: British Film Institute, 1986); Robert Murphy, *Realism and Tinsel: Cinema and Society in Britain 1939–1948* (London: Routledge, 1989); Lester Friedman, ed., *Fires Were Started: British Cinema and Thatcherism* (Minneapolis: University of Minnesota Press, 1993); Andrew Higson, *Waving the Flag: Constructing a National Cinema in Britain* (Oxford: Clarendon Press, 1995).
2. For the evacuation of the concept of class from academic discourse in the UK, see Patrick Joyce, ed., *Class* (Oxford: Oxford University Press, 1995). Among the few academic film works keeping the concept of class in operation, see John Hill, *Sex, Class and Realism: British Cinema 1956–1963* (London: British Film Institute, 1986) and David E. James and Rick Berg, eds, *The Hidden Foundation: Cinema and the Question of Class* (Minneapolis: University of Minnesota Press, 1996).
3. Robert E. Kapsis, *Hitchcock: The Making of a Reputation* (Chicago: University of Chicago Press, 1992).
4. See, for example, Janet Staiger, *Interpreting Films: Studies in the Historical Reception of American Cinema* (Princeton, NJ: Princeton University Press, 1992).

5. Alan Lovell, 'British Cinema: The Unknown Cinema' (London: British Film Institute Education Department seminar paper, 1967); Alan Lovell, 'British Cinema: The Known Cinema?', in *The British Cinema Book*, ed. Robert Murphy (London: British Film Institute, 2009), 5–12.
6. Tom Ryall, *Alfred Hitchcock and the British Cinema* (London/Atlantic Highlands, NJ: Athlone Press, 1996).
7. Barr, ed., *All Our Yesterdays*.
8. Ryall, *Alfred Hitchcock*, xi.
9. Charles Barr, 'Introduction: America and Schizophrenia', in *All Our Yesterdays*, ed. Barr, 20.
10. Julian Petley, 'The Lost Continent', in *All Our Yesterdays*, ed. Barr, 98–119.
11. David E. James and Rick Berg, eds, *The Hidden Foundation*, 1.
12. Patrick Joyce, ed., *Class*.
13. Ibid., 4.
14. See, for example, David Morley, *Family Television: Cultural Power and Domestic Leisure* (London: Comedia, 1986).
15. Forsyth Hardy, ed., *Grierson on the Movies* (London: Faber & Faber, 1981), 110.
16. Lindsay Anderson, 'Alfred Hitchcock', *Sequence*, no. 9 (1949), 113–24. The full article is reproduced at https://the.hitchcock.zone/wiki/Sequence_(1949)_-_Lindsay_Anderson:_Alfred_Hitchcock [accessed 19 October 2022].
17. Petley, 'The Lost Continent', 105.
18. See, for example, Eric Rohmer and Claude Chabrol, *Hitchcock: The First Forty-Four Films*, trans. Stanley Hochman (Headington: Roundhouse Publishing, 1992).
19. Robin Wood, *Hitchcock's Films Revisited* (New York: Columbia University Press, 1989); for a representative example of the wider British auteurist sub-paradigm referred to at this point, see V. F. Perkins, 'The British Cinema', *Movie*, no. 1 (June 1962), 2–7.
20. Ryall, *Alfred Hitchcock*, 177.
21. Donald Spoto, *The Dark Side of Genius: The Life of Alfred Hitchcock* (New York: Ballantine, 1983).
22. Ian Bradley, *The English Middle Classes are Alive and Kicking* (Glasgow: William Collins, 1982), 95.
23. Ibid., 97.
24. Spoto, *The Dark Side of Genius*, 477.
25. Ibid., 37.
26. Ibid., 55.
27. Ibid., 18.
28. Ibid., 16. In response to some naughty act as a child, Hitchcock was taken along to the local police station by his father, who had arranged for him to be locked up for several hours.
29. Ibid., 17.
30. Ibid., 17.

31. Quoted in Bradley, *The English Middle Classes*, 111.
32. François Bédarida, *A Social History of England: 1851–1990*, trans. A. S. Forester (London: Routledge, 1990), 220.
33. The term 'scopophilia' emerged in the literature of psychoanalysis, where it means the erotic pleasure of looking, whether at people or objects. Its entry to Film Studies was not 'innocent' or dispassionately academic, but closely tied to feminism with a strong tilt to the gender politics of viewing. See the foundational text of its importation into Film Studies: Laura Mulvey, 'Visual Pleasure and Narrative Cinema', *Screen* 16, no. 3 (1975), 6–18.
34. Anthony Anderson, *The Man Who Was H. M. Bateman* (Exeter: Webb & Bower, 1982).
35. Ibid., 122.
36. Ibid., 43.
37. Spoto, *The Dark Side of Genius*, 16–17.
38. For example, one of Hitchcock's pastimes as a young man was to attend murder trials at the Old Bailey and take notes of the proceedings and he had a particular fascination with the English mass murderer John Christie (1899–1953), whose murders, all of women, had a strong erotic dimension. See Ibid., 32–4.
39. Anderson, *The Man Who Was H. M. Bateman*, 13.
40. Kapsis and Anthony Anderson (both cited above) each describe this in detail.
41. Anderson, *The Man Who Was H. M. Bateman*, 157.
42. There are probably few feminist film texts which do not allude to Hitchcock, often in passing, but those which explicitly foreground his work include: Tania Modleski, *The Women Who Knew Too Much: Hitchcock and Feminist Film Theory* (London: Routledge, 1988); Susan White, '*Vertigo* and Problems of Knowledge in Feminist Film Theory', in *Alfred Hitchcock: Centenary Essays*, eds Richard Allen and S. Ishii-Gonzales (London: BFI Publishing, 1999), 279–98; and Florence Jacobowitz, 'Hitchcock and Feminist Criticism: From *Rebecca* to *Marnie*', in *A Companion to Alfred Hitchcock*, eds Thomas Leitch and Leland Pogue (Hoboken, NJ: Wiley-Blackwell, 2011), 452–72.
43. Virginia Wright Wexman, 'The Critic as Consumer: Film Study in the University, *Vertigo* and the Film Canon', *Film Quarterly* 39, no. 2 (Spring 1986), 32–41.
44. Stephen Shafer, *British Popular Films 1929–1939: The Cinema of Reassurance* (London: Routledge, 1997), 142–6.
45. John M. MacKenzie, *Imperialism and Popular Culture* (Manchester: Manchester University Press, 1986).
46. To a great extent the critical positions from which Hitchcock's films have been addressed can be traced in the yearly *Hitchcock Annual*, which began in 1992 and is currently published by Columbia University Press. One of the main strands is accounts of, and interviews with, (mainly) writers Hitchcock has worked with. There is, in *Hitchcock Annual* no. 17 (2011), a review article by James Naremore, 'Hitchcock Now', which does indeed become a survey

of Hitchcock criticism up to this point. Significantly, it does not mention the word 'race' (far less 'class'). There is, it seems, only one piece in the entire run of *Hitchcock Annual*s which is unambiguously about the question of race: Richard Allen, 'Sir John and the Half-Caste: Identity and Representation in *Murder!*', *Hitchcock Annual*, no. 13 (2004–5), 92–126. *Hitchcock Annual* no. 15 (2006–07) contains a dossier, 'Hitchcock and Hindi Cinema', which is less about the issue of race than Hitchcock's formal influence among Hindi filmmakers. Questions of race and class in relation to Hitchcock have been more extensively addressed outwith the *Hitchcock Annual*: for example, Homer B. Petley, 'Hitchcock, Class and Noir', in *The Cambridge Companion to Alfred Hitchcock*, ed. Jonathan Freedman (Cambridge: Cambridge University Press, 2015), 76–91; Jonathan J. Cavallero, 'Hitchcock and Race: Is the Wrong Man a White Man?', *Journal of Film and Video* 62, no. 4 (Winter 2010), 3–14; and David Greven, 'The Dark Side of Blondeness', *Screen* 59, no. 1 (Spring 2018), 59–79.
47. Virginia Wright-Wexman, *Creating the Couple: Love, Marriage, and Hollywood Performance* (Princeton, NJ: Princeton University Press, 1993).
48. Paul Fussell, *Class: Style and Status in the U.S.A.* (London: Arrow Books, 1984).
49. Emily Post, *Emily Post's Etiquette: The Blue Book of Social Usage* (New York: Funk & Wagnalls, 1955).
50. See, for example, William Rothman, *Hitchcock: The Murderous Gaze* (Cambridge, MA: Harvard University Press, 1982).
51. Staiger, *Interpreting Films*, 89.
52. Ryall, *Alfred Hitchcock*, 171.

CHAPTER 31

Caledonianising *Macbeth*, or, How Scottish is 'The Scottish Play'?*

Macbeth and Scotland: The Relevance of the Connection

Macbeth (*c*.1606) is habitually referred to as 'the Scottish play'. In but one of the innumerable examples of that phenomenon, the distributor's campaign book for a 1960 film adaptation of the play opined that, 'based in actual Scottish history, the film is a "natural" for Scots, wherever they may be – why not a Scottish Night complete with bagpipes and kilts?'[1] However, the central question with which this essay is concerned – how Scotland and the Scots are represented in William Shakespeare (*c*.1564–1616)'s original text and its subsequent (particularly cinematic) realisations – has only relatively recently become a possible topic of concern in the backwash of identity politics. The collective scholarly shift away from the politics of class to the politics of gender, sexual orientation, race and ethnicity, dating roughly from the late 1960s, has fed into every area of cultural activity, not least Shakespearean productions and Shakespeare Studies.[2]

Shakespearean criticism's historic lack of interest in questions of race and ethnicity (the figures of Shylock, Othello and Caliban excepted) has not precluded diverse versions of *Macbeth* from addressing such questions unconsciously. This essay argues that a few dominant discourses about Scotland and the Scots have lain, like deep-but-obscured foundations, within Shakespeare's original text and its diverse realisations. Those discourses have been activated only partially from case to case – in costume and/or scenic design here, in acting performance or incidental music there – all the way throughout history to the twentieth century's cinematic versions of *Macbeth*.

Asking how diverse versions of *Macbeth* constructed Scotland and the Scots exemplifies the core problem of any kind of ideological analysis: the interrogation of texts with regard to questions that they never set out

---

* Originally published in *Scottish Affairs*, no. 36 (2001), 12–39.

to answer. Consider, for instance, what is often spoken of as the first fine art representation of Scotland and the Scots: an early-sixteenth-century Italian fresco depicting a papal emissary, Enea Silvio Piccolomini (1405–64), addressing the court of Scottish king James I (1394–1437). Existing solely as a consequence of Piccolomini's subsequent status as Pope Pius II, the fresco was executed by the painter Pinturicchio (1454–1513) in 1505–07. Several commentaries have suggested that the impulse to represent Scotland as a distinctive place and Scots as a distinctive people was at least one factor in Pinturicchio's project.[3] However, more convincing Quattrocento scholarship has made clear that art production at this time, far from being concerned with 'realistic' representations, was determined primarily by factors intrinsic to the diverse regional cultures making up what we now call Italy. Most notable among such factors were the power of clients to control the content of the art work (including colours to be used and type of landscape to be incorporated), the religious function of art images and the intersection of time- and place-specific forms of cognition and art practice.[4]

In the centuries up to the Renaissance, Scotland and the Scots were less the subjects of a specific narrative than minor players in a Europe-wide discourse hinging on the opposition between 'the Settled' and 'the Wild', Scotland and the Scots being included in the latter. As Hayden White (1928–2018) has demonstrated, ideas about 'wildness' have circulated in every western culture from the Hebraic, through the Greek and Roman, to the Christian periods.[5] The idea of wildness was deployed dialectically, not out of an interest in the wild per se, but as a way of defining the 'not-wild', that is, the normal, the social, the orthodox. Around the fifteenth century the idea of wildness began to be dissociated in Europe from the monstrous Other of barbarism, heresy and madness and, under the sign of rising humanism, instead began to be considered more intrinsically. This process culminated in Romanticism's celebration of wildness in the late eighteenth and nineteenth centuries. Within that process, Shakespeare's *Macbeth* can be seen as partaking of the same construction of Scotland and the Scots as early travellers' tales. Maurice Lindsay (1918–2009) reviews several such accounts: although by no means uniform, they display several recurrent tropes: inhospitable terrain; unremitting weather; poverty and hard living, particularly of the peasantry; native querulousness and hatred of the English; and visitors' disposition to believe that the supernatural found a particularly congenial home in Scotland.[6] In short, these tropes collectively construct Scotland as a terrain exemplary of pre-modern Europe's 'wild versus not-wild' master narrative.

The scholarly work most singly dedicated to arguing for *Macbeth* as, indeed, 'the Scottish play', Arthur Melville Clark (1895–1990)'s *Murder Under Trust*, reaches much the same conclusion regarding the play's construction of Scotland:

> So Scotland is to be thought of as a country different from England [. . .] the reader and perhaps still more the spectator of *Macbeth* are made to envisage unmistakably a 'Caledonia stern and wild', a chilly and thinly-populated land of mountains and shaggy woods rather than ploughed fields, of barren moors and battlefields and grim fortresses rather than towns, villages and farms. The elements in this most atmospheric of plays accord with the wild setting and with the wild deeds occurring in it. The weather is unpredictable, more often than not stormy and boisterous [. . .] with dark nights or ominous half-light predominant over brief glimpses of the day and the sun.[7]

However, of all the pre-modern and modern discourses within which Scotland and the Scots have been constructed, Tartanry is the one which most impinges on productions of *Macbeth*, particularly in the area of costume and scenic design during the nineteenth century, although it continues into the twentieth century as well. A complex, many-sided discourse, one dimension of Tartanry was that late-nineteenth-century movement, including figures like Matthew Arnold (1822–88) and Ernest Renan (1823–92), to discriminate between the Teuton and the Celt.[8] The former figure was associated with rationality, and the latter with emotionality. It might be speculated that this opposition, albeit somewhat transformed, found its way into Shakespearean theatrical production to the extent that, at the level of dress and décor at any rate, there were Celtic, Teutonic, and hybrid *Macbeth*s. For example, Charles Kean (1811–68)'s programme note for his 1853 production of the play may be partaking of the same impulses which shaped Arnold and Renan's writings:

> I have introduced the tunic, mantle, cross-gartering and ringed byrnie of the Danes and Anglo-Saxons [. . .] retaining, however, the peculiarity of the 'striped and chequered garb' which seems to be generally admitted as belonging to the Scotch [. . .] together with the eagle feather in the helmet which, according to Gaelic tradition, was the distinguishing mark of a chieftain.[9]

Noting the popularity of winged helmets in late-nineteenth- and early-twentieth-century productions of *Macbeth*, one wonders about the influence of another great contemporary theatrical discourse – Wagnerism. However, whether Celtic, Teutonic or hybrid, productions of *Macbeth* have frequently been informed by the earliest ideology of Scotland as a wild and uncivilised terra incognita. Marvin Rosenberg (1912–2003) lists the various conceptions of the character of Macbeth which have existed throughout the play's history, one of which is precisely 'Macbeth the Barbarian'.[10] Rosenberg quotes Michael Redgrave (1908–85)'s account of the *Macbeth* he played in London and New York in 1947–48. Redgrave aimed: 'to reach back into a world of barbarism, to mirror accurately a primitive people who slept in their boots [. . . and] had no time for haircuts. Our Scotsmen will look what they were, a wild, violent, strange race'.[11] This lurking ideology of barbarism may help explain the fondness, in certain productions of *Macbeth*, for costumes made of animal skins (for example, the Old Vic in 1932 and 1937 and Orson Welles [1915–85]'s 1948 film). In the early twentieth century, the discourses within which diverse productions of *Macbeth* had been shaped were overlaid by yet another discourse, that of Modernism. Within Modernism's particular manifestations, albeit in a complexly tangled relationship with previous discourses, there are to be found Expressionist, Futurist and Constructivist *Macbeth*s.

Caledonianising *Macbeth* in the Pre-cinematic Period

There is, in the first illustrated edition (1709) of Shakespeare's plays, an image of Macbeth confronting the witches. The actor playing Macbeth wears the kind of elaborate wig, buckled shoes, silk hose and tricorn hat that would be worn in early-1700s court society. It is known that David Garrick (1717–79) also played the role in contemporary dress, wearing the uniform of the Foot Guards.[12] It would seem that the question of historical representation (and, within that, of representing *Macbeth* as Scottish) was simply not an issue in the early-to-mid-eighteenth century. A production was mounted in Edinburgh in 1757, however, with 'the characters entirely new dressed, after the manner of the Ancient Scots'[13] and records exist of a 1784 performance in which the male lead 'seems to have worn a Spanish dress with a piece of tartan drawn over the shoulder in the manner of the insignia of an order of knighthood'.[14] Why should these attempts to caledonianise *Macbeth* first occur, including in Scotland, at this historical moment? It is tempting to relate them to the publication of James Macpherson (1736–96)'s *Fragments of Ancient Poetry* (1760), ostensibly translations of Gaelic verse but probably composed by Macpherson himself. As Malcolm Chapman puts it: 'Macpherson's [work] was largely inauthentic with respect to any genuine Gaelic verse tradition, but it was the very voice of authenticity for the developing sentiments of Romanticism in Europe'.[15] Perhaps similar impulses were simultaneously at play in England, where actor Charles Macklin (1699–1797) is credited with having 'introduced the old highland military habit'[16] when producing and playing the title role in *Macbeth* in 1773. There are two striking prints of Macklin in the role: their difference (one shows Macklin in Highland dress and one does not) suggests that the costuming of *Macbeth* in the eighteenth century was in a process of transition.[17] Macklin further caledonianised the design of his *Macbeth*, putting the witches into 'Caledonian garments' and visualising 'a castle whose halls were adorned with helmets, swords, dirks, stuffed boars and wolves' heads'.[18]

The transition seems to have been complete by the middle of the nineteenth century. The fact that this period's most eminent tragedian, William Charles Macready (1793–1873), foregrounded the role of Macbeth in his repertoire may be an index of the extent to which Scotland had attained enhanced imaginative valency by this time. Alan Downer (1930–95), citing contemporary promptbooks, describes what a characteristic performance of Macready's *Macbeth* might have looked like and establishes that Macready was consistently in tartan Highland dress.[19] Downer's account bears testimony to the by now characteristic Victorian sumptuousness of British theatrical production, the very literalness of which required scenery and props indicating that the action was taking place in a specific time and place, namely, eleventh-century Scotland. Unconscious relaying of Tartanry is not incompatible with a wholly conscious attempt to think historically and to render the past 'authentically', a process well under way within British theatre (as with so many other areas of British culture) by the Victorian period.[20] While little is known about the details of scenery and props within productions of *Macbeth* during this period, evidence exists of the kinds of changes transforming British theatrical design since the early 1800s. Describing the designs for an 1814 production of *Macbeth*, Sybil Rosenfeld (1903–96) writes that they: 'might have served any melodrama of the time: a romantic landscape; rocky pass and bridge; Gothic screen; gallery in Macbeth's castle; banquet hall; cavern and car of clouds; Hecate's cave; castle gate and courtyard and castle exterior'.[21] Rosenfeld credits the change from Neo-Classical to Romantic scenic design primarily to the professional advent of painter and scenic designer Philip James de Loutherbourg (1740–1812) in 1772–73: 'He introduced grandeur in the form of mountains and torrents of natural wildness illuminated with dramatic light and shade with sublime effects'.[22]

The same sumptuous Romantic tropes which informed Macready's mid-Victorian *Macbeth* were still in place in late-Victorian theatre. Actor Sir John Martin-Harvey (1863–1944), for example, recalled a Henry Irving (1838–1905) production of *Macbeth* in 1888 as including 'the skirl of Arthur Sullivan's wild march'.[23] The reference to Arthur Sullivan (1842–1900)'s music suggests that the caledonianising of *Macbeth* in Victorian theatre extended to incidental music as well. But perhaps the most resplendently caledonianised images of *Macbeth* occur in the unexpected area of Toy or Juvenile Theatre. This latter phenomenon involved drawings of actors, props and scenery which, cut out, could be mounted on cardboard and fitted as movable pieces into miniature theatres. Toy Theatre's drawings – 'penny plain, tuppence coloured' – were often based on actual performers and productions: although tending to the lurid in their coloured versions, they nevertheless reflected actual costumes and scenery of the time.[24] Nor was the caledonianising of *Macbeth* restricted solely to the British stage. Reflecting Tartanry's international dimension, Rosenberg describes the great American tragedian Edwin Forrest (1806–72)'s 1845 Macbeth as being 'in Highland tartan, plumed Scotch cap, bare from knee to ankle, pointed shield on his arm'.[25]

Such explicitly 'Scottish' productions of *Macbeth* would be undermined partly by the attack on nineteenth-century theatrical realism associated with Modernism's arrival in the early twentieth century. Modernism in the theatre had the effect of de-historicising the contemporary treatment of particular plays, in that they might be mounted in a style which suggested that the action existed outside of historical time and geographical space, a suggestion often realised through abstraction of costume and décor and even the latter's virtual replacement by lighting effects. Such modernist productions, often based on the theories of Edward Gordon Craig (1872–1966) and Adolphe Appia (1862–1928), very much asserted their historicity in their modernity. The influence of the Modernist intervention in theatre was very uneven, strongest at the High Art end of the contemporary spectrum and weakest at the 'popular art' pole of pantomime and revue, where Victorian styles largely remained in place. Under the sign of Modernism, however, one can point to productions of *Macbeth* as disparate and as temporally and geographically distinct from each other as Arthur Hopkins (1878–1950)'s Symbolist 1921 version in New York with Lionel Barrymore (1878–1954) as Macbeth;[26] Les Kurbas (1887–1937)'s 1924 Constructivist version in Moscow;[27] Ingmar Bergman (1918–2007)'s 1940s Expressionist productions in Stockholm with Anders Ek (1916–79) as Macbeth; and Trevor Nunn's 1976 Stratford production with Ian McKellen as Macbeth, done in Victorian costume on a bare stage.[28] By obscuring precise references to the original time and place of the play's setting, such productions tended to de-caledonianise *Macbeth*. Curiously, however, Modernism might also allow the Scottish dimension to re-enter by the back door, so to speak. Barry Jackson (1879–1961) founded the Birmingham Repertory Company in 1911 with a view to presenting all plays, including Shakespeare's, in a much more contemporary naturalistic style.²⁹ It was within this conception that he mounted a disastrously received 1928 production of *Macbeth*. That production's central metaphor was the deep collective trauma of the Great War (1914–18), and it was precisely this which allowed the re-entry of *Macbeth*'s Scottish dimension. Eric Maturin (1883–1957) as Macbeth appeared in Highland dress – photographs of the production show him looking rather like a dummy in a Highland outfitter's window – and Malcolm's army, costumed in khaki tunics and kilts, looked like a Scottish regiment advancing on the Somme.

The orthodox English stage continued to mount productions of *Macbeth* which attempted to locate the play in eleventh-century Scotland, but these often betrayed a lack of certainty about how medieval Scotland ought to be represented. As has been suggested, perhaps the nineteenth-century debate which attempted to distinguish between Celt and Teuton had some relevance here, some twentieth-century English productions being Celtic and some being more clearly Teutonic. Michael Redgrave's 1947 *Macbeth*, at the level of its chain-mailed, cross-gartered costume at any rate, would appear to sit in the latter tradition, whereas Paul Rogers (1917–2013)'s kilted 1954 *Macbeth* probably sat in the former. The Celtic strain seemed still to be lurking in Peter O'Toole (1932–2013)'s 1978 version, the design of which he conceived as relating to the ninth-century *Book of Kells* and in which a fey kind of supernaturalism was dominant. This would, of course, connect with one of the earliest ideologies about Scotland: that which placed it as 'the wild' in relation to 'civilised' Europe's 'not-wild'. Two of the most intriguingly caledonianised productions of *Macbeth*, however, were those of George Rylands (1902–99) in 1939 and Lewis Casson (1875–1969)'s wartime touring version of 1940, both set in Scotland of 1745–46 at the moment of the last Jacobite Uprising. That event has been greatly romanticised in popular historiography and Rylands, as his programme note makes clear, set out to stage *Macbeth* as 'a romantic melodrama' of 'lost glamour'.³⁰ Why two quite unconnected productions should, at this precise moment, opt to set the play in Jacobite Scotland is puzzling. Perhaps they were a reaction to the grim mood of immediate pre-war and wartime Britain, harking back to another moment when the British state was under threat, but two other factors may have been pertinent. The 200th anniversary of the '45 was approaching and sentimental Jacobitism had been given some measure of currency throughout the 1930s in a play and several quasi-histories by Compton Mackenzie (1883–1972), a figure of enormous contemporary literary status and public profile.³¹

Thus far, the discussion of the caledonianising of *Macbeth* in the theatre has been primarily about costume and décor. Another element previously mentioned, acting performance style, is rather more difficult to research.

As far as can be established, none of the great Shakespearean tragedians from the eighteenth century to the twentieth played Macbeth consistently with a Scots accent, although the secondary character of the Porter, for obvious class reasons, is sometimes recorded as having been played thus.[32] However, Simon Callow gives an amusing account of Charles Laughton (1899–1962)'s preparation for the role of Macbeth in 1934, in which he tried for three days to play Macbeth as Scots before abandoning the attempt.[33] It would seem that several actors, while broadly maintaining Received Pronunciation, made certain concessions to Macbeth's Scottishness. Rosenberg, commenting on the speaking of the phrase ''Twas a rough night' in the Old Vic's 1937 production, indicates that '[Laurence] Olivier [1907–89] rode hard on the "r" of rough, with a touch of Scots brogue'.[34] He also mentions that Michael Redgrave deliberately roughened his voice for the role in 1947–48, but not whether this involved playing the role as Scots.[35]

As will be seen, however, the Scottish accents in one notable cinematic adaptation of *Macbeth* were to become the focus of considerable controversy.

Screening *Macbeth*

John Collick observes that between 1897 and 1989 Shakespeare's plays were the subject of upwards of 200 films and very likely many more television programmes. He goes on to note the curious fact that virtually all the major critical studies of Shakespearean cinema to that latter date confined themselves to a handful of sound films, almost all of which are British or American, with the rest being consigned to critical oblivion. His account of the reasons for that narrowness of critical interest has important implications for the argument of this essay. One key reason Collick cites – and one also alluded to in this essay's opening section – is the historically dominant Romantic orientation of Shakespearean criticism, whereby the meaning of any play is seen as having been wholly created and unchangingly residing within the text, waiting to be unlocked by the sensitive reader.[36] Translating this dominant literary critical tradition into the dominant film critical tradition with regard to Shakespearean film adaptations, '[a] film of a Shakespeare play is regarded in the same way as a reading, in other words the task of the director is to understand and articulate the values and truths that are supposedly embodied in the poetry'.[37] The only apparent debate within this film critical tradition is between the literary, anti-cinematic lobby who think Shakespeare's essential truths are corrupted by the cinema and those, more favourably disposed to cinema, who are on constant lookout for those rare adaptations which reconstitute, in cinematic terms, the same transcendental truths. Meanwhile, silent cinema's Shakespeare is dismissed because the dramatic text is of necessity excluded and a few foreign 'masterpieces' (for example, *Throne of Blood* [Akira Kurosawa, 1957] and *Hamlet* [Grigori Kozintsev, 1964]) are torn from their specific Japanese and Soviet contexts and celebrated instead for their intensely cinematic realisation of Shakespeare's 'essential' truths.

Collick adds that the development of auteurism within film criticism,[38] with its moving of the film director to the centre of critical concern at the expense of other film personnel and non-individualised factors such as genre, was entirely homologous with the celebration of the 'genius' of a Kurosawa or a Kozintsev and the attendant downplaying of the historical and cultural factors which shaped their work. The auteur question is particularly acute with regard to filmic adaptations of *Macbeth*, since the film versions by Orson Welles and Roman Polanski (1971) are among the few permitted entry to the Shakespearean cinematic canon, precisely on account of those filmmakers' status as auteurs. As will be seen, the central tenet of auteurism – that the personal style and 'philosophy' of the auteur is discernible across the entire range of their films – looms large in critical accounts of both Welles's and Polanski's adaptations of *Macbeth*.

Just as Collick's figure of upwards of 200 Shakespearean film adaptations between 1897 and 1989 is surprising, given the mere handful of such films accorded canonical status, so too is it surprising to learn that there had been at least sixteen filmic sallies at *Macbeth* during the twentieth century. These are: USA, 1905 (the duel scene from); USA, 1908; France, 1909 and 1910; UK, 1911; Germany, 1913; USA, 1918; Germany, 1922; UK, 1945 (famous scenes from); USA, 1946; USA, 1948; USA, 1950; Japan, 1957; UK, 1960; UK, 1971; and UK, 1998. Three film versions of *Macbeth* were available on video when the original version of this essay was written in 2001: Welles's 1948 version; Polanski's 1971 version; and a version by Cromwell Films in 1998. For reasons primarily of availability, these films form the core of the discussion here but all display contrasting relevance to the question of the construction of Scotland and the Scots in the filming of *Macbeth*.

Orson Welles's *Macbeth* (1948)

Orson Welles has been greatly celebrated in the history of film criticism. His oeuvre as a whole, and individual films within it, figure in quite diverse critical paradigms, from *Citizen Kane* (1941) being hailed as the apotheosis of cinematic realism by André Bazin (1918–58) in the 1950s on account of its deep focus cinematography to *Touch of Evil* (1958) being anatomised from a postcolonial perspective by Homi Bhabha in the 1980s.[39] Before the rise of auteurist criticism in 1950s France, Welles had already been celebrated in no small measure because of his difficulty in functioning in Hollywood, this being taken as a sign of his artistic integrity. However, with the development of the auteur theory, whereby all of a director's films are scrutinised to reveal stylistic and thematic recurrences – with the latter being seen as the touchstone of the 'true' auteur – Welles's entire oeuvre was subjected to this more Hollywood-friendly kind of analysis. From this point of view, 'Welles's films often centre on a powerful figure and an outsider, the latter being caught up in the former's search for a lost past'.[40] Critical observations of this kind, ostensibly illuminating the whole oeuvre rather than individual films, and Welles's own much-related anecdote of the scorpion begging a ride across a river from a frog, stinging the frog halfway across and thereby ensuring both their deaths, and then explaining that it was 'in his nature', indicate his attraction to monsters and tyrants, figures which Shakespeare supplies in abundance. Having played, produced and directed Shakespeare in the theatre and on radio, Welles went on to make three Shakespearean films: his 1948 *Macbeth*, *Othello* (1952) and *Chimes at Midnight* (1966), the last based on the Falstaff scenes from *Henry V* (c.1599) and *The Merry Wives of Windsor* (1602).

Serious artist though he was, Welles had a tub-thumping, hucksterish, melodramatic streak which invariably drove him to foreground style, spectacle and visual effect rather than the literary texts he so often used as his starting points. Such was the case with his extensive engagement with *Macbeth*. This is most evident in his so-called 'Voodoo *Macbeth*', produced at the Lafayette Theatre, Harlem in 1936. Mounted with an all-black cast and set on the island of Haiti in the early 1800s, it had voodoo priestesses as the witches, characters dazzlingly uniformed like Napoleonic officers, a sense of tropical lushness in the design, and a score by Virgil Thomson (1896–1989) consisting of early-nineteenth-century waltzes. Only four of the cast were professional actors including, as Macbeth, Jack Carter (c.1902–67), the original Porgy in *Porgy and Bess* (1927), and Canada Lee (1907–52), a former professional lightweight boxing contender, as a cigar-smoking Banquo.[41] Hailed as politically radical in some quarters, Welles's 1936 production could equally be viewed as exemplary of the chic Africanism which pervaded liberal interwar New York.[42] Not only did Welles cut and rewrite Shakespeare's text extensively, but he expunged every reference to Scotland from his Voodoo *Macbeth*.

However, Welles was to some extent to reinsert *Macbeth* into its original historico-geographical context in a theatrical version he put on at the Utah Centennial Festival in Salt Lake City in 1947, which he saw as a 'dry run' for his 1948 film. Although neither the décor nor the costumes were particularly Scottish, Welles did caledonianise the Utah production in one respect – the use of Scots accents to differentiate his production from the characteristic modern way of speaking blank verse.[43] Welles caledonianised his Utah *Macbeth* not primarily as a way of representing Scotland and the Scots, but as a technical device to circumvent the dominant way of speaking Shakespeare. He carried the same device over into his 1948 film version, but in the latter the Scots accent was apparently used primarily to create a sense of Otherness. Nevertheless, whatever his intention, Welles's reinsertion of the play's action back into Scotland makes it legitimate to ask how Scotland is represented: Within which pre-existing narratives did Welles construct his cinematic *Macbeth*? Earlier, it was suggested that the successively emerging historical narratives of Scotland did not simply displace each other. Rather, they became interpenetrated to produce a kind of Scottish discursive palimpsest, the diverse tropes of which might be mobilised by anyone seeking to create images, tell stories or, indeed, make any kind of utterance about Scotland and the Scots.[44] Such seems to have been the case with Welles's cinematic *Macbeth*. Pointing to some of the differences between Shakespeare's and Welles's respective conceptions of the play, James Naremore observes that the latter 'chooses to set *Macbeth* in the heart of darkness'.[45] Significantly, one of the many original Shakespearean textual passages Welles cut was that in which Duncan describes the pleasant ambience of Inverness Castle. Naremore goes on:

> In Welles' film, when the king and his entourage enter the gates at Inverness, they have to scatter aside a milling crowd of dogs and swine. The castle itself seems to have been hewn out of solid rock, its battlements vaguely reminiscent of Stonehenge. The sky overhead is always either black or steel grey while the courtyard is damp or mottled with ice. Inside, bedrooms resemble the caves of bears, water runs freely down the sides of a wall and the corridors, as Jean Cocteau [1889–1963] has said, look like an abandoned coal mine. Even the banquet hall where Macbeth sees the vision of the slain Banquo is more suitable to *Beowulf* than to the Renaissance. If the decor of the film is deliberately simple and primitive, so are the characterisations [. . .] Welles looks more like Attila the Hun [d. AD 453] than a courtier, and he goes through the entire picture with a crazed, somnambulistic expression.[46]

In fact, Naremore – in order to heighten the grimness of Welles's film – credits Shakespeare's text with being much less bleak than it actually is. Recalling the Melville Clark quote cited above about the view of Scotland offered in Shakespeare's original text, it might be argued that Welles's images constitute an entirely appropriate objective correlative to the foreboding mood Melville Clark discerns within the play.

As well as cost and access, another difficulty in researching cinema (one not unknown to literary scholars) is that any given film may exist in diverse forms: this version produced under the exigencies of studio interference, that version by the intervention of censorship bodies, and so on. The version of *Macbeth* discussed by Naremore apparently opens with a voiceover written and spoken by Welles which, together with the visual images accompanying it, mobilises the pre-Renaissance trope of Scotland as wild Other. This version of the film opens with a Celtic cross on a desolate moor, with Welles's voiceover telling us that Christianity is 'newly arrived' in Scotland and that the unfolding story takes place 'between recorded history and legend'. However, yet another version of the film begins instead with swirling mists which eventually part to reveal the three witches, who – in a Wellesian innovation probably deriving from his Voodoo *Macbeth* – construct a clay model of Macbeth which, at the film's end, they decapitate at the same moment as Macduff (Dan O'Herlihy) strikes Macbeth's head from his body. The powerful opening image of swirling mist illustrates how a trope from the earliest discourse Scotland figured in, the pre-Renaissance one, may be taken up in subsequent narratives of Scotland. *Brigadoon* (Vincente Minnelli, 1954), constructed primarily within the discourse of Tartanry, begins with a precisely similar image, swirling mist which parts to reveal a Scottish Highland landscape, as do two later Scottish films with a more ironic take on Tartanry, *Scotch Myths* (Murray Grigor, 1982) and *Local Hero* (Bill Forsyth, 1983). The same device also seems to have been a feature of William Charles Macready's mid-Victorian theatrical staging.[47]

The overall style of Welles's cinematic *Macbeth* has rightly been described as Expressionist, realised in semi-darkness with great slabs of light emanating from hidden, off-screen sources and deliberately catatonic performances from several actors.[48] Welles's Hollywood career, which ran from 1941 to 1956 with a few breaks, is homologous with what the dominant critical view sees as the moment of the American film noir. Indeed, *Touch of Evil* is often cited as an exemplary instance of that generic form.[49] It is therefore not altogether fanciful to describe all Welles's Hollywood films, including *Macbeth*, as film noirs. The costuming of Welles's *Macbeth* is a delirious pot-pourri of historical styles, the helmets alone including the Tartar, the Viking, the Anglo-Saxon and the Crusader (certain images recall *Alexander Nevsky* [Sergei Eisenstein, 1938]). But, as we have seen, such historical indeterminacy had been a feature of many productions of *Macbeth* from the Victorian period onwards. Nevertheless, overlaid upon this pot-pourri is a substantial element of Tartanry in the costuming. Although this often veers from the primitive (animal skins) to Renaissance-era styles, almost every character wears tartan. Macbeth himself at various times wears a tartan cape, a tartan suit and a tartan cowl under his crown, and Malcolm (Roddy McDowall) consistently wears kilt and plaid, as does Macduff's child (Christopher Welles).

It is, however, the Scottish accents in Welles's *Macbeth* which have elicited most comment. The film was savaged by the critics on its initial release in 1948. One of the points made was that the Scots accents rendered the film incomprehensible (an accusation levelled many years later against *Gregory's Girl* [Bill Forysth, 1980] and *Trainspotting* [Danny Boyle, 1996]). Republic, the film's production company, withdrew it from distribution in the United States but permitted its showing, to a much warmer critical reception, in certain European cities. It has been suggested that about 60 per cent of Welles's original soundtrack was redubbed before the film's re-release in 1951.[50] But if the Scottish accents were perceived as a major problem, they remain surprisingly intact in the version(s) of the film currently circulating, not only with regard to the principals such as Welles himself and Jeanette Nolan (1911–98), but also among the supporting players. Inevitably, this means that a considerable variety of Scots regional accents are at play in the film, but a common feature, particularly among the major characters, is their tendency (although not always maintained) to inflect the dialogue in a Highland manner, as though signifying that it was spoken by native Gaelic speakers. In my view, the sneering dismissal of the Scots accents in Welles's *Macbeth* is unwarrantable and probably emanates from a mixture of bardolatry (excessive veneration for Shakespeare) and a High Art distaste for Hollywood. The ultimate paradox is that Welles – albeit with quite other intentions – delivered the most discernibly caledonianised *Macbeth* up to that point in time.

Roman Polanski's *Macbeth* (1971)

If 'Expressionist' is an appropriate description of Welles's *Macbeth*, Roman Polanski's version evokes the adjective 'Surrealist', but only in a specifically defined sense of that term. Polanski's film is Surrealist in the same sense as René Magritte (1898–1967)'s paintings, in that bizarre, scarcely imaginable events are played out almost naturalistically and that sexuality, rather than politics, is the film's driving force. As with the Welles film, cinephiles had no problem relating both the circumstances of this production and the finished film itself to Polanski's wider oeuvre, central themes of which had been sexual dementia (*Repulsion* [1965]) and sexual abuse (*Rosemary's Baby* [1968]). As befitted a film coming in the Swinging Sixties' wake, the project had assertive sexual liberation written all over it.

The bulk of the financing came from the Playboy Organization, whose top management at the time were seeking to edge the company upmarket, and the script, partly by Polanski himself, was co-written with Kenneth Tynan (1927–80). Tynan's involvement was double-edged. On the one hand, it conferred further intellectual prestige on the project: Tynan had been theatre critic for *The Observer* newspaper and was currently literary manager of the National Theatre. But, on the other hand, he had devised *Oh! Calcutta!* (1970), the notoriously sexually explicit theatrical revue. The impulse to sexualise this *Macbeth* was apparent in the unusual youth of its leads, Jon Finch (1942–2012) and Francesca Annis, and their physical beauty; in depicting the three witches as part of an orgiastic coven (very reminiscent of that in *Rosemary's Baby*), one of whom displays her genitalia to Macbeth; in having Francesca Annis play Lady Macbeth's sleepwalking scene nude; and in Polanski's characteristic practice of rendering acts of violence in sexual terms. Polanski's Macbeth murders Duncan (Nicholas Selby) by pulling back the bedcover from his naked body, sitting astride him and stabbing him repeatedly. This sexualisation of the violence was picked up by several critics.[51] Like Welles, Polanski renders the murder of Lady Macduff (Diane Fletcher) and her children onscreen, but the manner of the killings is quite different, with the sexualisation being much more explicit in Polanski's version.[52] Such sexualisation of violence recurs in many Polanski films: the gasps of terror uttered by the central figure of *Repulsion* are an exact copy of her sister's coital gasping earlier in the film and the woman in *Death and the Maiden* (1995), having fettered her erstwhile torturer, gags him by slipping off her panties and stuffing them in his mouth. The discourse of 'liberated' sexuality, then, was a constant point of reference in reviews of the film as was its intense violence, the latter often being related to the tragic events in California some years before when Polanski's pregnant wife, the actress Sharon Tate (1943–69), and several friends were murdered by the so-called Manson family. The fact that devil worship figured among the latter was also suggested as a reason for Polanski's being drawn to *Macbeth*.[53] Certainly, Polanski's version is the goriest to have reached the cinema screen, but this also has to be seen against the wider backdrop of the constant extension of the permissible in screen violence, which can perhaps be dated from *Psycho* (Alfred Hitchcock, 1960) and to which Polanski himself had contributed with *Repulsion*, a project often linked to the Hitchcock film.[54]

In terms of the national specificity of the film's narrative setting, it has been suggested that 'Roman Polanski's film version of *Macbeth* [. . .] is not so much Scotland as Golgotha'.[55] Certainly, it is clear that at no time in the production did the question of representing Scotland and the Scots ever become a concern. George Schaefer (1920–97)'s 1960 film version of *Macbeth* was shot on location in Scotland and both Polanski's version and the unrealised 1950s project of Laurence Olivier had involved scouting for locations there. However, so remote was Polanski's concern with the Scottish dimension that he shot his exteriors in Wales and at Bamburgh Castle and Holy Island in Northumberland. Put in the recurrent terminology of this essay, Polanski constructed his *Macbeth* entirely outside the dominant discourses within which Scotland and the Scots have historically been constructed. This is well illustrated by the film's opening. As has already been indicated, many representations of Scotland begin with swirling mist, often lifting to reveal a Highland landscape. This trope was reprised, for example, in the opening of *Braveheart* (Mel Gibson, 1995), which begins with clouds parting to reveal a rugged Highland landscape (clearly signifying 'Scottishness') even though the action of the film takes place in an eastern sector of the Scottish Central Lowlands.[56] Polanski's opening scene in his *Macbeth* is starkly different, occurring on a flat, sandy beach with no particular geographical location. Eschewing any obvious reference to Scotland, it is nevertheless the kind of landscape to which Polanski had been drawn previously, most notably in his graduation film at the Polish Film School, *Knife in the Water* (1962), and his black comedy (also shot on Holy Island), *Cul de Sac* (1966). This jettisoning of the Scottish discourse is continued in the film's costuming, which unfailingly suggests the English late-Norman period. Here there are no winged helmets, targes, animal skins or tartan plaids. Rather, there are fluttering standards, sheet armour, resplendent robes and heraldic devices such as might be seen in cinematic medieval epics like *Ivanhoe* (Richard Thorpe, 1952) and *The Black Shield of Falworth* (Rudolph Maté, 1954).

If Polanski turned his back on available discourses about Scotland, what master narrative did he then opt for instead? Some hint is given in one critic's account of how Polanski fills his cinematic frame:

> In the Orson Welles *Macbeth*, it will be remembered, the great hall was little more than a cave, a hideout for eleventh-century Scots pirates. Polanski makes Inverness if not a Florentine ducal palace [. . .] then at least a shadow of the Elizabethan court at Whitehall or Windsor. Brilliant costumes, golden goblets, hovering serving louts, and so forth.[57]

This, rather misleadingly, suggests that Polanski's film partakes of the 'Merrie England' construction of the Middle Ages. In fact, taken as a whole, it partakes of what is far and away the dominant discourse within which the Middle Ages are constructed in the modern world, a discourse that might be called Dark Ageism. That discourse – in which the key tropes are religiosity and/or supernaturalism; grinding poverty and filth; physical deformity and disfiguring disease; and, above all, unrestrained and unspeakable cruelty – can be followed through many films, whether popular or art-house: *The Private Life of Henry VIII* (Alexander Korda, 1933), in which Charles Laughton's wife-beheadings and messy eating are key tropes; *Day of Wrath* (Carl Dreyer, 1943); *The Seventh Seal* (Ingmar Bergman, 1957), *The Virgin Spring* (Ingmar Bergman, 1960) and *The Vikings* (Richard Fleischer, 1958); to the cinematic adaptation of Umberto Eco (1932–2016)'s *The Name of the Rose* (Jean-Jacques Annaud, 1986). *Braveheart* is a veritable blueprint for this discourse. In effect, Polanski's *Macbeth*, exploring thematic and stylistic concerns paramount to its director, opts primarily for the violent trope, particularly in its sexual dimension.

Polanski's *Macbeth* provides a useful sounding board for the project of this essay. So manifestly lacking any reference to Scotland and the Scots (aside from a few Lion Rampant banners), it throws into relief those adaptations of *Macbeth* which do partake of 'the Scottish discourse'. Another such might have been Laurence Olivier's cherished project of a cinematic *Macbeth* following his 1957 triumph in the role at Stratford. There seems little doubt that he intended it to be heavily caledonianised. Apparently, he had intended taking 'stalwart Scottish actors, like John Laurie [1897–80] and Andrew Cruickshank [1907–88], to Scotland to sup full of the horrors of the blasted heath'.[58] As things stand, however, the only version to challenge Welles's in its 'Scottishness' is the one to have hit the screen at the twentieth century's end.

Cromwell Films's *Macbeth* (1996)

The most active partner in this tripartite production, Cromwell Films (the other two were Scottish-based set-ups, La Mancha Productions and Grampian Television), has been noted more for its entrepreneurial originality than for its cinematic accomplishment. Having developed some kind of track record producing material primarily on World War II for cable channels, Cromwell seemed for a while to have taken upon itself the mission of representing Scottish history to the wider world. Execrable in filmic terms, *Chasing the Deer* (Graham Holloway, 1994), about the 1745 Jacobite Uprising, and *The Bruce* (David McWhinnie and Bob Carruthers, 1996), about the fourteenth-century Scottish king Robert the Bruce (1274–1329), attracted considerable attention due to the peculiar terms of their financing. For a stake of £1,000, an investor could buy a share in one of the projects and appear in it as an extra. A similar investment opportunity – a

£500 stake, a role as an extra, tickets for the world premiere and a share in any net profits – was offered for *Macbeth*. Cromwell's mission as Scottish cinematic historiographer was to some extent dented by the appearance of *Rob Roy* (Michael Caton-Jones, 1995) and *Braveheart* in 1995, the latter in particular setting certain ground rules regarding how Scottish history was to be represented in late-twentieth-century mainstream commercial cinema. It is said, for example, that the battle scenes of *The Bruce* were reshot to meet the gore quotient established by *Braveheart*.[59]

Its historic mission thwarted, Cromwell to some extent changed tack while still retaining a lingering association with the filmic representation of Scotland. Still operating in the shadow of *Braveheart*, although without quite attaining that film's demented vulgarity, Cromwell latterly seemed to be slipstreaming the near-contemporaneous Kenneth Branagh/Ian McKellen Shakespeare adaptations such as *Henry V* (Kenneth Branagh, 1989) and *Richard III* (Richard Loncraine, 1995), or perhaps to be contributing to the Shakespeare mania trailing *Shakespeare in Love* (John Madden, 1998) and *William Shakespeare's Romeo + Juliet* (Baz Luhrman, 1996). Cromwell – latterly ensconced in Stratford-upon-Avon – intended its *Macbeth* to be the first in a series of Shakespearean adaptations. As Cromwell shaped up to its new mission of filmic presenter of Shakespeare, its previous identity, like a snake's half-discarded skin, still clung to its *Macbeth*. Documentation issued by Cromwell reveals that the prime motivation for this production was 'a desire to do justice to this great work and at the same time give it a truly Caledonian hallmark'.[60] In what sense, then, was this *Macbeth* caledonianised? Firstly (and importantly, given its long-term historical proscription under the ideology of Received Pronunciation), the Scottish accent is central to this production. All the characters, with the exception of the English ones, speak with a great diversity of genuine Scots accents, although Helen Baxendale as Lady Macbeth – partly as a result of the non-rhetorical, conversational playing of the more intimate scenes – comes across less as a demented harpy than as the head girl of a posh West of Scotland girls' school. Welles's *Macbeth* was attacked for the incomprehensibility (and, in Scotland, the inauthenticity) of its accents. No such charge can be made against the Cromwell *Macbeth*. The film is also caledonianised by associating the Connery name with the production, albeit that of son Jason, as Macbeth, rather than his father, Sean (1930–2020). Nevertheless, the father's increasing profile in late-twentieth-century Scottish cultural and political life and the fact that he played every one of his cinematic roles, irrespective of the character's origins, with a Scots accent, resulted in his becoming an international icon of Scottishness. Additionally, the cadences of Sean Connery's voice are echoed in that of his son, albeit without the former's gravitas and surfeit of sibilants. The presence of the name 'Connery' on the hoardings, therefore, lends the Cromwell production of *Macbeth* a Caledonian resonance.

Interestingly, the costuming of the Cromwell *Macbeth* wholly eschews Tartanry, a surprising fact given the extent to which this film shadows the contemporary template established by *Braveheart*. Recalling the extent to which historical productions of *Macbeth* could be categorised broadly as Teutonic or Celtic (although signs from both traditions might coexist in particular productions), this *Macbeth* is emphatically Celtic, in keeping with its main production company's stated aims. The costumes, made of soft, naturally dyed, flowing material, recall Victorian images of the ancient Celts and Britons. Similarly, the designs round the costumes' edges, and the brooches holding cloaks in place, recall snake-like Celtic designs. Connery's long, wild hair and beard are suggestive of the same tradition. The heavy, plated armour of the Polanski version, more appropriate to a Norman joust, is here replaced by studded leather (a feature also of the Welles *Macbeth*). The Celtic strain is even more evident in the published screenplay than in the Cromwell film as realised. The former's introduction implicitly criticises the Welles and Polanski films because 'neither sought to steep the play in the Celtic flavour of eleventh-century Scotland',[61] an early stylistic direction speaks of a 'mix through from titles to a map of Scotland in celtic style',[62] and the introduction of King Duncan (John Corvin) indicates that:

> as King of Scotland, his position is marked by the Lion Rampant Emblem, he also wears the same Lion Rampant on his chest. The symbolism of the Royal Crest of Scotland is important as it will recur throughout the film.[63]

Several of the exteriors were shot in Scotland, although English locations were also used, but there is no attempt to represent Scotland as the dark, mountainous terrain so beloved of Romanticism and Tartanry. The final element which caledonianises the Cromwell *Macbeth*, and restates its shadowing of the *Braveheart* template, is the involvement of the Wallace Clan Trust in the choreographing and playing of the film's battle scenes.[64]

However, Cromwell's impulse to caledonianise *Macbeth* existed in some degree of tension with its new mission as cinematic renderer of Shakespeare. There are some signs in the film as realised that it was aimed at school audiences. Unlike both the Welles and Polanski versions, it did not cut Shakespeare's text extensively. Its UK censor's certificate allowed it to be shown to those aged twelve and over, doubtless on account of its sexual restraint. Compared with Polanski's version it is chaste beyond belief. However, it is perhaps characteristically Anglo-American that circumspection on matters sexual may be accompanied by a more permissive view of violence, especially within a literary classic. Partly due to the involvement of the Wallace Clan Trust, the Cromwell *Macbeth*'s battle scenes are suitably gory, as is the murder of Duncan. The influence of the contemporary horror movie is writ large in the latter: Lady Macbeth, having returned to the murder scene with the bloody daggers, is seized by the apparent corpse of Duncan, a reprising of the double ending in contemporary horror films whereby the monster, presumed dead, rises once more from the depths to clasp the arm or leg of the hero or heroine. Aside from the extensive battle scenes and a few effective moments – a particularly sinister, scar-faced Seyton (Kern Falconer) and the 'phantom dagger' rendered naturalistically as the shadow of a crucifix on the floor – the Cromwell *Macbeth* is much less cinematically adventurous than the Welles and Polanski versions. Its most characteristic strategy is the tight close-up on the speakers, testimony perhaps to its being aimed at schools and to the involvement of Grampian Television in its funding.

Conclusion

A newspaper article appeared in 1999 to the effect that the Scottish Consultative Council on the Curriculum had recommended that *Macbeth* be excluded from the compulsory Scottish section of the new secondary school Higher qualification in English and Communication on account of its not being Scottish enough.[65] Almost no one made the connection between that event and the extreme historical volatility of the perception of *Macbeth*'s 'Scottishness' as traversed in this essay – a changing perception often homologous with significant developments in the discourses within which Scotland and the Scots more generally are constructed. Most of the productions referred to above have had aims other than the representation of Scotland and the Scots, the delivery of which has often been little more than a by-product of other concerns. However, it is precisely because production personnel have not been conscious of how they are representing Scotland that historically deep-seated narratives and discourses such as Tartanry and Scotland as terra incognita have come into play, almost on automatic pilot, so to speak. With regard to cinematic versions of *Macbeth*, the creative personnel involved in the production side of cinema often have a complex and multi-layered conception of the text they are constructing. This is not always so for those who market and promote films. Indeed, as this essay's opening quotation from a 1960 distributor's campaign book indicates, the 'purest' perception of *Macbeth* as a text about and for Scotland and the Scots comes, paradoxically perhaps, from this sector.

I will close, without further comment, by quoting another section of that document:

> Every care must be taken not to cheapen the theme of your campaign. Stunting, however, is always effective if it suits the mood of the picture and here, highlighting *Macbeth*, are a few suggestions:
>
> Place a large rock (to resemble the famed 'Coronation Stone') outside your theatre – with a show card thereon – 'LOANED ESPECIALLY FOR THE SHOWING OF THE SCOTTISH TRAGEDY "*MACBETH*" SHOWING HERE ALL NEXT WEEK.'
>
> A collection of Scottish 'oddities' in either your foyer or a local window will all add interest – with genuine Kilts, Bagpipes, Tartans and ceremonial wear – add a touch of humour with a mock haggis or an empty whisky bottle, etc.
>
> A notice in your nearest wine store to the effect that 'PLENTY OF GENUINE SCOTCH FOR EVERYONE at the . . . Cinema all next week' will add to your coverage.
>
> OVER TO YOU, MR SHOWMAN![66]

Notes

1. Marketing advice in the distributor's campaign book for the 1960 film version of *Macbeth*.
2. A glance at the annual *Shakespeare Survey* will indicate the extent to which identity politics has shaped Shakespearean criticism post-1968. I mention Scottishness as a 'possible' area of concern only, since this identity-based criticism has been heavily weighted towards gender and sexuality.
3. See, for example, Evelyn March Phillipps, *Pinturicchio* (London: George Bell & Sons, 1901), 125; James Holloway and Lindsay Errington, *The Discovery of Scotland* (Edinburgh: National Galleries of Scotland, 1978), 1.
4. See, for example, Michael Baxandall, *Painting and Experience in Fifteenth-Century Italy* (Oxford: Oxford University Press, 1972).
5. Hayden White, 'The Forms of Wildness: Archaeology of an Idea', in Hayden White, *Tropics of Discourse: Essays in Cultural Criticism* (Baltimore, MD: Johns Hopkins University Press, 1978), 150–82.
6. Maurice Lindsay, *The Discovery of Scotland* (London: Robert Hale Ltd, 1964).
7. Arthur Melville Clark, *Murder Under Trust, or, The Topical Macbeth and Other Jacobean Matters* (Edinburgh: Scottish Academic Press, 1981), 32. Clark's argument for the 'Scottishness' of *Macbeth* is scholarly and wide-ranging, alluding, among other things, to James VI (1566–1625)'s recent accession to the English throne as James I; his alleged descent from Banquo and known fascination with witchcraft; and the extensive references to Scotland and the Scottish terrain in the play.

8. Malcolm Chapman, *The Gaelic Vision in Scottish Culture* (London: Croom Helm, 1978), 81–112.
9. Quoted in Dennis Bartholomeusz, *Macbeth and the Players* (Cambridge: Cambridge University Press, 1969), 18.
10. Marvin Rosenberg, *The Masks of* Macbeth (Newark/Toronto/London: University of Delaware Press, 1978), 76.
11. Ibid., 76.
12. F. M. Kelly, *Shakespearean Costume for Stage and Screen* (London: A&C Black, 1938), 13.
13. James C. Dibdin, *The Annals of the Edinburgh Stage* (Edinburgh: R. Cameron, 1888), 95.
14. Ibid., 191.
15. Chapman, *The Gaelic Vision in Scottish Culture*, 42.
16. James Laver, *Costume in the Theatre* (London: George G. Harrap & Co., 1964), 98–9.
17. William W. Appleton, *Charles Macklin: an Actor's Life* (Cambridge, MA: Harvard University Press, 1961), 175.
18. Ibid., 171.
19. Alan Downer, *The Eminent Tragedian: William Charles Macready* (Cambridge, MA: Harvard University Press, 1961), 311–38.
20. See Nancy J. Doran Hazelton, *Historical Consciousness in Nineteenth-Century Shakespearean Staging* (Ann Arbor: UMI Research Press, 1987); James Chandler, *England in 1819: The Politics of Literary Culture and the Case of Romantic Historicism* (Chicago: University of Chicago Press, 1998).
21. Sybil Rosenfeld, *Georgian Scene Painting and Scene Painters* (Cambridge: Cambridge University Press, 1981), 150.
22. Ibid., 75.
23. Sir John Martin-Harvey, *The Autobiography of Sir John Martin-Harvey* (London: Sampson, Low, Marston & Co., 1933), 106.
24. Phyllis Hartnoll, ed., *The Oxford Companion to the Theatre* (Oxford: Oxford University Press), 834–5.
25. Rosenberg, *The Masks of* Macbeth, 119.
26. Orville K. Larson, *Scene Design in the American Theatre from 1915 to 1960* (Fayetteville: University of Arkansas Press, 1989). Larson reproduces many of the designs for this production.
27. Konstantin Rudnitsky, *Russian and Soviet Theater: 1905–1932* (New York: Harry N. Abrams Inc., 1988).
28. Dennis Kennedy, *Looking at Shakespeare: A Visual History of Twentieth-Century Performance* (Cambridge: Cambridge University Press, 1993).
29. Ibid., 109.
30. Bartholomeusz, *Macbeth and the Players*, 229; 246.
31. Andro Linklater, *Compton Mackenzie: A Life* (London: Hogarth Press, 1992).
32. Cumberland Clark, *Shakespeare and Costume* (London: Mitre Press, 1937), 24.
33. Simon Callow, *Charles Laughton: A Difficult Actor* (London: Methuen, 1987), 75.

34. Rosenberg, *The Masks of* Macbeth, 364.
35. Ibid., 77.
36. John Collick, *Shakespeare, Cinema and Society* (Manchester: Manchester University Press. 1989), 3.
37. Ibid., 4.
38. See, for example, John Caughie, ed., *Theories of Authorship* (London: Routledge & Kegan Paul, 1981); Jim Hillier, ed., Cahiers du cinéma, *the 1950s: Neo-Realism, Hollywood, New Wave* (London: Routledge & Kegan Paul, 1985).
39. André Bazin, *Orson Welles: A Critical View* (New York: Harper & Row, 1978); Homi K. Bhabha, 'The other question: stereotype, discrimination and the discourse of colonialism', in Homi K. Bhabha, *The Location of Culture* (London: Routledge, 1994), 66–84.
40. Edward R. O'Neill, 'Orson Welles' in *The Oxford History of World Cinema*, ed. Geoffrey Nowell-Smith (Oxford: Oxford University Press, 1996), 455.
41. Richard France, *The Theatre of Orson Welles* (London: Associated University Presses, 1977), 54–73.
42. See W. Kalaidjian, *American Culture Between the Wars: Revisionary Modernism and Postmodern Critique* (New York: Columbia University Press, 1993); James Naremore, *The Films of Vincente Minnelli* (Cambridge: Cambridge University Press, 1993).
43. Frank Brady, *Citizen Welles* (London: Hodder & Stoughton, 1989), 409.
44. Elsewhere, I have called this phenomenon 'the Scottish Discursive Unconscious' precisely on account of its systemic, 'automatic pilot' features. See, for example, Colin McArthur, 'Scotland and the *Braveheart* Effect', *Journal for the Study of British Cultures* 5, no. 1 (1998), 27–39.
45. James Naremore, 'The Walking Shadow: Welles' Expressionist *Macbeth*', *Literature/Film Quarterly* 1, no. 4 (Fall 1973), 361.
46. Ibid., 362–3.
47. Bartholomeusz, Macbeth *and the Players*, 158.
48. Naremore, 'The Walking Shadow'.
49. See, for example, Foster Hirsch, *Film Noir: The Dark Side of the Screen* (New York: Da Capo Press, 1983), 11; Nicholas Christopher, *Somewhere in the Night: Film Noir and the American City* (Emeryville CA: Shoemaker and Hoard, 2006), 70.
50. Barbara Leaming, *Orson Welles: A Biography* (London: Weidenfeld & Nicholson, 1985), 359.
51. See, for example, John Russell Taylor, '*Macbeth*', *The Times*, 4 February 1972, no page ref; Gavin Millar, '*Macbeth*', *The Listener*, 10 February 1972, no page ref.
52. Kenneth S. Rothwell, 'Roman Polanski's *Macbeth*: Golgotha Triumphant', *Literature/Film Quarterly* 1, no. 1 (January 1973), 74.
53. See, for example, Molly Haskell, '*Macbeth*', *Village Voice*, 30 December 1971, no page ref.; Pauline Kael, 'The Current Cinema: Killers and Thieves',

New Yorker, 5 February 1972, no page ref.; Tony Palmer, 'Notes from the Underground', *The Spectator*, 7 November 1970, no page ref.
54. See, for example, James Naremore, 'Remaking *Psycho*', *Hitchcock Annual*, no. 8 (1999), 3–12.
55. Rothwell, 'Roman Polanski's *Macbeth*', 71.
56. For accounts of *Braveheart*'s aesthetic and ideological impoverishment, and its pernicious effects in Scotland and elsewhere, see McArthur, 'Scotland and the *Braveheart* Effect'; Colin McArthur, '*Braveheart* and the Scottish Aesthetic Dementia', in *Screening the Past: Film and the Representation of History*, ed. Tony Barta (Westport, CT: Praeger, 1998), 167–87, and also reproduced elsewhere within the present volume.
57. Rothwell, 'Roman Polanski's *Macbeth*', 73.
58. Laurence Olivier, *On Acting* (London: Weidenfeld & Nicholson, 1986), 213.
59. M. McBain, 'Bruce has his bloody encore', *Scotland on Sunday*, 14 January 1995, 1.
60. Bob Carruthers, Macbeth: *The Screenplay* (Stratford-upon-Avon: Cromwell Productions, 1996), unpaginated introduction.
61. Ibid.
62. Ibid., 3.
63. Ibid., 6.
64. It seems the Wallace Clan Trust was set up in the mid-1980s by one Seoras Wallace, its central aim being to bring back clanship to Scotland and to secure 'the traditional Wallace lands' for use once more by the Clan Wallace. Seoras Wallace, animated by his twin passions for Scottish history and martial arts, also founded the Scottish Clan Battle Society in 1986, in which he and his fellow 'clansmen' re-enact, in the costume and bearing the arms of 'the Scottish warrior', the great battles of Scottish history. This interest led to the Clan/Society being engaged to stage the battle scenes in *Highlander* (Russell Mulcahy, 1986) and *Chasing the Deer*, which in turn led to their involvement in *Braveheart*. It was during the making of the latter film that they became close to Mel Gibson (apparently sharing certain ideological predispositions) and at certain moments, for example at the European premiere of *Braveheart* in Stirling, became a kind of Praetorian Guard to the actor. The Wallace Clan Trust is also funded by certain Scottish local authorities to provide adventure training for unemployed youngsters.
65. Jane Hughes, 'Daggers out for the not-so-Scottish play', *The Independent on Sunday*, 1 August 1999, 3.
66. Distributor's campaign book for the 1960 film version of *Macbeth*.

CHAPTER 32

Two Steps Forward, One Step Back: Cultural Struggle in the British Film Institute*

Introduction

In a 1992 volume on *The Big Heat* (Fritz Lang, 1953), as well as including sections on the film's origins as a *Saturday Evening Post* serial, the production milieu of Columbia Pictures, changing critical discourses surrounding the film and an analysis of the film itself, I included a section on the internal politics of the British Film Institute (BFI), primarily in the decade and a half from 1968.[1] Among other reasons, I did so in order to illustrate the extent to which, as Stuart Hall (1932–2014) has argued in another context:

> [Popular] culture is one of the sites where [the] struggle for and against the culture of the powerful is engaged: it is also the stake to be won or lost *in* that struggle. It is the arena of consent and resistance. It is partly where hegemony arises, and where it is secured.[2]

The version of Hall's argument made in my book about *The Big Heat* – that the inclusion of a section on the BFI's internal politics was relevant since critical disagreement about the film reflected, in microcosm, the kind of issues which underlay cultural policy debate in and around the BFI – was well received by film academics and by those sections of the press (particularly *Time Out* magazine) which engaged regularly with the politics of the BFI, but it provoked bafflement among those journalists whose conception of film culture begins and ends with the latest popular releases.[3] That the section could be included at all within the book was due to the presence in key posts within the BFI of figures who were themselves no strangers to the concept of cultural struggle, and who appreciated the overriding importance of institutions therein.[4]

---

* Originally published in *Journal of Popular British Cinema*, no. 4 (2001), 112–27.

The BFI was central during the period covered by this essay, since Film and Media Studies had not yet become institutionalised within the educational system and publishing in these areas was merely a trickle compared with the torrent it is today. The BFI was almost the sole source of materials, information, critical discussion and support for those British teachers at all levels who were trying to introduce Film and Media Studies to the curriculum.

Like the section in my book on *The Big Heat*, this essay is less an objective history of cultural struggle in the BFI and more a personal memoir. Nevertheless, it will point to the nature and source of the primary documentation necessary for the writing of an objective history (if such a notion retains any credibility in postmodern times). As a personal memoir, it considers the shock waves which came across my own desk. It has little to say about the important struggles which took place in associated milieux of the time, such as the Society for Education in Film and Television (1959–89) and its journals *Screen* (1969–) and *Screen Education* (1960–69; 1974–82), the Independent Film-makers' Association (1974–90) and the BFI Members' Action Group. The reasons for writing this memoir (it was originally published in 2001) were partly to reassert the importance of institutions as sites of struggle in a time when such spaces had once more become quiescent, and, more particularly, to ensure that the cultural work of the BFI Education Department and its allies in other departments (henceforth referred to collectively as BFI Education) did and does not get written out of history. At the time of the essay's original publication, there had already emerged a Grand Narrative about the development of 'left culturalism' – a rubric under which, with important qualifications, the work described herein might be bracketed. This narrative, doubtless with some justice, massively privileges the work of the Birmingham Centre for Contemporary Cultural Studies (1964–2002). It is also often couched in binary terms, true to the structuralist formation of many of its architects, with the role of the dark Other being assigned to *Screen*. The narrative is sometimes further binarised as Antonio Gramsci (1891–1937) versus Jacques Lacan (1901–81), Lacan being central to *Screen*'s feminist/psychoanalytic intervention and Gramsci being equally so in moving the Birmingham Centre further along the road to a Marxism more concerned with the cultural superstructures of societies than with their politico-economic bases. These central facets of the Grand Narrative elide certain important facts: both the Birmingham Centre and *Screen* were never wholly monolithic and BFI Education interfaced regularly with both.[5] Focusing on BFI Education also opens up other important sites of cultural struggle.[6]

The concept of cultural struggle is not nowadays extensively deployed by teachers of Film and Media Studies, so some explanation of what we thought we were doing in and around the BFI between the 1960s and the 1980s might be in order. For example, the quotation from Stuart Hall with which this essay opens speaks of (popular) culture's centrality as a site for the contesting of wider political power. This was undoubtedly a factor in our minds. Diversely and non-monolithically of the political Left, some of us in BFI Education were from working-class backgrounds, part of the first British generation to have gone on to higher education in significant numbers. Very much influenced by Richard Hoggart (1918–2014) and Raymond Williams (1921–88), we had a stronger impulse than these writers not to proscribe popular culture (including popular cinema), but to sift, clarify and validate what we thought to be the best of it. This was in contrast to a powerful tendency towards proscription within the BFI and, indeed, the wider British Establishment, at the time. Class loyalty figured centrally in our position, the *locus classicus* of which was Stuart Hall and Paddy Whannel (1922–80)'s 1964 book *The Popular Arts*, which became the 'bible' of our generation of aspiring film teachers.[7] To promote discussion of authorship and genre centred on popular Hollywood cinema was to us as much a political as an aesthetic act, endorsing as it did part at least of the taste of our own class. However, important as this wider political dimension was to our work, it was not the whole story. We also argued for the integrity of film culture itself against what we saw as the moribund state of a hegemony fiercely resistant to new ideas and centred on the BFI and its allies, particularly among the reviewers of the broadsheet press. Our political and aesthetic commitments did not always pull in the same direction. If the former threatened to draw us towards the Scylla of populism, the latter (particularly in their more theoretical dimensions) edged us towards the Charybdis of elitism. We tried to resolve the contradiction by making our commitments explicit and lucid, but I daresay it remains evident in our writings of the time.

The BFI Education Department

I joined the BFI Education Department in the *annus mirabilis* of 1968. The key operational figures at the time were Paddy Whannel (Education Officer), Jim Kitses (Deputy Education Officer), Alan Lovell (1935–2021; Editor of Film Study Materials) and Peter Wollen (1938–2019; Editor of Publications). I joined initially as Teacher Adviser to replace Victor Perkins (1936–2016), who had taken up an academic post. At the same time, Jim Hillier (1941–2014) was appointed Film Research

Officer of the Humanities Curriculum Project,[8] working closely with a BFI Education Department which had more than doubled in size within the previous four years. Three figures were particularly conducive to this remarkable growth: the Labour government which came into office in 1964 included the first minister with specific responsibility for the arts, Jennie Lee (1904–88), who was prepared to back the BFI financially, particularly with regard to its work outside London; a BFI Director, Stanley Reed (1911–96), who had himself been a teacher and a former Education Officer of the BFI; and Paddy Whannel, who had the rare capacity to function equally well as film critic, educationist and administrator. As early as 1968, however, that progressive coalition of forces was beginning to unravel and signs of confrontation and struggle were becoming visible. Some of the symptoms of this may be discernible in the Minutes of the BFI Executive and the BFI Board of Governors of the time. My recollection, however, is that a number of factors came together to set BFI Education in conflict with the wider Institute's Directorate, some powerful Heads of Department and some Governors. Being primarily about cultural struggle, this essay concentrates mainly on questions of policy. Details of questions of finance – occasionally the engine of, but more usually the brake on, policy – can be found in the BFI *Annual Reports and Financial Statements* quoted herein.

BFI Education had become increasingly critical of what it saw as the totally ad hoc expansion into the regions so lavishly funded by Jennie Lee, an expansion driven more by the availability of money than by cultural policy. An Education Department joke of the time was that anyone ringing up for a catalogue of BFI Distribution Library holdings would be asked if they would like a regional film theatre at the same time. The same powerful BFI department which controlled regional expansion, Film Services, also had responsibility for the BFI's Film Library and for the Institute's emergent production section. Another factor which enraged the Education Department at the time was Film Services having brought in swingeing increases on the hire fees for Film Library holdings, which hit the educational constituency, a main user of the Library. In addition – and here the May 1968 events in Paris were both a symptom and an example – the BFI, being non-unionised at the time, had a Staff Association which was beginning to flex its muscles. That Association was partly undertaking the steps which would lead to BFI staff being formally unionised in the Association of Scientific, Technical and Managerial Staff (ASTMS), and partly expressing staff anger at what was seen as the increasingly erratic management of the BFI. A third factor within BFI Education's increasingly critical stance on regional expansion was entirely cultural. The appointment of Victor Perkins and Peter Wollen to BFI Education began to be perceived as a hostile act by the Directorate, some Governors and Heads of Department and certain (mostly broadsheet) film journalists. Perkins, a founder editor of the journal *Movie* (1962–2000), had expressed in its first issue his distaste for British cinema as a whole and his contempt for the BFI's own house journal, *Sight and Sound*; and the publication in 1969 of Wollen's book *Signs and Meaning in the Cinema* provoked a hysterical response from Kenneth Tynan (1927–80), doyen of British theatre critics, who was to go on to become the influential film critic of *The Observer*.[9]

Perkins and Wollen's respective work illustrates BFI Education's increasing divergence from the largely unspoken conception of film culture dominant at that time within the wider BFI. This dominant conception could be seen as having two strands, the older of which Alan Lovell has described as follows:

> Up until about 1960 film education was an adjunct of the 1930s Documentary movement, at least of the 'academic' wing of the movement which emerged in the immediate post-war years and whose position is representatively presented in books like Roger Manvell [1909–87]'s widely read Penguin publications, *Film* [1944] and *[The] Film and the Public* [1950], and Ernest Lindgren [1910–73]'s *Art of the Film* [1948]. The basic educational assumption was that films were a decisive influence in the formation of false social and moral values by children and young people [. . .] Following from this, the task of film educationists was to protect children from such influences by teaching them to understand how the cinema worked and so leading them to appreciate good films rather than bad ones. The workings of the cinema were to be understood on the basis of aesthetic principles derived from [Sergei] Eisenstein [1898–1948] (an Eisenstein both simplified and abstracted from the cultural context of the Soviet Union in the 1920s) by way of [John] Grierson [1898–1972]. The basic principles were that editing was the key act in the creation of a film; that a direct analogy could be made between film and language such that a shot equalled a word, a sequence a sentence, and so on; and that the cinema was inherently a realistic medium. These principles led to the valuing of the Soviet films of the 1920s, British documentary films of the 1930s, British feature films of the late 1940s (principally the work of Carol Reed [1906–76] and David Lean [1908–91] plus Ealing comedies) and Italian neo-realist films.[10]

The emergence of the second (and later) strand within the dominant conception of film within the BFI is described by John Ellis:

> From the attempt to create a 'quality film' for the mass audience emerges the defence of the 'art cinema' of the 1950s [. . . and] the fundamental conundrum of the creative artist was resolved. The director became recognised as the creator. Specialised cinema films were categorised in terms of a set of known world authors: [Ingmar] Bergman [1918–2007], Satyajit Ray [1921–92], [Michelangelo] Antonioni [1912–2007] appear instead of the old categorisation of 'this sensitive film from Sweden/ India/Italy'.[11]

It is this shifting paradigm – the earlier strand represented by ageing senior officers of the BFI such as Stanley Reed, Ernest Lindgren and John Huntley (1921–2003) and the emergent strand increasingly represented by *Sight and Sound*, the broadsheet reviewers and their readers up and down the country – which Alan Lovell glimpsed in his 1971 description of the BFI-funded regional film theatres:

> The BFI view was that the decline of the cinema was partly due to the bad films shown in the cinema. The Institute could recover or create a new audience for the cinema by showing good films. So the Regional Theatres were seen as the basis for a 'high quality' circuit which would eventually replace the traditional ABC and Rank circuits. Since the strategy was never discussed openly, the naïveté of the assumptions it was based on didn't become immediately apparent [. . .] the distinction between good and bad films is not such an easy one to make; in practice the regional theatres have simply expressed a particular aspect of contemporary taste, providing mainly contemporary European films with a few classic films (a Buster Keaton [1895–1966] or a *Grapes of Wrath* [John Ford, 1940]) and the odd controversial choice (an underground movie or a film rejected by the circuits) thrown in.[12]

The 'we know what's good and don't need to spell it out' attitude underlying this paradigm, and its implicit hostility towards Hollywood narrative cinema, were utterly at odds with BFI Education's call for explicitness of critical and policy criteria and its increasing interest (by way of French, British and American auteurism and studies of popular culture) in Hollywood.

This concatenation of factors – some political, some cultural – increasingly cast BFI Education as a thorn in the flesh of BFI management and provoked a backlash in the form of a 1970–71 Governors' Sub-Committee of Enquiry into the department, chaired by the historian Asa Briggs (1921–2016). The central recommendations of this Sub-Committee's report – in an almost parodic assertion of English empiricism over 'foreign theory' – were that the department should be renamed the Educational Advisory Service, should cease to be concerned with ideas, and should simply respond to the expressed needs of teachers with regard to services and materials. Six members of the department, including Paddy Whannel and Alan Lovell (then Deputy Education Officer following Jim Kitses's departure to an academic post in the United States), resigned in protest.[13] Relationships between Stanley Reed and the rump of the department reached such a low ebb that all dealings with the BFI Directorate were conducted through Ernest Lindgren, Curator of the National Film Archive. The task of those senior officers remaining (myself as Acting Head, Jim Hillier and Christopher Williams, who had earlier replaced Peter Wollen as Editor of Publications) was to sustain the work of the department such as advice-giving, materials provision, an annual summer school and the running of the London University extra-mural courses in film and editorial input to the *Cinema One* series of books. There was a particularly bitter battle over our continuing involvement in this series. At its inception, editorial responsibility had been divided between the Education Department and *Sight and Sound*, with each selecting its own writers and titles. The Directorate now proposed to cede control entirely to *Sight and Sound*. Although our resistance was important in the thwarting of this plan, other contingent factors were probably decisive. Stanley Reed was himself ousted by the Board of Governors in 1971, partly on account of the vocal criticisms of staff and BFI members about the management of the Institute, and individual Governors who might have wished to continue the vendetta against the Education Department had by this time seen out their terms of office. Reed died in 1996, and the most substantial of his obituaries alluded to the circumstances of his departure from the BFI:

> In 1971 there was an attempt to have him removed by the combined efforts of an action committee, of John Davis [1906–93] of Rank who was a governor, and of two film-makers, Lindsay Anderson [1923–94] and Karel Reisz [1926–2002] who were also governors. Reed, it seemed, had set himself on a collision course with the aims of the education department. One member of its staff was heard to say that he would prefer people not to see a film than not to understand why they liked it. Reed would have disagreed with this intimidating view. John Davis, on a different tack, was no supporter of the expansion of regional theatres, while the filmmaker governors wanted a change of personnel at the BFI's film magazine *Sight and Sound* edited by Penelope Houston [1927–2015]. They felt the magazine did not support British film-makers enough. Reed would not budge on any of these issues.[14]

This quotation indicates the complexity of the political forces swirling around the BFI at the time. The anonymous obituary was probably written by a broadsheet film critic and reflects the writer's readiness to demonise BFI Education as soullessly elitist, a charge which would surface regularly throughout the 1970s.[15]

Before his departure, Reed had made it clear that existing members of the Education Department were *persona non grata* as far as the vacant Department headship was concerned. He headhunted Douglas Lowndes for the job, assuming that Lowndes's distinguished track record as a teacher of practical filmmaking would make him sympathetic to the BFI Directorate's plan to oust ideas from what was now the Educational Advisory Service. As it happened, Lowndes was much too sophisticated to make such a hard and fast distinction between theory and practice and, in common with many film teachers in the early 1970s, was himself going through a process of political and cultural reorientation which left him much better informed about, and sympathetic to, those discourses which BFI management most wanted to purge: auteurism, structuralism and semiotics (cine-psychoanalysis had not yet arrived on the scene).

Reed was eventually replaced as BFI Director by Keith Lucas (1924–2012), formerly Professor of Film at the Royal College of Art and a much less proactive figure than Reed. Insofar as there remained an anti-Education Department bias at directorial and gubernatorial level, Lowndes did much to shield the department from it and ensure that something close to its traditional work remained intact – in particular, those two mechanisms which were so crucial for the education of that generation of film teachers which emerged in the 1960s and 1970s, the annual summer schools and the University of London Extra-Mural Department classes in film.[16] It had been a quid pro quo that the BFI Governors precluding the Education Department from behaving – as they saw it – like a university department would be accompanied by a new budget to pump-prime lectureships in Film and Television Studies at British universities. Keele, Warwick, Essex and Stirling were among the first beneficiaries of this mechanism. It fell to me to draw up and administer the policy for this budget and to represent the BFI on interview panels. The policy, which stressed BFI Education's aim to facilitate 'a debate-based film culture', might have become a site of struggle but in most cases proved homologous with the universities' own aims. All the institutions involved with this mechanism (and the amounts they received) are set out in successive BFI *Annual Reports and Financial Statements* of the time.

Film Availability Services (FAS) and the BFI Distribution Division

Arguments about the efficient management of the BFI as a whole, and of particular departments within it, continued throughout the 1970s, one of the outcomes being that the powerful Head of Film Services, John Huntley, was retired in 1974. As well as supervising the BFI Production Fund and the development of regional film theatres (including the deployment of a substantial capital budget called the Housing the Cinema Fund), Huntley's department had purchase on the programming of the RFTs and the acquisition of films for the BFI Distribution Library, the erratic running and pricing policy of which had been a recurrent complaint of BFI Education. On Huntley's departure, Keith Lucas and his formidable Deputy Director, Alan Hill, decided that the Huntley empire had been too large and powerful. They therefore created three separate departments out of it: the Production Department; the Regional Department, with control over virtually all regional funding, including capital building, grants to film activity in regional arts associations and grants towards running costs and programming in RFTs; and Film Availability Services (FAS), with purchase on programming policy in RFTs and the running of the Distribution Library.

At the same time, Douglas Lowndes and the rest of us in the Education Department had made an analysis of the reasons why BFI management and Governors had been able to come so close to obliterating the cultural positions represented by the department. The key factors, we decided, were those positions' lack of purchase on senior post-holders on the BFI Executive and the absence of the vocal support of a well-mobilised constituency outside the BFI. The outcome of this analysis was the decision that I should apply for the post of Head of FAS, to which I was appointed in the summer of 1974.[17] I used to refer to the reshaping of FAS only half-jokingly as the cleansing of the Augean Stables. There were about fifty members of staff, from senior programme officers to technical and secretarial staff, none of whom had a job description and all of whom, it seemed to me, reported directly to the Head of Department. In the financially flush Jennie Lee years, staff had been appointed on a completely ad hoc basis. The duties of one officer, for example, related solely to the movements of one film, *The War Game* (Peter Watkins, 1966). I reorganised the department into three units, one relating to the programming of RFTs, one relating to the running of the Distribution Library, and one relating to booking services for the National Film Theatre, the RFTs, the nationwide educational constituency and film societies, and its financial affairs were recast on a more prudent basis.

It was very much a minority of the staff who were suitable for the jobs they held when the new FAS department was created. Fortunately, the BFI at that time had the capacity and the decency to carry its more elderly and diversely wounded staff until they reached retirement, in ways that would not damage either them or the Institute, and I took advantage of this. The most markedly inept and/or corrupt had to go, and yet others, unsympathetic to the new cultural policy, moved on, usually to well-paid jobs in television. Departing staff were gradually replaced by figures such as Ian Christie, Jane Clarke, John Stewart, Nigel Algar, Steve Jenkins, Susan Barrowclough, Paul Willemen (1944–2012), Roma Gibson and Behroze Gandhy, who, with the good people already in the department, such as Joy Wong, David Meeker and Edith Cobbett, brought a much greater cultural sophistication to the job, although I felt that we never got the mix of cultural intervention and administrative efficiency (the Paddy

Whannel dream ticket model) altogether right. The process of departmental change was thrown into disarray by the ASTMS union calling a strike in 1974 over the sacking of a senior figure in another department within weeks of my appointment.[18] Change was clearly going to have to be very slow in terms of changing personnel, but there was one area of activity where change could be made relatively quickly – acquisitions to the Distribution Library.

Like so many other areas of the BFI, the Distribution Library had grown in a totally ad hoc way. In the immediate period before the formation of FAS, some BFI staff (mainly from Education, the National Film Archive and the Information Department) had been so outraged at the way in which the Distribution Library was being run that they forced the creation of an interdepartmental acquisitions committee which formulated two broad criteria: that each acquisition should have a body of critical writing on it, and that it should not be available from any other film library. FAS being set up, we produced an interim Distribution Library catalogue in 1975, but it was the ambitious, culturally driven catalogue of 1978 which most clearly signals the changing identity of the Library (and, by extension, the changing one of FAS itself). To quote from the 1978 catalogue's foreword:

> Historically, and for the best possible motives, the BFI's Distribution Library did not define its identity very clearly. It grew piecemeal, a few early American films here, a few films about science there, with the odd Russian silent classic and some films about canoeing taken in on the way, the idea being to serve the widest possible film needs [. . . T]he decision was taken to make the Library more specialised. Much of the material it held might more appropriately be housed in other equally specialised libraries. The decision taken was to shift the Library's holdings progressively towards material relevant to the art and history of film and television, a key condition imposed on the [British Film] Institute through its Articles of Association and increasingly reflecting the needs of the two major parts of the Library's constituency, the film society movement and formal education, particularly those concerned with the study of film and television *per se*.[19]

It was also in relation to Distribution Library acquisitions that the content of the debate-based policy which had been gestating, since Paddy Whannel's time, in the Education Department, its successor, the Educational Advisory Service, and FAS was first formally articulated: 'the present catalogue [. . .] has sought where possible to foreground important critical debates and organise the holdings under these debates (e.g. Realism and Documentary, the Avant-Garde[s], etc)'.[20] The 1978 catalogue was written by a relatively recent graduate, Julian Petley, who went on to become a distinguished film teacher and critic. As well as providing accounts of particular films, Petley wrote brief contextualising essays, the titles of which bear witness to the seriousness and interrogatory tone of the enterprise, including: 'Lumière and Méliès: The Documentary and the Fantastic'; 'Soviet Cinema, 1919–1930: New Politics, New Forms'; and 'American Cinema: Critical Contexts'. Limited acquisition funds, instead of being dispersed across a series of individual, ad hoc titles, were instead targeted at groups of films on which serious critical writing existed, or which might prompt such writing – for example, a group of RKO films from the 1930s to the 1950s, which included *The Informer* (John Ford, 1935), *Out of the Past* (Jacques Tourneur, 1947), *Crossfire* (Edward Dmytryk, 1947), *They Live By Night* (Nicholas Ray, 1947) and *Beyond a Reasonable Doubt* (Fritz Lang, 1956), and a group of German feature films of the Third Reich.

The differences between the old Distribution Library acquisition policy and the new can best be gauged by comparing the policy/activity statements in the BFI *Annual Reports and Financial Statements* up to 1974 with, for example, the 1976 *Report*. The unfocused nature and catch-up policy of the former found space for individual acquisitions (for example, several German silent films of the Weimar period and some early American films, including titles by D. W. Griffith [1875–1948]) which would have sat happily within the later policy, but other acquisitions are also liable to fly off in every direction. The 1972 *Report*, for example, speaks of 'films on industrial archaeology [. . .] a selection of London scenes [. . .] a collection of popular science films of the early part of the century [. . .] a compilation on British Dance Bands of the 1930s'.[21] Now, if limitless funds had been available such acquisitions would have been perfectly valid in relation to that part of the BFI's Articles of Association which oblige it to be concerned with film and television as 'record of contemporary life'. The new policy, however, stressed that our key constituencies were film teachers in formal education, the film societies and the regional film theatres, all of whom were much more interested in that other part of the Articles relating to 'art and entertainment'. Reflecting this new policy, the 1976 *Report* mentions a second group of fiction films from the Third Reich – the most substantial acquisition of the year – and a collection of Goldwyn Productions films: *Ball of Fire* (Howard Hawks, 1941), *Barbary Coast* (Howard Hawks, 1935), *The Hurricane* (John Ford, 1937), *Stella Dallas* (Henry King, 1925 and King Vidor, 1937), *The Westerner* (William Wyler, 1940), *Nana* (Dorothy Arzner and George Fitzmaurice, 1934), *The Little Foxes* (William Wyler, 1941), *Dead End* (William Wyler, 1937), *The Best Years of Our Lives* (William Wyler, 1946), *A Song Is Born* (Howard Hawks, 1948) and *The Winning of Barbara Worth* (Henry King, 1926).

Film teachers will recognise the extent to which this list relates to existing critical concerns of the 1970s such as Howard Hawks (1896–1977), John Ford (1894–1973), the Western, the gangster movie and the writings of André Bazin (1918–58), but also to emergent concerns such as Dorothy Arzner (1897–1979) and the melodrama, which feminist film teachers in particular were moving up the agenda. This indicates that our conception of the 'key debates' was not like some mosaic tablet etched in stone which would remain unaltered to the end of time, but rather like a set of evolving concerns responsive to initiatives such as feminism. It seemed to us that the Distribution Library was now beginning to function as it ought to, closely following the contours of debate within film culture as a whole and Film Studies in particular. As well as giving details of the acquisitions, the 1976 *Report* goes into some detail about the policy criteria underlying the choices, it having been our view that these should be publicly available for debate and amendment.

The 1976 *Report* goes on to refer to two other dimensions of policy-building. Marking the arrival of Ian Christie and Paul Willemen, as Head of Regional Programming and Regional Documentation and Publicity Officer respectively, the *Report* also mentions the short-term appointment of Steve Neale (1950–2021), 'who is producing a "bank" of critical documentation on about three hundred films much used in RFTs'.[22] This underlined our commitment to producing documentation and discussion around the films shown in RFTs. The other key dimension – mentioned above in relation to BFI management's relatively free hand in its purging of the Education Department – was our building of a tight-knit and supportive constituency which would not only join us in formulating and revising policy, but which would also support us should we once more become the target of a directorial or gubernatorial purge. The key forum here was the Annual Conference of Regional Film Theatres (which, as regional bodies concerned with film education and film production emerged, would mutate into the BFI Regional Conference). The 1976 *Report* speaks of the annual conference at which:

> Film Availability Services argued against the concept of regional film theatres as separate and autonomous units and posed as an alternative, by way of a consultative document which had the full support of the FAS Advisory Committee, a situation within which the BFI and the theatres agree common aims and policies.[23]

The *Report* then goes on to describe that conference's endorsement of the 'key debates' policy and the acceptance of the RFTs as having an 'educative' role. It was one thing, however, to have a policy of 'democratic centralism' assented to, and quite another to have it carried out. Although a substantial number of RFT directors were enthusiastic proponents of the policy (the number grew through our representation on the interview panels for such posts) and made good use of the critical documentation and subsidy we provided to encourage lectures and educational events, others were more interested in using their theatres simply for amenity and entertainment (which, we agreed, were perfectly laudable aims within an agreed cultural policy). A minority, however, were actively hostile, invoking pressure from their local MPs and successive Ministers for the Arts to remove what they saw as metropolitan interference in their affairs and regularly going to the Director of the BFI and the Chair of the Board of Governors to have the policy nullified. We were perfectly prepared to switch funding away from such theatres towards those which were implementing the 'key debates' policy, and weather the resultant outcry on the basis of the general support for the policy secured at Conference. However, this stance was weakened by two factors. Formal control of both the Housing the Cinema Fund (a capital budget) and the RFT Support Fund (a revenue budget) lay not with FAS but with the Regional Department, which was much less committed to the 'key debates' policy. In addition, the BFI Director at this time, Keith Lucas, who had suffered a public mauling over the ASTMS strike, and successive Chairs of the Board of Governors (particularly John Freeman [1915–2014] and Sir Basil Engholm [1912–90]) had no stomach for public controversy, and, on several occasions, pulled the rug out from under FAS when lobbied by recalcitrant RFT directors.[24]

The generality of the concept of 'key debates' was given concrete applied form at the level of what actually went on in the RFTs, in the phrase 'structured programming'. By the latter we meant an abandoning of the traditional practice whereby films tended to stand as autonomous units, and its replacement by a system wherein relationships were posed among the programmed films which, where possible, would be grouped into seasons and supported with critical documentation, speakers who would introduce and lead discussion of the films, and more formal educational events such as day and weekend schools. BFI Governors were profoundly suspicious of the concept of 'structured programming'. Their disquiet, which had been fanned by certain RFT and Regional Arts Associations directors, first surfaced on the agenda of a policy review meeting involving the Board of Governors, the Directorate and the Heads of Departments on 20 and 21 November 1976. The overarching question of whether FAS (and, by extension, the BFI as a whole) ought to have an explicit cultural policy and the extent to which it should be actively promoted, particularly at regional level, appeared on the agenda in coded form as 'BFI and the Relationship of Initiation and Response' and 'BFI and Unity versus Diversity of Intent'.[25] Keith Lucas opened the discussion by indicating that 'the most heated area [. . .] was regional programming'. The greatest scepticism about FAS's policy was expressed by Michael Relph (1915–2004) and Colin Young (1927–2021), and the greatest support by Nicholas Garnham. This two-day meeting was followed up by a policy paper from Keith Lucas, entitled 'Unity/Diversity and Initiation/Response', which was discussed at the Governors' Meeting of 19 April 1977 and which, rather typically, appeared to want the BFI to face two ways simultaneously. The Minute summarising the Governors' discussion can be read as expressing irritation at the Director's failure to be more proactive, and concluded with the clear implication that Governors would enter any power vacuum which might exist.

The continuing struggle between FAS and the Regional Department provoked Governors to demand from the Director a policy paper entitled 'Programming of Regional Film Theatres', which was discussed at the Governors' Meeting of 15 November 1977. Unusually, the Director's paper was accompanied by an FAS paper, bearing the names of myself and Ian Christie, and a Regional Department paper under the names of Alan Knowles (Head of Department), Richard Rhodes and Barrie Ellis-Jones, setting out the incompatible departmental positions. The FAS paper reiterated our commitment to the 'key debates' and 'structured programming' policies, pointed towards the 'Film Centres in major conurbations' concept of BFI-subsidised regional work and implicitly called for an end to the separation of policy and finance manifest in the existing division of responsibility between the two departments. The Regional Department paper argued for the status quo, hinted darkly at the widespread suspicion of FAS in the regional constituency and, quoting from one of my *Tribune* columns, asserted that: 'Whilst FAS, in promulgating an insistence on "key debates", would appear to be encouraging broad discussion, the very notion of "key debates" is the product of a "materialist" approach to the cinema'.[26] This passage dredges to the surface a factor which lay for the most part like a concealed iceberg under much opposition to both Education Department and FAS activity – the suspicion that they amounted to some kind of leftist conspiracy to 'take over' the BFI. Such suspicions particularly missed the mark with regard to the 'key debates' policy. While we regarded it as only fair that Marxist aesthetics (so long silently proscribed in BFI discourse) should come onto the agenda, we saw the 'key debates' policy as entirely liberal – indeed, the only responsible policy for a publicly funded body in a democratic, pluralist society. In short, every seriously argued position had the right of inclusion within the 'key debates'; the point was to bring them into collision with each other.

In the Minutes of this same 15 November 1977 Governors' meeting the Director's views are summarised: '[T]here was strong criticism that the BFI was trying to dominate regional culture. In their zeal, FAS was in danger of moving too far and too fast. Progress could only be made by sensible reciprocal negotiations'.[27] Although clearly critical of FAS's handling of policy intervention, the Director stopped short of suggesting that FAS abandon its commitment to the 'key debates' policy and 'structured programming'. Once more, the Minutes can be read as the Governors entering the power vacuum at the top of the Institute, in their proposal to set up a working group of Governors 'to undertake a practical review of several film theatres'. Before leaving the papers of the November 1977 meeting, it is useful to quote at some length from the Director's paper:

> Structured programming should, in my view, remain the major thrust of FAS's work. However, it is important that it is recognised that this is a controversial policy and as yet not proven in practice [. . .] it is controversial [because] the criteria it applies to the choices of programmes are considered by many people both inside and outside the Institute as being doctrinaire and largely deny considerations of quality, standards or aesthetic excellence. While many of the new initiatives applied by FAS, particularly those designed to bring order and coherence to their work and which bring new criteria into play have great value, I strongly favour a wider interpretation of 'structured programming', i.e. one which contrives to give due consideration not only to Authorship, Genre, Realism, Movement, National Cinema, Ideology, Film History, Modernism and Institutions of Film (and TV), but *also* acknowledges (even if we continue to question the basis on which we evaluate merit) standards of excellence and creativity and the distinction between a work of art or the simple use of the medium.[28]

This passage could be read as Keith Lucas's counterposing the concreteness of the 'key debates' model with the vague commitment to 'good movies' which Alan Lovell discusses above as having vitiated previous BFI regional policy and which also marked much of the BFI's other activities. For example, around the same time, we challenged the meaningfulness of the National Film Theatre slogan, 'the best of world cinema'.

The Governors' Sub-Committee on Regional Film Theatres did indeed go on to visit several theatres, and its final report was discussed at the Governors' Meeting of 24 October 1978. We in FAS were pleased that the report endorsed our interventionist policy, recommended that the Standard Agreement (the quasi-legal document setting out the relationship between the BFI and a RFT) be rewritten to bring out the educative nature of RFTs and pointed towards the Film Centres conception. At the same time, Governors recommended the strengthening of consultative mechanisms for fear that our interventionist policy would be seen as imposition. Governors also asked FAS for another policy paper which, entitled 'Film Availability Services: The Next Five Years', was discussed at the Governors' Meeting of 9 March 1979. Reaffirming our commitment to the interventionist policy (based on the 'key debates' model) which had been the source of so much argument over the past half-decade, the paper nevertheless stressed that our work over the coming five years would be largely a servicing operation within this policy and the recently strengthened consultative mechanisms. The tone of the Governors' response to this paper was much milder, the Minute concluding with the Chairman's observation that 'it was encouraging to note that within a programme of phased expansion, the department appeared to be broadening its horizons'.[29] 'Film Availability Services: The Next Five Years' is particularly useful for those wishing to know in detail what we were doing at this time, containing appendices on: individual films subsidised into distribution; acquisitions made to the Distribution Library; critical documentation produced for RFTs; and contributions made by FAS staff to BFI publications, National Film Theatre seasons and other activities. The five-year struggle between FAS and the Regional Department over purchase on regional policy and finance was resolved by Anthony Smith (1938–2021), Keith Lucas's successor as Director of the BFI. Shortly after taking office in 1979, Smith merged the two departments into the Distribution Division with myself as head. Characteristically of British public life, the resolution of an often bitter power struggle was represented as a simple administrative rearrangement.[30]

It might be thought that FAS's 'victory' over the Regional Department would have put an end to the clear struggle between ourselves and the BFI Governors over the issue of cultural intervention, but this was not to be so. All my subsequent papers to Governors – 'Building an Active Audio-Visual Culture: BFI Partnerships in the Regions' (discussed at the Governors' Meeting of June 1980); 'BFI Funding and the Grant-in-Aid Bodies', which recommended enhanced funding for the Society for Education in Film and Television and reduced funding for the British Universities Film Council and the British Federation of Film Societies (discussed at the same meeting); and the 'Distribution Division Five Year Plan' (discussed at the January 1983 Governors' Meeting) – elicited opposition from Governors, as the Minutes of these meetings testify. It is for others to decide whether that opposition constituted Governors exercising their constitutional function of overseeing the operation of the BFI and touching the rudder from time to time, or whether it revealed a group of cultural and political conservatives terrified of an upfront, interventionist cultural policy. The last policy paper I submitted to Governors was 'The BFI and Ethnic Provision' (discussed at the Governors' Meeting of May 1984), which deployed the concept of 'institutional racism' to explain the sparse presence, within the BFI and its affiliates, of people from ethnic minority backgrounds. Characteristically, Governors viewed the concept with suspicion.

Conclusion

Sir Roy Shaw (1918–2012), sometime Director General of the Arts Council of Great Britain, countered the assertion that his organisation, like the BFI of the time, had no clear policy with these words:

> We *have* a policy even though it is perhaps not worked out in a schematic and logical way as, say, the French might have done it, and it has 'just growed' like Topsy. The many decisions taken in the arts field in the past, and still being taken, do amount to a policy and a fairly clear, and I dare to say, impressive one at that.[31]

Two elements of this are relevant to the present essay. Sir Roy's reference to 'the French' perhaps evokes echoes of the suspicion of 'foreign theory' which figures so largely in the purges of the 1960s and 1970s. Such sentiments, although largely unspoken, lurked (like the suspicion of leftist conspiracy) underneath the opposition to our attempts to articulate an explicit and interventionist cultural policy on the basis of the 'key debates'. In addition, and unusually for an English arts apparatchik, Sir Roy was prepared to concede that the ACGB's cumulative responses (rather than initiatives) amounted to a policy, but he stopped short of spelling out that policy's cultural content. Much of the BFI gubernatorial and wider opposition to our intervention referred to our alleged aim to 'impose' and 'dominate'. Our reply, that the unspoken BFI policy – as revealed in the analyses of Lovell and Ellis and in Keith Lucas's policy paper, all quoted above – was a form of dominance all the more insidious for being unspoken, went largely unacknowledged. So, too, did our contention (again, referred to above) that to identify – in collaboration with our constituency – the 'key debates', and build a set of policies around them, was precisely the kind of open and democratic activity that a publicly funded body such as the BFI should be engaging in.

Clearly our intervention went against the grain of 'the way things are done' in British arts organisations. What, therefore, was its long-term effect? Taking the BFI Education Department of the 1960s, the Educational Advisory Service of the 1970s and FAS/Distribution of the 1970s/1980s as working from within the same basic idea of a 'debate-based film culture', the main accomplishments were: the provision of advice; film study materials and books which helped the burgeoning constituency shape course structures; and the London University extra-mural courses and summer schools which helped form that cadre of educationists who subsequently occupied senior positions in Film and Media Studies and supervised the institutionalisation of these disciplines in the educational system. There are probably few figures from this cadre whose interest in their subject was not initially sparked by these BFI Education mechanisms.

Paradoxically, therefore, our struggle may ultimately have had more effect outside the BFI than inside. However, bearing in mind that few organisations, least of all the BFI, are monolithic, the struggle's legacy is still discernible in certain aspects of the BFI's activities, particularly education, publishing and distribution. However, another internal effect in the late 1970s, when Governors were still expressing unease about 'key debates' and 'structured programming', was that they were forced to go out and find a successor to Keith Lucas who would not only deliver on, for example, the PR and private funding fronts, but who would also, they thought, contain intellectually the interventionist 'threat'. That figure was Anthony Smith, an absolutely first-rate liberal who, rather in the manner of Douglas Lowndes a decade earlier, developed some measure of sympathy for the intellectual position he had been brought in partly to contain. As mentioned earlier, one of his first acts was to merge FAS and the Regional Department into the Distribution Division with myself as head and, sometime later, he appointed Colin MacCabe as BFI Head of Production. I have referred elsewhere[32] to Smith's stout defence of the BFI's intellectual freedom in the face of Thatcherite pressure during the 1980s, and he personally defended me when officers of the Scottish Film Council complained to BFI Governors about my public criticism of a 'sister body'.[33] Smith's remarkable capacity to attract private sponsorship to the BFI without vulgarising its activities was also an important counter to Thatcherite financial pressure. My impression, however, is that subsequent BFI Directors have shown little interest in articulating an explicit and interventionist cultural policy and have been largely content to go along with the rhetoric of the government of the day. This, in the New Labour context of the late 1990s and early 2000s, meant a flaccid populism.[34] However, as the historical events recounted in this essay demonstrate, the lack of an explicit cultural policy is far from meaning the absence of such a policy, one that is often expressed negatively in a strong sense of what is not wanted. During the original writing of this piece, the latest issue of the journal *Screen* appeared. It contained an interview with

Colin MacCabe about his ten years as a senior BFI executive, culminating in his dismissal by BFI Director John Woodward and Chairman Alan Parker (1944–2020), on the grounds of differing visions of what the BFI should be.[35]

La lutta continua!

Notes

1. Colin McArthur, '*The Big Heat* and Critical Method', in Colin McArthur, *The Big Heat* (London: BFI Publishing, 1992), 35–49.
2. Stuart Hall, 'Notes on Deconstructing "the Popular"', in *People's History and Socialist Theory*, ed. Raphael Samuel (London: Routledge & Kegan Paul, 1981), 239. Emphasis in original.
3. For an illustrative example of a supportive review, see *Time Out*, 3–10 February 1993; for an illustrative one expressing confusion, see *Film Quarterly* 64, no. 4 (1993), 61.
4. Both Ed Buscombe and Colin MacCabe, for example, could be described as 'victims' of cultural struggle: Buscombe because of his resignation from the editorial board of *Screen* in 1975, primarily on account of that journal's problematic embracing of psychoanalysis, and MacCabe due to his much higher-profile ejection from the English Faculty of Cambridge University in 1981 over the content of the English Tripos. The latter event is recounted in MacCabe's *Theoretical Essays: Film, Linguistics, Literature* (Manchester: Manchester University Press, 1985).
5. Christine Geraghty (Geraghty, 'Across the Divide: Thinking About Theory and Practice in Media Studies', in *Future Perfect: Proceedings of the Association of Media, Cultural and Communication Studies Conference, 1998*, 1–6) has alluded both to the process of repression and the binarised narrative which has come to occupy the space. Both are discernible in Graeme Turner, *British Cultural Studies: An Introduction* (London: Unwin Hyman, 1990); David Morley, *Television Audiences and Cultural Studies* (London: Routledge, 1992); Jim McGuigan, *Cultural Populism* (London: Routledge, 1992); Shaun Moores, *Interpreting Audiences: The Ethnography of Media Consumption* (London: SAGE, 1993); and an American account, Patrick Brantlinger, *Crusoe's Footsteps: Cultural Studies in Britain and America* (London: Routledge, 1990). An exception to the general trend is David Morley and Charlotte Brunsdon, *The Nationwide Television Studies* (London: Routledge, 1999), which not only mentions the cultural centrality of the BFI, but also reveals that it part-funded the *Nationwide* studies – another example of the frequent contacts between the BFI and the Birmingham Centre. The argument is not that there is a conspiracy to write the BFI out of history, but rather that Cultural Studies writings tend to concentrate on issues of intellectual debate, rather than on the melange of cultural intervention, service provision and institutional politics represented by the BFI.

6. As well as working for the BFI, I devoted considerable time to two other sites of cultural struggle which I saw as related to my BFI work. I was film critic of the British socialist weekly, *Tribune* from 1972 to 1979. My column, selections from which are collected in Colin McArthur, *Dialectic! Left Film Journalism: A selection of articles from* Tribune (London: Key Texts, 1982), deployed many of the ideas traversed in this essay. I also served on the Photography Board of the Council for National Academic Awards (CNAA), set up in 1965 to validate degree proposals in the burgeoning non-university sector of higher education. The Minutes of that Board – albeit drafted with civil service discretion – offer substantial evidence of struggle over the content of courses, both between CNAA and the polytechnics/colleges, and within CNAA itself.
7. Stuart Hall and Paddy Whannel, *The Popular Arts* (London: Hutchinson Educational, 1964).
8. The HCP was a Schools Council-funded project set up in 1968 to establish protocols for the discussion of social and moral questions in secondary schools. Since films and television programmes often dramatised such questions, the project organisers wished to select extracts which would help discussion. BFI Education cooperated enthusiastically with the project, connected strongly with the work done by Jim Kitses and others in further education and outlined in Kitses's book *Teaching About the Cinema* (London: British Film Institute, 1966). But I recall our being to some extent critical of the HCP's use of film as overly privileging realist forms and reading off social and ethical issues somewhat reductively from them. The large number of extracts selected by the HCP passed into general availability through the BFI Distribution Library when the project had run its course by 1972.
9. Perkins had drafted, on behalf of the editorial board of *Movie*, a piece hostile to British cinema and British film criticism, particularly *Sight and Sound*: Anon, 'The British Cinema', *Movie*, no. 1 (1962), 2–7; Peter Wollen, *Signs and Meaning in the Cinema* (London: Secker & Warburg in association with the British Film Institute, 1969); Tynan's review of Wollen's book is untraced.
10. Alan Lovell, 'The BFI and Film Education', *Screen* 12, no. 3 (Autumn 1971), 14.
11. John Ellis, 'The Quality Film Adventure: British Critics and the Cinema 1942–1948', in *Dissolving Views: Key Writings on British Cinema*, ed. Andrew Higson (London: Cassell, 1996), 90.
12. Lovell, 'The BFI and Film Education', 20.
13. Their full reasons are set out in their 'An Open Letter to the Staff of the British Film Institute', *Screen* 12, no. 3 (Autumn 1971), 2–8.
14. Anon, 'Obituary: Stanley Reed', *The Times*, 15 May 1996.
15. See, for example, the remarks of Sir Basil Engholm, Chair of BFI Governors, in his introduction to the *BFI Annual Report and Financial Statements* for 1979.
16. Throughout the 1960s and the 1970s, there was a marked interpenetration among the topics of summer schools and extra-mural courses and the

published writings of the film education community. For example, my own book *Underworld U.S.A.* (London: Secker & Warburg in association with the British Film Institute, 1972) gestated within an extra-mural course run by Alan Lovell and Peter Wollen, entitled *Myth and Genre in the American Cinema*. An extract from the book in question is reproduced elsewhere in the present volume.
17. This makes it sound easier than it actually was. It was only after the Directorate's first choice – a senior figure from the BBC – withdrew that they reluctantly appointed me.
18. Lack of space precludes discussion of this event, but issues of cultural policy figured significantly in certain manoeuvres during the strike.
19. *BFI Distribution Library Catalogue*, ed. Julian Petley (London: British Film Institute, 1978), iv.
20. Ibid., iv.
21. *BFI Annual Report and Financial Statements, 1972*, 7.
22. *BFI Annual Report and Financial Statements, 1976*, 13.
23. Ibid., 13.
24. The ferocity of some responses might have been gleaned from certain letters to *BFI News* following my 'thinking aloud' about policy in its pages, but – the BFI never having been very good at archiving its own documentation – it seems that all copies of this short-lived publication have been thrown away.
25. Minutes of the BFI Governors'/Management meeting, 20–1 November 1976, 6.
26. Appendix B, BFI Governors' Papers, 15 November 1977, 6.
27. Minutes of the BFI Governors' Meeting, 15 November 1977, 3.
28. Director's paper, 'Programming of Regional Film Theatres', BFI Governors' Papers, 15 November 1977, 3. Emphasis in original.
29. Minutes of the BFI Governors' Meeting, 9 March 1979, 5.
30. The Director's Report (item 6105 in the Minutes of the BFI Governors' Meeting, 27 November 1979) states blandly that 'the new Distribution Department [sic] would rationalise a series of activities currently undertaken by two departments'.
31. Quoted in Robert Hutchison, *The Politics of the Arts Council* (London: Sinclair Browne, 1982), 152. Emphasis in original.
32. McArthur, *The Big Heat*, 40.
33. Those criticisms were made in Colin McArthur, 'Scotland and Cinema: The Iniquity of the Fathers', in *Scotch Reels: Scotland in Cinema and Television*, ed. Colin McArthur (London: British Film Institute, 1982), 67, and reproduced elsewhere in the present volume.
34. The cultural situation of the 1960s and 1970s was quite different from that of today. At that time, the largely implicit bias towards (mainly) European art cinema in the BFI and its affiliates, such as RFTs, was contested by our insistence on including authorship and genre among the key debates, thereby ensuring that engagement with Hollywood found a place on the agenda.

Nowadays, however, due to the presence of an 'anything goes' strand within postmodernism, the dumbing down of terrestrial television and the proliferation of downmarket cable channels and magazines (all connected with the catastrophic decline in popular critical discourse), the horizons of film journalism rarely extend beyond current mainline cinema. The BFI should reinforce its commitment to the preservation of the historical memory of cinematic diversity. The terms of such a commitment must be formulated carefully in order to distinguish it from the discourse of those whom Andreas Huyssen describes as 'the sirens of cultural decline' (Huyssen, *After the Great Divide: Modernism, Mass Culture, Postmodernism* [Bloomington: Indiana University Press, 1986], 4).

35. John Caughie and Simon Frith, 'The film institute and the rising tide: an interview with Colin MacCabe', *Screen* 41, no. 1 (Spring 2000), 51–66.

CHAPTER 33

Transatlantic Scots, Their Interlocutors and the Scottish Discursive Unconscious*

Consider the following quotations:

From the green saucer of Glenaladale, dipping down to Loch Shiel, Alexander Macdonald had taken one hundred and fifty men to serve in Clanranald's regiment. Within a century there was nothing there but the lone shieling of the song.[1]

[T]his is Glencoe, the village at the foot of that most dramatic of glens, where the waters run down the precipitous black rock-faces like tears of pain and shame at what happened 300 years ago.[2]

In Kildonan there is today a shadow, a chill of which any sensitive mind would, I am convinced, be vaguely aware, though possessing no knowledge of the clearances. We are affected strangely by any place from which the tide of life has ebbed.[3]

I'm tied to Uig Sands. I don't know why [. . .] Balnakiel just represents sort of the centre of the historical universe for me, and it is a particularly beautiful setting, and for me, if I were to picture my historic home, then it's going to be some place on Uig Sands, whether it's Carnish that sits on one side or Crowlista on the other side. That bay is a sort of 'ground zero' for me. It's strange that it didn't turn out to be Aird, but Aird to me is always a sort of removal place, some place that we went after we left the homeland.[4]

The first quotation is from the deracinated Canadian writer John Prebble (1915–2001)'s *Culloden* (1961), the second from indigenous Scots journalist Brian Pendreigh's 1992 newspaper account of the 300th anniversary of the 1692 massacre of Glencoe, the third from a 1935 essay by the Scots novelist Neil Gunn (1891–1973) and the fourth is a statement by a transatlantic Scot on her recent return to Scotland. Speaking generally, the four quotes illustrate the extent to which '[Cultural] identities are the names we give to the different ways we are positioned by, and position

---

*Originally published in *Transatlantic Scots*, ed. Celeste Ray (Tuscaloosa: University of Alabama Press, 2005), 339–56.

ourselves within, the narratives of the past'.[5] More specifically, a related factor worthy of investigation is the extent to which all four quotations, despite being produced at diverse moments and by both indigenous Scots and North Americans, sound the same elegiac note and/or display the same rhetorical trope of running, mantra-like, the names of people and places off the tongue. Wherever one looks within discourse relating to Scotland – whether produced by Scots or non-Scots is irrelevant – one is confronted by the same restricted range of images, tones, rhetorical tropes and ideological tendencies, often within utterances promulgated decades (and sometimes even a century or more) apart.

Another example: in 1953 the film *The Maggie* was made in Scotland by the London-based Ealing Studios. That it was directed by Alexander Mackendrick (1912–93), born of Scots parents in the USA but brought up in Scotland, is interesting but, as is suggested above, not crucially relevant. In the film an American executive (Paul Douglas), through a misunderstanding, has his valuable cargo of domestic effects, en route for his Hebridean holiday home, transferred to a beat-up Clyde 'puffer', the kind of small, usually coal-hauling, boat which plied the Clyde estuary. He then engages in a duel of wits with the vessel's cunning captain to retrieve his cargo. However, when the boat lands on the rocks the American, having been ultimately transformed through his encounter with Scotland and the Scots, orders his valuable effects to be jettisoned in order to save the puffer. Exposure to Scotland teaches him to let his heart rule his head.[6] Three decades later, the London-based Enigma Productions made *Local Hero* (1983) in Scotland, written and directed by indigenous Scot, Bill Forsyth. In this film, an American oil tycoon (Burt Lancaster) sends his aide to Scotland to conclude a deal to build an oil refinery in the Highlands. He comes to Scotland himself to iron out difficulties and both he and his aide, transformed through their encounter with Scotland and the Scots, jettison their plan for an oil refinery, opting instead for an observatory and a marine wildlife sanctuary. Like the executive in the earlier film, they too learn to let their hearts rule their heads. By all accounts Forsyth had not seen *The Maggie* before he came to make *Local Hero*. How should it be, therefore, that his film should land on precisely the same ideological mark as the earlier one?

The writings of Stuart Hall (1932–2014) on ideology and cultural identity have consistently struggled with the contradiction between individual human agency and trans-individual influence, if not determination. The above quotation from his work leans both ways in relation to what Hall terms 'the narratives of the past', implying individual agency by suggesting that we position ourselves within them but recognising the possibility of determination by suggesting that we are also positioned by them. As the above concrete examples of discursive repetition imply, when it comes to discourse relating to Scotland, I bend towards emphasising factors of determination (albeit complex over-determination) rather than agency. Having been preoccupied with this question for several decades, I have sought to fashion and elaborate a theoretical concept which will help explain the limited and repetitive repertoire of images and utterances relating to Scotland.[7] That concept is the Scottish Discursive Unconscious (SDU), the suggestion being that anyone setting out to describe, comment on or make images of Scotland and the Scots, rather than producing a novel 'personal' take on the subject, instead switches to automatic pilot, so to speak, and slots into a pre-existing and hegemonic bricolage of images, narratives, sub-narratives, tones and turns of phrase suspended in the aspic of the Scottish Discursive Unconscious. That said, the 'suspended in aspic' metaphor perhaps implies too high a level of fixity in the SDU. The metaphor of the kaleidoscope – with its infinite capacity to disassemble and reconfigure its constituent contents – might be more appropriate. Angela McRobbie, describing the rise of anti-essentialism within feminism, under the sign principally of Michel Foucault (1926–84), talks of 'gender discourses rush[ing] in to fill over the cracks of fragile, unstable sexual identities'.[8] We might talk in analogous terms of the Scottish Discursive Unconscious rushing to fill the cracks in (transatlantic) Scots cultural identities. Clearly the idea of the SDU relates to Foucault's general emphasis on discourse, has some affinities with Edward Said (1935–2003)'s idea of Orientalism, wherein the West constructs rather than describes the Orient, and also connects with the process anatomised by Frantz Fanon (1925–61) wherein blacks in a white world adopt masks fashioned by their exploiters.[9] The SDU also shares with the concept of Orientalism the fact that much of its elaboration has taken place outside the land which is its focus, for example, within the European vogue for things Scottish in the late eighteenth and nineteenth centuries and the construction of twentieth-century cinematic images of Scotland in London and Hollywood.

The Scottish Discursive Unconscious has been a long time in the making. It was precisely the vogue for things Scottish in nineteenth-century Europe which pushed Robert Louis Stevenson (1850–94), with some element of awareness of what he was doing, to slot into a version of the SDU when pressed for an account of his native land by German friends. In a letter of 1882 to his mother he writes:

> [A]nd thence, as I find is always the case, to the most ghastly romancing about the Scottish scenery and manners, the Highland dress and everything national or local

that I could lay my hands upon [. . .] There is one thing that burthens me a good deal in my patriotic garrulage, and that is the black ignorance in which I grope about everything [. . .] I am generally glad enough to fall back again [. . .] upon Burns, toddy and the Highlands.[10]

There is some measure of consensus regarding the key personnel 'responsible' for the originating articulation of the SDU and the key moments of its subsequent elaboration. These would include James 'Ossian' Macpherson (1736–96) in the 1770s, his writings being taken up as a European vogue; Sir Walter Scott (1771–1832) throughout his active life and beyond, his works likewise being taken up universally, not least in North America (Mark Twain [1835–1910] hyperbolically blamed Scott for the outbreak of the American Civil War); Queen Victoria (1819–1901) and Prince Albert (1819–61) and their placing of the royal imprimatur on the Highlands, resulting in the emergence of 'Balmorality'; those masters of Victorian regional sentimentality, the Kailyard writers (particularly J. M. Barrie [1860–1937], S. R. Crockett [1859–1914] and 'Ian McLaren', the pen name of John Watson [1850–1907]) and their popularity in the late nineteenth and early twentieth centuries, especially in North America; and Harry Lauder (1870–1950)'s rise to dominance in the Edwardian music hall and, from the early 1900s, his celebrity status in North America. As to why the ball should have been set rolling by Scotland's emerging cultural visibility two centuries ago, Malcolm Chapman offers a convincing, if partial, answer:

Perhaps the most significant intellectual trend of the eighteenth century was that towards what we now label 'Romanticism'. Within this often rather monstrous historical figment of retrospective definition, one of the commonest of theoretical concerns was to speculate on the nature of society, and on the nature of social development. Theories of Man's primitive nature blossomed, and the Romantics looked both to nature and to this primal human essence for their poetic and intellectual inspiration. At the same time as British intellectuals were becoming more and more interested in the nature of primitive man and primitive society, they had within their own national boundaries a fitting object for their attention. The Scottish Gael fulfilled this role of the 'primitive', albeit one quickly and savagely tamed, at a time when every thinking man was turning towards such subjects. The Highlands of Scotland provided a location for this role that was distant enough to be exotic (in customs and language) but close enough to be noticed; that was near enough to visit, but had not been drawn so far into the calm waters of civilisation as to lose all its interest.[11]

Listing the points of articulation of the Scottish Discursive Unconscious in no way conveys the nature of its operation, its mercurial, hydra-headed, shape-shifting quality; its capacity to reconfigure and rearticulate all or

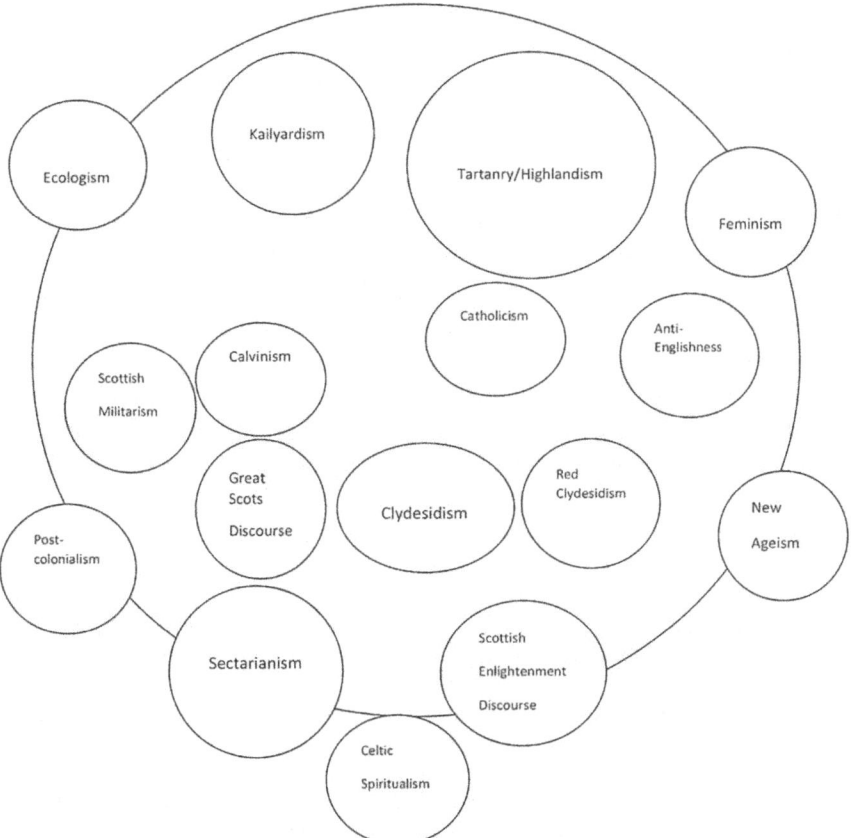

Figure 33.1 The Scottish Discursive Unconscious.

part of the sub-discourses from which it is constituted; and its ability to refurbish itself by appropriating parts of existing or emergent discourses. These qualities might best be conveyed in a (probably far from comprehensive) diagram: one should imagine disparate arrows potentially connecting each of these sub-discourses with all the others.

The sub-discourses constituting the SDU go some way beyond the specific discourse, variously labelled Tartanry and Highlandism, which this writer sees as hegemonic among transatlantic Scots. Indeed, part of this essay's purpose is to thicken the discursive soup in which Scots, whether transatlantic or indigenous, swim – to suggest that they are prey not only to Tartanry/Highlandism but also to some of the other sub-discourses making up the SDU. But first, some clarification of the nature of these sub-discourses. Many of them do, of course, have a conscious dimension – Catholicism or Calvinism, for example – but what I am concerned with here is their quotidian dimension, that part of them which is invoked unthinkingly in day-to-day utterances. Clearly, the sub-discourse of Tartanry/Highlandism is central to the SDU, a 'structure in dominance', to use the Althusserian terminology,[12] which is again problematic on account of the potentially misleading impression it gives of the SDU's fixity. Generally speaking, Tartanry/Highlandism is consistently well-recognised, unlike Kailyard (or, in the latter's discursive mode, Kailyardism). This is so despite the fact that Kailyard arguably forms the next most important sub-discourse in the SDU bricolage. That it tends to be overlooked may be due to the fact that, unlike Tartanry/Highlandism, which supplies the visual iconography of Scots 'identity', Kailyardism instead supplies a range of moods, tones and verbal registers. For example, Cairns Craig famously described Harry Lauder as 'Kailyard consciousness in tartan exterior'.[13] Thomas Knowles has offered a succinct account of that group of Kailyard novels and stories which flourished primarily in the decade 1888–98:

> In its 'classic' form the Kailyard is characterised by the sentimental and nostalgic treatment of parochial Scottish scenes, often centred on the church community, often on individual careers which move from childhood innocence to urban awakening (and contamination), and back again to the comfort and security of the native hearth. Typically thematic is the 'lad o' pairts', the poor Scottish boy making good within the 'democratic' Scottish system of education, and dying young as a graduated minister in his mother's arms with the assembled parish looking on. The parishioners themselves, their dialogue sometimes translated for an English audience, sprinkle their exchanges with native wit, and slip easily from the pettiness of village gossip to the profundities of rustic philosophising.[14]

My wish to foreground Kailyardism is due to its electrifying effect on North America at the turn from the nineteenth to the twentieth century and thereafter and its probable influence on transatlantic Scots, of which more presently.

Although closely associated with Tartanry/Highlandism, Scottish Militarism, another significant sub-discourse of the SDU, is not wholly to be identified with it. Scottish Militarism is discernible throughout Scotland as an exorbitant pride in the exploits of Scottish regiments, in periodic, well-supported campaigns to save them from amalgamation or extinction, in popular songs like 'A Scottish Soldier' (1961) and as a trope of verbal intercourse. I recall, for example, once being accosted by a drunk Orangeman in a Glasgow pub. Looking for trouble and judging me, mistakenly, to be of Irish extraction and therefore Catholic, he opened aggressively with: 'I say there's naebody like the wee Scots sodger.' On a closely related note, how should religion figure in the SDU? It should probably be represented as two separate traditions, Catholicism and Calvinism, albeit not in their theological but their ideological aspects, those elements of the traditions which translate into quotidian mental furniture that then emerge as oaths, sayings and saws and unthinking historical identifications. For example, the Catholicism of the Stuart dynasty seems to have been a strong attraction to latter-day Jacobites such as Compton Mackenzie (1883–1972) and to the handful of cranks who, even today, entertain the delusion of the Stuart dynasty being restored to the British throne. As for the Calvinist tradition, although almost wholly eroded among young Scots, its influence is still discernible in older generations, in the sense that the cadences of the Authorised Version may resonate within their heads and in their utterances. I suspect that such resonances are evident in my own writings and certainly my thoroughly secularised progeny roll their eyes when I refer to certain aspects of popular culture as 'a sounding brass and a tinkling cymbal' (1 Corinthians 13:1–2) or describe a particularly unctuous politician or media celebrity as 'a whited sepulchre' (Matthew 23:27).

The vestiges of religion in the SDU are somewhat separate from another significant component part of it, one that might be called the Sectarian Discourse and which Scotland shares with the north of Ireland. In the Scottish context this discourse ranges from bitter, violent insult ('We're up to our knees in Fenian blood!') to mild banter and jokes ('Did you hear about the Catholic window cleaner? The sash came down on his fingers'). Organised sectarianism was imported into North America by, primarily, the Ulster Scots. Although it survives in Scotland (sometimes as a lethal practice, but more usually as a historic narrative Scots still live within), it is doubtful whether it is nowadays significant in the identity narratives of transatlantic Scots. Yet another sub-discourse, and one which the sectarian discourse sometimes combines with, is Clydesidism. A heavily masculine and working-class discourse, its polar points are taciturnity, heavy drinking, devotion to football and the banishment of women to the margins of life. Clydesidism's historical evolution can be tracked from the myths generated by nineteenth-century urban planning and public health reports which revealed Clydeside to have the worst slums in Europe, through interwar popular journalism about razor gangs with picturesque names (the Baltic Fleet, the Cheeky Forty, the San Toy), to novels such as *No Mean City* (1935) and the 1970s and 1980s television plays of Peter McDougall.[15] The journalism and novels of William McIlvanney (1936–2015) are to some extent articulated within Clydesidism, but in a version inflected towards Red Clydesidism, itself a discourse within which the Clyde Valley has been, is and always will be a socialist-inclined place. It was this discourse which manifested itself in the 'Workers' City' movement, set up to counter the embourgeoisement of Glasgow implicit in the 'Glasgow's Miles Better' public relations campaign of the 1980s and the designation of Glasgow as European City of Culture in 1990.[16]

Turning attention to other areas of the SDU, the 'Great Scots' sub-discourse is one discernible in any Scottish antiquarian bookshop and its shelves of tomes celebrating Scots who have 'made it' in the world beyond Scotland. This discourse survives mainly in Scots journalism and, for much of the late twentieth and early twenty-first centuries, Sir Sean Connery (1930–2020) was the jewel in its crown. What could be called 'the Scottish Enlightenment' sub-discourse – sometimes appropriated, in terms of particular personalities, by the Great Scots counterpart – attempts to construct Scotland as rationalist, scientific and progressive. The Scottish Development Agency (now Scottish Development International) reanimated this discourse in its advertising campaigns of the early 1990s to lure industrial investment to Scotland. Clearly the SDA/SDI and the Scottish Tourist Board are caught in a contradiction, the Tartanry/Highlandism characteristically deployed within the latter's publicity materials and campaigns sending out quite the opposite message to that of the SDA/SDI. Finally, there is the sub-discourse of Anti-Englishness. Doubtless arising in the medieval Wars of Independence (1296–1346), it still flickers into life today, as with other discourses, showing itself in the lethal form of occasional physical violence against figures perceived to be English, but more usually at the level of banter among, for example, football supporters. It has to be said that an analogous anti-Scots discourse has deep roots in English culture, possibly peaking in 1902 with T. W. H. Crosland (1865–1924)'s book *The Unspeakable Scot*.[17] It is nowadays much less common than Scottish anti-Englishness although it survives in, for example, the late-1990s/early-2000s metropolitan murmurings about the disproportionate numbers of Scots holding high office in the Westminster government of Tony Blair.

These, then, are some of the most significant sub-discourses making up the Scottish Discursive Unconscious. Clearly some – particularly Tartanry/Highlandism and, I would argue, Kailyardism – are more pertinent to the identity narratives of transatlantic Scots, whereas others – for example, Sectarianism and Clydesidism – are more influential on (some) indigenous Scots. The unstable, mercurial nature of all discourse means that, like the Blob in the film of that name (Irvin Yeaworth, 1958), the SDU constantly assimilates parts of emergent discourses, even those most apparently in contradiction with it. Some contenders for assimilation are indicated in the diagram above. To take one illustrative example, certain breast-beating instances of the SDU have included a dash of ecologism. For instance, there is an ecological flavour to the ambitions of the Wallace Clan Trust – battle re-enactment group and Praetorian Guard to Mel Gibson during the making and premiering of *Braveheart* (Mel Gibson, 1995) – to reinhabit 'the traditional Wallace lands' as non-modern 'clansmen'. It is perhaps worth recalling here the not insignificant 'green' strain in German National Socialism.[18] Analogously, Paul Basu draws attention to the New Age rhetoric informing some of his informants' utterances and the following instance of these clearly appropriates the emphases of feminism:

> As the boat approached Lewis, I could almost 'see' years of Scottish women on the shores and bogs. I got my first real sense of the female side of the Scots [. . .] and I suddenly felt like I acquired a lineage of strong Scots women.[19]

A respect for the real gains of feminism should not blind us to the extent to which the stock phrase 'strong women' is the premier shibboleth of vulgar feminism, cranked out by virtually every female film director, screenwriter and actor to 'explain' what drew them to particular projects or characters – in other words, another example of a given discourse 'on automatic pilot'. It is the vulgar feminist equivalent of the 'positive images' phase of black discourse which, whatever its progressive historical role, is now somewhat discredited.[20] Celeste Ray has demonstrated the extent to which Tartanry/Highlandism may be merged with Celtic Spirituality.[21] I would hazard a guess that it will not be long before the subalternist preoccupation of certain post-colonialisms is brought to bear on the historic experience of that in all likelihood fanciful construction, the 'Celtic' peoples.[22]

Perhaps this is the point at which to tease out the implications of this essay. Celeste Ray, in her editorial Introduction to the book in which the original published version of this essay appeared, makes the following tactful observation:

> While some cultural studies scholars and anthropologists (especially those leaning towards ethnopoetics) would privilege what people *believe* about their past, the historian privileges 'facts' and the deconstruction of myths. If not through individual essays, then as a whole, this volume attempts to balance a respect for both and to offer both the 'natives'' perspectives and those of the outside observer.[23]

While appreciating the respect shown by ethnographers towards their informants' utterances and practices – a respect which always makes me feel guilty about my own writings as sanctimoniously judgemental – confronted with many of the utterances cited and practices described above, I feel akin to Tom Nairn (1932–2023) at that point within his

The Break-Up of Britain (1977) when he describes the interlocking of Kailyard and Tartanry:

> Kailyard is popular in Scotland. It is recognisably intertwined with that prodigious array of *Kitsch* symbols, slogans, ornaments, banners, war-cries, knick-knacks, music-hall heroes, icons, conventional sayings and sentiments (not a few of them 'pithy') which have for so long resolutely defended the name of 'Scotland' to the world. Annie S. Swan [1859–1943] and [A. J.] Cronin [1896–1981] provided no more than the relatively decent outer garb for this vast tartan monster. In their work the thing trots along doucely enough on a lead. But it is something else to be with it (e.g.) in a London pub on International night, or in the crowd at the annual Military Tattoo in front of Edinburgh Castle. How intolerably vulgar! What unbearable, crass, mindless philistinism! One knows that *Kitsch* is a large constituent of mass popular culture in every land: but this is ridiculous![24]

Clearly, most of the ethnographic work contained in the volume within which the originally published version of this essay appeared takes some distance from the North American version of Nairn's 'tartan monster', but this is not always the case. It is hard not to hear, in Jonathan Dembling's informants' accounts of Cape Breton fiddling, the macho tones of a kind of rural, North American version of Clydesidism.[25] I am not condemnatory of 'the tartan monster', and its centrality in transatlantic Scots' identity narratives, because it is popular. Rather, one is concerned about the heavy political cost of tolerating it, a cost recognised by some of the pieces in the volume. As Michael Vance's essay makes clear, it is principally the blacks of Nova Scotia who have had to pay the psychological price for the hegemony of 'Scottishness' there.[26] One wonders also what some transatlantic Scots' self-described 'webbing'[27] with other Scots distant in place and time implies for their capacity to 'web' with their ethnically diverse North American fellow-citizens in the here and now, and whether there might not be lurking under such filiopietistic utterances the kind of identity-shoring that Paul Gilroy condemns as 'ethnic absolutism'.[28] The present essay's reservations about certain aspects of ethnographic practice reflects the beady eye Anthropology and Cultural Studies have been keeping on each other for some decades. I have reason to be grateful to ethnographers: for example, my pillaging of Celeste Ray's work on Southern American Scots for my book on *Brigadoon* (Vincente Minnelli, 1954) and *Braveheart*.[29] But, *pace* Clifford Geertz (1926–2006) and others, I have a lingering suspicion that ethnography's humanism and empiricism remains, in many cases, largely unreconstructed, particularly in its fetishising of the concept of 'the field'.[30] Also, ethnography's tendency to political quietism is noted by that most ethnographically inclined of Cultural Studies practitioners, Paul Willis, in a book designed to promote dialogue between anthropology and cultural studies:

> [T]he approach to the field, the reasons you go to the field, the chain of logic that leads you to the field, what you admit to knowing and being before you're in the field – all these things are far more contingent and related to, in my own version of cultural studies, some form of intervention rather than to the continuing assumption that the field can stand by itself.[31]

Broadly sharing Willis's position – doubtless exacerbated by the indigenous Scot's exasperation at the flagrant invention of tradition at play – may help explain my impatience with the utterances of transatlantic Scots and their respectful transmission by some ethnographers. I see the revealing of the workings of the Scottish Discursive Unconscious as a political act, a necessary ground-clearing operation which will help both indigenous and transatlantic Scots form an identity adequate to the real.

Figure 33.2 1950s Scots-Americans wholly enmeshed in the Scottish Discursive Unconscious.

The specific proposition of this essay, then, is that however passionately transatlantic Scots experience their connection with Scotland, however much they feel their utterances and practices come out of the deepest core of their being, these practices and utterances are always already textual and discursive; and, if my argument is correct, emergent primarily from reconfigurations of the Scottish Discursive Unconscious. Although the fictive nature of these phenomena is recognised by many ethnographers, their respect for their informants, while not leading the former to credit the latter's utterances as proclamations from the Ark of the Covenant, tends to push that recognition to the background. Perhaps much ethnographic work is caught in the contradiction highlighted by Ella Shohat and Robert Stam: 'theory deconstructs totalising myths, activism nourishes them'.[32] Though not wholly analogous to ethnographic work in general, Annette Kuhn's work on the production of 'cinema memory' – based on interviews with cinemagoers of the 1930s – yields a model which more clearly foregrounds the fictive element in ethnography:

> [E]thnographic enquiry was undertaken in full recognition of the fact that, in dealing with events of 60 and more years earlier, informants' accounts are memory texts, or recorded acts of remembering and that particular questions arise concerning the evidential status of accounts which rely on remembering – and thus also on forgetting, selective memory and hindsight. However, memory is regarded here as neither providing access to, nor as representing, the past 'as it was'; the past, rather, is taken to be mediated, indeed produced, in the activity of remembering. When informants tell stories about their youthful film-going, they are producing memories in specific ways in a particular context, the research encounter. In other words, they are doing memory work; staging their memories, performing them.[33]

Mutatis mutandis, the process Kuhn outlines might also be applicable to what transatlantic Scots do in constructing their identity narratives, with the important addition, if my argument is correct, of the hegemonic positioning power of particular parts of the Scottish Discursive Unconscious, such as Tartanry/Highlandism.

What, then, might be the mechanisms whereby the SDU exercises this power continuously on the transatlantic Scots throughout their history in North America? What follows is a series of (doubtless far from comprehensive) notes for research into this question. Andrew Hook speaks of Sir Walter Scott being a model for indigenous American novelists and reveals that: '[I]n 1823 C. J. Ingersoll [1782–1862] asserted that "nearly 200,000 copies of the Waverly (sic) novels, comprising 500,000 volumes, have issued from the American press in the last nine years"'.[34] Ted Cowan (1944–2022) cites the even more startling statistic of 5 million copies of Scott's *Waverley* (1814) being printed in America between 1813 and

1823.[35] Although we have some sense of the overall effect of Scott's work on American sensibilities, particularly in the South, we are missing any sense of how the works circulated among transatlantic Scots and what effect they had on that group's identity narratives.

Even less documented is the considerable impact of the Kailyard novelists on North America, particularly in the decades spanning the nineteenth and twentieth centuries. Thomas Knowles has talked about 'a Kailyard fever' in America:

> For at least a six year period from 1891 until 1897, Barrie, McLaren and to a lesser extent Crockett ranked high on the lists of American best-sellers: *Beside the Bonnie Brier Bush* [1894] and *The Days of Auld Lang Syne* [1895] gave McLaren first and sixth place in 1895; the former novel was in tenth place in 1896, and *Kate Carnegie and Those Ministers* [1896] and Barrie's *Sentimental Tommy* [1895] in seventh and ninth places respectively; while in 1897 Barrie's tale of Tommy Sandys had risen to eighth position immediately after *Margaret Ogilvy* [1896] the story based on the author's mother.[36]

The same author cites the account, by the Chicago correspondent of the *New York Observer*, of McLaren's lecture performance in that city in 1896:

> 'Ian McLaren' has just closed his engagement in the city, and it is fair to say that no foreigner has been more popular in Chicago than he. People of all classes have sought to do him honour [. . .] The audience [. . .] was decidedly Scotch, who thoroughly appreciated the speaker's analysis of Scotch character. The gross receipts of those lectures are not below 8000 dollars.[37]

Another writer on the Kailyard has noted its influence in Canada:

> [T]he familiar authors are freely available second-hand in Ontario, in the districts settled by Scots, and among the most fascinating of Canadian novels of the early years of this century are those by such writers as Robert Knowles [1868–1946], Minister of Galt in Ontario, who reproduces the formula of Barrie and McLaren exactly, but applies it to rural Ontario.[38]

These passages suggest that transatlantic Scots were avid consumers of Kailyardism, but the wider research question is the extent to which the tones and values of the Kailyard helped shape the identity narratives of this community.

Although the strictly literary phenomenon of the Kailyard would be eclipsed by the turn of the nineteenth into the twentieth century, its influence lingered on. Barrie's success as a dramatist was initiated by an 1897 theatrical adaptation of his 1891 novel *The Little Minister* which, following its New York success, toured the United States. *The Little Minister*'s first cinematic adaptation was in 1912 (with subsequent adaptations in 1915, 1921, 1922 and 1934) and cinematic versions of *Beside the Bonnie Brier Bush* and *The Lilac Sunbonnet* appeared in 1921 and 1922. Throughout the twentieth century the cinema, particularly Hollywood, has appropriated several of the Scottish Discursive Unconscious's sub-discourses, both individually and in combination: Tartanry/Militarism – *The Black Watch* (John Ford, 1929), *Bonnie Scotland* (James W. Horne, 1935), *Wee Willie Winkie* (John Ford, 1937), *The Drum* (Zoltan Korda, 1938), *Gunga Din* (George Stevens, 1939); Tartanry – *Rob Roy* (Arthur Vivian, 1911; Harold French, 1953; Michael Caton-Jones, 1995), *Bonnie Prince Charlie* (Charles Calvert, 1923; Anthony Kimmins, 1948), *The Swordsman* (Joseph H. Lewis, 1948), *The Master of Ballantrae* (William Keighley, 1953), *Kidnapped* (Alan Crosland, 1917; Alfred L. Werker, 1938; William Beaudine, 1948; Robert Stevenson, 1960); Kailyardism – the numerous adaptations of the Kailyard novels referred to above, *The Green Years* (Victor Saville, 1946), *Bob, Son of Battle* (Louis King, 1947), the Disney films *Greyfriars Bobby* (Don Chaffey, 1961) and *The Three Lives of Thomasina* (Don Chaffey, 1964); plus that melange par excellence of Tartanry and Kailyard, *Brigadoon*. These titles – which exclude the extensive number of adaptations from Sir Walter Scott's works – are a mere fraction of the list, running from 1898 to 1990, compiled by Janet McBain.[39] Once again, the research question – ethnographic work on the model of Annette Kuhn's would be appropriate here – is: How did the transatlantic Scots relate to this diet of films representing Scotland and/or the Scots and to what extent did it shape their identity narratives?

There are three other phenomena which also require investigation in relation to the construction of these identity narratives. The first of these is Harry Lauder (Cairns Craig's above-quoted personification of 'Kailyard consciousness in tartan exterior'), who took North America by storm on his first visit in 1907 and was to return there twenty times. Lauder was never in any doubt about the role played by transatlantic Scots in his triumph:

> While the native Americans certainly rolled up in their thousands [. . .] there is no doubt in my mind that the exiled Scots in the States had more to do with my success than many people imagined [. . .] The expatriated Caledonians sure rallied to my support during my earlier trips to Dollar-land. Not only so, they turned up at my shows in all manner of Scottish costumes – in kilts, with Balmoral bonnets, wearing tartan ties. And many of them brought their bagpipes with them. They imparted an enthusiastic atmosphere to my appearances everywhere; their weird shouts and 'hoochs' and skirls provided good copy for the journalists, and next-day talking points for the natives. In the first twenty weeks I spent in the States I must have met personally ten thousand people who claimed acquaintance with me [. . .] I shook hands with them all [. . .] and presented signed postcards to one at least out of every fifty![40]

It is likely that Lauder's on-stage success translated into extensive sales of his recordings and, at a time when family music-making was still a significant social activity, sheet music of his songs, both among transatlantic Scots and beyond. Yet again, the research questions relate to the construction of Scotland offered by these songs and their role in shaping ideologically the transatlantic Scots community.

The second phenomenon requiring further investigation relates to the fact that in the period before extensive intercontinental travel and telephoning, the major means of contact between transatlantic and 'homeland' Scots was the letter and the postcard. The same questions posed about the other utterances and activities of transatlantic Scots might also be asked of their letters: To what extent are they always already textual and discursive and informed by the Scottish Discursive Unconscious? Postcards pose an additional question. As well as their written messages, which might be interrogated in terms similar to the letters, what visual messages did the cards carry? Austria in 1875 is usually cited as the point of origin of the picture postcard, although the period 1900 to 1918 is spoken of as its golden age, the period when postcard production, collection and transmission were at their height.[41] A significant number of 'Scottish' postcards were produced, collected and sent during the golden age, some manufactured within Scotland, many manufactured elsewhere. One particular postcard genre is especially interesting in relation to transatlantic Scots: the 'Hands across the Sea' card. Although not restricted solely to 'Scottish' cards (there are also English and Irish variants), this genre is a significant presence in the Scottish context and there is even a sub-genre which specifically foregrounds the Scotland–North America connection. I have written elsewhere of 'Scottish' postcards frequently displaying 'semiotic overkill', that is, the insistent signification of 'Scottishness' being carried out redundantly in several dimensions.[42] The central point, however, is the hegemony of Tartanry and Kailyard in 'Scottish' postcards and the research question is, yet again: What was their circulation in the transatlantic Scots community and their contribution to the formation of identity narratives?

Finally, the re-articulation of discourses relating to Scotland in mass circulation magazines should also be considered, assuming that the magazine-buying habits of transatlantic Scots did not differ significantly from those of other hyphenate communities in North America. The leading critical work on *National Geographic* describes its rise to mass circulation status since its founding in 1888 as 'a "slim, dull and technical" journal for gentleman scholars [evolving] into a glossy magazine whose circulation is the third largest in the United States',[43] reaching a peak of nearly eleven million in the mid-1970s. *National Geographic* has offered constructions of Scotland in two ways. Virtually since its inception, it has run intermittent pieces on Scotland (sixteen substantial articles, always lavishly illustrated, between 1917 and 1996 in my own personal collection of the journal). It would be an oversimplification to suggest that Tartanry and Kailyardism are indisputably hegemonic in these pieces, but they are substantially present and construct Scotland as an exotic Other, the delivery of which to bourgeois Americans is the journal's central function. Also, apart from its articles on Scotland, *National Geographic* has, at least since the 1930s, carried adverts for Scottish tourism which invariably invoke Tartanry. Other North American mass circulation magazines (*Life, Saturday Evening Post, Colliers*) have also been a channel for the circulation of discourse relating to Scotland, occasionally in their articles (for example, 'They *Like* To Dress That Way' [*Saturday Evening Post*, 1944] and 'Robert Burns: These Scottish Scenes Inspired His Poems' [*Life*, 1949]), but more centrally in their adverts. Apart from the frequent (but not invariable) recourse to Tartanry in these magazines' adverts for Scotch whisky, they consistently offer the common melding of Tartanry and Kailyardism. An enormous number of their adverts invoke the legendary thrift of the Scots. Within Scotland itself this is a Lowland discourse, with jokes being made about the meanness of people from places on the east coast such as Aberdeen and Fife ('It taks a lang spoon tae sup wi' a Fifer'). As such, it is a Kailyardesque discourse. This Lowland linguistic element is retained in many of these North American adverts, but so hegemonic is Tartanry in the worldwide representation of things Scottish, that they invariably include a tartan-clad, Lauderesque figure, or some splash of tartan, to reinforce the message that the product is keenly priced. I have counted over thirty products in the period 1930 to 1960 deploying this strategy. Once again, the research question is: To what extent did transatlantic Scots partake of these magazines and to what effect?

An essay by Margaret Bennett on the Quebecois Scots displays both the sophistication of some ethnographic work and its key potential lacuna. On the one hand, Bennett is entirely aware of the fictive, performative dimensions of the transatlantic Scots' identity narratives:

> In the New World, descendants of immigrants keep alive images of Old World identity constructed from descriptions perpetuated in oral tradition (usually of individual characters and their specific traits); from written accounts in popular books and journals; and also from stereotypical images such as Scotland's mountain glens, heather, tartan, whisky and oatcakes.[44]

On the other hand, however, Bennett cites with approval the words of Alan Dundes (1934–2005):

> I am interested in folklore because it represents a people's image of themselves. The image may be distorted but at least the distortion comes from the people, not from some outside observer armed with a range of *a priori* premises. Folklore as a mirror of culture provides unique raw material for those eager better to understand themselves and others.[45]

The material of folklore is, in my view, far from 'raw'. It is highly processed and, in the case of the transatlantic (and, indeed, the indigenous) Scots, the key blender is the Scottish Discursive Unconscious. I am reluctant to deny the transatlantic Scots the dignity of agency and the support of cultural identity. But so compelling, in my view, is the evidence of the SDU's shaping power that this concession has to be provisional, interrogatory and denying of fixity. Having opened with a quotation from Stuart Hall, let me therefore close with another:

> Identities are [. . .] constituted within, not outside representation. They relate to the invention of tradition as much as to tradition itself [. . .] not the so-called return to roots but a coming to terms with our 'routes'.[46]

Notes

1. John Prebble, *Culloden* (London: Penguin, 1961), 315.
2. Brian Pendreigh, 'Myth and mystique in a cruel glen', *The Scotsman*, 19 February 1992, 15.
3. Neil M. Gunn, 'Caithness and Sutherland' (1935), reproduced in *Landscape and Light: Essays by Neil M. Gunn*, ed. A. McCleery (Aberdeen: Aberdeen University Press, 1987), 32.
4. Quoted in Paul Basu, 'Pilgrims to the Far Country: North American "roots-tourists" in the Scottish Highlands and Islands', in *Transatlantic Scots*, ed. Celeste Ray (Tuscaloosa: University of Alabama Press, 2005), 299.
5. Stuart Hall, 'Cultural Identity and Diaspora', in *Identity: Community, Culture, Difference*, ed. Jonathan Rutherford (London: Lawrence & Wishart, 1990), 225.
6. Colin McArthur, Whisky Galore! *and* The Maggie (London: I.B. Tauris, 2003).
7. See Colin McArthur, 'Scottish Culture: A Reply to David McCrone', *Scottish Affairs*, no. 4 (1993), 95–106, and reproduced elsewhere in the present volume; Colin McArthur, 'The Scottish Discursive Unconscious', in *Scottish Popular Theatre and Entertainment*, eds Alasdair Cameron and Adrienne Scullion (Glasgow: Glasgow University Library Studies, 1996), 81–9, and reproduced elsewhere in the present volume; McArthur, Whisky Galore! *and* The Maggie; Colin McArthur, Brigadoon, Braveheart *and the Scots: Distortions of Scotland in Hollywood Cinema* (London: I.B. Tauris, 2003).
8. Angela McRobbie, *In the Culture Society: Art, Fashion and Popular Music* (London: Routledge, 1999), 78.

9. Edward Said, *Orientalism* (London: Routledge & Kegan Paul, 1978); Frantz Fanon, *Black Skin, White Masks* (New York: Grove Press, 1968).
10. Quoted in Andrew Noble, 'MacChismo in Retrospect', *Bulletin of Scottish Politics*, no. 2 (Spring 1981), 72.
11. Malcolm Chapman, *The Gaelic Vision in Scottish Culture* (London: Croom Helm, 1978), 19.
12. Louis Althusser (1918–90) was a French Marxist philosopher. Among his most influential writings was his critique of the traditional Marxist view of the relationship between the economic base (the means and relations of production) of any social formation and its superstructure (which he described as consisting of the Repressive State Apparatuses such as the military and the police and the Ideological State Apparatuses such as the family, religion, education and the arts). The core of his critique was that the traditional Marxist view allowed too little autonomy to the elements of the superstructure. Althusser saw the central function of these elements as reconciling people to the dominant power structure. However, while canvassing the autonomy of the superstructure, Althusser also saw that autonomy as provisional and relative. That is, in any social formation there was always a structure in dominance which shaped the precise nature of the superstructure.
13. Cairns Craig, 'Myths Against History: Tartanry and Kailyard in 19th-Century Scottish Literature', in *Scotch Reels: Scotland in Cinema and Television*, ed. Colin McArthur (London: British Film Institute, 1982), 13.
14. T. D. Knowles, *Ideology, Art and Commerce: Aspects of Literary Sociology in the Late Victorian Scottish Kailyard* (Gotenborg: Acta Universitatis Gothoburgensis, 1983), 13–14.
15. Ian Spring, *Phantom Village: The Myth of the New Glasgow* (Edinburgh: Polygon, 1990).
16. Ibid.
17. Thomas W. H. Crosland, *The Unspeakable Scot* (London: Grant Richards, 1902).
18. Janet Biehl and Peter Staudenmaier, *Ecofascism: Lessons from the German Experience* (Edinburgh: AK Press, 1995).
19. Quoted in Basu, 'Pilgrims to the Far Country', 292.
20. Stuart Hall, 'New Ethnicities', in *Stuart Hall: Critical Dialogues in Cultural Studies*, eds David Morley and Kuan-Hsing Chen (London: Routledge, 1996), 441–9.
21. Celeste Ray, 'Scottish Heritage Southern Style', *Southern Cultures* 4, no. 2 (1998), 28–45; Celeste Ray, *Highland Heritage: Scottish Americans in the American South* (Chapel Hill, NC: University of North Carolina Press, 2001).
22. Homi K. Bhabha, 'The Other Question: The Stereotype and Colonial Discourse', *Screen* 24, no. 6 (1983), 18–36; Gayatri Chakravorty Spivak, 'Can the Subaltern Speak?', in *Marxism and the Interpretation of Culture*, eds

Cary Nelson and Lawrence Grossberg (London: Macmillan, 1988), 271–313; Malcolm Chapman, *The Celts: The Construction of a Myth* (Basingstoke: Macmillan, 1992).
23. Celeste Ray, 'Introduction', *Transatlantic Scots*, ed. Ray, 10.
24. Tom Nairn, *The Break-Up of Britain: Crisis and Neo-Nationalism* (London: New Left Books, 1977), 162.
25. Jonathan Dembling, 'You Play It as You Would Sing It: Cape Breton, Scottishness and the Means of Cultural Production', in *Transatlantic Scots*, ed. Ray, 180–97.
26. Michael Vance, 'Powerful Pathos: The Triumph of Scottishness in Nova Scotia', in *Transatlantic Scots*, ed. Ray, 156–79.
27. Quoted in Basu, 'Pilgrims to the Far Country', 296.
28. See, for example, Paul Gilroy, *The Black Atlantic: Modernity and Double Consciousness* (London: Verso, 1993).
29. Ray, 'Scottish Heritage Southern Style'; Ray, *Highland Heritage*.
30. James Clifford, *The Predicament of Culture: Twentieth-Century Ethnography, Literature and Art* (Cambridge, MA: Harvard University Press, 1988); Clifford Geertz, *Works and Lives: The Anthropologist as Author* (Stanford: Stanford University Press, 1988).
31. Paul Willis, 'TIES: Theoretically Informed Ethnographic Study', in *Anthropology and Cultural Studies*, eds Stephen Nugent and Cris Shore (London: Pluto Press, 1997), 187.
32. Ella Shohat and Robert Stam, *Unthinking Eurocentrism* (London: Routledge, 1994), 342.
33. Annette Kuhn, *An Everyday Magic: Cinema and Cultural Memory* (London: I.B. Tauris, 2002), 8–9.
34. Andrew Hook, *Scotland and America: A Study of Cultural Relations, 1750–1835* (Glasgow/London: Blackie, 1975), 145.
35. Edward J. Cowan, 'Tartan Day in America', in *Transatlantic Scots*, ed. Ray, 323.
36. Knowles, *Ideology, Art and Commerce*, 66.
37. Ibid., 79–80.
38. Ian Campbell, *Kailyard: A New Assessment* (Edinburgh: Ramsay Head Press, 1981), 119.
39. Janet McBain, 'Scotland in Feature Film: A Filmography', in *From Limelight to Satellite: A Scottish Film Book*, ed. Eddie Dick (London/Glasgow: British Film Institute/Scottish Film Council, 1990), 233–53.
40. Harry Lauder, *Roamin' in the Gloamin'* (Philadelphia/London: J. P. Lippincott Company, 1928), 160–1.
41. Anthony Byatt, *Picture Postcards and Their Publishers* (Malvern: Golden Age Postcards Books, 1978).
42. Colin McArthur, 'Breaking the Signs: *Scotch Myths* as Cultural Struggle', *Cencrastus*, no. 7 (Winter 1981/2), 21–5, and also reproduced elsewhere in the present volume.

43. Catherine A. Lutz and Jane L. Collins, *Reading* National Geographic (Chicago: University of Chicago Press, 1993), 16.
44. Margaret Bennett, 'From the Quebec-Hebrideans to "les Écossais-Québécois": Tracing the Evolution of a Scottish Cultural Identity in Canada's Eastern Townships', in *Transatlantic Scots*, ed. Ray, 125.
45. Quoted in Ibid., 127.
46. Stuart Hall, 'Who Needs Identity?', in *Questions of Cultural Identity*, eds Stuart Hall and Paul du Gay (London: SAGE, 1996), 4.

CHAPTER 34

Scotch Myths, Scottish Film Culture and the Suppression of Ludic Modernism*

Scottish moving image culture has produced three masterpieces of ludic modernism: John McGrath (1935–2002) and John Mackenzie (1928–2011)'s *The Cheviot, the Stag and the Black, Black Oil* (1974), Ian Pattison and Colin Gilbert's BBC Television series *Rab C. Nesbitt* (1988–2014) and Murray Grigor's *Scotch Myths* (1982), funded by Channel 4. Having celebrated the two former, I now wish to remedy the scandalous lack of critical attention accorded to the latter.[1] That lack is itself symptomatic of the effective suppression of *Scotch Myths* and of modernism (ludic or otherwise) within Scottish film culture. Indeed, to address *Scotch Myths* is to wade knee-deep into the debates which traversed Scottish film culture in the 1970s and 1980s. Yet until now a film constituting one of the key reference points in these debates has had no adequate description, far less analysis, of its subject matter and style. But first, what is meant by 'ludic modernism'? The phrase recalls, and perhaps lies silently within, the increasingly prevalent concept of ludic postmodernism. The assertion underlying the latter is that once there was this monolithic phenomenon, modernism, which was austere, all-embracing, elitist, lacking the common touch and, above all, humourless. Ludic postmodernism, the argument runs, has swept all this away. Unable to say anything useful about the real world – if indeed, as postmodernism has it, the latter even exists at all – postmodern discourse has recourse only to the complex glissandi of its own operations. The only appropriate stance is one of ludic irony. We may be going to hell in a handcart, but let's have fun on the way! (Ludic) postmodernism, unaware of the structuralist binarism of its own position, sets itself in opposition to its self-projected grim-faced predecessor, modernism, and

---

*Originally published in *Scottish Cinema Now*, eds Jonathan Murray, Fidelma Farley and Rod Stoneman (Newcastle upon Tyne: Cambridge Scholars Publishing, 2009), 39–55.

in the process travesties the latter. Justus Nieland, in his editorial introduction (appropriately entitled 'Modernism's Laughter') to a 2006 issue of *Modernist Cultures*, writes:

> This special issue [. . .] is animated by two claims. First, that modernism is funny, and the moderns [are] inveterate laughers, gigglers, joke-pullers and devastating wags. Second, that modernism's ubiquitous laughter is overlooked, under-theorised, and downright gagged by the aura of high seriousness that still infuses critical descriptions of modernism.[2]

This could serve as a rubric for *Scotch Myths* (and for Murray Grigor's work more generally). This essay seeks to locate the film within the ludic modernist tradition of the Surrealists, James Joyce (1882–1941) and Samuel Beckett (1906–89), arguing that it is simultaneously playful and politically serious and that its effective suppression within Scottish film culture is massively retrogressive.

The Exhibition

Several strands went into the making of what was to become the film *Scotch Myths*, the central one being Grigor's exhibition of the same name (co-conceived and -curated with his wife, Barbara [1944–94]) which ran in a small St Andrews gallery in 1981 before transferring to the Edinburgh Festival. On each occasion the press and public response was substantial and generally sympathetic. Both the exhibition's wit and its serious political purpose were recognised: ludic modernism is, it would seem, acceptable in the gallery if not on film and television.[3] The exhibition, which included postcards, labels from whisky bottles and orange crates, tea towels, popular songs and the detritus of Scottish souvenir shops, was mounted with considerable imaginative flair and a very light touch: one of the key installations was a version of Fingal's Cave with a pianola pounding out Felix Mendelssohn (1809–47)'s famous *The Hebrides* overture (1830) and spouting water at the piece's climax. Grigor had clearly been influenced by the writings of Tom Nairn (1932–2023), particularly his essay 'Old and New Scottish Nationalism'.[4] This, in its scathing account of certain aspects of Scottish popular culture, had characterised the latter as pathological precisely because, unlike the popular cultures of other European countries, it had never been mobilised within the drive to create a nation. This, Nairn argued, was because the British polity (including Scotland) had been settled with the Act of Union in 1707, almost a century before the rise of popular nationalism in Europe and its colonial outposts. It was the exhibition's deconstruction of Scottish popular culture, its anatomising of the main figures (James Macpherson [1736–96], Sir Walter Scott [1771–1832], Harry Lauder [1870–1950], and so on) who had projected internationally a pathological view of Scotland, and its implication that Scotland needed a radically different culture more attuned to the modern world which constituted its political import.

The Film

In order for *Scotch Myths* to become a television film the static nature of the exhibition had to some extent to become animated. Grigor achieved this by conjoining the former with a theatrical piece he had written, *Breeksadoon* (*c*.1979). That title's play on *Brigadoon* (Vincente Minnelli, 1954), the cinematic representation of Scotland most loathed by Scots intellectuals of the late 1970s and early 1980s, is characteristic of Grigor's ludic modernism. The pun (a montage within a word) is one of modernism's most favoured verbal strategies, deployed most deliriously by James Joyce in *Ulysses* (1922) and *Finnegan's Wake* (1939). *Scotch Myths* being commissioned by Channel 4 and transmitted on Hogmanay 1982 was itself a political act, a throwing down of the gauntlet to those characteristic annual New Year's Eve broadcasts from Scotland that were constructed within the very discourses *Scotch Myths* took apart. That the film found a home on the newly created Channel 4 was partly due to that channel's first Chief Executive, Jeremy Isaacs, being a Glaswegian well able to understand (and, one suspects, highly sympathetic to) the argument *Scotch Myths* was making. Additionally, the film's aesthetic innovation was precisely in line with Channel 4's original remit to cater for minorities, a remit increasingly abandoned by the Chief Executives who succeeded Isaacs.

Scotch Myths is modernist above all in its refusal of classical Hollywood narrative structure. It does, however, gesture towards such narrative structure via the plot devices of a lost tourist bus and its discovery by a Scots aristocrat. Both these gestures earn their place in the film by referring to what is perhaps the most resonant date in Scottish history, 1745–46, the date of the last Jacobite uprising which sought to wrest the British Crown back to the Stuart dynasty. A source of lachrymose nostalgia for many indigenous Scots, 'the '45' is perhaps the key shaping mechanism in the identity narratives of transatlantic and other diasporic Scots.[5] In Grigor's film, a tourist bus, festooned with Scottish Tourist Board brochures referencing Scottish history, is lost on a heath which turns out to be Culloden Moor, the site of the famous 1746 battle which saw the defeat of Charles Edward Stuart (1720–88), who, as Bonnie Prince Charlie, is one of the key dramatis personae in Romantic discourse about Scotland. The tourists are 'rescued' by Sir Johnny Stalker (Walter Carr) who, greasing the palm of the tour guide (Freddie Boardley) with banknotes bearing the faces of Sir Walter Scott and Robert Burns (1759–96) (Grigor is acutely sensitive to the circulation of Scots icons in the quotidian Scottish world), induces him to reroute the tourists to Castle Dundreich so that they might partake of 'the Dundreich Experience'. This narrative strategy ties together what are perhaps the two key sites of regressive discourse about Scotland: whisky and tourism. Sir Johnny's name and apparel (short, red hunting coat) evoke a prominent brand of Scotch whisky while his surname carries the whiff of the grouse moor and the reactionary role of the Scots aristocracy in fashioning images of Scotland. Given that *Scotch Myths* is primarily about international perceptions of Scotland and the Scots, Grigor's invocation of whisky (which forms a continuing motif in the film) is an inspired narrative device. Not only is whisky the phenomenon which foreigners immediately allude to when thinking about Scotland or meeting a Scot, it also has profound implications for many Scots' self-identity, touching on questions of health, aggressive sociability and rites of passage to manhood.[6] The other dimension, tourism, reflects the recurrent propensity of the Scottish Tourist Board (and its present-day successor, VisitScotland) to render national history as diverse 'experiences'. Within this framework, for example, the area round Stirling will now forever be '*Braveheart* country'.

Another gesture within *Scotch Myths* towards classical Hollywood narrative is the very brief scene of the arrival at Castle Dundreich of the actors who will embody the historical figures in the Dundreich Experience. The minibus they arrive in bears the words '17:45 Theatre Company'. At one level a simple joke about 7:84, the (then) most politically radical Scottish theatre group and one with which several of the actors in *Scotch Myths* were associated, at another level it joins with the film's earlier evocation of the 1745 uprising. This fact reconfirms that *Scotch Myths* will not just be about Scottish culture, but also its most internationally resonant moments and historical figures. The film's third gesture towards classical Hollywood narrative is less clearly motivated but it too earns its place in the film by creating different resonances. This gesture has the famous Hollywood director Sam Fuller (1912–97) appear in the film 'as himself', upbraiding his assistant for being unable to find Castle Dundreich on the map. This is firstly an act of homage to a great director, an assertion of cinephilia. However, Fuller was not just any film director: he was a talismanic figure beloved of the *Cahiers du cinéma* generation of critics who themselves went on to become directors (Fuller also appeared 'as himself' in Jean-Luc Godard's *Pierrot le Fou* [1965]).

He was the touchstone of a certain kind of anti-literary, pro-image kind of cinema: to love Fuller was to love cinema.

Additionally, Fuller's presence in *Scotch Myths* asserts the continuity between filmmaking and film criticism. Murray Grigor had been director of the Edinburgh International Film Festival from 1967 to 1972. His first major retrospective in that role had been one of Fuller's works and, crucially, it inaugurated the policy whereby EIFF retrospectives would be accompanied by books of critical essays on the figure or the topic of the retrospective, a policy continued until the early 1980s.[7] From its inception in 1947, the EIFF had a *politique* of cinema, an assertion that certain kinds of cinema were preferable to others and a corresponding wish to argue and debate that assertion publicly. Initially very much under the influence of John Grierson (1898–1972) and Forsyth Hardy (1910–94), the Festival had stressed documentary and realist cinema. Grigor inflected this towards auteurist and, to some extent, modernist cinema.[8] Culturally important as Fuller's presence in *Scotch Myths* is, then, the most important meaning of the scene in which he berates his aide for being unable to locate Castle Dundreich lies in its dramatic situation and *mise-en-scène*. Scots and cinephiles would immediately recognise two men lost in the

Figure 34.1 Scotland meets Hollywood once again: Murray Grigor directs Sam Fuller in *Scotch Myths*.

Scottish Highlands and discussing a place which does not appear on the map as referencing the opening of *Brigadoon*, the 1947 Broadway musical and subsequent Hollywood film most often cited as the nadir of debased Romanticism as it relates to Scotland.[9] The fact that mist swirls round the characters reinforces the *Brigadoon* connection, asserting that Grigor's film will not only be about Scotland and its history, but also about their construction in discourse. Underlining Grigor's lack of interest in classical narrative, Fuller and his hapless assistant quickly disappear from the film, only to reappear in its final moments within Grigor's pointedly perfunctory gesture towards classical narrative resolution. The meaning of *Scotch Myths* lies altogether elsewhere.

One of the most stable features of classical narrative cinema is coherence between actor and role, the individual actor embodying a single character throughout the running time of the film. Different theatrical and cinematic traditions have, however, posed other relationships between actors and roles, some ancient and non-western (such as Noh, Kabuki and Bunraku), others western and modern(ist) (such as the practices of Bertolt Brecht [1898–1956], Antonin Artaud [1896–1948] and Jerzy Grotowski [1933–99]). The use of actors and their playing style in *Scotch Myths* probably draws most from Brechtian practice in that there is no attempt to provoke identification with or sympathy for any of the protagonists, who are instead present within the film to further a particular historico-cultural argument. In this, as in much else, *Scotch Myths* is close to aspects of *The Cheviot, the Stag and the Black, Black Oil*. Screening them together would illustrate starkly what has been lost to Scottish moving image culture. While the actors playing the tour guide, the bus driver and Fuller's assistant, plus Fuller himself, could be said to be performing broadly within the conventions of Euro-American naturalism, those embodying the historical personages of the Dundreich Experience use a heightened, declamatory mode of address quite alien to that tradition. Additionally and crucially, as individuals that second set of actors are not coterminous with single historical figures with the film. As its credits show, several actors migrate from playing one historical or mythical figure to another: Alex Norton (James Boswell [1740–95], Robert Burns, Napoleon Bonaparte [1769–1821], Felix Mendelssohn, Prince Albert [1819–1861], John Brown); John Bett (James Macpherson, Ossian, Sir Walter Scott, Lord Byron [1788–1824], William McGonagall [1825–1902]); Juliet Cadzow (Malvina Farquharson-Smith, Miss Moffat 1770, Bonnie Jean); Sorel Johnson (Queen Victoria [1819–1901], Mary Rose); and Bill Paterson (Samuel Johnson [1709–84], Harry Lauder). In one scene Sir Walter Scott and Lord Byron (both in the body of actor John Bett) argue the merits of the former's construction of Scotland. Another clearly Brechtian device (also much used in *The Cheviot*) is the punctuation of the action by songs, most of them composed and performed by Ron Geesin, who as the Bonnie Hieland Laddie (here represented as a gap-toothed, grotesquely ugly, but convivial character), provides a musical commentary throughout the film. Geesin, like the other actors, shape-shifts to appear as a bizarre cross between Bonnie Prince Charlie and Liberace (1919–87). Playing a white piano, he disappears beneath the foaming billows of Fingal's Cave, a kind of Surrealist transposition of the foaming grotto of the original *Scotch Myths* exhibition of 1981.

In the cinematic *Scotch Myths* Murray Grigor is a postmodernist before postmodernism had achieved its current high profile, particularly in his obliteration of the distinction between high and low art. So central has this particular strategy come to be seen in the definition of postmodernism[10] that it is often forgotten how recurrent it also was in modernism itself. *Scotch Myth*'s endless jokes are often demotic, as in the bus driver's take on Culloden Moor ('MAMBA country: miles and miles of bugger all') and if historical figures such as Macpherson, Johnson and Scott are often regarded today as fixtures of high art, they exist cheek by jowl in this film with buffoons of popular Scottish culture such as Lauder and McGonagall. At one moment Scott declaims *The Lady of the Lake* (1810); at another he cuts his arse on the wine glass which, inveterate royal sycophant that he was, he had pocketed at the ceremony welcoming George IV to Edinburgh in 1822. It is *Scotch Myths*'s melding of high and low art which particularly links it to *Rab C. Nesbitt*, as does its unremittingly comic tone. The tone apart, the visual look of and use of actors in *Scotch Myths* links it to that other great modernist film, Hans-Jürgen Syberberg's *Ludwig: Requiem for a Virgin King* (1972). But, whereas *Scotch Myths* provides (almost literally) a laugh a minute, Syberberg's film – like his *Karl May* (1974), *Hitler: A Film from Germany* (1977) and *Parsifal* (1982) – is sombrely didactic. However, their shared engagement with history, their interrogation of Romanticism and their indifference to classical narrative set these films in opposition to mainstream cinema.

Finally, *Scotch Myths* is also modernist in being a multi-discourse film, ranging outside the unities of time, space and action. The bus trip and the Fuller episodes exist in present-day 'real' time and, at a pinch, the historical charades could be said to be so motivated (as part of the performance of the Dundreich Experience being witnessed by the tourists). Yet from time to time the charades erupt into historical reconstruction (another connection with *The Cheviot*), as when James Macpherson is seen riding through the Highlands and collecting his 'fragments of ancient poetry'. In addition, the charades sometimes segue into animation sequences, one of which is perhaps the most notable moment in the entire film. Sir Walter Scott and his faithful manservant (played by the Buster Keaton-faced Scots comedian Chic Murray [1919–85], who also plays the whisky blender, Sir Rhosis Hue McRose of Glen Liver) are discussing the arrangements for George IV's visit to Edinburgh, which Scott choreographed. Describing the tartans which will be worn at the event, Scott deploys what has come to be called 'the invention of tradition'.[11] Informed that the tartan chosen for the kilt George IV will wear is known in the pattern books simply as Number 137, Scott, with increasingly rhetorical gestures, renames it successively as 'Stuart', 'Royal Stuart', 'Ancient Royal Stuart', 'Ancient Royal Hunting Stuart' and 'Ancient Royal Hunting Dress Stuart'. As he then declaims, 'Bring furrit the tartan and we'll tartan the kingdom', the screen explodes into festoons of tartan of every hue and the Scottish landscape itself becomes tartanised.

The Suppression

Given the quite extensive press coverage of the *Scotch Myths* exhibition, the meagre coverage of the *Scotch Myths* film is puzzling. Even making allowance for the Hogmanay transmission (no newspapers published on New Year's Day) the coverage is scant, just one press piece, by the *Glasgow Herald*'s Julie Davidson, in the British Film Institute cuttings file.[12] Davidson appreciates both the film's political import and aesthetic innovation – 'possibly the most creative and discreetly bitter piece of self-analysis to come out of Scotland in years' – and recognises its likely difficulty for a general television audience. This point may help explain the lack of press cuttings, but is not an absolute guarantee that no such coverage exists. Rather, it simply demonstrates that *Scotch Myths*'s transmission was not covered by the BFI's designated list of titles (broadly speaking, the major English, Scottish and some American daily papers and journals). The only other material in the BFI cuttings file (apart from a Channel 4 press announcement) are three letters to *The Scotsman* newspaper, one by P. H. Scott (a prominent Scottish nationalist and sometime spokesperson on culture for the Scottish National Party) attacking the film and two others (one by the present writer) defending it. Scott is the author of a book on his famous namesake, Sir Walter, in which he unambiguously celebrates the extent to which Scott's writings had brought Scotland to the attention of the world while being blind to the pernicious romanticism relating to Scotland that they also engendered, as a review of the book by David Daiches (1912–2005) pointed out.[13] P. H. Scott's hostility to *Scotch Myths* may be partly explicable by

Daiches's citing of Grigor's original exhibition as making good the lack in Scott's book.

Given workaday factors such as the absence of newspapers around New Year, to call the press response to *Scotch Myths* 'suppression' would be to overstate the case. However, the term begins to have some validity in relation to the response of the institutions of moving image culture that one would have most expected to engage with the film. This had already been true in the setting-up of the project, with the main sponsor of film production in Scotland at the time, Films of Scotland (1954–82), and Scottish Television and Grampian Television all turning it down. BBC Scotland had funded an early version of the script in the mid-1970s but did not follow through into production, it being left to Channel 4 (for the reasons outlined above) to bring it to the screen. *Scotch Myths* was also screened at the Festival of Film and Television in the Celtic Countries in 1984, but it is instructive to compare its programming there with that of another of Channel 4's Scottish feature film projects, *Ill Fares the Land* (Bill Bryden, 1983), a historical account of the state-enforced evacuation of the island of St Kilda in the 1930s.[14] Bryden (1942–2022)'s film, an orthodox, quasi-Hollywood exercise much influenced by the films of John Ford (1894–1973), was given three primetime weekend screenings at the Festival, while *Scotch Myths* was given only one midweek lunchtime screening. Clearly, this represented the Festival organisers' judgement of the kinds of audiences likely to be attracted to both films and perhaps indicates their own mainstream tastes, the Celtic Film Festival always having followed closely the contours of the dominant aesthetics of the film and television industries in the Celtic countries.

It is the behaviour of the Scottish Film Council (1934–97), however, which most fully validates use of the term 'suppression' in relation to *Scotch Myths*. The SFC flatly refused to acquire the film for its Central Film Library or, amazingly, for the Scottish Film Archive, on the grounds that it was not important enough.[15] No documentary evidence exists to confirm this assertion, but the chilly response to the film by the SFC as a whole was evident to me in the conversations I had with SFC personnel at the time. *Scotch Myths* would at this point have sunk without trace had I not been in a position (as Head of the Distribution Division of the BFI at the time) to ensure that it was acquired for the BFI Distribution Library and later to have it included in a Critic's Choice season at the National Film Theatre. I also used it as an aesthetic/political countermodel for a putative Scottish cinema in a review of the film *Local Hero* (Bill Forsyth, 1983) for a 1983 edition of the Channel 4 film programme, *Visions* (1982–85). *Scotch Myths* would be publicly screened intermittently thereafter, on Channel 4 as a 1985 St Andrew's Night offering and at some of the publicly subsidised regional film theatres in the major Scottish cities. Some material relating to it (hopefully enough to strike a new print or DVD from) eventually found its way into the Scottish Film Archive, but it arrived there by bequest of Murray Grigor himself and not as a result of any policy decision by the Scottish Film Council. As the present essay makes clear, there was never at any time a concerted attempt to discuss and analyse *Scotch Myths* and assess its place in Scottish moving image culture. The Scottish Film Council's suppression of *Scotch Myths* in the spheres of distribution, exhibition, archiving and education was fully matched by its grudging and meagre support for Grigor's subsequent projects through its production mechanisms, the Scottish Film Production Fund (1982–97) and the wider body which later enveloped it, Scottish Screen (1997–2010). The extent of these bodies' chasing of the chimeras of, first, a European-style art cinema and, subsequently, a full-blown 'Hollywood on the Clyde' orthodox narrative cinema, and the consequent suppression of the kind of (ludic) modernism represented by a work like *Scotch Myths*, can be followed in outline by reference to the writings of the key personnel (John Brown [1944–2006], Ian Lockerbie [1930–2021], Allan Shiach, Eddie Dick and Steve McIntyre) controlling public production financing in Scotland between the early 1980s and mid-1990s.[16]

However, Scottish film culture's putative suppression of (ludic) modernism in fact predates the SFC's early-1980s entry into film production. It might be said that every film culture operating in a market economy suppresses or marginalises modernism: not usually in a direct, upfront way, but by implication in the (often unspoken) policies they adopt. Film critics dealing with issues of gender and sexuality have talked about the 'heterosexual presumption' underlying most mainline cinema.[17] There is, too, an analogous classical narrative presumption, the (usually) unspoken belief that the 'true' nature of cinema manifests itself in the two-hour narrative feature film, with protagonist(s) and antagonist(s), coherent characters and an arc of action leading to narrative closure.[18] Aside from those opting for documentary and animation (forms which may themselves display many of the features of classical narrative fiction), cineastes in every market-driven culture gravitate towards the narrative norm. Scottish cineastes are no exception to this general rule. At collective gatherings, such as the annual Film Bang events in the 1970s, the cry was invariably raised that Scotland must have its own feature films. This was particularly poignant, since virtually the only film-producing mechanism in the country at that time, Films of Scotland, had grown out of the Griersonian documentary movement, and was predicated (for political, aesthetic and economic reasons) upon the making of sponsored documentaries. The more imaginative cineastes working under its auspices, such as Murray Grigor, Laurence Henson, Eddie McConnell (1936–2018), Douglas Eadie and Brian Crumlish (1944–94), stretched the documentary form to breaking point. When something approaching a feature film, *The Duna Bull* (Laurence Henson, 1972), was prised out of Films of Scotland, it was entirely orthodox in narrative terms. Moreover, it also echoed the ideological stance of Ealing Studios about Scotland in films such as *Whisky Galore!* (Alexander Mackendrick, 1949) and *The Maggie* (Alexander Mackendrick, 1954) and Ealing-type films such as *Laxdale Hall* (John Eldridge, 1953) in having a range of couthy Highland characters outwit imperious southerners. In *The Duna Bull*'s case, the southern incomers are civil servants of the Scottish Office in Edinburgh. The history of the development of publicly funded film production in Scotland is ably described by Duncan Petrie.[19] That history can be read not only as an accelerating suppression of (ludic) modernism but also of any kind of art cinema, although this reading is one Petrie chooses not explicitly to foreground. All the key officers in the diverse public funding bodies and mechanisms of the 1980s and first half of the 1990s (John Brown, Ian Lockerbie, Allan Shiach, Eddie Dick and Steve McIntyre) made concordats with the market and with classical narrative cinema, albeit some more reluctantly than others. Steve McIntyre seems to have been the most conflicted of these officers, because he was also the most sensitive among them to the contradictions and absences within the industrial model Scotland had opted for.[20]

Scottish film culture's long march to the industrial model was largely a question of individual choice and taste (during his time in charge of film production and thereafter, John Brown was writing classical narrative screenplays for series such as *Taggart* (STV, 1983–2010) and *Inspector Morse* (ITV, 1987–2000) and was submitting scripts to film production set-ups in Hollywood and elsewhere). But it was also heavily over-determined by external forces. Two such forces – one economic, the other aesthetic, but both ultimately very much interpenetrated – were particularly important. The first was the neoliberal economic policy first espoused by the Thatcherite Tory government from 1979, within which the market was king and every public body had to pay its way or, at the very least, 'give value for money'. Up until 1979 the Scottish Film Council had balanced commerce and aesthetics uneasily, but one always felt that their endorsement of the classical narrative feature film, whether in its European art-house or Hollywood form, was primarily for aesthetic rather than financial reasons. During the mid-1990s, however, the financial discourse came yet further to the fore with the report commissioned by the then Tory Secretary of State for Scotland, Michael Forsyth, following the Republic of Ireland's poaching of the shooting of *Braveheart* (Mel Gibson, 1995) from Scotland by use of such devices as tax incentives and the provision of the Irish Army as extras. The report led to the setting-up of Scottish Screen in 1997 and unambiguously installed the industrial model for Scottish film production, relegating culture to a decidedly secondary role.[21] Subsequent changes in the Scottish polity arising from devolution in 1997 have resulted in the industrial model being tinkered with to add social criteria.

Virtually contemporaneous with the rise of British governmental neoliberalism was the emergence of what might be called story-structure discourse. Its generative mechanisms were the DIY screenwriting manuals of Syd Field (1935–2013) and the three-day story structure seminars of Robert McKee, which themselves ultimately emerged in book form.[22] To simplify somewhat, Field and McKee argued that every 90-to-120-minute narrative feature film script conformed to the same basic structure involving: set-up, development and resolution; characters who were goal-driven (in simpler scripts, having an external drive such as finding a lost object or person and, in more complex scripts, having both an external and an internal drive such as purging a past mistake); and antagonists seeking to thwart the protagonists' aims. Field and McKee were quickly cloned, the provision of DIY screenwriting manuals mushroomed and soon aspiring scriptwriters, directors, producers, agents and actors were all spouting the story-structure-speak of plots, sub-plots, action arcs, turning points, false endings and so on. As I wrote the original version of this essay in 2009, I could see no less than twenty-four such manuals on my bookshelf (a mere fraction of those available), the title of one boiling down what story-structure discourse delivers: 'conflict, action and suspense'.[23]

I was comforted, however, that alongside the tiresomely repetitive DIY screenwriting manuals on my shelf there also lay the most trenchant critique of story-structure discourse published to that point in time, Jean-Pierre Geuens's *Film Production Theory*.[24] Geuens demolishes the ideas underpinning classical narrative cinema: that the self is coherent, seamless and autonomous as opposed to fractured, fluctuating and prey to the unconscious; that it acts on the world rather than the world acting on it; that human actions have entirely predictable consequences; and that the individual life is a plot rather than a chronicle. The emergence in the early 1990s of the Scottish production mechanism Movie Makars ('makar' is an old Scots word for 'writer'), designed explicitly to introduce story-structure discourse to Scotland, can be mapped onto both of the over-determining economic and aesthetic forces referred to above, or, perhaps better, can be read as a local distilling of the latter. Movie Makars marked the emergence into the Scottish film production limelight of Allan Shiach, who became the first Chair of Scottish Screen in 1997. Shiach incarnated perfectly both the economic and aesthetic master currents of the time. As Allan Shiach, he was co-Chair of the Macallan whisky firm and, as Allan Scott, he was a practicing Hollywood screenwriter – a Jekyll and Hyde for the late twentieth century except that, in this case, the two personalities were not in contradiction but were pulling in exactly the same direction: the further industrialising and narrativising of Scottish cinema. Lest there be any doubt where Scottish cinema was headed, one guest of honour at Movie Makars was the eminent Hollywood screenwriter William Goldman (1931–2018).

It would be tedious to relate the Gradgrindian detail – economic, social and cultural (in the anthropological sense) – with which Scottish Screen implemented its industrial model during the thirteen years of its existence between 1997 and 2010. Collectively, the Scottish Screen website's policy guidelines and application forms for its innumerable schemes at every level of production and training constituted a manual for how to crush the life out of a creative project. Fortunately some, albeit a minority, of cineastes were able to reanimate the corpse at the moment of production. It goes without saying that a ludic modernist work such as *Scotch Myths* would have had little chance of being funded under Scottish Screen's policies, a fact confirmed by the virtual absence of Murray Grigor's name from its funding rosters. Like that other great British modernist, Peter Greenaway, Grigor raised the money for his projects, which during the 1990s were mainly about modernist architects, from continental Europe and to some extent North America.

What is to be Done?

So entrenched did the industrial, classical narrative model in Scottish film production become by the late 2000s that it was by that point a waste of time and energy to continue railing against it and proposing alternatives, even though one had a cultural and moral duty to remind younger cinephiles of what they have lost and to honour the best examples of suppressed traditions such as *Scotch Myths*. There was, however, one battle that was (and is) still worth fighting. Scottish Screen still had – however marginalised and attenuated – a cultural remit, still housing within itself most of the mechanisms of a complete film culture, including film education and a national film archive. Around my original time of writing, the latter relocated to become part of the National Library of Scotland. Unlike its sister organisation, the British Film Institute, Scottish Screen never aspired to produce a substantial critical journal on the model of *Sight and Sound*. Instead, Scottish Screen functioned primarily as an enabling facility for the production of 'Scottish' films, the term being in inverted commas since the definition of nationality internal to Scottish Screen was economic rather than historico-aesthetic. As an enabling house, it did not venture far into the marketing of the films it funded, perhaps with the exception of the entry of films to international festivals. More generally, Scottish Screen apparently saw marketing as the job of the individual production companies it funded. Although its ethos was that of a traditional production company, in its adoption of the industrial model, both economically and aesthetically, it did not follow through into marketing in the way that a traditional production company would.

Aside from billboards, radio and television advertising and trailers, the central marketing mechanism in the film business has been the campaign book on each individual film which would be sent to every local cinema manager. Perfectly understandably, these books made little claim to cultural enlightenment but were primarily mechanisms to maximise ticket sales. To take a concrete example, the campaign book for *The Big Heat* (Fritz Lang, 1953) issued by Columbia Pictures's British subsidiary in 1954 runs to four pages. The first page gives key information such as credits, synopsis, certification details and running time, the second page a more detailed account of the film and short anecdotes primarily about the stars. The anecdotes continue on the third page, which begins to make clear who exactly the campaign book is aimed at: individual cinema managers. A reference to the novel on which the film is based urges managers to ensure that local bookshops stock and display the novel prior to playdate. About half of page three is taken up with a section headed 'Exploitation', which offers suggestions for drumming up business, and page four details the diversity of posters, stills and trailers to be had from Columbia's branch offices in major British cities.

Needless to say, such campaign books show no evidence of any attempts to induce audiences to reflect on the film in question, far less on wider issues of film culture. But Scottish Screen was ostensibly not simply a money-making machine. Were Scottish Screen to have upped its profile in the marketing of the films it funded, Scottish film culture could reasonably have demanded that the former's promotional discourse be culturalist as well as commercial. Where, then, might Scottish film culture and its key public institutions, such as Scottish Screen's present-day successor, Screen Scotland, look for a cultural model of film promotion?

Good historical examples to ponder include the magazines and brochures produced by the film exporting arms of the former socialist republics of Central and Eastern Europe, in which commercial promotion took second place to raising the profile of communism in general and the individual producing states in particular. For instance, Sovexportfilm (1945–91) produced a bulky brochure on *Lenin in Poland* (Sergei Yutkevich, 1966), the USSR's entry to that year's Cannes Film Festival. It runs to twelve large-format pages, mostly comprising stills, but also includes a substantial critical essay on the film. More impressive – in intellectual if not presentational terms – is the bi-monthly *Hungarofilm Bulletin*, produced very cheaply in A4 format, almost like a *samizdat* production. Characteristically, it ran to forty pages in English and tended to be devoted primarily to one film. One issue, for example, was given over to *The Round-Up* (Miklós Jancsó, 1966), the celebrated film about the Kafkaesque methods of the Habsburg secret police in identifying the ringleaders of an abortive uprising by Hungarian patriots in the mid-nineteenth century. The publication contains a Jancsó filmography; three pages of stills; a twelve-page analysis of the film by a noted Hungarian film critic; a nine-page interview with Jancsó; and bio-filmographies of the film's Director of Photography and its leading actor. Both the critical essay and interview with Jancsó are substantially concerned with the philosophical, moral and formal aspects of cinema. The bulletin is exemplary in the seriousness with which it approaches cinema, even if its production is austere by western standards.

In many respects, however, the most attractive publication to come out of communist East Europe was *Film Polski*, the regular magazine (in French and English) of the Polish film industry. It managed to adopt several features of contemporaneous western film magazines while retaining a serious discourse about cinema. A characteristic issue of 1965 has photographs of Polish actors on the back and front covers; three pages of photographs of and statements from participants at the Krakow Film Festival; a double-page spread on a new Polish feature film; a double-page spread on the films of Andrzej Wajda (1926–2016); and three double-page spreads on his then-latest film, *Ashes* (1965). There are briefer sections on films in production, industry news and new Polish films being set up. *Film Polski* remained serious about cinema: its lavish illustration and generally short articles achieved a good balance between criticism and promotion without becoming a vehicle for fragmented bits of industry information and gossip. Finally in this specific regard, what is perhaps the most aspirational model of all for Scotland comes not from the communist East but from the non-communist West, the quarterly *German Films*. Established in 1954 and with (at time of original writing in 2009) an annual production budget of €5.7 million, it runs to over eighty full-colour pages. Issue 2 of 2005 contained a ten-page article on documentary film in Germany; four double-page features on German film personnel (directors, producers, an actor); five pages of industry news; ten pages on films in production; thirty pages, each one devoted to a new German film; and four pages which are part of an ongoing discussion of key German films of the past. *German Films* represents an exemplary mobilisation of stakeholders, supporters and institutions around the common purpose of promoting German cinema in a non-hucksterish, intellectually serious manner.

Much of the hype emanating from Scottish Screen was about the efflorescence and international success of Scottish cinema between the late 1990s and late 2000s. Some of this was justified, but most of it was empty tub-thumping. An equally significant development contemporaneous with the various historical events and processes discussed by this essay was the growth of Film Studies at all levels of the Scottish educational system. It is unclear the extent to which the personnel making up this development see themselves as a collective. If and when they ever do, they will have every right to demand not only that national public institutions like Scottish Screen continue allocating a significant amount of their resources to Film Studies, but that its publications adhere to the highest intellectual standards. Part of the demand might be for a publication along the lines of the better models discussed above. As well as promoting Scottish cinema in the here and now it might, like *German Films*, retain the memory of Scottish cinema past. Who knows, it might even recall lost masterpieces like *Scotch Myths*.

Notes

1. Colin McArthur, *Television and History* (London: British Film Institute, 1978); Colin McArthur, 'The Exquisite Corpse of Rab(elais) C(opernicus) Nesbitt', in *Dissident Voices: The Politics of Television and Cultural Change*, ed. Mike Wayne (London: Pluto Press, 1998), 107–26, and reproduced elsewhere in the present volume.
2. Justus Nieland, 'Editorial Introduction: Modernism's Laughter', *Modernist Cultures* 2, no. 2 (2006), 80.
3. Colin McArthur, 'Breaking the Signs: *Scotch Myths* as Cultural Struggle', *Cencrastus*, no. 7 (Winter 1981/2), 21–5, and reproduced elsewhere in the present volume.
4. Tom Nairn, *The Break-Up of Britain: Crisis and Neo-Nationalism* (London: New Left Books, 1977), 126–95.
5. For the indigenous response, see Colin McArthur, 'Culloden: A Pre-emptive Strike', *Scottish Affairs*, no. 9 (1994), 97–126, and also republished elsewhere

in the present volume; for the transatlantic counterpart, see Celeste Ray, *Highland Heritage: Scottish Americans in the American South* (Chapel Hill, NC: University of North Carolina Press, 2001).

6. See Colin McArthur, 'A Dram for All Seasons: The Diverse Identities of Scotch', in *Scots on Scotch*, ed. Phillip Hills (Edinburgh: Mainstream, 1991), 87–102, and reproduced elsewhere in the present volume; Colin McArthur, *Whisky Galore! and The Maggie* (London: I.B. Tauris, 2003).
7. David Will and Peter Wollen, eds, *Samuel Fuller* (Edinburgh: Edinburgh International Film Festival in association with Scottish International Review, 1969).
8. Colin McArthur, 'The Rises and Falls of the Edinburgh International Film Festival', in *From Limelight to Satellite: A Scottish Film Book*, ed. Eddie Dick (London/Glasgow: British Film Institute and Scottish Film Council, 1990), 91–102, and reproduced elsewhere in the present volume.
9. Colin McArthur, *Brigadoon, Braveheart and the Scots: Distortions of Scotland in Hollywood Cinema* (London: I.B. Tauris, 2003).
10. See, for example, Terry Eagleton, *After Theory* (London: Penguin, 2004), 46; Andreas Huyssen, *After the Great Divide: Modernism, Mass Culture, Postmodernism* (Bloomington: Indiana University Press, 1986), x.
11. Eric Hobsbawm and Terence Ranger, eds, *The Invention of Tradition* (Cambridge: Cambridge University Press, 1983).
12. Julie Davidson, '*Scotch Myths*', *Glasgow Herald*, 28 December 1982, no page ref.
13. P. H. Scott, *Sir Walter Scott and Scotland* (Edinburgh: William Blackwood, 1981); David Daiches, 'Scott's Double Vision', *The Scotsman*, 19 September 1981, no page ref.
14. Colin McArthur, 'Tendencies in the New Scottish Cinema', *Cencrastus*, no. 13 (1983), 33–5.
15. At time of writing in 2022, a celluloid print of *Scotch Myths* is now held within the National Library of Scotland's Moving Image Archive: for further details, see https://movingimage.nls.uk/film/6382 [accessed 21 July 2022].
16. For full bibliographical details of those writings, see Jonathan Murray, *That Thinking Feeling: A Research Guide to Scottish Cinema 1938–2004* (Edinburgh/Glasgow: Edinburgh College of Art and Scottish Screen, 2004).
17. See, for example, Claire Pajaczkowska, 'The Heterosexual Presumption: A Contribution to the Debate on Pornography', *Screen* 22, no. 1 (1981), 79–94; Richard Dyer, *Now You See It: Studies in Lesbian and Gay Film* (London: Routledge, 1990).
18. John Ellis, *Visible Fictions: Cinema: Television: Video* (London: Routledge, 1982); David Bordwell, Janet Staiger and Kristin Thompson, *The Classical Hollywood Cinema: Film Style and Mode of Production to 1960* (London: Routledge, 1985).
19. Duncan Petrie, *Screening Scotland* (London: British Film Institute, 2000).
20. Steve McIntyre, 'Vanishing Point: Feature Film Production in a Small Country' in *Border Crossing: Film in Ireland, Britain and Europe*, eds John

Hill, Martin McLoone and Paul Hainsworth (London/Belfast: British Film Institute and Institute of Irish Studies, 1994), 88–111; Steve McIntyre, 'Art and Industry: Regional Film and Video Policy in the UK During the 1980s', in *Film Policy: International, National and Regional Perspectives*, ed. Albert Moran (London: Routledge, 1996), 215–33.
21. Hydra Associates, *Scotland on Screen: The Development of the Film and Television Industry in Scotland* (Glasgow: Scott Stern Associates, 1996).
22. Syd Field, *Screenplay: The Foundations of Screenwriting* (New York: Dell, 1979); Syd Field, *The Screenwriter's Workbook* (New York: Dell, 1984); Robert McKee, *Story: Substance, Structure, Style and the Principles of Screenwriting* (London: Methuen, 1998).
23. William Noble, *Conflict, Action & Suspense* (Cincinnati, OH: F&W Publications, 1994).
24. Jean-Pierre Geuens, *Film Production Theory* (Albany, NY: State University of New York Press, 2000).

CHAPTER 35

Bring Furrit the Tartan-Necks! Nationalist Intellectuals and Scottish Popular Culture*

Advancing a position unpopular in contemporary Scotland, Fred Halliday (1946–2010) permits himself a volcanic eruption of principled feeling about nationalism in an otherwise sober essay based on his Ernest Gellner [1925–95] Memorial Lecture:

> Yes, we welcome the diversity and the legitimacy which nationality brings, but we should also recognise the down side – not just the wars, the massacres, the intolerance, but the everyday nastiness of much nationalism, its petty-mindedness, its mean-spiritedness, the endless self-serving arguments, the vast culture of moaning, whingeing, kvetching, self-pity, special pleading, that 'narcissism of small differences' that Freud rightly denounced.[1]

In both quoted extract and full essay alike, Halliday probes the implicitly and explicitly normative claims of nationalism on a number of fronts: national self-determination, the national in relation to the supranational, nationalism's moral agenda, and its uses of history. In all these areas Halliday poses substantial questions: whether national self-determination is always worth the cost in terms of social upheaval (Kosovo is his most recent example); whether it always delivers more humane state formations (Chechnya being a case in point); whether the national, as a given, should invariably trump the supranational (the routine flouting of the United Nations charter and aims by national interests, nuclear proliferation argued on the basis of national defence); whether loyalty to the nation state should always supersede other loyalties (class, gender, faith); and whether nationalism's relaxed attitude to its own diverse 'imaginings' needs to be challenged (Ernest Renan [1823–92]'s famous belief that 'Getting your history wrong is part of being a nation').

Halliday's timely reminder that nationalism is not a natural but a historical phenomenon challenges those in Scotland and elsewhere who

---

*Originally published in *Scottish Affairs*, no. 69 (2009), 75–92.

would regard scepticism about nationalism as tantamount to treason. His piece should be read as a backdrop to this essay, which is about some of the cultural dimensions of the collective turn to nationalism of a significant section of the Scots intelligentsia. In particular, this essay emphasises the silences and deformations that this turn imposes on them with regard to their position on certain popular Scottish cultural phenomena, most notably, what has come to be known as Tartanry or Highlandism.[2] At a stretch, and with considerable provisos, this could be interpreted as what Halliday calls 'a carnival of mendacity',[3] it being virtually a structural necessity of nationalism that its local intellectual vanguards mouth something less than the truth about their own popular culture. Also, and as will be seen in the following discussion of certain nationalist Scots intellectuals' utterances, the much-vaunted, cool, 'civic' nationalism of Scotland can take on an altogether hotter 'ethnic' quality, especially in relation to the perceived 'treachery' of those critical of these same traditions. What, then, is at stake in this discussion? Why is it necessary to re-traverse terrain already well-trampled in the 1980s? It is so firstly due to the ethnicist drift of some prominent recent Scottish cultural nationalist writings and the dubious ethics of some cultural nationalists' prevarication about Scottish popular culture. Secondly, it is also so because of a contemporarily quite widespread, and arguably mistaken, assumption that this same culture is either benign, part of the quotidian cement that holds the 'nation' together, or else entirely devoid of ideological significance and therefore unworthy of serious analysis.[4] I have argued elsewhere that, far from being either benign or neutral, much Scottish popular culture is suffused with ideologically, and therefore politically, regressive impulses which inhibit or displace more progressive alternatives.[5] This point of view is being increasingly challenged or sidestepped by present-day cultural nationalists. The appropriate response to Scottish (or any other national) popular culture is neither benign acceptance nor populist celebration, but detailed analysis.

We have to begin with Tom Nairn (1932–2023). Consider the following statements made upwards of two decades apart:

> It is almost as difficult for a Scots intellectual to get out of the Kailyard as to live without an alias. The dilemma is not just an intellectuals' one [. . .] the whole thing is related to the much larger field of popular culture. For Kailyard is popular in Scotland. It is recognisably intertwined with that prodigious array of *Kitsch* symbols, slogans, ornaments, banners, war-cries, knick-knacks, music-hall heroes, icons, conventional sayings and sentiments (not a few of them 'pithy') which have for so long defended the name of 'Scotland' to the world. Annie S. Swan [1859–1943] and [A. J.] Cronin [1896–1981] provided no more than the decent outer garb for this vast

tartan monster. In their work the thing trots along doucely enough, on a lead. But it is something else to be with it (e.g.) in a London pub on International night, or in the crowd at the annual Military Tattoo in front of Edinburgh Castle. How intolerably vulgar! What unbearable, crass, mindless philistinism! One knows that *Kitsch* is a large constituent of mass popular culture in every land: but this is ridiculous![6]

[Culture] must [. . .] be faked, with whatever materials come to hand. It is in this sense that the fakelore of Gaelicism and assumed Highland identity is by no means accidental, or simply the consequences of bad faith and culpable romantic escapism. Phoniness is its unavoidable accompaniment, of course, as is the kind of uneasy half-belief which most Scottish Lowlanders have half-indulged in about it since Victorian times. However, all that really means is that since [. . .] 'real' identity cannot be deployed for certain important purposes, a display identity is needed to fill the gap. Intellectuals are often terribly sanctimonious about the results, but should waste less breath on it. I speak as one who has in the past expended all too much of the precious stuff on the follies of tartanry. A cure will be found in politics, not in aesthetic disdain or a stand-off intellectualism.[7]

Clearly Nairn no longer shares (if, indeed, he ever did) Halliday's queasiness about the liberties that nationalism takes with history. But the main point of interest here is that he draws back from his earlier ferocious critique of Tartanry and its sub-discourses, which he now sees simply as 'whatever materials come to hand' in providing 'a display identity' which will hold the nation together. It might be argued that Nairn has always been more interested in political structures rather than in Tartanry itself, but the change of tone between the two quotations is startling and has political implications. It is not a huge step from recognising to celebrating inevitability and the kind of 'national' culture it embodies. To his credit, unlike some other commentators, this is a step Nairn hesitates over. Far from celebrating Tartanry, he avers in passing within the 1997 passage quoted above that it requires a 'cure'. What is surprising, however, is that the same passage apparently depoliticises questions of aesthetics despite the fact that Nairn's whole argument hinges on the central mobilising and identity-sustaining role of 'aesthetic' discourses such as Tartanry. Needless to say, to resist the depoliticising of aesthetics is not to evacuate the distinctions between politics and aesthetics.

I do not wish here to venture too far into Nairn's millennial position on the inevitability and desirability of nationalism. Characteristically, it is highly sophisticated, persuasive and expressed with his customary rhetorical flair, but is far from uncontested.[8] There are, however, in some of his writings of that period passages which make one's hair stand on end. Critiquing the influential Gellnerian position on the centrality of modernity in the rise of nationalism,[9] for example, Nairn goes on:

> There has to be more to the view than modernisation doctrine allows: but what? The most obvious answer remains 'the blood' in the familiar metaphorical sense of transmission or inheritance from the past in either a biological or a socio-cultural sense.[10]

Nairn then immediately concedes the sullied inheritance of the concept of 'the blood' but earlier in the same text he celebrates a poem by Douglas Dunn, about the connection between Pictish and modern Scotland, in a way which invites a 'blood and soil' reading.[11] Such provocative sailing close to the wind earned Nairn a reproof from fellow nationalist intellectual Pat Kane.[12] Perhaps chastened by the alarm engendered by his unwise flirtation with 'the blood', Nairn has since been more explicitly condemnatory of this tradition ('Ethno-cultural or blood-descent nationalism is today the preserve of cranks and ideological gangsters in Scotland'[13]) but his later work still shows signs of drifting into the ethnicist mist:

> A modern nation has first and foremost to be a 'community of citizens' [. . .] Democratic citizenship must be its principal armature; but it has to be a community too – social survival and reproduction, from which there is no escape, demands that it be simultaneously a 'felt' association resting upon deeper and longer-range motifs linked to culture, emotion and transmissible 'instincts'.[14]

A symptomatic reading in the style of Pierre Macherey of Nairn's post-Marxist writings (that is, a reading of 'Nairn' the text, not Nairn the man) would be likely to reveal, under the Dr Jekyll of civic nationalism, the snarling ethnicist Mr Hyde.[15]

More generally still, the present essay (originally published in 2009) reflects my dismay at what I at that time read as the ethnicist tendencies in the writings of certain Scots intellectuals I respect. It was also conceived as being a response to critiques from within that tendency of some of my own earlier writings. A particular object of attack has been *Scotch Reels*, a 1982 collection of essays I edited and contributed to and which, to oversimplify somewhat, argued that cinematic representations of Scotland and the Scots are determined by certain historically hegemonic discourses such as Tartanry, Kailyard and a more recent addition, Clydesidism.[16] The book is often conjoined with *Scotch Myths*, a 1981 exhibition mounted by Murray and Barbara Grigor (1944–94), and the two routinely referred to as 'the Scotch Myths position'. Setting aside the flatly abusive responses,[17] *Scotch Reels* has been intelligently critiqued from virtually every position in the Cultural Studies repertoire: feminism;[18] comparative cinematics;[19] anti-Marxism;[20] reader response theory;[21] post-structuralism;[22] populism;[23] anti-structuralism;[24] and post-nationalism.[25] Some of those critiques are hard to pin down since their overall arguments may be articulated within one set of terms and their judgements on *Scotch Reels* in quite another.

Craig Beveridge and Ronald Turnbull, for instance, make their critique within their influential cultural nationalist essay entitled 'Inferiorism', but their specific remarks are formulated in reader response terms: 'meanings are never passively consumed, but always subject to selection and adjustment to other discourses'.[26] This is a substantial point, even if it implies (as in much reader response criticism) that the audience consists of hermetically sealed identity boxes uninflected by the encounter with the specifics of any text. In fact, the options any reader has in the textual encounter have less to do with individual readerly identity or capability than with a range of historically determined reading formations. For instance, before the 1960s few readers, unlike today, would have been likely to deploy a feminist reading strategy.

Quite pointed as some criticisms of *Scotch Reels* are, they pale into insignificance beside the writings of Cairns Craig. He emerges as the Witchfinder General of Scottish cultural nationalism, scouring the pages of Scottish criticism to root out any signs of anti-nationalist heresy and denounce them in a tone Halliday would recognise as all too historically audible among nationalists. Sometime between the early 1980s and the mid-1990s, Craig underwent a Damascene conversion, abandoning Karl Marx (1818–83) for Friedrich Nietzsche (1844–1900) and displaying his new cultural nationalist position in an influential 1996 collection of essays.[27] Here the story becomes rather complicated, for one of the main targets of Craig's ire is Tom Nairn's seemingly Marxist explanation for the poverty of Scottish (popular) culture in his 1977 essay cited above. However, Craig is at pains to point out that it is the Nairn position of the 1970s that he is taking issue with, not Nairn's later, more cultural nationalism-friendly, writings. This is quite understandably so, since the latter writings reveal Nairn to be an ally of Craig in the contemporary nationalist project. Craig then swiftly extends his critique to a group of texts and events much influenced by Nairn's earlier writings, including (by implication, since the guilty are sleekitly unnamed) the present writer's work. He writes:

> What the Scotch Myths debate pointed to was not the tawdriness of Scottish culture – that was no more tawdry than any other popular culture anywhere in the world – but to the profound hatred of the intellectuals for the culture they inhabited, the profound embarrassment they suffered by being unable, any more, to identify themselves with some universalist truth that would redeem them from Scottishness. They did not want to carry the burden of the Scottish past; they did not want to negotiate with the actualities of Scottish culture; they wanted to abolish it and create it anew in their own image.[28]

Here is the true voice of the (cultural) nationalist. It is not sufficient to valorise one's own national culture: the logic of nationalism demands that (constructed) internationalist or cosmopolitan enemies also be identified and pilloried. In fact, the violence of the denunciation may act as a smokescreen for Craig's (like Nairn's) doubts about the popular indigenous culture his nationalism requires that he publicly support. To say that one's own popular culture is 'no more tawdry than any other popular culture anywhere' is hardly a ringing endorsement.

Craig's tone subsequently became even more bitterly denunciatory during the first decade of the 2000s. In a 2009 essay consisting largely of a perceptive riff round the opposition 'home' and 'away' in two Scottish feature films (art-house rather than popular films, significantly) and the wider Scottish culture, he describes adherents to 'the Scotch Myths position' as exhibiting 'an abnormal fear or dislike of home amounting to nostophobia'.[29] This neologism is based on the word 'nostalgia', coined by a Swiss physician, Johannes Hofer (1669–1752), in the late seventeenth century to describe the profound homesickness experienced by Swiss mercenaries serving abroad.[30] The modern usage of the term means yearning for another time; the original usage meant yearning for another place. It is this earlier usage that Craig rhetorically inverts in 'nostophobia'. In terms of the respective metaphors for which they reach in their common valorisation of Scotland, it might therefore be said that Craig supplies the 'soil' to go along with Tom Nairn's 'blood'. Anything short of complete submission to the primacy of Scottish culture is treachery. To make a (so far) disproportionate comparison, one begins to understand how it might have felt to be a Jew or a communist in the early days of the Third Reich. Craig claims, disingenuously, that by deploying the term 'nostophobia' and designating certain Scots intellectuals as 'nostophobes', he is simply naming a discernible phenomenon. He must surely be aware, however, that 'nostophobia', formed on the analogy of bigoted beliefs such as 'homophobia' and 'Islamophobia', goes way beyond an act of naming to become one of vilification and, incidentally, embodies that bleating about victimhood which Halliday identifies as characteristic of nationalist ideologies. Most tellingly, Craig's 'nostophobe' is analogous to 'self-hater', the pejorative label slung round the necks of those Jews critical of the actions of the state of Israel. The conjoining of self-hatred with a sceptical view of Scottish cultural nationalism also lurks within the writings of another prominent contemporary redeemer of Tartanry, Murray Pittock.[31]

Craig's thinking seems to have been much influenced by that of Beveridge and Turnbull or, perhaps more accurately, all of them have bought into aspects of the postcolonial theoretical discourse, versions of which are manna from heaven for those wishing to formulate a victim-centred cultural nationalist agenda, despite the highly contested idea of

Scotland as a postcolonial society.[32] In two books Beveridge and Turnbull fashioned and developed the concept of 'inferiorism', alluded to above, whereby Scottish culture had allegedly been told – largely by English or Anglocentric Scots intellectuals – that it was barren and impoverished.[33] As well as traducing the traducers (the early work of Tom Nairn figures here yet again) Beveridge and Turnbull's remedy was to seek positive elements within primarily Scots cultural, intellectual and institutional traditions. Their 1989 book foregrounds the ideas of Scots intellectuals such as George Elder Davie (1912–2007) and Alasdair Macintyre on specifically Scottish conceptions of education and philosophy respectively. Their 1996 book, while referring once more to these figures, is more centrally concerned to dispute (and in one case, that of Murray Pittock's favourable rereading of Jacobitism,[34] to commend) the constructions of Scotland offered by Scots historians and sociologists.

This strategy of finding the positive primarily within indigenous national traditions was subsequently adopted by Craig in his 1999 study, *The Modern Scottish Novel: Narrative and the National Imagination*,[35] and made particularly explicit in a 2004 essay:

> To imply that it is only through the ideas of Russian or American intellectuals that one can grasp the real nature of the Scottish condition is to continue Scotland's submission to cultural imperialism rather than fulfil its 'post-colonial' identity, reproducing the inferiorism by which Scotland is always the *object* of an understanding that can only come from outside Scotland itself, never a *subject* capable of understanding itself.[36]

A seemingly moderate statement, its profoundly immoderate implications are revealed when set alongside a description by Aijaz Ahmad (1941–2022) of certain tendencies in his native India:

> There is a powerful political movement in India which says that Indian Muslims and Christians are not true Indians because they subscribe to religions that did not *originate* in India; that Indian socialists are not true Indians because Marxism *originated* in Europe; that the Indian state should not be a secular state because secularism is a western construct. There are influential social scientists who argue that parliamentary democracy does not suit Indian conditions, and that India should invent indigenous social sciences and indigenous political forms.[37]

Not the least of the contradictions in Craig's writings is, on the one hand, the ethnicist impulse to harry those less than fulsome about cultural nationalism and, on the other, his oft-repeated obeisance to the structuring presence of hybridity and heterogeneity in Scottish culture. Looking more closely at the Craig quotation above, it is quite complicated to separate out what is correct and what is deformed by nationalism. To be sure, there are hegemonic discourses, both external and internal to Scotland, which shape the way it has been and is seen by the world and the way most Scots see themselves. The most central of these discourses are Tartanry and Kailyard, the very discourses that Craig and other (cultural) nationalists would seek to valorise as Scottish popular culture but, significantly, would not wish to get too close to (of which more presently). However, what is most striking about this passage is the extent to which it embodies the defining qualities of nationalism Halliday anatomises within the quote with which the present essay began ('the endless self-serving arguments, the vast culture of moaning, whingeing, kvetching, self-pity, special pleading').

Partly because of its ambitiousness, Craig's *The Modern Scottish Novel* is a markedly uneven book. Paradoxically (for this is a cultural nationalist text), it is at its most brilliantly insightful when engaging with the high art end of Scottish culture and the formal aspects of texts. Compare the laser precision of Craig's comments on Patrick Doyle's discussion with his parents in James Kelman's novel *A Disaffection* (1989):

> 'Ye' and 'you' are mixed in this speech, as are traditional Scottish words – 'weans' – with the demotic pronunciation of English: 'canni' [. . .] what Kelman has done is to allow the language to fuse together with his own narrative voice so that [. . .] the distinction between the language of narration and the language of dialogue is dissolved.[38]

with the unfocussed generality of his attempt to incorporate John Buchan (1875–1940)'s work within the Calvinist-based concept of 'fearful selves' that Craig claims to be a significant current within Scottish culture:

> Buchan's role as one of the inventors of the 'thriller' genre is perhaps the result of the fear which is fundamental to his perception of the world, with his fearless heroes in continual flight across a world riddled with fear.[39]

Craig's violent yoking everything together under the conceptual rubric 'fear', sustaining his argument by rhetoric rather than analysis, is reminiscent of the thematic strand of auteurist film criticism between the 1950s and 1970s which – unlike the simultaneous *mise-en-scène* strand – tended to make the work of all Hollywood directors sound alike.[40] I write as one who has deployed both strands (and genre analysis) within the same book[41] and been an egregious offender with regard to thematic analysis. Craig's historical centrality in the institutionalisation of Scottish literary studies, the range of his scholarship and the subtlety of his judgements seem to have dazzled younger critics, blinding them to the contradictions of his work and its ethnicist tendencies. That said, it has had an emancipatory effect on the best of Scottish academic film criticism and Scottish postcolonial studies.[42] Indeed, Graeme Macdonald casts Craig as the Moses who will lead Scots postcolonialists out of the arid deserts of textuality to the promised land of political progressiveness. Craig's work has also stiffened the spines of other critics in their commendable defence of internationalism and cosmopolitanism, discourses peremptorily dismissed by Tom Nairn in relation to politics and (more contradictorily) by Craig in relation to aesthetics.[43]

To restate one of this essay's main arguments, (Scottish cultural) nationalists are caught in a particular contradiction. On the one hand, nationalism demands that they be (or pretend to be) populist, that they embrace the 'culture of the people'. But, on the other hand, they can, precisely because they are intellectuals, see through the sentimentality, simple-mindedness and lack of appreciation of the world's complexity so characteristic of much popular culture. This is emphatically not to argue that no popular culture has value or that nuanced judgements cannot be made between one piece of popular culture and another (for example, *Rab C. Nesbitt* [BBC Scotland, 1988–2014] versus *The White Heather Club* [BBC Scotland, 1958–68] or, in the area of the comic Scots postcard, Cynicus [aka Martin Anderson, 1854–1932] versus Lawson Wood [1878–1957]). This contradiction may help explain Nairn's and Craig's (at best) lukewarm support for Scottish popular culture and the lack of its detailed discussion within their work. In this they are within the great tradition of nationalist intellectual cynicism with regard to ostensibly nationalist popular art. Joseph Goebbels (1897–1945), erstwhile admirer of Impressionism and certain aspects of modern art, then ardent persecutor of '*Entartete Kunst*' as an affront to National Socialist cultural policy, in the privacy of his diaries denounced as 'terrible bullshit' and 'Nordic Kitsch' the kind of official German art that set Hitler's pulse racing.[44] While Craig's influential work on the Scots novel might imply that there are riches within the Kailyard tradition by drawing attention (in a footnote) to 'sympathetic'[45] accounts of it, his own discussion, aside from some remarks on J. M. Barrie (1860–1937), whom he contrives to relocate within the anti-Kailyard tradition, is primarily of the anti-Kailyard work of George Douglas Brown (1869–1902) rather than, say, that of the more mainstream S. R. Crockett (1859–1914). To be sure, he incorporates into that ghostly paradigm of 'the Scots tradition' the middlebrow fiction of John Buchan and Ian Rankin, but *The Modern Scottish Novel* is heavily weighted towards 'high art' (dare one even say, quasi-modernist) figures such as Lewis Grassic Gibbon (1901–1935), Alasdair Gray (1934–2019), James Kelman and Muriel Spark (1918–2006).

There is another factor which may have inhibited Scottish cultural nationalists such as Nairn and Craig from getting to grips with the real down-and-dirty aspects of Scottish popular culture which, strictly speaking, the nationalist project should demand of them. They are both of the generation which predates postmodernism, memorably and synoptically defined by Terry Eagleton:

> By 'postmodern', I mean, roughly speaking, the contemporary movement of thought which rejects totalities, universal values, grand historical narratives, solid foundations to human existence and the possibility of objective knowledge. Postmodernism is sceptical of truth, unity and progress, opposes what it sees as elitism in culture, tends towards cultural relativism, and celebrates pluralism, discontinuity and heterogeneity.[46]

Cultural and political nationalists may flirt with postmodernism when they assert that Enlightenment and Marxist internationalism are dead, but they themselves remain committed to the grand historical narratives of their own individual nations. The aspect of Eagleton's definition most relevant to this essay's argument is postmodernism's opposition to cultural elitism, its evacuating of the distinction between high and popular art, the 'great divide' which, according to Andreas Huyssen, we are now living 'after'.[47] As Eagleton puts it: 'students once wrote uncritical, reverential essays on Flaubert, but all that has been transformed. Nowadays they write uncritical, reverential essays on *Friends*.'[48] A glance at the range of literary references in Craig and Nairn's respective works will indicate the extent to which they are discernibly more sympathetic to the high art side of the opposition.

However, there is another group of contemporary Scottish cultural nationalist intellectuals for whom this does not seem to be so. David Goldie, for example, has made a thoroughly justifiable attack on Hugh MacDiarmid (1892–1978)'s monolithic, unnuanced condemnation of Scottish popular culture while, on the other hand, simultaneously offering a more questionable celebration of Harry Lauder (1870–1950), MacDiarmid's particular Scottish popular cultural bugbear, largely on the grounds that Lauder was able to communicate with (or manipulate?) popular audiences.[49] Goldie's methodology is curious. Arguing that the nature of Lauder's performances is inaccessible to us, he cites contemporary accounts of Lauder's winning ways with audiences, including one by H. V. Morton (1892–1979), whom Goldie describes as 'the much-celebrated *Daily Express* countryside writer and author of the best-selling 'In Search of . . .' series of books'.[50] In fact, Morton was a crypto-fascist hack wholly complicit with the most regressive discourses about a whole series of romanticised Others (including the Scots) and who, disgusted with the election of a Labour government in 1945, emigrated to and ended his days in Apartheid-era South Africa. Morton's account of his visit to the Scottish National War Memorial in Edinburgh illustrates the extent to which he had bought into the most lurid tropes of 'Scottish' discourse and perhaps helps explain his sympathetic response to Lauder:

> When the gate was declared open Scots pipers mounted high on the ramparts played 'The Flowers o' the Forest' [. . .] It seemed to me, as I stood in Scotland's Shrine, that the sound of this lament had flown home to crystallise in stone upon the rock of Edinburgh. The shrine is a lament in stone, the greatest of all Scotland's laments, with all the sweetness of pipes crying among hills, with all the haunting beauty of a lament, all the pride, all the grandeur. I think the Cenotaph in London and the National Shrine in Edinburgh are the most remarkable symbols in existence of the temperamental difference between the two nations. One is Saxon and inarticulate; the other is Celtic and articulate. Grief locks the English heart, but it opens the Scottish. The Celt has a genius for the glorification of sorrow. All his sweetest songs are sad; all his finest music is sad; all his finest poetry springs from tragedy. That is why Scotland has built the finest war memorial in the world. The 'Flowers of the Forest' have all turned to stone.[51]

In fact, Lauder's performances are less inaccessible than Goldie allows. The Scottish Screen Archive holds almost twenty minutes of footage of Lauder singing 'I Love a Lassie', 'Oh Sing To Me the Old Scotch Songs', 'My Ain Dear Nell', 'Roamin' in the Gloamin'' and interrelating with the audience. In addition there are available several CDs of Lauder's original recordings, many of the songs (for example, 'The Waggle o' the Kilt', 'Breakfast in Bed on Sunday Morning') including extensive sections of 'patter', suggesting that the recordings are very much as he delivered the songs to live audiences. A thematic analysis of the songs reveals a rather juvenile conception of romance, veiled allusions to the problematic nature of marriage, a sentimental attachment to place and former times, and a mainly British (rather than Scottish) patriotism. However, ideologically dubious as much of the content of Lauder's songs is, it is his performance of them that sets the teeth on edge: his unctuous wheedling and cajoling interspersed with phoney laughter; and the voice itself, which is creepy at best and, in its upper registers (as in 'Stop Your Ticklin', Jock'), verging on the demented.

Curiously, given our diametrically opposed critical evaluations, my own view of Lauder partly agrees with that of Goldie, who writes:

> It is true that [Lauder] chose, with a degree of understanding of his audience that amounted almost to cynicism, to make for himself a naïve persona whose primary

appeal was to sentiment and to a regressive stereotype of highlandism. But it is also true that he had a much wider tonal range and formal sophistication than this.[52]

Amen to the nature of the Lauder persona, but what of his 'wider tonal range and formal sophistication'? Relying, as he does, on second-hand accounts of Lauder's performances, Goldie is decidedly light on the analysis of them. In an ironic twist, the definitive summing-up of Lauder was delivered elsewhere by none other than Cairns Craig in an earlier, pre-cultural nationalist identity:

> [The] turning of the back on the actuality of modern Scottish life is emblematically conveyed in the figure of Harry Lauder – Kailyard consciousness in tartan exterior – who evacuates from his stage persona, indeed from his total identity, the world of the Lanarkshire miners from which he began.[53]

One is tempted to conclude that, like Nairn and Craig, Goldie, as a cultural nationalist, is ideologically impelled to celebrate Scottish popular culture but is also disinclined to get too close to it. The same criticism can be made of Ian Brown, who makes sweeping claims for Lauder's 'progressiveness' without once engaging with the detail of a Lauder performance.[54] This is odd since Brown has in other contexts shown himself more than capable of close textual analysis.[55] Without referencing its generative or diffusionary texts,[56] both Goldie and Brown subscribe to that fetishising of the popular which Anglo-American Cultural Studies – terrified that 'the people' might be constrained by regressive aesthetic/discursive or economic factors – has rendered hegemonic.[57]

It might be useful to recall, shorn of its elitist implications, one of T. S. Eliot (1888–1965)'s maxims: 'the greatness of literature cannot be determined solely by literary standards; though we must remember that whether it is literature or not can be determined only by literary standards'.[58] Bringing the matter back onto Scottish turf, this is close in spirit to the *politique* enunciated within the editorial of the first issue of the *International Journal of Scottish Literature*:

> This journal is not exclusively or even mainly interested in reading Scottish literature in terms of what Laurence Nicoll once called 'the cultural nationalist paradigm': the persistent sense, as Gavin Miller and Eleanor Bell have it [. . .] that 'literature from Scotland must firstly be explained in terms of its Scottishness, rather than in terms of its literary or aesthetic qualities' [. . .] Christopher Whyte rejects, on similar grounds, 'the illusion that the primary function of poetic texts lies in identity building, and that they are capable of resolving identity issues'. This is not to say, of course, that issues surrounding cultural identity are uninteresting or unimportant, or that a critical moratorium should be declared on the question of 'Scottishness'. Rather, there is no compelling *literary* reason why identity issues

should be the primary critical consideration when encountering a new poem or play or novel by a Scottish writer.[59]

Welcome as Eliot and the *IJSL* are in the face of cultural nationalist reductiveness, I would canvass a critical method which still privileges ideological analysis but also locates it within detailed textual analysis, a method I have attempted to deploy in some of my later writings.[60] Ideological analysis on its own tends to operate with a broad brush, revealing hegemonic discourses here (McArthur) or alleged national traditions there (Craig). It needs to be supplemented with close readings of texts, ideally to find the ideology within the formal features of any given text, as Craig does so successfully with James Kelman's writing. Without being wholly reductive, I want a form of cultural analysis which bears some relationship to (among other things) the following: that a mortgaging policy formulated in New York can lead to house repossessions in New Malden; that a democratically elected government can, against the wishes of the majority of its electors, embark on wars in distant corners of the world; and that a powerful political lobby in one country can determine the fate of the powerless in quite another. The kind of analysis I am canvassing is close in spirit to that Berthold Schoene dubs 'rooted cosmopolitanism',[61] although for historical reasons I would prefer the term 'internationalism'. Schoene quotes a definition of this type of analytical model offered by Steven Vertovec and Robin Cohen. It:

> (a) transcends the seemingly exhausted nation-state model; (b) is able to mediate actions and ideals oriented both to the universal and the particular; (c) is culturally anti-essentialist; and (d) is capable of representing seriously complex repertoires of allegiance, identity and interest.[62]

I am not convinced that such analysis is best realised by concentrating on 'the nation' or 'national cultural traditions', however dialogically conceived. Such concentration may lead to the types of critical blindness and exorbitant feelings alluded to above. In particular, the incompatibility of Tartanry and Kailyard with this kind of analysis must constantly be reasserted, as should the telling prevarication of cultural nationalist Scots intellectuals with regard to these discourses.

Contemporary nationalism in Scotland has bent over backwards to prove that it is 'civic' rather than 'ethnic'. If Fred Halliday is correct, however, that distinction is flawed, with every nationalism having a fatal tilt to the 'ethnic'. Tom Nairn admits as much in his ongoing metaphor of nationalism as Janus, one face turned to the future, the other to the past. As this essay has demonstrated, this 'ethnic' tilt is discernible in certain Scottish cultural nationalist writings with their argument that those Scots sceptical about the nationalist project are heretics, traitors and haters of the land of their birth.

Hopefully there is room in Scottish cultural criticism for a hundred thistles to bloom.

Notes

1. Fred Halliday, 'The Perils of Community: Reason and Unreason in Nationalist Ideology', *Nations and Nationalism* 6, no. 2 (2000), 158–9.
2. For Tartanry, see Colin McArthur, ed., *Scotch Reels: Scotland in Cinema and Television* (London: British Film Institute, 1982); Colin McArthur, Brigadoon, Braveheart *and the Scots: Distortions of Scotland in Hollywood Cinema* (London: I.B. Tauris, 2003); for Highlandism, see T. M. Devine, *The Scottish Nation: A History 1700–2000* (London: Allen Lane, 1999); Neil Davidson, *The Origins of Scottish Nationhood* (London: Pluto Press, 2000).
3. Halliday, 'The Perils of Community', 167.
4. See, for example, Tom Nairn, *Faces of Nationalism: Janus Revisited* (London: Verso, 1997); Ian Brown, *Performing Scottishness: Enactment and Identities* (London: Palgrave Macmillan, 2020).
5. McArthur, Brigadoon, Braveheart *and the Scots*; Colin McArthur, Whisky Galore! *and* The Maggie (London: I.B. Tauris, 2003).
6. Tom Nairn, *The Break-Up of Britain: Crisis and Neo-Nationalism* (London: New Left Books, 1977), 162.
7. Nairn, *Faces of Nationalism*, 207.
8. Neil Davidson, 'In Perspective: Tom Nairn', *International Socialism*, no. 82 (1999), 97–136; J. Cocks, *Passion and Paradox: Intellectuals Confront the National Question* (Princeton, NJ: Princeton University Press, 2002).
9. Ernest Gellner, *Nations and Nationalism* (Oxford: Blackwell, 1983).
10. Nairn, *Faces of Nationalism*, 9.
11. Ibid., 6–7.
12. Pat Kane, *Tinsel Show: Pop, Politics, Scotland* (Edinburgh: Polygon, 1992), 98.
13. Tom Nairn, *After Britain: New Labour and the Return of Scotland* (London: Granta Books, 2000), 244.
14. Ibid., 252.
15. Pierre Macherey, *A Theory of Literary Production* (London: Routledge & Kegan Paul, 1978).
16. McArthur, *Scotch Reels*.
17. See, for example, Andrew Noble, 'Bill Douglas' *Trilogy*', in *From Limelight to Satellite: A Scottish Film Book*, ed. Eddie Dick (London/Glasgow: British Film Institute/Scottish Film Council, 1990), 133–50.
18. Douglas Bain, Ouainé Bain and Gillian Skirrow, 'Woman, Women and Scotland: *Scotch Reels* and Political Perspectives', *Cencrastus*, no. 11 (1983), 3–6.
19. Susan Barrowclough, 'A Critique of *Scotch Reels*', *Framework*, no. 21 (Summer 1983), 57.

20. John Brown, 'Letter', *Cencrastus*, no. 14 (Autumn 1983), 47–8.
21. Craig Beveridge and Ronald Turnbull, *The Eclipse of Scottish Culture: Inferiorism and the Intellectuals* (Edinburgh: Polygon, 1989); Tim Edensor, *National Identity, Popular Culture and Everyday Life* (Oxford: Berg 2002).
22. John Caughie, 'Representing Scotland: New Questions for Scottish Cinema', in *From Limelight to Satellite*, ed. Dick, 13–30.
23. Pam Cook, *Fashioning the Nation: Costume and Identity in British Cinema* (London: British Film Institute, 1996); Jeffrey Richards, *Films and British National Identity: From Dickens to* Dad's Army (Manchester: Manchester University Press, 1997).
24. Philip Kemp, *Lethal Innocence: The Cinema of Alexander Mackendrick* (London: Methuen, 1991).
25. David McCrone, *Understanding Scotland: The Sociology of a Stateless Nation* (London: Routledge, 1992).
26. Beveridge and Turnbull, *The Eclipse of Scottish Culture*, 14.
27. Cairns Craig, *Out of History: Narrative Paradigms in Scottish and British Culture* (Edinburgh: Polygon, 1996).
28. Ibid., 107.
29. Cairns Craig, 'Nostophobia', in *Scottish Cinema Now*, eds Jonathan Murray, Fidelma Farley and Rod Stoneman (Newcastle: Cambridge Scholars Publishing, 2009), 62.
30. Fred Davis, *Yearning for Yesterday: A Sociology of Nostalgia* (New York: The Free Press, 1979).
31. Murray Pittock, *The Myth of the Jacobite Clans* (Edinburgh: Edinburgh University Press, 1995), 117–18.
32. Davidson, *The Origins of Scottish Nationhood*, 90–111.
33. Beveridge and Turnbull, *The Eclipse of Scottish Culture*; Craig Beveridge and Ronald Turnbull, *Scotland After Enlightenment* (Edinburgh: Polygon, 1996).
34. Murray Pittock, *The Invention of Scotland: The Stuart Myth and the Scottish Identity, 1638 to the Present* (London: Routledge, 1991).
35. Cairns Craig, *The Modern Scottish Novel: Narrative and the National Imagination* (Edinburgh: Edinburgh University Press, 1999).
36. Cairns Craig, 'Scotland and Hybridity', in *Beyond Scotland: New Contexts for Twentieth-Century Scottish Literature*, eds Gerard Carruthers and David Goldie (Amsterdam: Rodopi, 2004), 241.
37. Aijaz Ahmad, 'The Politics of Literary Postcoloniality', in *Contemporary Postcolonial Theory: A Reader*, ed. Padmini Mongia (London: Routledge, 1996), 279.
38. Craig, *The Modern Scottish Novel*, 100–1.
39. Ibid., 44.
40. John Gibbs, Mise-en-scène: *Film Style and Interpretation* (London: Wallflower Press, 2002).
41. Colin McArthur, *Underworld U.S.A.* (London: Secker & Warburg for the British Film Institute, 1972).
42. See, for example, Duncan Petrie, *Screening Scotland* (London: British Film Institute, 2000); Graeme Macdonald, 'Postcolonialism and Scottish Studies', *New Formations*, no. 59 (2006), 116–31.

43. See, for example, Christopher Whyte, 'Occasional Paper: The Debt to Theory', *International Journal of Scottish Literature*, no. 3 (Autumn/Winter 2007), 82–8; Berthold Schoene, 'Cosmopolitan Scots', *Scottish Studies Review* 9, no. 2 (2008), 71–92.
44. Glenn R. Cuomo, 'The Diaries of Joseph Goebbels as a Source for the Understanding of National Socialist Cultural Politics', in *National Socialist Cultural Policy*, ed. Glenn R. Cuomo (New York: St Martin's Press, 1995), 211.
45. Craig, *The Modern Scottish Novel*, 243.
46. Terry Eagleton, *After Theory* (London: Penguin Books, 2004), 13.
47. Andreas Huyssen, *After the Great Divide: Modernism, Mass Culture, Postmodernism* (Bloomington: Indiana University Press, 1986).
48. Eagleton, *After Theory*, 5.
49. David Goldie, 'MacDiarmid, Harry Lauder and Scottish Popular Culture', *International Journal of Scottish Literature*, no. 1 (Autumn 2006), available at https://www.ijsl.stir.ac.uk/issue1/goldie.htm [accessed 19 October 2022].
50. Ibid.
51. H. V. Morton, *In Search of Scotland* (London: Methuen, 1929), 54.
52. Goldie, 'MacDiarmid, Harry Lauder and Scottish Popular Culture'.
53. Cairns Craig, 'Myths Against History: Tartanry and Kailyard in 19th-Century Scottish Literature', in *Scotch Reels*, ed. McArthur, 13.
54. Ian Brown, 'Penguins and Flowers: Failure of Nerve, Cultural Complexity and Tartanry', *Scottish Studies Review* 8, no. 2 (Autumn 2007), 69–88.
55. Ian Brown, 'Alternative Sensibilities: Devolutionary Comedy and Scottish Camp', in *The Edinburgh Companion to Contemporary Scottish Literature*, ed. Berthold Schoene (Edinburgh: Edinburgh University Press, 2007), 319–27.
56. Michel de Certeau, *The Practice of Everyday Life* (Berkeley/Los Angeles: University of California Press, 1984); John Fiske, *Understanding Popular Culture* (London: Unwin Hyman, 1989); Paul Willis, *Common Culture: Symbolic Work at Play in the Everyday Cultures of the Young* (Buckingham: Open University Press, 1990).
57. Jim McGuigan, *Cultural Populism* (London: Routledge, 1992); Francis Mulhern, *Culture/Metaculture* (London: Routledge, 2000).
58. T. S. Eliot, 'Religion and Literature', in T. S. Eliot, *Selected Prose* (Harmondsworth: Penguin, 1953), 32.
59. Anon, 'Editorial: Internationalism Now?', *International Journal of Scottish Literature*, no. 1 (Autumn 2006), 1.
60. McArthur, *Brigadoon, Braveheart and the Scots*; McArthur, *Whisky Galore! and The Maggie*.
61. Schoene, 'Cosmopolitan Scots', 85.
62. Ibid., 76. The original source of the quotation is: Steven Vertovec and Robin Cohen, 'Introduction: Conceiving Cosmopolitanism', in *Conceiving Cosmopolitanism: Theory, Context, and Practice*, eds Steven Vertovec and Robin Cohen (Oxford: Oxford University Press, 2002), 4.

CHAPTER 36

Vanished or Banished? Murray Grigor as Absent Scots Auteur*

Although the following words were written about Charles Rennie Mackintosh (1868–1928), they are perhaps equally applicable to this essay's subject, Murray Grigor, given the uncanny resemblance between Grigor's career and that of Mackintosh:

> He soon discovered that the reputation he had acquired abroad made not the slightest difference to his status in Glasgow and the applause [. . .] had no effect whatever on the stolid, unimaginative men-of-the-world with whom he had to do business.[1]

It is not that Grigor is wholly unknown in Scotland. He has, for example, collaborated with prominent Scots in mounting exhibitions and sociocultural public advocacy campaigns, including ones aiming to bring to greater public attention the architectural heritage of Glasgow in the buildings of Rennie Mackintosh and Alexander 'Greek' Thomson (1817–75). Nor has the Scottish press been uniformly hostile to his work. The run-of-the-mill press often responded warmly, if somewhat bemusedly, and more politically and culturally alert commentators were positively enthusiastic. In Grigor's case, the equivalent of the 'stolid, unimaginative men-of-the-world' who had thwarted Mackintosh were the uncomprehending apparatchiks in certain Scottish arts, broadcasting and film institutions.

The title of this piece describes Grigor as 'auteur', a term formulated within French film criticism (particularly, the magazine *Cahiers du cinéma*) to describe the kind of film director whose stylistic and thematic identity is discernible across the whole range of their work.[2] This essay retains the 'auteur' idea of identity and coherence, but – while being centrally concerned with Grigor's films – extends it to include his journalism, public advocacy, graphic art and association with the Edinburgh International

---

*Originally published in *Directory of World Cinema: Scotland*, eds Bob Nowlan and Zach Finch (Bristol: Intellect Books, 2015), 58–65.

Film Festival. His directorship of the latter (1967–73) coincided with the importation into the UK of the cinephilia which had reanimated post-WWII French film culture. The ideas of authorship and *mise-en-scène* were taken up and applied by younger British critics primarily associated with the journal *Movie* (1962–2000) and the British Film Institute Education Department. Inheriting a festival which was well-established, thoroughly respectable but cripplingly limited by the realist and documentarist aesthetic of its co-founder and John Grierson (1898–1972) biographer, Forsyth Hardy (1910–94), Grigor entered into alliance with the *Movie*/BFI Education initiative and brought into the Festival younger figures like Lynda Myles and David Will. The result was a dazzling series of auteurist retrospectives, on Samuel Fuller (1912–97) and Douglas Sirk (1897–1987) among others, each accompanied by a book of essays. By the time (the early 1970s) that British critical auteurist interest had mutated into engagement with theoretical issues such as ideology and psychoanalysis, Grigor had handed the Festival over to his younger colleagues.[3]

Grigor meanwhile was embarking on his filmmaking career, the subject of his first two 'documentary' films, *Mackintosh* (1968) and *Scope: Mackintosh* (1970), being, appropriately, Charles Rennie Mackintosh. Today the phenomenon of Mackintosh (or, as Grigor derisively calls it, 'Mockintosh') is so omnipresent in Scotland that it requires an effort of historical will to recall that serious appreciation of his work had to be laboriously constructed: Grigor's films were part of that process. At the time the only film production funding mechanisms available in Scotland, apart from the broadcasters, were those associated with public institutions specialising in sponsored documentaries, such as Films of Scotland (1954–82) and the Highlands and Islands Development Board (1965–91). Grigor worked with these, his early films like *Travelpass* (1973) and *Suilven Spring* (1974) employing young Scots actors such as Bill Paterson, John Bett and Alex Norton. *Travelpass* looks not unlike a characteristic Scottish travelogue except that the soundtrack disdains the usual plaintive clarsach or fiddle music, opting instead for modern music in the folk tradition. However, it is 'folkish' and not *volkisch*. In the early 1970s Scots filmmakers also had access to two other funding mechanisms, the Scottish Arts Council (1967–2010) and the Arts Council of Great Britain (1946–94), both of which had film sections. It was here that Grigor's modernism and, in a non-pejorative sense, formalism were allowed freer rein, as in his *Blast* (1975), about Wyndham Lewis (1882–1957) and Vorticism, the early-twentieth-century art movement that Lewis co-founded. Grigor's modernism elicited immediate appreciation and reward, though mainly outside Scotland, *Blast* receiving awards at festivals in Melbourne, Tampere and Sydney.

I have described elsewhere much of Grigor's work as 'ludic modernism', the ludic element deriving from the Surrealists, Samuel Beckett (1906–89) and, above all, James Joyce (1882–1941).[4] This strain appeared early in his career, in two films he made with the Scots comedian Billy Connolly, *Clydescope* (1974) and *Billy Connolly: Big Banana Feet* (1977). The latter was a record of Connolly's recent Irish tour and, aesthetically speaking, very much resembles the celebrated documentary film of Bob Dylan's 1965 British tour, *Don't Look Back* (D. A. Pennebaker, 1967). However, *Clydescope* is a much more interesting work. With few exceptions, Scottish cinematic travelogues tended towards the po-faced and reverent, often drawing on regressive discourses about Scotland such as Tartanry and Kailyard. In *Clydescope*, Grigor upends this tradition. Funded by the Clyde Tourist Board, it follows Connolly down the River Clyde from its source. One could imagine such a project in other hands being constructed on the pattern of the Ur-Tartan Documentary with vistas of hills and lochs and a reverent commentary stressing the timelessness of the river and the 'proud and independent' people who inhabit its banks (see, for example, the Stakhanovite *Seawards the Great Ships* [Hilary Harris, 1961]). But instead of dwelling on 'views' of the Clyde, Grigor opts for a photographic studio and the complex Edwardian glasswork on the roof of Wemyss Bay railway station – a Scotland of culture rather than nature. Loch Lomond is a central trope in Tartanry, views of it being endlessly recycled and celebrated in popular song. Grigor demurs, drawing attention to a bear-garden on its shore and, against the image of the stately boat *Maid of the Loch* cruising into frame, Grigor adds the tune 'Loch Lomond', but played on a ship's siren.

Individual examples such as the one above suggest the extent to which Grigor's work is unremittingly political. His early project which most explicitly unites politics and culture is *The Hammer and the Thistle* (1977), a film on the Scots poet Hugh MacDiarmid (1892–1978). The apparent anomaly of its being funded by a north of England broadcasting company, Granada Television, is explained by the then presence, at a senior level in Granada, of Gus Macdonald, a Scot with leftist sympathies. This was the first of several instances in which Grigor's career was advanced by powerful émigré Scots. In 1977–78 Grigor lived in the United States on a UK/US Bicentennial Fellowship in the Arts, awarded to allow him to research a film on the American architect Frank Lloyd Wright (1867–1959). This would have a profound effect on his later career, spinning it off into the world of modernist architecture, the subject of many of his later films. Grigor's return to Scottish filmmaking, *Sean Connery's Edinburgh* (1982), was quite a low-key affair, funded by the City of Edinburgh District

Council and 'starring' Connery (1930–2020) himself. Less obviously political than many of Grigor's other projects, it nevertheless is less than reverent to certain venerable Scots institutions. A memorable moment has Connery driving off on a golf course followed by a golf ball striking the head of a statue of John Knox (*c*.1514–72), the historical lynchpin of Scottish Calvinism.

As has been indicated, Grigor is also active across a range of creative practices outside cinema. In this context it is appropriate to consider his graphic work, which invariably gives a humorous twist to phenomena often treated solemnly in Scottish writing. There is in Scottish, as in Irish, culture a strong vein of victimhood, a pleasurable scab-scratching attended by lachrymose nostalgia. One such generative event is the Massacre of Glencoe (1692), in which members of the Clan Campbell, on the orders of the British government, murdered several of the Clan MacDonald. While mainstream Scottish culture wrung its hands and wiped the tears from its eyes on the 300th anniversary of that event, Grigor's take on it was to construct a montage of Glencoe with on one side a Campbell's soup tin and on the other the logo of the fast-food giant McDonald's. On a postcard of Holyroodhouse, Scottish residence of the British monarch, Grigor added to the background hills, and in the style of the famous Los Angeles sign, the word 'Holyrood'.

The melding of the ludic and the political is at the heart of what, in the Scottish context, is arguably Grigor's most important work: *Scotch Myths* (1981–82). There was in 1979 a referendum on whether a devolved assembly would be set up in Edinburgh. Widely seen to have been gerrymandered, the referendum returned a negative vote but the paradoxical outcome was that the post-referendum energy which might have flowed into overtly political activity was channelled instead into culture. Grigor and other contemporary Scots intellectuals were familiar with Tom Nairn (1932–2023)'s essay 'Old and New Scottish Nationalism', which offered a scathing account of Scottish (popular) culture for not having been mobilised in the formation of the nation, as had been the case with other European nation-states.[5] To oversimplify somewhat, the dominant cultural discourses which instead emerged, under the sign of Romanticism, in Scotland from the eighteenth century on were Tartanry and Kailyard. *Scotch Myths* took these discourses apart. The project had begun in St Andrews in 1981 with an exhibition co-mounted by Grigor and his wife Barbara (1944–94), who, until her tragically early death, was a central organising and stabilising force on his work. The exhibition was primarily a delirious kaleidoscope of artefacts incarnating the dominant discourses of Tartanry and Kailyard:

postcards, tea towels, shortbread tins, whisky labels, souvenirs and popular songs. The Grigors identified the key historical figures who gave these discourses life: James 'Ossian' Macpherson (1736–96), Sir Walter Scott (1771–1832), Felix Mendelssohn (1809–47), Queen Victoria (1819–1901) and Prince Albert (1819–61), and Harry Lauder (1870–1950). It is significant that *Scotch Myths* transmogrified into a feature film version in 1982 less through the institutions of Scottish moving image culture than through yet another key Scots émigré in UK-wide broadcasting, Jeremy Isaacs, CEO of Channel 4. The filmic *Scotch Myths*, taking advantage of a special deal between the channel and the broadcast unions, was made for just £100,000, a perfect example of the kind of 'poor cinema' that contemporarily emergent Scottish film funding institutions such as the Scottish Film Production Fund (1982–97) might have encouraged, had their priorities not lain elsewhere.[6] The film's subsequent scheduling was itself a political act. Programmed round midnight on 31 December 1982 (Hogmanay is a key Scottish festival), it aired in deliberate competition and contrast with BBC Scotland and Scottish Television, both of which in this slot traditionally ran programmes constructed wholly within the discourses of Tartanry and Kailyard.

Classical Hollywood film narrative is of tangential interest to Grigor, who as a filmmaker is much more concerned with ideas, style, wit and texture. Such is the hegemony, however, of the classical Hollywood model that Grigor has on occasion made minimal gestures to it to allow projects to get off the ground. The ostensible story of *Scotch Myths* concerns a group of tourists lost on a Scottish moor which turns out to be Culloden Moor, site of the battle in 1746 which put paid to the pretensions of the House of Stuart to the British Crown. By foregrounding this icon of romantic Tartanry, Grigor signals the seriousness of his project. The tourists are side-tracked to Castle Dundreich to partake of 'the Dundreich Experience', Grigor's swipe at what may now be called the '*Braveheart*-isation' of Scotland, the impulse to render Scottish history as theme park. In a separate, equally tangential narrative strand, the famous Hollywood film director Samuel Fuller appears 'as himself' and upbraids his assistant for being unable to find Castle Dundreich on the map. This represents the other side of Grigor, his cinephilia. Appropriately enough in that regard, the scene in question also contains an additional film historical allusion. Anyone familiar with discussion of cinema in relation to Scotland would recognise that two figures lost in a mist-shrouded Scottish Highland landscape could refer only to *Brigadoon* (Vincente Minnelli, 1954). Grigor is telling his audience that his film is about not only Scottish history, but how that history is represented in discourse. Within the diverse historical charades of 'the Dundreich Experience', Grigor jettisons the classical narrative convention of the individual actor embodying a single character. Not only do the actors playing the diverse historical personages in most cases cover more than one role (Alex Norton, for example, variously plays James Boswell [1740–95], Robert Burns [1759–96], Napoleon Bonaparte [1769–1821], Felix Mendelssohn, Prince Albert and John Brown [1826–83]), but they adopt a declamatory style of delivery quite at odds with naturalistic acting. Its ludic elements apart, *Scotch Myths* is reminiscent of another great modernist, anti-naturalistic film, Hans-Jürgen Syberberg's *Ludwig: Requiem for a Virgin King* (1972). Like another non-naturalistic project nearer home, John McGrath (1935–2002)'s and John Mackenzie (1928–2011)'s *The Cheviot, the Stag and the Black, Black Oil* (1974), *Scotch Myths* is also Brechtian in its punctuation of narrative events with songs and is multi-discursive in accommodating naturalistic action, stylised performance and animation. The latter figures in one of the film's most accomplished sequences, in which Sir Walter Scott, with his faithful retainer (played by the Keaton-faced Scots comic, Chic Murray [1919–85]), 'tartans the kingdom', an imaginative rendering of the key role Scott played in what has been described as 'the invention of tradition'.[7]

I have described elsewhere, without too much exaggeration, the 'suppression' of *Scotch Myths* within Scotland, the officers of the Scottish Film Council (1934–97) dismissing it as irrelevant and banning its acquisition to their own film library and to the Scottish Film Archive.[8] A print of *Scotch Myths* would eventually find its way into the latter, not through the support of any of the indigenous film institutions, but by direct donation from Grigor himself. If *Scotch Myths* represents Grigor's engagement with the great internationally known discursive figures of Scottish (cultural) history, *Budgies Repaired Saturdays: A Wake for Bud Neill* (1993) marks his encounter with the most local and parochial of Scots artists. Bud Neill (1911–70) ran a comic strip in the *Glasgow Evening Times* from 1949 to 1955 entitled *Lobey Dosser*. Lobey Dosser (a Glasgow term for a rough sleeper who dossed rent-free in tenement lobbies) was the sheriff of Calton Creek, a mythical town ostensibly in the American West but whose denizens speak in the Glasgow idiom. Like so much else of Grigor's work, *Budgies* is a multi-discourse film made up of vox pop interviews, contemporary newsreels, animations of some of the original Neill strips and extracts from feature films (for example, those of actor William S. Hart [1864–1946]) Neill revered.

Some of Grigor's films (for example, *Clydescope* and *Scotch Myths*) have been given their due in that most even-handed critical account of Scottish cinema, Duncan Petrie's *Screening Scotland*.[9] The latter also moves deftly through the kaleidoscopic changes, from the early 1980s to the year 2000, within the public institutions supporting filmmaking in Scotland: Petrie provides a list of the feature films and shorts these funded over this period and an indication of the personnel involved. Grigor's name does not figure in this list. Part of the explanation for this is that he worked in the United States over the period 1983–86, first on an individual 1983 film on Frank Lloyd Wright and then on *Pride of Place*, an ambitious 1984 series of eight one-hour films on American architecture, both of which considerably enhanced his reputation in architectural circles. However, during the period covered by Petrie's list Grigor also worked on many projects in the UK, backed not by the indigenous Scottish film institutions but instead, most frequently, by Channel 4 (*E.P. Sculptor* [1987]; *The Demarco Dimension* [1989]; *The Great Wall of China* [1989]; *Irony Curtain: Art and Politics Between USA and USSR* [1990]; *The Why?s* Man [1990]; *Distilling* Whisky Galore! [1991]; *Carlo Scarpa* [1995]) and by Scottish Television (*The Why?s Man, The Fall and Rise of Mackintosh* [1991]; *Top Casting* [1993]; *Budgies*; *Fakelore: The Cultural Set-Aside (Scotland) Act* [1994]). A key element in Channel 4's and STV's respective support for Grigor's work at this time was the presence at senior levels within these organisations of figures who admired and understood that work, unlike analogous figures in the indigenous filmmaking institutions. Jeremy Isaacs remained as CEO of Channel 4 throughout much of this period and Gus Macdonald moved from Granada to Scottish Television, first as Director of Programmes, then as CEO. Throughout Grigor's CV there are only two mentions of the Scottish Film Production Fund. One is to its input to *Blue Black Permanent* (Margaret Tait, 1992), produced by Barbara Grigor, and the other to its modest input to *The Why?s Man*. Grigor also received small script development grants for *Green Fire*, about the Celtic Revival Scottish writer William Sharp (1855–1905) and his curious literary doppelganger (from 1893), Fiona Macleod, and another script, *Scotch Gothic*, but neither project received production funding.

The explanation for Grigor's name not otherwise figuring in Petrie's list of works supported by Scottish public film funding institutions between 1982 and 2000 is much more likely to have been structural rather than a matter of personal prejudice. Duncan Petrie traces the dialectic between culture and commerce within the Scottish filmmaking institutions of the period in question, culminating in the triumph of the commercial imperative.[10] Petrie, like many of the best people associated with public (part-) funding of national cinemas in different societies, remains cautiously optimistic that the culture/commerce dialectic can produce good results. The kind of films Petrie would offer as examples would be Peter Mullan's *Orphans* (1999) and Lynne Ramsay's *Ratcatcher* (1999). However, and here the argument reconnects with the question of Grigor's exclusion, both those films (and, indeed, the entire list of films Petrie outlines, with the possible exception of Timothy Neat's *Play Me Something* [1989]) subscribe in essential respects to the classical narrative norm. That implicit commitment is written across every policy initiative taken by the Scottish Film Production Fund and its successors, including: the setting-up of a script development fund; the drafting in of whisky magnate/Hollywood screenwriter Allan Shiach to senior roles within Scottish film culture; and the creation of short film mechanisms like Tartan Shorts to bring young filmmakers up in the faith, so to speak. Is it any wonder that the policy has been dubbed 'Hollywood on the Clyde'![11]

Scottish cinema's Gadarene rush to a financially, industrially and aesthetically Hollywoodean narrative model was not simply an aberration peculiar to Scotland. The process is discernible across the cultures of all developed countries, stemming, on the one hand, from an adoption of neoliberal economic policies within which every feature of society, including culture, must give 'value for money' and, on the other hand, the amoeba-like spread of what might be called 'story-structure' discourse. That discourse, emanating initially from the DIY screenwriting manuals and courses of Syd Field (1935–2013), Robert McKee and others, fetishises the 90-to-120-minute Hollywood feature film, asserting that the latter's characteristic structure (set-up, development and resolution; goal-driven protagonists and antagonists; plots and [often several] sub-plots; action arcs and false endings) constitutes a veritable definition of the essence of cinema. To opt for this structure carries discernible ideological costs, as Jonathan Murray demonstrates in his analysis of, among other 1990s Scottish films, *Rob Roy* (Michael Caton-Jones, 1995).[12] It is hardly surprising that some cinephiles, sated with the structured procrastination of this kind of cinema, should look to the cinemas of cultures (for example, Senegal, Iran) insulated from its economic and aesthetic determinants.

Cold-shouldered by Scottish filmmaking institutions, Grigor continued his cultural activism, mounting an exhibition entitled *Seeds of Change* (1992), timed to coincide with a European Economic Community summit in Edinburgh and (ironically) celebrating Scottish innovation and invention. His film *Nineveh on the Clyde – the Architecture of Alexander 'Greek' Thomson* (1999) did for its subject what Grigor's earliest films had done for Mackintosh and, like them, helped mobilise public opinion in support of threatened Thomson buildings in Scotland. Alongside these indigenous projects, Grigor embarked on a series of films on modernist architects, mostly funded outside Scotland. As was suggested at the outset, it would be wrong to suggest that Grigor has been wholly ignored in Scotland. On the one hand, he can be seen as a well-connected member of the Scottish arts establishment, not just Director but later Chair of the Edinburgh International Film Festival, a member of the board of Channel 4 from 1995 to 1999, appointed to the Scottish Broadcasting Commission in 2007, Fellow of the Royal Society of the Arts, Honorary Fellow of the Royal Incorporation of Architects in Scotland and the Royal Institution of British Architects, recipient of the Royal Television Society's Reith Award and, the final Establishment cachet, awarded the OBE in 2012 'for services to architecture and the film industry'. Set against all of these, however, is his relative absence from the funding rosters of the successive Scottish film funding institutions. These remain culpable in not providing production funding for Grigor's work. In particular, they missed the opportunity to develop with Grigor a progressive take on Scottish history, a gap filled by execrable films such as *Braveheart* (Mel Gibson, 1995). Germany has its Hans-Jürgen Syberberg, Italy its Luchino Visconti (1906–76), Hungary its Miklós Jancsó (1921–2014) and Greece its Theo Angelopoulos (1935–2012). But for the purblindness of successive indigenous film institutions, Grigor might have filled what remains the most egregious lacuna in Scottish cinema.

Notes

1. T. Howarth, *Charles Rennie Mackintosh and the Modern Movement* (London: Routledge & Kegan Paul, 1952), 193.
2. For further detail, see Jim Hillier, ed., Cahiers du cinéma, *the 1950s: Neo-Realism, Hollywood, New Wave* (London: Routledge & Kegan Paul in association with the British Film Institute, 1985); Emilie Bickerton, *A Short History of* Cahiers du cinéma (London: Verso Books, 2011).
3. For further detail, see Colin McArthur, 'The Rises and Falls of the Edinburgh International Film Festival', in *From Limelight to Satellite: A Scottish Film Book*, ed. Eddie Dick (London/Glasgow: British Film Institute/ Scottish Film Council, 1990), 91–102, and also reproduced elsewhere in the present volume.
4. Colin McArthur, '*Scotch Myths*, Scottish Film Culture and the Suppression of Ludic Modernism', in *Scottish Cinema Now*, eds Jonathan Murray, Fidelma Farley and Rod Stoneman (Newcastle: Cambridge Scholars Publishing, 2009), 39–55, and also reproduced elsewhere in the present volume.
5. Tom Nairn, *The Break-Up of Britain: Crisis and Neo-Nationalism* (London: New Left Books, 1977), 126–95.
6. Colin McArthur, 'In Praise of a Poor Cinema', *Sight and Sound* 3, no. 8 (August 1993), 30–2, and reproduced elsewhere in the present volume.

7. Eric Hobsbawm and Terence Ranger, eds, *The Invention of Tradition* (Cambridge: Cambridge University Press, 1983).
8. McArthur, '*Scotch Myths*'.
9. Duncan Petrie, *Screening Scotland* (London: British Film Institute, 2000), 118–9; 127–8.
10. Duncan Petrie, 'Cinema and the Economics of Representation: Public Funding of Film in Scotland', in *The Edinburgh Companion to Contemporary Scottish Literature*, ed. Berthold Schoene (Edinburgh: Edinburgh University Press, 2009), 362–70.
11. The present writer has used this term extensively, but it has also figured centrally in the press, both elite and popular. See, for example, Geoffrey Macnab, 'Hollywood on the Clyde: Why filmmakers love Glasgow', *The Independent*, 20 September 2011, 14–16.
12. Jonathan Murray, *The New Scottish Cinema* (London: I.B. Tauris, 2015).

Author's Afterword

Colin McArthur

Roland Barthes (1915–80) asserted that no text is a closed, stand-alone structure but rather a 'tissue of quotations'[1] endlessly open to connections with other texts. Put another way, every text is overdetermined, made as it is by other texts as much as (and perhaps even more than) by the conscious effort of its author. Barthes might have added that this multiply diverse parenthood extends also to institutions. Looking back over the essays in this book, I am struck by how heavily overdetermined many of them are. Within the period 1968–84, when I worked for the British Film Institute, the three institutional sites I concentrated on were the BFI itself (both in terms of policy and administration), the Council for National Academic Awards (1965–93), which, through its diverse subject boards, validated degree proposals from (mainly) the British polytechnics that would go on to join the new universities from 1992, and the socialist newspaper *Tribune*, on which I was film critic from 1972 to 1978. The ideas and interventions underpinning these essays were rehearsed across the terrain of those institutions.

This book's first piece, on *Ashes and Diamonds* (Andrzej Wajda, 1958), was written somewhat earlier, in 1966. While I was a student I had seen Andrzej Wajda (1926–2016)'s graduation film from the Łodz Film School, *A Generation* (1955), and been overwhelmed by it. This response was replicated by Lindsay Anderson (1923–94): British culture's taking-up of Wajda's work, and Polish cinema more generally, was greatly enhanced by Anderson's celebration of it, most notably in the *New Statesman*.[2] When I joined the Education Department of the BFI in 1968 there was already a strong commitment to Polish cinema in that milieu, especially from Paddy Whannel (1922–80) and Bolesław Sulik (1929–2012), who, himself Polish, was not a member of the department but very closely involved with it. That commitment would result in a publication I edited for the department in 1970, *Andrzej Wajda: Polish Cinema*.[3] As to the actual critical method deployed in the *Ashes and Diamonds* essay, as a student

I had been very much influenced by American New Criticism and its formalist attention to literary effects.[4] This was the first critical method I would apply when I started writing about cinema, a method which, as it happens, is particularly congenial to Wajda's kind of cinema (unlike, say, that of Jean Renoir [1894–1979]). Almost contemporaneous with this was the emergence of the journal *Movie* in 1962, like all of us at that time heavily influenced by the auteurism of *Cahiers du cinéma*. Several contributors to *Movie* (most notably, Victor Perkins [1936–2016]) would embrace a broadly similar critical method, arrived at not by way of New Criticism, but through exposure to the writings of F. R. Leavis (1895–1978). Crucially, unlike much of academia today, the film director as the prime artist of the cinema was regarded as axiomatic.

The immediate contexts of 'The Roots of the Western' were rather different. Originally published in *Cinema* (UK), one of the lively student-edited film magazines which emerged in the UK in the late 1960s and early 1970s, mostly at the new universities such as Sussex, Essex and (somewhat later) Warwick, this essay marks the (primarily British) inflection away from 'pure' auteurism towards an appreciation of the importance of genre in generating cinematic meaning.[5] The piece is also much less concerned with formal(ist) analysis of individual Westerns than with the American historical contexts which made the Hollywood Western possible. Crucially important here was a University of London Extra-Mural Department course run (probably in 1966–67) by Alan Lovell (1935–2021) and Peter Wollen (1938–2019), *Myth and Genre in the American Cinema*, a course which would also profoundly shape my 1972 book *Underworld U.S.A.*[6] It was this course that introduced me to Henry Nash Smith (1906–86)'s book *Virgin Land: The American West as Symbol and Myth*, which (with 'The Roots of the Western') I now see as foreshadowing the critical method of revealing ideology at play in particular films which would so mark our critical endeavours in the late 1970s and thereafter.[7] It might be added that the binarism of Nash Smith's critical/historical categories (for example, Garden versus Desert) would feed into the emergent structuralism in British film culture, most notably in the first edition of Peter Wollen's *Signs and Meaning in the Cinema*.[8]

The author and editor of the present collection had made an early decision to include within it mainly relatively substantial essays from film periodicals and academic journals. However, the anonymous reviewers engaged by Edinburgh University Press to consider the worth and viability of the project made specific reference to the historical importance of the author's first monograph, *Underworld U.S.A.*, and its being no longer in print, and suggested that some extracts from it be included in the collection. The decision was made to include in their entirety the book's first two chapters and summaries of its two subsequent chapters, thus covering the genre-based sections of that text. The summaries in particular offered a retrospective opportunity to signal some criticisms of the original text.

The essay on *Pickup on South Street* (Samuel Fuller, 1953) emerged out of yet another context of the late 1960s, the Edinburgh International Film Festival (EIFF). Since its setting-up in 1947, John Grierson (1898–1972) and his friend and biographer Forsyth Hardy (1910–94) being central figures, the Festival's prime emphasis had been on the tradition of British Documentary specifically and realist cinema more generally. While concern with Hollywood cinema was not absent in the Festival's first two decades, sustained and strategic engagement with more popular generic forms would move into the foreground with the appointment of Murray Grigor as Director in 1967. The *Pickup on South Street* piece was included in a book of essays supporting the first major retrospective of a Hollywood director's films, held at EIFF in 1969.[9] Clearly marked by the auteurism of the time, the retrospective/book of essays model would characterise Grigor's period as EIFF Director but was also retained in the subsequent exploration of theoretical issues which succeeded the model's original auteurist focus. The critical method of the *Pickup* essay is (given it supported the Sam Fuller retrospective) substantially marked by auteurism but, like 'The Roots of the Western', it retains the historical and cultural contextualisation which would become a permanent feature of my essays as the question of ideology moved to the centre of critical concern.

The three immediate contexts of 'Politicising Scottish Film Culture' (written for an edition of *New Edinburgh Review* edited by Murray Grigor and devoted to film in Scotland) were the increasing political agitation in the country which would lead to the failed 1979 devolution referendum, the first tentative moves of the Scottish filmmaking community to constitute themselves as a collective and, more remotely, the publication of the first UK writings on the interface between cinema and identity politics.[10] I had reported, in my *Tribune* column early in 1976,[11] on the first Film Bang event which brought Scottish filmmakers together and within the half-decade following 'Politicising Scottish Film Culture', identity-based writings on women, blacks and gays in film surfaced. The essay deplores the fragmented nature of film culture in Scotland and calls for it to be addressed holistically as in the post-revolutionary Soviet Union, post-WWII Italy and the France of the New Wave. It also calls for ideological analysis to be privileged, and this latter point reflects the then-current influence of the journal *Screen*, as does the specific example of ideological analysis offered within the essay, the seven-category framework by Jean-Louis Comolli (1941–2022) and Jean Narboni first published in *Cahiers du cinéma* and translated in *Screen* in 1971, but my essay substitutes examples drawn from Scottish films and television.[12] Although there is no extensive ideological analysis in the piece, that critical procedure would become a dominant theme of my subsequent writings,[13] as would the analysis of Scottish film culture.

'*Crossfire* and the Anglo-American Critical Tradition' was a contribution solicited by not quite a student magazine, but an independent film journal, *Film Form*, set up and edited by a recent graduate, Tony Harrild. Writing *Underworld U.S.A.* had familiarised me with the stylistic tropes of the film noir, so I was taken aback by the extent to which most writings on a film I greatly admired, *Crossfire* (Edward Dmytryk, 1947), had either ignored or traduced its noir elements and discussed it primarily as a tract against antisemitism. The essay's insistence that the noir tropes are as much up there on the screen as the dialogue relating to antisemitism and require as much analysis hints at a theme which would become much more explicit in my later writings – the contention that stylistic features may carry ideological meanings. There is a certain irony here: while this essay argues that most writings on *Crossfire* are too preoccupied with history and neglectful of formal concerns, my later 1995 essay on *Casablanca* (Michael Curtiz, 1942), also included in the present volume, traduces most recent writings on that film for their neglect of history.

'Breaking the Signs: *Scotch Myths* as Cultural Struggle' is at one level a review of the 1981 exhibition of that name by Murray and Barbara Grigor (1944–94). But it also floats the term 'semiotics', which was then becoming increasingly current in Cultural Studies writing, and makes explicit the idea of cultural struggle, also circulating on the Left at the time.[14] This essay's deployment of the terms 'Tartanry' and 'Kailyard' (first introduced in relation to cinema in my 1976 *Tribune* review of Film Bang) would become increasingly central in many of my succeeding writings, as in 'Scotland and Cinema: The Iniquity of the Fathers'. The contexts underpinning 'Breaking the Signs' were the increasing cultural activity (waging politics by other means?) following the failed 1979 devolution referendum, but also the wider sweep of identity politics which impinged increasingly on contemporary film writings. The immediate context for the 'Scotland and Cinema' essay was, of course, the *Scotch Reels* event at the 1982 Edinburgh International Film Festival. That event followed the characteristic model the Festival had used throughout the late 1960s and 1970s, namely, a retrospective (this time, of films representing Scotland and the Scots) plus a supporting book of essays.[15] The essay became influential, if not hegemonic, in discussions of Scotland and cinema until increasingly critiqued by the writings (many of them influenced by emergent postmodernism) of a new generation of Scots academics.[16] Following the *Scotch Reels* event the members of the group associated with it entered into a productive relationship with the journal *Cencrastus* (1979–2006), during which the critical framework of *Scotch Reels* was applied, refined and broadened to include, in particular, the feminist dimension. My essay on *The Maggie* was one such intervention in *Cencrastus*.

Three mid-1980s essays, 'TV Commercials: Moving Statues and Old Movies', 'Tele-history: *The Dragon Has Two Tongues*' and '*Scotland's Story*', all involve responses to television, which I had engaged with intermittently over the years. The first had been commissioned for a volume presenting itself as analogous to Roland Barthes's *Mythologies* (1957) but traversing UK television.[17] It explores the concept of intertextuality, increasingly deployed in cultural analysis at this time. The second essay is part of the *Cencrastus* intervention and, incidentally, the TV historical series which it analyses is one of the few creative endeavours to explicitly credit the influence of critical writing (in this case, my 1978 monograph *Television and History*) on its form. The third is a review of Scottish Television's mid-1980s historical series and deploys the critical categories adumbrated in the *Scotch Reels* essay.

The 1938 Glasgow Empire Exhibition essay reflects the increasing association of the Film Studies movement with other sites of cultural analysis, including the BBC, the Centre for Contemporary Cultural Studies (1964–2002) at Birmingham University and, in this case, the Popular Culture team at the Open University. In my own case this relationship began with the team running (in an earlier OU volume) a dossier entitled *History, Politics and Classical Narrative*, which included extracts from my *Television and History* monograph and my contribution in *Screen* to the debate surrounding *Days of Hope*, a 1975 four-part TV series by writer Jim Allen (1926–99), director Ken Loach and producer Tony Garnett (1936–2020) covering British working-class history over the period 1916 to 1926.[18] That dossier also included a piece by another *Scotch Reels* contributor, John Caughie. The 1938 Exhibition essay was included in a later OU anthology, *Popular Culture and Social Relations* (1986), within a section of that volume dealing with the historical application of the concept of hegemony associated with the Italian Marxist thinker Antonio Gramsci (1891–1937). The introduction to the volume by one of its co-editors refers to 'the turn to Gramsci', alluding to this figure's displacing of Louis

Althusser (1918–90) in British Marxist thought of the time and heralding a more flexible kind of Marxist analysis.[19] That said, such transitions do not involve one hermetically sealed method replacing another. The Empire Exhibition essay, for example, is as deeply marked by structuralist binarism as by Gramscian concepts. Indeed, the high-water mark of the influence of structuralism on my writing is the 1997 essay 'Chinese Boxes and Russian Dolls: Tracking the Elusive Cinematic City', which was commissioned by an urban geographer, David B. Clarke, for a volume entitled *The Cinematic City*.[20] The essay is constructed round the opposition city/country and follows this, and its accreted antinomies, primarily through Hollywood cinema and the cinema of Weimar Germany. It draws particular attention to the fragility of all structuralist oppositions, how one or other side of the binary may be valorised or traduced according to the discursive situation within which it is functioning. Importantly, this essay also defends the pedagogical usefulness of structuralism as a critical method in the face of criticism by poststructuralists, most notably, that one side of the binary is invariably privileged.

'The Rises and Falls of the Edinburgh International Film Festival', while still interlaced with concepts from what had come to be called 'the *Scotch Reels* position', inaugurates a new set of concerns within my writing, one centred on the institutions of (Scottish) film culture rather than analyses of individual films. Often highly polemical and unsparing about what I saw as the defects of such institutions, my essays exploring such concerns would at the same time throw up operative concepts such as 'Poor Cinema' as alternatives to the (often inexplicit) film policies of these institutions. The essays 'The New Scottish Cinema?', 'In Praise of a Poor Cinema', 'Artists and Philistines: The Irish and Scottish Film Milieux' and 'Two Steps Forward, One Step Back: Cultural Struggle in the British Film Institute' can, in broad terms, be seen as exemplifying this 'institutional turn' within my work.

My 1996 essay 'The Scottish Discursive Unconscious' marks both a new inflection and a 'pulling-together' of several of my essays from 'Scotland and Cinema: The Iniquity of the Fathers' onwards. That idea was first alluded to three years earlier, in my essay 'Scottish Culture: A Reply to David McCrone', but then subsequently filled out and given fuller discussion here. My take on Scottish culture had always been (albeit implicitly) holistic, seeing that culture as determined by a limited range of hegemonic discourses. The theoretical concept of the Scottish Discursive Unconscious represents my attempt to render that holistic quality explicit; it would be further deployed and extended in my subsequent essay, 'Transatlantic Scots, Their Interlocutors and the Scottish Discursive

Unconscious'. The 2001 essay 'Caledonianising *Macbeth*, or, How Scottish is the Scottish Play?' is also marked by the increasing centrality within my work of the concept of 'discourse', although it tends to be contextualised in relation to a piece, 'Out, damned Scot: A tale of sound and fury', that I wrote for the *New Statesman* in 1999 in response to a recent recommendation by the Scottish Consultative Committee on the Curriculum that *Macbeth* be excluded from the compulsory Scottish section of the new Scottish secondary school Higher qualification in English and Communication on account of its being 'not Scottish enough'.[21] The piece was therefore part of the (often heated) debate arising from that recommendation. That 'Caledonianising *Macbeth*' is seen as a longer version of the same argument relates to the differing timescales of journalistic and academic publishing. Although published in 2001, 'Caledonianising *Macbeth*' was in fact written before 'Out, damned Scot', in response to a conversation with a Scots academic contemplating editing a book on Shakespeare and Scotland. Finding his timetable rather too extended, I opted to publish the piece as a journal article. It is therefore altogether 'cooler' and less polemical than the associated *New Statesman* piece. 'Wake for a Glasgow Culture Hero', an enthusiastic review of Murray Grigor's film about the Glasgow newspaper cartoonist Bud Neill (1911–70), is the first of several homages to the work of this Scottish filmmaker and graphic artist who I identified as embodying the precepts of Poor Cinema. It can usefully be grouped with '*Scotch Myths*, Scottish Film Culture and the Suppression of Ludic Modernism' and 'Vanished or Banished? Murray Grigor as Absent Scots Auteur'. Most of the remaining essays are less tightly bound into the dominant 'Scottish film culture and its institutions' framework which forms the spine of this book, although both 'A Dram for All Seasons' and '*Braveheart* and the Scottish Aesthetic Dementia' could well fit into this. The former was a response to a request from the founder of the Scotch Malt Whisky Society, Phillip Hills, for a piece on the history of whisky advertising, and the latter a response to one from Australian historian Tony Barta, who was editing a collection of essays on the interface between history and cinema.

My friend and sometime colleague Richard Dyer once observed that if he ever again heard the words 'Gay' and 'Film' conjoined he would scream. He was, of course, referring to the plight of the academic who works recurrently on a particular topic and is thereafter stereotyped as 'the guy who [. . .]'. Several of the essays collected in this volume mark my own flight from the 'Scotland and Cinema' tag but were also penned out of enthusiasm or irritation in particular cases. 'The Exquisite Corpse of R(abelais) C(opernicus) Nesbitt' reflects my great affection for that character and the TV series which bears his name and argues (contra the

Scottish 'unco guid') that, far from being a blight on the city of Glasgow and Scotland more generally, it should be celebrated, not least for its progressive qualities. Likewise, '*Mise-en-scène* Degree Zero: Jean-Pierre Melville's *Le Samouraï*' reflects my admiration for this film and its director's work more generally. Elsewhere, when Ian Christie became Professor of Film at the University of Kent, one of his projects was the setting-up of the journal *Film Studies* and he solicited a contribution. As it happened, I had just been teaching, at the University of Warwick, a course on Alfred Hitchcock (1899–1980) that looked at the diverse critical paradigms within which his work had been discussed. I noted with irritation the absence of 'the class paradigm' and this irritation was further fuelled by my learning that at the 1989 conference of the leading US organisation of film and television academics, the decision had been taken to drop the term 'class' from the Task Force on Race and Class. This seemed to me symptomatic of the virtual abandonment of class as a critical category in recent writing about cinema. Irritation also fuelled the writing of 'Culloden: A Preemptive Strike', 'Bring Furrit the Tartan-Necks! Nationalist Intellectuals and Scottish Popular Culture' and '*Casablanca*: Where Have All the Fascists Gone?' The target of the first two essays was those Scots intellectuals who, for shabby political reasons, let Scottish popular culture too easily off the hook, and that of the third those who foreground discourses of romance at the expense of history when discussing *Casablanca*.

Although the wider Scottish culture – and within it, also some Scottish (film) academics – does not (or does no longer) agree with the arguments which recur throughout the essays in this book, I consider them still to pose important aesthetic and political questions for that culture. My final film column for *Tribune* in 1978 was entitled 'A Socialist Film Critic's Valedictory', part of which reads:

> Clearly my position has changed and developed over the years: the change could be summed up as a process of conscious and explicit politicisation. This obviously came about as much through impulses outside of film culture as within it: the shock waves of the events in Paris of May 1968 and their delayed repercussions in British education and culture; the necessity of having to take up a position on issues such as the escalating American involvement in Vietnam and the analogous escalation of British involvement in Ulster (and perhaps more importantly finding a theoretical framework within which these apparently disparate events related to each other); the spectacle of British capitalism falling apart and the necessity of understanding what was happening; the increased penetration into British culture of European Marxist writings (including writings on aesthetics); and, above all, an increasingly urgent wish to bring into relationship one's life in film and one's life in politics. Gradually I began to think of myself not as a film reviewer trying to do a more explicit and systematic job than the average

bourgeois film reviewer, but as a socialist film journalist describing and interrogating from a socialist perspective all the impulses, mechanisms and institutions of a complex film culture.²²

Plus ça change, plus c'est la même chose!

Notes

In too many (film) books the illustrations do not earn their place in the text, rather they lie inert within it, being little more than decorative. I have always tried to render illustrations active by ensuring that their captions anchor them firmly within the text, often by using quotations from the latter. I have tried to maintain this within this book.

Due to its unusual length, and associated budgetary constraints, it has not been possible fully to reproduce the extensive illustrations in some of the books and journals in which the essays and book chapters herein originally appeared. Perusing the following items in their original settings may offer readers an enhanced sense of the arguments being made as much by illustration as by text: *Crossfire and the Anglo-American Critical Tradition; Breaking the Signs: Scotch Myths as Cultural Struggle; The Dialectic of National Identity: the 1938 Glasgow Empire Exhibition; A Dram for All Seasons: the Diverse Identities of Scotch; Braveheart and the Scottish Aesthetic Dementia; The Critics Who Knew Too Little: Hitchcock and the absent Class Paradigm*; and *Culloden: a Pre-emptive Strike*. Readers sourcing the latter may be a little puzzled since the relevant pages in the original journal, though extensively illustrated, are bound in the wrong order.

1. Roland Barthes, 'The Death of the Author', in Roland Barthes, *Image, Music, Text*, trans. Stephen Heath (London: Fontana, 1977), 149.
2. See, for example, Lindsay Anderson, 'Anti-System', *New Statesman*, 12 October 1957, 460.
3. Colin McArthur, ed., *Andrzej Wajda: Polish Cinema – A BFI Education Department Dossier* (London: First Media Press, 1970).
4. See, for example, Cleanth Brooks, *The Well Wrought Urn: Studies in the Structure of Poetry* (Norfolk, CT: New Directions, 1947); John Crowe Ransom, *The New Criticism* (New York: Harcourt Brace, 1941).
5. For contemporaneous examples of that inflection, see Jim Kitses, *Horizons West* (London: Thames & Hudson in association with the British Film Institute, 1969); Ed Buscombe, 'The Idea of Genre in the American Cinema', *Screen* 11, no. 2 (1971), 33–45.
6. Colin McArthur, *Underworld U.S.A.* (London: Secker & Warburg for the British Film Institute, 1972).
7. Henry Nash Smith, *Virgin Land: The American West as Symbol and Myth* (Cambridge, MA: Harvard University Press, 1950).

8. Peter Wollen, *Signs and Meaning in the Cinema* (London: Secker & Warburg for the British Film Institute, 1969).
9. David Will and Peter Wollen, eds, *Samuel Fuller* (Edinburgh: Edinburgh Film Festival '69 in association with Scottish International Review, 1969), 28–31.
10. See, for example, Claire Johnston, *Notes on Women's Cinema* (London: Society for Education in Film and Television, 1973); Jim Pines, *Blacks in Films: A Survey of Racial Themes and Images in the American Cinema* (London: Studio Vista, 1975).
11. Colin McArthur, 'Building a Scottish Film Culture', in Colin McArthur, *Dialectic! Left Film Criticism from* Tribune (London: Key Texts, 1982), 64–5.
12. Jean-Louis Comolli and Jean Narboni, 'Cinema/Ideology/Criticism', in Screen *Reader 1: Cinema/Ideology/Politics*, ed. John Ellis (London: Society for Education in Film and Television, 1977), 12–35.
13. See, for example, Colin McArthur, *Television and History* (London: British Film Institute, 1978).
14. The term 'semiotics' had been first publicly circulated in British culture by Wollen's *Signs and Meaning in the Cinema*. The idea of cultural struggle moved to the centre of Left thinking with the increasing presence of Gramscian thought in the UK. The papers presented at, for example, the annual Communist University of London throughout the 1970s reflect this and a late example of its percolating into book form is: Tony Bennett, 'Hegemony, Ideology, Pleasure: Blackpool', in *Popular Culture and Social Relations*, eds Tony Bennett, Colin Mercer and Janet Woollacott (Milton Keynes: Open University Press, 1986), 135–53. Bennett's essay deals with the struggle between 'respectable' and 'popular' culture to 'own' Blackpool.
15. Colin McArthur, ed., *Scotch Reels: Scotland in Cinema and Television* (London: British Film Institute, 1982).
16. See, for example, John Caughie, 'Representing Scotland: New Questions for Scottish Cinema', in *From Limelight to Satellite: A Scottish Film Book*, ed. Eddie Dick (London/Glasgow: British Film Institute/Scottish Film Council, 1990), 13–30; Cairns Craig, 'Nostophobia', in *Scottish Cinema Now*, eds Jonathan Murray, Fidelma Farley and Rod Stoneman (Newcastle upon Tyne: Cambridge Scholars Publishing, 2009), 56–71; David Goldie, 'Don't Take the High Road: Tartanry and Its Critics', in *From Tartan to Tartanry: Scottish Culture, History and Myth*, ed. Ian Brown (Edinburgh: Edinburgh University Press, 2010), 232–45.
17. Len Masterman, ed., *Television Mythologies: Stars, Shows and Signs* (London: Comedia, 1984).
18. Colin McArthur, '*Days of Hope*', Screen 16, no. 4 (1975), 139–44.
19. Tony Bennett, 'Introduction: Popular culture and "the turn to Gramsci"', in *Popular Culture and Social Relations*, eds Bennett et al., xi–xix.
20. David B. Clarke, ed., *The Cinematic City* (London: Routledge, 1997).
21. Colin McArthur, 'Out, damned Scot: A tale of sound and fury', *New Statesman*, 18 October 1999, 43–4.
22. Colin McArthur, 'A Socialist Film Critic's Valedictory, in McArthur, *Dialectic!*, 24–5.

Select Bibliography

Books

Barthes, Roland. *Image, Music, Text*. Edited and translated by Steven Heath. London: Fontana, 1977.

Beveridge, Craig and Ronald Turnbull. *The Eclipse of Scottish Culture: Inferiorism and the Intellectuals*. Edinburgh: Polygon, 1989.

Blain, Neil and David Hutchison, eds. *The Media in Scotland*. Edinburgh: Edinburgh University Press, 2008.

Chapman, Malcolm. *The Gaelic Vision in Scottish Culture*. London: Croom Helm, 1978.

Craig, Cairns. *Out of History: Narrative Paradigms in Scottish and English Culture*. Edinburgh: Polygon, 1996.

Craig, Cairns. *The Modern Scottish Novel: Narrative and the National Imagination*. Edinburgh: Edinburgh University Press, 1999.

Dick, Eddie, ed. *From Limelight to Satellite: A Scottish Film Book*. London/Glasgow: British Film Institute/Scottish Film Council, 1990.

Fanon, Frantz. *Black Skin, White Masks*. New York: Grove Press, 1968.

Hall, Stuart and Paddy Whannel. *The Popular Arts*. London: Hutchinson, 1964.

Hardy, Forsyth. *Slightly Mad and Full of Dangers: The Story of the Edinburgh Film Festival*. Edinburgh: The Ramsay Head Press, 1992.

Hechter, Michael. *Internal Colonialism: The Celtic Fringe in British National Development*. London: Routledge, 1975.

Hill, John, Martin McLoone and Paul Hainsworth, eds. *Border Crossing: Film in Ireland, Britain and Europe*. London/Belfast: British Film Institute/Queen's University Institute of Irish Studies, 1994.

Hillier, Jim, ed. Cahiers du cinéma, *the 1950s: Neo-Realism, Hollywood, New Wave*. London: Routledge & Kegan Paul in association with the British Film Institute, 1985.

Hobsbawm, Eric and Terence Ranger, eds. *The Invention of Tradition*. Cambridge: Cambridge University Press, 1983.

Huyssen, Andreas. *After the Great Divide: Modernism, Mass Culture, Postmodernism*. Bloomington: Indiana University Press, 1986.

Lloyd, Matthew. *How the Movie Brats Took Over Edinburgh: The Impact of Cinephilia on the Edinburgh International Film Festival, 1968–1980*. St Andrews: St Andrews Film Studies, 2010.

McArthur, Colin, ed. *Andrzej Wajda: Polish Cinema – A BFI Education Department Dossier*. London: First Media Press, 1970.
McArthur, Colin. *Underworld U.S.A*. London: Secker & Warburg for the British Film Institute, 1972.
McArthur, Colin. *Television and History*. London: British Film Institute Educational Advisory Service, 1978.
McArthur, Colin. *Dialectic! Left Film Criticism from* Tribune. London: Key Texts, 1982.
McArthur, Colin, ed. *Scotch Reels: Scotland in Cinema and Television*. London: British Film Institute, 1982.
McArthur, Colin. *The Big Heat*. London: British Film Institute, 1992.
McArthur, Colin. *The* Casablanca *File*. London: Half Brick Images, 1992.
McArthur, Colin. Brigadoon, Braveheart *and the Scots: Distortions of Scotland in Hollywood Cinema*. London: I.B. Tauris, 2003.
McArthur, Colin. Whisky Galore! *and* The Maggie. London: I.B. Tauris, 2003.
McArthur, Colin. *Along the Great Divide: High Art, Mass Art and Classic Hollywood Narrative* (London: Independent Publication, 2020).
McCrone, David. *Understanding Scotland: The Sociology of a Stateless Nation*. London: Routledge, 1992.
Martin-Jones, David. *Scotland: Global Cinema*. Edinburgh: Edinburgh University Press, 2009.
Meir, Christopher. *Scottish Cinema: Texts and Contexts*. Manchester: Manchester University Press, 2015.
Murray, Jonathan. *That Thinking Feeling: a Research Guide to Scottish Cinema*. Edinburgh: Edinburgh College of Art and Scottish Screen, 2004.
Murray, Jonathan. *Discomfort and Joy: The Cinema of Bill Forsyth*. Oxford: Peter Lang, 2011.
Murray, Jonathan. *The New Scottish Cinema*. London: I.B. Tauris, 2015.
Murray, Jonathan, Fidelma Farley and Rod Stoneman, eds. *Scottish Cinema Now*. Newcastle: Cambridge Scholars Publishing, 2009.
Nairn, Tom. *The Break-Up of Britain: Crisis and Neo-Nationalism*. London: New Left Books, 1977.
Nairn, Tom. *Faces of Nationalism: Janus Revisited*. London: Verso, 1997.
Nairn, Tom. *After Britain: New Labour and the Return of Scotland*. London: Granta Books, 2000.
Nash Smith, Henry. *Virgin Land: The American West as Symbol and Myth*. Cambridge, MA: Harvard University Press, 1950.
Nowlan, Bob and Zach Finch, eds. *Directory of World Cinema: Scotland*. Bristol: Intellect Press, 2015.
Perkins, V. F. *Film as Film: Understanding and Judging Movies*. London: Penguin, 1972.
Petrie, Duncan. *Screening Scotland*. London: British Film Institute, 2000.
Petrie, Duncan. *Contemporary Scottish Fictions: Film, Television and the Novel*. Edinburgh: Edinburgh University Press, 2004.
Pittock, Murray. *The Invention of Scotland: The Stuart Myth and the Scottish Identity, 1638 to the Present*. London: Routledge, 1991.

Said, Edward. *Orientalism*. London: Routledge & Kegan Paul, 1978.
Spring, Ian. *Phantom Village: The Myth of the New Glasgow*. Edinburgh: Polygon, 1990.
Wollen, Peter. *Signs and Meaning in the Cinema*. London: Secker & Warburg in association with the British Film Institute, 1969.
Wollen, Peter and David Will, eds. *Samuel Fuller*. Edinburgh: Edinburgh Film Festival '69/Scottish International Review, 1969.

Articles and Chapters in Books

Cahiers du cinéma. 'John Ford's *Young Mr. Lincoln*'. In Screen *Reader 1: Cinema/Ideology/Politics*, edited by John Ellis, 113–52. London: Society for Education in Film and Television, 1977.
Caughie, John. 'Representing Scotland: New Questions for Scottish Cinema'. In *From Limelight to Satellite: A Scottish Film Book*, edited by Eddie Dick, 13–30. London/Glasgow: British Film Institute/Scottish Film Council, 1990.
Comolli, Jean-Louis and Jean Narboni. 'Cinema/Ideology/Criticism'. In *Screen Reader 1: Cinema/Ideology/Politics*, edited by John Ellis, 12–35. London: Society for Education in Film and Television, 1977.
Craig, Cairns. 'Myths Against History: Tartanry and Kailyard in 19th-Century Scottish Literature'. In *Scotch Reels: Scotland in Cinema and Television*, edited by Colin McArthur, 7–15. London: British Film Institute, 1982.
Craig, Cairns. 'Nostophobia'. In *Scottish Cinema Now*, edited by Jonathan Murray, Fidelma Farley and Rod Stoneman, 56–71. Newcastle: Cambridge Scholars Publishing, 2009.
Dick, Eddie. 'Poor Wee Scottish Cinema?'. *Scottish Film*, no. 10 (1994), 19–23.
Giulianotti, Richard. 'Scotland's Tartan Army in Italy: The Case for the Carnivalesque'. *Sociological Review* 39, no. 3 (1991), 503–27.
Goldie, David. 'Don't Take the High Road: Tartanry and Its Critics'. In *From Tartan to Tartanry: Scottish History, Culture and Myth*, edited by Ian Brown, 232–45. Edinburgh: Edinburgh University Press, 2010.
Hill, John. 'Revisiting British Film Studies'. *Journal of British Cinema and Television* 7, no. 2 (2010), 299–310.
Lovell, Alan. 'The BFI and Film Education'. *Screen* 12, no. 3 (Autumn 1971), 13–26.
McArthur, Colin. 'Samuel Fuller's Gangster Films'. *Screen* 10, no. 6 (1969), 93–101.
McArthur, Colin. '*Days of Hope*'. *Screen* 16, no. 4 (1975), 139–44.
McArthur, Colin. '*Scotch Reels* and After'. *Cencrastus*, no. 11 (New Year 1983), 2–3.
McArthur, Colin. 'British Film Reviewing, a Complaint'. *Screen* 26, no. 1 (1985), 79–85.
McArthur, Colin. 'Scotland and the *Braveheart* Effect'. *Journal for the Study of British Cultures* 5, no. 1 (1998), 27–39.
McArthur, Colin. 'Implementing Cultural Policy: The Case of the BFI Distribution Library'. *Cinema Journal* 47, no. 4 (Summer 2008), 147–52.

McBain, Janet. 'Scotland in Feature Film: A Filmography'. In *From Limelight to Satellite: A Scottish Film Book*, edited by Eddie Dick, 233–53. London/Glasgow: British Film Institute/Scottish Film Council, 1990.

Murray, Jonathan. 'Convents or Cowboys? Millennial Scottish and Irish Cinemas and *The Magdalene Sisters*'. In *National Cinemas and Beyond: Studies in Irish Film I*, edited by John Hill and Kevin Rockett, 149–60. Dublin: Four Courts, 2004.

Murray, Jonathan. 'Sibling rivalry? Contemporary Scottish and Irish cinemas'. In *Ireland and Scotland: Culture and Society, 1707–2000*, edited by Liam McIlvanney and Ray Ryan, 144–63. Dublin: Four Courts, 2005.

Murray, Jonathan. 'Straw or Wicker? Traditions of Scottish Film Criticism and *The Wicker Man*'. In *Constructing* The Wicker Man*: Film and Cultural Studies Perspectives*, edited by Jonathan Murray, Benjamin Franks, Stephen Harper and Lesley Stevenson, 11–36. Dumfries: University of Glasgow Crichton Publications, 2005.

Murray, Jonathan. 'Trainspotter's Delight: Issues and Themes in Scottish Film Criticism'. In *A Companion to British and Irish Cinema*, edited by John Hill, 490–509. Hoboken, NJ: Wiley-Blackwell, 2019.

Warshow, Robert. 'The Gangster as Tragic Hero'. In *The Gangster Film Reader*, edited by Alain Silver and James Ursini, 11–16. Pompton Plains, NJ: Limelight Editions, 2007.

Will, David. 'Edinburgh'. *Framework*, no. 20 (1983), 49–53.

Index of Names

Ahmad, Aijaz, 493
Akerman, Chantal, 118
Albert, Prince, 452, 507
Althusser, Louis, 94n, 466n
Álvarez, Santiago, 118
Anderson, Lindsay, 246, 388–9, 513
Angelopoulos, Theo, 118, 176, 178, 511
Arnold, Matthew, 260, 405
Arzner, Dorothy, 438
Ascherson, Neal, 339, 343–4, 348n
Aubrey, Douglas, 227, 239

Barr, Charles, 128, 386
Barrie, J. M., 100, 164, 352, 452, 461, 495
Barta, Tony, 519
Barthes, Roland, 8, 207, 262, 364, 513, 517
Bateman, H. M., 393–5
Bazin, André, 3, 35, 54, 411, 438
Beckett, Samuel, 470, 505
Benjamin, Walter, 307
Bertolucci, Bernardo, 118
Beveridge, Craig, 283, 491–3
Bhabha, Homi, 241, 306–7, 412
Blake, George, 103, 105
Boetticher, Budd, 38, 53
Bogart, Humphrey, 56, 140, 273, 275, 299, 354
Brecht, Bertolt, 72, 474
Bresson, Robert, 225, 237, 246
Briggs, Asa, 432
Brown, Ian, 498
Brown, John, 478–9
Bryden, Bill, 352, 477
Burns, Robert, 89, 356–7

Cagney, James, 56–7, 61–2, 140, 299, 354
Caughie, John, 11, 517
Chapman, Malcolm, 126, 152, 162, 174, 214, 241, 243, 281–2, 285, 338, 406, 452
Clark, Arthur Melville, 405, 413
Cocteau, Jean, 372
Cohen, Elliot, 82–3
Comolli, Jean-Louis, 72, 176, 179
Connery, Sean, 353–4, 419, 456, 506
Connolly, Billy, 93, 114–15, 357, 505
Conte, Richard, 56
Craig, Cairns, 20, 349, 355, 359, 454, 491–5, 498
Crockett, S. R., 452, 495
Crumlish, Brian, 225, 479
Cynicus (aka Martin Anderson), 91–2, 495

de Rochemont, Louis, 62
De Sica, Vittorio, 311
Dick, Eddie, 322, 478–9
Douglas, Bill, 225, 246
Dyer, Richard, 303, 519

Eadie, Douglas, 479
Eagleton, Terry, 496
Eisenstein, Sergei, 71, 237, 245
Eliot, T. S., 355–6, 498
Ellis, John, 431
Engholm, Sir Basil, 439

Fanon, Frantz, 127, 131n, 152, 163, 174, 199, 241, 282, 350, 451
Field, Syd, 222, 237, 480, 510
Fisher, Gregor, 360

Ford, John, 37, 51–3, 216n, 245, 438, 477
Forsyth, Bill, 116, 172, 174, 211, 221, 225, 242, 279–80, 319, 450
Forsyth, Michael, 320–1, 342, 480
Foucault, Michel, 207, 311n, 451
Fountain, Alan, 223
Freeman, John, 439
Freud, Sigmund, 231, 250
Friedrich, Caspar David, 89, 335
Fuller, Sam, 45–8, 49, 188, 472–4, 504

Gerz, Esther, 267–8
Gerz, Jochen, 267–8
Geuens, Jean-Pierre, 480
Gilbert, Colin, 353, 361–2, 469
Gilroy, Paul, 458
Giulianotti, Richard, 207, 345
Godard, Jean-Luc, 71, 118, 176, 179, 237
Goldie, David, 496–8
Goldman, William, 222, 237, 481
Gramsci, Antonio, 133, 138n, 358, 428 517–18
Gregson, John, 107–8
Grierson, John, 71, 107, 111–13, 182, 184, 187, 193n, 388–9, 473, 504, 515
Griffith, D. W., 99, 437
Grigor, Barbara, 5, 85, 114, 348n, 470, 490, 506, 509, 516
Grigor, Murray, 5, 13, 19–20, 74n, 85, 90, 94n, 114–15, 168, 186–7, 215, 225, 229–30, 286, 325, 469–75, 478–9, 481, 490, 503–12, 515–16, 519

Hall, Stuart, 187, 205, 215, 427, 429, 450, 465
Halliday, Fred, 487–8, 491–2, 499
Hardy, Forsyth, 108, 111, 115, 181–2, 184, 187, 190, 473, 504, 515
Harrild, Tony, 516

Harvey, David, 307
Has, Wojciech, 246
Hawks, Howard, 53, 216n, 438
Henson, Laurence, 112, 479
Heston, Charlton, 339
Hickey, Jim, 74n, 189, 191, 235
Higgins, Michael D., 321
Hill, Alan, 434
Hills, Phillip, 519
Hillier, Jim, 429, 432
Hitchcock, Alfred, 17–18, 129, 298, 385–402
Hitchcock, Emma Jane, 391, 393
Hitchcock, William, 389–90
Hofstadter, Richard, 45
Huillet, Danièle, 118

Isaacs, Jeremy, 359, 471, 507

James, David, 387
Jansco, Miklós, 178, 483, 511
Jarman, Derek, 225, 237
Joyce, James, 351, 470–1, 505
Joyce, Patrick, 387

Kane, Pat, 490
Kapsis, Robert E., 385
Kazan, Elia, 49, 364
Kefauver, Senator Estes, 45, 47, 65
Kelman, James, 350–1, 494–5
Kitses, Jim, 429, 432, 446n
Knight, Arthur, 77
Kracauer, Siegfried, 84n, 307
Kuhn, Annette, 460, 462

Lacan, Jacques, 428
Lang, Fritz, 49, 58, 245
Lauder, Harry, 93, 99, 169, 452, 454, 462–3, 471, 496–8, 507
Leavis, F. R., 51, 514
Lee, Jennie, 430, 435
Lenin, Vladimir, 252, 266
Leonard, Tom, 351
Lin, Maya, 252

Lindgren, Ernest, 432
Lochhead, Liz, 221, 351, 358
Lockerbie, Ian, 478–9
Longstaffe, Ernest, 89
Lovell, Alan, 54, 386, 429, 431–2, 514
Lowndes, Douglas, 433–5, 444
Lucas, Keith, 434, 439–44
Lye, Len, 246

MacCabe, Colin, 351, 444, 445n
McColl, Ranald, 229, 232
McConnell, Eddie, 112, 479
McCrone, David, 11, 205–17, 283
MacDiarmid, Hugh, 286, 356, 496
MacDonald, Flora, 157, 260–2
Macdonald, Gus, 505, 509
McGrath, John, 469
Macherey, Pierre, 145, 364–5, 490
McIntyre, Steve, 478–9
Mackay, James, 225, 244
McKee, Robert, 222, 237, 480, 510
Mackendrick, Alexander, 7, 102, 125, 127, 174, 279
Mackenzie, John, 469, 508
Mackintosh, Charles Rennie, 114, 503
McLaren, Norman, 246
MacLeod, Colin, 225
McLoone, Martin, 327
Macpherson, James, 87, 98, 168, 204n, 212, 255, 284, 337, 406, 452, 471, 507
McRobbie, Angela, 451
Makavejev, Dušan, 118, 237
Marwick, Eric, 169
Marx, Karl, 39, 491
Melville, Jean-Pierre, 17, 49, 327, 371–83
Minnelli, Vincente, 102, 245, 281
Mizoguchi, Kenji, 177, 246
Morgan, Edwin, 351, 356–7
Morton, H. V., 154, 259, 496–7
Mulloy, Phil, 118
Mulvey, Laura, 118
Murnau, F. W., 177, 309

Murray, Chic, 476, 508
Murray, Jonathan, 248n, 510
Myles, Lynda, 74n, 187, 221, 504

Nairn, Tom, 8, 15, 20, 110, 133, 160–1, 173, 240, 260, 283, 317, 336, 338, 351, 457, 470, 488–91, 493, 495, 499, 506
Napier, Theodore, 263–4
Narboni, Paul, 72
Neill, Bud, 13, 229–33, 356, 508, 519
Neuberger, Rabbi Julia, 350
Nietzsche, Friedrich, 491

Ōshima, Nagisa, 118, 246
Ozu, Yasujirō, 237, 245

Parker, Alan, 445
Paterson, Lindsay, 85
Pattison, Ian, 353, 358, 361, 366
Peckinpah, Sam, 41, 52
Pendreigh, Brian, 213, 344, 449
Perkins, V. F., 175, 179, 429, 431, 514
Petley, Julian, 386, 388, 436–7
Petrie, Duncan, 479, 508–10
Pittock, Murray, 258, 265, 492–3
Polanski, Roman, 411, 415–18, 420
Pudovkin, Vsevolod, 71, 246

Rainer, Yvonne, 118
Rand, Ayn, 296–7
Ray, Celeste, 457–8
Ray, Nicholas, 40, 49, 51, 53, 179
Ray, Robert B., 366
Reed, Stanley, 430, 432–3
Renan, Ernest, 260, 405, 487
Renoir, Jean, 514
Rieupeyrout, Jean-Louis, 35, 54–5
Robinson, David, 189–91
Robinson, Edward G., 56
Rossellini, Roberto, 170, 183, 237, 245, 310–11
Rotha, Paul, 51, 71, 77, 81, 182–3
Ryall, Tom, 386, 388–9, 398–9

Said, Edward, 127, 152, 163, 174, 199, 241, 276, 282, 350, 451
Salmond, Alex, 342–3
Sartre, Jean-Paul, 372–3
Shiach, Alan (aka Alan Scott), 222, 236–7, 322–3, 478–9, 481, 510
Schlesinger, Philip, 209
Schoene, Berthold, 499
Scott, Adrian, 83
Scott, P. H., 85, 476–7
Scott, Sir Walter, 87, 89, 98, 113–14, 156, 164, 195, 201, 240, 255, 332, 337, 364, 452, 460, 462, 471, 507–8
Shakespeare, William, 18, 201, 403
Siegel, Don, 49
Siodmak, Robert, 49
Sirk, Douglas, 72, 75n, 188, 504
Smith, Anthony, 442, 444
Smith, Henry Nash, 36, 38, 52–3, 514
Snow, Michael, 118, 245
Spoto, Donald, 389–94
Staiger, Janet, 398–9
Stevenson, Robert Louis, 86, 451–2
Stoneman, Rod, 223, 322–4
Straub, Jean-Marie, 118
Sulik, Bolesław, 513
Swan, Kate, 222, 228n
Syberberg, Hans-Jürgen, 118, 176, 188, 246, 475, 508, 511

Taylor, Dwight, 45
Telford, Thomas, 113–14

Thomas, Colin, 148
Thomas, Wynford Vaughan, 146–9
Thomson, Penny, 235
Turnbull, Ronald, 206, 283, 491–3
Turner, Frederick Jackson, 36–7

Vardell, Dr Charles Graves, 261–2
Vertov, Dziga, 71, 246
Victoria, Queen, 197, 199, 255–6, 318, 337, 452, 507
Vigo, Jean, 246
Visconti, Luchino, 511

Wajda, Andrzej, 2, 29–34, 176, 246, 483, 513–14
Wallace, Randall, 16, 340–1
Wallerstein, Immanuel, 173
Warshow, Robert, 54, 58, 63, 305
Welles, Orson, 411–15
Welsh, Irvine, 351
Wenders, Wim, 327
Whannel, Paddy, 187, 429–30, 432, 436, 513
White, Hayden, 212, 284, 404
Widmark, Richard, 47, 56
Will, David, 187, 504
Williams, Christopher, 432
Williams, Gwyn Alf, 146–50
Williams, Raymond, 142n, 145, 429
Wilson, Norman, 181–2, 185, 187
Wollen, Peter, 66n, 118, 216n, 248n, 302, 307, 429, 431–2, 514

Film Titles

Aîné des Ferchaux, L' (France 1963), 373, 376, 381
Al Capone (USA 1959), 57
Alexander Nevsky (USSR 1938), 414
An American in Paris (USA 1951), 303, 305
Armeé des ombres, L' (France 1969), 375–6
Angels with Dirty Faces (USA 1938), 61
Ashes (Poland 1965), 483
Ashes and Diamonds (Poland 1958), 2, 29–34, 513
Asphalt Jungle, The (USA 1950), 58, 62, 373
Assignment to Kill (USA 1968), 59

Baby Face Nelson (USA 1957), 57
Ball of Fire (USA 1941), 437
Barkleys of Broadway, The (USA 1949), 292
Barbary Coast (USA 1939), 437
Bend of the River (USA 1952), 53
Berlin: Symphony of a Great City (Germany 1927), 308–9
Beside the Bonnie Brier Bush (USA 1921), 99
Best Years of Our Lives, The (USA 1946), 437
Beyond a Reasonable Doubt (USA 1956), 437
Bicycle Thieves (Italy 1949), 311
Big Banana Feet (UK 1977), 505
Big Heat, The (USA 1954), 47, 57–9, 427, 482

Big Man, The (UK 1990), 212
Big Mill, The (UK 1963), 112
Big Store, The (USA 1946), 309
Blanche (France 1971), 336
Blast (UK 1975), 504
Blow-Up (UK 1966), 306
Blue Lamp, The (UK 1950), 306
Bonnie Prince Charlie (UK 1923), 99
Bonnie Prince Charlie (UK 1948), 101
Brave Don't Cry, The (UK 1952), 107–8
Braveheart (USA 1995), 7–8, 16, 320, 326, 331–48, 417–19, 457, 480, 511
Brazil (UK 1985), 307
Brigadoon (USA 1954), 102, 241, 280–1, 303, 414, 462, 474, 507
Broken Arrow (USA 1950), 53
Broken Blossoms (USA 1919), 305
Brothers Rico, The (USA 1957), 47, 57
Bruce, The (UK 1995), 418
Brute Force (USA 1947), 48
Budgies Repaired Saturdays (UK 1994), 508

Cabaret (USA 1972), 305
Caledonian Account, The (UK 1976), 73, 113, 209, 241
Carabiniers, Les (France 1963), 179, 225, 246
Casablanca (USA 1942), 14, 273–7, 342
Cecilia, La (1975), 176, 179
Chagrin et la pitié, Le (France 1970), 375

Chasing the Deer (UK 1994), 418
Cheviot, the Stag and the Black, Black Oil, The (UK 1974), 73, 469, 508
Chimes at Midnight (Spain/Switzerland 1966), 412
Clydescope (UK 1974), 113–15, 209, 505
Commitments, The (Ireland 1991), 326
Cook, the Thief, His Wife and Her Lover, The (UK 1989), 307
Covered Wagon, The (USA 1924), 37, 42, 52, 54
Criss Cross (USA 1949), 62
Crossfire (USA 1947), 5, 64, 77–84, 437, 516
Crowd, The (USA 1928), 296
Cul de Sac (UK 1966), 417

Dark Corner, The (USA 1946), 59
Dark Eyes of London (UK 1937), 305
Day of Wrath (Denmark 1943), 337, 418
Dead End (USA 1957), 437
Death and the Maiden (UK/USA/France 1995), 416
deuxième souffle, Le (France 1966), 60, 275, 372, 374–6, 378–9, 381
Don't Look Back (USA 1967), 505
Double Indemnity (USA 1944), 373
doulos, Le (France 1962), 372, 374, 376, 378–80
Driver, The (USA 1978), 380
Drums Along the Mohawk (USA 1940), 37
Du rififi chez les hommes (France 1954), 374
Duna Bull, The (UK 1971), 115–16, 479

Far Country, The (USA 1954), 41, 53
Five Boys from Barska Street (Poland 1952), 311
Fixed Bayonets! (USA 1951), 46
Floodtide (UK 1949), 103–7, 309
Flying Down to Rio (USA 1933), 303

42nd Street (USA 1933), 303
Fountainhead, The (USA 1949), 296–8
Frenzy (USA/UK 1972), 395
Funny Face (USA 1957), 303, 305

'G' Men (USA 1936), 61
Garment Jungle, The (USA 1957), 59
Gaslight (UK 1944), 305
Generation, A (Poland 1955), 513
Germany, Year Zero (Italy 1947), 311
Gigi (USA 1958), 303
Gorbals Story, The (UK 1950), 310
Gregory's Girl (UK 1980), 226, 415
Guns in the Afternoon (aka *Ride the High Country*) (USA 1962), 38, 41, 53

Hammer and the Thistle, The (UK 1977), 114, 505
Hangover Square (USA 1945), 305
Harder They Fall, The (USA 1956), 55, 59–60
Heart of Scotland (UK 1961), 112
High Noon (USA 1952), 40, 53
Homecoming (Hong Kong 1984), 310
House of Bamboo (USA 1955), 47
Hud (USA 1961), 41
Hue and Cry (UK 1946), 311
Hurricane The (USA 1937), 437

I Confess (USA 1953), 395
Ill Fares the Land (UK 1983), 285, 477
In the Name of the Father (Ireland/UK 1993), 326
Informer, The (USA 1935), 437
Iron Horse, The (USA 1924), 40, 53

Jetée, La (France 1963), 225, 246
Johnny Guitar (USA 1954), 53, 179–80
Juarez (USA 1939), 335

Killing, The (USA 1956), 62
Kiss of Death (USA 1948), 47, 58
Knife in the Water (Poland 1962), 417

Last of England, The (UK 1987), 225, 307
Last Train from Gun Hill (USA 1959), 40
Last Wagon, The (USA 1956), 39
Laura (USA 1944), 373
Law and Jake Wade, The (USA 1958), 39
Lenin in Poland (Poland 1966), 483
Leopard, The (Italy 1964), 338
Lethal Weapon (USA 1987), 339
Lilac Sunbonnet, The (USA 1922), 99, 462
Little Caesar (USA 1930), 55, 57, 60–1, 299
Little Foxes, The (USA 1941), 437
Little Minister, The (USA 1934), 100
Local Hero (UK 1983), 131, 152, 174, 211, 242, 248n, 279–81, 295, 414, 450, 477
London Can Take It! (UK 1940), 306
Lonely Are the Brave (USA 1962), 41, 295
Lost Weekend, The (USA 1945), 373
Ludwig: Requiem for a Virgin King (Germany 1972), 225, 246, 475, 508

Macbeth (USA 1948), 18, 411–15
Macbeth (UK 1971), 18, 415–18
Macbeth (UK 1996), 18, 418–21
Machine-Gun Kelly (USA 1958), 59
Mackintosh (UK 1968), 113–14, 209, 504
Mad Max cycle (Australia 1979–2015), 339
Maggie, The (UK 1953), 7, 102, 116, 121–32, 174, 241–2, 279–80, 450, 517
Maltese Falcon, The (USA 1941), 61
Man with a Movie Camera (USSR 1929), 309
Man Without a Star (USA 1955), 37
Manhattan (USA 1921), 309

Manhattan (USA 1979), 303–4
Marnie (USA 1964), 396
Mary Poppins (USA 1964), 306
Metropolis (Germany 1927), 58, 140, 308
Michael Collins (USA/Ireland 1996), 326
Misfits, The (USA 1961), 41
Monty Python and the Holy Grail (UK 1975), 337
Moving Target, The (USA 1966), 59
Mr. and Mrs. Smith (USA 1941), 397
Mr. Deeds Goes to Town (USA 1936), 292–3, 308
Mrs Brown (UK 1997), 318
Murder, Inc. (USA 1951), 57, 62
My Beautiful Laundrette (UK 1985), 307
My Darling Clementine (USA 1946), 37, 54
My Left Foot (Ireland/UK 1989), 326

Naked Kiss, The (USA 1964), 47
Name of the Rose, The (West Germany/France/Italy 1986), 337, 418
Nana (USA 1934), 437
New York Confidential (USA 1955), 48
Night and Fog (aka *Nuit et Brouillard*) (France 1955), 225, 246
Night and the City (USA 1950), 47, 305
Nineveh on the Clyde: the architecture of Alexander "Greek" Thomson (UK 1999), 510
North by Northwest (USA 1959), 395

Oldest Son, The (South Korea 1985), 310
Olvidados, Los (Mexico 1950), 309
On Dangerous Ground (USA 1952), 301
On the Town (USA 1949), 303
On the Waterfront (USA 1954), 55
Orphans (UK 1999), 510
Othello (USA 1952), 412
Out of the Past (USA 1947), 437

Paisan (Italy 1946), 183, 310
Paradine Case, The (USA 1947), 395–6
Phantom Lady (USA 1944), 48, 79
Pickup on South Street (USA 1953), 3, 45–8, 515
Pierrot le fou (France 1966), 472
Play Me Something (UK 1989), 209, 222, 238, 325, 510
Prague (UK 1990), 219–20, 238
Pride of Place (USA 1984), 509
Private Life of Henry VIII, The (UK 1933), 101, 337, 418
Professionals, The (USA 1966), 41
Psycho (USA 1960), 391
Public Enemy, The (USA 1931), 57, 59, 61

Quiet Man, The (USA 1953), 241

Ratcatcher (UK 1999), 510
Rear Window (USA 1954), 398
Rebecca (USA 1940), 395
Red River (USA 1948), 38
Repulsion (UK 1965), 415–16
Riders of Death Valley (USA 1941), 39
Rob Roy (USA 1996), 221, 324, 335, 419, 510
Rocco and His Brothers (Italy 1960), 309
Roman Spring of Mrs. Stone, The (USA 1961), 305
Rosemary's Baby (USA 1968), 415
Round-Up, The (Hungary 1966), 483
Run of the Arrow (USA 1957), 47

Samouraï, Le (France 1967), 371–83
Scarface (USA 1932), 57–9, 61
Scope: Mackintosh (UK 1970), 504
Scotch Myths (UK 1982), 19, 168, 241, 324, 414, 469–86, 484, 507–8
Sean Connery's Edinburgh (UK 1982), 505
Seawards the Great Ships (UK 1959), 112–13, 187, 505

Seven Guns for the MacGregors (Italy 1966), 97–8
Seventh Seal, The (Sweden 1957), 337, 418
Shadow of a Doubt (USA 1943), 298
Shane (USA 1957), 37–8, 52
Silence de la Mer, Le (France, 1947), 376
Singin' in the Rain (USA 1952), 303
Sleeping with the Enemy (USA 1991), 295, 298
Steel Helmet, The (USA 1951), 46
Stella Dallas (USA 1925), 437
Stella Dallas (USA 1937), 437
Street with No Name, The (USA 1948), 47, 57
Suilven Spring (UK 1975), 504
Sunrise: A Song of Two Humans (USA 1927), 291–2

Telefon (USA 1977), 305
They Live By Night (USA 1947), 437
Three Coins in the Fountain (USA 1954), 305
3:10 to Yuma (USA 1957), 38, 40
Tony Rome (USA 1967), 55
Touch of Evil (USA 1954), 411, 414
Tragedy of the Switchboard Operator, The (Yugoslavia 1967), 178–9, 225, 246
Trainspotting (UK 1995), 326, 415
Travelling Players, The (Greece 1975), 178
Travelpass (UK 1973), 504
Trou, Le (France 1960), 374, 381
True Story of Jesse James, The (USA 1957), 38, 40, 51–2
Turning Point, The (USA 1977), 47

Under Capricorn (USA 1949), 395
Underworld U.S.A. (USA 1961), 47, 57, 59, 62, 300
Union Pacific (USA 1939), 40, 53

Verdict, The (USA 1946), 305
Vertigo (USA 1958), 395
Vikings, The (USA 1958), 337, 418
Virgin Spring, The (Sweden 1960), 337, 418

Wake for Bud Neill, A (UK 1993), 229–33
War Lord, The (USA 1965), 336
Waterloo Road (UK 1945), 306
Wee Willie Winkie (USA 1937), 101, 318, 462
Westerner, The (USA 1940), 37, 52, 437
Wild Bunch, The (USA 1969), 41
Winning of Barbara Worth, The (USA 1926), 437
Witness (USA 1985), 301
Work, Rest and Play (UK 1994), 227, 239
Wrong Man, The (USA 1956), 396

Young and Innocent (UK 1937), 396–7
Young Lochinvar, The (UK 1923), 99
Young Mr. Lincoln (USA 1939), 176, 364–5

Ideas, Institutions and Non-Film Texts Index

Act of Union (1707), 122, 470
Alfred Hitchcock and the British Cinema (book), 386
All Our Yesterdays (book), 386
American Jewish Committee, 82
americanophilia, 371–3, 377–8
Ancient Monuments Protection Act (1882), 259
Anti-Socialist Alliance, 389
Arts Council of Great Britain, 443, 504
auteur theory, 54, 188, 412
auteurism, 49, 411, 432, 434, 503–4, 514–15

balmorality, 452
baronialism, 99
Barrie and the Kailyard School (book), 103
BBC Scotland, 70, 74n, 93, 227, 239, 351, 477, 507
BFI (British Film Institute), 18–19, 27n, 138n, 192, 245, 427–48, 513
'BFI and Ethnic Provision, The' (policy paper), 443
BFI Board of Governors, 430, 432–3
BFI Distribution Division, 434–48
BFI Distribution Library, 434–6, 477
BFI Distribution Library Catalogue (1973), 436
BFI Education Department, 18, 428, 429–34, 443
BFI Executive, 430, 435

BFI Film Services, 430, 434
'BFI Funding and the Grant-in-Aid Bodies' (policy paper), 442
BFI Governors Sub-Committee on Regional Film Theatres, 441
BFI Members' Action Group, 428
BFI Regional Department, 435, 439–40, 442, 444
Birmingham Centre for Contemporary Cultural Studies, 428, 445, 517
Breeksadoon (play), 471

Cahiers du cinéma, 3, 72, 83n, 175–6, 179, 351, 381–2, 472, 503, 514, 516
Calvinism, 454–5, 506
cartoons of H. M. Bateman, 394
Catholicism, 392, 454–5
Cencrastus (magazine), 169, 283, 517
Channel 4, 145, 172, 223, 245, 324–5, 329n, 471, 477, 507, 509, 511
Charter for the Moving Image in Scotland (policy statement), 223, 236
cinema of process, 17, 373–5, 377, 379–80
Cinema (UK) (magazine), 514
cinephilia, 372, 472, 504, 507
city as utopia, the, 303–4
city/country opposition, the, 291–3, 308, 518
city in the gangster film and film noir, the, 57–8, 300

IDEAS, INSTITUTIONS AND NON-FILM TEXTS INDEX 537

city in Weimar cinema, the, 307–8, 518
city/small town opposition, 294–5, 298
city symphonies, 309
class, 14, 17, 230, 340–2, 387–93, 396–7, 399n, 520
Clydesidism, 6, 215, 455–6, 458, 490
core/periphery opposition, the, 151–2, 161–3, 173, 369n
Council for National Academic Awards, 446n, 513
Culloden cairn, 13, 253–4, 258, 263–6
Culloden, Battle of (1746), 13, 243, 249, 507
cultural institutions, 9, 94n, 210
cultural nationalism, 20, 491–3, 496, 498–9
cultural struggle, 18, 427–30, 516, 521n
Cultural Studies, 9, 189, 490, 516

Dark Ageism discourse, 337, 417–18
debate-based culture, 210, 434, 444
Days of Hope (TV series), 17, 517
differential temporality, 196–7
discourse, 118n, 148, 152–5, 157, 165, 168–9, 196, 199–200, 202, 211, 222, 224, 240–2, 249–50, 280–2, 289–91, 304–5, 307–8, 311n, 414, 417, 450–1, 491–2, 519
Documentary Cinema, 180, 182, 306, 479
Doon the Watter (Scottish postcard series), 92

Ealing Studios, 102, 122, 127, 280, 450, 479
Edinburgh International Film Festival, 10, 70–2, 114, 117, 181–94, 235, 473, 503–4, 511, 515–17
elegiacism, 212–13, 215, 249, 268, 284
essentialism, 399, 451
ethnic absolutism, 458
existentialism, 371–3
expressionism, 66, 415

feminist/psychoanalytic paradigm, 387, 392–5, 428
'Film Availability Services: the Next Five Years' (policy paper), 442
Film Bang, 70, 72, 74n, 117, 478, 515
Film Form (journal), 516
film journalism, 7, 12–13, 122–5, 339, 342
film noir, 49, 61–8, 77–84, 299–300, 371–2, 382, 414, 516
film policier, 78, 299–300, 381
Film Polski (magazine), 226, 483
Film Production Theory (book), 480
Films of Scotland, 74n, 108–15, 118, 184–5, 187, 191, 207, 210, 224, 246, 477–9, 504
Film Studies, 5, 17, 29, 385–6, 438, 484, 517
First Reels, 245
'Flower of Scotland' (song), 265

Gaelic Vision in Scottish Culture, The (book), 152, 162, 204n
gangster film, the, 47–8, 49–67, 299–301
genre, 3–4, 40, 49–55, 65n, 334, 514
German Films (magazine), 483–4
Glasgow, 103–7, 229–33
Glasgow discourse, 285–6, 289–91, 358–9
Glasgow Empire Exhibition (1938), 159–70
Glasgow's Miles Better (PR campaign), 290, 358–9, 456
Glencoe, 213–15, 243, 285–6
Great Scots (sub-)discourse, 197, 456
Griersonianism, 112–17, 210
Group 3, 107–8, 184

high art and mass art, 231, 300, 314n, 332, 398, 415, 475, 496
High Culture, 90, 196–7, 231, 356–7
Highland Clearances, the, 153, 243

Highlands and Islands Development Board, 504
historiography, 8, 9, 133, 143–50, 151–8, 212, 254, 259–60, 271n, 284, 331–3, 346n, 511, 516–17
Hollywood on the Clyde, 219, 243, 478, 510
Hollywood/Mosfilm, 246, 248n
homo africanus, 241
homo celticus, 151–2, 240–3, 282
homo oeconomicus, 151, 158n, 164, 240–1, 281–2
homo pacificus, 241
Humanities Curriculum Project, 430, 446n
Hungarofilm Bulletin, 483

iconography, 55–61
identity politics, 272n, 387, 403, 515–16
ideology, 8, 72–3, 90, 93, 94n, 129, 143, 255, 279, 332, 336, 351, 403, 409, 499, 504, 514–16
imperialism, 155, 202–3, 318
In the Good Old Summertime (Scottish postcard series), 92
Independent Film-Makers' Association, 428
Industrialism, 36, 39, 40–2, 301
inferiorism, 122, 131n, 491, 493
institutional racism, 443
International Journal of Scottish Literature, 498–9
interpellation, 94n
intertextuality, 139–42, 342, 344–5, 517
invention of tradition, 254–5, 259, 341, 450, 459, 476, 508
Irish Film Board, 322–3

Jacobitism, 157, 260–3, 265–6, 409, 493
jus primae noctis, 336, 347n

Kailyard, 85–7, 89–90, 92, 99–101, 103, 108–11, 113, 116–17, 164, 206–7, 209–10, 215, 352–3, 452, 454, 456, 458, 463–4, 490, 499, 506, 516
'key debates' policy, 438–44
kitsch, 86, 94n, 458

Lobey Dosser (strip cartoon), 229–33, 508
London discourse, 305–7
longue durée, 265, 271n

Macbeth (play), 6, 18, 403–10, 421
Marxism, 21, 117, 149, 211, 387, 428, 517–18
Massacre of Glencoe Tercentenary, the (1992), 213, 243, 249, 285
memorialisation, 249–50, 257, 259, 265
Merrie England discourse, 417
Middle Class Defence League, the, 389
mise-en-scène, 10, 128–9, 175, 179, 281, 338–9, 376, 393, 473, 504
Modernism, 114, 117, 168, 297–8, 406, 408, 469, 471, 504–5, 508
monuments, destruction of, 250, 252, 272n
monuments, non-permanent, 266–8
Movie (journal), 10, 175, 187, 431, 504, 514
Movie Makars (event), 222, 237–8, 480–1
Mythologies (book), 517

National Geographic (magazine), 463–4
national identity, 7–8, 35, 133–8, 159–70, 214, 253, 321, 362, 369n
national-popular, 133, 138n
nationalism, 20, 133–8, 160–1, 260, 264, 276, 317–18, 362, 488, 499
nationalism, ethnic, 490
Neorealism, 193n, 226, 243, 310–11

New Criticism, 514
New German Cinema, 172, 329n
nostophobia, 492
Nouveau Roman, 373, 382n

Open University, the, 517
Orientalism, 451
Ossianism, 87, 101, 240
Othering, 241, 281–2, 304
Oxford Opinion (magazine), 175, 187

Panorama du film noir américain, (book), 54
'Paranoid Style in American Politics, The' (essay), 45
petty bourgeoisie, 390–1
politique des auteurs, 188
Poor Cinema, 13, 180, 219–28, 232n, 238–48, 507, 518–19
Poor Theatre, 232n
The Popular Arts (book), 187, 429
popular culture, 206, 274, 429, 432, 495
postmodernism, 208, 210, 231, 300, 469, 475, 496, 517
'Programming of Regional Film Theatres' (policy paper), 440
Prohibition, 54, 63

Rab C. Nesbitt (TV series), 16, 215, 349–70, 469, 475
race in Alfred Hitchcock's films, 396–7
reading formations, 491
reception studies, 398
Regional Film Theatres, 189, 432, 434, 438, 441
RKO, 437
Romanticism, 87, 89, 98, 103, 129, 151, 161, 168, 211, 254, 260, 317–18, 338, 341, 404, 406–7, 452, 506
rooted cosmopolitanism, 499

scopophilia, 393–4, 401n
scopophobia, 18, 393–5

Scotch Myths (exhibition), 5–6, 85–95, 470–1, 490, 506, 516
Scotch Myths position, 490, 492
Scotch Reels (book), 23n, 119n, 207, 209–11, 241, 282–3, 490–1
scotch whisky, 195–204
Scotland on Screen (report), 320
Scotland on the Move discourse, 111–13, 117, 210
Scottish Arts Council, 109, 117, 169, 210, 325, 504
Scottish Central Film Library, 109, 246
Scottish Discursive Unconscious, 12, 19, 211, 215, 242–3, 249, 265, 268, 279–87, 359, 449–68, 518
Scottish Film Archive, 477–8, 508
Scottish Film Council, 74n, 109, 117–18, 191–2, 210, 219, 235–6, 239, 322, 444, 477–9, 508
Scottish film culture, 69–75, 118, 119n, 121, 175, 181, 238–9, 469–86, 510, 516
Scottish Film Production Fund, 178, 210–11, 219, 235, 239, 319, 322, 478, 507, 510
Scottish intelligentsia, 173, 487–502
Scottish militarism, 87, 90, 454
Scottish National Party, 341–3
Scottish National War Memorial, 154, 497
Scottish popular culture, 356, 470, 487–502, 520
Scottish Screen, 237, 320, 322–5, 478, 480–2, 484
Scottish screen acting, 353–5, 474–5
Screen (journal), 10, 17, 175, 428, 444, 516
Screen Scotland, 482
Sectarian Discourse, 105–6, 365–6, 455–6
semiotics, 89, 95n, 175, 196, 206, 516
sentimental Jacobitism, 260–3, 265–6, 268, 409

'Significance of the Frontier in American History, The' (essay), 36–7
Sight and Sound (magazine), 431–3, 482
Signs and Meaning in the Cinema (book), 431, 514
Society for Education in Film and Television, 428, 442
Sovexportfilm, 483
space-time compression, 254, 259, 307
Spaghetti Westerns, 97
spectatorialism, 397
stairheid nostalgia, 352
stereotype, 90, 94n, 118n
story-structure discourse, 237, 379, 480, 510,
structuralism, 4, 94n, 151, 207–8, 216n, 312n, 364, 514, 518
structured programming, 439–41, 444
structuring absence, 364–6
STV (Scottish Television), 153, 229, 509
surrealism, 366, 371–3
symbolic appropriation, 98, 125–7, 241, 255, 282, 338

Tartan Army, 207–8, 345
Tartan Shorts, 226–7, 239
Tartanry, 85–7, 89–90, 92, 99, 101, 103, 108–11, 113, 117, 164, 206–7, 209, 210, 239, 337, 405, 408, 414, 420–1, 453–8, 460, 463–4, 488, 490, 499, 505–7, 516

technology in the western and gangster film/thriller, 39–41, 58–9
Thatcherite/Churchillian rhetoric, 134
Transactions of the Gaelic Society of Inverness, 261
Tribune (newspaper), 69, 446n, 513, 515–16, 520

Unconscious, the, 211
Unifrance (magazine), 226
United Kingdom Property Owners Association, 389
Ur-Tartan Documentary, 110, 113, 115, 505

Vietnam Memorial, 252, 258, 263
Virgin Land: the American West as Symbol and Myth (book), 36, 52–3, 514
Voodoo *Macbeth*, 412, 414

Wagnerism, 405
Wallace Clan Trust, 420–1, 425n, 457
Weimar Germany, 300, 305, 307–9, 312n
West as Desert, the, 38–9
West as Garden, the, 36–9
West as Pasture, the, 38
the Western, 35–43, 52–4, 97, 514
wildness, 404–9
Workers' City (political campaign), 456
Workmen's Compensation Act (1897), 389

EU representative:
Easy Access System Europe
Mustamäe tee 50, 10621 Tallinn, Estonia
Gpsr.requests@easproject.com

www.ingramcontent.com/pod-product-compliance
Lightning Source LLC
Chambersburg PA
CBHW061339300426
44116CB00011B/1924